Networking, Models and Methods of Cloud Computing

Networking, Models and Methods of Cloud Computing

Edited by **Michelle Vine**

WILLFORD PRESS

New York

Published by Willford Press,
118-35 Queens Blvd., Suite 400,
Forest Hills, NY 11375, USA
www.willfordpress.com

Networking, Models and Methods of Cloud Computing
Edited by Michelle Vine

International Standard Book Number: 978-1-68285-267-5 (Hardback)

Printed in the United States of America.

Contents

Preface

Over the recent decade, advancements and applications have progressed exponentially. This has led to the increased interest in this field and projects are being conducted to enhance knowledge. The main objective of this book is to present some of the critical challenges and provide insights into possible solutions. This book will answer the varied questions that arise in the field and also provide an increased scope for furthering studies.

Cloud computing has provided the state-of-the-art platform for storing and sharing information and databases between multiple users. This book explores the latest developments in cloud computing technology. It attempts to understand the multiple branches that fall under the discipline of cloud computing as well as the vast framework of cloud infrastructure which includes various networks, models and algorithms of cloud computing. The chapters included in this book cover topics such as cloud storage and distribution of data, cloud security and trust management, data allocation and management, cloud computing applications, etc. With advanced inputs by acclaimed experts of this field, it targets students and professionals alike.

I hope that this book, with its visionary approach, will be a valuable addition and will promote interest among readers. Each of the authors has provided their extraordinary competence in their specific fields by providing different perspectives as they come from diverse nations and regions. I thank them for their contributions.

Editor

Cache performance models for quality of service compliance in storage clouds

Ernest Sithole[1*], Aaron McConnell[1], Sally McClean[2], Gerard Parr[2], Bryan Scotney[2], Adrian Moore[2] and Dave Bustard[2]

Abstract

With the growing popularity of cloud-based data centres as the enterprise IT platform of choice, there is a need for effective management strategies capable of maintaining performance within SLA and QoS parameters when responding to dynamic conditions such as increasing demand. Since current management approaches in the cloud infrastructure, particularly for data-intensive applications, lack the ability to systematically quantify performance trends, static approaches are largely employed in the allocations of resources when dealing with volatile demand in the infrastructure. We present analytical models for characterising cache performance trends at storage cache nodes. Practical validations of cache performance for derived theoretical trends show close approximations between modelled characterisations and measurement results for user request patterns involving private datasets and publicly available datasets. The models are extended to encompass hybrid scenarios based on concurrent requests of both private and public content. Our models have potential for guiding (a) efficient resource allocations during initial deployments of the storage cloud infrastructure and (b) timely interventions during operation in order to achieve scalable and resilient service delivery.

Keywords: Storage cloud, Enterprise applications, Cache performance, Optimisation

Introduction

The cloud computing paradigm is emerging as a mainstream approach in the design and implementation of enterprise computing solutions [1-3]. The principal factors favouring the adoption of cloud-based technologies in business computing environments are: (a) the ease with which IT infrastructure deployments and expansions can be achieved when bringing together multiple and heterogeneous computing resources, typically scattered across wide geophysical locations, and (b) the simplified mechanisms by which users can access and utilise hosted IT services.

Based on the specific needs of target user environments, which cloud based technologies are intended to serve, business IT service solutions can be crafted and made available in a variety of offerings, which can be Software-as-a-Service (SaaS), Platform-as-a-Service (PaaS) or Infrastructure-as-a-Service (IaaS) computing

capabilities. The adoptions of the SaaS solutions [1,2] present hosted applications to user environments customers as usable service entities for business computing needs; the PaaS-based solutions [4-7] present for use by application routines executing at the SaaS level, service capabilities that are derived from the integration of Operating System and virtualisation functionalities; the IaaS solutions [3,8-10] bring together the operational hardware elements such as data centre equipment, processor and storage servers, and networking devices into functional capabilities that can be plugged into and utilised by user routines executing at both the SaaS and PaaS levels of the cloud stack.

Depending on the nature of the affinity groups that are served by cloud-based IT environments, there are four main categories of clouds - Private, Community, Public or Hybrid, which can serve user environments according to their access entitlements. Private clouds are exclusively for intra-organisational needs; Community clouds result from federations of resources that serve the interests of select user groups with common objectives; Public clouds offer on-demand services to anyone with

*Correspondence: esithole@infc.ulst.ac.uk
[1] Networking and Computing Technologies Laboratory, University of Ulster at Coleraine, Coleraine - BT52 1SA Northern Ireland, United Kingdom
Full list of author information is available at the end of the article

service-provider-authenticated web access over the standard Internet connection; Hybrid clouds fulfill requirements that can only met through services derived from combinations of in-house and off-premises resources. The delivery of cloud computing service according to above mentioned implementations enables reduced setup times for the deployments of outsourced business computing solutions, with little or no requirement being imposed on the customers to understand and manage the underlying technologies operating in the infrastructure.

Despite the enormous strides that have been achieved in developing functional capabilities for cloud computing systems, challenges still remain that present formidable barriers to the reliable performance and therefore effective use of cloud-based IT infrastructures. Performance related issues in the cloud domain encompass a range of considerations such as how to maintain Key Performance Indicators (made up of throughput and response time metrics), on-demand resource and service availability, continuity and scalability of IT services at competitive SLA and QoS levels that will enable business customers to meet performance goals. In order for the management-driven strategies and interventions to meet required levels of service reliability and availability and, thus maintain infrastructure operations within specified SLA and QoS targets, in-depth knowledge is required for establishing quantitative trends that are associated with principal performance indicators such as throughput rates, response times and load-scalability as the levels of user requests being sent to the cloud infrastructure vary. Thus, in quantitative terms, the ability to provide SLA and QoS-capable resource management in cloud-based IT environments requires accurate characterisations of the load response patterns, based on the interplay of factors such as the resource infrastructure's service capacity, the levels of applied user workloads and their resource consumption needs in the cloud service environment.

Given the lack of intimate knowledge that can lead to mature capabilities for establishing the quantitative relationships between user requests and performance in precise detail, the allocations of resources in cloud-based IT infrastructures are largely conducted in a reactive manner, with the assignment of resource entities being carried out statically in response to any changes in user demand. As a result, the fulfilment of SLAs and QoS contracts for outsourced IT services essentially relies on either excess provisioning that leads to inefficiencies or, limited allocation of infrastructure resources that has carries the risk of SLA violations. Hence, instead of having in place proactive technical interventions that can immediately respond by reassigning resources to keep performance levels within acceptable thresholds, any QoS breaches that occur in the infrastructure are handled largely by follow up admin negotiations with a view to settling any business losses

that may result from service interruptions through compensation. It is therefore worth exploring approaches by which performance trends in the cloud infrastructure can be determined with sufficient accuracy to enable proactive resource management for QoS compliant delivery of IT services. In our work, we isolate for study the resource utilisation trends of the storage subsystems on server hardware, an aspect that has not been given sufficient consideration in the context of supporting SLA-capable resource management mechanisms in storage clouds.

Proposed strategy for QoS compliance support in storage clouds

As has been highlighted, the challenge of achieving SLA-awareness in cloud environments is a multifaceted research issue with a number of dimensions stemming from it such as determining the levels of resource availability, service continuity rates and scalability trends of performance that will be able to satisfy QoS constraints. As a starting point towards addressing the vital issues pertinent to QoS maintenance in storage cloud infrastructures, this paper focuses on developing characterisations of cache performance trends, an aspect which we consider to have potential for serving as an important source of guidance for informed decisions on the provisioning of scalable data storage services in enterprise IT environments. Our approach, thus aims to support QoS readiness in resource allocation management strategies for storage clouds through accurate modelling of content availability levels at individual cache entities in the infrastructure, and the modelled scalability trends can serve as a feed into the management strategies for storage space provisioning.

In order to establish the validity of the modelled cache performance, a data centre facility with cloud-based storage elements is used. As a key contribution of this paper, we present and validate scalability trends of cache performance at individual nodes, and the derived theoretical models can be a foundation upon which the considerations for infrastructure sizing can proceed and decisions are made in accord with the applications' resource needs and the service capabilities of the resources in enterprise computing environments on the following: (a) initial sizes of the storage deployments for cloud-based services, (b) re-calibration of the scale of storage resource integrations an ongoing basis in order to preempt SLA violations that could arise from short-term increases in demand and, (c) storage capacity upgrades based on anticipated margins of permanent increases in user demand.

Given that the accuracy of cache performance characterisations is the critical component underpinning the ability of our proposed strategy to quantify the scale of resource allocations required to fulfil performance goals in storage clouds, the next section proceeds with a detailed consideration of cache performance trends, with the focus primarily on the analytical derivations of the scalability response patterns of content retention rates at individual storage server nodes in the cloud domain. In Section "Experimental facility for validations of cache performance Trends" we describe the key components of the practical facility used for conducting experimental validations of the models. Sections "Validations of cache performance trends for user requests of private data" and "Validations of cache performance trends for user requests of public data" respectively feature the sets of experiments conducted to establish the validity of the modelled cache performance for private and public data requests. Section "Performance characterisations for concurrent accesses to private and public content" extends the analytical models to scenarios that are based on concurrent requests going to private and public data. A brief evaluation of our cache performance characterisations is provided in Section "Discussion" through the consideration of the implications of the results on the ability to provide support for service continuity, scalability and SLA compliance in the management of storage resources. Section "Related research" provides a summary review of other research initiatives that are aimed at developing SLA support strategies for clouds by addressing aspects that are adjacent to our area of focus. The ninth section concludes the paper by highlighting further issues to be investigated in future work so that viable techniques are developed for QoS-ready deployments in the storage cloud infrastructure.

Derivations of cache performance models

We begin our consideration of cache performance trends in storage clouds by developing theoretical models of data availability levels based on the scalability response to rising numbers user of requests for content. In developing quantitative estimates of cache hit ratios at storage caches, four principal factors and their impact on cache performance are considered. These factors are (a) the respective sizes of the storage capacities of the local cache and source storage devices, C_L, and C_S (b) the user loading levels in terms of the average number and average sizes of input files to satisfy each received request, N_F and S_F, (c) the mean service time period for the execution of the requests, $\frac{1}{\lambda_{App}}$, during which a cached file is used by a runtime process at the CPU and (d) the affinities of user patterns to the individual files that they request in the cache. Table 1 provides a complete list of the basic input and output parameters that are used in the derivations of the cache models and practical experiments.

Cache performance analysis of user requests for private data

Based on the interplay of these factors, the overall cache performance in terms of the average cache hit ratio, P_L,

Table 1 Input and output parameters for the local cache node

Parameter	Description	Value
N_{Users}	Number Active Users	10 - 250
$(\frac{1}{\lambda_{App}})$	Application Request Inter-repetition Time (sec)	exp (2.5)
J_{Limit}	Transaction Limit for Received Jobs	Infinite
J_{Policy}	Job Instance Limit Policy	Queue
$J_{Priority}$	Priority assigned for	Regular 5
$(\frac{1}{\mu_{CPU}})$	Average CPU Service Time (sec)	exp (1.5)
N_F	Average I/O File Read Count	Constant (1)
S_F	Average Read File Size (MB)	Constant (1)
S_{CPUMem}	Average Size of Memory (MB)	Uniform (0- 10)
C_L	Capacity of Local Cache (GB)	40 - 200
C_S	Capacity of Remote Storage (GB)	1000
L	Local Cache Capacity (users)	10 - 50
S	Remote Storage Capacity (users)	400
P_L	Overall Local Cache Hit Ratio	0 - 1

at each local storage can thus be summarized by the basic expression, $P_L = f(C_L, C_S, S_F, N_F, \frac{1}{\lambda_{App}})$. We make the assumption that the interplay of these input parameters impacts the local cache performance by predominantly generating capacity misses.

The analysis of cache performance that we consider first applies to application routines that have rigid affinities between user requests and target files i.e. cases where $User_1$ will always request $File_1$ with $User_2$ requesting $File_2$ etc. The criterion of rigid affinity to content is pertinent to situations where each customer using the business computing infrastructure accesses his own master data [11], which he can view and edit. Thus, ignoring the impact of conflict and compulsory misses on cache performance trends and assuming uniform file sizes, S_F, for cached content, then the cache hit ratio or the probability, P_L, of satisfying data requests in the local cache, follows the relationship:

$$P_L = \begin{cases} 1 & \text{if } S_F N_F N_{Users} \leq C_L \\ \dfrac{C_L}{S_F N_F N_{Users}} & \text{if } S_F N_F N_{Users} > C_L. \end{cases} \quad (1)$$

Assuming that the theoretical analysis applies to those cases where the data request cycles have gone beyond the point of start up misses, the model derivation shows that the hit cache ratio remains at 100% before and upon matching the storage capacity, C_L. Whenever the applied user load given by storage space requirements of the generated, $S_F N_F N_{Users}$, exceeds the storage capacity of the local cache, C_L, the cache hits begin falling asymptotically toward zero. Conversely, the local cache capacity miss ratio, M_L, is described by the relationship:

$$M_L = \begin{cases} 0 & \text{if } S_F N_F N_{Users} \leq C_L \\ 1 - \left(\dfrac{C_L}{S_F N_F N_{Users}}\right) & \text{if } S_F N_F N_{Users} > C_L. \end{cases} \quad (2)$$

Next, we consider cache performance in scenarios where users generate dispersed requests i.e. unrestricted access is allowed to all the publicly available files that are kept on the remote storage device of capacity, C_S.

Cache performance analysis of user requests for public data

Unrestricted data access patterns apply to publicly hosted content, which many users will likely have an interest in obtaining, whether from the public internet or in-house data sources [11,12]. We make two assumptions for dispersed file requests: one that the master storage is at least equal or greater to the local cache space i.e. $C_S \geq C_L$, and the other that the time period for considering the cache performance is sufficiently long for the users to cycle their requests over the entire collection of files kept on the master storage device, i.e. $S_F N_F N_{Users} \geq C_S$. Since the access to all the content on the remote storage is unrestricted, each of the N_{Users} can thus request any of the files at master storage device with equal chance so that the probability of requesting one of the stored $\frac{C_S}{S_F}$ files becomes $\frac{S_F}{C_S}$. If the start up cache misses are disregarded by taking into account the $\frac{C_L}{S_F}$ files that are already in the local cache node, then the cache hit ratio, P_L, which is equivalent to the probability that a requested file can be found in the cache node, is equal to $\frac{C_L}{C_S}$. Thus, regardless of the actual number of user requests coming onto the IT infrastructure, the cache performance is given by the relationship:

$$P_L = \begin{cases} \left(\dfrac{C_L}{C_S}\right) & \text{if } C_L < C_S \\ 1 & \text{if otherwise.} \end{cases} \quad (3)$$

Apart from the fact that load levels of input user requests are irrelevant to cache performance, it also follows that for scenarios where user requests are uniformly scattered over the remotely stored files, the trends for local node cache miss ratios in such cases are given by the expression:

$$M_L = \begin{cases} 1 - \left(\dfrac{C_L}{C_S}\right) & \text{if } C_L < C_S \\ 0 & \text{if otherwise.} \end{cases} \quad (4)$$

The following section provides an introduction to the setup for the experiments that were conducted to establish the practical validity of the modelled scalability trends of the cache hit rates derived for the two cases of data access patterns considered above.

Experimental facility for validations of cache performance Trends

As shown in Figure 1, the practical setup for our experiments employs four Virtual Machines: the User Load Generator, Application Server, File Manager and Remote Storage Manager VMs, all of which comprise the software elements for the experiments.

The Load Generator program initiates the operations in the Application Server, File Manager and Remote Storage VMs in readiness for the start of measurements and results collection. As a preparatory step, an initial start signal is sent by the generator to both the File Manager and Remote Storage VMs so that the cache optimisation algorithm and storage partitions are provisioned with target files to be requested by users are set up. After a delay of appropriate duration, a second start signal is generated to initiate first user request, $Request_1$, which will be followed by a train of arrivals, $Request_2 \ldots Request_N$, at the Application Server according to the predefined arrival process rate, λ_{App}. The File Manager VM responds to the initial start signal by setting aside the required storage space in the local cache and activating the algorithm selected for optimising cached content.

In addition to retaining cached content according to the selected optimisation criterion, the cache algorithm functionality in the File Manager VM responds directly to the data requests by compiling a record of the Request, Hit and Miss events occurring in the local cache. The Remote Storage VM ensures that permanent copies of all the file objects to be requested by the users are kept on its storage partition, ready to be copied across to the local cache partition should any misses occur at the latter. Upon the lapse of the predefined duration of the experimental measurements, a stop signal is emitted by Load Generator to the Application Server, File Manager and Remote Storage VMs.

The number of users, N_{Users}, that generate data requests at runtime is varied from 0 to 250, and the user sessions execute concurrently in the form of thread instances spawned off from the invoked work process instance. Thus, for each active user session, the runtime execution is in the form a VM instance at the application server. The consumptions of processor hardware resources (CPU and memory), $\frac{1}{\mu_{CPU}}$ and S_{CPUMem}, are according to the requests generated by the application routine generated inside the VM instance. The average number of input data files, N_F, requested by each user routine, is fixed to 1, with each file being 1000 KB in size and, the reserved cache space on the storage node, C_L, is varied from 40 GB to 200 GB for the two cases for data request patterns. The accessed files are indexed as database objects in the MySQL backend database entries, and the file retrievals into cache space are handled as block data transfers of

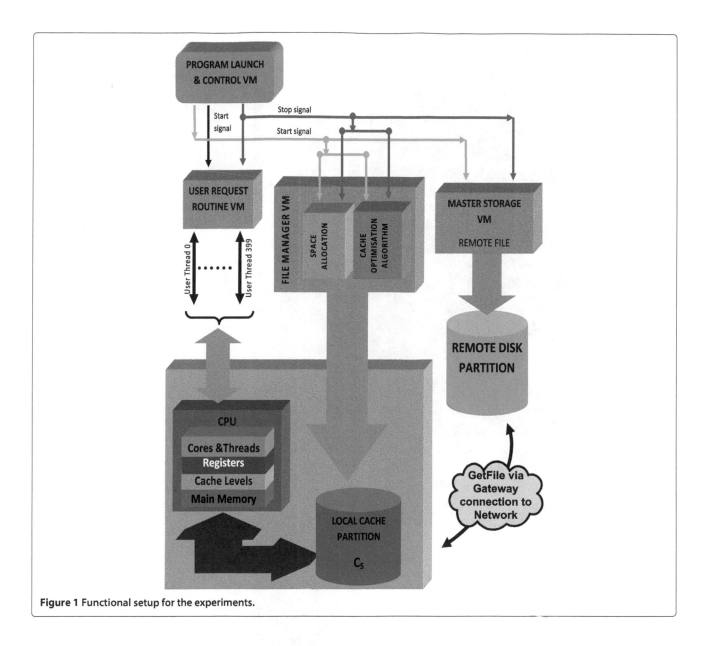

Figure 1 Functional setup for the experiments.

the database table entries. The cached content is hosted on a local Dell R515 node, whose hardware is made up of an AMD 12-core 4170 HE, 2.1 GHz processor, 128 GB Memory and 25 TB storage. The functional configuration for Dell server is based on the Tier 2 settings so that both the application's CPU executions and the data access services are colocated in the same machine. The inter-arrival time, $\frac{1}{\lambda_{App}}$, for the data requests occurring inside each cycle of user operations is assumed to follow the exponential distribution with a mean of 2.5 seconds. The mean service durations of computation operations when interacting with cached files is set to 1.5 seconds also following the exponential distribution, and the duration of the experiments is 10 minutes. We base the parameter values and the distribution patterns for service times

on the workload scenarios described in [11]. The run-in period before the experiment begins recording results data lasts for 2 minutes from the instant at which the experimental run is launched. For each data point that is presented by the graphs in the experimental scenarios that were featured in our studies, the result value was obtained from computing a running average of ten output readings as shown in the screenshot in Figure 2. Before the ten experimental runs for each result are conducted, the input parameters are fed into both the File Manager (which enforces the cache policies) and the User Emulator (which generates requests for files). Reference can be made to Table 1 for a complete list of the input parameters that were used in setting up the practical experiments.

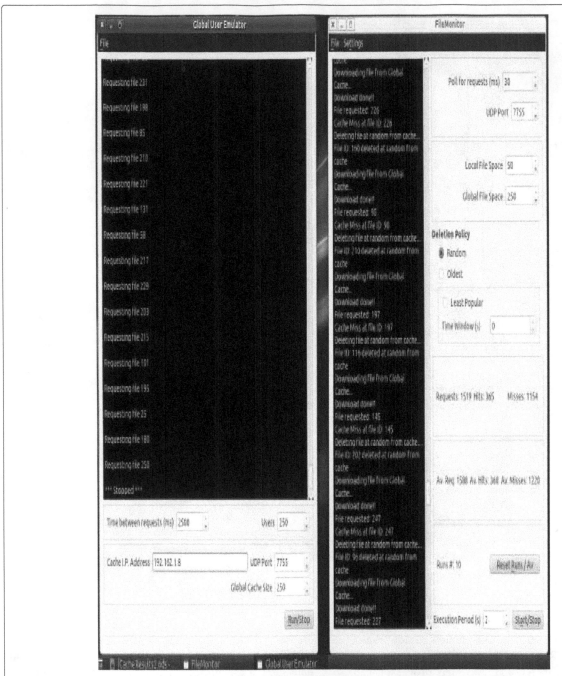

Figure 2 Screenshot of the input and output parameters of the experiments for cache performance analysis.

Definitions of scenarios for the experimental study

A simplification is made to Equations 1 - 4, developed in 2.1 and 2.2 so that the experimental analyses of the impact of user runtime behavior on the local cache hits and miss ratios can be carried out by expressing the local cache and remote storage capacities in terms of the maximum users that fill up the cache and master storage respectively. Thus, the formula, $L = \frac{C_L}{S_F N_F}$, represents the maximum number of users that can use cache storage before capacity

misses occur, and the equation, $S = \frac{C_S}{S_F N_F}$, relates to the maximum users whose data are kept on the remote storage space. Figure 3 shows the experimental setup of the scenarios based on the use of simplified input parameters for user load levels, local cache and remote storage capacities.

Therefore, in situations where user requests for the experiments are defined according to each user having a unique file set for exclusive access, L becomes relevant

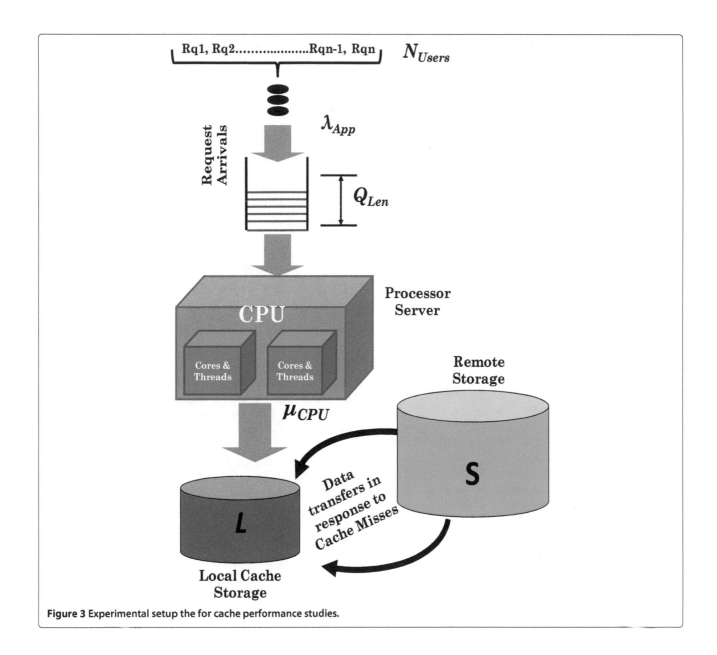

Figure 3 Experimental setup the for cache performance studies.

to the analysis of cache performance according to the expression,

$$P_L = \begin{cases} 1 & \text{if } N_{Users} \leq L \\ \dfrac{L}{N_{Users}} & \text{if } N_{Users} > L. \end{cases} \quad (5)$$

The cache performance analysis associated with requests for private data is thus considered in terms of the number of active users, N_{Users}, generating data requests and the number of users, L, that fill up local cache capacity. Similarly, when public data objects are requested randomly from the list of shared data objects that are kept in the remote storage, the respective sizes of the

local cache and remote storage affect cache performance according to the equation,

$$P_L = \begin{cases} \left(\dfrac{L}{S}\right) & \text{if } L < S \\ 1 & \text{if otherwise.} \end{cases} \quad (6)$$

It is important to reiterate that the specific definitions for the scenarios considered in the experimental studies take into account the fact that the levels of content availability at storage nodes in the cloud are governed by the interplay of the principal factors considered in the derivations of cache hit ratios, which are the data request patterns in terms of whether they specify private or shared data, the amounts of storage space in both the cache and remote nodes, the applied user load according to volumes of data requests and file sizes associated with each request, and the efficacy of the storage management and cache replacement policies in keeping content that closely matches the needs of anticipated user requests. Hence, we define scenarios for experimental investigations to bring out the impact the respective factors to cache performance by setting the key experimental parameters as follows:

- Scenario 1 considers Cache Performance with User Requests accessing Private Data
- Scenario 2 considers Cache Performance with User Requests accessing Public Data
- Within each of the two primary scenarios, three separate studies of cache performance are conducted based on cache optimisation policies for Random, Popularity and Age-based File Evictions.
- The applied user load, based on the number of users and the average file sizes per request, is uniformly increased to levels that are beyond the assigned cache storage, C_L, and the resulting scalability patterns for cache misses and hits are recorded for comparisons with the theoretical ones.

Validations of cache performance trends for user requests of private data

The arrival and service processes for the user requests received at the local cache nodes server are assumed to be Poisson, and in order to ensure a stable queue on the storage node, the relationship, $\frac{1}{\lambda_{App}} > \frac{1}{\mu_{CPU}}$, must hold for the respective magnitudes of the mean arrival and service times. Reference can be made to the list of input parameters shown in Table 1 for the actual values of arrival and service intervals. To investigate the sensitivity of the local cache ratios to user load, the local cache and remote storage capacities are assigned fixed values of $L = 50$, and $S = 400$ respectively. The applied user load parameter, N_{Users}, is increased uniformly from 10 to 250 with each active user accessing his own set of data whenever requests are sent to the local cache.

Random eviction criterion

The pseudocode representing key functional features of the cache optimisation program is presented in Algorithm 1. It is important to point out that for the purpose of providing a complete summary of the experimental operations, Algorithm 1 also includes the primary functionalities of the Load Generator and Storage Manager programs. Once all start up misses have been dealt with and the cache is space is filled up, the Random Cache Eviction algorithm responds to any further misses by choosing the victim files in the local cache that are marked for deletion. The victim files are then replaced

with the requested content, which is brought from the remote storage in order to satisfy the cache miss event. The durations of inter-arrival and service times of the user requests follow the exponential distribution with mean values of $\frac{1}{\lambda_{App}} = 2.5$ and $\frac{1}{\mu_{CPU}} = 1.5$ seconds respectively.

The results in Figure 4 showing both the measurements and theoretical trends confirm a decrease in the cache miss ratio, P_L, as the applied user load, N_{Users}, is increased. Even more significant from the graphs is the observation that the practical results track the modelled trends very closely, with the cache performance levels of the measurement results being higher than the theoretical ones.

An important factor leading to better performance for the measurement results is that the analytical models are based on the worst-case situations, in which the consideration of excess requests within each average cycle of user requests by N_{Users} does not take into account the possibility that some of the requests generated in the practical scenarios would be accessing data already in the cache. Hence because of the inability of the performance analysis to quantify exactly the extent of improvement in cache hits caused by the repeat requests that can occur within the $\{N_{Users} - L\}$ excess requests inside each average load cycle, there are lower cache hit ratios for the theoretical trends.

The use of the Random Eviction criterion in selection of the files for deletion in the cache is another factor contributing to the better cache performance achieved in the practical measurements. Since the identities of requested files is determined by the Load Generator according to the probability, $(\frac{1}{N_{Users}})$, and that of the files to be deleted according to the probability, $(\frac{1}{L})$, identical strategies are thus used for the respective actions of file requests and cache optimisation. Having such alignment in the Load Generator and Caching Algorithm functional patterns therefore helps improve the cache hit ratios obtained from practical measurements. Despite the consistently lower performance levels for the modelled cache hit ratios, the comparisons in Figure 4 nonetheless show that the theoretical trends can be a reliable indicator of achievable cache performance in practice.

Least frequently used criterion

The LFU Algorithm is structurally similar to the Random Eviction criterion, the important difference as shown in the program module below, being that update and sort functions on the popularity list are performed according to the frequencies of the requests for the cached files. The lowest ranked file on the list is marked for deletion and its place in the cache is taken by the newly requested content brought into the local cache from the remote storage.

Algorithm 1 : *Cache Eviction Simulator* (N_{Users}, *L*, *S*)

1: *Measurement.start ← true*

   Beginning program execution

2: $((|LocalCache| ← L) \land (|RemoteStore| ← S)) \mid (LocalCache \subsetneq RemoteStore)$

   Setting the cardinalities for, Local Cache and Remote Storage

3: **for** $j ← 1$ to N_{Users} **do**

4:     *StorageFile[j].Popularity ← default*

      Initialising file popularity parameters to default value.

5: **end for**

6: $(t_i ← t_{(i-1)} + t_w) \mid (Pr(t_w) ← exp(\lambda_{App}))$

   Setting the waiting time for next user request, t_i

7: $i ← \{0 + \%rand(N_{Users})\}$

   Fixing User ID associated with next request, *i*

8: *Listen.Request[i] ← StorageFile[i].[Content]*

   Setting the affinity between User ID and Target File ID

   Execution of File Manager upon resolving startup misses

9: **while** $((\neg Measurement.stop) \land (CacheMiss.EventType \neg Compulsory))$ **do**

10:    **if** $(Request[i].Content \in LocalCache)$ **then**

11:       *LocalCacheRequest.Total.Update*

12:       *LocalCacheHit.Total.Update*

13:    **else**

14:       *LocalCacheRequest.Total.Update*

15:       *LocalCacheMiss.Total.Update*

16:       $m ← \{0 + \%rand(L)\}$

        Local Cache position ID, *m*, marked for Random Deletion.

17:       *LocalCache.Position[m] ← Request[i].Content*

18:    **end if**

19:    $(CPUTime.Request[i] ← t_{CPU}) \mid (Pr(t_{CPU}) ← exp(\mu_{CPU}))$

    Setting the service time for current request

20:    *Request[i].execute*

21:    return *Request[i].Result*

22: **end while**

In order to perform the comparisons for cache performance trends, two graphs are used in the validations: one based on measurement results and the other on the derived theoretical trends. The trends for the analytical characterisations are based on capacity misses occurring on the local cache space assuming that fully-associative mapping policies are enforced i.e. cached objects brought in from external nodes can reside anywhere within the entire cache storage area, *L*, that is set aside for local caching service. Apart from compulsory misses, the impact of conflict misses on the cache performance is also disregarded in the analysis, the assumption being that the incidence of predictive errors of cache policies (i.e. whenever the algorithms evict content that should have been retained) will have a negligibly low impact on the overall cache ratio, P_L.

1: **if** $(Request[i].[Content] \in LocalCache)$ **then**

2:    *LocalCacheRequest.Total.Update*

3:    *LocalCacheHit.Total.Update*

4:    *Popularity.List.Update ← Request[i].Content.*

5: **else**

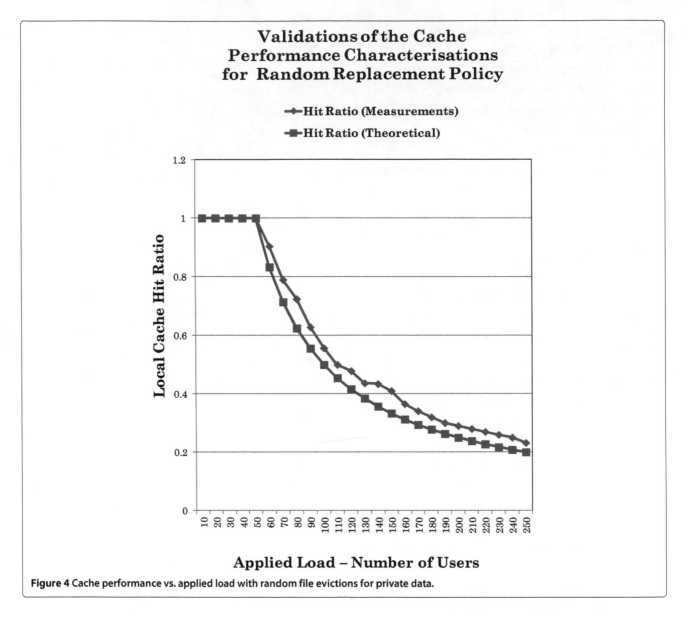

Figure 4 Cache performance vs. applied load with random file evictions for private data.

6:      *LocalCacheRequest.Total.Update*

7:      *LocalCacheMiss.Total.Update*

8:      *Popularity.List.Update ← Request[i] .Content.*

9:      *Popularity.Rank.Consult*

10:     *m ← Lowest.Rank.CachePosition.Get*
        Local Cache Position, *m*, marked for deletion
        according to LFU criterion.

11:     *LocalCache.Position[m] ← Request[i] .Content*

12: **end if**

As in Figure 4, the overall cache hit ratio trend in Figure 5 shows a decrease according to the relationship, $P_L = (\frac{L}{N_{Users}})$ whenever the data requirements of user requests exceed the capacity of the local cache space.

Measurements for scenarios based on the popularity of cached data produce lower cache hits than in the case of optimisation techniques that use the Random Eviction policy. As can be seen in Figure 5, the practical values of cache hit ratios are much nearer to the theoretical ones than those shown in Figure 4. The reduced level of cache performance using the popularity based criteria suggests that the LFU algorithm is less efficient than the random deletions of cached files in response to cache misses. The performance knock resulting from the LFU algorithm is likely accounted for by the fact that mechanisms, which rank cached files by virtue of the frequencies of previous requests are not employing the relevant strategy given that the identities of requested files are in fact specified by the Load Generator at random, based on uniform probability of occurrence of magnitude, $(\frac{1}{N_{Users}})$. Hence, the LFU approach for ranking cached content only produces nonexistent patterns of file popularity, which in turn, results in reductions of cache hit events.

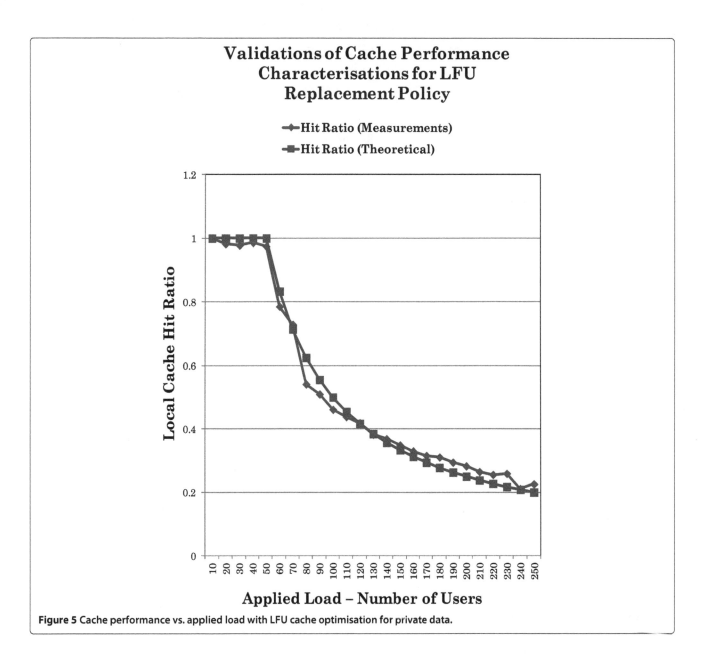

Figure 5 Cache performance vs. applied load with LFU cache optimisation for private data.

Least recently used criterion

The LRU algorithm is based on rating cached files according to age so that file objects that have been kept in the local cache the longest are assigned the lowest indices of usefulness with respect to data needs of future requests. The oldest files are thus selected for deletion whenever cache miss events occur and the victim files are replaced by the newly requested content, which is transferred from the master storage.

The trends shown in Figure 6 for the comparisons of both the theoretical and measurement results confirm that there is a drop in local cache ratio performance as the load is increased beyond the local cache capacity. The results for the LRU algorithm are almost identical to those associated with the LFU criterion presented in Figure 5.

As load levels exceed the local capacity cache corresponding to L files, the cache hit ratios track the modelled trends very closely according to the analytical formula, $P_L = (\frac{L}{N_{Users}})$.

As in the case of the LRU, the lower cache hit ratio performance is probably an outcome of the mismatch between the cache optimisation strategy and the patterns associated with data requests coming onto the cache. The age-based approach of quantifying the likelihood of experiencing repeat requests in the future for cached files is not a useful optimisation technique given the random manner in which requested files are specified by users. Thus, any apparent difference in the ages of stored files that may be computed by the LRU provides no predictive value on the likely patterns of future file requests, which

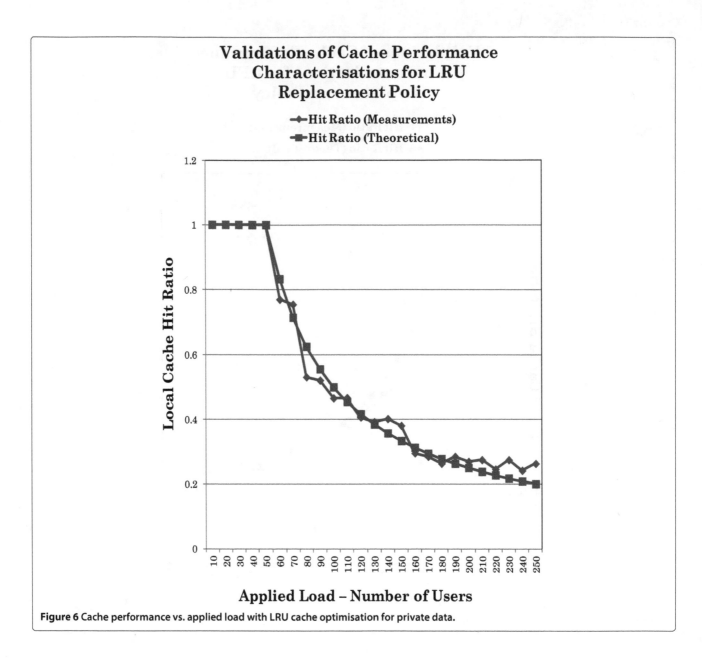

Figure 6 Cache performance vs. applied load with LRU cache optimisation for private data.

according to Algorithm 1, are stochastic and follow a discrete uniform distribution with probability, $(\frac{1}{N_{Users}})$, for each request action.

Summary of validation experiments for private data requests

The practical measurements that were conducted using the three cache optimisation algorithms produced results that were closely matched to the modelled theoretical trends. In terms of the actual cache hit ratios, the use of the Random Cache Eviction criterion resulted in better cache performance over the age and popularity-based LRU and LFU policies respectively. The inefficiencies in the LRU and LFU Cache Eviction criteria are due to the non-existence of age and popularity-based behavioural

patterns in the requests for cached content. Since each of the public data objects, like private content, are requested with identical probability, the next set of validations of cache performance models for the requests for public data are therefore carried out on the basis that our initial results show superiority of Random Eviction policy over LRU and LFU by considering the scenarios involving use of the Random Cache Eviction policy only.

Validations of cache performance trends for user requests of public data

In conducting the practical measurements, we simplify the cache performance models for public data requests developed in Subsection "Cache performance analysis of user requests for public data" by expressing the storage capacities of the local cache and external storage in terms of L and S, which are the respective numbers of active user requests that can fill up the storage entities. Content access patterns to the S publicly available files on the remote storage are thus governed by the discrete uniform distribution with the probability, $\frac{1}{S}$, applying to each file request. Consequently, when the requested data objects can be specified randomly from the list of shared data objects that are kept in the remote storage, the respective sizes of the local cache and remote storage capacities impact on cache performance according to Equation 3.

To ensure that user requests cycle through all the S files in the remote storage device, the duration of the experiment runs should be sufficient to cover at least S unique file requests from active users. If the assumption is made that no repeat requests are generated in each request cycle, the minimum time period for the experiment should equal $\frac{S}{\mu_{CPU} - \lambda_{App}}$. Hence, the duration of the experiments for publicly hosted content can be expressed by the equation, $T_{Exp} = \frac{MS}{\mu_{CPU} - \lambda_{App}}$, where $M \geq 1$. Figure 7 shows the setup for the cache performance studies of accesses generated in M request cycles.

Based on the setup shown in Figure 7, the derivation and practical evaluations of cache performance emanating from scattered requests take into account that of the S possible files that can be specified by each user request with equal probability, $\frac{1}{S}$, there are L files already in the cache if compulsory misses are ignored. Hence, assuming that the M request cycles are sufficient to produce a record of data accesses to all the S files, the probability that a requested data object is found inside the local cache is given by equation,

$$P(L)|(T_{Exp} >> \{\frac{S}{\mu_{CPU} - \lambda_{App}}\}) \approx \left(\frac{L}{S}\right). \qquad (7)$$

As an input parameter the practical validation of cache performance trends, the applied load based on N_{Users} is increased from 10 to 250 in uniform incremental steps as shown in Figure 8. Since the LRU and LFU algorithms proved ineffective in tracking file request patterns that are associated with the File Generator, our use of the cache optimisation techniques in the second practical study is confined to the technique of Random Eviction of least useful data in the cache. Figure 8 also presents three cases of modelled cache performance based on the ratio, $\frac{L}{S}$, which were chosen for comparison. The theoretical performance trends featured in the validations are based on the predefined hit ratios, $\frac{L}{S}$ =0.25, $\frac{L}{S}$ =0.5, and $\frac{L}{S}$ =0.75.

The results from the three scenarios confirm that in the event of data requests predominantly going to publicly hosted content, which all active users are free to access the overall cache performance is independent of load in accord with the theoretical approximation. Another important observation from the graphs in Figure 8 is that for the modelled cache performances of 25 and 50%, the theoretical and measurement results are very similar, with the practical results marginally better than the theoretical estimates in some places for cache hit ratio of 25%. As the size of the local cache is increased to 75% of the remote storage, the practical performance also goes even though it stays within the 70% range. We attribute the lower values of cache hit ratios in the measurements at high cache capacity to a further need for calibrating the number of user request cycles, M, that governs the duration for the measurements to capture the events so that the impact data of the requests to all S files is accurately reflected by practical observations. Despite the discrepancies in the modelled and practical results shown in the graphs, particularly for higher values of hit ratios, the theoretical approximations of cache performance (in terms the respective sizes of local cache and remote storage capacities) is a reliable guide of cache performance for file requests that are spread across publicly available content.

Section "Performance characterisations for concurrent accesses to private and public content" follows the theoretical derivations of cache performance patterns with scenarios where mixed requests are generated simultaneously by users to access both public and private content.

Performance characterisations for concurrent accesses to private and public content

The analysis of simultaneous requests patterns to public and private data considers two cases of cache space allocation, one which features separate cache partitions for private and public data and the other involving the use of a common cache partition that is shared by both types of content. In both cases of cache space assignment, the sizes of input parameters used in the performance analysis remain the same, i.e. N_{Users} is uniformly varied from 10 to 250, while L is equal to 50, and the remote storage space for public data, S, is 200. The list of input and output parameters used in the derivations of cache performance models that are associated with the simultaneous requests of private and public is provided in Table 2.

Data access patterns for content on separate caches

We define separate cache partitions, L_1 and L_2, for private and public data respectively on the local cache storage. The cache partitions are both equal to 50 and the respective probabilities of each active user requesting private and public data are P_1 and P_2 i.e. a generated data request either specifies personal user or publicly available content, which means $P_1 + P_2 = 1$. Figure 9 shows the setup involving data requests going to separately allocated cache spaces.

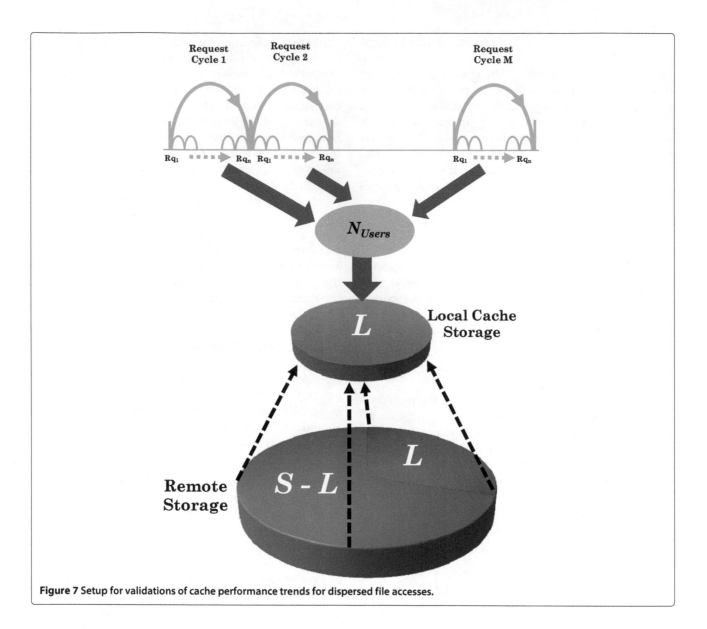

Figure 7 Setup for validations of cache performance trends for dispersed file accesses.

We recall that the local cache hit performance, P_{HitL1}, on the cache partition assigned for private user content, L_1, is given by the expression:

$$P_{HitL1} = \begin{cases} 1 & \text{if } N_{Users} \leq L_1 \\ \dfrac{L_1}{N_{Users}} & \text{if } N_{Users} > L_1. \end{cases} \quad (8)$$

Similarly, the local cache performance, P_{HitL2}, on the cache space that is set aside for hosting public content is given by the expression,

$$P_{HitL2} = \begin{cases} \left(\dfrac{L_2}{S_2}\right) & \text{if } L_2 < S_2 \\ 1 & \text{if otherwise.} \end{cases} \quad (9)$$

Hence, taking into account the preference weights associated with user request patterns to both sets of cached data, the cache hit ratio for private data accesses becomes:

$$P_{HitPrivate} = \begin{cases} P_1 & \text{if } N_{Users} \leq L_1 \\ \left(\dfrac{P_1 L_1}{N_{Users}}\right) & \text{if } N_{Users} > L_1. \end{cases} \quad (10)$$

The cache hit ratio associated with requests to public data is given by equation,

$$P_{HitPublic} = \begin{cases} \left(\dfrac{P_2 L_2}{S_2}\right) & \text{if } L_2 < S_2 \\ 1 & \text{if otherwise.} \end{cases} \quad (11)$$

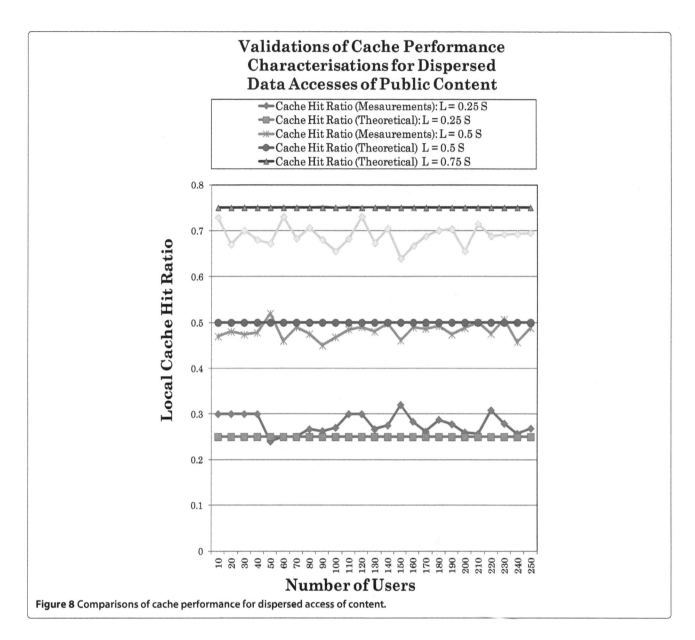

Figure 8 Comparisons of cache performance for dispersed access of content.

The overall cache hit ratio for data accesses over the both cache partitions is then given by the expression,

$$
P_L = \begin{cases} P_1 + \left(\dfrac{P_2 L_2}{S_2} \right) & \text{if } N_{Users} \leq L_1 \\ (\dfrac{P_1 L_1}{N_{Users}}) + \left(\dfrac{P_2 L_2}{S_2} \right) & \text{if } N_{Users} > L_1. \end{cases} \quad (12)
$$

The overall trends for the cache hit and miss ratios associated with the requests to both sets of hosted data are shown in Figures 10 and 11 respectively.

As shown by both Figures 10 and 11, the Private Access Ratios i.e. the preference weights associated with requests to private data, P_1, are varied in uniform steps of 0.1 from 0 to 1. Conversely, the access weights for public data, P_2, vary in reverse order from 1 to 0 for the featured scenarios in the graphs, given that the request events to public

Table 2 Parameters for concurrent requests of private and public data

Parameter	Description
P_1	Probability of Requesting Private Data
P_2	Probability of Requesting Public Data
L_1	Capacity of Cache Partition for Private Data (users)
L_2	Capacity of Cache Partition for Public Data (users)
S_1	Capacity Remote Storage Partition for Private Data (users)
S_2	Capacity Remote Storage Partition for Public Data (users)
$P_{HitPrivate}$	Cache Ratio from the requests of Private Data
$P_{HitPublic}$	Cache Ratio from the requests of Private Data
P_L	Overall Hit Ratio on the Local Cache

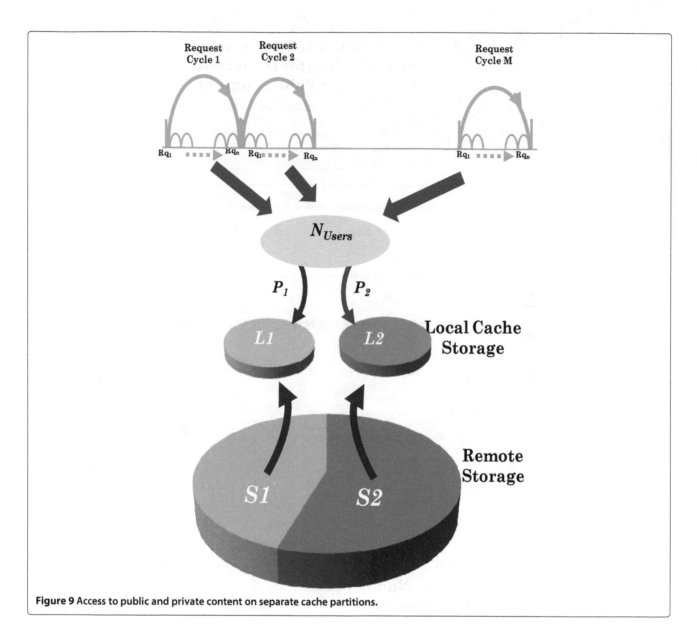

Figure 9 Access to public and private content on separate cache partitions.

and private content are mutually exclusive. Hence, when Private Access Ratio is 0, the cache hit and miss trends solely emanate from requests that are directed at public content. It also follows that when Private Access Ratio is equal to 1, the cache performance complete derives from the requests for private user content. Between the two extremes as P_1 is raised gradually, the cache performance patterns associated with private data requests become more dominant.

It can be deduced from the equation of the overall cache hit ratio, P_L, that the assignment of separate cache partitions provides the ability to isolate and individually control the respective cache performance trends associated with private and public data requests. Thus, within the boundary fixed by P_1, there is the ability in the spilt cache configuration to tune L_1 and fix the cut-off point,

at which cache performance begins to fall exponentially with increase in N_{Users} for requests of private data. Within the bounds of P_2, the cache capacity, L_2, can similarly be adjusted with respect to S_2 to determine the average cache performance associated with the requests of public data.

The trends for overall cache misses, M_L, shown in Figure 11 can have serious QoS implications, should there be considerable delays associated with data retrievals from external source storage whenever requested content is not found in the local cache. If the respective data access times that are experienced in the event of cache hits are also taken in account, the tuning of cache performance can be carried out to deliver output performance that keeps average storage access within SLA thresholds. With the allocation of split caches providing the flexibility of enabling individual adjustments of cache sizes,

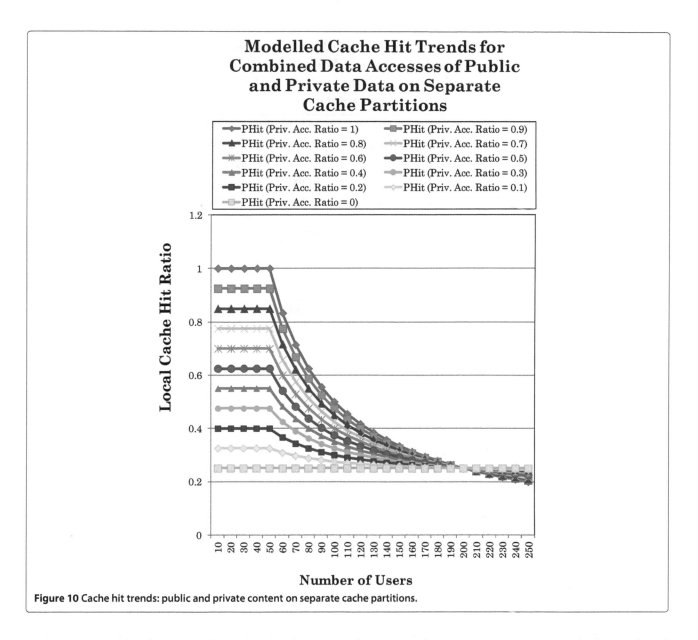

Figure 10 Cache hit trends: public and private content on separate cache partitions.

performance can thus be managed in a way that discriminates between different sets of content according to their desired QoS ratings.

Data access patterns for content on a shared cache partition

We begin the analysis of cache performance trends for mixed data access patterns on a shared cache partition by assigning a value of 50 to the common cache space, L, which is made up of L_1 and L_2 as the component caches for holding the private and public data respectively. The preference weights associated with the data request patterns to L_1 and L_2 are P_1 and P_2. The remote storage capacity for S_2 is set to 200 and the parameter, N_{Users}, for number of active users that generate data requests increases uniformly from 0 to 250. Figure 12 shows the

basic setup for user requests accessing data on a shared cache partition.

Given that the total cache space, L, is divided up between public and data requests, we can express the amount of space allocated to L_1 as follows:

$$L_1 = \begin{cases} P_1 N_{Users} & \text{if } N_{Users} \leq L \\ P_1 L & \text{if } N_{Users} > L. \end{cases} \tag{13}$$

Thus, the cache space for private data is a subset of the data requested by active users according to the proportional factor which is equivalent to probability, P_1, if the number of users does not exceed L. Whenever N_{Users} becomes greater than L, the average space occupied by public data is $P_1 L$. Similarly, the amount of cache

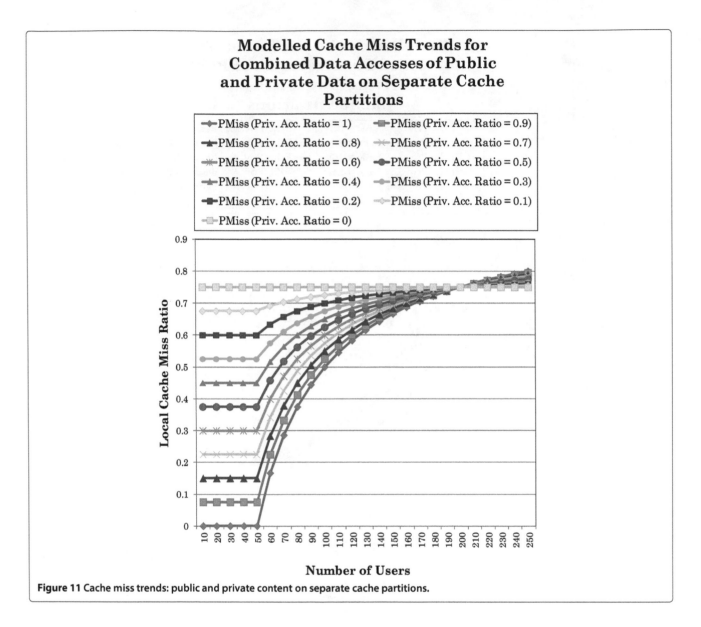

Figure 11 Cache miss trends: public and private content on separate cache partitions.

space, L_2, that is occupied by public data is given by the expression:

$$L_2 = \begin{cases} (L - P_1 N_{Users}) & \text{if } N_{Users} \leq L \\ P_2 L & \text{if } N_{Users} > L. \end{cases} \quad (14)$$

Since S_2 is greater than L, the cumulative requests for public content will inevitably fill all space (equivalent to $L - P_1 N_{Users}$) that is left by public data requests if the number of active users remains lower than L. Once N_{Users} goes beyond the cache capacity, L, the storage space is shared proportionally according to the ratios P_1 and P_2.

The expression for the cache performance associated with private data requests becomes,

$$P_{HitPrivate} = \begin{cases} P_1 & \text{if } N_{Users} \leq L \\ \dfrac{P_1^2 L}{N_{Users}} & \text{if } N_{Users} > L. \end{cases} \quad (15)$$

For the data accesses to public content the cache trends are given by the expression,

$$P_{HitPublic} = \begin{cases} \dfrac{(L - P_1 N_{Users})P_2}{S_2} & \text{if } N_{Users} \leq L \\ \dfrac{P_2^2 L}{S_2} & \text{if } N_{Users} > L. \end{cases} \quad (16)$$

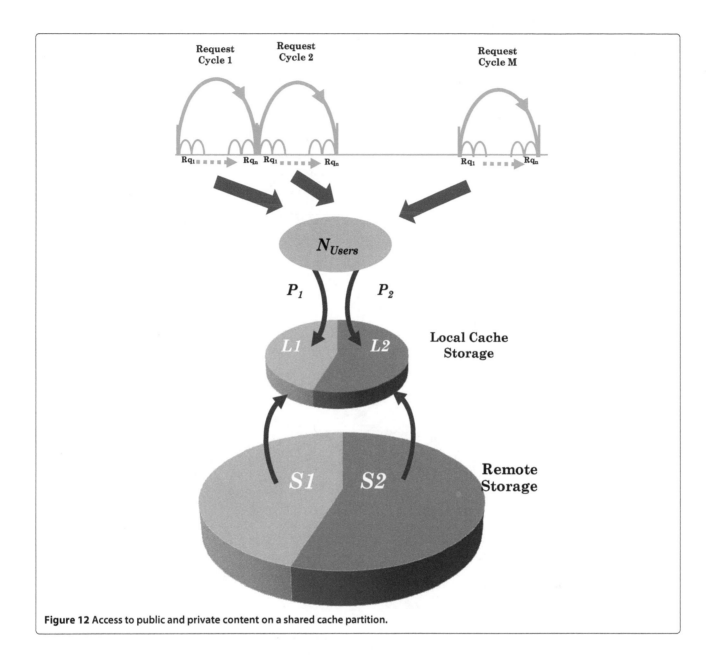

Figure 12 Access to public and private content on a shared cache partition.

From the constituent cache performance trends of the public and private data requests, the overall cache hit ratio is therefore given by the expression,

$$P_L = \begin{cases} P_1 + \dfrac{(L - P_1 N_{Users})P_2}{S_2} & \text{if } N_{Users} \leq L \\[2ex] \dfrac{P_1^2 L}{N_{Users}} + \dfrac{P_2^2 L}{S_2} & \text{if } N_{Users} > L. \end{cases}$$

(17)

Figure 13 shows the overall cache hit trends on a common cache partition as the access weight, P_1, that is assigned for private data is uniformly increased from 0 to 1.

As in the case of separate cache partitions, the cache hit ratios trends for the scenario, $P_1 = 0$, correspond to data requests that are going to completely public content, while that for $P_1 = 1$, applies solely to accesses to private content. Between these two extremes, the cache hit ratios fall more steeply compared to the corresponding scenarios considered for split caches as shown in Figure 12. The rate of performance drops as P_1 is raised from 0.1 to 0.9 is due to limited space on L_1, which is divided up between the two sets of cached content.

The impact of having a shared cache can be further emphasised by Figure 14, which shows the corresponding cache miss ratios as P_1 varies between 0 and 1. Comparisons with Figure 10, which has the family of cache miss

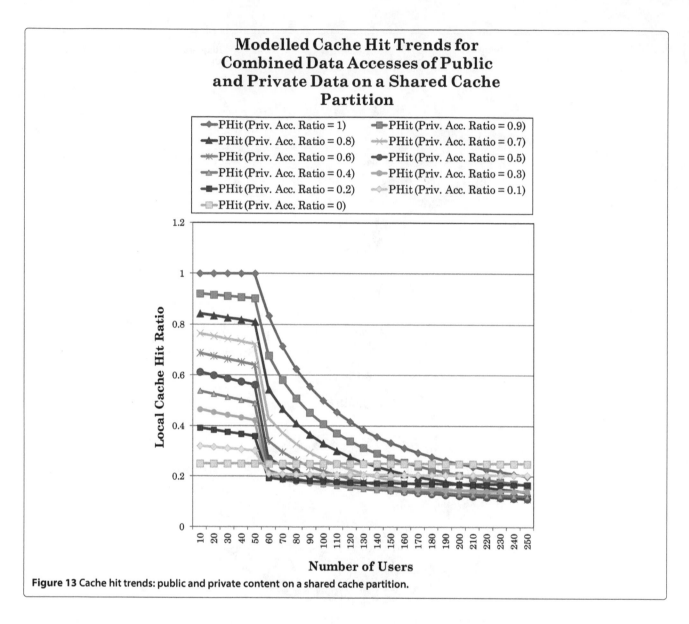

Figure 13 Cache hit trends: public and private content on a shared cache partition.

ratio trends for corresponding scenarios of P_1, reveal that with N_{users} reaching the value of 250, the cache miss ratios associated with the shared cache partition range between 75 and 90% , while those for split cache configuration are between 75 and 80%. The impact of the higher cache misses on overall performance is amplified if the data access operations that are associated with content transfers from external storage are subject to huge delays.

The equations for cache performance trends of private and public data requests are subject to the size of the available space, *L,* in the common cache. As such it is not possible to individually change the storage allocations for given sets of content without affecting other cached datasets. Hence, even though the shared cache configuration is simpler to implement and is less computationally expensive because of having all the cached datasets on a

single global list for cache optimisation, the design does not permit flexible allocation of cache space that would grade various sets of content according their assigned QoS categories.

Discussion

We began the discussion by highlighting the need for having capabilities for scalable solutions in storage cloud domains so that infrastructure-based responses can be achieved for maintaining performance within SLA thresholds in the event of such challenges as increases in user demand or, interruptions to the operating states of the service entities making up the cloud resource fabric. We went on to argue that for SLA-compliant services to be provided consistently over a wide range of load levels, an in-depth understanding of the performance trends associated with storage cache resource

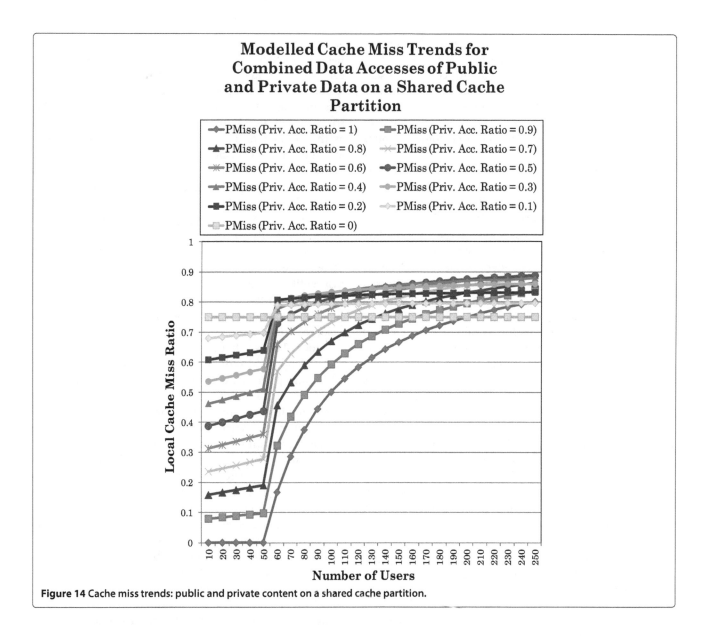

Figure 14 Cache miss trends: public and private content on a shared cache partition.

entities in the cloud infrastructure, is an important foundation on which to base QoS-ready solutions. It was further pointed out that from the performance characterisations of storage cache entities, storage resource management decisions on infrastructure sizing can be made, which are relevant to important stages of resource deployment such as initial roll-outs, short-term expansions to deal with overflow requests, and permanent upgrades.

Theoretical models were proposed for estimating performance trends occurring at individual cache entities as the levels of user demand for content increase. In order to validate the derived theoretical trends, three suites of experiments (based on Random, LFU and LRU eviction policies) were defined for studying the sensitivity of cache performance to applied loads. A noteworthy

observation from the results was that whenever the data request patterns are characterised by rigid affinity to content (i.e. each user accessing only its own data) and with the requested data objects being of comparable popularity, the decay trends for the measured cache hits exhibit high fidelity to the theoretical characterisations. Additionally, the Random Cache replacement algorithm provides better results than the LFU and LRU algorithms, which although still conforming to theoretical estimates, have lower levels of cache hit ratio performance. Thus, the LFU algorithm is more effective if there are distinct categories of data popularity from the users generating the requests. Similarly, the LRU algorithm performs better for cases where the usefulness of cached content is indexed by age, and thus the algorithm is not equipped deal with the even scatter of requests over a wide range of file objects.

Overall, the results for private data requests demonstrate the potential utility of the models for estimating the cache storage needs associated with computing scenarios involving enterprise application routines such as Sales and Distribution (SD), Assembly-to-Order (ATO) or Employee Self-Service Portal (EP-ESS), whereby user requests work with their own sets of customer account data [11].

Another important observation from the results was the confirmation of the validity of trends for the second set of cache performance models that is associated with data requests for wide selections of files [12], where there is loose coupling between users and public content. The cache performance levels in such cases characterised by dispersed requests are independent of the levels of input user load i.e. the local cache hit ratio can be expressed as a function of the respective ratios of the local cache and remote storage capacities, $P_L = \frac{L}{S}$. The accuracy of performance measurements for scattered file requests is based on setting the durations of the observation time window for the experiments long enough to cover data requests to the all the S files kept in the remote storage. Additionally, the measurement results of the three cases of predefined cache performance (corresponding to P_L = 0.25, 0.50 and 0.75) show that the actual values of cache hit ratios obtained from practical investigations are close to the theoretical estimates. However performance from results is slightly lower than the theoretical one when the size of the local cache is increased to $0.75S$. It therefore has to be emphasised that the potential usefulness of second set of characterisations in predicting cache performance trends in scenarios where users interact with public content (to which there is unrestricted access) is subject to durations of the observation time window.

The cache model extensions for the characterisations of concurrent requests to private and public data were developed in Sections "Validations of cache performance trends for user requests of public data" and "Performance characterisations for concurrent accesses to private and public content", the modelled trends derived for mixed requests apply to scenarios of shared and separate storage cache partitions holding the cached content.

Related research

A number of initiatives are being pursued towards maturing performance management capabilities in cloud computing infrastructures so that scalable, secure and reliable IT services can be delivered to computing environments, most of which run business-critical applications. Below, we briefly highlight some of the work that is underway to develop SLA-based strategies for supporting firm guarantees of performance delivery.

In [13], estimates of output performance based on the levels of applied user loads and the mean service rates at the resource entities are used and, from applying the Laplace Stieltjes Transform, the overall response times at each service node in the cloud infrastructure are calculated, with SLA mappings being derived from probability distributions of the calculated response service times. The study in [14] also features use of input parameters such as the number of service requests from the consumers and the service capacities offered by deployed resource entities in developing SLA indices and, a trust model is then obtained for performing predictive estimates of the levels of resource and service availability in the cloud infrastructure. The strategy for SLA enforcement that is presented in [15] categorises workload instances that are despatched to server entities into four basic classes of resource consumption of the processor, memory and disk entities, and from taking into account the service constraints in the cloud infrastructure, the optimisation function determines the number of VM instances of each resource consumption class, which can be hosted by the provider. The work that is presented in [16] features fault tolerant and redundancy techniques for identifying and filtering out compromised resource elements in the infrastructure in order to ensure service availability and continuity in the cloud. Apart from applying redundancy strategies on the matrix-mapped resource collections, the SLA enforcement in [16] also employs predefined performance constraints on the constituent resource entities in the cloud together with integer linear programming methods that eliminate faulty and malicious elements with the greatest likelihood of compromising service quality.

By making high-level considerations regarding the overall resource capabilities in developing strategies for SLA guarantees, the approaches described above thus treat the runtime operations of CPU execution, memory and storage data access as a single composite service functionality, which differs from our work, whose focus is exclusively on establishing internal cache performance trends pertaining to storage access.

The studies in [17-19] have a similar focus to our approach of isolating subsystems of server hardware in order to characterise their resource consumption patterns for SLA and QoS support, the difference being that the strategies presented in all the three contributions consider CPU and memory utilisations associated with processor-bound workloads. Specifically, the strategy in [17] aims to guarantee CPU QoS delivery by overcoming the common problem of runtime interference effects that usually arises when running multiple instances of applications that are derived from virtualisation technologies. The interferences between the active VM application instances are minimised through the control of the working set sizes of allocated memory pages, thereby ensuring predictability of memory fetch times, CPU utilisations and ultimately, processor QoS support. In [18], the standardised metric,

EC2 Compute Unit (ECU), developed by Amazon is used for rating available computing power on various CPU hardware architectures. Based on the ECU metric, thresholds margins can be defined for identifying the resource utilisation levels, at which SLA violations are approached and the reallocation of the CPU resources can be initiated to protect SLA contracts. The framework presented in [19] features a dynamic SLA template that is designed to deal with changing user requirements by mapping consumer requirements to existing capabilities in the cloud infrastructure, with the focus also being on the allocation of processor cores as the primary resource entities of user interest.

In a related contribution on data caching mechanisms featured in [20], models have been developed for cache hit performance, with emphasis however being on the performance of multilevel cache configurations based on hierarchical and cooperative models for data sharing across distributed environments. Another endeavour on developing caching solutions for improve data availability is in the form of the Tuxedo caching framework presented in [21], which is based on the use of protocols to enhance traditional CDN and local caching strategies and thereby ensure that user requests for both personalised and public content are fulfilled incurring minimum latency. While the objectives behind Tuxedo are very similar to the motivations for our work particularly as considered in Section "Performance characterisations for concurrent accesses to private and public content", the approach taken in the former approach is different from ours in that the emphasis of Tuxedo is on an architecture-based solution as opposed to the quantitative analyses for cache performance that we consider in this paper.

Future directions

It has been highlighted that the relative inadequacies of LRU and LFU cache algorithms in the scenarios that were featured in our studies, stem from the inherent bias of the cache optimisation logic to index the usefulness of cached content according to age and popularity respectively. It is therefore necessary to build within our cache algorithms the ability to capture and respond to the complexity in the behaviours of user requests. Hence, one strand of further work will proceed in the direction of establishing and characterising the relevant dynamics affecting the likelihood of repeat requests of cached content based on both popularity and passage of time. A significant part of proposed investigations on this aspect will consider developing strategies for breaking down the cached content into principal categories of popularity (such as High, Moderate and Low popularity) and building time profiles for the request events so that the decay of content popularity is defined as a function of time. The proposed extension will be a further step in the study

of the heterogeneity of data access patterns, which in our current models involves two broad classes of data requests; private and public content requests. From the results of this study, we intend to calibrate the cache replacement algorithms on the basis of hybrid criteria that employ adjustable time windows for rating content value.

The allocation of storage cache space for accessed data in our initial studies was simplified through the choice of uniform file sizes. In the next phase of the study, we will therefore also investigate approaches, by which cached content is classified according file sizes. In working towards the overall estimates of the required cache capacity, it will be important to investigate how to characterise patterns of the variability of the range of all file sizes grouped together within each category.

Another dimension worth exploring in the future work is employing the utilisation of the strategy proposed in [22] to harness the cloud infrastructure as a data gathering and dissemination engine to achieve ready availability of context information in supporting informed caching decisions. The information collection and dissemination technique considered in [22] is predicated on the idea that context data exhibits predominantly temporal trends. Hence, cache optimisation mechanisms (most likely in the form of enhanced versions of the LRU policy) can be developed for characterising the time-related properties of cached items in such a way that their values are indexed and, the eviction and retention of content can then follow formal criteria. An additional aspect of scoring the cached files would determine how to categorise the rates of expiration of cached objects based on the frequency of modifications to original files. Typically, the public content which becomes stale more quickly would be based on volatile updates such as live sports news and business feeds.

As has been highlighted in Section "Experimental facility for validations of cache performance Trends", our experimental scenarios employ the Tier 2 configuration i.e. application executions and data fetch operations are conducted on the same physical server. In the next phase, part of the focus will involve deployments based on the Tier 3 setting, whose configuration is such that application routines and data transfer operations are handled in server entities. Based on the outcome of the experiments conducted so far, we consider network delays that are associated with the transfers of requested data to be the most likely factor that can impact the accuracy of the future experiments. Hence, an important aspect of the work on analysing cache performance in Tier 3 server settings will involve characterisations of the network delays so that the time windows for the measurement epochs are properly calibrated according to prevailing conditions on the data transfer paths such as available bandwidth, propagation and congestion delays. And since our current theoretical models basically apply to standalone cache configurations, the Tier 3 scenarios can also be considered in the context of more complex caching environments based on redundant and hybrid physical deployments. Thus, the follow up work will study of the joint use of network management and replica location services on our infrastructure-monitoring framework in order to characterise service performance profiles associated with wide-area data accesses in cloud environments.

Competing interests
The author declare that they have no competing interests.

Author's contributions
ES and GP designed the basic caching strategies for the experimental studies and the combined data scenarios that were featured in the paper. SM and BS developed the analytical models for characterising the caching scenarios that were considered. AM developed the test cloud infrastructure and the code that was deployed in the User Request, File Manager and Master Storage Virtual Machines. DB and AM helped with the structure and the Introduction of the paper. All authors read and approved the final manuscript.

Acknowledgements
The authors acknowledge support for this work from the Engineering and Physical Sciences Research Council (Grant References EP/G051674/1 and EP/J016748/1). Any views or opinions presented herein are those of the authors and do not necessarily represent those of IU-ATC, their associates or their sponsors.

Author details
[1]Networking and Computing Technologies Laboratory, University of Ulster at Coleraine, Coleraine - BT52 1SA Northern Ireland, United Kingdom.. [2]School of Computing and Information Engineering, University of Ulster at Coleraine, Coleraine - BT52 1SA Northern Ireland, United Kingdom.

References
1. Oracle Inc. Oracle platform for SaaS. http://www.oracle.com/us/technologies/saas/index.html. Accessed 12 December 2012
2. SAP Inc. On-demand solutions from SAP that fit your needs now. http://www.sap.com/solutions/technology/cloud/index.epx
3. Varia J (2010) Amazon Web Services., Architecting for the cloud: best practices, AWS white paper, (January 2010), pp 1–21. https://aws.amazon.com/whitepapers/
4. VMWare Inc. (2010) Architecting a vCloud, technical white paper, version 1.0, pp 1–30. http://www.vmware.com/solutions/cloud-computing/index.html
5. Piech M (2009) Oracle Corporation., Platform-as-a-service private cloud with oracle fusion middleware, oracle whitepaper (October 2009), pp 1–20. http://www.oracle.com/us/technologies/cloud/index.htm
6. VMware Inc. (2010) VMware vSphere - The best platform for building cloud infrastructures. http://www.vmware.com
7. VMware Inc. (2009) vSphere basic system adminstartion VCenter server 4.0, (2009), pp 1–370. http://www.vmware.com
8. Rackspace Hosting, Hosting solutions for business. http://www.rackspace.co.uk/managed-hosting/solutions-for-business/. Accessed 12 December 2012
9. Mozy, Mozy products for business. http://mozy.co.uk/products. Accessed 12 December 2012
10. Eucalyptus Systems, Eucalyptus open source cloud computing infrastructure - an overview, Euclayptus Whitepaper. http://www.eucalyptus.com/. Accessed 12 December 2012
11. Alexa - Site Inforamtion. http://www.alexa.com/siteinfo. Accessed 14 December 2012
12. Finkelstein S, Brendle R, Jacobs D, Hirsch M, Marquard U (2008) The SAP transaction model: know your applications. In: ACM. SIGMOD. Conference
13. Xiong K, Perros H (2009) Service performance and analysis in cloud computing. In: SERVICES '09 proceedings of the 2009 congress on Services - I, Los Angeles, CA, USA, July 6-10, 2009
14. Kim H, Lee H, Kim W, Kim Y (2010) A trust evaluation model for QoS guarantee in cloud systems. Int J Grid Distributed Comput 3(1): 1–10
15. Tordsson J, Montero RS, Moreno-Vozmediano R, Llorente (2012) IM cloud brokering mechanisms for optimized placement of virtual machines across multiple providers. Future Generation Comput Syst 28(2): 358–367
16. Deng J, Huang SCH, Han YS, Deng JH (2010) Fault-tolerant and reliable computation in cloud computing. In: Globecom Workshops (GC Wkshps 2010), Miami Florida (December 2010)
17. Nathuji R, Kansal A, Ghaffarkhah A (2010) Q-Clouds: managing performance interference effects for QoS-Aware clouds. In: Proceeding EuroSys '10 proceedings of the 5th European conference on computer systems, Paris, France, 13-16 April 2010
18. Goiri I, Julia F, Fito JO, Macias M, Guitart J (2010) Resource-level QoS metric for CPU-based guarantees in cloud providers. In: GECON'10 proceedings of the 7th international conference on economics of grids, clouds, systems, and services, Ischia, Italy, August 31, 2010
19. Maurer M, Emeakaroha VC, Brandic I, Altmann J (2012) Cost-benefit analysis of an SLA mapping approach for defining standardized cloud computing goods. In: GECON'10 proceedings of the 7th international conference on economics of grids, clouds, systems, and services. Vol.28, No.1, Jan. 2012
20. Dykes SG, Robbins KA (2001) A viability analysis of cooperative proxy caching. In: IEEE INFOCOM, Anchorage, Alaska, USA, April 2001
21. Shi W, Shah K, Mao Y, Chaudhary V (2003) Tuxedo: a peer-to-peer caching system. In: Intl Conf on Parallel and Distributed Processing Techniques and Applications (PDPTA) 2003
22. Kiani SL, Anjum A, Antonopoulos N, Munir K, McClatchey R (2011) Towards Caching in the Clouds. In: International Workshop on Intelligent Techniques and Architectures for Autonomic Clouds (ITAAC 2011) co-located with 4th IEEE/ACM international Conference on Utility and Cloud Computing (UCC 2011), Melbourne, Australia, 8th December, 2011

2

Experiences in building a mOSAIC of clouds

Dana Petcu[1*], Beniamino Di Martino[2], Salvatore Venticinque[2], Massimiliano Rak[2], Tamás Máhr[3], Gorka Esnal Lopez[4], Fabrice Brito[5], Roberto Cossu[6], Miha Stopar[7], Svatopluk Šperka[8] and Vlado Stankovski[9]

Abstract

The diversity of Cloud computing services is challenging the application developers as various and non-standard interfaces are provided for these services. Few middleware solutions were developed until now to support the design, deployment and execution of service-independent applications as well as the management of resources from multiple Clouds. This paper focuses on one of these advanced middleware solutions, called mOSAIC. Written after the completion of its development, this paper presents an integrated overview of the mOSAIC approach and the use of its various software prototypes in a Cloud application development process. We are starting from the design concepts and arrive to various applications, as well as to the position versus similar initiatives.

Introduction

The story of mOSAIC (Open-source API and Platform for Multiple Clouds) starts in Spring 2009 when its idea emerged. The main challenges for Cloud Computing identified to that moment, as shown in [1,2], were application and data interoperability and portability, governance and management, metering and monitoring, as well as security. In the meanwhile some partial solutions addressing these challenges have proposed, however, according to a recent report [3], these challenges still exist. The key goal of mOSAIC is to offer a solution for application portability and interoperability across multiple Clouds. However, the complete mOSAIC' solution addresses partially also the other challenges, management, governance, and security, as will be revealed in what follows.

The mOSAIC' solution is a result of a multi-national team effort as part of a grant agreement with the European Commission in the frame of FP7-ICT programme [4] (details on the project web site [5]). The implementation has started in September 2010 and the final software was released in March 2013. The promises made in the early stage of development were described in the position paper 'Building a mOSAIC of Clouds' [6]:

1. Design a language- and vendor-agnostic application programming interface for using multi-Cloud resources and Cloud usage patterns.

2. Design a generic agent skeleton for representing various stakeholders, e.g. Cloud vendors and their resources, Cloud users of various types, and a collection of modules that can be used to adapt agent skeleton to support needed functionalities.

3. Design user-centric service level agreements, a Cloud ontology, and mechanisms for dynamic negotiation of resources based on multi-agent technologies and semantic data processing.

4. Build an open-source and portable platform for using Cloud services based on the proposed API and Cloud usage patterns.

5. Build proof-of-concept applications with a special emphasis on data intensive applications.

These scientific and technical goals were related with the time's lack of (a) common programming model for Cloud-oriented applications, (b) of tools for easy deployment of scalable applications and (multi)-Cloud-based services, (c) of standard representation for Cloud resources, (d) of adequate service level agreements and their dynamic negotiation, (e) of application portability due to different APIs for Cloud services from different providers.

A variety of reports on mOSAIC's particular software solutions have been presented at recent scientific conferences and in journal papers. The current paper intends to provide an overview of the full and integrated solution with exhaustive references to literature where details can be found. Therefore the main contribution of this paper consists in the high-level description of the mOSAIC's approach and the answers to the current challenges in

*Correspondence: petcu@info.uvt.ro
[1] Institute e-Austria Timişoara and West University of Timişoara, Timişoara, Romania
Full list of author information is available at the end of the article

the Cloud computing domain by the mOSAIC's technical solutions.

The paper is organized as follows. The first part is a description of the overall mOSAIC's approach for solving the current problems of using multiple Clouds. The second part concerns the mOSAIC's positioning in the landscape of Cloud computing services. The third part is dedicated to a discussion of the possible future developments and improvements.

The mOSAIC's approach

This section explains in details how the mOSAIC solution matches the key scientific and technical goals that were outlined in the introduction.

APIs and patterns

Several open API are already available (like jclouds, libcloud, OpenStack, most of them develop in parallel with mOSAIC) offering a management layer for the resources of same type from multiple Clouds (based on a common denominator of their APIs). However the services are restricted to a specific language (like Java), a specific architectural style (like REST oriented) or specific type of resources (like virtual machines).

Component-based programming

The component model provides a natural abstraction for programming and execution of Cloud applications, since is lightweight and flexible in terms of APIs, according [7]. However, component frameworks that are expected to provide design-time and run-time infrastructures in Clouds are few. A short preliminary analysis of the existing solutions was done for mOSAIC positioning purpose and is reported in [8]. This analysis revealed that a proof-of-concept implementation of a component framework for Clouds only for Java [9] was developed in parallel with mOSAIC.

The mOSAIC's API offers a simple way to develop components which run on the top of its platform. The programming model of mOSAIC is based on using loosely coupled components. A mOSAIC component represents an entity controlled by the user: the entity is configurable, exhibits a well defined behavior, implements application dependent functionalities and exposes them to other components. When an instance of a mOSAIC component runs in a Cloud environment, it consumes hardware or software resources, e.g. state-full resources hosted by Cloud service provider and accessible through dedicated APIs. The communication among moSAIC components takes place through message queues, e.g. using the AMQP [10] protocol or the Amazon's SQS [11].

The mOSAIC's basic component is the *Cloudlet* (first introduced in [12]). A Cloudlet is an event-driven and stateless component whose functionalities do not depend

on the number of its instances at run-time (has a degree of autonomy). The Cloudlets can get automatic support for their life-cycle from the mOSAIC's platform including initialization, configuration and bindings to the needed hardware and software resources. Moreover, Cloudlets should be able to run in a Cloud environment independently from other components. Furthermore, Cloudlets are started, stopped, replaced, or multiplied at run-time for the application performance improvement. Multiple instances of the same Cloudlet are therefore expected to be supported by an application. Consequently, the elasticity concept, specific for Cloud computing, is applied at the level of application in the mOSAIC approach.

The Cloudlets are able to access Cloud services through Connectors. The concept of Connector is introduced to ensure the independence from the Cloud service interfaces. A Connector is a concrete class that abstract the access to Cloud resources and defines the set of events to which the Cloudlet should react; its behavior is similar to a remote procedure call, and it offers the functionality of the common denominator of a certain type of Cloud service. For example, in the mOSAIC library for Java there is only one Connector for key-value stores.

The Connectors access Cloud services using Drivers. The Drivers are implementing the Cloud services interfaces. They can be interpreted as wrappers of native resource APIs or uniform APIs, like OpenStack. These wrappers are able to send and receive messages from the mOSAIC's message queues.

The components of a mOSAIC application can be written in several different languages (Java, Python, Erlang, Node.js) and are able to communicate with each other using a component bus (similar to CORBA's one) and asynchronous communications (as being loosely coupled). In particular, Connectors and Drivers can be written in different languages. However, the Cloudlets that are expressing the behavior of the applications are calling the Connectors – therefore the Connectors are expected to be written in the same language as the Cloudlets (further details are provided in [13]).

A simple example

We assume that a software developer intends to built an application which is able to receive requests from the Web (e.g. an XML file) to perform an analysis of the document (e.g. XML parsing) and to store the results in a Cloud storage.

Such an application will be built easily using a predefined mOSAIC component which manages the HTTP protocol and offers the REST interfaces (the HTTP gateway, *HTTPgw*, in mOSAIC terms), and a Cloudlet that receives the XML files from the gateway, process them, and store the results in the Cloud storage using a key-value store Connector.

Once the application is developed it is possible to deploy it it and use a Cloud storage service offered by a Cloud Provider (e.g. Amazon S3) or a platform's internal component (like Riak-based service). The decision which one should be use can be taken at application deploy time (*not during the development*) and can be even dynamically changed at runtime. Moreover if the application needs to scale-up due to the high number of requests, the developer can just add at runtime new Cloudlet or other component instances to manage the newly incoming requests.

Event-driven programming

mOSAIC's API was designed to be event-driven. There are few implementations of event-driven approaches in Cloud computing, but the most known are Amazon's SNS, Microsoft's Azure, and the open-source Node.js.

The main reasons for such an approach are [14]: avoidance of expensive pooling on Cloud resources; opportunity to deal with an unlimited number of messages; adaptability that is naturally event-driven; rare changes in the state of long-running Cloud applications; integration with Internet of Things.

The event-driven approach has also drawbacks. The application developer needs to write the callbacks and the data cannot be provided with these callbacks due to the access rights. The states of a resource should be well defined to trigger a call to the API by the resource provider. Therefore, a dependence on the provider can be created for the callback. To overcome these problems, mOSAIC has proposed an abstraction layer (Cloudlets and Connectors) that allows the application developer to follow the concepts of event-driven architecture, while the low level components of the platform (Drivers) are treating the cases of demand-driven approach in the connection with the specific Cloud services. An interoperability component of the platform (between the Connectors and Drivers) acts as a proxy between the instances following the two different models of interactions (further details can be found in [15]).

Patterns

Currently, four pattern categories are used in mOSAIC: (1) programming patterns; (2) platform patterns; (3) service usage patterns; (4) application patterns.

The programming patterns are related to 'component-based' and 'event-driven' approaches. The patterns that are supported by the mOSAIC's platform are 'just-in-time-scalability' and 'event-based execution'.

The classical Cloud service usage patterns, as introduced in [16], are: end user to Cloud, enterprise to Cloud, Private Cloud, changing of Cloud vendors, Hybrid Cloud and so on. mOSAIC is mainly supporting the 'changing of Cloud vendors', and partially the 'Hybrid Cloud'.

Basic application patterns that can be used for quick application prototyping in mOSAIC were presented in an early paper [17]. Web, databases or application servers are supported. The proof-of-concept applications developed in the frame of mOSAIC project showed the approach usefulness for scientific applications. Therefore, Cloud related patterns for scientific applications were analyzed in details and are reported in [18].

Cloud agency

Role

The mOSAIC's Cloud Agency is a service for the deployment and execution of mOSAIC application. It is in charge for provisioning, from different providers, a collection of Cloud resources, which fulfill at best the user's requirements, to be consumed by mOSAIC applications.

The selection of the Cloud resources to be consumed is nowadays a challenging task for the developer or user of Cloud applications due to different business models associated with resource consumptions as well as due to the variety of features that the Cloud providers are offering. The IaaS commercial provider is interested in proposing a technological solution that is differentiating it from the others providers. This differences have the drawback of locking the customers as no alternative are provided. Also open source technologies for setting up Private Clouds are not compliant with each other. In this context, the Cloud Agency addresses the interoperability problem by proposing an uniform interface for accessing multiple IaaSs.

In the Cloud computing service market there are thousands of options which are different in terms of characteristics of the service, general terms and conditions and service levels that providers ensure. Their current Service Level Agreements (SLAs) use proprietary metrics that make difficult to evaluate properly each offer and to compare different offers among them. Moreover, the customer must trust twice its provider: because the agreed SLA, and because the provider's proprietary monitoring service. That is why the Cloud Agency aims at advancing the state of art of using the Clouds by providing a decision making support to the user for discovery and decision about the best Cloud solution that satisfies his requirements.

The Cloud customers need to detect under-utilization and overload conditions, and also to take decisions about load balancing and resource reconfiguration. In both the cases it is necessary to dimension the Cloud resource to avoid useless expenses and to not fail to satisfy the service requirements when workloads change dynamically. The Cloud Agency aims at providing a monitoring service that run on IaaS under the control of the customer.

Autonomic optimization of Cloud is widely investigated at provider side, but is not perceived by the customer as its own benefit, because it aims at maximize the provider's utility in terms of utilization of physical resource business improvement. That is why the Cloud Agency approach is based on autonomic agents, which enforce well defined policies to provide the perceived utility to their owners. The user is able to delegate to the Cloud Agency the necessary checks of SLA fulfillment, the monitoring of resource utilization, and, eventually, necessary re-negotiations.

The preliminary concept of the Cloud Agency architecture is detailed in [19], while the implementation layers to support Cloud applications were presented in [20]. The Cloud Agency is a step forward towards the implementation of the recent vision of Autonomic Cloud (as discussed in [21]).

Interfacing

Implemented as a multi-agent system, the Cloud Agency is based on asynchronous messaging as other mOSAIC software prototypes. The message-passing architecture was exposed in [22].

The Cloud Agency can act as a standalone and independent component or as an integrated platform component. In the first case it can be used to book Cloud resources and eventually monitor and reconfigure them (scale up, scale out, change providers), without the need of other mOSAIC components. Several user-friendly and programmatic interfaces can be used for interaction (a list and their descriptions can be found in [23]). In the second case, the Cloud Agency offers services to the core components of the platform (e.g. in the case of reconfiguration at application level). A RESTful interface can be used for the interaction [24]. It is compliant with OCCI.

While multi-agent based Cloud management architectures or frameworks were proposed before mOSAIC (like in the proposal exposed in [25]), we consider that mOSAIC's Cloud Agency is the most complete implementation of the concepts that has been tested in the context of complex scientific and commercial applications.

Resource management: provisioning and monitoring

The Cloud Agency provisions resources which should be consumed by the applications. Through its interfaces, detailed in [26], the Agency Client can start a Call-for-Proposal, based on a component description of the application and the policy specifications (a HTTP POST message embedding an SLA is sent to the Agency). The availability of a result triggers an event (using a HTTP POST message), after which the Cloud Agency Client is able to accept or reject the proposal.

The brokering of the best collection of Cloud resources has been modeled as a multi-criteria optimization problem, with hard and soft constraints that can be included by the user in the Call-for-Proposals, as it is described in [27]. With regards to a computing service, such constraints can

be required for service properties, like CPU architecture, minimum amount of memory, CPU speed, I/O speed or number of cores. The level of the service availability can be set over a threshold. Multiple objectives can be defined by the user to choose the cheaper proposal and/or to optimize the performance of I/O-bound or memory-bound application.

Beyond the provisioning role, the Cloud Agency has also other resource management functionalities, like monitoring, that is related to the parameters specified in SLAs (monitorinf the quality of service). Details about this role implementation can be found in [28,29].

Vendor modules

A Cloud provider offer is represented in a brokering or negotiation process by a Vendor Module; details about the module architecture and interaction with the Cloud Agency were exposed in [30]. A simple template was designed to offer a mechanism for new Cloud providers to connected their services to the Cloud Agency; the template was first documented in [31].

Until now mOSAIC' software repository includes Vendor Modules for more than ten Public Clouds. Among these mOSAIC supports well known providers like Amazon, Rackspace [32], and GoGrid [33], as well as European Cloud providers including Flexiant [34] (UK), CloudSigma [35] (Switzerland), NIIFI [36] (Hungary), Arctur [37] and Hostko [38] (Slovenia), latest two using VMware's vCloud [39], respectively OnApp [40]. Moreover, Private Clouds built by using open-source technologies, like Eucalyptus [41], OpenNebula [42], CloudStack [43], or OpenStack [44], can be also represented in the brokering process by their corresponding Vendor Modules and managed by the Cloud Agency's uniform interface.

User-centric SLA management and dynamic negotiation
SLA management

Service Level Agreements (SLAs) are the basics of a common language for agreements between the Cloud clients and the Cloud service providers. Due to the self-service approach, typical for Cloud computing, a SLA for a Cloud service has from user perspective a relevant role in defining what the service effectively grants. mOSAIC supports SLA both at brokering level and at API level. In the first case, SLAs are used for the brokering mechanisms through the Cloud Agency and through a SLA client with respect to provider's offer. In this second case, mOSAIC acts as an SLA provider: the offered services are enriched with SLAs.

The API offers to the application developer a framework which helps in building custom SLA, as well as in seamless integration of their management in service provisioning. At state of art few frameworks exists that offers such kind of functionalities: the one produced by SLA@SOI [45-47], which proposed a solution for building SLA managers to be integrated in service oriented architectures, or WSAG4j [48] which is a Java library compliant with the WS-Agreement standard (that defines protocol and format for SLA representation and management). Such frameworks are complex and expected to be integrated by Cloud providers: SLA are defined by the provider and the users can access only a set of predefined templates.

The SLA management in mOSAIC is considered to be different from such predecessors in its concept: the main goal of mOSAIC' SLA framework is to enable a developer to easily integrate a single application with an SLA life cycle, so instead of offering a single and static general purpose solution for SLA management for any application, a set of micro-functionalities is offered to be integrated with the application in order to build up a dedicated solution for the application developer problem. Due to the component-based approach of the API, it is possible to build up applications enriched with user-oriented SLA management, from the very early development stages. Example of such microfunctionalities are the *SLAgw* which offers a REST-based interface to submit and sign SLAs, the *SLAstore* which maintain the SLA life cycle or the *SLApolicy* which is adopted to automate the enforcement of SLA policies.

Following such approach SLAs can be defined both by the developers (offering SLA templates like with other solutions) or defined by the users (following the standard WS-Agreement format); in such latter case it is up to the application to parse and eventually accept or refuse the submitted SLA. mOSAIC' SLA framework offers the tools to access the submitted request and templates for building custom *decision components*, which have the role of making decisions on the basis of the SLA submitted. Such user-centric service level management is further discussed in details in [49].

Note that the SLA parameters to be supported in such solution are strictly dependent on the application and their management is delegated to the application developer. The SLA framework was applied further for the management of security-based SLA (in [50-53]) and has been integrated in simulation engines able to predict the evolution of the developed application [54,55].

SLA-based brokering and negotiations

The mOSAIC's brokering mechanism is an intermediary between the resource consumers and the resource providers. The best SLA from the point of view of consumer is identified [56]. The policies that can be used are presented in [57], the basic one being the 'lowest cost'. SLA-based brokering mechanisms for 'lowest cost' strategy were detailed in [58].

Exploiting the event-driven architecture, a SLA condition violation triggers an event that can lead to a reconfiguration. A reconfiguration mechanism was therefore conceived, and it is based on rules and a reasoner [59].

Assuming that the Cloud providers are willing to negotiate the costs of the resources, a more complex mechanism with stages for negotiations can be conceived, as the one presented in [60].

Semantic processing and ontology
Semantic engine

The Semantic Engine is a mOSAIC component helping the user in selecting APIs components and functionalities needed for building new Cloud applications as well as in identifying the proper Cloud resources to be consumed. It introduces a new level of abstraction over the Cloud APIs, by providing semantic based representation (in the OWL language of the Semantic Web) of functionalities and resources, related by properties and constraints. The detailed architecture of the solution is presented in [61].

Using the Semantic Engine the developer of Cloud applications can semantically describe and annotate the developed components, specify application domain related concepts and application patterns, potentially using application domain ontologies, as explained in details in [62].

The Semantic Engine overcomes the syntactical differences between Cloud services, resources or their programming models. Automatic analysis of Cloud Vendor APIs is therefore possible, as demonstrated in [63]. Moreover, the semantic representation of Cloud APIs combined with automated algorithmic concept recognition in object-oriented code, augmented with structural based matchmaking techniques, can be a strong basis for porting existing applications towards Clouds [64].

The semantic techniques are used for describing application requirements. The Semantic Engine infers the infrastructural requirements from the application description and from other information, and produces a vendor agnostic SLA template [65].

Cloud ontology

While several Cloud ontologies were developed before mOSAIC (like the one proposed in [66]), the mOSAIC's one is built upon existing standards and proposals analysis through annotation of documents, as described in depth in [67]. It is used in the mOSAIC's semantic processing.

The mOSAIC's Cloud ontology has been developed in OWL. It has been populated with instances of Cloud provider APIs. The knowledge base can be extended with new Cloud provider APIs in the future. The initially proposed ontology was first exposed in [68]. Later on it was augmented with services specific terms – a list of enhancements is presented in [69].

Integration platform

For the purpose of this paper, the collection of individual components that represent mOSAIC's proof-of-concept prototype solutions are depicted in Figure 1. Individual components, like API implementations, application developing tools, vendor modules and so on are part of the integration platform (named here the mOSAIC's PaaS).

Core components of the software platform

Core components are aiming to enable the run-time and deployment functionalities offered by the platform. These include: mOS, Deployer, Container, Components-of-the-Shelf (COTS) and Drivers. They are responsible for the platform control, scheduling, scaling, monitoring, application deploying and so on.

mOS is a customized Linux kernel running in virtual machines. It is used to host and control the platform and the application components. The Deployer is a core component which deploys software modules on mOS:

the packaged component is retrieved by the Deployer from the named location and installed into an appropriate execution environment inside the instantiated Virtual Machines. A Container is a component which hosts Cloudlets, and is responsible for meeting the requirements of elasticity and fault tolerance. The Drivers access specific API of external Cloud services, and are built, for example, for message queue mechanisms like RabbitMQ [70], for key-value stores provided by Amazon S3 [71] or Riak [72], or for distributed file system HDFS [73].

The functionality of the core components was described for the first time in [74]. Aspects like reliability or fault-tolerance support are treated in later papers like [75].

Commercial off-the-shelf components

A number of software components were adapted, so that they can interoperate with the mOSAIC platform and facilitate seamless application development and deployment. Examples of components off-the-shelf (COTS) that

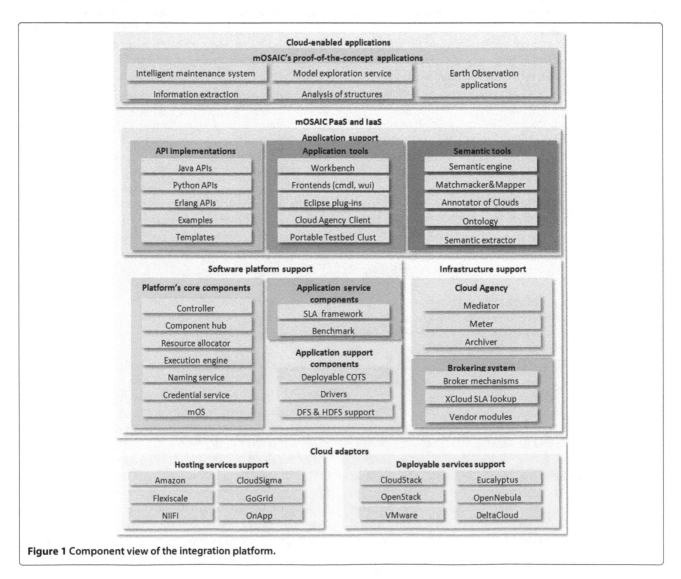

Figure 1 Component view of the integration platform.

are currently available are: RabbitMQ Server, Riak Server, CouchDB server [76], Jetty web application server [77], MySQL server.

In mOSAIC, COTS are viewed as Cloud software resources, based on open source technologies and reusable. These components are deployed as any other component and can be managed, monitored, and accessed via specific Drivers.

Application development and deployment tools

Several tools are offered to enable the seamless development of new applications or the deployment of the existing applications. Eclipse plug-ins, for example, allow the development, deployment, debugging and control of the components written in Java. A Web interface and a command line interface are available to monitor the status of the deployed components (including analysis of the logs) and to control the life-cycle of the running applications. Configuration tools and editors are provided so that, for example, it is possible to build Call-for-Proposals, which may be directly submitted to the Cloud Agency.

The Portable Testbed Cluster (PTC) is a specific component that allows for application testing on the developer's desktop computer. The PTC simulates a Cloud environment using VirtualBox [78]. Its also uses a simple resource allocator, a credential service (which stores the credentials for a specific user for a specific Cloud provider), and the storage of the application components in a Web accessible location. Through its graphical interface the PTC allows the seamless movement of the locally developed application into a Public or Private Cloud.

Open-source and portability of the integrated platform

A large part of the integrated platform is offered as open-source in the mOSAIC's Bitbucket collection [79]. Tables 1 and 2 map the components to the corresponding repositories. The open source part makes it possible to design and execute a variety of Cloud applications.

The platform is theoretically deployable on any Linux-based virtual machine. mOS needs to be first installed to make available the core components. For several providers (e.g. Amazon, Flexiant), virtual machine images, with mOS already installed on top, are publicly available.

The fact that the mOSAIC's platform is deployable makes the difference from other PaaS, like Google Application Engine [80] or Microsoft Azure [81]. An open-source and deployable PaaS, developed in the same time with mOSAIC, is the VMware's Cloud Foundry [82]. Compared with this one, an advantage is the complete openness of the mOSAIC's API.

Platform-as-a-Service characteristics

As discussed earlier, by using mOSAIC, the developer of a Cloud application can postpone the selection of a Cloud infrastructure provider, from the development to the deployment phase. Through the usage of the application tools, a seamless deployment of the application in various Public Clouds is possible after its development and debugging in a Private Cloud or on a local computer. This is more than a Platform-as-a-Service can currently offer – usually the application is deployed immediately on the infrastructure that the PaaS owner provides.

A classical PaaS is not exposing the infrastructure services that are used, while in mOSAIC its user is aware and able to control the resource services. From this point of view mOSAIC distinguishes from other PaaS, as being a portable and lightweight management software for IaaS.

Proof-of-concept applications

The concept of a mOSAIC Cloud application

A mOSAIC compliant application is built from loosely coupled components. Its execution is expected to have no limits in time. It may be expected that some of the components would be elastic, i.e. able to scale up and down in number. The most common cases of Cloud applications are Web applications, which fully fit into this behavioral model. However, the mOSAIC API and platform are suitable for building and deploying also other applications which can have the same behavior.

There are two basic scenarios of using the mOSAIC set of solutions:

1. Developing a new application from scratch. In this case the developer has the possibility to use most of the software tools provided by mOSAIC, starting with the API implementation and the application tools. The Semantic Engine can be used to find proper design patterns. Application tools can be used to prepare a Call-for-Proposal for the Cloud Agency and to approve one of its responses. Software platform services are responsible to deploy, control and monitor the executing application.
2. Migration of an existing application. In this case the application owner may be interested in finding a proper place to deploy the application, and the Cloud Agency is the main tool which is used in the process. The application owner may use the application tools to properly describe the application and to make a Call-for-Proposal to the Cloud Agency. Only a part of the platform is used to control the application after its deployment.

Benefits of using mOSAIC

The main reason of using the mOSAIC solution may be its vendor-agnosticity. The application developer and owner can select at run-time the Cloud services to be consumed (usually this decision need to be made at design phase).

Table 1 Open-source codes in Bitbucket repository (Part I)

Component	Description	Sub-repository
API implementations		
Java API	Provides the developer with an asynchronous API for managing a customized Component and allowing the access to various data sources and backends	Mosaic-java-platform
Python API	Similar with Java API, but for Python	Mosaic-python-platform
Erlang	Tools for Erlang	Mosaic-erlang-tools
NodeJS	NodeJS implementation	nodejs-libraries
DFS Java Connector	Java Connector for distributed file systems	Mosaic-java-connectors-dfs
Realtime feeds	Allows interested users to receive live updates of various ATOM feeds, via a Web interface	Mosaic-examples-realtime-feeds
Application tools		
Workbench	A set of functionalities implemented inside the EclipseRCP that permits to have a fully functional Eclipse workbench to work with the mOSAIC platform	Mosaic-workbench
Frontends	Allow the user to interact with the actual tool implementations (the backends) via various interfaces like CLI (Command Line Interface) or graphical UI's	Mosaic-node-wui
Eclipse plugins - Editors	Provides the end user a way to edit the configuration files in a completely visual way	Mosaic-workbench
CA Connector	Cloud Agency Connector	Mosaic_ca-connectors
Portable Testbed Cluster	Local virtual cluster environment that simulates a IaaS	ftp.info.uvt.ro/mosaic/ptc/
Application service components		
SLAgw	SLA REST interface	Mosaic-java-SLAgw
SLA-components	SLA storage management component	components-SLA
Benchmark-SLA	SLA Policy Component	components-benchmarks
Benchmarks	Java benchmarks	Mosaic-java-benchmarks
Vendor modules (in mosaic-vendormodule-)*		
Amazon	Amazon vendor module	-amazon
CloudSigma	CloudSigma vendor module	-cloudsigma
Eucalyptus	Eucalyptus vendor module	-eucalyptus
Flexiscale	Flexiscale vendor module	-flexiscale
GoGrid	GoGrid vendor module	-gogrid
NIIFI	Vendor module for Hungarian IaaS	-niifi
OpenNebula	OpenNebula vendor module	-opennebula
OpenStack	OpenStack vendor module	-openstack
PTC	Module for mOSAIC's PTC	-ptc
VMware	VMware 's vCloud vendor module	-vmware

A side effect is the possibility to migrate applications from one Cloud provider to another. Therefore mOSAIC can be used to port applications between Clouds. Other reasons for using mOSAIC may be more technical:

1. Ability to ensure the elasticity at component level (usually done to a lower level of granularity, at virtual machines level).
2. Integration in one set of solutions of application development tools with deployment and control tools, as well as with Cloud brokering mechanisms.

3. Open-source technology that allows extensions as needed for special applications or embedding of other technologies.
4. Deploy-ability that allows to use on-premises resources in development phase and to build Private or Hybrid Clouds enabled applications.

Demo applications for the API usage

Simple applications, like the 'Hello world', producer-consumer, ping-pong messaging and so on, are provided for the Java implementation of the API. The example

Table 2 Open-source codes in Bitbucket repository (Part II)

Component	Description	Sub-repository
Platform's core components		
Controller	Allows the developer to observe and control the running components (either Cloudlets, Drivers, Resources, etc.)	Mosaic-node
Component hub	Intermediates communication between the components, and other various needed services (eg. logs)	Mosaic-node
Resource allocator	Resource provisioner based on existing credentials	Included in PTC
Execution engine	Container: Component responsible for instantiating linux containers (LXC) from mosaic bundles (containing all required data for running an application)	Mosaic-execution-engine
	Agent: Running inside the Containers providing application setup, startup and monitoring	Mosaic-execution-engine-agent
Naming service	Allows the registration of new components and their discovery by other components	Mosaic-node
Deployer	A Python RPC implementation based on JSON-RPC2, providing introspection, Unix socket based protocol, standard Http protocol support and a simple CLI application implementing the protocol	mjsrpc2
Packager	Packaging utilities and repositories	Mosaic-packages-repositories
Scheduler & Scaler	Scheduling and scaling components	Mosaic-scheduler
Credentials service	Provides secure access to various credentials or secret tokens needed by various libraries or components to access external resources	Mosaic-credentials-service
mOS	mOSAIC operating system: the system includes the platform's core services	Mosaic-mos
Deployable COTS and Drivers		
RabbitMQ component	Customized variant of RabbitMQ which makes it behave like a managed component	Mosaic-components-rabbitmq
Riak component	Customized variant of Riak which makes it behave like a managed component	Mosaic-components-riak-kv
CouchDB component	Customized variant of CouchDB which makes it behave like a managed component	Mosaic-components-couchdb
HTTP Gateway component	Intermediates HTTP requests between clients on the Internet and components handling those requests. Provides routing and load balancing	Mosaic-components-httpg
mHTTP Gateway component	Routes HTTP messages on queue and enable access to a key value store. Renders HTML pages	Mosaic-components-mhttpgw
AMQP driver component	Message Queue driver for the AMQP protocol	Mosaic-java-platform
Riak driver component	Key value driver for the Riak component	Mosaic-java-platform
HDFS driver component	Distributed File System driver for Hadoop	Mosaic-java-drivers-hdfs
MySQL component	A component for handling (starting/stopping) a MySQL database engine	Mosaic-components-mysql

applications as well as various Cloudlet templates are available in the open-source repository.

A more complex application that combines COTS and developed Cloudlets, is a so-called real-time-feed application. It is small a RSS feed alerter. A classical implementation supposes a poll mechanism that constantly fetches content and makes a comparison with the previous version of the retrieved content to see what is new. On contrary, the demo application implements a push method which identifies the changes and announces them to the event listeners. It uses Twitter' streams of updates to subscribed applications. A first-time description is available in [83].

Proof-of-concept scientific and commercial applications
In the context of mOSAIC project, a variety of applications were developed. These include:

1. an Earth observation application where IaaS is procured for processing satellite data in emergency situations (e.g. earthquakes);

2. an Intelligence Maintenance System allowing maintenance of devices from different industrial scenarios through early diagnosis of faults in critical components and real-time monitoring of key variables;

3. a Model Exploration Service, an online service to run agent-based simulation, requiring scalability;

4. a port to the Cloud of a legacy application for the information extraction from scientific papers;

5. a port to the Cloud of an engineering application for analysis of structures under static loading, with the intention to make it available on the Internet without the need for special licenses or environmental settings.

The Earth observation application prototype dealing with big sets of large-sized data is based on GMTSAR, an open source processing system. It uses the mOSAIC Cloud Agency as independent component for the provisioning of computational resources to create Virtual Clusters to run an OpenGIS Web Processing Service server and a Hadoop framework. The main benefit of using the mOSAIC approach is related to vendor-agnosticity. The prototype is described in [84].

The Intelligent Management System intends to manage easily and rapidly large amounts and continuous streams of information. It has been written using the mOSAIC API specifications. Two main groups of components are used: components provided by the platform (message queues, storage systems, HTTP gateway, etc) and specific components implemented as Cloudlets (for sensor data management, knowledge extraction dispatcher, etc). The main benefits of using mOSAIC are: the elasticity of the application depending on the required computation capacity, and the usage of fault tolerance features. A preliminary description is provided in [85].

The Model Exploration Service is an online service to run agent-based simulations in the Cloud. Cloud resources are used to run large parameter sweeps of the models. The initial application has already run using Amazon's AWS. The porting of the application by applying the mOSAIC approach has not involved only the change of calls from the Amazon API to the mOSAIC API. The internal architecture of the application was changed to adopt mOSAIC design principles (the Cloudlet model) to facilitate scalability, portability and autonomous reconfiguration. By avoiding vendor lock-in, the new version of the application can be moved across 'Cloud borders', or the application can be Multi-Cloud in the sense that certain parts run on different provider infrastructures. The application architecture was first presented in [86].

Information extraction from scientific papers is a part of the ReReSearch project that aims to build a knowledge base about research. It is a computationally expensive task and, as the number of papers to be processed varies considerably in time, there is a need for elasticity of the Cloud (the preliminary study [87] lists the requirements). The legacy Python code implementing the extraction algorithms was split into components and wrapped into Cloudlets. These Cloudlets, managed by the mOSAIC platform, make the application elastic and portable. The Cloudified extractor is exposed as a RESTful web service which can be used as needed by ReReSearch control system. Implementation details are exposed in [88].

The Analysis of Structures under Static Loading application is based on a specific Finite Element formulation, which allows the modeling of a desired structure by beam elements. It is based on the NoDeK software which is written in Matlab and used by small number of construction engineers, due to the required Matlab licenses for running the simulation. The application has scalability problems and its user-friendly interface could be considerably improved. There are several reasons to use Cloud computing technology, e.g. offering the application as a service has the target of widening the customer base. The reasons of selecting mOSAIC is related to the expectations of faster calculation in Clouds than on the local desktops, as well as to deal with the dynamic change in the number of concurrent users. The design of the Cloudified version of the application is available in [89]. Matlab-based Cloudlets were designed and are presented in further details in [90]. The use of Semantic Engine usage in the development phase of the application is exposed in [91].

Benchmarking

A mOSAIC application is developed without taking into account the target provider, however when the application needs to run and consume resources, the choice of the infrastructure provider may significantly affect the application performances and costs of using the infrastructure. The evaluation and prediction of such performances for applications is a complex task, due for example, to the elasticity offered by Cloud resources, or the high number of layers involved.

In order to face the problem of choosing appropriate infrastructure provider, mOSAIC provides a Benchmarking Framework. The framework contains a set of components that can be used in order to setup a custom benchmark which measures the performances of the target application under well known workloads. Such benchmarks are built "ad-hoc" for each different application, even if a set of stable application for common resources and application are available and can be used as kernel benchmark to compare different providers [92]. Moreover, through the adoption of simulation techniques it is possible to use benchmark results to predict the behavior of application in different execution conditions, as proposed and demonstrated in [93].

Scientific applications support

While being partially an open-source solution, it is expected that mOSAIC is interesting especially for the academic communities. As pointed above, mOSAIC has prove its utility for several scientific applications with different requirements. Therefore, the opportunity for mOSAIC to be a science facilitator was investigated recently in [94]. An early study of migration from Grid to Cloud using mOSAIC concepts is provided in [95] for a platform intended for high education activities in Earth observation. The support for scientific legacy applications through self-configuration is exposed in [96]. For the particular case of engineering application, a comprehensive study can be found in [97].

Beyond the promises

Security

Security is a critical issue for the Cloud adoption. While mOSAIC has not promised initially to deal with this topic, in order to offer a complete solution, the problem of security in multiple Clouds was studied in order to define, develop and adopt a mOSAIC-specific security approach. Taking into account the target of mOSAIC for multiple Clouds, the available solutions for Cloud Federations were analyzed in deep in [98], establishing the basic requirements. The research activities acquired experiences from previous work related to Cloud and Grid integrations, as exposed in [99]. The main security problem that was treated is related to the access control solutions, as presented in [100]. The mOSAIC's SLA framework was integrated into an automated access control mechanism for the Cloud and Grid, as proved in [53]. The FP7 project SPECS (Secure Provisioning of Cloud Services based on SLA management [101]), starting in Autumn of 2013, will continue to enhance the mOSAIC's SLA framework.

Due to the Cloud elasticity and auto-scalability features, denial of services was considered one major threat. Therefore denial of service attacks, specially targeted to Cloud systems, were were studied in [50,52]. A mOSAIC based solution for protecting Cloud applications against such attacks was proposed in [51]. Finally, a special service was designed based on SLAs: Intrusion tolerance as a Service [102].

Another research direction considered the secure authentication negotiation in Cloud. The first results are exposed in [103].

Governance

Cloud governance comes as the next development step after Cloud management. It provides the ability to set policies within the environment in order to ensure the system's wide security, privacy and compliance. It is provide also the business level missing in Cloud management solutions. While the Cloud management is providing an execution environment, according [104], the Cloud governance is in charge of decision making in order to achieve objectives that meet its customers' needs.

As shown in [105] the multi-agent systems are fit to build a Cloud governance solution due to the autonomous nature, fault tolerant behavior and ability to self-organize. Therefore the mOSAIC which is based partially on multi-agent systems provides a convenient environment to study the merge of Cloud management and Cloud governance. To do so, the requirements in order to achieve Cloud governance in mOSAIC were established in [106], most importantly being the ones related to service lifecycle control and governance bus.

Cloud service lifecycle in a Multi-Cloud needs to take into account the distribution of services across different provider sites and the ability of services to scale. The core aspects of a service lifecycle, including service template, offering, contract, provisioning service, runtime maintenance, and end of service, are extended in the mOSAIC's governance architecture, first time presented in [107].

A Cloud governance bus needs to handle messages, security, exceptions, protocol conversion and to provide an adequate level of quality of services. The bus proposed in [108] implements enterprise integration patterns as well as data integration services which enables easy access to datastores.

Particular attention was given in mOSAIC to the data services as part of the proof-of-concept applications which are dealing with big data (static and streaming). Data-stores and the appropriate services were studied and developed in conjuction with the mOSAIC's Cloud governance solution [109,110]. Another issue that was treated in the same context is the security of the data [111].

The Cloud governance can lead to an unitary ecosystem, where applications can be easily created, managed, discovered and can easily interact one another. This is aligned with the idea of InterCloud and Cloud Blueprint, introduced in [112]. The grounds for such an ecosystem based on mOSAIC's approach were put in [113].

Resource management: scheduling and application monitoring

Scheduling mechanisms are widely used in distributed systems. However the particularities of Clouds impose a reconsideration of these mechanisms. In order to come with a practical offer, the scheduling problem in Clouds and Multi-Clouds was studied. An initial proposal for the particular case of workflows and based on multi-agent systems was presented in [114]. Starting from this proposal and exploiting the capacity of multi-agent systems for regeneration, a self-healing scheduling mechanism was later on presented in [115].

A large category of Cloud applications are long-running and their high availability is essential. In this context and taking into account the design of mOSAIC application based on components, in [116] is proposed a scheduling mechanism of replicated components aiming to reach the objective of highly availability despite multiple faults in Multi-Cloud. Another scheduling mechanism based on cost constraints was presented in [117], while a novel P2P scheduling scheme has been introduced in [118].

Monitoring services are usually referring to the infrastructure delivery indicators and are in relationship with service level agreements and quality of services. However, the user is highly interested in the behavior of particular applications deployed in Clouds. Therefore an important topic should be the Cloud application monitoring. Taking into account the component based architecture of the mOSAIC applications (including the communication system as a component), the component monitoring can be considered. This approach for the monitoring services was first presented in [119].

Model-driven engineering

In mOSAIC a Cloud application consists of loosely coupled components, which in particular can wrap legacy software. In this context, the paper [120] investigates the possibilities to introduce a model-driven architecture which support composition, customization, flexibility, maintenance and reusability of Cloud application components in the particular case of scientific and engineering applications. The approach is illustrated through the design and operation of the application for analysis of structures under static loading.

A methodology, named MetaMORP(h)OSY, that uses model-driven engineering and model transformation techniques to analyse Cloud services was introduced in [121]. Due to the complexity of the systems to analyse, when modeling profiles are built with MetaMORP(h)OSY, the mOSAIC Ontology is used as being able to specify Cloud domain-related properties. Following the methodology, a proof-of-concept for a particular Cloud use case is provided in [122].

Related projects, prototypes or applications
Related projects

mOSAIC has a strong relationship with two national projects: the Italian Cloud@Home [123] and the Romanian AMICAS [124].

The primary goal of Cloud@Home is to implement a volunteer Cloud, by which both the commercial/business and the volunteer/scientific viewpoints coexist. Several topics that are treated by Cloud@ Home and are not primary targets to mOSAIC have lead to common proposals. Two topics are in this context relevant: performance management exposed in [125], and quality of services exposed in [126]. Moreover the SLA-based mechanisms for brokerage are common to mOSAIC and Cloud@Home [127].

CHASE [128], Cloud@Home's Automatic Service Engine is designed to optimize the scheduling of virtual machines in a Cloud environment based on the a performance prediction service and a forecast service.

The primary goal of AMICAS is to offer a solution for Automatic Clouds. Opposite to mOSAIC which is targeting the Cloud users, AMICAS is targeting the Cloud providers, intending to offer them an easy manageable middleware (Cloudware) for Multi-Cloud. It starts from the mOSAIC's software platform and enhances it with facilities of interest to Cloud providers. An important topic that is tackled by AMICAS, using the mOSAIC experimental platform, is the programmability of services for multiple Clouds. The steps to reach a high level of programmability were discussed in [129], while the programmatic management of services from multiple Clouds using mOSAIC was described in [130]. Another subject is the auto-scaling mechanisms, essential in Cloud computing environment. Currently most of such mechanisms that are used by Cloud providers are centralized. Taking into account the perspective of the Multi-Cloud, such centralized approach is not appropriate. A decentralized auto-scaling mechanism was therefore proposed in [131] for the case of homogeneous systems, and was extended for the heterogeneous systems in [132]. Theoretical analysis of the background algorithm correctness is presented in [133].

mOSAIC's software platform is used as a Multi-Cloud resource management middleware in another current project funded by the European Commission: more precisely, it plays the role of run-time environment in the model-driven engineering project named MODAClouds [134]. Its role in the architecture is explained in the early position paper [135].

Moreover, the Earth Observation application can be viewed as a preliminary study for the Earth Observation Use Case scheduled in the frame of the Helix Nebula project (Science Cloud initiative funded by the European Commission [136]).

Related prototypes

As stated earlier, mOSAIC is interested to support scientific applications running in Clouds. A large category of scientific applications are based on parallel computing simulations.

mJADES is a prototype for concurrent simulations in Clouds, using the mOSAIC's SLA framework. It is the result of Italian PerfCloud project (building an environment for IaaS provision based on Cloud and Grid integration). Its architecture is explained in [55]. Using this prototype several performance prediction studies of Cloud-based parallel simulations were done [54,137].

The mOSAIC software platform is used by the prototypes of services delivering HPC-in-the-Cloud in the frame of HOST project [138] funded by European Commission in the frame of FP7 Capacities programme [139].

The mechanism used in Clouds and Grids for resource identification and brokering are close. Key ideas that were the basis for mOSAIC Ontology and Brokering systems were used recently in the Grid context. An Ontology for contract negotiations was presented in [140], while negotiations in an agent-based grid resource brokering system are exposed in [141].

An adaptive and semantic database model for RDF data stores [142] was also conceived following mOSAIC data service examples.

Related software products

Olaii [143] is a commercial product emerged as side effect of developing the dynamic semantic discovery service of mOSAIC. Information extraction library developed under the umbrella of mOSAIC's dynamic semantic discovery service is focused on extraction of the semantic descriptors for REST APIs, but can be extended to cover other use cases. The product is an application which will help discovering events or finding friends to go out with. The semantic extractor developed in mOSAIC is modified to extract the events instead of REST operations. Machine learning techniques applied in the semantic extractor to classify REST operations and to find irregular operations are applied for the events for building a recommendation system based on users' Facebook or Twitter profiles.

mOSAIC is currently used to provide an information service to the citizens of the third largest town of Romania. More precisely in the frame of SEED project [144], funded by European Commission through the CIP programme [145], a particular information service was build using mOSAIC API and platform and continuously extracts feeds from governmental sites (European, national and regional) as well as public service institutions (theaters, public transportation etc) and display them on in- and out-door large devices. The application is similar to the real-time-feed demo application.

mOSAIC positioning

Position as a solution for interoperability and portability in multiple Clouds usage scenarios

Generally speaking, the interoperability problem has three dimensions in the case of Cloud computing domain:

1. a design dimension, that deals with the need to abstract the programmatic diverse interfaces of various services,
2. a dynamic run-time dimension, that deals with the need to support migration of the Cloud application from one provider Cloud to another provider Cloud, and

3. a policy dimension, that deals with the need to support communication and federation among the Cloud providers.

mOSAIC is dealing mainly with the first dimension, ensuring an abstraction level for vendor-agnosticity. While is not tackling explicitly the migration or federation, it allows on-demand re-deployment of the supported application in various Clouds.

The portability problem has also three dimensions (all tackled by mOSAIC):

1. a functional dimension, that refers to the application functionality in an environment-agnostic manner,
2. a service dimension, that refers to the on-the-fly adding, reconfiguration and removal of resources, and
3. a data dimension, that refers to the import and export of data in different formats.

The main requirements of portability (following the comprehensive list from [146]) are met by the mOSAIC solution as indicated in Table 3.

There are currently several technical approaches to deal with portability and interoperability: open APIs and protocols (like jclouds [147], libcloud [148], OpenStack, OCCI [149] or δ-Cloud [150]), standards (like OVF [151], CDMI [152] or CIMI [153]), frameworks (like for SLAs from SLA@SOI project), semantic repositories (like UCI [154]), or domain specific languages (like CloudML [155]). mOSAIC is an *integrated solution* that offers an open API with a high level of abstraction, and uses OCCI, SLA@SOI framework and semantic processing.

Position as enabler for Multi-Cloud, Federations and InterCloud

There are several reasons for the use of services from multiple Clouds. The ones motivating mOSAIC are the following two: (1) ensure the avoidance of vendor lock-in by relaying upon the services from two or more providers; (2) support Hybrid Clouds build from Private and Public Clouds in order to deal with peaks or customer requirements.

According to the NIST report [156], multiple Clouds can be used sequentially or simultaneous. The sequentially usage is related to the migration from one Cloud to another driven from economic reasons (e.g. cost reductions, emergencies, back-ups etc). The simultaneous usage of services from different Clouds can also have several benefits like high availability and fault tolerance. mOSAIC is mainly targeting the first scenario, while is not excluding the second one.

According to [157], two delivery models can distinguished for multiple Clouds. The first one, the Federated

Table 3 Portability requirements (five most important ones in of the six category) and their degree of fulfillment by mOSAIC

Requirement	Fulfillment	Requirement	Fulfillment
Market		*Monitoring*	
Economic models	Model of a component-based market	SLA and performance monitoring	SLA compliance checks, component monitoring
License flexibility	Open-source	Sets of benchmarks	Benchmarks for component based applications
Negotiated SLAs	Through Cloud Agency	Load balance monitor	Through Containers
Cost-effectiveness	Broker mechanism	Service audit	—
Leasing mechanisms	—	QoS aware services	—
Application		*Deployment*	
Data portability and exchange	Unique API for same type of data services	Deploy in multiple Clouds with single tool	PaaS' Deployer
Scale-in and -out	Elasticity of Cloudlets	Service discovery	Based on semantics
Location-free	No location restriction	Automated provisioning	Requires user consensus
Workflow management	Components started in requested order	Navigation between services	—
Span on multiple Clouds	If no communication	Behavior prediction	—
Programming		*AA & Security*	
Minimal reimplementation when move	Re-deployment	Trust mechanisms	Intrusion-detection as a service
Common set or standard APIs	Use AMQP, OCCI	Authentication	Credential service
Same tools for cloud and entreprise appls	Eclipse and Web GUIs	Security standards	Use Cloud vendor certificates
Ontology of Cloud	Own Cloud Ontology	Single sign-on	—
High level modelling	—	Digital identities	—

Cloud, assumes a formal agreement between the Cloud providers. The second model, of Multi-Cloud, assumes that there is no priori agreement between the Cloud providers. mOSAIC is targeting mainly the Multi-Cloud, establishing only at deployment phase the needs in terms of services and the contacts with the Cloud providers.

According to [158], the term Multi-Cloud denotes the usage of multiple and independent Clouds by a client or a service. Clients or their software representatives are responsible for managing resource provisioning. In the same paper Multi-Clouds are classified in two categories. The first category is that of libraries allowing the usage of multiple clouds in a uniform way (including brokers that directly take care of provisioning of services across Clouds). The second category is that of services for provisioning resources which are hosted either externally or in-house by the clients, and which usually includes a broker. In this case the clients are entitled to specify a service level agreement or a set of provisioning rules and the service performs accordingly the deployment and execution. As the authors of [158] have correctly noted, mOSAIC can be mapped to the second category, of services.

We should remind that in the category of libraries, the most known products are the Python library Libcloud, the Java library jclouds, the REST API δ-Cloud, the PHP API Simple Cloud [159], or C++/ Python/Java API SAGA [160]. These libraries can be used as Drivers in mOSAIC. Moreover, mOSAIC's API libraries are available for Java, Python, Erlang and Node.js.

In what concerns the Multi-Clouds based on services, we consider that there are two categories: hosted services and deployable services. mOSAIC belongs to the deployable category.

Three hosted services are most relevant in this moment: RightScale, Enstratius and Kaavo. RightScale [161] offers a Private Cloud management platform for control, administration, and life-cycle support of deployments across multiple Clouds (it supports Amazon, Eucalyptus, GoGrid, VMware and FlexiScale); server templates are available to automatically install software on supported Cloud infrastructures. Enstratius [162] allows configuration management, monitoring, governance and automation and it supports Amazon, CloudStack, CloudSigma, Eucalyptus, GoGrid, Joyent Cloud, OpenStack, Rackspace, vCloud, Azure and others. Kaavo [163] allows also the deployment and management of distributed applications, workloads, and environments in various Clouds enabling resource management across Public, Private, and Hybrid Clouds (it supports Amazon, Rackspace, OpenStack, Eucalyptus, Cloud.com, Terremark, Logicworks, HP Cloud and IBM Cloud).

In terms of number of Cloud providers that are supported, mOSAIC is similar with the above mentioned hosted services, but with a clear preference for the support of European Cloud providers. In terms of GUIs the mOSAIC Web oriented one is considerably different, as designed to serve applications, not resource management: the user does not control the resources distribution or consumption (provider interfaces can be used for this purpose), but instead controls the processes of the application that are running (an application oriented view, instead a resource provider view).

The current deployable services for Multi-Cloud are in prototype phases as results of different research projects. Two main competitors for mOSAIC are currently available: Aoleus and Optimis. The RedHat's Aoleus [164] is an open-source Cloud management software written in Ruby for Linux systems. It allows users to choose between Private, Public or Hybrid Clouds, using δ-Cloud library. The Optimis Toolkit [165], result of the project with the same name and funded by the European Commission in the same work-programme as mOSAIC (in parallel with it), offers a platform for Cloud service provisioning that manages the lifecycle of the service and addresses issues like risk and trust management. Compared with Aoleus, mOSAIC has the advantage of including more than a resource management middleware (not restricted to the δ-Cloud list of providers). Compared with Optimis, mOSAIC is weaker in terms of trust and risk management, or even in brokerage process due to the reduced set of policies; however the semantic processing support, the SLA-based negotiation mechanisms, or the application tools are the main comparative advantages of mOSAIC.

A comprehensive analysis of mOSAIC positioning versus the research prototypes for Federations and Multi-Clouds, complementary to the above one that is mentioning software products, was recently exposed in [166].

A Cloud Federation or a Multi-Cloud that includes at least one Cloud Broker and offers dynamic service provisioning is an Inter-Cloud. In the case of Multi-Cloud, the Broker is often part of the service or library. This is the case also for mOSAIC. According [158], the brokering mechanisms are: SLA-based, i.e. requirements are specified by clients in the form of a service level agreements; or trigger-action, i.e. rules are becoming active, triggering an action, when a predefined condition considering the externally visible application performance indicators

becomes true. Evidently, mOSAIC has a SLA-based brokering mechanism. However, taking into account its event-driven orientation, part of its behavior is based on rules and triggered-actions.

The most relevant representatives for SLA-based brokers for Multi-Clouds are SpotCloud and Stratos. SpotCloud [167] provides a marketplace where service providers sell the extra capacity they have and the clients can select the 'best' service provider at a certain moment. WSO2 Stratos [168] provides core services and building blocks for federated identity and single sign-on, data-as-a-service and messaging-as-a-service, and monitors SLAs, CPU, memory and bandwidth utilization and automatically scales up or down depending on the load. The mOSAIC brokering, monitoring, scaling or messaging mechanisms are rather simpler compared with Spot-Cloud and Stratos ones. However, its component-based and open-source design has the comparative advantage of easy updates and customization according to user's needs.

mOSAIC has not been yet able to establish a market place, as SpotCloud, but it does not exclude the idea. A Cloud platform supporting applications composed of software components can come with a component store which provides components for common tasks. Using such a store, developers should be able to build new applications and services by configure and compose the existing components, or by extending them with new functionalities. Moreover, a dynamic recomposition of software during execution, i.e. adding, removing or reconfiguring components within an application at runtime, should be possible. A case study of using mOSAIC and a component market for the design of a Bussiness-Process-as-a-Service is sketched in [169].

Position as PaaS

As described earlier, mOSAIC exhibits some characteristics of a PaaS. Despite the fact that is not a hosted service, but a deployable one, it offers several tools and facilities to develop, deploy and control at run-time new applications. We consider here only two significant PaaSs to be compared with mOSAIC's PaaS. While the PaaS offer is quite diverse, the selection is based on the usage spread, respectively closeness to mOSAIC.

Google's Application Engine (GAE) is one of the most known PaaS. While the deployment facilities are more complicated in mOSAIC due to the need of the user final decision in selecting the Cloud provider, several limitations of GAE are avoided by mOSAIC. For example file-system write access are forbidden in GAE; applications are not allowed to make arbitrary network connections to the Internet and HTTP requests must be made only through a special library. All data handled by GAE must be stored in a columnar database, and even though the developer has a query language resembling SQL, it is very limited in what concerns filters. Moreover, in GAE the requests should be handled within one minute or less. All of these restrictions are not encountered in mOSAIC approach.

From the long list of hosting PaaS, Heroku [170] is the most closest to mOSAIC concepts. Its features have inspired not only mOSAIC, but also most of the recently emerged PaaSs. The reason is its simple scheme to handle development, configuration, deployment, and management. It supports a variety of programming languages (Ruby, Python, Node.js, Scala and Clojure), as well as arbitrary executables either as binary or scripts. However, there are several improvements that mOSAIC has been able to provide. For example, it is actually impractical to mix multiple languages in the same Heroku application, while in mOSAIC components can be written in various languages if they are able to use a message passing system. Any update of component of a Heroku application needs the complete shutdown of the application. In mOSAIC components can be stopped, started or updated during the execution of the application, as the messages are waiting in the queues. Several other advantages are comprehensively discussed in [171].

Position in open-source community

As earlier mentioned, mOSAIC is included in the category of services for Multi-Cloud. However there are other open-source middlewares that are deployable, while not necessary designed with the Multi-Cloud in mind, still able to deal with homogeneous distributed resources. A comprehensive comparisons of them and mOSAIC positioning is presented in [172], including ConPaaS, the Contrail [173] solution for Federations. In the same paper are provided a series of criteria that can be used to compare PaaSs.

We mention here only VMware's Cloud Foundry and Red Hat's OpenShift [174], developed in the same time as mOSAIC. Both are dedicated to Web applications, while mOSAIC scope is more broader. mOSAIC is stronger also in terms of data support, the number of Cloud providers that are supported, the interfacing variants, the SLA and brokerage mechanisms, as well as portability on other Linux system than VMware or RedHat provided ones. However is weaker in terms of performance analytics or integration with other development environments than Eclipse.

Position in the landscape of Cloud Computing projects funded by the European Commission

Beyond Optimis, Contrail and MODAClouds that were mentioned earlier, there are several other Cloud computing projects that have run in parallel with mOSAIC and have provided close related solutions. A snapshot of the landscape covered by these projects in the late 2011

was provided with mOSAIC contribution in [175] in the book [176] that collects reports on the states of more than twelve such projects. The positioning of mOSAIC in relationship with several Multi-Cloud projects was expressed more recently in [177].

We remind here only few projects offering alternatives to mOSAIC approach or complementing it. 4CaaSt [178] is building a BluePrint for registering Cloud services in an e-Market. Cloud4SOA [179] is dealing with semantic based interoperability at platform level. Cloud-TM [180] is proposing another programming paradigm for Clouds. Remics [181] is dealing with migration of legacy applications to Clouds through model-driven engineering. TClouds [182] is offering security, privacy and resilience mechanisms for Multi-Clouds. Vision Cloud [183] is looking in details to the issues of data management in Federations and Multi-Clouds.

Conclusions and future developments

Drawing the line at the end of project, the mOSAIC's multi-national team is checking the degree of fulfillment of the initial promises. Shortly these were:

 (i)   a set of APIs for application portability between Clouds,
 (ii) agent technologies supporting dynamic negotiations with multiple Cloud providers,
 (iii) user-centric service level agreements,
 (iv) Cloud ontology and semantic data processing,
 (v)   an open-source and portable platform-as-a-service,
 (vi) proof-of-concept applications.

Targeting to provide an innovative solution in these fields, mOSAIC approach has proven its uniqueness and advantages over other existing approaches in what concerns:

 (a) deployable and portable services of platform type on top of IaaS;
 (b) brokering system based on customizable service level agreements and agent technologies;
 (c) portability of Cloud applications supported by semantic processors and multi-layered API;
 (d) usefulness for porting scientific and commercial applications towards the Cloud;
 (e) a stable, complete and innovative middleware for building, deploying and controlling applications following Multi-Cloud usage scenarios.

While disparate proofs of the innovations are dispersed in various mOSAIC-related articles, the present report tried to offer a general overview of the main achievements and advantages of mOSAIC. However it highlights also some weaknesses in relationship with other approaches, subject to improvements in the next years:

(1) the event-driven programming style of mOSAIC applications is considered to be complex by less skilled programmers; the templates collections as well as the workbench and wizzards should be improved to better assist the application developers;

(2) the deployment of special libraries still require manual intervention; the deployment procedures are therefore expected to be improved;

(3) the mechanism of the brokerage system allow complex policies to be applied; however, simple policies are currently used and the full potential was not yet exploited;

(4) semantic processing is used currently at design phase; the potential of the dynamic discovery services, for example, has not yet been fully exploited.

(5) several software prototypes have been developed as proof-of-concept and a considerable part of them, yet functional, are not ready for a production phase; according to the interest expressed by the community surrounding mOSAIC, particular components (like the PTC simulator and resource allocator) will be further improved to offer production-level quality of service;

(6) commercial products developments has underline the need of enlarging the number of COTS that are wrapped to work with mOSAIC platform;

(7) the proof-of-concept applications developed in the frame of the project are expected to be improved to satisfy the requirements of their external users.

Several topics that were not in the main focus of mOSAIC project are expected to be pursued in the near future relying on the mOSAIC approach and software repositories. We have already mentioned some of them in this paper: model-driven engineering for Clouds, Cloud security or automated management of Cloud resources. With certainty this will happen in the frame of the research, development and collaborative projects that already rely upon the mOSAIC's specific components. We remind here some of them:

FP7 projects: MODAClouds in model-driven engineering direction, SPECS in security direction, HOST in scientific application support direction, Helix Nebula in Earth observation application field; National projects: AMICAS, in the direction of automated management of multiple Cloud resources, or Cloud@Home in the direction of Volunteer Cloud.

The fact that the mOSAIC architecture is built from loosely coupled components enhance the chances for the open-source software prototypes to be adopted and enhanced in other contexts that mOSAIC initial scenarios. This is the case of the commercial product Olaii that was mentioned in this paper, which has started from the semantic extractor developed in the frame of mOSAIC project.

Competing interests
The authors declare that they have no competing interests.

Authors' contributions
The paper presents a comprehensive overview of the mOSAIC approach for Multi-Cloud. It offers the first integrated image of the full set of solutions, at the end of the development cycle. It also position the approach versus other currently available ones, from multiple points of view (Multi-Cloud, open-source, PaaS, related initiatives). All authors read and approved the final manuscript.

Acknowledgements
The research and development reported in this article was partially supported by the European Commission grant no. FP7-ICT-2009–5-256910 (mOSAIC). The development of the mOSAIC approach was sustained by a large multinational team that is far from being reflected in the list of the authors of this paper: the paper's authors are the key persons from each team that have drive the approach development. They are taking this opportunity to express their gratitude to the team members of mOSAIC project that are not in the author list:

- from Second University of Naples: Alba Amato, Giuseppe Aversano, Rocco Aversa, Antonio Bagarolo, Daniele Bove, Pasquale Cantiello, Giuseppina Cretella, Vincenzo De Crescenzo, Massimiliano Diodati, Massimo Ficco, Loredana Liccardo, Francesco Moscato, Manuela Serrao, Luca Tasquier;
- from Institute e-Austria Timişoara: Bogdan Alexandru Căprărescu, Adrian Copie, Ciprian Dorin Crăciun, Teodor-Florin Fortiş, Marc Eduard Frîncu, Georgiana Macariu, Victor Ion Munteanu, Marian Neagul, Viorel Negru, Silviu Panica, Călin Şandru;
- from AITIA: Rajmund Bocsi, Gabor Ferschl, László Gulyás;
- from Tecnalia: Unai Antero, Imanol Padillo Cruz, Gorka Mikel Echevarria Velez, Iñigo Lazkanotegui Larrate, Miguel Loichate, Asier Sesma;
- from TerraDue: Hervé Caumont, Pedro Gonçalves, Simone Tripodi;
- from ESRIN-ESA: Claudio Di Giulio, Fulvio Marelli;
- from Xlab: Mariano Cecowski, Gregor Pipan, Boris Savič;
- from Brno University of Technology: Petr Škoda, Pavel Smrž;
- from University of Ljubljana: Peter Češarek, Jernej Južna, Matija König, Aleš Kroflič, Gašper Stegnar.

Author details
[1]Institute e-Austria Timişoara and West University of Timişoara, Timişoara, Romania. [2]Second University of Naples, Aversa, Italy. [3]AITIA International Inc, Budapest, Hungary. [4]Industrial Systems Unit, Tecnalia, San Sebastian, Spain. [5]Terradue SRL, Rome, Italy. [6]Earth Observation Science, Applications and Future Technologies Department, ESRIN, European Space Agency, Frascati, Italy. [7]XLAB d.o.o., Ljubljana, Slovenia. [8]Brno University of Technology, Brno, Czech Republic. [9]University of Ljubljana, Ljubljana, Slovenia.

References
1. Armbrust M, Fox A, Griffith R, Joseph AD, Katz RH, Konwinski A, Lee G, Patterson DA, Rabkin A, Zaharia M (2009) Above the clouds: A berkeley view of cloud computing. Tech. rep., EECS Department, U.C. Berkley, UCB/EECS-2009–28. http://www.eecs.berkeley.edu/Pubs/TechRpts/2009/EECS-2009-28.pdf
2. Buyya R, Yeo CS, Venugopal S, Broberg J, Brandic I (2009) Cloud computing and emerging it platforms: Vision, hype, and reality for delivering computing as the 5th utility. Future Generation Comput Syst 25(6): 599–616. doi:10.1016/j.future.2008.12.001

3. Schubert L, Jeffery Ke (2012) Above the clouds: A berkeley view of cloud computing. Tech. rep., European Commission, Expert Group on Cloud Computing. http://cordis.europa.eu/fp7/ict/ssai/docs/future-cc-2may-finalreport-experts.pdf

4. Ict – information and communication technologies. http://cordis.europa.eu/fp7/ict/

5. mOSAIC project. http://www.mosaic-cloud.eu

6. Di Martino B, Petcu D, Cossu R, Gonçalves P, Máhr T, Loichate M (2011b) Building a mosaic of clouds. In: Guarracino MR, Vivien F, Täff JL, Cannataro M, Danelutto M, Hast A, Perla F, Knüpfer A, Martino B, Alexander M (eds) Euro-Par 2010 Parallel Processing Workshops, Lecture Notes in Computer Science, vol 6586. Springer, pp 571–578. doi:10.1007/978-3-642-21878-1_70, http://dx.doi.org/10.1007/978-3-642-21878-1_70

7. Malawski M, Meizner J, Bubak M, Gepner P (2011) Component approach to computational applications on clouds. Procedia Comput Sci 4(0): 432–441. doi:10.1016/j.procs.2011.04.045, http://dx.doi.org/10.1016/j.procs.2011.04.045

8. Petcu D, Şandru C (2012) Towards component-based software engineering of cloud applications In: WICSA/ECSA 2012 Companion Volume. ACM, pp 80–81. doi:10.1145/2361999.2362013, http://doi.acm.org/10.1145/2361999.2362013

9. Kächele S, Domaschka J, Hauck FJ (2011) Cosca: an easy-to-use component-based paas cloud system for common applications In: 1st International Workshop on Cloud Computing Platforms (CloudCP 2011). ACM, pp 4:1–4:6. doi:10.1145/1967422.1967426, http://doi.acm.org/10.1145/1967422.1967426

10. Advanced message queuing protocol. http://www.amqp.org/

11. Amazon simple queue service. http://aws.amazon.com/sqs/

12. Petcu D, Crăciun C, Rak M (2011c) Towards a cross platform cloud api - components for cloud federation. In: Leymann F, Ivanov I, van Sinderen M, Shishkov B (eds) 1st International Conference on Cloud Computing and Services Science (CLOSER 2011). SciTePress, pp 166–169

13. Petcu D, Macariu G, Panica S, Crăciun C (2012b) Portable cloud applications—from theory to practice. Future Generation Comput Syst 29(6): 1417–1430. doi:10.1016/j.future.2012.01.009, http://dx.doi.org/10.1016/j.future.2012.01.009

14. Petcu D, Panica S, Şandru C, Crăciun CD, Neagul M (2012c) Experiences in building an event-driven and deployable platform as a service. In: Wang XS, Cruz I, Delis A, Huang G (eds) Web Information Systems Engineering (WISE 2012), Lecture Notes in Computer Science, vol 7651. Springer, pp 666–672. doi:10.1007/978-3-642-35063-4_51, http://dx.doi.org/10.1007/978-3-642-35063-4_51

15. Petcu D, Crăciun C, Neagul M, Lazcanotegui I, Rak M (2011a) Building an interoperability api for sky computing In: International Conference on High Performance Computing and Simulation (HPCS 2011). IEEE Computer Society Press, pp 405–411. http://dx.doi.org/10.1109/HPCSim.2011.5999853

16. Cloud Computing Use Case Discussion Group (2010) Cloud computing use cases, version 4.0. Tech. rep. http://opencloudmanifesto.org/Cloud_Computing_Use_Cases_Whitepaper-4_0.pdf

17. Petcu D (2010) Identifying cloud computing usage patterns In: IEEE International Conference on Cluster Computing Workshops and Posters (Cluster Workshops 2010). IEEE Computer Society Press, pp 1–8. http://dx.doi.org/10.1109/CLUSTERWKSP.2010.5613106

18. Fortiş TF, Lopez GE, Cruz IP, Ferschl G, Máhr T (2012b) Cloud patterns for mosaic-enabled scientific applications In: International Conference on Parallel Processing (Euro-Par 2011). Springer, Lecture Notes in Computer Science, vol 7156, pp 83–93. doi:10.1007/978-3-642-29737-3_10, http://dx.doi.org/10.1007/978-3-642-29737-3_10

19. Aversa R, Di Martino B, Rak M, Venticinque S (2010) Cloud agency: A mobile agent based cloud system In: International Conference on Complex, Intelligent and Software Intensive Systems (CISIS 2010). IEEE Computer Society Press, pp 132–137. http://dx.doi.org/10.1109/CISIS.2010.143

20. Şandru C, Venticinque S (2013) Agents layer to support cloud applications. In: Fortino G, Badica C, Malgeri M, Unland R (eds) Intelligent Distributed Computing VI, Studies in Computational Intelligence, vol 446. Springer, pp 281–286. doi:10.1007/978-3-642-32524-3_35, http://dx.doi.org/10.1007/978-3-642-32524-3_35

21. Cuomo A, Rak M, Venticinque S, Villano U (2012) Enhancing an autonomic cloud architecture with mobile agents In: International Conference on Parallel Processing (Euro-Par 2011). Springer, Lecture Notes in Computer Science, vol 7156, pp 94–103. doi:10.1007/978-3-642-29737-3_11, http://dx.doi.org/10.1007/978-3-642-29737-3_11

22. Venticinque S, Aversa R, Di Martino B, Petcu D (2011a) Agent based cloud provisioning and management - design and prototypal implementation. In: Leymann F, Ivanov I, v Sinderen M, Shishkov B (eds) 1st International Conference on Cloud Computing & Services Science (CLOSER 2011). SciTePress, pp 184–191

23. Tasquier L, Venticinque S, Aversa R, Di Martino B (2012) Agent based application tools for cloud provisioning and management. In: Yousif M, Schubert L, Jeffery K (eds) 3rd International Conference on Cloud Computing (CloudComp 2012). pp 24–30. http://www.itutility.ac.uk/outputs/CloudComp_Wien_Sept2012/USB-cloudcomp2012/file-storage/papers/134555472397963.pdf

24. Venticinque S, Amato A, Di Martino B (2012a) An occi compliant interface for iaas provisioning and monitoring. In: Leymann F, Ivanov I, van Sinderen M, Shan T (eds) 2nd International Conference on Cloud Computing and Services Science (CLOSER 2012). SciTePress, pp 163–166

25. Cao BQ, Li B, Xia QM (2009) A service-oriented qos-assured and multi-agent cloud computing architecture In: 1st International Conference on Cloud Computing (CloudCom 2009). Springer-Verlag, pp 644–649. doi:10.1007/978-3-642-10665-1_66, http://dx.doi.org/10.1007/978-3-642-10665-1_66

26. Venticinque S, Tasquier L, Di Martino B (2012c) Agents based cloud computing interface for resource provisioning and management In: 6th International Conference on Complex, Intelligent & Software Intensive Systems (CISIS 2012). IEEE Computer Society, pp 249–256. http://dx.doi.org/10.1109/CISIS.2012.139

27. Amato A, Venticinque S, Di Martino B (2012b) Evaluation and brokering of service level agreements for negotiation of cloud infrastructures In: International Conference for Internet Technology and Secured Transactions (ICITST-2012). Infonomics Society, pp 144–149

28. Aversa R, Tasquier L, Venticinque S (2012) Management of cloud infrastructures through agents In: 3rd International Conference on Emerging Intelligent Data and Web Technologies (EIDWT 2012). IEEE Computer Society Press, pp 46–53. http://dx.doi.org/10.1109/EIDWT.2012.57

29. Ficco M, Venticinque S, Di Martino B (2012) Mosaic-based intrusion detection framework for cloud computing. In: Meersman R, Panetto H, Dillon T, Rinderle-Ma S, Dadam P, Zhou X, Pearson S, Ferscha A, Bergamaschi S, Cruz I (eds) On the Move to Meaningful Internet Systems: OTM 2012. Springer-Verlag, Lecture Notes in Computer Science, vol 7566, pp 628–644.

30. Amato A, Tasquier L, Copie A (2013b) Vendor agents for iaas cloud interoperability. In: Fortino G, Badica C, Malgeri M, Unland R (eds) Intelligent Distributed Computing VI Studies in Computational Intelligence, vol 446. Springer, pp 271–280. doi:10.1007/978-3-642-32524-3_34, http://dx.doi.org/10.1007/978-3-642-32524-3_34

31. Şandru C, Petcu D, Munteanu V (2012) Building an open-source platform-as-a-service with intelligent management of multiple cloud resources In: 5th IEEE/ACM Internat. Conference on Utility & Cloud Computing (UCC 2012). IEEE Computer Society, pp 333–338. http://dx.doi.org/10.1109/UCC.2012.54

32. Rackspace. http://www.rackspace.com

33. GoGrid. http://www.gogrid.com

34. Flexiant. http://www.flexiant.com

35. CloudSigma. http://www.cloudsigma.com

36. NIIFI Cloud. http://www.cloudsigma.com

37. Arctur vCloud. https://vcloud.arctur.si/cloud/

38. Hostko. http://www.hostko.si

39. VMware vCloud. http://vcloud.vmware.com

40. OnApp. http://onapp.com

41. Eucalyptus. http://www.eucalyptus.com

42. OpenNebula. http://opennebula.org

43. CloudStack. http://cloudstack.apache.org

44. OpenStack. http://www.openstack.org/

45. SLA@SOI project. http://sla-at-soi.eu/

46. Theilmann W, Yahyapour R, Butler J (2008) Multi-level sla management for service-oriented infrastructures. In: Mähönen P, Pohl K, Priol T (eds) Towards a Service-Based Internet, Springer Berlin, Lecture Notes in Computer Science, vol 5377, pp 324–335. http://dx.doi.org/10.1007/978-3-540-89897-9_28

47. Comuzzi M, Kotsokalis C, Rathfelder C, Theilmann W, Winkler U, Zacco G (2010) A framework for multi-level sla management. In: Dan A, Gittler F, Toumani F (eds) ICSOC/ServiceWave 2009 Workshops, Springer Berlin. Lecture Notes in Computer Science, vol 6275, pp 187–196. http://dx.doi.org/10.1007/978-3-642-16132-2_18

48. WS-Agreement for Java framework. http://wsag4j.sourceforge.net

49. Rak M, Aversa R, Venticinque S, Di Martino B (2012a) User centric service level management in mosaic applications. In: Alexander M, D'Ambra P, Belloum A, Bosilca G, Cannataro M, Danelutto M, Di Martino B, Gerndt M, Jeannot E, Namyst R, Roman J, Scott S, Traff J, Vallée G, Weidendorfer J (eds) Euro-Par 2011: Parallel Processing Workshops, Lecture Notes in Computer Science, vol 7156, Springer, pp 106–115. doi:10.1007/978-3-642-29740-3_13, http://dx.doi.org/10.1007/978-3-642-29740-3_13

50. Ficco M, Rak M (2011) Intrusion tolerant approach for denial of service attacks to web services In: International Conference on Data Compression, Communications and Processing (CCP 2011). IEEE Computer Society Press, Los Alamitos, pp 285–292. http://dx.doi.org/10.1109/CCP.2011.44

51. Ficco M, Rak M (2012a) Intrusion tolerance in cloud applications: The mosaic approach In: 6th International Conference on Complex, Intelligent and Software Intensive Systems (CISIS 2012). IEEE Computer Society Press, pp 170–176. http://dx.doi.org/10.1109/CISIS.2012.202

52. Ficco M, Rak M (2012b) Intrusion tolerance of stealth dos attacks to web services. In: Gritzalis D, Furnell S, Theoharidou M (eds) SEC 2012, Springer, IFIP Advances in Information and Communication Technology, vol 376, pp 579–584. http://dx.doi.org/10.1007/978-3-642-30436-1_52

53. Rak M, Liccardo L, Aversa R (2011b) A sla-based interface for security management in cloud and grid integrations In: 7th International Conference on Information Assurance and Security (IAS 2011). IEEE Computer Society Press, pp 378–383. http://dx.doi.org/10.1109/ISIAS.2011.6122783

54. Rak M, Cuomo A, Villano U (2012b) Cloud-based concurrent simulation at work: Fast performance prediction of parallel programs In: 21st IEEE International Workshop on Enabling Technologies: Infrastructure for Collaborative Enterprises (WETICE 2012). IEEE Computer Society Press, pp 137–142. http://dx.doi.org/10.1109/WETICE.2012.74

55. Rak M, Cuomo A, Villano U (2012c) Mjades: Concurrent simulation in the cloud. In: Barolli L, Xhafa F, Vitabile S, Uehara M (eds) 6th International Conference on Complex, Intelligent and Software Intensive Systems (CISIS 2012). IEEE Computer Society Press, pp 853–860. http://dx.doi.org/10.1109/CISIS.2012.134

56. Amato A, Venticinque S (2013) Multi-objective decision support for brokering of cloud sla In: 27th IEEE International Conference on Advanced Information Networking and Applications Workshops (WAINA 2013). IEEE Computer Society, pp 1241–1246. http://dx.doi.org/10.1109/WAINA.2013.149

57. Venticinque S, Negru V, Munteanu VI, Şandru C, Aversa R, Rak M (2012b) Negotiation policies for provisioning of cloud resources. In: Filipe J, Fred ALN (eds) 4th International Conference on Agents and Artificial Intelligence (ICAART 2012), SciTePress, pp 347–350

58. Amato A, Liccardo L, Rak M, Venticinque S (2012a) Sla negotiation and brokering for sky computing. In: Leymann F, Ivanov I, van Sinderen M, Shan T (eds) 2nd International Conference on Cloud Computing and Services Science (CLOSER 2012). SciTePress, pp 611–620

59. Venticinque S (2012) Agent based services for negotiation, monitoring and reconfiguration of cloud resources In: European Research Activities in Cloud Computing. Cambridge Scholars Publishing, pp 178–202. http://www.c-s-p.org/Flyers/European-Research-Activities-in-Cloud-Computing1-4438-3507-2.htm

60. Venticinque S, Aversa R, Di Martino B, Rak M, Petcu D (2011b) A cloud agency for sla negotiation and management. In: Guarracino MR, Vivien F, Träff JL, Cannatoro M, Danelutto M, Hast A, Perla F, Knüpfer A, Di Martino B, Alexander M (eds) Euro-Par 2010 Parallel Processing Workshops, Lecture Notes in Computer Science, vol 6586. Springer, pp 587–594.

doi:10.1007/978-3-642-21878-1_72, http://dx.doi.org/10.1007/978-3-642-21878-1_72

61. Cretella G, Di Martino B (2012a) Towards a semantic engine for cloud applications development In: 6th International Conference on Complex, Intelligent and Software Intensive Systems (CISIS 2012). IEEE Computer Society Press, pp 198–203. http://dx.doi.org/10.1109/CISIS.2012.159

62. Cretella G, Di Martino B (2012) Semantic web annotation and representation of cloud apis In: 3rd International Conference on Emerging Intelligent Data and Web Technologies (EIDWT 2012). IEEE Computer Society Press, pp 31–37. http://dx.doi.org/10.1109/EIDWT.2012.61

63. Cretella G, Di Martino B (2012b) Towards automatic analysis of cloud vendors apis for supporting cloud application portability In: 6th International Conference on Complex, Intelligent and Software Intensive Systems (CISIS 2012). IEEE Computer Society Press, pp 61–67. http://dx.doi.org/10.1109/CISIS.2012.162

64. Di Martino B, Cretella G (2012) Semantic and algorithmic recognition support to porting software applications to cloud. In: Bibi S, Moschitti A, Plank B, Stamelos I (eds) Joint Workshop on Intelligent Methods for Software System Engineering (JIMSE 2012), pp 24–30. http://www2.lirmm.fr/ecai2012/images/stories/ecai_doc/pdf/workshop/W26-jimse2012.pdf

65. Amato A, Cretella G, Di Martino B, Venticinque S (2013a) Semantic and agent technologies for cloud vendor agnostic resource brokering In: 27th International Conference on Advanced Information Networking and Applications Workshops (WAINA 2013). IEEE Computer Society, pp 1253–1258. http://dx.doi.org/10.1109/WAINA.2013.163, http://www.odysci.com/article/1010113019663301/semantic-and-agent-technologies-for-cloud-vendor-agnostic-resource-brokering

66. Youseff L, Butrico M, Da Silva D (2008) Toward a unified ontology of cloud computing In: Grid Computing Environments Workshop (GCE 2008), pp 1–10. doi:10.1109/GCE.2008.4738443, http://dx.doi.org/10.1109/GCE.2008.4738443

67. Moscato F, Aversa R, Di Martino B, Fortiş T, Munteanu V (2011) An analysis of mosaic ontology for cloud resources annotation In: Federated Conference on Computer Science and Information Systems (FedCSIS 2011), pp 973–980. http://fedcsis.eucip.pl/proceedings/pliks/154.pdf

68. Aversa R, Di Martino B, Moscato F, Petcu D, Rak M, Venticinque S (2011b) An ontology for the cloud in mosaic. In: Wang L, Ranjan R, Chen J, Benatallah B (eds) Cloud Computing: Methodology Systems, and Applications. CRC Press, pp 467–486. http://www.crcpress.com/product/isbn/9781439856413

69. Fortis TF, Munteanu VI, Negru V (2012) Towards an ontology for cloud services In: 6th International Conference on Complex, Intelligent, and Software Intensive Systems (CISIS 2012). IEEE Computer Society Press, Washington, pp 787–792. doi:10.1109/CISIS.2012.138, http://dx.doi.org/10.1109/CISIS.2012.138

70. RabbitMQ. http://www.rabbitmq.com/

71. Amazon Simple Storage Service. http://aws.amazon.com/s3/

72. Riak. http://basho.com/riak/

73. Hadoop Distributed File System. http://hadoop.apache.org/docs/r1.0.4/hdfs_design.html

74. Petcu D, Crăciun C, Neagul M, Panica S, Di Martino B, Venticinque S, Rak M, Aversa R (2011b) Architecturing a sky computing platform. In: Cezon M, Wolfsthal Y (eds) Towards a Service-Based Internet. ServiceWave 2010 Workshops, Lecture Notes in Computer Science, vol 6569. Springer, pp 1–13. doi:10.1007/978-3-642-22760-8_1, http://dx.doi.org/10.1007/978-3-642-22760-8_1

75. Petcu D (2012b) How to build a reliable mosaic of multiple cloud services In: 1st European Workshop on Dependable Cloud Computing (EWDCC 2012). ACM, pp 4:1–4:2. doi:10.1145/2365316.2365320, http://doi.acm.org/10.1145/2365316.2365320

76. CouchDB. http://couchdb.apache.org/

77. Jetty. http://www.eclipse.org/jetty/

78. VirtualBox. https://www.virtualbox.org/

79. mOSAIC's open-source code repository. https://bitbucket.org/mosaic

80. Google App Engine. https://appengine.google.com

81. Windows Azure. http://www.windowsazure.com

82. Cloud Foundry. http://www.cloudfoundry.com/

83. Petcu D, Frîncu ME, Crăciun C, Panica S, Neagul M, Macariu G (2011d) Towards open-source cloudware In: 4th IEEE International Conference

on Utility and Cloud Computing (UCC 2011). IEEE Computer Society Press, pp 330–331. http://dx.doi.org/10.1109/UCC.2011.53

84. Cossu R, Di Giulio C, Brito F, Petcu D (2013) Cloud computing for earth observation. In: Kyriazis D, Voulodimos A, Gogouvitis S, Varvarigou T (eds) Data Intensive Storage Services for Cloud Environments, IGI Global, chap 12, pp 256–277. http://dx.doi.org/10.4018/978-1-4666-3934-8

85. Panica S, Petcu D, Lazkanotegi Larrate I, Máhr T (2012) Sky computing platform for legacy distributed application In: International Symposium on Parallel and Distributed Computing (ISPDC 2012). IEEE Computer Society Press, pp 293–300. http://dx.doi.org/10.1109/ISPDC.2012.47

86. Ferschl G, Máhr T (2012) Migrating a simulation framework from the cloud to the sky In: WoSS-4, CLASS Conference, Slovenia, pp 25–27

87. Škoda P, Šperka S, Smrž P (2012) Extracting information from scientific papers in the cloud In: 6th International Conference on Complex, Intelligent and Software Intensive Systems (CISIS 2012). IEEE Computer Society Press, pp 775–780. http://dx.doi.org/10.1109/CISIS.2012.176

88. Šperka S, Škoda P, Smrž P (2012) Cloudification of legacy information extraction system In: WoSS-4, CLASS Conference, Slovenia, pp 9–14. http://www.kc-class.eu/datoteke/proceedings-woss-4.pdf

89. Stankovski V, König M (2012) A sustainable building application design based on the mosaic api and platform In: 8th International Conference on Semantics, Knowledge and Grid (SKG 2012), pp 249–252. doi:10.1109/SKG.2012.13, http://dx.doi.org/10.1109/SKG.2012.13

90. Južna J, Češarek P, Stankovski V (2013) Porting existing matlab applications to the cloud by using the mosaic platform. In: Topping BHV, Iványi P (eds) 3rd International Conference on Parallel, Distributed, Grid and Cloud Computing for Engineering (PARENG 2013). Civil-Comp Press. paper 30. http://dx.doi.org/10.4203/ccp.101.30

91. Cretella G, Di Martino B, Stankovski V (2012) Using the mosaic's semantic engine to design and develop civil engineering cloud applications. In: Taniar D, Pardede E, Steinbauer M, Khalil I (eds) 14th International Conference on Information Integration and Web-based Applications & Services (iiWAS2012). ACM, pp 378–386. http://dx.doi.org/10.1145/2428736.2428805

92. Rak M, Aversano G (2012) Benchmarks in the cloud: The mosaic benchmarking framework In: 14th International Symposium on Symbolic and Numeric Algorithms for Scientific Computing (SYNASC 2012). IEEE Computer Society, pp 415–422. http://dx.doi.org/10.1109/SYNASC.2012.41

93. Cuomo A, Rak M, Villano U (2013b) Simulation-based performance evaluation of cloud applications. In: Fortino G, Badica C, Malgeri M, Unland R (eds) Intelligent Distributed Computing VI Studies in Computational Intelligence, vol 446. Springer, pp 263–269. doi:10.1007/978-3-642-32524-3_33, http://dx.doi.org/10.1007/978-3-642-32524-3_33

94. Petcu D (2012a) Cloudware support for scientific applications In: RO-LCG 2012. IEEE, Romania, pp 70–73

95. Petcu D, Panica S, Neagul M (2010) From grid computing towards sky computing. case study for earth observation In: 10th Cracow Grid Workshop (CGW 2010). Academic Computer Center, Poland, pp 11–20

96. Panica S, Neagul M, Crăciun C, Petcu D (2011) Serving legacy distributed applications by a self-configuring cloud processing platform In: 6th IEEE International Conference on Intelligent Data Acquisition and Advanced Computing Systems (IDAACS 2011), vol 1. IEEE Computer Society Press, pp 139–144. http://dx.doi.org/10.1109/IDAACS.2011.6072727

97. Stankovski V, Južna J, Petcu D (2012) Enabling legacy engineering applications for cloud computing: Experience with the mosaic api and platform In: 3rd International Conference on Emerging Intelligent Data and Web Technologies (EIDWT 2012). IEEE Computer Society Press, pp 281–286. http://dx.doi.org/10.1109/EIDWT.2012.49

98. Rak M, Ficco M, Luna J, Ghani H, Suri N, Panica S, Petcu D (2012d) Security issues in cloud federation. In: Villari M, Brandic I, Tusa F (eds) Achieving Federated and Self-Manageable Cloud Infrastructures: Theory and Practice. IGI Global, pp 176–194. http://dx.doi.org/10.4018/978-1-4666-1631-8.ch010

99. Casola V, Cuomo A, Rak M, Villano U (2013) The cloudgrid approach: Security analysis and performance evaluation. Future Generation Comput Syst 29(1): 387–401. doi:10.1016/j.future.2011.08.008, http://dx.doi.org/10.1016/j.future.2011.08.008

100. Casola V, Cuomo A, Villano U, Rak M (2012) Access control in federated clouds: The cloudgrid case study. In: Villari M, Brandic I, Tusa F (eds) Achieving Federated and Self-Manageable Cloud Infrastructures: Theory and Practice. IGI Global, pp 395–417. doi:10.4018/978-1-4666-1631-8.ch020, http://dx.doi.org/10.4018/978-1-4666-1631-8.ch020

101. SPECS project. http://www.fp7-specs.eu

102. Rak M, Ficco M (2012) Intrusion tolerance as a service - a sla-based solution. In: Leymann F, Ivanov I, van Sinderen M, Shan T (eds) 2nd International Conference on Cloud Computing and Services Science (CLOSER 2012). SciTePress, pp 375–384

103. Rak M, Liccardo L, Aversa R (2012e) A sla-based interface for secure authentication negotiation in cloud. J Inf Assur Secur 7(2): 137–146. http://www.mirlabs.org/jias/secured/Volume7-Issue3/vol7-issue3.html

104. Bennett T, Stephen an Erl, Gee C, Laird R, Manes AT, Schneider R, Shuster L, Tost A, Venable C (2011) SOA Governance: Governing Shared Services On-Premise & in the Cloud. Prentice Hall/Pearson PTR

105. Munteanu VI, Fortiş T F, Negru V (2012b) An event driven multi-agent architecture for enabling cloud governance. IEEE Computer Society Press. http://dx.doi.org/10.1109/UCC.2012.50

106. Fortiş T, Munteanu V, Negru V (2012a) Steps towards cloud governance. a survey In: 34th Internat. Conference on Information Technology Interfaces (ITI 2012), pp 29–34. http://dx.doi.org/10.2498/iti.2012.0374

107. Copie A, Fortis TF, Munteanu VI, Negru V (2012b) Datastores supporting services lifecycle in the framework of cloud governance. Scalable Comput: Pract Exp 13(3): 251–267. https://www.scpe.org/index.php/scpe/article/view/796

108. Munteanu VI, Fortiş TF, Copie A (2012a) Building a cloud governance bus. Int J Comput Commun Control 7(5): 900–906. http://journal.univagora.ro/download/pdf/642.pdf

109. Copie A, Fortis T, Munteanu V, Negru V (2012a) Service datastores in cloud governance In: 10th IEEE International Symposium on Parallel and Distributed Processing with Applications (ISPA 2012). IEEE Computer Society Press, pp 473–478. http://dx.doi.org/10.1109/ISPA.2012.69

110. Copie A, Fortis TF, Munteanu VI (2013b) Datastores in cloud governance. Int J Comput Commun Control 8(1): 42–49. http://univagora.ro/jour/index.php/ijccc/article/view/167/

111. Copie A, Fortis TF, Munteanu VI (2013a) Data security perspectives in the framework of cloud governance In: EuroPar 2012 Workshops – BDMC 2012, no. 7640 in Lecture Notes in Computer Science. Springer, pp 24–33. http://dx.doi.org/10.1007/978-3-642-36949-0_4

112. Bernstein D, Vij D, Diamond S (2011) An intercloud cloud computing economy - technology, governance, and market blueprints In: Annual SRII Global Conference (SRII 2011), pp 293–299. doi:10.1109/SRII.2011.40, http://dx.doi.org/10.1109/SRII.2011.40

113. Fortiş TF, Munteanu VI, Negru V (2012c) Towards a service friendly cloud ecosystem In: 11th International Symposium on Parallel and Distributed Computing (ISPDC 2012). IEEE Computer Society Press, pp 172–179. http://dx.doi.org/10.1109/ISPDC.2012.31

114. Frîncu ME (2010) Scheduling service oriented workflows inside clouds using an adaptive agent based approach. In: Furht B, Escalante A (eds) Handbook of Cloud Computing. Springer, pp 159–182. doi:10.1007/978-1-4419-6524-0_7, http://dx.doi.org/10.1007/978-1-4419-6524-0_7

115. Frîncu ME, Villegas NM, Petcu D, Muller HA, Rouvoy R (2011) Self-healing distributed scheduling platform In: 11th IEEE/ACM International Symposium on Cluster, Cloud and Grid Computing (CCGrid 2011). IEEE Computer Society Press, pp 225–234. doi:10.1109/CCGrid.2011.23, http://dx.doi.org/10.1109/CCGrid.2011.23

116. Frîncu ME (2012) Scheduling highly available applications on cloud environments. Future Generation Comput Syst 29. doi:10.1016/j.future.2012.05.017, http://www.sciencedirect.com/science/article/pii/S0167739X12001136

117. Frîncu ME, Crăciun C (2011) Multi-objective meta-heuristics for scheduling applications with high availability requirements and cost constraints in multi-cloud environments In: 4th IEEE International Conference on Utility and Cloud Computing (UCC 2011). IEEE Computer Society Press, pp 267–274. doi:10.1109/UCC.2011.43, http://dx.doi.org/10.1109/UCC.2011.43

118. Di Martino B, Aversa R, Venticinque S, Buonanno L (2011a) Competitive p2p scheduling of users' jobs in cloud In: 2nd Internat. Conference on Cloud Computing, Grids, & Virtualization (Cloud Computing 2011). IARIA, pp 105–112. http://www.thinkmind.org/download.php?articleid=cloud_computing_2011_4_40_20137

119. Rak M, Venticinque S, Máhr T, Echevarria G, Esnal G (2011c) Cloud application monitoring: The mosaic approach In: 3rd IEEE International Conference on Cloud Computing Technology and Science (CloudCom 2011). IEEE Computer Society Press, pp 758–763. http://dx.doi.org/10.1109/CloudCom.2011.117

120. Stankovski V, Petcu D (2013) Developing a model driven approach for engineering applications based on mosaic. Cluster Computing. http://dx.doi.org/10.1007/s10586-013-0263-x

121. Moscato F, Di Martino B, Aversa R (2012b) Enabling model driven engineering of cloud services by using mosaic ontology. Scalable Comput: Pract Exp 13(1): 29–47. http://www.scpe.org/index.php/scpe/article/download/765/345

122. Moscato F, Aversa R, Amato A (2012a) Describing cloud use case in metamorp(h)osy In: 6th International Conference on Complex, Intelligent, and Software Intensive Systems (CISIS 2012). IEEE Computer Society Press, pp 793–798. doi:10.1109/CISIS.2012.143, http://dx.doi.org/10.1109/CISIS.2012.143

123. Cloud@Home project. http://cloudathome.unime.it/

124. Amicas project. http://amicas.hpc.uvt.ro

125. Aversa R, Bruneo D, Cuomo A, Martino B, Distefano S, Puliafito A, Rak M, Venticinque S, Villano U (2011a) Cloud@home: Performance management components. In: Guarracino M, Vivien F, Träff J, Cannataro M, Danelutto M, Hast A, Perla F, Knüpfer A, Di Martino B, Alexander M (eds) Euro-Par 2010 Parallel Processing Workshops, Lecture Notes in Computer Science, vol 6586. Springer, pp 579–586. doi:10.1007/978-3-642-21878-1_71, http://dx.doi.org/10.1007/978-3-642-21878-1_71

126. Distefano S, Puliafito A, Rak M, Venticinque S, Villano U, Cuomo A, Di Modica G, Tomarchio O (2011) Qos management in cloud@home infrastructures In: International Conference on Cyber-Enabled Distributed Computing and Knowledge Discovery (CyberC 2011). IEEE Computer Society Press, pp 190–197. http://dx.doi.org/10.1109/CyberC.2011.40

127. Cuomo A, Di Modica G, Distefano S, Puliafito A, Rak M, Tomarchio O, Venticinque S, Villano U (2013a) An sla-based broker for cloud infrastructures. J Grid Comput 11: 1–25. http://dx.doi.org/10.1007/s10723-012-9241-4

128. Rak M, Cuomo A, Villano U (2011a) Chase: An autonomic service engine for cloud environments In: 20th IEEE International Workshops on Enabling Technologies: Infrastructure for Collaborative Enterprises (WETICE 2011). IEEE Computer Society Press, pp 116–121. http://dx.doi.org/10.1109/WETICE.2011.21

129. Petcu D (2012e) Towards programmable infrastructures: the steps made by cloud computing and their technical support In: WoSS-4, CLASS Conference. Slovenia, pp 19–21. http://www.kc-class.eu/datoteke/proceedings-woss-4.pdf

130. Petcu D, Frîncu ME, Panica S, Neagul M (2012a) Towards programmatic management of services from multiple clouds In: 4th International Conference on Intelligent Networking and Collaborative Systems (INCoS 2012). IEEE Computer Society Press, pp 487–488. http://dx.doi.org/10.1109/iNCoS.2012.77

131. Calcavecchia NM, Căprărescu BA, Di Nitto E, Dubois DJ, Petcu D (2012) Depas: A decentralized probabilistic algorithm for auto-scaling. Computing 94: 701–730. doi:10.1007/s00607-012-0198-8, http://dx.doi.org/10.1007/s00607-012-0198-8

132. Căprărescu BA, Petcu D (2012) Decentralized probabilistic auto-scaling for heterogeneous systems In: 4th International Conference on Adaptive and Self-Adaptive Systems and Applications (Adaptive 2012), pp 7–12. http://www.thinkmind.org/download.php?articleid=adaptive_2012_1_20_50022

133. Căprărescu BA, Kaslik E, Petcu D (2012) Theoretical analysis and tuning of decentralized probabilistic auto-scaling. CoRR abs/1202.2981, http://arxiv.org/abs/1202.2981

134. MODAClouds project. http://www.modaclouds.eu

135. Ardagna D, di Nitto E, Mohagheghi P, Mosser S, Ballagny C, D'Andria F, Casale G, Matthews P, Nechifor CS, Petcu D, Gericke A, Sheridan C (2012) Modaclouds: A model-driven approach for the design and execution of applications on multiple clouds In: ICSE Workshop on Modeling in Software Engineering (MISE 2012), pp 50–56. doi:10.1109/MISE.2012.6226014, http://dx.doi.org/10.1109/MISE.2012.6226014

136. Helix Nebula project. http://helix-nebula.eu

137. Aversa R, Di Martino B, Rak M, Venticinque S, Villano U (2011c) Performance prediction for hpc on clouds In: Cloud Computing. John Wiley & Sons, Inc, pp 437–456. doi:10.1002/9780470940105.ch17, http://dx.doi.org/10.1002/9780470940105.ch17

138. HOST project. http://host.hpc.uvt.ro

139. Research potential of convergence regions. http://cordis.europa.eu/fp7/capacities/convergence-regions_en.html

140. Drozdowicz M, Wasielewska K, Ganzha M, Paprzycki M, Attaoui N, Lirkov I, Olejnik R, Petcu D, Bădică C (2011) Ontology for contract negotiations in an agent-based grid resource management system. In: Iványi P, Topping BHV (eds) Trends in Parallel, Distributed, Grid and Cloud Computing for Engineering. Saxe-Coburg Publications, pp 335–354. doi:10.4203/csets.27.15

141. Wasielewska K, Ganzha M, Paprzycki M, Drozdowicz M, Petcu D, Badica C, Attaoui N, Lirkov I, Olejnik R (2011) Negotiations in an agent-based grid resource brokering system. In: Iványi P, Topping BHV (eds) Trends in Parallel, Distributed, Grid and Cloud Computing for Engineering. Saxe-Coburg Publications, pp 355–374. doi:10.4203/csets.27.16

142. Šperka S, Smrž P (2012) Towards adaptive and semantic database model for rdf data stores In: 6th International Conference on Complex, Intelligent and Software Intensive Systems (CISIS 2012). IEEE Computer Society Press, pp 810–815. http://dx.doi.org/10.1109/CISIS.2012.137

143. Olaii. http://www.olaii.com

144. SEED project. http://www.seed-project.eu

145. Competitiveness and Innovation Framework Programme. http://ec.europa.eu/cip/

146. Petcu D (2011) Portability and interoperability between clouds: Challenges and case study. In: Abramowicz W, Llorente IM, Surridge M, Zisman A, Vayssière J (eds) Towards a Service-Based Internet, Lecture Notes in Computer Science, vol 6994. Springer, pp 62–74. doi:10.1007/978-3-642-24755-2_6, http://dx.doi.org/10.1007/978-3-642-24755-2_6

147. Jclouds. http://www.jclouds.org

148. Libcloud. http://libcloud.apache.org

149. OCCI. http://occi-wg.org

150. Deltacloud. http://deltacloud.apache.org

151. Open Virtualization Format. http://www.dmtf.org/standards/ovf

152. Cloud Data Management Interface. http://cdmi.sniacloud.com

153. Cloud Infrastructure Management Interface – Common Information Model. http://dmtf.org/sites/default/files/standards/documents/DSP0264_1.0.0.pdf

154. Unified Cloud Interface Project. http://code.google.com/p/unifiedcloud

155. CloudML. http://www.cloudml.org

156. Hogan M, Liu F, Sokol A, Tong J (2011) Nist cloud computing standards roadmap-version 1.0. Tech. rep. NIST Special Publication 500–291. http://www.nist.gov/customcf/get_pdf.cfm?pub_id=909024

157. Ferrer AJ, Hernández F, Tordsson J, Elmroth E, Ali-Eldin A, Zsigri C, Sirvent R, Guitart J, Badia RM, Djemame K, Ziegler W, Dimitrakos T, Nair SK, Kousiouris G, Konstanteli K, Varvarigou T, Hudzia B, Kipp A, Wesner S, Corrales M, Forgó N, Sharif T, Sheridan C (2012) Optimis: A holistic approach to cloud service provisioning. Future Generation Comput Syst 28(1): 66–77. doi:10.1016/j.future.2011.05.022, http://dx.doi.org/10.1016/j.future.2011.05.022

158. Grozev N, Buyya R (2012) Inter-cloud architectures and application brokering: Taxonomy and survey. Softw Pract Exp. doi:10.1002/spe.2168, http://dx.doi.org/10.1002/spe.2168

159. Simple Cloud API. http://www.simplecloud.org

160. SAGA – a simple api for grid applications. http://saga-project.github.com

161. RightScale. http://www.rightscale.com

162. Enstratius. http://www.enstratius.com/

163. Kaavo. http://www.kaavo.com

164. Aeolus. http://www.aeolusproject.org

165. OPTIMIS Toolkit v2. http://www.optimis-project.eu/Toolkit_v2

166. Petcu D (2012d) A panorama of cloud services. Scalable Computing:
     Pract Exp 13(4): 303–314
167. SpotCloud. http://spotcloud.com
168. WSO2 Stratos. http://wso2.com/cloud/stratos
169. Petcu D, Stankovski V (2012) Towards cloud-enabled business process
     management based on patterns, rules and multiple models In: 10th IEEE
     Internat. Symposium on Parallel & Distributed Processing with
     Applications (ISPA 2012). IEEE Computer Society, pp 454–459. http://dx.
     doi.org/10.1109/ISPA.2012.66
170. Heroku. https://www.heroku.com
171. Crăciun CD (2012) Building Blocks of Scalable Applications. Master's
     thesis, West University of Timişoara, Computer Science Department.
     https://github.com/downloads/cipriancraciun/masters-thesis/thesis.pdf
172. Petcu D, Rak M (2013) Open-source cloudware support for the
     portability of applications using cloud infrastructure services. In:
     Mahmood Z (ed) Cloud Computing: Methods and Practical Approaches,
     Computer Communications and Networks. Springer, chap 15,
     pp 323–341. http://dx.doi.org/10.1007/978-1-4471-5107-4_15
173. Contrail project. http://contrail-project.eu
174. OpenShift. https://www.openshift.com
175. Petcu D (2012c) Invitation to a journey in the era of cloud computing In:
     European Research Activities in Cloud Computing. Cambridge Scholars
     Publishing, pp 1–20. http://www.c-s-p.org/Flyers/978-1-4438-3507-7-
     sample.pdf
176. Petcu D, Vasquez-Poletti JL (2012) European Research on Cloud
     Computing. Cambridge Scholars Publishing, Cambridge
177. Bessani A, Kapitza R, Petcu D, Romano P, Gogouvitis SV, Kyriazis D,
     Cascella RG (2012) A look to the old-world sky: Eu-funded dependability
     cloud computing research. SIGOPS Oper Syst Rev 46(2): 43–56.
     doi:10.1145/2331576.2331584, http://doi.acm.org/10.1145/2331576.
     2331584
178. 4CaaSt project. http://4caast.morfeo-project.org/
179. Cloud4SOA project. http://www.cloud4soa.eu
180. Cloud-TM pproject. http://www.cloudtm.eu
181. REMICS project. http://www.remics.eu
182. TClouds project. http://www.tclouds-project.eu
183. VISION Cloud project. http://www.visioncloud.eu

3

Data management in cloud environments: NoSQL and NewSQL data stores

Katarina Grolinger[1], Wilson A Higashino[1,2*], Abhinav Tiwari[1] and Miriam AM Capretz[1]

Abstract

Advances in Web technology and the proliferation of mobile devices and sensors connected to the Internet have resulted in immense processing and storage requirements. Cloud computing has emerged as a paradigm that promises to meet these requirements. This work focuses on the storage aspect of cloud computing, specifically on data management in cloud environments. Traditional relational databases were designed in a different hardware and software era and are facing challenges in meeting the performance and scale requirements of Big Data. NoSQL and NewSQL data stores present themselves as alternatives that can handle huge volume of data. Because of the large number and diversity of existing NoSQL and NewSQL solutions, it is difficult to comprehend the domain and even more challenging to choose an appropriate solution for a specific task. Therefore, this paper reviews NoSQL and NewSQL solutions with the objective of: (1) providing a perspective in the field, (2) providing guidance to practitioners and researchers to choose the appropriate data store, and (3) identifying challenges and opportunities in the field. Specifically, the most prominent solutions are compared focusing on data models, querying, scaling, and security related capabilities. Features driving the ability to scale read requests and write requests, or scaling data storage are investigated, in particular partitioning, replication, consistency, and concurrency control. Furthermore, use cases and scenarios in which NoSQL and NewSQL data stores have been used are discussed and the suitability of various solutions for different sets of applications is examined. Consequently, this study has identified challenges in the field, including the immense diversity and inconsistency of terminologies, limited documentation, sparse comparison and benchmarking criteria, and nonexistence of standardized query languages.

Keywords: NoSQL; NewSQL; Big data; Cloud computing; Distributed storage; Data management

Introduction

In recent years, advances in Web technology and the proliferation of sensors and mobile devices connected to the Internet have resulted in the generation of immense data sets that need to be processed and stored. Just on Facebook, 2.4 billion content items are shared among friends every day [1]. Today, businesses generate massive volume of data which has grown too big to be managed and analyzed by traditional data processing tools [2]. Indeed, traditional relational database management systems (RDBMS) were designed in an era when the available hardware, as well as the storage and processing requirements, were very different than they are today [3]. Therefore, these solutions have been encountering many challenges in meeting the performance and scaling requirements of this "Big Data" reality.

Big Data is a term used to refer to massive and complex datasets made up of a variety of data structures, including structured, semi-structured, and unstructured data. According to the Gartner group, Big Data can be defined by 3Vs: volume, velocity, and variety [4]. Today, businesses are aware that this huge volume of data can be used to generate new opportunities and process improvements through their processing and analysis [5,6].

At about the same time, cloud computing has also emerged as a computational paradigm for on-demand network access to a shared pool of computing resources (e.g., network, servers, storage, applications, and services) that can be rapidly provisioned with minimal management effort [7]. Cloud computing is associated with service provisioning, in which service providers offer computer-based services to consumers over the network. Often these

* Correspondence: whigashi@uwo.ca
[1]Department of Electrical and Computer Engineering, Faculty of Engineering, Western University, London, ON N6A 5B9, Canada
[2]Instituto de Computação, Universidade Estadual de Campinas, Campinas, SP, Brazil

services are based on a pay-per-use model where the consumer pays only for the resources used. Overall, a cloud computing model aims to provide benefits in terms of lesser up-front investment, lower operating costs, higher scalability, elasticity, easy access through the Web, and reduced business risks and maintenance expenses [8].

Due to such characteristics of cloud computing, many applications have been created in or migrated to cloud environments over the last few years [9]. In fact, it is interesting to notice the extent of synergy between the processing requirements of Big Data applications, and the availability and scalability of computational resources offered by cloud services. Nevertheless, the effective leveraging of cloud infrastructure requires careful design and implementation of applications and data management systems. Cloud environments impose new requirements to data management; specifically, a cloud data management system needs to have:

- Scalability and high performance, because today's applications are experiencing continuous growth in terms of the data they need to store, the users they must serve, and the throughput they should provide;
- Elasticity, as cloud applications can be subjected to enormous fluctuations in their access patterns;
- Ability to run on commodity heterogeneous servers, as most cloud environments are based on them;
- Fault tolerance, given that commodity machines are much more prone to fail than high-end servers;
- Security and privacy features, because the data may now be stored on third-party premises on resources shared among different tenants;
- Availability, as critical applications have also been moving to the cloud and cannot afford extended periods of downtime.

Faced with the challenges that traditional RDBMSs encounter in handling Big Data and in satisfying the cloud requirements described above, a number of specialized solutions have emerged in the last few years in an attempt to address these concerns. The so-called NoSQL and NewSQL data stores present themselves as data processing alternatives that can handle this huge volume of data and provide the required scalability.

Despite the appropriateness of NoSQL and NewSQL data stores as cloud data management systems, the immense number of existing solutions (over 120 [10]) and the discrepancies among them make it difficult to formulate a perspective on the domain and even more challenging to select the appropriate solution for a problem at hand. This survey reviews NoSQL and

NewSQL data stores with the intent of filling this gap. More specifically, this survey has the following objectives:

- To provide a perspective on the domain by summarizing, organizing, and categorizing NoSQL and NewSQL solutions.
- To compare the characteristics of the leading solutions in order to provide guidance to practitioners and researchers to choose the appropriate data store for specific applications.
- To identify research challenges and opportunities in the field of large-scale distributed data management.

NoSQL data models and categorization of NoSQL data stores have been addressed in other surveys [10-14]. In addition, aspects associated with NoSQL, such as MapReduce, the CAP theorem, and eventual consistency have also been discussed in the literature [15,16]. This paper presents a short overview of NoSQL concepts and data models; nevertheless, the main contributions of this paper include:

- A discussion of NewSQL data stores. The category of NewSQL solutions is recent; the first use of the term was in 2011 [17]. NewSQL solutions aim to bring the relational data model into the world of NoSQL. Therefore, a comparison among NewSQL and NoSQL solutions is essential to understand this new class of data stores.
- A detailed comparison among various NoSQL and NewSQL solutions over a large number of dimensions. By presenting this comparison in a table form, this paper helps practitioners to choose the appropriate data store for the task at hand. Previous surveys have included comparisons of NoSQL solutions [11]; nonetheless, the number of compared attributes was limited, and the analysis performed was not as comprehensive.
- A review of a number of security features is also included in the data store comparison. According to the surveyed literature [10-14], security has been overlooked, even though it is an important aspect of the adoption of NoSQL solutions in practice.
- A discussion of the suitability of various NoSQL and NewSQL solutions for different sets of applications. NoSQL and NewSQL solutions differ greatly in their characteristics; moreover, changes in this area are rapid, with frequent releases of new features and options. Therefore, this work discusses the suitability of NoSQL and NewSQL data stores for different use cases from the perspective of core design decisions.

The rest of this paper is organized as follows: the "Background and Related Work" section describes background concepts and studies related to this survey. The methodology used in this survey is presented in the "Methodology" section. The "Data Models" section presents the NoSQL and NewSQL data models and categorizes the surveyed data stores accordingly. Querying capabilities are discussed in the "Querying" section, while the "Scaling" section describes the solutions' scaling properties and the "Security" section their security features. The suitability of NoSQL and NewSQL data stores for different use cases is discussed in the "Use Cases" section. The challenges and opportunities identified in this study are described in the "Opportunities" section, and the "Conclusions" section concludes the paper.

Background and related work

This section introduces relevant concepts and positions this paper with respect to other surveys in the NoSQL domain.

Cloud computing

Cloud computing is a model for enabling ubiquitous, convenient, on-demand network access to a shared pool of configurable computing resources (e.g., network, servers, storage, applications, and services) that can be rapidly provisioned and released with minimal management effort or service provider interaction [7]. It denotes a model in which a computing infrastructure is viewed as a "cloud", from which businesses and individuals can access applications on demand from anywhere in the world [18]. Essential characteristics of the cloud-computing model, according to the U.S. National Institute of Standards and Technology (NIST), include [7]:

- On-demand self-service, enabling a user to access cloud provider services without human interaction;
- Broad network access that enables heterogeneous thick and thin client applications to access the services;
- Pooling of service provider computing resources to serve multiple consumers;
- Automatic, rapid, and elastic provisioning of resources;
- Measured service in which resource usage is monitored and controlled.

Overall, a cloud computing model aims to provide benefits in terms of lesser up-front investment in infrastructure during deployment, lower operating costs, higher scalability, ease of access through the Web, and reduced business risks and maintenance expenses [8].

The CAP theorem

In order to store and process massive datasets, a common employed strategy is to partition the data and store the partitions across different server nodes. Additionally, these partitions can also be replicated in multiple servers so that the data is still available even in case of servers' failures. Many modern data stores, such as Cassandra [19] and BigTable [20], use these and others strategies to implement high-available and scalable solutions that can be leveraged in cloud environments. Nevertheless, these solutions and others replicated networked data stores have an important restriction, which was formalized by the CAP theorem [21]: only two of three CAP properties (consistency, availability, and partition tolerance) can be satisfied by networked shared-data systems at the same time [21,22].

Consistency, as interpreted in CAP, is equivalent to having a single up-to-date instance of the data [22]. Therefore, *consistency* in CAP has a somewhat dissimilar meaning to and represents only a subset of *consistency* as defined in ACID (Atomicity, Consistency, Isolation and Durability) transactions of RDBMSs [22], which usually refers to the capability of maintaining the database in a consistent state at all times. The *Availability* property means that the data should be available to serve a request at the moment it is needed. Finally, the *Partition Tolerance* property refers to the capacity of the networked shared-data system to tolerate network partitions. The simplest interpretation of the CAP theorem is to consider a distributed data store partitioned into two sets of participant nodes; if the data store denies all write requests in both partitions, it will remain consistent, but it is not available. On the other hand, if one (or both) of the partitions accepts write requests, the data store is available, but potentially inconsistent.

Despite the relative simplicity of its result, the CAP theorem has had important implications and has originated a great variety of distributed data stores aiming to explore the trade-offs between the three properties. More specifically, the challenges of RDBMS in handling Big Data and the use of distributed systems techniques in the context of the CAP theorem led to the development of new classes of data stores called NoSQL and NewSQL.

NoSQL and NewSQL

The origin of the NoSQL term is attributed to Johan Oskarsson, who used it in 2009 to name a conference about "open-source, distributed, non-relational databases" [23]. Today, the term is used as an acronym for "Not only SQL", which emphasizes that SQL-style querying is not the crucial objective of these data stores. Therefore, the term is used as an umbrella classification that includes a large number of immensely diverse data stores that are not based on the relational model, including some solutions designed for very specific applications such as graph storage. Even though there is no agreement on what exactly constitutes a NoSQL solution, the following set of characteristics is often attributed to them [11,15]:

- Simple and flexible non-relational data models. NoSQL data stores offer flexible schemas or are sometimes completely schema-free and are designed to handle a wide variety of data structures [11,12,24]. Current solution data models can be divided into four categories: key-value stores, document stores, column-family stores, and graph databases.
- Ability to scale horizontally over many commodity servers. Some data stores provide data scaling, while others are more concerned with read and/or write scaling.
- Provide high availability. Many NoSQL data stores are aimed towards highly distributed scenarios, and consider partition tolerance as unavoidable. Therefore, in order to provide high availability, these solutions choose to compromise consistency in favour of availability, resulting in AP (Available/ Partition-tolerant) data stores, while most RDBMs are CA (Consistent/Available).
- Typically, they do not support ACID transactions as provided by RDBMS. NoSQL data stores are sometimes referred as BASE systems (Basically Available, Soft state, Eventually consistent) [25]. In this acronym, *Basically Available* means that the data store is available all the time whenever it is accessed, even if parts of it are unavailable; *Soft-state* highlights that it does not need to be consistent always and can tolerate inconsistency for a certain time period; and *Eventually consistent* emphasizes that after a certain time period, the data store comes to a consistent state. However, some NoSQL data stores, such as CouchDB [26] provide ACID compliance.

These characteristics make NoSQL data stores especially suitable for use as cloud data management systems. Indeed, many of the Database as a Service offerings available today, such as Amazon's SimpleDB [27] and DynamoDB [28], are considered to be NoSQL data stores. However, the lack of full ACID transaction support can be a major impediment to their adoption in many mission-critical systems. For instance, Corbert *et al.* [29] argue that it is better to deal with performance problems caused by the overuse of transactions rather than trying to work around the lack of transaction support. Furthermore, the use of low-level query languages, the lack of standardized interfaces, and the huge investments already made in SQL by

enterprises are other barriers to the adoption of NoSQL data stores.

The category of NewSQL data stores, on the other hand, is being used to classify a set of solutions aimed at bringing to the relational model the benefits of horizontal scalability and fault tolerance provided by NoSQL solutions. The first use of the term is attributed to a report of the 451 group in 2011 [17]. The Google Spanner [29] solution is considered to be one of the most prominent representatives of this category, as is also VoltDB [30], which is based on the H-Store [31] research project. Clustrix [32] and NuoDB [33] are two commercial projects that are also classified as NewSQL. All these data stores support the relational model and use SQL as their query language, even though they are based on different assumptions and architectures than traditional RDBMSs. Generally speaking, NewSQL data stores meet many of the requirements for data management in cloud environments and also offer the benefits of the well-known SQL standard.

Related surveys

Several surveys have addressed the NoSQL domain [10-14]; nevertheless, this survey is different because it focuses on the comparison of available NoSQL and NewSQL solutions over a number of dimensions. Hecht and Jablonski [11] presented a use case-oriented survey, which, like this one, compares features of several NoSQL solutions, including the data models, querying capabilities, partitioning, replication, and consistency. However, for a large number of features, they use a "black and white" (+/−) approach to indicate that the solution either does or does not have the feature. This survey adopts a different approach by expressing degrees, aspects, and details of each solution's features. Moreover, this survey includes security features and NewSQL solutions, which are not addressed in their work.

Pokorny [13], Cattell [12], and Sakr *et al.* [14] have also reviewed NoSQL data stores. They portrayed a number of NoSQL data stores, describing their data models and their main underlying principles and features. However, in contrast to this work, they did not perform direct feature comparison among data stores. Sadalage and Fowler [15] described the principles on which NoSQL stores are based and why they may be superior to traditional databases. They introduced several solutions, but they did not compare features as is done in this work.

In addition, existing surveys have not described the rationale or method for choosing the specific data stores to include in their studies [11-14]. For example, Sakr *et al.* stated, "...we give a brief introduction about some of those projects" [14], or Hecht and Jablonski "The most prominent stores are ..." [11]; however, the method for choosing the data stores included in their studies were not presented. In contrast, this work uses a systematic approach to choose which data stores to include in the study. Additionally, this survey includes different data stores than the existing surveys [11-14].

Methodology

Due to the large number of NoSQL and NewSQL solutions, it was not feasible to include all of them in this survey. While other NoSQL surveys did not specify the methodology for choosing the data stores to be included in their studies [11-14], this survey makes use of a systematic approach to select the solutions.

DB-Engine Ranking [34] ranks database systems according to their popularity by using parameters such as the number of mentions on Web sites, general interest according to Google Trends, frequency of technical discussions on the Web, number of job offers, and number of professional profiles in which the solutions are mentioned. As can be seen, the DB-Engine Ranking estimates overall popularity of a data store on the Web. Nevertheless, this work is also interested in popularity within the research community; therefore, it also considers how often each system has been mentioned in research publications. Even though various research repositories could have been used, this study focuses on the IEEE as it is one of the most prominent publishers of research papers in computer science and software engineering. Hence, the initial list of NoSQL solutions was obtained from DB-Engine Ranking [34] and includes all NoSQL solutions listed by DB-Engine Ranking. Next, the IEEE Xplore database was searched to determine how many times each data store was mentioned in the indexed publications. For each NoSQL category, the most often cited data stores were chosen to be included in this survey. The key-value category was further divided into in-memory and disk-persistent key-value stores, and the most prominent solutions within each subcategory were chosen.

The prevalent data stores found in IEEE publications are similar to the data stores ranked high by DB-Engine Ranking. In the document category, the same three data stores, MongoDB [35], CouchDB [26], and Couchbase [36] are the most popular according to DB-Engine Ranking and IEEE publications. Both popularity estimation approaches rank Cassandra [19] and HBase [37] as the most prominent in the column-family category. SimpleDB [27] and DynamoDB [28] are ranked high by both approaches. While DB-Engine Ranking considers them key-value stores, this work categorizes them as column-family stores because of their table-like data model. In the remaining two categories, key-value data stores and graph databases, a large number of solutions rank high in popularity according to both approaches, including Redis [38], Memcached [39], Riak [40], BerkeleyDB [41], and Neo4J [42].

The selection of NewSQL data stores followed a similar approach. Nevertheless, because most of these solutions are very recent, only VoltDB and Spanner had a significant number of hits in the IEEE Xplore database. Therefore, in order to include a larger number of solutions in this survey, Clustrix and NuoDB were also selected because of their unique architectural and technical approaches.

The selected NoSQL and NewSQL solutions were compared with a focus on the data model, querying, scaling, and security-related capabilities. The categorization according to data model was used because the data model is the main factor driving other capabilities, including querying and scaling. In the querying context, support for MapReduce, SQL-like querying, REST (representational state transfer) and other APIs was considered. With regard to scaling, the study considered scaling read and write requests, or scaling data storage and analyzed four concepts closely related: partitioning, replication, consistency, and concurrency control. Finally, the following security related features were analyzed: authentication, authorization, encryption, and auditing.

Data models

The family of data stores belonging to the NoSQL category can be further sub-classified based on their data models. Many authors have proposed distinct interpretations for NoSQL categories, which has led to different sub-classifications [10,12]. In this paper, the classification provided by Hecht and Jablonski [11] has been used, which divides the various NoSQL data stores into four major categories: key-value stores, column-family stores, document stores, and graph databases. Figure 1 shows representations of these models. This study also reviews NewSQL as a hybrid between NoSQL stores and relational databases.

Key-value stores

Key-value stores have a simple data model based on key-value pairs, which resembles an associative map or a dictionary [11]. The key uniquely identifies the value and is used to store and retrieve the value into and out of the data store. The value is opaque to the data store and can be used to store any arbitrary data, including an integer, a string, an array, or an object, providing a schema-free data model. Along with being schema-free, key-value stores are very efficient in storing distributed data, but are not suitable for scenarios requiring relations or structures. Any functionality requiring relations, structures, or both must be implemented in the client application interacting with the key-value store. Furthermore, because the values are opaque to them, these data stores cannot handle data-level querying and indexing and can perform queries only through keys. Key-value stores can be further classified as *in-memory key-value stores* which

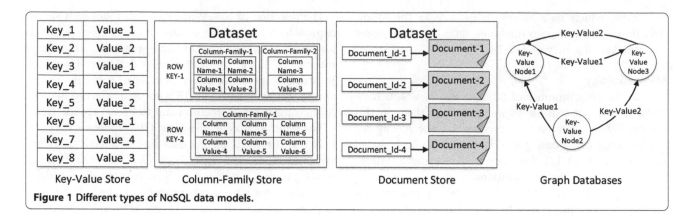

Figure 1 Different types of NoSQL data models.

keep the data in memory, like Memcached [39] and Redis [38], and *persistent key-value stores* which maintain the data on disk, such as BerkeleyDB [41], Voldemort [43], and Riak [40].

Column-family stores

Most column-family stores are derived from Google Bigtable [20], in which the data are stored in a column-oriented way. In Bigtable, the dataset consists of several rows, each of which is addressed by a unique row key, also known as a *primary key*. Each row is composed of a set of column families, and different rows can have different column families. Similarly to key-value stores, the row key resembles the key, and the set of column families resembles the value represented by the row key. However, each column family further acts as a key for the one or more columns that it holds, where each column consists of a name-value pair. Hadoop HBase [37] directly implements the Google Bigtable concepts, whereas Amazon SimpleDB [27] and DynamoDB [28] have a different data model than Bigtable. SimpleDB and DymanoDB contain only a set of column name-value pairs in each row, without having column families. Cassandra [19], on the other hand, provides the additional functionality of super-columns, which are formed by grouping various columns together.

In column-family stores, a column family in different rows can contain different columns. Occasionally, SimpleDB and DynamoDB are classified as key-value stores [34]; however, this paper considers them as column-family stores due to their table-like data model in which each row can have different columns. Typically, the data belonging to a row is stored together on the same server node. However, Cassandra offers to store a single row across multiple server nodes by using composite partition keys. In column-family stores, the configuration of column families is typically performed during start-up. However, a prior definition of columns is not required, which offers huge flexibility in storing any data type.

In general, column-family stores provide more powerful indexing and querying than key-value stores because they are based on column families and columns in addition to row keys. Similarly to key-value stores, any logic requiring relations must be implemented in the client application.

Document stores

Document stores provide another derivative of the key-value store data model by using keys to locate documents inside the data store. Most document stores represent documents using JSON (JavaScript Object Notation) or some format derived from it. For example, CouchDB [26] and the Couchbase server [36] use the JSON format for data storage, whereas MongoDB [35] stores data in BSON (Binary JSON). Document stores are suitable for applications in which the input data can be represented in a document format. A document can contain complex data structures such as nested objects and does not require adherence to a fixed schema. MongoDB provides the additional functionality of grouping the documents together into collections. Therefore, inside each collection, a document should have a unique key.

Unlike an RDBMS, where every row in a table follows the same schema, each document inside these document stores can have a different structure. Document stores provide the capability of indexing documents based on the primary key as well as on the contents of the documents. This indexing and querying capability based on document contents differentiates this data model from the key-value stores model, in which the values are opaque to the data store. On the other hand, document stores can store only data that can be represented as a document. Like key-value stores, they are inefficient in multiple-key transactions involving cross-document operations.

Graph databases

Graph databases originated from graph theory and use graphs as their data model. A graph is a mathematical concept used to represent a set of objects, known as vertices or nodes, and the links (or edges) that interconnect these vertices. By using a completely different data model than key-value, column-family, and document stores, graph databases can efficiently store the relationships between different data nodes. In graph databases, the nodes and edges also have individual properties consisting of key-value pairs. Graph databases are specialized in handling highly interconnected data and therefore are very efficient in traversing relationships between different entities. They are suitable in scenarios such as social networking applications, pattern recognition, dependency analysis, recommendation systems and solving path finding problems raised in navigation systems [11,44].

Some graph databases such as Neo4J [42] are fully ACID-compliant. However, they are not as efficient as other NoSQL data stores in scenarios other than handling graphs and relationships. Moreover, existing graph databases are not efficient at horizontal scaling because when related nodes are stored on different servers, traversing multiple servers is not performance-efficient.

NewSQL

These solutions are by definition based on the relational model. VoltDB [30], Clustrix [32], and NuoDB [33] offer their clients a pure relational view of data. On the other hand, Google Spanner [29] is based on a semi-relational model in which tables are seen as mappings from the primary-key columns to the other columns. In its model, hierarchies of tables are created so that users can specify locality relationships between tables [29].

Even though clients interact with these data stores in terms of tables and relations, it is interesting to note that NewSQL solutions might use different data representations internally. For example, NuoDB can store its data into any compatible key-value store.

Querying

Similar to the selection of a data model, the querying capabilities of data stores play an important role when choosing among them for a particular scenario. Different data stores offer different APIs and interfaces to interact with them. This is directly dependent upon the data model that a particular data store possesses. For example, a key-value store cannot provide querying based on the contents of the values, because these values are opaque to the data store. On the other hand, a document store can do so because its data model provides the capability to index and query the document contents.

Another important query-related feature of NoSQL and NewSQL data stores is their level of support for MapReduce. MapReduce, which was first developed by Google, is a programming model and an associated implementation for processing large datasets [45]. It has now become a widely accepted approach for performing distributed data processing on a cluster of computers.

Because one of the primary goals of NoSQL data stores is to scale over a large number of computers, MapReduce has been adopted by most of them. Similarly, SQL-like querying has been a preferred choice because of its widespread use over the past few decades, and it has now also been adopted in the NoSQL world. Therefore, some of the prominent NoSQL data stores like MongoDB [35] offer a SQL-like query language or similar variants such as CQL [46] offered by Cassandra and SparQL [47] by Neo4j and Allegro Graph [48].

As for the NewSQL category, the use of SQL as a query language is one of its defining characteristics, but the level of SQL support varies considerably. Clustrix [32] and NuoDB [33] are the most SQL-compliant of the solutions analyzed, having only minor incompatibilities with the standard. On the other hand, Corbett et al. state that the Google Spanner query language "looks like SQL with some extensions to support protocol-buffer-value fields" [29], but they do not provide details about the language. Finally, VoltDB [30] has a larger number of restrictions in place: it is not possible to use the *having* clause, tables cannot join with themselves, and all joined tables must be partitioned over the same value. It is also worth mentioning that the recommended way of interacting with VoltDB is through Stored Procedures. These procedures are written in Java, where programming logic and SQL statements are interspersed.

On the other hand, a command-line interface (CLI) is usually the simplest and most common interface that a data store can provide for interaction with itself and is therefore offered by almost all NoSQL and NewSQL products. In addition, most of these products offer API support for multiple languages. Moreover, a REST-based API has been very popular in the world of Web-based applications because of its simplicity [49]. Consequently, in the NoSQL world, a REST-based interface is provided by most solutions, either directly or indirectly through third-party APIs. Table 1 provides a detailed view of the different APIs support provided by the most prominent NoSQL and NewSQL solutions along with other querying capabilities offered.

Scaling

One of the main characteristics of the NoSQL and NewSQL data stores is their ability to scale horizontally and effectively by adding more servers into the resource pool. Even though there have been attempts to scale relational databases horizontally, on the contrary, RDBs are designed to scale vertically by means of adding more power to a single existing server [3].

With regard to what is being scaled, three scaling dimensions are considered: scaling read requests, scaling write requests, or scaling data storage. The partitioning, replication, consistency, and concurrency control strategies used

Table 1 Querying capabilities

NoSQL data stores		Querying					License
		Map reduce	REST	Query	Other API	Other features	
Key-value stores	**Redis** http://redis.io	No	Third-party APIs	Does not provide SQL-like querying	CLI and API in several languages	Server-side scripting support using Lua.	Open source: BSD (Berkeley Software Distribution).
	Memcached http://memcached.org	No	Third-party APIs	Does not provide SQL-like querying	CLI and API in several languages. Binary and ASCII protocols for custom client development	No server-side scripting support.	Open source: BSD 3-clause license.
	BerkeleyDB http://www.oracle.com/us/products/database/berkeley-db/overview/index.html	No	Yes	SQLite	CLI and API in several languages.	No secondary indices, no server-side-scripting support.	Closed source: Oracle sleepycat license.
	Voldemort http://www.project-voldemort.com/voldemort	Yes	Under development	No	Clients for several languages		Open source: Apache 2.0 license.
	Riak http://basho.com/riak	Yes	Yes	Riak search, secondary indices	CLI and API in several languages	Provides filtering through key filters. Configurable secondary indexing. Provides Solr search capabilities. Provides server-side scripting.	Open source: Apache 2.0 license.
Column family stores	**Cassandra** http://cassandra.apache.org	Yes	Third party APIs	Cassandra query language	CLI and API in several languages. Supports Thrift interface	Secondary indexing mechanisms include column families, super-columns, collections.	Open source: Apache 2.0 license.
	HBase http://hbase.apache.org	Yes	Yes	No, could be used with Hive	Java/Any Writer	Server-side scripting support. Several secondary indexing mechanisms.	Open source: Apache 2.0 license.
	DynamoDB (Amazon service) http://aws.amazon.com/dynamodb	Amazon Elastic MapReduce	Yes	Proprietary	API in several languages	Provides secondary indexing based on attributes other than primary keys.	Closed source: Pricing as pay-per-use basis.
	Amazon SimpleDB (Amazon service) http://aws.amazon.com/simpledb	No	Yes	Amazon proprietary	Amazon proprietary API	Automatic indexing for all columns.	Closed source: Pricing as pay-per-use basis.
Document stores	**MongoDB** http://www.mongodb.org	Yes	Yes	Proprietary	CLI and API in several languages	Server-side scripting and secondary indexing support. A powerful aggregation framework.	Open source: Free GNU AGPL v3.0 license.
	CouchDB http://couchdb.apache.org	Yes	Yes	SQL like UnQL, under development	API in several languages	Server-side scripting and secondary indexing support.	Open source: Apache 2.0 license.
	Couchbase server http://www.couchbase.com	Yes	Yes	No	Memcached API + protocol (binary and ASCII) in several languages.	Server-side scripting and secondary indexing support.	Open source: Free community edition. Paid enterprise edition.
Graph databases	**Neo4J** http://www.neo4j.org	No	Yes	Cypher, Gremlin and SparQL	CLI and API in several languages	Server-side scripting and secondary indexing support.	Open source license: NTCL + (A)GPLv3.
	HyperGraphDB www.hypergraphdb.org/	No	Yes	SQL like querying	Currently has Java API. Could be used with Scala.	Provides a search engine and Seco scripting IDE.	Open source license: GNU LGPLv3.

Table 1 Querying capabilities (*Continued*)

	Allegro graph http://www.franz.com/agraph/allegrograph	No	Yes	SparQL and Prolog	API in several languages	Support for Solr indexing and search.	Closed source: free, developer and enterprise versions.
NewSQL	**VoltDB** http://voltdb.com/	No	Yes	SQL	CLI and API in several languages. JDBC support	Stored procedures are written in Java. Tables cannot join with themselves, and all joined tables must be partitioned over the same value.	Open source AGPL v3.0 license.Commercial enterprise edition.
	Spanner	Yes	NA	SQL like language	NA	Tables are partitioned into hierarchies, which describe locality relationship between tables.	Google internal use only.
	Clustrix http://www.clustrix.com/	No	No	SQL	Wire protocol compatible with MySQL.		Closed source. Available as a service in the AWS marketplace, as an appliance, and as standalone software.
	NuoDB http://www.nuodb.com/	No	No	SQL	CLI and drivers for most common data access APIs (JDBC, ODBC, ADO.NET). Also provides a C++ API.	No support for stored procedures.	Closed source. Pro and developers editions. Available as a service in the AWS marketplace.

by the NoSQL and NewSQL data stores have significant impact on their scalability. For example, partitioning determines the distribution of data among multiple servers and is therefore a means of achieving all three scaling dimensions.

Another important factor in scaling read and write requests is replication: storing the same data on multiple servers so that read and write operations can be distributed over them. Replication also has an important role in providing fault tolerance because data availability can withstand the failure of one or more servers. Furthermore, the choice of replication model is also strongly related to the consistency level provided by the data store. For example, the master–slave asynchronous replication model cannot provide consistent read requests from slaves.

Finally, another influential factor in scaling read and write requests is concurrency control. Simple read/write lock techniques may not provide sufficient concurrency control for the read and write throughput required by NoSQL and NewSQL solutions. Therefore, most solutions use more advanced techniques, such as optimistic locking with multi-version concurrency control (MVCC).

In the following subsections, partitioning, replication, consistency, and concurrency control strategies of NoSQL and NewSQL data stores will be compared; an overview is presented in Table 2.

Partitioning

Most NoSQL and NewSQL data stores implement some sort of horizontal partitioning or sharding, which involves storing sets or rows/records into different segments (or shards) which may be located on different servers. In contrast, vertical partitioning involves storing sets of columns into different segments and distributing them accordingly. The data model is a significant factor in defining strategies for data store partitioning. For example, vertical partitioning segments contain predefined groups of columns; therefore, data stores from the column-family category can provide vertical partitioning in addition to horizontal partitioning.

The two most common horizontal-partitioning strategies are range partitioning and consistent hashing. *Range partitioning* assigns data to partitions residing in different servers based on ranges of a partition key. A server is responsible for the storage and read/write handling of a specific range of keys. The advantage of this approach is the effective processing of range queries, because adjacent keys often reside in the same node. However, this approach can result in hot spots and load-balancing issues. For example, if the data are processed in the order of their key values, the processing load will always be concentrated on a single server or a few servers. Another disadvantage is that the mapping of ranges to partitions and nodes must

be maintained, usually by a routing server, so that the client can be directed to the correct server. BerkeleyDB, Cassandra, HBase, and MongoDB implement range partitioning as depicted in Table 2.

In *consistent hashing*, the dataset is represented as a circle or ring. The ring is divided into a number of ranges equal to the number of available nodes, and each node is mapped to a point on the ring. Figure 2 illustrates consistent hashing on an example with four nodes N1 to N4. To determine the node where an object should be placed, the system hashes the object's key and finds its location on the ring. In the example from Figure 2, object *a* is located between nodes N4 and N1. Next, the ring is walked clockwise until the first node is encountered, and the object gets assigned to that node. Accordingly, object *a* from Figure 2 gets assigned to node N1. Consequently, each node is responsible for the ring region between itself and its predecessor; for example, node N1 is responsible for data range 1, node N2 for data range 2, and so on. With consistent hashing, the location of an object can be calculated very fast, and there is no need for a mapping service as in range partitioning. This approach is also efficient in dynamic resizing: if nodes are added to or removed from the ring, only neighbouring regions are reassigned to different nodes, and the majority of records remain unaffected [16]. However, consistent hashing negatively impacts range queries because neighbouring keys are distributed across a number of different nodes. Voldemort, Riak, Cassandra, DynamoDB, CouchDB, VoltDB, and Clustrix implement consistent hashing.

The in-memory stores analyzed, Redis and Memcache, do not implement any partitioning strategy and leave it to the client to devise one. Amazon SimpleDB, the NoSQL solution which is provided as a service, offers its clients simple, manual mechanisms for partitioning data, as described in Table 2. However, the service provider might implement additional partitioning to achieve the throughput capacity specified in the service level agreement.

Partitioning graph databases is significantly more challenging than partitioning other NoSQL stores [50]. The key-value, column-family, and document data stores partition data according to a key, which is known and relatively stable. In addition, data are accessed using a lookup mechanism. In contrast, graphs are highly mutable structures, which do not have stable keys. Graph data are not accessed by performing lookups, but by exploiting relations among entities. Consequently, graph partitioning attempts to achieve a trade-off between two conflicting requirements: related graph nodes must be located on the same server to achieve good traversal performance, but, at the same time, too many graph nodes should not be on the same server because this may result in heavy and concentrated load. A number of graph-partitioning algorithms have been proposed [50], but their adoption in practice

Table 2 Partitioning, replication, consistency, and concurrency control capabilities

NoSQL data stores		Partitioning	Replication	Consistency	Concurrency control
Key-value stores	Redis	Not available (planned for Redis Cluster release). It can be implemented by a client or a proxy.	Master–slave, asynchronous replication.	Eventual consistency. Strong consistency if slave replicas are solely for failover.	Application can implement optimistic (using the WATCH command) or pessimistic concurrency control.
	Memcached	Clients' responsibility. Most clients support consistent hashing.	No replication Repcached can be added to memcached for replication.	Strong consistency (single instance).	Application can implement optimistic (using CAS with version stamps) or pessimistic concurrency control.
	BerkeleyDB	Key-range partitioning and custom partitioning functions. Not supported by the C# and Java APIs at this time.	Master–slave	Configurable	Readers–writer locks
	Voldemort	Consistent hashing.	Masterless, asynchronous replication. Replicas are located on the first R nodes moving over the partitioning ring in a clockwise direction.	Configurable, based on quorum read and write requests.	MVCC with vector clock
	Riak	Consistent hashing.	Masterless, asynchronous replication. The built-in functions determine how replicas distribute the data evenly.	Configurable, based on quorum read and write requests.	MVCC with vector clock.
Column family stores	Cassandra	Consistent hashing and range partitioning (known as order preserving partitioning in Cassandra terminology) is not recommended due to the possibility of hot spots and load balancing issues.	Masterless, asynchronous replication. Two strategies for placing replicas: replicas are placed on the next R nodes along the ring; or, replica 2 is placed on the first node along the ring that belongs to another data centre, with the remaining replicas on the nodes along the ring in the same rack as the first.	Configurable, based on quorum read and write requests.	Client-provided timestamps are used to determine the most recent update to a column. The latest timestamp always wins and eventually persists.
	HBase	Range partitioning.	Master–slave or multi-master, asynchronous replication. Does not support read load balancing (a row is served by exactly one server). Replicas are used only for failover.	Strong consistency	MVCC
	DynamoDB	Consistent hashing.	Three-way replication across multiple zones in a region. Synchronous replication	Configurable	Application can implement optimistic (using incrementing version numbers) or pessimistic concurrency control.
	Amazon SimpleDB	Partitioning is achieved in the DB design stage by manually adding additional domains (tables). Cannot query across domains.	Replicas within a chosen region.	Configurable	Application can implement optimistic concurrency control by maintaining a version number (or a timestamp) attribute and by performing a conditional put/delete based on the attribute value.
Document stores	MongoDB	Range partitioning based on a shard key (one or more fields that exist in every document in the collection). In addition, hashed shard keys can be used to partition data.	Master–slave, asynchronous replication.	Configurable Two methods to achieve strong consistency: set connection to read only from primary; or, set *write concern* parameter to "Replica Acknowledged".	Readers–writer locks

Table 2 Partitioning, replication, consistency, and concurrency control capabilities *(Continued)*

		Partitioning	Replication	Consistency	Concurrency control
	CouchDB	Consistent hashing.	Multi-master, asynchronous replication. Designed for off-line operation. Multiple replicas can maintain their own copies of the same data and synchronize them at a later time.	Eventual consistency.	MVCC. In case of conflicts, the winning revision is chosen, but the losing revision is saved as a previous version.
	Couchbase server	A hashing function determines to which bucket a document belongs. Next, a table is consulted to look up the server that hosts that bucket.	Multi-master.	Within a cluster: strong consistency. Across clusters: eventual consistency.	Application can implement optimistic (using CAS) or pessimistic concurrency control.
Graph databases	**Neo4J**	No partitioning (cache sharding only).	Master–slave, but can handle write requests on all server nodes. Write requests to slaves must synchronously propagate to master.	Eventual consistency.	Write locks are acquired on nodes and relationships until committed.
	Hyper GraphDB	Graph parts can reside in different P2P nodes. Builds on autonomous agent technologies.	Multi-master, asynchronous replication. Agent style communication based on Extensible Messaging and Presence Protocol (XMPP) .	Eventual consistency.	MVCC.
	Allegro graph	No partitioning (federation concept which aims to integrate graph databases is abstract at the moment).	Master–slave.	Eventual consistency.	Unclear how locking is implemented "100% Read Concurrency, Near Full Write Concurrency".
NewSQL	**VoltDB**	Consistent hashing. Users define whether stored procedures should run on a single server or on all servers.	Updates executed on all replicas at the same time.	Strong consistency.	Single threaded model (no concurrency control).
	Spanner	Data partitioned into tablets. Complex policies determine in which tablet the data should reside.	Global ordering in all replicas (Paxos state machine algorithm).	Strong consistency.	Pessimistic locking in read-write transactions. Read-only transactions are lock-free (versioned reads).
	Clustrix	Consistent hashing. Also partitions the table indices using the same approach.	Updates executed on all replicas at the same time.	Strong consistency.	MVCC.
	NuoDB	No partition. The underlying key-value store can partition the data, but it is not visible by the user.	Multi-master (distributed object replication). Asynchronous.	Eventual consistency.	MVCC.

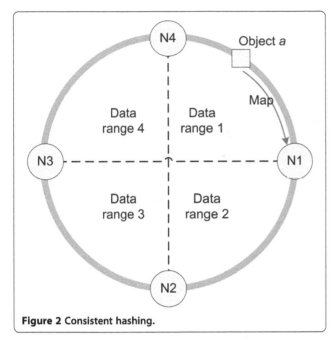

Figure 2 Consistent hashing.

has been limited. One of the reasons is the rapid pace of changes in graphs, which may trigger intensive rebalancing operations. For this reason, the graph databases investigated, Neo4J, HypergraphDB, and AllegroGraph, do not offer partitioning in the traditional sense. However, Neo4J offers cache sharding, while HypergraphDB relies on autonomous agents to provide communication among graphs residing in different peer nodes, as summarized in Table 2.

The NewSQL data stores investigated also use diverse partitioning strategies. VoltDB uses a traditional approach in which each table is partitioned using a single key and rows are distributed among servers using a consistent hashing algorithm. Stored procedures can be executed on a single partition or on all of them; however, the drawback is that the user is responsible for selecting between these options. The Clustrix data store also partitions the data using a consistent hashing algorithm over a user-defined primary key. In addition, Clustrix also partitions the table indices using the indexed columns as the keys. Theoretically, this strategy enables parallel searches over these indices, leading to faster query resolution.

Google's Spanner uses a different partitioning model. A Spanner deployment contains a set of servers known as *spanservers*, which are the nodes responsible for serving data to clients. A *spanserver* manages hundreds to thousands of *tablets*, each of which contains a set of directories. A directory is basically a set of rows that shares a common key prefix, as specified by the user-defined table hierarchy mentioned in section "Data Models". A directory is also considered to be the basic unit of placement configuration, which is used to define constraints for data partitioning and replication among the available tablets.

Some of the criteria that can be defined are the datacentres where replicas should reside, the number of replicas, the distance of the data to their clients, and the distance among replicas. The data store automatically moves the directories among the *spanservers* to respect these criteria and to improve general data access performance.

NuoDB is another NewSQL solution that uses a completely different approach for data partitioning. A NuoDB deployment is made up of a number of Storage Managers (SM) and Transaction Managers (TM). The SMs are the nodes responsible for maintaining the data, while the TMs are the nodes that process the queries. Each SM has a complete copy of the entire data, which basically means that no partitioning takes place within the SM. Nevertheless, the underlying key-value store used by the SMs can partition the data by itself, although this is neither controllable nor viewable by the user.

Replication

In addition to increasing read/write scalability, replication also improves system reliability, fault tolerance, and durability. Two main approaches to replication can be distinguished: master–slave and multi-master replication.

In *master–slave replication*, shown in Figure 3.a, a single node is designated as a master and is the only node that processes write requests. Changes are propagated from the master to the slave nodes. Examples of data stores with master–slave replication are Redis, BerkeleyDB, and HBase. In *multi-master replication*, illustrated in Figure 3b, multiple nodes can process write requests, which are then propagated to the remaining nodes. Whereas in master–slave replication the propagation direction is always from master to slaves, in multi-master replication, propagation happens in different directions. CouchDB and Couchbase Server are examples of *multi-master data stores*. Three other data stores, Voldemort, Riak, and Cassandra, support *masterless* replication, which is similar to multi-master replication as multiple nodes accept write requests, but as highlighted by the term *masterless*, all nodes play the same role in the replication system. Note that all three of the data stores with masterless replication use consistent hashing as a partitioning strategy. The strategy for placing replicas is closely related to node position on the partitioning ring, as shown in Table 2.

NewSQL replication schemes can be considered as multi-master or masterless schemes because any node can receive update statements. In VoltDB and Clustrix, a transaction/session manager receives the updates, which are forwarded to all replicas and executed in parallel. On the other hand, Google Spanner uses the Paxos state-machine algorithm [29] to guarantee that a sequence of commands will be executed in the same order in all the replica nodes. Note that Paxos is a distributed algorithm

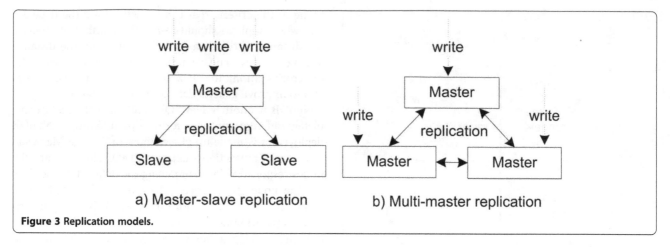

a) Master-slave replication   b) Multi-master replication

Figure 3 Replication models.

without central arbitration, which differs significantly from the other solutions. Finally, in NuoDB, the table rows are represented as in-memory distributed objects which communicate asynchronously to replicate their state changes.

The choice of replication model impacts the ability of the data store to scale read and write requests. Master–slave replication is generally useful for scaling read requests because it allows the many slaves to accept read requests – examples are BerkeleyDB and MongoDB. However, some data stores such as HBase do not permit read requests on the slave nodes. In this case, replication is used solely for failover and disaster recovery. In addition, *master–slave data stores* do not scale write requests because the master is the only node that processes write requests. An interesting exception is the Neo4J database, which is able to handle write requests on the slave nodes also. In this case, write requests are synchronously propagated from slaves to master and therefore are slower than write requests to master. Finally, *multi-master* and *masterless* replication systems are usually capable of scaling read and write requests because all nodes can handle both requests.

Another replication characteristic with a great impact on data stores throughput is how write operations are propagated among nodes. Synchronization of replicas can be synchronous or asynchronous. In *synchronous* or *eager replication*, changes are propagated to replicas before the success of the write operation is acknowledged to the client. This means that synchronous replication introduces latencies because the write operation is completed only after change propagation. This approach is rarely used in NoSQL because it can result in large delays in the case of temporary loss or degradation of the connection. In *asynchronous* or *lazy replication*, the success of a write operation is acknowledged before the change has been propagated to replica nodes. This enables replication over large distances, but it may result in nodes containing inconsistent copies of data. However, performance can be greatly improved over synchronous replication. As

illustrated in Table 2, the majority of the data stores studied use asynchronous replication. Typically, NoSQL solutions use this approach to achieve the desired performance, yet CouchDB uses it to achieve off-line operation. In CouchDB, multiple replicas can have their own copies of the same data, modify them, and then synchronize these changes at a later time.

Consistency

Consistency, as one of the ACID properties, ensures that a transaction brings the database from one valid state to another. However, this section is concerned with consistency as used in the CAP theorem, which relates to how data are seen among the server nodes after update operations. Basically, two consistency models can be distinguished: strong and eventual consistency. *Strong* or *immediate consistency* ensures that when write requests are confirmed, the same (updated) data are visible to all subsequent read requests. Synchronous replication usually ensures strong consistency, but its use can be unacceptable in NoSQL data stores because of the latency it introduces. Among the observed NoSQL data stores with replication, HBase is the only one exclusively supporting strong consistency. In the *eventual consistency* model, changes eventually propagate through the system given sufficient time. Therefore, some server nodes may contain inconsistent (outdated) data for a period of time. Asynchronous replication, if there are no other consistency-ensuring mechanisms, will lead to eventual consistency because there is a lag between write confirmation and propagation. Because NoSQL data stores typically replicate asynchronously, and eventual consistency is often associated with them, it was expected that the reviewed NoSQL solutions provide eventual consistency. Nevertheless, as illustrated in Table 2, the majority of these data stores allow configuration of the consistency model using alternate consistency-ensuring mechanisms; however, choosing strong consistency may have a performance impact.

The data stores with consistent hashing and masterless replication, specifically Voldemort, Riak, and Cassandra, use a quorum approach in their consistency models. In this approach, a read or write quorum is defined as the minimum number of replicas that must respond to a read or write request for it to be considered successful and confirmed to the requestor. Even though these data stores are designed for eventual consistency, they can achieve strong consistency by choosing *(read quorum + write quorum)* larger than the number of replicas.

MongoDB can achieve strong consistency using two different techniques. First, a connection can be set to read-only from the master, which removes the data-stores' ability to scale read requests. The second option is to set the *write concern* parameter to *"Replica Acknowledged"*, which ensures that a write succeeds on all replicas before being confirmed. This makes the data store into a synchronous replication system and degrades its performance.

Finally, it is important to note that the NewSQL solutions analyzed, with the exception of NuoDB, are strongly consistent, fully transactional data stores.

Concurrency control

Concurrency control is of special interest in NoSQL and NewSQL data stores because they generally need to accommodate a large number of concurrent users and very high read and/or write rates. All the solutions studied facilitate concurrency by implementing partitioning and replication. However, this section focuses on concurrency control as a means of achieving simultaneous access to the same entity, row, or record on a single server node.

The main concurrency-control schemes can be categorized as pessimistic or optimistic. *Pessimistic concurrency control*, or *pessimistic locking*, assumes that two or more concurrent users will try to update the same record or object at the same time. To prevent this situation, a lock is placed onto the accessed entity so that exclusive access is guaranteed to a single operation; other clients trying to access the same data must wait until the first one finishes its work. The entity that is locked depends on the underlying data model. For example, key-value stores lock records consisting of key-value pairs, column-family stores lock rows, and document stores enforce locking at document level. In graph databases, specifically in Neo4J, locks are acquired on nodes and their relationships. BerkeleyDB and MongoDB implement readers-writer locks which allow either multiple readers to access data or a single writer to modify them. Pessimistic locking techniques can lead to performance degradation, especially in write-intensive scenarios.

Optimistic concurrency control or *optimistic locking* assumes that conflicts are possible, but rare. Therefore,

instead of locking the record, the data store checks at the end of the operation to determine whether concurrent users have attempted to modify the same record. If a conflict is identified, different conflict-resolution strategies can be used, such as failing the operation immediately or retrying one of the operations. Several of the data stores investigated, including Voldemort, Riak, HBase, CouchDB, Clustrix, and NuoDB, implement optimistic concurrency control with *multi-version concurrency control* (MVCC). In MVCC, when the data store needs to update a record, it does not overwrite the old data, but instead adds a new version and marks the old version as obsolete. Multiple versions are stored, but only one is marked as current. With the MVCC approach, a read operation sees the data the way they were when it began reading, even if the data were modified or deleted by other operations in the meantime.

A number of NoSQL solutions allow applications to implement optimistic concurrency control by providing primitives such as *check and set* (CAS) in Memcached and Couchbase Server. The CAS method ensures that a write will be performed only if no other client has changed the record since it was last read. In Redis, the WATCH primitive performs a similar function. Optimistic concurrency-control implementations use various approaches to determine whether a record has been changed. For example, Memcached uses version stamps and AmazonDB incrementing version numbers. Often it is hard to tell which approach a data store uses internally to achieve check and set functionality based solely on the system documentation.

Cassandra has been recognized for its ability to handle large numbers of write requests [19], and therefore architecture characteristics contributing to Cassandra's write scalability are highlighted. Although the storage structure in typical relational databases and a number of NoSQL data stores including MongoDB and CouchDB relies on a B-Tree, Cassandra takes advantage of a log-structured merge tree. When a write occurs, Cassandra stores the changes in two places: in the memory structure called memtable, and in the commit log on disk by appending to the existing data. When the memtable reaches a threshold, the memtable data are flashed to SSTables (sorted string tables) on disk, and data in the commit log corresponding to the flushed memtable are purged. When flashing the memtable, Cassandra writes entire sectors to disk using sequential I/O instead of modifying rows in place. This approach eliminates locking of data on disk for concurrency control because write operations only append data and do not modify existing data on disk. Consequently, Cassandra is especially suitable for applications with high write volume or those that require very fast writes.

Some of the NewSQL solutions analyzed also implement innovative approaches to concurrency control. For example, Google's Spanner uses a hybrid approach in which read-write transactions are implemented through read-write locks, but read-only transactions are lock-free. This is possible because Spanner stores multiple versions of data, and a read transaction is basically a read at a "safe" timestamp. On the contrary, VoltDB implements an interesting alternative to concurrency control. This data store assumes that the total available memory is large enough to store the entire data store. Moreover, it also assumes that all user transactions are short-lived and can be very efficiently executed over in-memory data. Based on these assumptions, all transactions are then executed sequentially in a single-threaded, lock-free environment.

Security

Security is an important aspect of data stores that is overlooked by many NoSQL implementations. In this section, the data stores surveyed are compared with regard to the following features:

- Authentication: mechanisms that enable verification of the identity of users who are accessing the data. This is usually achieved through a password associated with a user's login, but more sophisticated mechanisms are also possible, such as user certificates. For many enterprises, an important requirement for authentication is the capacity of integration with enterprise user-directory systems such as Lightweight Directory Access Control (LDAP)/Active Directory and Kerberos servers.
- Authorization: this refers to the capability to ensure access control to the data-store resources. Authorization is usually performed through association of each user with a set of permissions. For example, some data stores might require specific permissions for read and write requests on tables, creation of users, and execution of administrative functions. Authorization information might also be included in directory systems.
- Encryption: this refers to mechanisms that encrypt data so that they cannot be read by attackers and others unauthorized parties. A complete encryption solution should be present in at least three different levels:
  - ○ Data at rest: data stored on disks can be read if an attacker has access to the servers' file systems. A data-at-rest encryption mechanism guarantees that the users' data are automatically encrypted when written to these files and unencrypted when retrieved.
  - ○ Client-to-server communication: Most data stores allow remote connections of users and applications so that stored data can be obtained.

This data flow must also be encrypted to guarantee private and secure communication.
  - ○ Server-to-server connections: because many NoSQL and NewSQL data stores include some sort of replication and distributed processing functionalities, communications among the server nodes can also be eavesdropped to obtain unauthorized access to data. A server-to-server encryption mechanism guarantees that these flows cannot be read.
- Auditing: auditing functionalities are usually related to the creation of an audit trail that logs records of events that occurred in a data stores. This is especially important in forensic analysis of security events. Many security standards, such as PCI-DSS [51] and HIPAA [52], require the existence of audit trails.

Table 3 shows a summary of the security features found in the solutions surveyed. It is worth mentioning that very often the system documentation mentions nothing about some of the criteria analyzed, especially server-to-server communication and data-at-rest encryption. In these cases, the corresponding cells in the table contain "NA".

Generally speaking, it is possible to affirm that the security features of NoSQL solutions are not as mature as those included in traditional RDBMSs. Many solutions, such as Redis, Memcached, Voldemort, and Riak, are designed to be used in secure networked environments only. Therefore, they assume that it is the network administrator's responsibility to ensure that only authorized applications have access to the data store, using mechanisms such as firewalls, operating system configurations, or the adoption of virtual private networks (VPN). In these cases, there is no fine-grained access control to the data store. Furthermore, audit features are not present in most cases, and when present, they are very simple and not customizable. For example, VoltDB can log all the queries executed on its data, but it cannot constrain this logging to only a subset of the tables.

Another interesting observation is that MongoDB and Cassandra offer additional security functionalities in their enterprise editions, acknowledging the fact that security is a particularly relevant concern for large companies. For instance, data-at-rest encryption and auditing functionalities are available only in Cassandra Enterprise Edition.

Among the NewSQL solutions, Clustrix and NuoDB use the authorization and authentication schemes of traditional RDBMS by supporting the GRANT/REVOKE statements. In its turn, VoltDB implements access control to execution of stored procedures, and no information regarding Google Spanner security could be found.

Cloud data management systems may also need to handle other security related concerns, such as legal issues

Table 3 Security features

NoSQL data stores		Encryption			Authentication	Authorization	Auditing
		Data at rest	Client/Server	Server/Server			
Key-value stores	Redis	No	No	No	Admin password sent in clear text for admin functions. Data access does not support authentication.	No	No
	Memcached	NA, Memcache does store data on disk.	No	No	Binary protocol supports Simple Authentication and Security Layer (SASL) authentication.	No	No
	BerkeleyDB	Yes, the database needs to be created using encryption.	NA, embedded data store.	No	No	No	No
	Voldemort	Possibly if BerkeleyDB is used as the storage engine.	No	No	No	No	No
	Riak	No	REST interface supports HTTPS. Binary protocol is not encrypted.	Multiple data-centre replication can be done over HTTPS	No	No	No
Column family stores	Cassandra	Enterprise Edition only. Commit log is not encrypted.	Yes, SSL based.	Yes, configurable: all server-to-server communication, only between datacentres or between servers in the same rack	Yes, store credentials in a system table. Possible to provide pluggable implementations.	Yes, similar to the SQL GRANT/REVOKE approach. Possible to provide pluggable implementations.	Enterprise Edition only. Based on log4j framework. Logging categories include ADMIN, ALL, AUTH, DML, DDL, DCL, and QUERY. Possible to disable logging for specific keyspaces.
	HBase	No, planned for future release.	Yes	Communication of HBase nodes with the HDFS and Zookeeper clusters can be secured. Not clear whether the HBase nodes communicate via a secure channel.	Yes, RPC API based on SASL, supporting Kerberos.REST API uses a HTTP gateway, which authenticates with the data store as one single user, and executes all operations on his/her behalf.	Yes, permissions include read, write, create and admin. Granularity of table, column family, or column.	No, planned for future release.
	Amazon DynamoDB	No	Yes, HTTPS	NA	Integration with Identity and Access Management (IAM) services. The requests need to be signed using HMAC-SHA256.	Allow the creation of policies that associate users and operations on domains. Possible to define policies for temporary access.	Integrates with Amazon Cloud Watch service. Access. information about latencies for operations, amount of data stored, and requests throughput.
	Amazon SimpleDB	See DynamoDB					
Document stores	MongoDB	No, a third-party partner (Gazzang) provides an encryption plug-in.	Yes, SSL-based	Yes	Yes, store credentials in a system collection. REST interface does not support authentication. Enterprise Edition supports Kerberos.	Yes, permissions include read, read/write, dbAdmin, and userAdmin. Granularity of collections.	No

Table 3 Security features *(Continued)*

CouchDB	NA	Yes, SSL-based	Possible using HTTPS connections	Yes, HTTP authentication using cookies or BASIC method. Oauth supported	Three levels of users: server admin, database admin, and database member. Complex authorization can be done in validation functions.	No
Couchbase server	No	No	No, planned for future release	Yes, SASL authentication – each bucket is differentiated by its name and password. REST API for administrative function uses HTTP BASIC authentication.	No	No
Graph databases						
Neo4J	No	Yes, SSL-based	No	No, developers can create a SecurityRule and register with the server.	No	No
Hyper graphDB	No	NA, embedded data store	No	No	No	No
Allegro graph	No	Yes, HTTPS	NA	Yes	Yes, permissions include read, write, and delete. Predefined user attributes are used to define special administration capabilities.	A structure audit log can be used to record specific changes. Not clear what types of changes are logged, nor how to customize this process.
NewSQL						
VoltDB	No	No	No	Yes, users are defined in a deployment file that needs to be copied to each node.	Yes, roles are defined at the schema level, and each stored procedure defines which roles are allowed to execute it.	Yes, logging categories include connections, SQL statements, snapshots, exports, authentication / authorization, and others.
Spanner	NA					
Clustrix	NA	Yes	NA	Yes, SQL-like	Yes, SQL-like	NA
NuoDB	Native store does not support it. Theoretically, it could use a pluggable store that supports it.	Yes	Yes	Yes, SQL-like	Yes, SQL-like	Yes, logging categories include SQL statements, security events, general statistics, and others.

associated to the data location, and the complete disposal of sensitive data [53], but they are out of scope of this survey.

Use cases

Due to the diversity of NoSQL and NewSQL solutions, making the choice of the most appropriate data store for a given use case scenario is a challenging task. This section discusses some general guidelines that can be used in this task and shows examples of applications that use different data stores. The following discussion is mostly focussed on selecting a specific data model over others, but when relevant, we also examine the appropriateness of specific data stores.

Key-value stores

Generally speaking, key-value data stores are appropriate for scenarios in which applications access a set of data as a whole using a unique value as the key. Sadalage and Fowler [15] use three examples for this category: storing Web session information, user profiles and configurations, and shopping cart data. In all three cases, the data are always accessed through user identification and are never queried based on the data content. The Web session and shopping cart examples are also representatives of another common key-value use case: the stored information is needed for a limited period of time only (the duration of the user session). Indeed, in many simple Web applications, these types of data are kept in the application server's memory because of their transient nature. Nevertheless, the use of a key-value store may be appropriate in scenarios where multiple application servers access the same session information. This is a commonly used strategy to make application servers stateless and to implement high availability and scalability requirements.

Similarly, key-value data stores are useful in content providing applications. The Riak documentation [54] uses as examples of this use case an advertisement platform that provides ads based on a campaign identifier and a content provider application that retrieves images and videos based on IDs.

Key-value data stores are also suitable for object caching, especially in-memory implementations. In this case, they are used to store the results of processing intensive requests such as database queries, page rendering, and API calls. For example, Memcached is used as a caching layer for large clusters of MySQL databases in Facebook [55]. The LinkedIn service also uses a key-value data store (Voldermort) as a cache on top of their primary storage and also to store the results of intensive algorithms [43]. The use of these data stores as a caching layer is very common and is often considered an integral part of cloud applications [56,57].

It is important to note that some key-value data stores provide enhanced functionalities that may increase their applicability. For example, Redis can interpret stored values as specific data types, such as lists, sets, and strings, and also provides many primitives to manipulate these types. On the other hand, Riak enables the integration of search engines to index the stored values and the attachment of tags on keys to facilitate complex searches. These extra functionalities are also relevant when choosing the most appropriate key-value store for a particular scenario.

Finally, it is essential to recognize that key-value data stores have limitations when dealing with:

- Highly interconnected data, because all relationships need to be explicitly handled in the client applications.
- Operations that manipulate multiple items, as data are often accessed using a single key and most data stores do not provide transactional capabilities.

Document stores

Document stores can be seen as key-value stores in which the value is not completely opaque and therefore can be examined [15]. As mentioned in the "Data Model" section, these data stores manage data that can be represented as documents, which are self-describing hierarchical data structures which may contain nested objects and list attributes and do not require adherence to a fixed schema.

The first use cases for document stores are for applications dealing with data that can be easily interpreted as documents, such as blogging platforms and content management systems (CMS). Both Sadalage and Fowler [15] and the MongoDB documentation [35] use these applications as canonical examples. A blog post or an item in a CMS, with all related content such as comments and tags, can be easily transformed into a document format even though different items may have different attributes. For example, images may have a resolution attribute, while videos have an associated length, but both share name and author attributes. Moreover, these pieces of information are mainly manipulated as aggregates and do not have many relationships with other data. Finally, the capability to query documents based on their content is also important to the implementation of search functionalities.

A second significant use case for document data stores is for storing items of similar nature that may have different structures. For example, document data stores can be used to log events or monitor information from enterprise systems. In this case, each event is represented as a document, but events from different sources log different information. This is a natural fit for the flexible document data model and enables easy extension to new log formats. This contrasts with the relational approach, in which a new table needs to be created for each new format or new columns needs to be added to existing tables. As an example, Liu *et al.* [58] used CouchDB for storing and analyzing log data from a Platform as a Service (PaaS). Similarly, document data stores have also been used to store sensor network data, as suggested by Ramaswamy *et al.* [59].

Document data stores have also been chosen in scenarios in which high development productivity and low maintenance cost are essential. The flexibility of the data model mentioned in the previous paragraphs, in tandem with easy mapping of documents to object oriented constructs [60], makes these data stores especially suited for fast application development. Moreover, many modern applications provide services using REST interfaces based on JSON representations that can be directly mapped to document data stores.

Finally, it is also worth mentioning that CouchDB has been used in scenarios, such as in Havlik *et al.* [61], which specifically explore its off-line replication capabilities. CouchDB allows the co-existence of multiple instances of a database that can be updated independently and be synchronized only when the instances can communicate with each other. This characteristic is explored in applications where servers and clients are not always on-line and also to provide low latency and local data access to remote clients.

Document data stores have similar limitations to key-value data stores, such as the lack of built-in support for relationships among documents and transactional operations involving multiple documents.

Column-family stores

Due to differences in the data models of the analyzed column-family stores, the use cases for this category will be discussed in two groups. The first group contains data stores which do not use the column-family concept, namely SimpleDB and DynamoDB, and the second group consists of HBase and Cassandra.

SimpleDB and DynamoDB are both based on a schema-free tabular model, in which each row can have different columns and a column can possibly contain more than one value. The expressiveness of this model is similar to the document-store model, but with the additional limitation that nested objects are not allowed. Therefore, SimpleDB and DynamoDB are appropriate for use cases comparable to those mentioned in the previous section - document stores. In addition, both data stores are managed services, which make them especially suitable for scenarios where the users want to avoid the cost and complexity of managing a data store.

Regarding the second group of column-family stores, both HBase and Cassandra have flexible data models,

and it is difficult to choose only a few applications as representatives of their use cases. Sadalage and Fowler [15] cite event logging, CMS, and blogging platforms as column-family use cases, which are once again similar to document store examples. On the other hand, we opt to show applications and benchmarks which are diverse, but which help to show the strengths and limitations of these data stores.

As mentioned in the "Concurrency Control" section, Cassandra is a data store optimized for handling a large number of write requests, and different benchmarks have confirmed this capability. In Cooper *et al.* [62], Cassandra achieved the highest update throughput on an update heavy workload in comparison to HBase, MySQL, and Yahoo's PNUTS [63]. Similarly, Rabl *et al.* [64] showed that Cassandra can achieve good throughput on 50%/50% read-write workloads and 99% write workloads, and most importantly, can scale linearly as a function of the number of nodes in the cluster. On this benchmark, HBase had similar scalability results, but at the cost of a much smaller throughput rate. In addition, both Cooper *et al.* [62] and Rabl *et al.* [64] stated that generally HBase can handle write requests with latency orders of magnitude faster than Cassandra, even though the opposite happens when comparing read latency. Nevertheless, a different performance comparison performed by Altoros Systems [65] showed that Cassandra and HBase had similar latency and throughput in both reads and writes and that HBase had slightly better results in most cases.

The flexibility, scalability, and high performance of these data stores, in conjunction with MapReduce support, make them a good fit for analytics scenarios. For example, Chang *et al.* [20] demonstrated the use of BigTable in two applications that are representative of this use case: Web analytics and personalized search. In the first application, webmasters instrument their pages to keep track of how visitors use them. All user actions are logged to the database, and a MapReduce task is run to aggregate and transform these data into statistics useful for the Web page administrator. In the personalized search application, all user searches and actions in diverse Google services are stored, and a MapReduce task generates profiles that are used to personalize the user interaction experience.

It is also worth mentioning that Cassandra was originally designed to fulfill the storage requirements of the inbox search application [19], which Facebook's users can use to search for conversations with specific friends or using specific terms. This application also has a write-intensive workload, but at the same time requires low-latency results when these indices are queried. More recently, Facebook has revealed that they are using HBase in applications that require high write throughput and efficient random reads [55], but they do not discuss the limitations of Cassandra in addressing these requirements. They justify the choice of HBase based on their confidence in addressing missing features using their own engineering team and in the resiliency of the system against disk failures.

Finally, the limitations of column-family data stores are similar to those of other NoSQL categories, such as the lack of built-in support for relationships and transactional operations that involve more than one row. In addition, HBase and Cassandra are not very appropriate for scenarios where queries are highly dynamic because changes in queries may impact the column-family design.

Graph databases

Graph databases are a suitable choice for the following types of applications: location-based services, recommendation engines, and complex network-based applications including social, information, technological, and biological networks [15,66]. For instance, user location history data which are used to generate patterns that associate people with their frequently visited places could be efficiently stored and queried using Neo4J in location-based socio-spatial network applications [67]. Similarly, recommendation-based systems in which users are provided directed content based on their preferences could be efficiently built using graph databases. As an example, news broadcasters could create an aggregated global profile of a user, link it with their preferences for events and news, and effectively feed personalized RSS feeds to users using a graph database like Allegrograph [68].

Moreover, graph databases are being increasingly used since the rise of large social computing platforms like YouTube, Flicker, LiveJournal, and Orkut [69]. These solutions offer graph data storage and a graph processing system which provides indexing on nodes and edges, making them very efficient in storing closely related data and performing highly complex queries similar to those involving multiple joins in relational databases [69]. Another interesting application of graph databases was proposed by Sor and Srirama [70] for memory leak detection in distributed applications. To detect memory leaks, a leak cause analysis was required, which involved finding the shortest path from leaking objects to garbage collection roots with the intention of detecting the object responsible for holding the references which are no longer used. However, their use case required implementing custom graph database solutions over existing ones due to the high reliance on shortest-path search over other kind of traversals.

NewSQL

Generally speaking, the use of NewSQL data stores is appropriate in scenarios in which traditional DBMS have been used, but which have additional scalability and performance requirements.

First, NewSQL data stores are appropriate for applications which require the use of transactions that manipulate more than one object, or have strong consistency requirements, or even both. The classical examples are applications in the financial market, where operations such as money transfers need to update two accounts automatically and all applications need to have the same view of the database. Most of the analyzed NoSQL data stores do not support multi-object transactions, and many of them are eventually consistent solutions, which make them inappropriate for these use cases.

Second, the relational model is appropriate in scenarios where the data structure is known upfront and unlikely to change. The overhead of creating a schema beforehand is compensated by the flexibility of querying the data using SQL [60], a very powerful mechanism that can be used to implement almost any kind of data manipulation.

Finally, when selecting the most appropriate solution for an application, it is essential to consider the investment already made in tools and personnel training. In this regard, NewSQL data stores are especially attractive because they are compatible with most DBMS tools and use SQL as their main interaction language.

Opportunities

Although NoSQL and NewSQL data stores deliver powerful capabilities, the large number and immense diversity of available solutions make choosing the appropriate solution for the problem at hand especially difficult. Moreover, such diversity presents challenges in obtaining a perspective on the field and establishing directions for future research. Analysis and comparison of a number of NoSQL and NewSQL solutions in this study has revealed the following opportunities for future research in the field:

A common terminology needs to be established, at least for data stores having the same data model. Different terminology makes comparison of solutions challenging. An example of a terminology discrepancy is Riak's quorum read and write requests, which are referred to as routing parameters in Voldemort. Establishing a common terminology will not only help in comparing different data stores, but will also help in understanding the concepts of a new data store when a user is switching between different NoSQL products.

It is important to create a clear distinction between the term *consistency* as used in the ACID acronym and *consistency* as used in "eventual consistency". The overloading of this term has led to the general belief that an eventual-consistency data store cannot be ACID, which Bailis *et al.* [71] have already shown is not true.

Possibilities for establishing a standard SQL-like querying mechanism need to be explored, at least for data stores having the same data model. Today, with NoSQL data stores, performing even a simple query requires significant programming expertise and often solution-specific code. Therefore, switching to another data store may require changing the majority of the application code. Solutions such as Hive [72] have provided a great help in this direction, but their use is still limited to only a few data stores such as HBase and Cassandra. Additionally, some NoSQL data stores such as Cassandra, MongoDB, and Neo4J natively provide SQL-like querying. Standardizing querying mechanisms based on the capabilities of their data models would increase adoption of NoSQL in practice and would ease migration among different solutions.

- Standardized performance benchmarking is required. The popularity of NoSQL stores for cloud data management has been growing, especially in the Big Data domain. However, little has been done to compare the performance of different solutions under different processing loads. Although there have been some attempts to establish benchmarking standards, for example the Yahoo Cloud Serving Benchmark (YCSB) [62], the adoption of these standards in practice has been limited. Establishing a benchmarking standard would help in comparing different data stores with a view to selecting one for a particular application.
- Another consideration arises from modern-day business needs. Businesses now rely heavily on business intelligence (BI) tools. Although an analysis platform called Pig [73] provides some basic analytical functionalities for NoSQL data stores, it is not yet as powerful as the BI tools available for RDBMSs. Therefore, BI tools need to provide support for NoSQL data stores to obtain the most benefit from them.
- Sophisticated security and privacy provisions are needed. The review of the security properties offered by NoSQL solutions has revealed that in comparison to relational databases, the security capabilities of NoSQL solutions are limited. It is expected that future development in this area will increase adoption of NoSQL in practice.
- Use of more than one NoSQL data store in a single application needs to be explored. This consideration arises from the fact that NoSQL is not just one product, but encompasses several different data stores, each offering features specific to a particular type of use case or data need. Therefore, to cover a wider range of application scenarios, a solution might need to incorporate more than one NoSQL data store to address the need for different kinds of data. Sadalage and Fowler [15] use the term *polyglot persistence* to refer to the use of different data stores

for different purposes within the same application. As an example of this type of work, Atzeni *et al.* [74] recently proposed a common interface for accessing key-value, document, and column-family data stores.

This list includes the prominent opportunities and illustrates the great potential for future research in this domain. It can be expected that further research, together with the use of NoSQL and NewSQL in practice, will lead to emergence of preferred solutions for specific requirements. It is also important to note the significance of documentation and a user community: better documentation, a more active user community, or both may be the deciding factors because they can effectively support application development and ease data store administration.

Conclusions

In recent years, cloud computing has emerged as a computational paradigm that can be used to meet the continuously growing storage and processing requirements of today's applications. This study has focused on the storage aspect of cloud computing systems, in particular, NoSQL and NewSQL data stores. These solutions have presented themselves as alternatives to traditional relational databases, capable of handling huge volumes of data by exploiting the cloud environment.

Specifically, this paper has reviewed NoSQL and NewSQL data stores with the objectives of providing a perspective on the field, providing guidance to practitioners and researchers to choose appropriate storage solutions, and identifying challenges and opportunities in the field. A comparison among the most prominent solutions was performed on a number of dimensions, including data models, querying capabilities, scaling, and security attributes. Use cases and scenarios in which NoSQL and NewSQL data stores have been used were discussed and the suitability of various solutions for different sets of applications was examined. The discussion of the use cases, together with the comparison of data stores, will assist practitioners in choosing the best storage solution for their needs. In addition, this work has identified challenges in the domain, including terminology diversity and inconsistency, limited documentation, sparse comparison and benchmarking criteria, occasional immaturity of solutions and lack of support, and non-existence of a standard query language.

Abbreviations
ACID: Atomicity consistency isolation durability; API: Application programming interface; BASE: Basically available soft-state eventually consistent; BI: Business intelligence; BSON: Binary JSON; CAP: Consistency availability partition tolerance; CAS: Check and set; CLI: Command line interface; CMS: Content management system; CQL: Cassandra query language; JSON: JavaScript object notation; LDAP: Lightweight directory

access control; MVCC: Multi-version concurrency control; NIST: National institute of standards and technology; PaaS: Platform as a service; RDBMS: Relational database management system; REST: Representational state transfer; SM: Storage manager; SQL: Structured query language; TM: Transaction manager; VPN: Virtual private network; YCSB: Yahoo cloud serving benchmark.

Competing interests

The authors declare that they have no competing interests.

Authors' contributions

KG contributed towards defining the survey methodology and establishing the relation of this survey with other cloud data management surveys. Also, KG studied the scaling aspect of NoSQL stores and participated in identifying the challenges and opportunities of the cloud data management. WAH contributed towards the selection and study of the NewSQL data stores. WAH studied the security aspects of all the data stores included in this study and also developed the Use Cases section. Finally, WAH worked on the contextualization of the study in the cloud computing field, and participated into the discussions about the challenges and future opportunities of the cloud data management solutions. AT contributed towards the work of choosing the NoSQL data stores included in the study and carried out the studies of cloud computing. AT studied various NoSQL data stores, their data models, and their querying capabilities in detail and also contributed towards exploring the challenges and future opportunities regarding NoSQL data stores. MAMC provided direction and advice, participated in the critical and technical revision of the manuscript. All authors read and approved the final manuscript.

References

1. Facebook Newsroom A New data center for Iowa. http://newsroom.fb.com/News/606/A-New-Data-Center-for-Iowa. Accessed 29 Sep 2013
2. Ohlhorst FJ (2013) Big Data Analytics: Turning Big Data into Big Money. John Wiley & Sons, Inc, Hoboken, New Jersey, USA
3. Stonebraker M, Madden S, Abadi DJ, Harizopoulos S, Hachem N, Helland P (2007) The end of an architectural era: (it's time for a complete rewrite). Proc 33rd Int Conf Large Data Bases:1150–1160
4. Beyer MA, Laney D (2012) The Importance of "Big Data": A Definition. http://www.gartner.com/id=2057415. Accessed 29 Sep 2013
5. Agrawal D, Das S, El Abbadi A (2011) Big data and cloud computing: Current State and Future Opportunities. Proceedings of the 14th International Conference on Extending Database Technology - EDBT/ICDT'11. ACM Press, New York, NY, USA, pp 530–533
6. Bughin J, Chui M, Manyika J (2010) Clouds, big data, and smart assets: Ten tech-enabled business trends to watch. McKinsey Quarterly 2010:1–14
7. Mell P, Grance T (2011) The NIST definition of cloud computing. NIST special publication 800–145. http://csrc.nist.gov/publications/nistpubs/800-145/SP800-145.pdf. Accessed on 29 Sep 2013
8. Zhang Q, Cheng L, Boutaba R (2010) Cloud computing: state-of-the-art and research challenges. J Intern Serv Appl 1:7–18. 10.1007/s13174-010-0007-6
9. Venters W, Whitley EA (2012) A critical review of cloud computing: researching desires and realities. J Info Technol 27:179–197. 10.1057/jit.2012.17
10. Tudorica BG, Bucur C (2011) A comparison between several NoSQL databases with comments and notes. 2011 10th International Conference RoEduNet. IEEE:1–5
11. Hecht R, Jablonski S (2011) NoSQL evaluation: A use case oriented survey. Proc 2011 Int Conf Cloud Serv Computing:336–341
12. Cattell R (2011) Scalable SQL and NoSQL Data Stores. ACM SIGMOD Record 39(4):12–27
13. Pokorny J (2011) NoSQL Databases: a step to database scalability in Web environment. Int J Web Info Syst 9(1):69–82
14. Sakr S, Liu A, Batista DM, Alomari M (2011) A survey of large scale data management approaches in cloud environments. IEEE Commun Surv Tutorials 13(3):311–336
15. Sadalage PJ, Fowler M (2013) NoSQL distilled: a brief guide to the emerging world of polyglot persistence. Addison-Wesley, Upper Saddle River, NJ
16. Abiteboul S, Manolescu I, Rigaux P, Rousset M-C, Senellart P (2012) Web Data Management. Cambridge University Press, New York
17. Aslett M (2011) How will the database incumbents respond to NoSQL and NewSQL? https://451research.com/report-short?entityId=66963. Accessed 29 Sep 2013
18. Buyya R, Yeo CS, Venugopal S, Broberg J, Brandic I (2009) Cloud computing and emerging IT platforms: Vision, hype, and reality for delivering computing as the 5th utility. Future Gen Computer Syst 25(6):599–616. http://dx.doi.org/10.1016/j.future.2008.12.001
19. Lakshman A, Malik P (2010) Cassandra: a decentralized structured storage system. ACM SIGOPS Operating Syst Rev 44(2):35–40. 10.1145/1773912.1773922
20. Chang F, Dean J, Ghemawat S, Hsieh W, Wallach D, Burrows M, Chandra T, Fikes A, Gruber R (2006) Bigtable: A distributed structured data storage system. 7th OSDI 26:305–314
21. Gilbert S, Lynch N (2002) Brewer's conjecture and the feasibility of consistent, available, partition-tolerant web services. ACM SIGACT News 33(2):51–59. 10.1145/564585.564601
22. Brewer E (2012) CAP twelve years later: How the "rules" have changed. Computer 45:23–29. 10.1109/MC.2012.37
23. NOSQL meetup. Eventbrite, San Francisco. http://nosql.eventbrite.com/. Accessed 29 Sep 2013
24. Konstantinou I, Angelou E, Boumpouka C, Tsoumakos D, Koziris N (2011) On the elasticity of NoSQL databases over cloud management platforms. Proceedings of the 20th ACM international conference on Information and knowledge management - CIKM '11. ACM Press, New York, NY, USA, pp 2385–2388
25. Pritchett D (2008) BASE: An ACID Alternative. Queue 6:48–55. 10.1145/1394127.1394128
26. Apache CouchDB. http://couchdb.apache.org/. Accessed 29 Sep 2013
27. Murty J (2008) Programming Amazon Web Services: S3, EC2, SQS, FPS, and SimpleDB. O'Reilly Media, Inc
28. DeCandia G, Hastorun D, Jampani M, Kakulapati G, Lakshman A, Pilchin A, Sivasubramanian S, Vosshall P, Vogels W (2007) Dynamo: Amazon's highly available Key-value store. ACM SIGOPS Operating Syst Rev 41:205. 10.1145/1323293.1294281
29. Corbett JC, Dean J, Epstein M, Fikes A, Frost C, Furman JJ, Ghemawat S, Gubarev A, Heiser C, Hochschild P, Hsieh W, Kanthak S, Kogan E, Li H, Lloyd A, Melnik S, Mwaura D, Nagle D, Quinlan S, Rao R, Rolig L, Saito Y, Szymaniak M, Taylor C, Wang R, Woodford D (2012) Spanner: Google's globally-distributed database. Osdi 2012:1–14
30. VoltDB Inc (2013) VoltDB Technical Overview. 1–4. http://voltdb.com/downloads/datasheets_collateral/technical_overview.pdf. Accessed 29 Sep 2013
31. Kallman R, Kimura H, Natkins J, Pavlo A, Rasin A, Zdonik S, Jones EPC, Madden S, Stonebraker M, Zhang Y, Hugg J, Abadi DJ (2008) H-store: a high-performance, distributed main memory transaction processing system. Proc VLDB Endowment 1(2):1496–1499
32. Clustrix Inc (2012) A New Approach: Clustrix Sierra Database Engine. 1–10. http://www.clustrix.com/wp-content/uploads/2013/10/Clustrix_A-New-Approach_WhitePaper.pdf. Accessed 29 Sep 2013
33. NuoDB Greenbook Publication (2013) NuoDB Emergent Architecture. 1–20. http://go.nuodb.com/rs/nuodb/images/Greenbook_Final.pdf. Accessed 29 Sep 2013
34. DB-Engines Ranking. http://db-engines.com/en/ranking. Accessed 29 Sep 2013
35. MongoDB.. http://www.mongodb.org/. Accessed 29 Sep 2013
36. Couchbase Server The NoSQL document database. http://www.couchbase.com/couchbase-server/overview. Accessed 29 Sep 2013
37. Apache HBase. http://hbase.apache.org/. Accessed 29 Sep 2013
38. Redis. http://redis.io/. Accessed 29 Sep 2013
39. Memcached. http://memcached.org/. Accessed 29 Sep 2013
40. Klophaus R (2010) Riak Core: building distributed applications without shared state. Proceedings of CUFP'10 - ACM SIGPLAN Commercial Users of Functional Programming. ACM Press, New York, NY, USA, p 1
41. Oracle Berkeley DB 12c. http://www.oracle.com/technetwork/products/berkeleydb/overview/index.html. Accessed 29 Sep 2013
42. Neo4j - What is a Graph Database? http://www.neo4j.org/. Accessed 29 Sep 2013
43. Auradkar A, Botev C, Das S, De Maagd D, Feinberg A, Ganti P, Gao L, Ghosh B, Gopalakrishna K, Harris B, Koshy J, Krawez K, Kreps J, Lu S, Nagaraj S,

Narkhede N, Pachev S, Perisic I, Qiao L, Quiggle T, Rao J, Schulman B, Sebastian A, Seeliger O, Silberstein A, Shkolnik B, Soman C, Sumbaly R, Surlaker K, Topiwala S, Tran C, Varadarajan B, Westerman J, White Z, Zhang D, Zhang J (2012) Data Infrastructure at LinkedIn. Proceedings of 2012 IEEE 28th International Conference on Data Engineering. IEEE:1370–1381

44. Buerli M (2012) The current state of graph databases. http://www.cs.utexas.edu/~cannata/dbms/Class%20Notes/08%20Graph_Databases_Survey.pdf. Accessed 29 Sep 2013

45. Dean J, Ghemawat S (2008) MapReduce: simplified data processing on large clusters. Comm ACM 51(1):107–113. 10.1145/1327452.1327492

46. Cassandra Query Language (CQL) v3.1.1. http://cassandra.apache.org/doc/cql3/CQL.html. Accessed 29 Sep 2013

47. Harris S, Seaborne A (2013) SPARQL 1.1 Query Language. http://www.w3.org/TR/2013/REC-sparql11-query-20130321/. Accessed 29 Sep 2013

48. AllegroGraph 4.11. http://www.franz.com/agraph/allegrograph/. Accessed 29 Sep 2013

49. Battle R, Benson E (2008) Bridging the semantic Web and Web 2.0 with Representational State Transfer (REST). Web Semantics: Sci Serv Agents World Wide Web 6:61–69. 10.1016/j.websem.2007.11.002

50. Soni Madhulatha T (2012) Graph partitioning advance clustering technique. Int J Computer Sci Eng Surv 3(1):91–104. 10.5121/ijcses.2012.3109

51. PCI Security Standards Council (2010) Payment card industry (PCI) data security standard - requirements and security assessment procedures - version 2.0. https://www.pcisecuritystandards.org/documents/pci_dss_v2.pdf. Accessed 29 Sep 2013

52. Health insurance portability and accountability Act of 1996 (HIPAA). http://www.cms.gov/Regulations-and-Guidance/HIPAA-Administrative-Simplification/HIPAAGenInfo/downloads/hipaalaw.pdf. Accessed 29 Sep 2013

53. Gonzalez N, Miers C, Redígolo F, Simplício M, Carvalho T, Näslund M, Pourzandi M (2012) A quantitative analysis of current security concerns and solutions for cloud computing. J Cloud Computing: Adv Syst Appl 1:11. 10.1186/2192-113X-1-11

54. Basho Technologies (2012) From relational to riak. http://basho.com/assets/RelationaltoRiak.pdf. Accessed 11 Dec 2013

55. Borthakur D, Rash S, Schmidt R, Aiyer A, Gray J, Sen SJ, Muthukkaruppan K, Spiegelberg N, Kuang H, Ranganathan K, Molkov D, Menon A (2011) Apache hadoop goes realtime at Facebook. Proc 2011 Int Conf Manage Data - SIGMOD '11 1071. 10.1145/1989323.1989438

56. Petcu D, Macariu G, Panica S, Crăciun C (2012) Portable cloud applications—from theory to practice. Future Gen Computer Syst 29(6):1417–1430. 10.1016/j.future.2012.01.009

57. Vaquero LM, Rodero-Merino L, Buyya R (2011) Dynamically scaling applications in the cloud. ACM SIGCOMM Computer Comm Rev 41(1):45–52. 10.1145/1925861.1925869

58. Liu Z, Wang Y, Lin R (2012) A novel development and analysis solution to PaaS log by using CouchDB. 2012 3rd IEEE Int Conf Network Infrastr Digital Content:251–255

59. Ramaswamy L, Lawson V, Gogineni SV (2013) Towards a quality-centric Big data architecture for federated sensor services. 2013 IEEE Int Congr Big Data:86–93. 10.1109/BigData.Congress.2013.21

60. Redmond E, Wilson JR (2013) Seven databases in seven weeks: a guide to modern databases and the NoSQL movement. O'Reilly Media. 978-1-934356-92-0

61. Havlik D, Egly M, Huber H, Kutschera P, Falgenhauer M, Cizek M, et al. (2013) Robust and Trusted Crowd-Sourcing and Crowd-Tasking in the Future Internet. In: IFIP Advances in Information and Communication Technology, 413th edition, pp 164–176

62. Cooper BF, Silberstein A, Tam E, Ramakrishnan R, Sears R (2010) Benchmarking cloud serving systems with YCSB. Proceedings of the 1st ACM Symposium on Cloud Computing. 154:143–154

63. Cooper BF, Ramakrishnan R, Srivastava U, Silberstein A, Bohannon P, Jacobsen H-A, Puz N, Weaver D, Yerneni R (2008) PNUTS: Yahoo!'s hosted data serving platform. Proc VLDB Endowment 1(2):1277–1288

64. Rabl T, Gómez-Villamor S, Sadoghi M, Muntés-Mulero V, Jacobsen HA, Mankovskii S (2012) Solving big data challenges for enterprise application performance management. Proc VLDB Endowment 5(12):1724–1735

65. Bushik S (2012) A Vendor-independent Comparison of NoSQL Databases: Cassandra, HBase, MongoDB, Riak. http://www.networkworld.com/news/tech/2012/102212-nosql-263595.html. Accessed 11 Dec 2013

66. Angles R, Gutierrez C (2008) Survey of graph database models. ACM Computing Surv 40:1–39. 10.1145/1322432.1322433

67. Doytsher Y, Galon B, Kanza Y (2012) Querying socio-spatial networks on the world-wide web. Proceedings of 21st international conference companion on world wide web - WWW'12 Companion. ACM Press, New York, NY, USA, pp 329–332

68. Mannens E, Coppens S, Pessemier T, Dacquin H, Deursen D, Sutter R, Walle R (2011) Automatic news recommendations via aggregated profiling. Multimed Tools Appl 63:407–425. 10.1007/s11042-011-0844-8

69. Ho L-Y, Wu J-J, Liu P (2012) Distributed graph database for large-scale social computing. 2012 IEEE Fifth Int Conf Cloud Computing:455–462

70. Sor V, Srirama SN (2012) Evaluation of embeddable graph manipulation libraries in memory constrained environments. Proceedings of the 2012 ACM Research in Applied Computation Symposium - RACS'12. ACM Press, New York, NY, USA, pp 269–275

71. Bailis P, Fekete A, Ghodsi A, Hellerstein JM, Stoica I (2013) HAT, not CAP: highly available transactions. arXiv preprint arXiv:1302.0309

72. Thusoo A, Sarma J, Sen JN, Shao Z, Chakka P, Anthony S, Liu H, Wyckoff P, Murthy R (2009) Hive: a warehousing solution over a Map-reduce framework. Proc VLDB Endowment 2(2):1626–1629

73. Olston C, Reed B, Srivastava U, Kumar R, Tomkins A (2008) Pig latin: a not-so-foreign language for data processing. Proceedings of the 2008 ACM SIGMOD International Conference on Management of Data - SIGMOD'08. ACM Press, New York, NY, USA, pp 1099–1110

74. Atzeni P, Bugiotti F, Rossi L (2013) Uniform access to NoSQL systems. Information systems (in press). 10.1016/j.is.2013.05.002

4

A simple, adaptable and efficient heterogeneous multi-tenant database architecture for ad hoc cloud

Sanjeev Kumar Pippal* and Dharmender Singh Kushwaha

Abstract

Data management and sharing is the challenge being faced by all the IT majors today. Adds over it, is the challenge faced by the cloud service providers in terms of multi-tenancy of data and its efficient retrieval. It becomes more complex in a heterogeneous computing environment to provide cloud services. A simple, robust, query efficient, scalable and space saving multi-tenant database architecture is proposed along with an ad hoc cloud architecture where organizations can collaborate to create a cloud, that doesnt harm their existence or profitability. An ad hoc cloud fits very well to the scenario where one wants to venture into remote areas for providing education services using a cloud. The results of the proposed multi-tenant database show 20% to 230% improvement for insertion, deletion and updation-queries. The response of the proposed approach is stable as compared to other system which degrades in terms of response time by 384% for increased number of attributes up to 50. The proposed approach is also space efficient by almost 86%. Dynamically changing cloud configurations requires adaptable database and mechanism to persist and manage data and exploit heterogeneous resources. The proposed ad hoc cloud handles heterogeneity of the involved nodes and deals with node specific granularity while decomposing workloads for efficient utilization of resources.

Keywords: Ad hoc Cloud, Heterogeneity, Multi-Tenant database

Introduction

Cloud computing is a computing paradigm where services and data reside in common space in scalable data centers, which are accessible via authentication. Cloud has three delivery models namely IaaS (Infrastructure as a Service), PaaS (Platform as a Service) and SaaS (Software as a service). Cloud computing [1] services can form a strong infrastructural and service foundation framework to provide any kind of service oriented computing environment. Ad hoc clouds [2,3] enable existing infrastructure as cloud compliant and the available resources in the system are utilized non-intrusively. An Ad hoc cloud is very efficient solution to problems faced by organizations to venture into remote areas for their IT infrastructure and support needs. Ad hoc cloud proliferate stakeholders to provide competitive services in a collaborative way.

Most existing business entities refrain from spreading their reach to remote geographical regions because of concern of huge upfront investment and profitability. The same is true for establishing institutes in these areas where the admission seekers exist but the location is so remote or hostile that many of the professionals would be reluctant to work. For these scenarios, Ad hoc cloud holds huge potential and promise in starting these ventures. The resources of parent or fixed education cloud initially act as a feeder for this new establishment. Once the system is working and matures with time, this ad hoc infrastructure gradually translates into persistent setup. Ad hoc education-cloud, where a cloud computing framework is harnessed to manage information system of an educational institution would be highly efficient in terms of accessibility, manageability, scalability and availability. An ad hoc cloud would enable us to harness services offered by fixed education-cloud[4] and services created and composed within an ad hoc cloud.

*Correspondence: sanpippalin@gmail.com
Department of Computer Science and Engineering, MNNIT Allahabad, Allahabad, India

Multi-tenancy implies that a single instance of application satisfies the requests of multiple clients. Each individual educational organization is considered as a tenant and all such organizations collaborate to create and participate in data-store building process. We propose a multi-tenant database for such a scenario where more than one tenants (Educational Institutions) collaborate to build the distributed database and use it by authorization [5]. In this scenario the tenants are free to join or leave. Providing dynamically adaptable multi-tenant database [6] with transactional level guarantee for the distributed data base to be used as a data store in the cloud formed with heterogeneous resources is our concern.

The major goal of this work is to implement multi-tenant database for an ad hoc cloud at remote location and provide the following sub goals to:

1. Provide an architecture that supports multi-tenancy in shared database shared schema scenario.
2. Find the best granularity level at which the work decomposition is to be done for heterogeneous environment.
3. Manage heterogeneity in terms of varying attributes, database technology and resources.
4. Optimize scheduling criteria and also provide load balancing.
5. Manage scalability and performance.

In order to meet the above goals we have developed a simple architecture that supports multi-tenancy and which work at optimum granularity with support for scalability and data management.

The rest of the paper is organized as follows. Section 'Related work' explains the related work done earlier. The details about the proposed architecture are elaborated in Section 'Proposed approach'. Section 'Results' presents the results obtained for the proposed architecture and section 'Conclusion & future work' provides the future scope of the work and concluding remarks.

Related work
Heterogeneity related work
Heterogeneity in terms of the cloud resources implies differences or variations in computing power of resources that could create further issues of performance and reliability. Some of the significant related work concerning Heterogeneity, Granularity, Replication, Load balancing and Scalability are:

A significant amount of work on load-balancing has emphasized on cluster based distributed systems. Condor [7] and Mosix [8] depend on check pointing and process migration to do load balancing in a cluster based distributed system. The heterogeneity of the cluster of workstations is managed by dynamically collecting load information and migrating active processes between cluster nodes to balance the load. This kind of load balancing techniques can be complementary to our work allocation techniques that focus on initial allocation of tasks according to capabilities of a node. Clusters of workstations have also been employed to host Web and Internet servers. A large amount of work on such cluster-based network servers has focused on request distribution as a means for handling the load imbalance in the cluster. Load-aware request distribution [9,10] use content-based request distribution which considers the locality of data and the load on the cluster nodes. Aron et al. [11] emphasizes on request isolation and resource management on cluster based distributed systems while [12] proposes cluster load balancing policies for fine grain network services. Load sharing in heterogeneous systems has been widely researched. [13] Evaluates and compare different load sharing algorithms for heterogeneous multicomputer systems. Goswami et al. [14] propose dynamic load sharing heuristics which manage workload in a distributed system by judging the resource requirements of processes. The author in [15] uses a proactive load sharing scheme for distributed systems which prevents the occurrence of load imbalance by collecting load and task execution behavior information in advance.

Karatza et al. [16] analyze load sharing policies for heterogeneous distributed systems to study the effect of load sharing on different classes of jobs. Berman et al. [17] explain an application specific scheduling approach for scheduling data parallel applications on a heterogeneous distributed system. Nieuwpoort et al. [18] elaborates load balancing strategies specifically for divide and conquer applications on a hierarchically organized distributed system. Kondo et al. [19] take into consideration a similar system model as ours and propose techniques for resource selection for short-lived applications on enterprise desktop Grids with the aim of minimizing the overall execution elapsed time of a single application. We consider a similar scenario but propose algorithms and heuristics for deciding the decomposition of tasks in order to load balance in a heterogeneous set of computation resources. Such scheduling algorithms have also been an active area of research in the field of divisible load scheduling. [20] Provides an overview of the research done in this field for master/worker architectures. Many approaches for scalability and data management services have been proposed like big table [21] and dynamo [22], but lacks in providing transactional level guaranty.

Multi-tenancy related work
Various approaches for multi-tenancy have been proposed depending on the degree of isolation. Three broad approaches are:

1. Separate database: In this approach, a separate database is used to store the data of an individual tenant.
2. Shared database, separate schema: This approach requires multiple tenants to be accommodated into a single database.
3. Shared database, shared schema: This approach involves same database and schema to be shared by all tenants.

Some of significant related work for providing multi-tenancy is as follows:

Universal table layout

A universal table [23] contains pre-specified number of fields. It consists of a Tenant_id column, a table column and all the data columns. Tenant_id is used to uniquely identify the data of a tenant whereas the table column refers to the id of the table for that tenant. This approach has been originated from Universal Relation where a table holds all the columns from all the tables. This approach is relatively easy to implement and queries are applied directly to the table.

Chunk folding

Chunk folding is a technique discussed in [24]. It vertically divides the logical tables into chunks and those are folded together into various physical tenants and are joined as needed. One table is used to store the base account information and other table is used to hold the extensions. This approach works by containing the heavily used parts of the schema into base tables and the rest part is mapped into the extensions.

Extension tables

The concept of extension tables came into picture after the development of decomposed storage model described in [24]. It divides a table of n-columns into n 2-column tables that are merged together. One problem with this approach is how to partition the table so that after joining these tables no extra information is generated.

Pivot tables

In this approach, a pivot table is created for a single column [25]. This table is shared by various tenant's tables. Each pivot table consists of a tenant column, Table column, a col column and a row column. Tenant column refers to the particular tenant. Table refers to the particular table for that tenant.

Multi-tenant shared table

In this approach, common contents from tenant information are separated as in [25]. This technique introduces the concept of tenants at database layer so that database engine can select an appropriate area for storage of data for that tenant.

An approach that deals with scalability issue is discussed in [26]. Two main problems are resolved; one is to resolve the sparseness of the universal table approach and second is to provide an indexing scheme for multi-tenant database. Three different approaches shared machine, shared process and shared table are discussed by Jacobs in [27]. In [28], a simulation study is done which analyzes the performance of different approaches to implement the multi-tenant databases. An approach for multi-tenant architecture supporting the SaaS model is discussed in [29]. The authors have proposed a cloudio software platform that is concerned with the flexibility of data model and managing the large data sets in the database.

Different challenges in multi-tenant applications are discussed in [27] such as scalability, security, performance, zero downtime and replication in [30].

Proposed approach

An ad hoc cloud is proposed with data persistence model along with task allocation and load balancing system, which works at best granularity. An efficient multi-tenant data base is also proposed. The load allocation system supports node specific granularity calculation for optimum allocation of resources in the environment. Ad hoc cloud architecture scenario is shown in Figure 1 along with its data center model which includes an efficient multi-tenant database.

An Ad hoc cloud derives data and cloud services from fixed cloud, further they are connected using an ad hoc link (V-SAT). The S, P and V nodes in the ad hoc data center represents Super-node (Permanent node at remote location with ad hoc connectivity with the fixed cloud to facilitate cloud formation at remote site), Persistent-node (organizations hosting cloud and data services) and Volunteer-nodes (other participating nodes within an organization). The S nodes promote the stake holders to establish their own collaborative dispersed data center. The P nodes within a data center provide reliability and availability through replication of services and data. The V nodes can voluntarily cache data and provide availability and performance in the absence of persistent node and large number of requests. The nodes participating in data center can be heterogeneous in terms of computing resources, database technology. All nodes participating in the data center are logically hierarchically organized and communication between them is encrypted with key shared and provided by hierarchically common parent node.

Data persistency

An ad hoc Data-center is proposed having some Super (S) nodes, some Persistent (P) nodes and other Volunteer (V) nodes. S nodes are permanent; P nodes are persistent node that store data on ad hoc basis and V

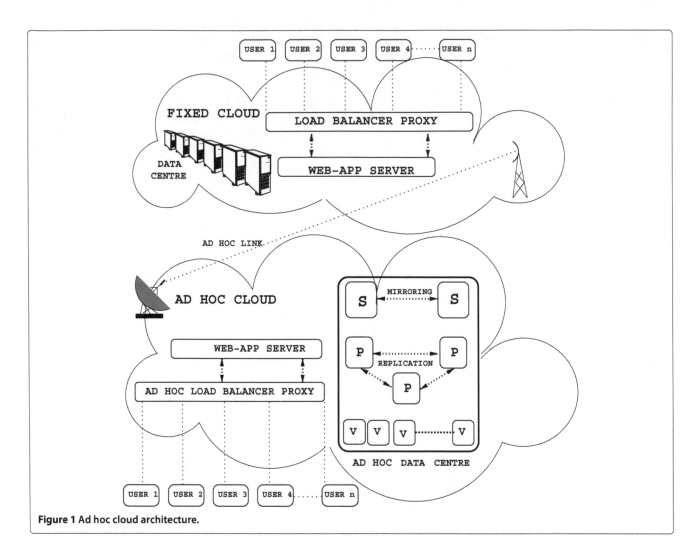

Figure 1 Ad hoc cloud architecture.

nodes voluntarily participate in Data-center. Mirroring is performed between S nodes to provide reliability, replication is performed between P nodes to increase availability and improve reliability further V nodes acts as new data sources or cache data for performance as shown in Figure 2. Data consistency is maintained for replicas using eager update protocol for frequent updates and lazy protocol is used for infrequent updates.

As shown in Figure 2 the OLTMs (Organizational Level Transaction Managers) are resource manager application pertaining to specific organizations. OLTM manage transaction within organizations whereas cross organization transactions are managed with help of HLTMs (High Level Transaction Managers). Each and every node participating in the data center is logically hierarchically organized with S node taking the root of the tree position with mirror support, P nodes as intermediate nodes in the tree and V nodes taking the leaf levels. Various issues arising out in data persistency like replication, granularity, failure handling and data domain are explained in the following sections.

Replication strategy, schema and data usage

The replication approach vary with the types of nodes and their characteristics as shown in Table 1. A nonvolunteer user does not replicate or store anything, it just uses the system whereas a volunteer node always replicate on demand and while quiting submits all at site updations to the hierarchical parent node or nearest neighbor node.

The persistent nodes always replicate to increase availability maintaining data consistency. The super nodes between themselves implement mirroring periodically so as to provide reliability. The S, P, V, nodes always downloads the schema in first use. The data population if V node is done on demand basis, whereas P and S nodes always update their data as consistency requirements.

Data domain and replication granularity

The data semantics of every type of user is bounded by boundaries as shown in the Table 2.

The V nodes data requirements are user need specific, P nodes data requirements are organizational specific whereas the S node data requirements are administration,

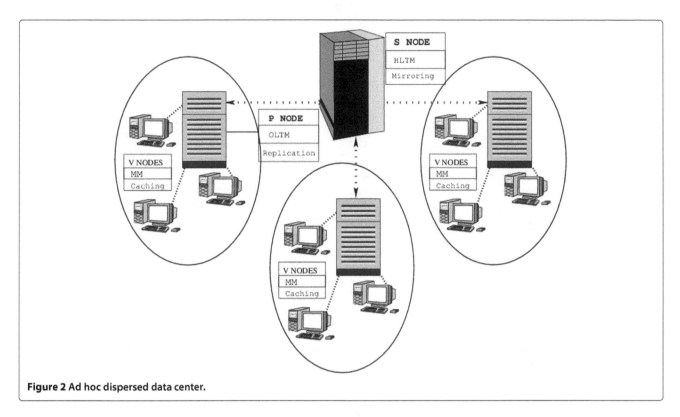

Figure 2 Ad hoc dispersed data center.

system support and management specific. The replication granularity for V node is record level dump task specific, for P node first complete dump is copied and further differential dump is used based on check pointing and for S nodes complete copy of the database dump is used among them.

We propose a simple application level check pointing approach for finding the differential dump that is records modified after a time stamp.

Tables 3 and 4 are used to manage the process of finding record level modifications. Table 3 is shown having R_id as primary key in all related tables along with other attributes and CKP_F being a flag field to denote the modification of records. Initially the field is set to F (false) indicating no modification, it is set to T (true) when there is a modification by itself or a replication update from some other node is received. Table 4 stores modified record ids and time stamp of recording the checkpoint in a table called checkpoint table.

Failure handling strategy

For the various classification of nodes the specific failure handling strategy in case of node failure is given. A proactive approach is used by the failed nodes, after recovering from failure the V nodes and S nodes populate themselves using a differential dump.

Application level Check-pointing is used to calculate difference. Further as shown in Table 5. S nodes use complete dump from mirror sites.

Load balancing

At primary level load balancing is done by the DNS using a round robin scheduling among the p nodes available in the working set. For load balancing in a heterogeneous environment the important decision parameters are granularity of sub-task, application requirements, computation, communication resources available and task dependency. In our solution to this problem we develop a heuristic

Table 1 Replication approach, schema and data use

Type of user	User characteristics	Schema & data population
Non Volunteer	User have no contribution in data center	No & never
Volunteer	User allows sharing but can exit anytime	Yes & when in use
Persistent	User are stake holders	Yes & always
Super	Super users	Yes & always

Table 2 Data domain and replication granularity

Type of user	Data domain	Replication granularity
Non Volunteer	Only surfing	Not required
Volunteer	Need Specific	Difference dump (record level)
Persistent	Organizational specific	First Complete then Difference dump
Super	Administration specific	Complete dump (database dump)

Table 3 Tenant table with check-pointing

R_id	....	CKP_F
1	—	F
2	—	T
3	—	T
4	—	F
5	—	F

that works upon the above mentioned parameters and also takes into account the total number of nodes available in the working set and the total size of the task. Generic granularity for a task (participation in data center) can be calculated as follows.

$$Generic_{Granularity} = Total_{Tasksize}/Total_{Numberofnodes}$$
$$(1)$$

We improve the granularity calculation by inculcating computation and communication resources available respectively. We redefine this generic granularity to be as specific heuristic granularity w.r.t. specific nodes. We take into account the last successful subtask execution and also history of such executions to calculate granularity.

For the entire network, Min_granularity is defined as per Min_bandwidth , Min_memory and Min_CPU available. Similarly Max_granularity is defined.

Algorithm 1 WORKLOAD DECOMPOSITION($Task_{size}$, $History_{decomp}$)
Require: $Task_{size}$ and $History_{decomp}$.
Ensure: Optimal granularity selection.

1:   $Current_{decomp} \leftarrow History_{decomp}$
2:   $Old_{granularity} \leftarrow Task_{size}/History_{decomp}$
3: **while** TRUE **do**
4:     $Current_{decomp} \leftarrow (Current_{decomp} + Hi_{decomp})/2$
5:     $Current_{decomp} \leftarrow (Current_{decomp} + Hi_{decomp})/2$
6:     **if** Task executed at $New_{granularity}$ **then**
7:        $History_{decomp} \leftarrow Current_{decomp}$
8:        $Best_{size} \leftarrow New_{granularity}$
9:        **return** WORKLOADDECOMPOSITION
      ($Best_{size}, History_{decomp}$)
10:     **else**
11:        **return** $Best_{size}$
12:     **end if**
13: **end while**

Table 4 Checkpoint table

CKP_id	TS (Time Stamp)	R_id
1	1.0	2,3
2	1.1	1,3
3	1.2	0

Table 5 Failure handling approach

Type of user	Replication approach	Failure handling
Non Volunteer	Not required	Not required
Volunteer	Submits before it switches off	Populate from previous timestamp
Persistent	Replicate always	Copy nearest replica (record level)
Super	Mirror always	Copy attached mirror (database dump)

The execution capability of a system is subjective and depends upon factors like $CPU_{available}$, $Memory_{available}$, $Network_{bandwidth}$, $Disk_{available}$. Therefore to objectively decide the specific node for execution for specific task, a heuristic is needed to assign task to a specific node. To do this the resources like CPU, Memory and Network bandwidth are graded from 0 to 1. Any request for execution is mapped to best fit node as per required resources for execution. The nearest match to request is allocated and the task is scheduled to execute on the matched node. The normalized node profile table for 10 nodes is shown in Table 6. Where each resources is graded between 0 to 1. The grades are decided as per the min and max unit of the resource present in the environment and, min is assigned 0 and max is assigned 1 and all intermediate nodes are graded accordingly.

The Table 6 shows resource statistics for a partial working set among the nodes, Table 7 grades and normalizes them between 0 to 1 for all resource instances.

Further Table 8 is calculated from Table 7 to provide a grid that enables us to take decision regarding task scheduling linked with execution node id. The task is allocated to a node which is just almost capable for execution. The Assign Exec. flag in the table indicates the node being assigned for task execution of size equal to or less than its RAM size.

Table 6 Node resource profile

NODE ID	RAM (MB)	CPU (MHz)	N/W (Kbps)	HDD (MB)
N1	400	600	60	6000
N2	700	1800	70	5000
N3	100	600	50	4000
N4	1000	400	70	1000
N5	100	1600	90	5000
N6	700	2000	50	4000
N7	100	1400	40	2000
N8	100	1800	30	2000
N9	200	1400	40	2000
N10	600	1800	40	3000

Table 7 Node profile normalized data

NODE ID	RAM	CPU	N/W	HDD
N1	0.4	0.6	0.6	0.6
N2	0.7	0.9	0.7	0.5
N3	0.1	0.3	0.5	0.4
N4	1.0	0.2	0.7	0.1
N5	0.1	0.8	0.9	0.5
N6	0.7	1.0	0.5	0.4
N7	0.1	0.7	0.4	0.2
N8	0.1	0.9	0.3	0.2
N9	0.2	0.7	0.4	0.2
N10	0.6	0.9	0.4	0.3

The following rules are used while making decision:

1. JOB_{size} is equal to RAM_{size}.
2. Free $Disk_{space}$ is ten times of RAM_{size}.
3. If RAM_{size} vs $Disk_{space}$ ratio is less than 1 : 10. THEN alter RAM_{size} by $DISK_{size}/10$ in the Table 6.
4. If $N/W_{bandwidth} < (1/6)$ of RAM_{size} implies discard node for participation in data center.
5. If $CPU_{available} < 2$ times of RAM_{size} implies discard node for participation in data center.
6. If cumulative sum of the normalized grades is less that 1 unit discard the node for participation in data center.

Following rules are used to assign values in Table 8 and decide about task assignment:

> NODE ID: Node id of nodes involved.
> RAM vs HDD: if Ratio of $RAM_{size} VsHDD_{size}$ more than 1:10 then TRUE else FALSE.
> N/W:Thresh hold >: $Task_{size}/6$ kbps implies TRUE.
> CPU: If available CPU is greater than equal to $2*Task_{size}$ implies TRUE.
> TOTAL: Total sum of grades < 1 implies no assignment.
> ASSIGN EXEC.: * implies RAM_{size} Altered.

The heuristics were developed after many iterations of execution with different values of the proportion factor and finally these values were experimentally determined and found to produce reasonable results.

Scalability and data management

We propose a light weight data store capable of providing transactional level guaranty. Our data store would have Organizational level transaction manager (OLTM) and Higher level transaction manager (HLTM) as shown in Figure 3. The transactions within an organization would be handled by OLTM and between organizations would be handled by HLTM. Elasticity at data store level is important as it would not limit upper layers for scalability. The Meta-data Manager (MM) implementation provides decoupling of database and transaction manager and it also provides mapping of distributed database partitions into OLTM. Synchronous replication of MM is required for fault tolerance. Storage layer takes care of replication of data and fault tolerance. Slower nodes can use meta data caching for improved performance. Since HTLM are stateless therefore to improve performance during scalability spawning a new HTLM is easy. Further data base migration between data-store or in cloud can be done as discussed in Albatross [31].

Maintaining a working set

In ad hoc cloud nodes can be joining and leaving randomly, so it is important to formulate a mechanism to find out live donation based or volunteer resources, which can be exploited for task execution. To solve this issue we maintain a working or live set of processors. Table 9. below show different scenarios which different types of node may exhibit. The hierarchically parent node always keeps track of live and volunteering to donate resources and keeps propagating this information up in the hierarchy. As soon as a node quits it is immediately removed from the working set of processors. A node may also be removed due to node or communication failure. The node resuming after failure initiates for updating of its local database. When a (P) persistent node joins the working set for the first time it downloads the schema, and data is replicated in entirety within domain, only if a threshold number of requests are received. If a node rejoins it calculates difference using check-pointing and does a record level differential replication.

Before quitting it either submits to hierarchical node or replicates to nearest neighbor. In case of a (S) super node, complete backup of database is replicated to the new node. A super node never shuts down randomly or

Table 8 Decision grid for task assignment

NODE ID	RAM vs HDD	N/W	CPU	TOTAL	ASSIGN EXEC.
N1	T	T	T	1.9	TRUE
N2	F	T	T	2.8	*
N3	T	T	T	1.3	
N4	T	T	F	2.0	FALSE
N5	T	T	T	2.3	TRUE
N6	F	T	T	2.6	*
N7	T	T	T	1.4	TRUE
N8	T	F	T	1.5	FALSE
N9	T	T	T	1.5	
N10	F	T	T	2.2	*TRUE

*in Table 8 implies representation of RAM_{size} is altered.

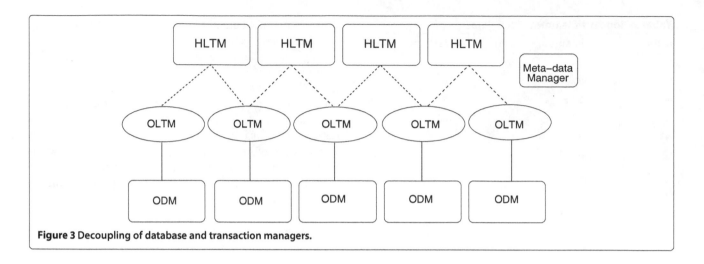

Figure 3 Decoupling of database and transaction managers.

frequently, for maintenance related shut down, differential backups may be used for consistency requirements. The (V) Volunteer node rarely gets a replicated copy, if there are no persistent node nearby and for temporal requirement a volunteer node may also act as a replica, but as soon as the requirements are satisfied it submits back, or if the persistent nodes are up, the persistent nodes bully the volunteer nodes and all further requests are served by the persistent node after handover.

Multi-tenant architecture

The Proposed approach for multi-tenant database is designed over the shared database shared schema technique. We decided for shared database and shared schema approach as it is suitable for Large number of tenants with lesser data and hence entries (as required by our application) and thus minimizing cost and leverage benefit of using same h/w, s/w, database, schema and table for all tenants and at the same time guaranteeing them isolation and security. In case we go for shared database approach we would be limited by the number of instances of database supported by the DB server. So adding more tenants will add more cost. In case, if we go for separate schema approach then in case of failure, schema restore from backup will be forced on other users also with different schema on the same data base (if no replica for the

same schema is present), also (which is a time consuming task). Our proposed approach makes use of extension table.

Extension table approach

In the universal table model it is a big challenge to decide the number of custom fields (columns in table). Providing less number of columns might restrict the tenants who wish to use a large number of custom fields. A large number of such fields may result in large number of NULL values in the database table. Second problem is of differing data types of these columns [32].

In recent times, the use of multi-tenant database systems increased multi-fold. In multi-tenant database a data center is hosted by a service provider and the tenants subscribe to the services provided by the service provider [26,33]. Figure 4 shows three tables used in the basic approach that makes use of extension table. The primary table keeps the Tenant_id and record_id and some other fields. record_id field uniquely identifies the transaction made by a particular tenant. By extracting the value of record_id field, one can extract the values from the extension table. For a single record_id, there are number of rows in the extension table.

The number of rows for a particular record_id is the number of columns in the logical table of that tenant. The Meta Data table tells about the data types of these fields.

Whenever a tenant inserts data into its table, Meta Data table is accessed to match the given values against the data types of the Meta data table. An Extn_ID in extension table is associated with an Extn_ID field of Meta Data table. This extension-id is unique for each column and is used to know the data type and external label of that field in the logical table for that tenant. An extension table contains the actual data for all the tenants. In case of universal table structure, columns, which are not used by a particular tenant, contain the NULL value, this results in wastage

Table 9 Events and associated actions of a participating user

Events	Action
New user joins	Schema download
User re-joins	If require schema update (schema populated with exported XML) check pointing used to find difference
Daemon user	Regularly schema and data exports updated
User quits	Submit, replicate, mirror as applicable

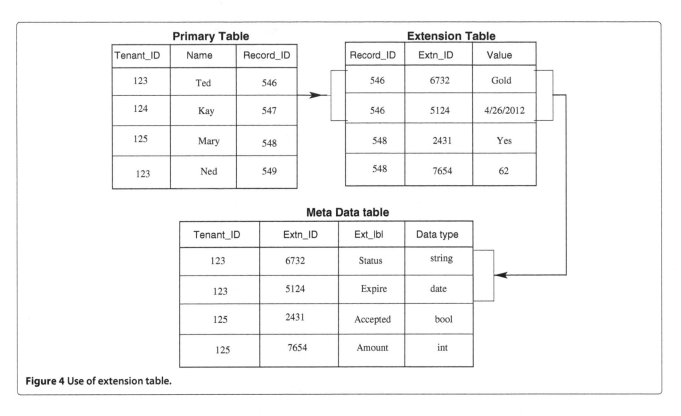

Figure 4 Use of extension table.

of space. Extension table concept overcomes this problem. Figures 4 and 5 shows an extension table and a Meta Data table.

In the basic approach of extension table discussed above, following drawbacks can be observed:

1. Extension table contains a lot of information for Meta Data i.e. for a single row of table of a tenant that consists of four columns, The Record_ID and Extn_ID are repeated four times this information introduces a kind of redundancy.
2. Whenever a query for insertion, deletion or update is performed three tables are accessed which increases the query processing time. In our proposed approach following concepts are introduced and implemented:

Tenant_ID	Record_ID	XML_Ext	Table_ID
123	546		1
123	546		2
125	548		5
125	548		4

```
<Status>Gold</Status>
<Expire>2012-04-25</Expire>
```

Figure 5 Modified extension table.

3. Concept of XML object into a database is used that helps to reduce the size of extension table as well as eliminates the need of a primary table.
4. An approach that achieves multiple table creation for a tenant is proposed and successfully implemented. Figure 5 shows the proposed approach where extension table consists of a Tenant_id, a Record_id, an XML attribute and a Table_id. Tenant_id and Record_id uniquely identify a particular record. A Record_id is used to associate each transaction with a unique record number. XML object contains the data for an entire row of a Tenants logical table. Tags in a single XML object refers to the name of a particular field in the corresponding table. Table_id field represents the id of the table in which a particular record is inserted for the specified tenant. The tenant specifies the name of the table and our proposed system generates unique id for that table for that tenant.

A table that maintains the information about all the tables of all tenants is created. This table maps the Table_id field of the extension table to the name of the table which a tenant is referring to.

Creation of Table

A tenant is free to use any number of custom fields assuming that service provider has created sufficient number of fields in the main database schema. A tenant is free

Table 10 A metadata table

Tenant$_I$D	Tbl$_N$ame	Table$_I$D
123	Employee	1
123	Purchase	2
125	Customer	5
125	Funds	4

to create any number of tables and use any data type (supported by that DBMS) for its fields.

Whenever a tenant specifies a new table name, this name is stored in the table_meta_data table. Table 10 shows the structure of table_meta_data table.

Insertion in the Table

A tenant specifies the name of the table and supplies the values. Our proposed architecture follows a sequence of steps to insert the values in the main extension table as follows:

1. The table id of a particular table for that tenant is extracted from the table_meta_data table.
2. Meta_data table is accessed to know the data types of the fields.
3. A Record_id, identifying this particular transaction, is generated and is inserted into the Record_ID column.
4. An XML document with inserted values is created whose tags are the column names in the table.
5. This XML document is inserted into XML_Ext column of the extension table.
6. Table_Id extracted from the table_meta_data is inserted into the Table_Id column of extension table.

Updating the information in the database

The table name and the name of the field is specified, and following steps are followed:

1. It accesses the table_meta_data table from where it retrieves the id of the table for that tenant
2. In extension table, it finds out the rows corresponding to that table id and tenant.
3. From the XML documents, which are related to the Table_ID, it makes a Xquery that gives field names.
4. It modifies the value in the XML document and stores it back in the extension table with the same record id.

Deleting records The name of the table along with indicative key is for a specific record is provided. Similar to the update process, the table_meta_data is accessed to know the Table_ID of the table. Later extension table is accessed to know the rows corresponding to that Table_ID. The entire row, containing The XML document in which the specified value for the given field is found, is deleted.

Results

To implement the proposed approach, MySQL database in Ubuntu has been used. Ubuntu is installed over VMware and all involved nodes (computers) are configured with heterogeneity. Factors of heterogeneity are allocated CPU power, allocated RAM and disk space and network bandwidth. To test and generate report python is used as scripting language. The test bed comprise of 90 nodes for the distributed multi-tenant data base. The processing capability ranges from 500 MHz to 2.4 GHz for processor, 500MB to 1500MB for RAM and 10-30 GB of free disk space as shown in Table 4.

The proposed approach has been successfully implemented and queries like selection, insertion and deletion have been experimented. For more added attributes in a table the performance is slightly better, and saves a lot of space as compared to the extension table approach. This benefit comes from the use of XML in the attributes.

Test bed Configurations: A sampled 10 nodes configuration is shown in the Table 4. and depicted in the following graph in Figure 6. The graph for test bed configuration shows heterogeneity among processors in terms of speed, among RAM in terms of size of primary memory, among HDD in terms of size and space available for secondary

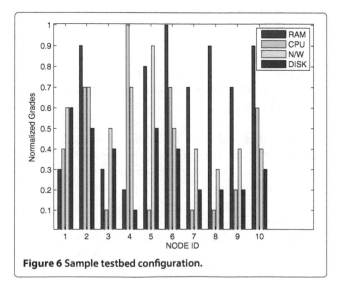

Figure 6 Sample testbed configuration.

Table 11 No. of Queries executed per sec

Type of query	Proposed approach	Extension table approach
Insertion	804	665
Deletion	804	238
Updation	662	197
Selection	747	1026

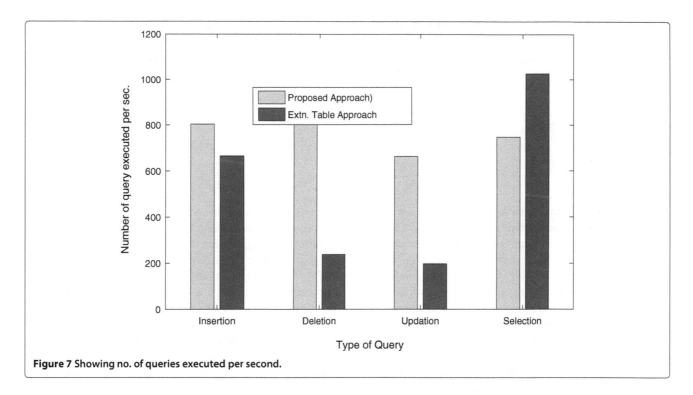

Figure 7 Showing no. of queries executed per second.

storage, among network bandwidth in terms of data rate available.

Comparison with extension table approach

The number of rows in the original extension table depends upon the number of fields in a tenants table. But in our approach it contains only a single entry for a row. Therefore a lot of space savings and also solves the NULL value problem with the extension table approach.

In Table 11 and Figure 7 it can be seen that except for select query all other query outperform the extension table approach. As shown in Figure 7 Statistically for

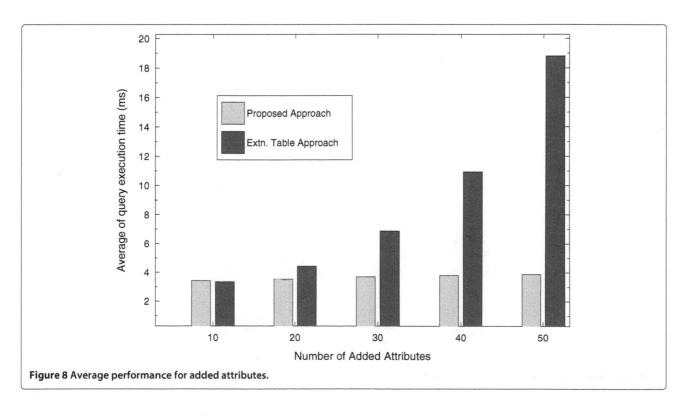

Figure 8 Average performance for added attributes.

Table 12 Avg. performance (time taken) for added attributes

Number of added attributes	Proposed approach (ms)	Extension table approach (ms)
10	3.427	3.345
20	3.532	4.435
30	3.712	6.874
40	3.804	10.932
50	3.884	18.809

Table 13 Comparison for space requirements (bytes) for added attributes

Number of added attributes	Proposed approach (ms)	Extension table approach (ms)
0	2048	15360
2	2048	16384
4	2560	17408
8	3072	19456
16	4096	23552

insertion, deletion and updation query there is a gain in number of query execution per second of 20%, 230% and 236% respectively and there is drop by 27% for selection query, which is slow due to parsing of XML file. The gain is due to less number of joins involved in the schema.

The average response time for query execution for added attributes is almost constant for our approach as shown in Figure 8 and Table 12, but for extension table approach it increases exponentially. Figure 8 shows there is exponential rise in the response time with increase in number of attributes in the extension table approach where as our approach yields a constant response time approximately. The response time in the extension table approach degrades varying from 2.45% to 384.5% in five consecutive increases in step size of 10 attributes. The increase in attributes involves creation of new tables therefore more number of joins are required to satisfy a query. Therefore in the extension table approach the

response time increases with added attributes. Since in the proposed approach due to the use of XML attribute the number of tables created would be less therefore resulting in lesser number of joins required for query execution.

The better performance in response time in our approach is due to the use of XML filed, which accommodates and adjusts extra added attributes in the XML filed.

Figure 9 show the increase in space requirements in the extension table approach, with the increase in number of attributes, whereas in our approach the space requirement increases linearly. This is again due to the adjustment of group of attributes into one field in for of XML file.

In Table 13 we consider in the implementation model that a total of 10 common attributes are present in the multi-tenant database along with this 20 tenant specific attributes are there. The size of a field is 512 bytes. Maximum allowed attributes in an XML file is 4. The efficiency gained in space on an average is 86%. It could be greater

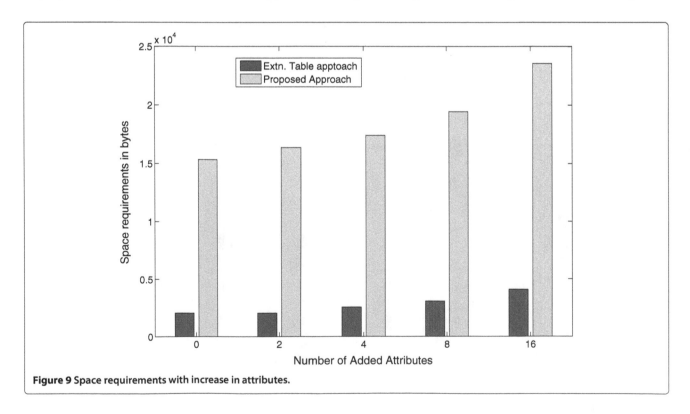

Figure 9 Space requirements with increase in attributes.

Table 14 Comparison for concurrent queries

No. of concurrent queries	Proposed approach (time in ms)	Extension table approach (time in ms)
10	11.44	11.05
20	24.55	23.04
50	66.98	62.98
100	140.86	132.45
200	292.37	262.34
500	604.42	535.67

if more than 4 attributes could be allowed in a field. In our approach we are only limited by the size of XML file that can fit in field as constraint by the native database technology used.

Table 14 lists the response time for concurrent queries as the number of concurrent queries increases the graph in Figure 10 depicts that after the number of concurrent queries crosses the 200 mark the performance of our approach slightly degrades but does not affect the applications response substantially. The response time for concurrent query execution is within comparable range with the extension table approach.

Conclusion & future work

In this paper, an attempt has been made to implement the Multi-tenant database for an ad hoc cloud that offers operational advantages over the existing ones. It fits very well in scenarios where SaaS cloud services are to be delivered between multiple clients (institutions). The proposed multi-tenant database accommodates larger number of tenants because a single database instance is used to store the data of multiple tenants. Another advantage of the proposed work is that the tenants are allowed to create multiple tables which add flexibility in terms of having varied set of attributes as specifically required for its application. It is evident from the result that our approach performs much better in terms of space saving in terms of solving the NULL value problem as compared to other multi-tenant approaches. With increase the number of attribute in the table the query performance drops with the extension table approach as compared to our approach, which is due to more number of attribute and more number of joins required to execute query. The multi-tenant database architecture proposed is highly efficient in terms of query execution, space saving and change in number of attributes. The performance is moderate and comparable with extension table approach for concurrent requests. The results of the proposed work show 20% to 230% improvement for insertion, deletion and updation-queries. The response of the proposed approach is stable as compared to other system which degrades in terms of response time by 384% for increased number of attributes up to 50. The proposed approach is also space efficient by average of 86% for 2 to 16 more added attributes. Further the work decomposition algorithm proposed optimally calculates the node specific granularity, which helps in performance and better resource utilization by optimizing

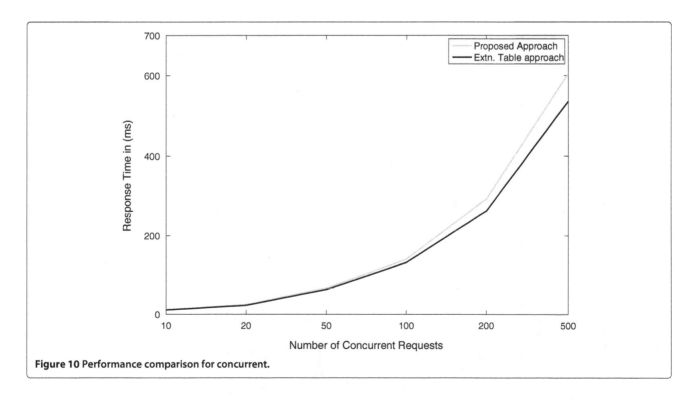

Figure 10 Performance comparison for concurrent.

the resource allocation policy. The data management and scalability approach discussed is simple to implement and proves to be practically efficient due to the concept used for decoupling the database manager and the transaction manager. The replication scheme discussed uses a simple approach to calculate change in database state. It further improves availability and strengthens reliability and uses a simple application level check-pointing to find differential updates. Further work can be done to remove the limitation imposed by database attribute field so as to include a sufficiently large XML file.

Competing interests
The authors declare that they have no competing interests.

Authors' contributions
SKP and DSK designed the research (project conception, development of overall research plan and study oversight). SKP conducted research (hands-on conduct of the experiments and data collection). SKP and DSK analyzed data or performed statistical analysis and wrote paper. SKP had primary responsibility for final content. Both authors read and approved the final manuscript.

Acknowledgements
A special thank you goes to those who contributed to this paper: Mr. Manu Vardhan for his valuable comments and sharing his knowledge. Prof. Saurabh Raina for proof reading the paper. The Lab staff, JRE Group of Institution and MNNIT Allahabad for hosting the research.

References
1. Mell P, Grance T (2009) The NIST definition of cloud computing, version 15, NIST. Retrieved January 2010. http://www.nist.gov/itl/csd/cloud-102511.cfm
2. Kirby G, Dearle A, Macdonald A, Fernandes A (2010) An approach to ad hoc cloud computing. In: DBLP: CoRR, Volume abs 1002.4738
3. Chandra A, Weissman J (2009) Nebulas: Using distributed voluntary resources to build clouds. In: Proceedings of the 2009 conference on Hot topics in cloud computing. ACM id 1855535, USENIX Association
4. Pippal S, Kushwaha DS (2012) Architectural design of education cloud framework extendible to ad hoc clouds. In: IEEE 2nd International Conference on Recent Advances in Information Technology (RAIT)
5. Chapin PC, Skalka C, SeanWang X (2008) Authorization in trust management: features and foundations. Comput Surv 40(3): 1–48
6. Das S, Agrawal D, El Abbadi A (2009) ElasTraS: An elastic transactional data store in the cloud. In: Proceedings of the conference on Hot topics in cloud computing (HotCloud'09)
7. Litzkow MJ, Livny M, Mutka MW (1988) Condor : A hunter of idle workstations. In: 8th International Conference on Distributed Computing Systems. IEEE Computer Society Press, Washington, pp 104–111
8. Barak A, Guday S, Wheeler RG (1993) The MOSIX Distributed Operating System, Load Balancing for UNIX. In: Lecture Notes in Computer Science, vol 672. Springer-Verlag, Berlin; New York
9. Pai VS, Aron M, Banga G, Svendsen M, Druschel P, Zwaenepoel W, Nahum E (1998) Locality-aware request distribution in cluster-based network servers. SIGOPS Oper Syst Rev 32(5): 205–216
10. Aron M, Sanders D, Druschel P, Zwaenepoel W (2000) Scalable content aware request distribution in cluster-based network servers. In: Proceedings of the USENIX 2000 Annual Technical Conference, San Diego
11. Aron M, Druschel P, Zwaenepoel W (2000) Cluster reserves: a mechanism for resource management in cluster-based network servers. In: Proceedings of the ACM SIGMETRICS Conference on Measurement and Modeling of Computer Systems
12. Shen K, Yang T, Chu L (2002) Cluster load balancing for fine-grain network services. In: Proceedings of the 16th International Parallel and Distributed Processing Symposium, (IPDPS'02), Fort Lauderdale FL
13. Banawan SA, Zeidat NM (1992) A comparative study of load sharing in heterogeneous multicomputer systems. In: Proceedings of the 25th Annual symposium on Simulation
14. Goswami KK, Devarakonda M, Iyer RK (1993) Prediction based Dynamic Load-Sharing Heuristics. In: IEEE Transactions on Parallel and Distributed Systems
15. Anane R, Anthony RJ (2003) Implementation of a Proactive Load Sharing Scheme. In: Proceedings of the 2003 ACM symposium on Applied computing
16. Berman F, Wolski R, Figueira S, Schopf J, Shao G (1996) Application Level Scheduling on Distributed Heterogeneous Networks. In: Proceedings of the 1996 ACM/IEEE conference on Supercomputing
17. Karatza HD, Hilzer RC (2002) Load Sharing in Heterogeneous Distributed Systems. In: Proceedings of the 2002 Winter Simulation Conference
18. van Nieuwpoort RV, Kielmann T, Bal HE (2001) Efficient load balancing for wide-area divide and conquer applications. In: Proceedings of the eighth ACM SIGPLAN symposium on Principles and practices of parallel programming
19. Kondo D, Chien AA, Casanova H (2004) Resource Management for Rapid Application Turnaround on Enterprise Desktop Grids. In: Proceedings of the 2004 ACM/IEEE conference in Supercomputing
20. Beaumont O, Casanova H, Legrand A, Robert Y, Yang Y (2005) Scheduling Divisible Loads on Star and Tree Networks:Results and Open Problems. IEEE Trans Parallel Distributed Syst (TPDS) 16(3): 207–218
21. Chang F, Dean J, Ghemawat S, Hsieh WC, Wallach DA, Burrows M, Chandra T, Fikes A, Gruber RE (2006) Bigtable: a distributed storage system for structured data. In: OSDI. pp 205–218
22. DeCandia G, Hastorun D, Jampani M, Kakulapati G, Lakshman A, Pilchin A, Sivasubramanian S, Vosshall P, Vogels W (2007) Dynamo: Amazon's highly available key-value store. In: SOSP. pp 205–220
23. Maier D, Ullman JD (1983) Maximal objects and the semantics of universal relation databases. In: ACM Trans. Database System. p 114
24. Copeland GP, Khoshafian SN (1985) A decomposition storage model. In: The Proc. of 1985 ACM SIGMOD International conference on Management of Data. ACM Press, pp 268–279
25. Grund M, Schapranow M, Kruege J, Schaffner J, Bog A (2008) IEEE Symposium on Advanced Management of Information for Globalized Enterprises. pp 1–5
26. Hui M, Jiang D, Li G, Zhou Y (2009) Supporting Database Applications as a service. In: IEEE 25thInternational Conference on Data Engineering. pp 832–843
27. Jacobs D, Aulbach S (2007) Ruminations on Multi-Tenant Databases, Datenbanksysteme. In: Bro, Technik undWissenschaft (German Database Conference) BTW. pp 514–521
28. Wang ZH, Guo CJ, Gao B, Sun W, Zhang Z, Hao W (2008) Study and Performance Evaluation of the Multi-Tenant Data Tier Design Patterns for Service Oriented Computing. In: IEEE International Conference on e-Business Engineering. pp 94–101
29. Domingo EJ, Nino JT, Lemos AL, Lemos ML, Palacios RC, Berbis JMG (2010) A cloud computing-oriented multi-tenant architecture for business information systems. In: IEEE 3rd International Conference on Cloud Computing. pp 532–533
30. Vardhan M, Verma S, Bhatnagar P, Kushwaha DS (2012) Eager computation and lazy propagation of modifications for reducing synchronization overhead in file replication system. In: IEEE 3rd International Conference on Computer and Communication Technology (ICCCT-2012)
31. Das S, Nishimura S, Agrawal D, El Abbadi A (2011) Albatross: Lightweight Elasticity in Shared Storage Databases for the Cloud using Live Data Migration. In: 37th International Conference on Very Large Data Bases (VLDB)
32. Aulbach S, Grust T, Jacobs D, Kemper A, Rittinger J (2008) Multi-tenant databases for software as a service:schema-mapping techniques. In: The proc. of International Conference on Management of Data - SIGMOD. pp 1195–1206
33. Hacigumus H, Iyer B, Mehrotra S (2002) Providing database as a service. In: 18th International Conference on Data Engineering. pp 29–38

5

User-controlled resource management in federated clouds

Marc Mosch[1,2*], Stephan Groß[1] and Alexander Schill[1]

Abstract

Virtualization and broadband Internet connections enabled what is known today under the term cloud. Benefits like scalability and cost reduction by pay per use agreements are accompanied by potential harm to the users data. Since existing cloud solutions can be considered synonymous with unknown locations and potentially hostile environments security protection objectives can not be guaranteed. Motivated by cloud's potential we propose a way to get rid of this drawback. We present π-Cloud, a personal secure cloud, that enables users to benefit from cloud computing and retain data sovereignty by federating the users own resources. More precisely we present a cloud resource manager that is able to keep control on the devices forming the user's π-Cloud as well as the services running on them.

Keywords: Cloud computing; Federated clouds; Cloud resource management; User-control

Introduction

Catchwords like scalability, on demand self service, pay per use, availability everywhere and any time describe an even bigger catchword: cloud computing. Cloud computing has evolved from technologies like utility and grid computing or the Internet of services. The progress in the area of virtualization and the availability of broadband Internet connections even for average consumers enabled cloud computing. It allows the outsourcing of computing and storage and involves the renting of virtualized hardware as well as of software running on it.

The cloud computing paradigm focuses on offering services and differentiates between three service levels [1]: As a foundation, the Infrastructure as a Service (IaaS) layer offers pure virtualized hardware like computing, network and storage. On top of this, the Platform as a Service layer (PaaS) provides a development platform for software which can then be utilised as Software as a Service (SaaS). Orthogonally to these service layers, four types of clouds are defined based on their consumer groups. The type mostly referred to when talking about clouds is the public cloud. Users of public clouds share the same resources under control of a cloud provider. In contrast, the users of private clouds are provided with resources that are maintained by themselves or at least for them alone. Hybrid clouds are a combination of public and private clouds while community clouds are a combination of several private clouds. Furthermore, we define federated clouds in contrast to other work such as [2] not only as synonymous to hybrid clouds but as a special mixture of hybrid and community clouds. To be more precise, a federated cloud is formed by an individual combination of public and private cloud resources as defined by an arbitrary participant of a community cloud.

With the outsourcing comes the cost reduction as it is no longer necessary to run data centres that are dimensioned for maximum peak loads and that run most of the time underutilized. However, these benefits are accompanied by a severe drawback that unsettles companies and prevents them from using cloud solutions: the decrease of data control. Data once outsourced is exposed to loss, abuse and manipulation. Cloud users are not able to determine where their data is located and who has access to it. The three security protection objectives availability, integrity and confidentiality are endangered in cloud environments. This is where our approach of a personal secure cloud sets.

The π-Cloud approach

The FlexCloud research group [3] aims to enable users to outsource their data and benefit from cloud computing

*Correspondence: marc.mosch@tu-dresden.de
[1] Technische Universität Dresden, Department of Computer Science, Chair of Computer Networks, D-01062 Dresden, Germany
[2] Technische Universität Dresden, Faculty of Civil Engineering, Institute of Construction Informatics, Dresden, Germany

without losing data control. This is achieved by dividing the used resources within a federated cloud into trustworthy and non-trustworthy ones. The devices under complete control of the user are per definition trustworthy whereas foreign resources are assumed to be non-trustworthy until further classification. This personal secure cloud, or π-Cloud is controlled by the so called π-Box, a security gateway that manages the separation of sensitive from public data. The former is stored preferably on trustworthy resources although it might be outsourced if necessary. An automatic encryption beforehand ensures data protection. Public data can be outsourced unencrypted. While this approach ensures integrity and confidentiality of important data the usage of information dispersal mechanisms ensures availability as well. See [4] for further details regarding the implementation of this feature. Similar mechanisms apply for the distribution of services. So services processing critical data should be bound to trusted resources only.

Thus, the π-Cloud's major objective is to put the user in a position to externalize his IT-infrastructure without losing the control over his data [5]. Therefore we form the π-Cloud consisting of all resources, services and data under the complete control of the user. The user is able to adjust his π-Cloud to his actual demands by secure inclusion of foreign resources. In doing so, data flow as well as service execution has to be controlled. Cloud setup and control, data flow as well as service distribution are regulated by the π-Box. The π-Box is composed of four main components, as depicted in Figure 1: (1) the Cockpit, (2) the Service Controller, (3) the Data Controller and (4) the Resource Manager.

The Cockpit provides the user interface. Although we are aiming to include as much intelligence in our π-Box as possible, to disburden the user from cumbersome administration tasks, it would be exaggerated to claim that the π-Cloud is able to maintain itself. In order to prevent the user from becoming the weakest link in the security chain, the cockpit has to put him into a position to supervise and manage his π-Cloud even if he is not an expert [6,7].

The Service Controller is responsible for secure service execution. As complete homomorphic encryption is not yet real-time capable, we realize secure service execution by decomposing services into critical and non-critical sub-services. Critical sub-services process high-confidential data and are executed strictly on trustworthy resources, whereas non-critical sub-services are allowed to compute on arbitrary resources.

The Service Controller's counterpart, the Data Controller, takes care of secure cloud storage. We split each file into several slices and place each slice encrypted and attached by an authentication code on a different resource. Since only a subset of these slices is required to restore the original information, a high availability is realized [4].

Last but not least, the π-Box Resource Manager is responsible for managing the set of all available resources and services.

Contributions and outline

In this work we focus on the development of this Resource Manager. The remainder of this paper is structured as follows. Before actually analysing necessary requirements for the design of the Resource Manager, we first discuss drawbacks of existing cloud resource management approaches. Going on, we present our three-fold design concept that covers service description as well as device and service coordination. We then present an overview of our prototype implementation and discuss first evaluation results. We conclude with a final discussion of our achievements as well as future work.

Our main contributions are:

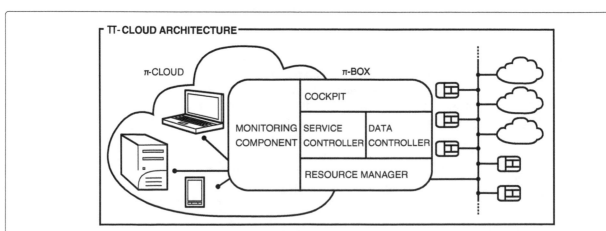

Figure 1 The π-Box. Architectural layout of the π-Cloud with a subdivision of the π-Box into Service and Data Controller, Cockpit, Monitoring Component and Resource Manager.

- The conceptional and technical development of fundamental system components for the setup of user-controlled federated clouds.
- This includes the development of CRDL, a Cloud Resource Description Language, that leverages the existing Open Cloud Computing Interface (OCCI) standard for the PaaS and SaaS layer.

A preliminary version of this work has already been presented at the Utility and Cloud Computing Conference in 2012 [8]. This revised version provides more details and insight in all aspects of our work. Furthermore, we have added two sections to discuss drawbacks of current cloud resource management solutions and to present first evaluation results of our Resource Manager prototype respectively.

Drawbacks of existing cloud resource management solutions

To gain an understanding, which functionality the Resource Manager has to provide, we start with an analysis of already existing solutions. In order to compare them with each other, we first of all define following reasonable evaluation criteria.

Availability as open source In order to prevent lock-in effects and to enhance security/trustworthiness, only Open Source solutions or such based on open standards are considered suitable.

Ability to integrate services from a user's devices Furthermore according to the π-Cloud idea presented in the previous section it is mandatory that the sought solution is able to integrate services from a user's own devices.

Ability to integrate arbitrary cloud providers The same applies for the integration of services and devices from different cloud providers. This includes community clouds.

Ad hoc migration of the managing component Additionally, we aim at enabling the ad hoc migration of the managing component itself between different parts of the π-Cloud due to stability, performance or trustworthiness reasons.

Support for IaaS, PaaS and SaaS Last but not least, our solution should support the whole bandwidth of cloud platforms, i. e. IaaS as well as PaaS and SaaS platforms.

For our investigation we concentrated on open source solutions and those proposed by academia. Industry solutions like *Akitio MyCloud* [9], *mydlink Cloud* [10], *Synology Cloud Station* [11] and *LenovoEMC Personal Cloud* [12] as well as *Samsung HomeSync* [13] and *myQ-NAPCloud* [14] have not been considered as they are proprietary, focussed solely on storage service and are bound to the respective companies' storage devices.

OwnCloud [15] is a promising open source solution which unfortunately does not support computing or platform services either and nearly no software services yet.

Most scientific approaches like the *Anzere* project [16], *PCP* [17] and *Cloud@Home* [18] are mainly storage centred, offer sometimes groupware functionality but not more and are therefore not suitable. Some scientific approaches like the *Clouds@Home* [19] project seem promising but are still work in progress.

Table 1 summarizes how the mentioned cloud resource management solutions match our evaluation criteria. Obviously, none of them fully meets our requirements which motivates the development of our own solution.

Requirements analysis

We start our requirements analysis by detailing the general tasks a cloud Resource Manager has to perform. Basically, these can be divided in three parts. On the on hand, the user's devices must be coordinated in order to combine them into a π-Cloud. On the other hand, there are the requirements from the other π-Box components. Specifically, the description of services to be run within the π-Cloud as well as their storage and management. Thus, we come to a high-level architectural overview of the Resource Manager presented in Figure 2.

The connector is more or less a straight forward component that encapsulates all necessary functionality for connecting the Resource Manager with the remaining parts of the π-Box as well as with the user's own devices or with external cloud resources. As it only contains technically state of the art mechanisms we skip a more detailed description here. Instead, we concentrate on the device and service coordination respectively.

Device coordination requirements

For coordinating the access to all relevant user devices in the π-Cloud the Resource Manager first has to recognize the (re)appearance of devices whose status has then to be maintained by a specific device directory. For this purpose, we distinguish between three general communication scenarios as depicted in Figure 3.

Intra-π-cloud scenario In this first scenario a resource wants to establish a connection to the π-box and both are inside a local area network. In such a situation as low operational effort as possible should be necessary. In ideal case the resource detection and interconnection between resource and π-box should work automatically. Furthermore the π-box should be safely identifiable and the communication should take place in a secure manner in order to prevent unauthorized access to the user's communication and data.

Table 1 Comparison of existing cloud resource management solutions

Approach	Open source	Integration of services from user's devices	Integration of arbitrary clouds	Ad hoc migration of the managing component	IaaS, SaaS and PaaS
Industry Solutions	No	No	No	No	No
OwnCloud	Yes	No	Yes	No	No
Sparkle Share	Yes	No	No	No	No
Aero FS	Yes	No	No	No	No
Anzere [16]	Yes	Yes	Yes	No	No
PCP [17]	Yes	?	?	?	No
[20]	Yes	Yes	No	?	?
[21]	Yes	Yes	No	No	Yes
Cloud CDI [22]	Yes	Yes	?	No	No
Social Cloud [23]	Yes	Yes	No	No	No
Cloud@Home [18]	Yes	Yes	Yes	No	?
Clouds@Home [19]	Yes	?	Yes	?	?
Cloud4Home [24]	Yes	Yes	Yes	No	No

The solutions are evaluated by means of the criteria defined above. If a matching is not certain due to no or imprecise information, a question mark is entered in the corresponding field.

Remote Intra-π-cloud scenario In this second scenario a resource tries to establish the connection to the π-box from the outside of the local network. Here it is necessary for that resource to know how to establish the connection to its own π-box. The requirements regarding identifiability and secure communication are just the same as in the Intra-π-cloud scenario.

Inter-π-cloud scenario If all the user's resources are registered – and with them the services – the user might want to use a service. In order to find an appropriate one he will send a query to the own π-Box. If the desired service is not available in the own repository the user can try to use the service of somebody else. Every π-Box runs its own repository. In order to use foreign services the π-Box has to connect to at least one other π-Box. This third scenario is the Inter-π-Cloud scenario where one or more π-Boxes interconnect to share information and resources.

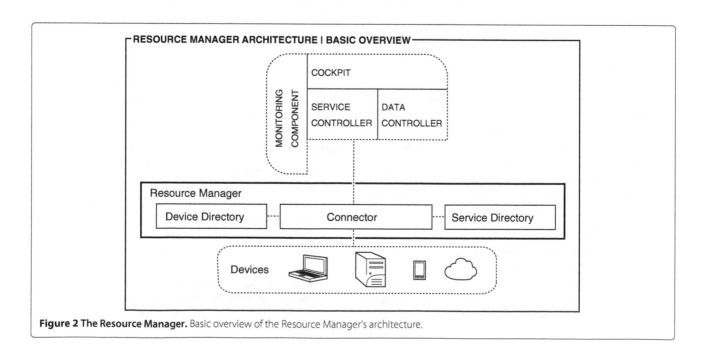

Figure 2 The Resource Manager. Basic overview of the Resource Manager's architecture.

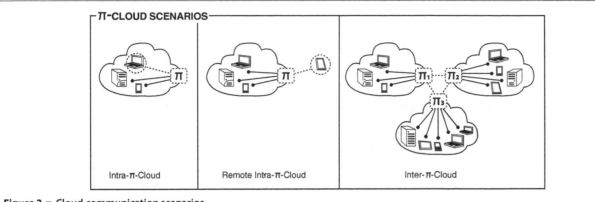

Figure 3 π-Cloud communication scenarios.

For each scenario the device directory has to be able to store all necessary information about available resources. It must be possible to search a device based on these information. Thus, the following two basic requirements are retrieved from the striven functionalities of the device directory.

Storing The information about devices might either be stored as a file directly into the file system or they might be stored in a storage system of any kind like for example in a relational database.

Searching Either a device initiates a search – for example to find the current π-Box – or other components of the π-Box incorporate the search function as a subroutine for other tasks. The result of a request is a set of attributes of the node.

Besides these functional requirements our system should also satisfy several non-functional requirements as follows.

Platform independence According to the π-Cloud idea every device might get the π-Box status which basically means that the same π-Box software has to run on all of them independent of their software and hardware platform.

Resource conservation To enable all devices to gain π-Box status, the Device Directory as well as the other π-Box components have to be lightweight enough to run – at least in small scenarios with a low double-digit number of devices – even on a smart phone if necessary without affecting its main functionalities. This means that a resource conserving architecture has to be chosen.

Security The device coordinator must support the user's wish for confidentiality, integrity and availability of his data when migrating it to the cloud. Therefore, strong security mechanisms must be integrated to protect the data traffic carried out by the device coordinator.

Scalability The number of the devices within the corresponding π-Cloud could vary from half a dozen in a home office to several hundred thousands in a big company. The device directory has to show a high scalability to manage such a large number of devices with satisfying performance.

Responsiveness Besides scalability another important aspect for the acceptance of such a system is its responsiveness. It is important to keep waiting times for search results as low as possible.

Service coordination requirements
Service description format requirements

During the handshake between device and π-Box the device has to publish its services. To describe them a service interface description format has to be found that is extensible, widely distributed, easy usable and that supports the description of non-functional properties. These requirements have to be meet for the following reasons:

1. *Extensibility:* For the description of cloud services they have to be differentiated based on the before mentioned service levels IaaS, PaaS and SaaS. Since PaaS and SaaS show a broad range of properties that differ from provider to provider and from service to service a fixed basic set of properties is not powerful enough to describe the services. For example the description of functional properties of a routing planner differ fundamentally from that of an office product. Even IaaS providers need the flexibility to extend the basic feature set. Although it might be assumed that a basic set of computing, storage and network properties is sufficient for them and that only units may change from time to time (the measure for computing power may for example change from GigaFlops to TerraFlops) a closer inspection shows that essential infrastructural changes occur. It just takes longer time periods for

changes that are fundamental enough to require the descriptiveness of new properties.

General-purpose computing on graphics processing units (GPGPU) is such a fundamental change. Powered by computing engines and interfaces like CUDA (Compute Unified Device Architecture) [25] and OpenCL (Open Computing Language) [26] users were provided with a huge performance boost that came with the utilization of GPUs (graphic processing units) for former CPU tasks. Amazon for example offers GPU computing instances since 2011 [27]. With this change came the need to extend the given set of property descriptions.

2. *Non-functional properties:* Given a set of services with similar functional properties the non-functional properties become important for the selection of the most appropriate service. That is why the description language has to be able to describe them as well. Non-functional properties include the functional description, costs, quality and safety.

3. *Distribution:* The distribution of the service interface description language plays another important role. In order to be able to integrate as much existing services as possible a widespread language has to be used.

4. *Ease of use:* Last but not least the ease of use is a major feature that should allow service providers to easily extend the basic set of property descriptions without being discouraged by to complex handling. Therefore the service interface description language has to be of as low complexity as possible while being as complex as necessary.

Service directory requirements

To manage all available services within the π-Cloud we further introduce a service directory. It has to be able to store service descriptions and extract information from them to build search indexes. It furthermore has to be able to deliver whole service descriptions or specific information about them if users request so. Hence, the following requirements are retrieved from the striven functionalities of the service directory:

Storing The service descriptions might either be stored directly into the file system or they might be stored as a string in a storage system of any kind like for example in a relational database. Furthermore the storage subsystem has to be able to store extracted elements and attributes in a way that future extensions of the service description format can be handled. For management reasons meta data like IDs have to be stored in the same place as the information extracted from the service descriptions.

Parsing After storing a new service description, the system has to extract relevant data from it. Due to the fact that it can not be foreseen which data might be requested by users and which not, all the elements and attributes have to be considered relevant. The whole content of the service description is therefore extracted and in the following referred to as relevant data. Since the service description format might be extended, the parser should be able to deal with new elements.

Searching It is not only the user that should be enabled to initiate a search. Other components of the π-Box might incorporate the search function as a subroutine for other tasks. The data controller might for example run a background task that searches for suitable storage services to disperse the data to. For a broad access to the stored information the ability to cope with syntax variety is important. The use of a lexical analyser that can for example handle fuzzy queries and replace synonyms can make the search for users more intuitive and flexible. π-Box components that have to access the service directory are better suited with a machine readable query language. To face this demand the service directory has to be provided with an interface that allows to couple a variety of query modules to it. The result of a request is however a list of suitable services. These might be ordered according to a rating either based on information from a monitoring system or on user decisions. Although the rating system necessary for this task is out of focus of this work, the service directory has to be designed open enough to be easily extended with such a system.

Retrieval If the user chooses one of the offered services from the list, additional detailed information and the whole service description might have to be retrieved. Authorisation and authentication rules have to be part of an other subsystem of the π-Box or should be encapsulated in a library that all π-Box components can use.

In addition, the same non-functional requirements already stated for the device directory apply here, too. Concerning the scalability a maximum amount of 500,000 devices for big companies was estimated. Assumed that not all devices provide services, an average of two services per device is likely which sums up a total amount of 1,000,000 service descriptions. With the amount of managed service descriptions the response time increases and it becomes increasingly complicated to keep users patient if the search is executed directly on the descriptions. So the responsiveness of the system has to be high enough to react within 3 to 4 seconds or faster [28]. For the adding of service descriptions this can be achieved with caching mechanisms if necessary. In contrast the retrieval of information has to rely on an efficient indexing technology, e. g.

with binary search trees. Since service descriptions can describe different resources, they contain various, sometimes unrelated data. That implies the need for multi tree indexes. A search combining different parameters results in the utilisation of the same amount of search trees. There is the need for a manager for different binary trees and for the trees themselves. But instead of creating them from scratch it seems to be more economically to consider only such existing storage systems that are able to generate the trees and manage them. The storage system therefore has to analyse the service descriptions and generate binary search trees based on extracted elements and attributes. Furthermore it has to have mechanisms to organise the search over multiple trees.

Designing the resource manager

In the following we discuss the conceptual design of the Resource Manager based on the requirements determined in the previous section.

Device coordination

The design of the device coordinator architecture is presented according to the three scenarios introduced in the last section.

Intra-π-Cloud In the previous section low operational effort was defined as a requirement when a resource wants to establish a connection to the π-Box in a local network. During this initial handshake phase resource and π-Box meet each other for the first time. The resource shares information about its available services and gets an ID. For the automatic resource discovery Zero Configuration Networking (Zeroconf) [29] seems promising since it is a configuration-free network approach that proposes techniques to build up an Internet Protocol without intervention from human operators. Participating resources can automatically connect to the network and get network addresses assigned. The two most common implementations are Bonjour [30] from Apple and Avahi [31]. Bonjour is an implementation not limited to Apple OS X and iOS. It also works on Linux and Microsoft Windows. Unfortunately Bonjour is only partially open source under Apache 2.0 license and partially closed source under an Apple license. We aim to offer the π-Box as open source. That is why we prefer Avahi which is an open source implementation developed under GNU Lesser General Public License. The needed identifiability could for example be ensured with a PIN code that is shown at a diplay at the π-Box. Other ways to safely identify the π-Box involve for example certificates and a Public Key Infrastructure (PKI) to check these certificates or recommendation or reputation

systems might be utilized. A hybrid encryption will ensure a secure communication that is more efficient than a asymmetric one. Therefore the π-Box first sends its public key to the resource. In case of an successful identity check the resource generates a symmetric key, encrypts it with the π-Box's public key and hands it over to the π-Box. Which for its part decrypts the symmetric key with the private key only known to the π-Box. After this the whole communication (which includes the remote Intra-π-Cloud communication) can take place encrypted in a lightweight manner with the symmetric key that is now only known to the resource and the π-Box. Since we are in an early state regarding the communication protocol we can not offer deeper conceptional insight or implementations. The essence is that Zeroconf would enable automatic interconnection between resource and π-Box as desired and that the identifiability might be ensured via PIN code, PKI or recommendation or reputation systems while the secure communication should be realized with a hybrid encryption approach.

Remote Intra-π-Cloud In general it can be assumed that a remote connection to the π-Cloud follows an initial resource registration like discussed in the Intra-π-Cloud scenario. If so the necessary information like a constant IP and a port to contact the π-Box from the outside were already handed over to resource by the π-Box. If not for example because the user got in possession of a new device and is eager to test it before he enters his home network he has to know these information from memory. The solutions for identifiability and secure communication can be based on the solutions for the Intra-π-Cloud scenario.

Inter-π-Cloud The Inter-π-Cloud scenario is conceivable in two forms. Either all π-Boxes are part of a friend of a friend (FOAF) network. In this case it can be assumed that the users π-Box is in possession of the connection information to all the users friends' π-Boxes. Then a directed multicast might be the best way to query for a desired service. Then again if it is assumed that the user does not have such a FOAF at least one other π-Box has to be known. In this case a structured peer-to-peer network can be the solution. If a user enters such a network where he only knows one other π-Box the communication is not limited to the known instance. In fact directly addressed π-Boxes should be able to forward failed service queries or to introduce other instances to the new π-Box. To cope with π-Boxes that are leaving the network unattended because of faulty internet connections or hardware failures the network has to be robust. That is the network should be able to heal itself and replace information that are missing due to the unannounced absence of the peer. Furthermore it should be fault-tolerant and highly effective to ensure successful routing of messages.

Given these scenarios, we have identified several options for the general architecture of the device directory as depicted in Figure 4.

Going on, we analysed the use cases for the Intra-π-Cloud scenario (see Figure 5).

Join π-cloud The first use case captures the contact initiation between a device and the π-Box. A successful attempt results in the π-Box revealing itself and sending information to the device how to connect from the outside of the personal network. Furthermore a certificate has to be generated and handed over to the device to enable it to identify itself as an authorised member of the π-Cloud.

Create connection This use case deals with the creation of a secure connection between a device and the π-Box. It is required that the π-Box is clearly identifiable and that the communication takes place in a secure manner in order to prevent unauthorised access to the user's data. The device sends information about itself to the π-Box. After a authorisation check the π-Box generates a session key for the ongoing communication. Afterwards the Device Directory marks the device is as connected and stores the session key.

Delete device record If a device has to be finally dismissed from the network – for example because it is broken – it has to be deleted from the list of managed devices in order to keep the data base up-to-date and slim.

Set disconnected For management tasks it is sometimes necessary to know if a device is available or not. Therefore it must be possible to set an entry in the data base that marks a device as disconnected.

Set π-box info The π-Box software should potentially run on all π-Cloud devices. The π-Box status can change from one to another. This means that the Resource Manager has to provide a way to assign π-Box status to a specific device.

Get π-box info If a member of the π-Cloud wants to contact its π-Box it has to be provided with a method to get to know which other member of the π-Cloud is the current π-Box.

Revoke certificate It has to be ensured that certificates once handed out by the π-Box can be revoked to exclude devices from the π-Cloud if they are responsible for access violations or other harmful behaviour. The revoking has to be initiated by a component of the π-Box which sends the ID of the device that has to be excluded from the π-Cloud. After the Device Directory added the certificate of the corresponding device to the revoke certification list, a list of the connected devices is requested which leads the Device Directory to return a list of them. A request should then be send to all devices of the list

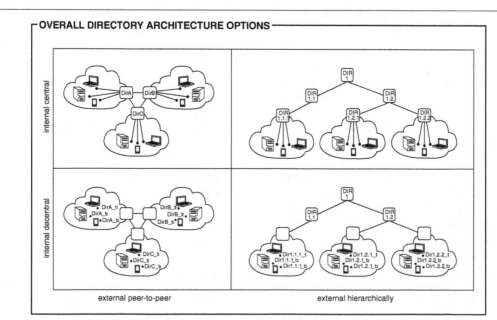

Figure 4 Architectural options of internal and external π-Cloud device directories.

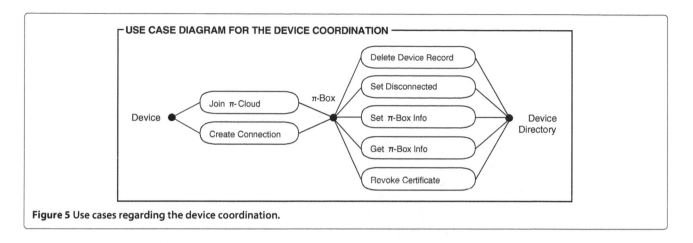

Figure 5 Use cases regarding the device coordination.

in order to cause each of them to add the undesired device to the own revoke certification list.

Service coordination
Service description

As the analysis shows there are four main features the service interface description language has to provide. It has to be easily extensible and support the description of non-functional properties while being widely distributed and of low complexity in order to achieve a good ease of use. Existing service interface description languages are either easily extensible and support the description of non-functional properties (like USDL and OWL-S) or they are widely distributed and show a good ease of use (like WSDL, WADL) as to be seen in Table 2.

To the best of our knowledge there is no approach that is fulfilling all four requirements in one solution. Here is where a meta model comes in hand that was designed to describe cloud resources. It is the so called Open Cloud Computing Initiative (OCCI) [32] powered by the Open Grid Forum [33]. At the moment it consists of a core model [34] and an infrastructure extension [35]. A combined diagram of both models is depicted in Figure 6. The graphic except the grey parts represents the OCCI core model with an infrastructure extension according to the specifications v1.1. Among other things this modularisation makes the model easily extensible. Well known open source cloud attempts like OpenNebula, Openstack and Eucalyptus already implement OCCI [36]. Given this

high distribution and the simple but easily extensible model OCCI seems to be an appropriate base for an own implementation to describe services.

Service directory

The design of our service directory is based on the use cases depicted in Figure 7.

Add service description To be able to describe cloud resources, CRDL, a Cloud Resource Description Language, was developed. It leverages the existing Open Cloud Computing Interface (OCCI) standard for the PaaS and SaaS layer. To publish the services of a device an appropriate CRDL file has to be added to the Service Directory. Therefore the file is sent to the to the Resource Manager. The Resource Manager checks the file's validity and adds some meta data like the user's id. The file is then translated in a format that can be understood by the Resource Manager's Service Directory where it is sent next. In the Service Directory a file id is generated and added as meta data. Furthermore the CRDL file has to be parsed to extract relevant data. All information will then be stored in the Service Directory's own storage. Finally an acknowledgement and the newly generated id will be sent back to the device.

Search service To search a service a device sends a respective search request to the π-Box. The request is handled by Service Directory's Storage module. As a result the Service Directory returns a list of CRDL files matching the search criteria. The Resource Manager as well as

Table 2 Comparison of service description formats

	USDL	WSDL	WADL	OWL-S	WSMO	OCCI
NFP Support	Very good	Existing	Existing	Existing	Existing	Existing
FP extensibility	Existing	No/bad	No/bad	Good	Good	Very good
NFP extensibility	Very good	No/bad	No/bad	Very good	Very good	Very good
Distribution	No/bad	Very good	Existing	No/bad	Existing	Existing
Ease of use	Existing	Very good	Very good	No/bad	No/bad	Good

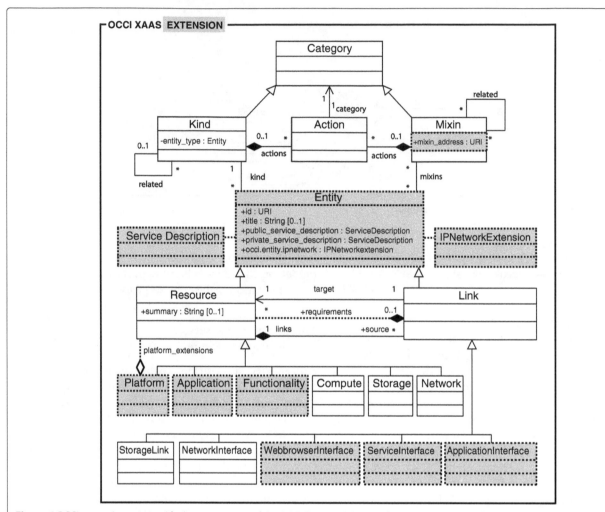

Figure 6 OCCI extensions. A simplified representation of the OCCI Core Model with infrastructure extension for the IaaS domain according to the specifications v1.1. The grey parts mark an additional extension for the integration of existing service description formats as well as additional extensions for non-functional properties, platform and software extension for the XaaS domain and required interface extensions.

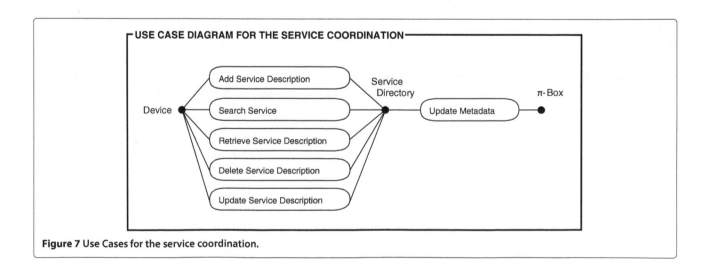

Figure 7 Use Cases for the service coordination.

other components of the π-Box can filter and reorder the results, for example according to the knowledge of a rating module, before they are resend to the inquiring system.

Retrieve service description Retrieve a CRDL file based on the ID assigned during the addition of the service description.

Delete service description Delete a CRDL file based on the ID assigned during the addition of the service description.

Update service description Update a CRDL file based on the ID assigned during the addition of the service description.

Update metadata Update a CRDL file's metadata based on the ID assigned during the addition of the service description.

Overall architecture

A schema of the Resouce Manager's architecture is shown in Figure 8. It consists of three main modules, one for each directory and one – the Connector – as an interface. This Connector itself again contains three modules. The Internal Call Manager is responsible for the communication with other π-Box components while Listener and External Call Manager cover the communication with external resources. The Device Directory consists of two modules. The Core module encapsulates management

functionalities and the Storage module offers storage functionalities. In addition to two similar modules, the Service Directory contains a parser module, which is responsible for the parsing of the CRDL files.

Prototype implementation
Device directory

According to the π-Cloud idea, the π-Box software is intended to run on a variety of hardware platforms. That is why the prototype is based on the platform-independent programming language Java. With future migration in mind, devices and π-Box should run different instances of the same program. Migrating the π-Box from one device to another then just involves a change of the status of both devices and a transfer of administrative tasks, information and rights. It seems appropriate to use RMI the Remote Method Invocation protocol for the communication. It is Java's version of an RPC (Remote Procedure Call). An RPC enables one program to execute procedures in the foreign address space of another program on a different machine. The Java RMI API allows to invoke Java methods remotely from another (JVM) (Java Virtual Machine). The machine which is in possession of the remote object registers it at the RMI-registry with a unique name. The machine that strives for remote access uses the object's name to retrieve an object reference from

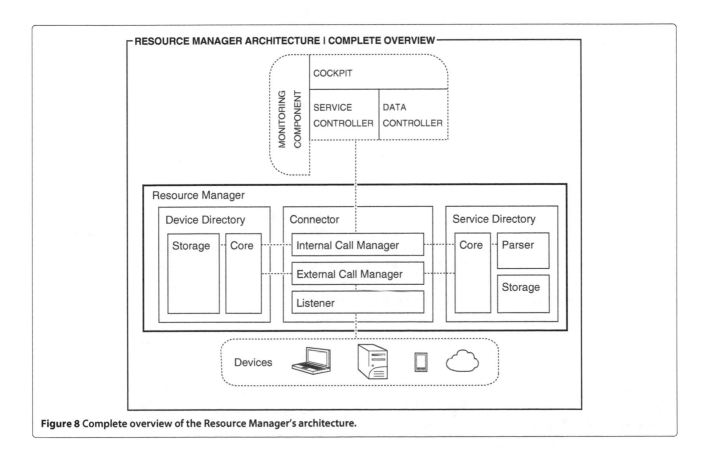

Figure 8 Complete overview of the Resource Manager's architecture.

the RMI-registry. The object reference has to correspond with its remote interface. If the machine that strives for remote access invokes a method from the object reference of the machine which is in possession of the remote object, the method on the remote object is executed. In this process external code might be loaded dynamically for usage. As a result of the invocation return values or an error message are sent back. This response is useful in the communication process between client and π-Box since in most cases it is initiated by the client which relies on a response. In seldom cases the communication is initiated by the π-Box and is then sent to all connected clients in the network. But this is a rare event. It is so rare, that RMI overhead compared with publish subscribe mechanisms is acceptable.

The most obvious storage solution for data sets is storing them in the file system. But if the data to be stored are well structured, data bases can be a faster solution. Data bases that are able to store the data completely in main memory have to be preferred. They utilise high throughput and low response times of main memory and achieve a much better performance than common data bases, which work mostly on comparatively slow hard disks. With HSQLDB (HyperSQL DataBase) [37] one of the most popular Java-based open source databases is used which is able to run completely in-memory.

Service description

The base of the π-Box service description is the OCCI core specification with some extensions implemented as XML Schema. The class resource is complemented by a complex data type converter specifications that consist of:

- a classification of the service description of the service provider as Enum (e.g. WSDL, WADL and OWL-S)
- the corresponding service description address in form of an URI
- the address of the converter for the extraction of the needed data from the service providers service description in form of an URI
- an execution instruction for the converter (e.g. XSLT for WSDL/WADL/OWL-S converter in XSL)

This converter specifications are stored in a separate local file and can therefore be easily extended by the user for other forms of service descriptions. The core class Link is extended by inheritance for diverse interface types of the services in addition to existing specifications of the OCCI infrastructure model. The resulting interface class structure is integrated into the resource class as an abstract element. Its ascertainment of goods can be generated at runtime – together with other resource elements – from the providers service description by means of the converter specification. The class resource uses the extensions for infrastructure services of the OCCI infrastructure model. With Software and Platform own extensions for software and platform services are added in form of ascertainments of goods of the resource class. The class Platform is composed of one or more instantiations of each of the following: Compute, Storage and software. Non-functional extensions (e.g. for quality and safety features) as well as individual extensions of the service description by the π-Box users are integrated via Mixins. Mixins allow to extend Ressource with additional arbitrary attributes. For reasons of manageability and clarity of the service description the class Mixin is extended by the address of the Mixin in form of the URI of the XML source file which is integrated at runtime.

Service directory

For the implementation of the service directory we have existing basic technologies that are open source and therefore compatible with the π-Cloud idea. Table 3 summarizes the results of our analysis. We have chosen Lucene as our founding implementation component since it fulfils all our functional requirements. The fulfilment of non-functional requirements is only of interest for the complete Service Directory. For a basic technology like Lucene it is only important to be platform independent, resource conserving, scalable, responsive and able to cope with CRDLs inherent complexity. According to the Apache project [38] all these requirements are fulfilled.

Evaluation and discussion

In this section we describe our evaluation of the Resource Manager's efficiency. After introducing the evaluation methodology, our results are presented and discussed.

Table 3 Comparison of basic technologies for the service directory

	LDAP	RDBMS	File system	XML Query Languages	Digester	Lucene
Parsing	Impossible	Impossible	Impossible	Intended	Intended	Intended
Storing files	Possible	Intended	Intended	Impossible	Possible	Possible
Storing data	Intended	Intended	Possible	Impossible	Possible	Intended
Searching	Intended	Possible	Possible	Impossible	Impossible	Intended
File retrieving	Intended	Intended	Impossible	Impossible	Impossible	Intended

Methodology

In order to validate sufficient performance in real-world scenarios, several test scenarios are applied. As already discussed the π-Box and thereby also the Resource Manager have to be scalable to manage even big usage scenarios with up to 500,000 devices and 1 million CRDL files. At the same time the response of the system should not exceed 4 seconds to provide a good user experience [28]. The tests cover this big scenario with 1 million CRDL files and a middle size scenario with 100,000 CRDL files. Even smaller scenarios are indirectly included in the middle size scenario.

Service Directory and Device Directory are accessed by only one Connector and therefore have to handle requests only sequentially. The Connector can be accessed by several devices at the same time. Therefore in theory it has to manage parallel requests and is responsible for the execution order. However, the prototype takes no care of this. Since for the tests only one client sends requests they enter the connector one by one and are executed sequentially. So the scalability can just be assumed.

Four test parameters can be used to judge the performance of the developed Resource Manager. The parameter which represents the efficiency of the Resource Manager the most is the *response time* (t_{resp}). It is defined as the period between the moment when the device sends the request and the moment when it receives the response. The period starting with the point when the Listener module receives the query and ending when it sends the response is the period which defines the execution time. Thus, the response time equals the execution time (t_{exe}) plus twice the network delay (t_{nd}):

$$t_{resp} = t_{exe} + 2t_{nd}$$

Another important parameter is the *CPU load*. As already mentioned the π-Box may run on a device which has another original purpose. If a smart phone acts as a π-Box, it should for example still be able to make and accept calls. That is why the CPU should be used economical – at least in smaller π-Clouds. In case of bigger π-Clouds, it seems plausible that the π-Box is hosted by a dedicated server, rendering CPU load less relevant, as long as it is not excessive.

The *memory consumption* is a further parameter which may also interfere with using the host system in smaller scenarios for its original purpose. It is hard to find an objective requirement regarding the acceptable amount of utilised memory. That is why it is only possible to rely on subjective estimation.

Last but not least the *size* of the Device Directory's *database* and the Service Directory's *index* are important parameters. They have to be within reasonable limits.

Our **test cases** have been designed with all processes in mind which involve a waiting user. These are:

- join π-Cloud
- create connections
- add new CRDL files
- search services
- retrieve CRDL files
- delete CRDL files
- update CRDL files

Furthermore these processes have to be evaluated under different sizes of π-Clouds according to the before mentioned usage scenarios. The evaluation covers a middle size π-Cloud with 0 to 100,000 CRDL files and 50,000 devices and a big π-Cloud with 10,000 to 1,000,000 files and 500,000 devices.

To reflect conditions of real world personal clouds, the client server communication takes place inside a local network. Apart from that, the systems differ for the two π-Cloud sizes. The middle size scenario involves a laptop computer with the following characteristics hosting the π-Box:

- Model: Lenovo G550
- CPU: 2.1 GHz Intel Core 2 Duo
- Memory: 3072 MB RAM
- Architecure: 32 bit
- HDD: WesternDigital 500 GB 5400 rpm (ATA WDC WD5000BEVT-22ZAT0)
- OS: Debian 6.7 Squeeze
- Runtime Environment: Oracle JDK 7

The laptop computer itself was the server and a QEMU-KVM 0.12.5 based virtual machine with 1 CPU core and 128 MB of RAM was used as client. The server for the big scenario is a virtual machine with the following specifications:

- CPU: 4 × 2.4 GHz (only one core used)
- Memory: 8192 MB RAM
- Architecure: 64 bit
- OS: Debian 6.7 Squeeze

The client virtual machine shows the following characteristics:

- CPU: 1 × 2.0 GHz
- Memory: 500 MB RAM
- Architecure: 64 bit
- OS: Debian 6.7 Squeeze

Both virtual machines run on a host system with the following characteristics:

- Model: Fujitsu Primergy RX300S6
- CPU: 2 × Xeon E5620 2,4 GHz 4C/8T 12 MB
- RAM: 4 × 12 GB
- HDD: Fujitsu ETERNUS DX APAK 6x750 GB (Raid5)
- Virtualisation Environment: VMWare vSphere 4.1

The measurements presented in the following should provide a coarse comparison of the performance of the two systems. They were taken with the GNU/Linux file copy and conversion command dd.

The CRDL files for the test were generated based on four main structure types – one for storage, one for compute, one for platform and one for software descriptions. To achieve good diversity which means a huge set of unique CRDL files, parameters were changed randomly within each of the four groups – always within predefined limits.

The queries were generated at runtime. There are four query types: the fastest possible without parameters which retrieves all services; the normal one, a query for storage, with different sizes and status online; the slowest, a query for compute services with close restrictions for all five possible parameters; a query which searches for storage with unsatisfiable demands.

Results
Response time

Join π-cloud In the middle size scenario run on the laptop computer the fulfilment of join requests on server side (execution time) took 2.25 milliseconds in average with a maximum of 202 milliseconds. 98.9 percent of the request where processed within 2 to 8 milliseconds. And 99.9 percent took not longer then 64 milliseconds. The overall network delay with an average of 2.25 milliseconds leads to an average response time of 4.89 milliseconds and a maximum response time of 206 milliseconds on client side. 98.2 percent of the responses reached the inquiring client within 2 to 8 milliseconds. And 99.9 percent took not longer then 68 milliseconds. Since the overall network delay is constant and negligible small the execution time on server and the response time are almost identical. We found that the response time is independent from the amount of already joined devices. This result was expected. It reflects the fact, that information about already registered nodes is not retrieved during the join process.

In the big scenario executed on the virtual machine the fulfilment of join requests on server side took 1.04 milliseconds in average with a maximum of 2179 milliseconds. The second longest join was executed within around 1 second. 99.994 percent of the request where processed within less then 10 milliseconds. And only 10 of 500,000 joins took longer then 100ms. The overall network delay with an average of 1.04 milliseconds added to a total average execution time of 1.73 milliseconds. 99.988 percent of the responds reached the inquiring client within less then 10 milliseconds. As in the mid-size scenario, we found that the response time for join

requests is independent from the amount of already joined devices.

Create connections In the middle size scenario the response time grows almost at a linear rate with the amount of registered devices. After each 10,000 join operations the time for connecting the according clients was measured. After joining the last 10,000 clients to the π-Cloud each of the subsequent connections took around 38.5 milliseconds in average from sending the request to receiving the acknowledgement. The drop at the beginning is the result of initial just-in-time compilation of the JVM. In the big scenario the response time also grows almost at a linear rate with the amount of registered devices. After each 100,000 join operations the time for connecting the according clients was measured. After joining the first 100,000 clients to the π-Cloud each of the subsequent connections took around 34 milliseconds in average while the last 100,000 connections took around 264 milliseconds from sending the request to receiving the acknowledgement.

Add new CRDL files In the middle size scenario run on the laptop computer the fulfilment of an add request on server side took 262 milliseconds in average with the four slowest responses between 6 and 11 seconds. 88 percent of the requests were answered in less than 0.3 seconds and 99.8 percent took less than 2 seconds. Since the overall network delay is similar to the delay in the join case the execution time can be considered almost equal to the response time.

In the big scenario, run on the virtual machine the fulfilment of an add request on server side took 29 milliseconds in average which is almost ten times faster than on the laptop computer. The four worst results reached from 20 to 45 seconds. Nevertheless, 99.83 percent of the requests were answered within less than 300 milliseconds and 99.99 percent within less then 1 second. Since the overall network delay is similar to the delay in the join case the execution time can be considered almost equal to the response time.

Search services As it can be seen in Figure 9 the response time for search requests depends on the size of the index and grows with a linear rate.

Retrieve CRDL files After each 1,000 added CRDL files the retrieval of 100 files was measured. The retrieval took an average of 6.7 milliseconds. The slowest request took 71 milliseconds. 99 percent of the requests took not more than 14 milliseconds. 99.9 percent of the retrieve requests took less than 39 milliseconds and 99.99 percent less than 45 milliseconds. We found that the response time grows only negligibly for the mid-size scenario.

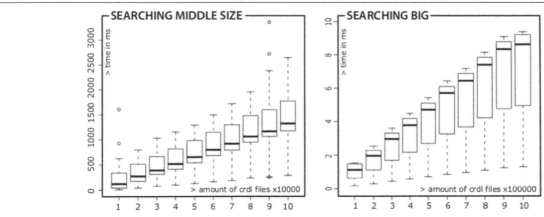

Figure 9 Response time for the search a service request. The abscissae show respectively the amount of already added CRDL files and are therefore like time-lines. The ordinates both show the response time in milliseconds. For the response times for every 10,000 requests maximum, 75%, median, 25% and minimum are shown. The circles mark faulty measured values not considered for the determination of these quantiles.

After each 10,000 added CRDL files the retrieval of 1,000 files was measured. The retrieval took an average of 9.3 milliseconds. The slowest request took 40 milliseconds. 99 percent of the requests took not more than 14 milliseconds. 99.9 percent of the retrieve requests took less than 28 milliseconds and 99.99 percent less than 37 milliseconds. Just as in the mid-size scenario the response time for the big scenario grows negligibly.

Delete CRDL files After each 1,000 added files 10 of them were deleted for this test. The response time for the deleting requests took 121.9 milliseconds in average. 90 percent of the requests took not longer than 146 milliseconds. The longest request took 302 milliseconds. Up to 100,000 added files the response time grows with the size of the index – but not considerably.

After each 10,000 added files 10 of them were deleted for the big scenario test. The response time for the deleting requests took 20.5 milliseconds in average. The longest request took 331 milliseconds. 90 percent of the requests did not take longer than 25 milliseconds. Up to 1,000,000 added files the response time grows with the size of the index. Nevertheless the response time is superior considering that the average value is in the range of black-white-black response times of LCD displays. And even the worst result with 331 milliseconds corresponds with the duration of a blink of the human eye.

Update CRDL files For this test 10 files were updated every 1,000 added files. The response time for the updating took 371,6 milliseconds in average. The longest update took 2,773 milliseconds. 90 percent of the requests were answered within a maximum of 438 milliseconds. The growing of the request time with the amount of files in the index is negligible.

The same applies for the big scenario where 10 files were updated every 10,000 added files. The response time for the updating took 55.2 milliseconds in average. This is almost 7 times faster compared with the middle size scenario – the result of the more powerful host system. The longest update took 780 milliseconds. 90 percent of the requests were answered within a maximum of 79 milliseconds.

Scalability assumptions It can be assumed that the response time will increase with the number of parallel requests. Given the almost consistent low response times for the different processes this increase can be assumed marginal. Except for the search process, it is most likely that the response time will not exceed the critical 4 seconds mentioned before. However, referring to this 4 second threshold, the search process only performed well for up to 300,000 stored service descriptions. The number of manageable descriptions will decrease with the growing number of parallel requests, since the regular expressions used for the search are very resource intensive. However, it is likely that companies big enough to depend on hundreds of thousands of service descriptions will have powerful dedicated π-Box servers to speed up the response times to a bearable extent. Furthermore it has to be pointed out that the developed architecture only covers service brokering. Regarding performance the service brokering is far less important then the actual service usage. The usage is responsible for the main traffic and takes place between the clients only. No server is involved.

Index and database size

The generated CRDL files have a size between 2 KB and 9 KB with an average of 6 KB. Figure 10 shows that the

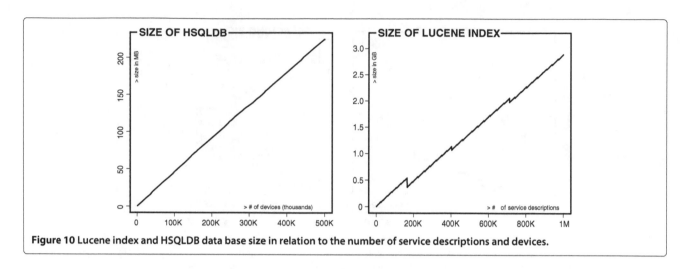

Figure 10 Lucene index and HSQLDB data base size in relation to the number of service descriptions and devices.

size of the index grows at a linear rate with the amount of files. The index including CRDL files plus extracted data and meta data is 1.6 to 1.9 times smaller than the storage space needed by the original CRDL files. 590 MB for 100,000 CRDL files mean a Lucene index of 361 MB. In the big scenario the compression is even more efficient most likely due to a higher rate of reusable patterns for Lucene's compression algorithms. With growing index the compression induced perennial index size reduction shows as a spiky graph. The storage space of 5,896 MB for 1,000,000 CRDL files is reduced to 3,019 MB if the files are stored and described in the index. Extensions of the description via meta data will increase the size of the index but the growing will be negligible. The size of the database also grows at a linear rate. 50,000 joined devices occupy 22.6 MB if they are all connected. 500,000 devices use

219 MB. The size of the data base depends on the number of joined and connected nodes and on the amount of revoked certificates.

CPU load and memory consumption

Table 4 shows CPU load as well as memory and hard disk consumption for the different use cases. The adding process depends more on the hard disk than on the CPU or the memory. On the laptop computer there were for example only 10 to 20 percent CPU usage. The comparison of the adding process for laptop computer and virtual machine shows that a fast hard disk can shift the bottleneck. Since the virtual machine's host was a server with 6 fast SAS disks in RAID5 mode the CPU became fully utilised. In contrast searching requests demanded full processing power on both, server and laptop

Table 4 Utilisation of processor, memory and hard disk for the specific use cases

Use case	CPU	RAM	HDD
Laptop computer			
Join and connect	60%–70%	78 MB–84 MB	Low load
Add	10–20	Grows linear	High load
Search	100%	330 MB–360 MB	Low load
Retrieve	100%	ca. 300 MB	Low load
Delete	20%–30%	ca. 200 MB	High load
Update	30%–50%	ca. 350 MB	High load
VMWare			
Join and connect	73%–75%	140 MB–190 MB	Low load
Add	100%	Grows linear	High load
Search	100%	up to 2 GB per request	Low load
Retrieve	100%	up to 2 GB per request	Low load
Delete	up to 100%	up to 1.5 GB	Medium load
Update	50%–60%	ca. 400 MB	Medium load

The values for processor and memory are based on observations during the evaluation while the content of the last column is based on theoretical assumptions.

computer. The memory consumption did not exceed 360 MB on the laptop computer while the virtual machine had to provide the π-Box with up to 2 GB per request when the index held 1 million service descriptions. After the request the size of the program in memory fell below 200 MB.

Summary

The developed prototype works well for networks with a file amount of up to around 300,000 CRDLs with the given virtual test server and with a sequential order of requests. Larger amounts of service descriptions lead to response times for search requests of 4 seconds and more, at least with the given virtual test server. Anyhow, is likely that such large π-Clouds are managed by powerful dedicated π-Box servers, which would be capable of handling more service descriptions. Then again, the tested program was only a prototype. Not all designed features were included. The communication channel was for example not encrypted and was furthermore based on a local area network. Additional encryption will add overhead and increase the response time. Communication over the Internet can be substantially slower then our LAN-based tests, depending on the quality of the user's connection. But there are also possibilities to enhance the prototype with regard to its performance. The Lucene based Storage module of the prototype is single threaded and therefore only utilises one core. But since the design of the Resource Manager is modular, Lucene could be exchanged for example with ElasticSearch [39] – an extension of Lucene which enables distributed indexes. This would allow multi threading and therefore decrease the response time with the growing number of distributed indexes. The response time for the search requests could also be reduced if regular expression queries would be replaced by less resource intense query types. During the parsing process frequently searched properties could be extracted and added as meta data to the service records. Since this would prevent browsing indexes for whole CRDL files at run time, it will speed up the search process.

Conclusion

Cloud computing attracts, inter alia, with scalability and cost reduction. However, cloud's benefits are accompanied by potential harm to the users data. Existing cloud solutions can be considered synonymous with unknown locations and potentially hostile environments. Therefore security protection objectives can not be guaranteed in the cloud. Motivated by cloudâĂŹs potential we proposed a way to get rid of this drawback. We presented π-Cloud, a personal secure cloud, that enables users to benefit from cloud computing and retain data sovereignty by federating the users own resources. More precisely we presented the prototypic implementation of a Resource Manager for personal secure clouds. This includes the coordination of devices which form this cloud as well as the description of the services they provide and the description of external services. For this description an intermediary format, the Cloud Resource Description Language (CRDL) was developed as an extension of the Open Cloud Computing Infrastructure (OCCI). Since OCCI is currently limited to infrastructure services the approach has been extended to support PaaS and SaaS services as well. Furthermore, an architecture for the coordination and management of CRDL service descriptions and the respective services was developed. As a foundation for the π-Box the Resource Manager enables users to (re)gain their data sovereignty when going to the cloud. Scalability and usability of our prototype have been empirically demonstrated by extensive lab tests.

Future work

Until now we have neglected the need for a trust management system although it represents an inevitable requirement for real life scenarios. However, the estimation of trust in services, resources and provider implies manifold research challenges from different scientific disciplines. Thus, we have postponed this issue for future work.

More technical aspects for further development include distribution support, temporary fragmentation or interconnecting several π-Clouds in order to form a community cloud. As each component of the π-Box can be considered to be a service, it should be possible to distribute them throughout the π-Cloud. This implies mechanisms to handle abrupt disconnections of devices which host services, intelligent replication of services, service redundancy and so on. The scientific area of peer-to-peer protocols offers a variety of potentially suitable basic technologies for this challenge.

For scenarios like business trips it seems plausible that a user would benefit from a mobile π-Box. Building up on already implemented basic π-Box status functionalities, intelligent hand over mechanisms can be developed. Depending on the amount of data necessary for a business trip, it might be wise to migrate the π-Box and relevant data in advance. Particularly interesting is the question which criteria can be used to predict such user behaviour and how this data can be aggregated, utilised and secured.

Finally, in community cloud scenarios every participating π-Box would provide at least partial access to its resources for friendly π-Boxes in addition to its own devices. This entails authentication checks during search, update, delete and retrieval processes.

Competing interests
The authors declare that they have no competing interests.

Author's contributions
All the listed authors made substantive intellectual contributions to the research and manuscript. Specific details are as follows: MM: Led the work on requirements gathering and analysis, design, development and evaluation of

the Resource Manager. Carried out the analysis of related work. Wrote the main part of the paper based on his PhD thesis. Contributed to the editing and preparation of the paper as well as the overall architecture of the π-Box. SG: FlexCloud project lead. Responsible for the overall technical approach and architecture, editing and preparation of the paper. Contributed to requirements gathering for the Resource Manager. AS: Principal investigator of the FlexCloud project. All authors read and approved the final manuscript.

Acknowledgements
This work has received funding under project number 080949277 by means of the European Regional Development Fund (ERDF), the European Social Fund (ESF) and the German Free State of Saxony. The information in this document is provided as is, and no guarantee or warranty is given that the information is for any particular purpose. The authors would like to acknowledge the contributions of Hartmut Schweizer in the initial version of this paper [8] and his support in the design and development of CRDL. Furthermore, we appreciate the assistance of Ievgenii Maksymiuk in the development and evaluation of the Resource Manager prototype.

References
1. Mell P, Grance T (2011) The NIST definition of cloud computing. Technical Report 800-145. National Institute of Standards and Technology (NIST), Gaithersburg, MD, http://csrc.nist.gov/publications/nistpubs/800-145/SP800-145.pdf
2. Rochwerger B, Breitgand D, Eliezer L, Galis A Nagin K, Llorente IM, Montero R, Wolfsthal Y, Elmroth E, Cáceres J, Emmerich W, Galán F (2009) The reservoir model and architecture for open federated cloud computing. IBM J Res Dev 53(4):4:1–4:11
3. Flexible Service Architectures for Cloud Computing, FlexCloud project web site. http://flexcloud.eu/. Accessed 2014-06-12
4. Strunk A, Mosch M, Groß S, Thoß Y, Schill A (2012) Building a flexible service architecture for user controlled hybrid clouds In: 7th International Conference on Availability, Reliability and Security, AReS 2012. IEEE, Prague, CZ
5. Groß S, Schill A (2012) Towards user centric data governance and control in the cloud. In: Camenisch J, Kesdogan D (eds) Open Problems in Network Security. Lecture Notes in Computer Science, vol 7039. Springer, Berlin/Heidelberg, pp 132–144
6. Moltkau B, Thoß Y, Schill A (2013) Managing the cloud service lifecycle from the user's view. In: Proceedings of the 3rd International Conference on Cloud Computing and Services Science (CLOSER). SCITEPRESS Digital Library, Aachen
7. Spillner J, Schad J, Zepezauer S (2013) Personal and federated cloud management cockpit. PIK – Praxis der Informationsverarbeitung und Kommunikation 36(1):44
8. Mosch M, Schweizer H, Groß S, Schill A (2012) Automated federation of distributed resources into user-controlled cloud environments. In: 5th IEEE/ACM International Conference on Utility and Cloud Computing (UCC 2012), 2nd International Workshop on Intelligent Techniques and Architectures for Autonomic Clouds (ITAAC 2012). IEEE, Chicago, Il, USA, pp 321–326
9. Akitio My Personal Cloud Server Product web site. http://www.akitio.com/information-center/personal-cloud-server. Accessed 2014-06-12
10. mydlink^{TM}. Product web site. http://www.dlink.com/de/de/home-solutions/mydlink/what-is-mydlink. Accessed 2014-06-12
11. Synology Cloud Services. Product web site. http://www.synology.com/dsm/home_file_sharing_cloud_station.php. Accessed 2014-06-12
12. LenovoEMC Personal Cloud. Product web site. http://www.iomegacloud.com/landing_page.php. Accessed 2014-06-12
13. Samsung Tomorrow. Samsung Electronics Official Global Blog. Samsung HomeSync creates connected media experience for the whole family. http://global.samsungtomorrow.com/?p=22348. Accessed 2014-06-12
14. myQNAPcloud Product web site. https://www.myqnapcloud.com/. Accessed 2014-06-12
15. ownCloud. Project web site. http://owncloud.org/. Accessed 2014-06-12
16. Riva O, Yin Q, Juric D, Ucan E, Roscoe T (2011) Policy expressivity in the anzere personal cloud. In: Proceedings of the 2nd ACM Symposium on Cloud Computing (SOCC '11). ACM, New York, pp 1–14
17. Ardissono L, Goy A, Petrone G, Segnan M (2009) From service clouds to user-centric personal clouds. In: Cloud Computing (CLOUD-II), 2009 IEEE International Conference On. IEEE, Bangalore, India, pp 1–8
18. Cunsolo VD, Distefano S, Puliafito A, Scarpa M (2009) Volunteer computing and desktop cloud: The cloud@home paradigm. In: Network Computing and Applications, 2009. NCA 2009. Eighth IEEE International Symposium On. IEEE, Cambridge, MA, USA, pp 134–139
19. Andrzejak A, Kondo D, Anderson DP (2010) Exploiting non-dedicated resources for cloud computing. In: Network Operations and Management Symposium (NOMS), 2010 IEEE. IEEE, Osaka, Japan, pp 341–348
20. Marinos A, Briscoe G (2009) Community cloud computing. In: Proceedings of the 1st International Conference on Cloud Computing (CloudCom'09). Springer, Berlin, Heidelberg, pp 472–484
21. Barraca JP, Matos A, Aguiar RL (2011) User centric community clouds. Wireless Personal Commun 58(1):31–48
22. Ning W, De X, Baomin X (2010) Collaborative integration and management of community information in the cloud. In: E-Business and E-Government (ICEE), 2010 International Conference On. IEEE, Guangzhou, China, pp 1406–1409
23. Chard K, Caton S, Rana O, Bubendorfer K (2010) Social cloud: Cloud computing in social networks. In: Cloud Computing (CLOUD), 2010 IEEE 3rd International Conference On. IEEE, Miami, Florida, USA, pp 99–106
24. Kannan S, Gavrilovska A, Schwan K (2011) Cloud4home – enhancing data services with @home clouds. In: Distributed Computing Systems (ICDCS), 2011 31st International Conference On. IEEE, Minneapolis, Minnesota, USA, pp 539–548
25. NVIDIA CUDA Parallel Programming and Computing Platform. http://www.nvidia.com/object/cuda_home_new.html. Accessed 2014-06-12
26. Khronos Group. OpenCL - The open standard for parallel programming of heterogeneous systems. http://www.khronos.org/opencl/. Accessed 2014-06-12
27. Amazon Web Services Homepage. Announcing Cluster GPU Instances for Amazon EC2. http://aws.amazon.com/about-aws/whats-new/2010/11/15/announcing-cluster-gpu-instances-for-amazon-ec2/. Accessed 2014-06-12
28. Brutlag JD, Hutchinson H, Stone M (2008) User preference and search engine latency. In: JSM Proceedings, Qualitiy and Productivity Research Section. IEEE, Alexandria, VA, USA
29. IETF Zeroconf Working Group homepage. http://www.zeroconf.org/. Accessed 2014-06-12
30. Apple Bonjour support homepage. http://www.apple.com/support/bonjour/. Accessed 2014-06-12
31. Avahi project web site. http://www.avahi.org/. Accessed 2014-05-10
32. Open Cloud Computing Interface. Project web site. http://www.occi-wg.org/. Accessed 2014-06-12
33. Open Grid Forum. Project web site. http://www.ogf.org/. Accessed 2014-06-12
34. Metsch T, Edmonds A, Nyrén R (2010) Open cloud computing Interface-Core. In: Open Grid Forum, OCCI-WG, Specification Document. http://forge.gridforum.org/sf/go/doc16161, Online publication
35. Metsch T, Edmonds A (2010) Open cloud computing Interface-Infrastructure. http://ogfweb.pti.iu.edu/Public_Comment_Docs/Documents/2010-12/ogf_draft_occi_infrastructure.pdf, Online publication, Accessed 2012-11-08
36. Open Cloud Computing Interface. OCCI implementations. http://www.occi-wg.org/community/implementations/. Accessed 2014-06-12
37. HyperSQL database. Project web site. http://hsqldb.org. Accessed 2014-06-12
38. Apache Lucene. Project web site. http://lucene.apache.org/core/. Accessed 2014-06-12
39. elasticsearch. Project web site. http://www.elasticsearch.org/. Accessed 2014-06-12

6

An adaptive framework for utility-based optimization of scientific applications in the cloud

Martin Koehler

Abstract

Cloud computing plays an increasingly important role in realizing scientific applications by offering virtualized compute and storage infrastructures that can scale on demand. This paper presents a self-configuring adaptive framework optimizing resource utilization for scientific applications on top of Cloud technologies. The proposed approach relies on the concept of utility, i.e., measuring the usefulness, and leverages the well-established principle from autonomic computing, namely the MAPE-K loop, in order to adaptively configure scientific applications. Therein, the process of maximizing the utility of specific configurations takes into account the Cloud stack: the application layer, the execution environment layer, and the resource layer, which is supported by the defined Cloud stack configuration model. The proposed framework self-configures the layers by evaluating monitored resources, analyzing their state, and generating an execution plan on a per job basis. Evaluating configurations is based on historical data and a utility function that ranks them according to the costs incurred. The proposed adaptive framework has been integrated into the Vienna Cloud Environment (VCE) and the evaluation by means of a data-intensive application is presented herein.

Keywords: Cloud; Cloud stack; Adaptive; Autonomic computing; Utility

Introduction

Executing scientific applications in a Cloud-based environment requires dynamic allocation of computing resources, provisioning of the underlying programming environments and the applications themselves. In addition, these applications are often Cloud-enabled by following the Software as a Service approach. Cloud computing [1,2] offers researchers the illusion of virtually infinite resources that can be allocated on demand and are accessible via the Internet. Nevertheless, researchers usually have to pay for the utilized resources when using a public Cloud environment [3,4] or, in case of a private Cloud, resources are not disposable for other experiments. Consequently, a shared goal of service providers and clients is the optimization of resource utilization while keeping costs and runtime of potentially time-consuming applications low. In general, researchers want to obtain results in a given period of time and they want to spend as little money as possible on compute resources. Cloud providers aim at serving as many researchers as possible in order to increase earnings and thus strive to optimize the utilization of resources.

This work presents an adaptive framework optimizing the utilization of Cloud computing resources as well as the runtime of an application. Within this context, the two main and at the same time contradicting objectives are the allocation of as little computing resources as possible and the minimization of runtime. The adaptive framework tackling this challenge on a per-job-basis relies on well-known concepts from autonomic computing [5,6], particularly on the MAPE-K loop containing a monitor, analyzer, planner, executor, and knowledge component. By accessing knowledge about historical jobs, the adaptive framework is able to effect the configuration of a specific job.

This approach represents knowledge by means of the concept of *utility* [7] known from economics, which measures the usefulness from the researchers' and the service providers' perspective. Utility takes into account the utilization of Cloud computing resources as well as the runtime of an application. For maximizing the utility of a

Correspondence: martin.koehler@ait.ac.at
Mobility Department, Austrian Institute of Technology (AIT), Giefinggasse 2, 1210 Vienna, Austria

specific job it is necessary to consider the configuration of all three layers of the Cloud service model: (1) the application layer where applications are provisioned based on the Software-as-a-Service (SaaS) concept, (2) the programming and execution environment layer, also referred to as Platform-as-a-Service (PaaS) layer, and (3) the resource layer, also known as Infrastructure-as-a-Service (IaaS) layer. Therefore, a comprehensive and generic model enabling the configuration of different implementations of the Cloud service model layers is needed. This paper presents a Cloud stack configuration model tackling this challenge by supporting the specification of layer-specific parameters to be taken into account during the utility optimization process.

The runtime of an application depends on the hardware characteristics and the amount of computing resources available or allocated (e.g. number of processors used). The programming environment layer (e.g. MapReduce programming model [8]) provides multiple configuration parameter sets which may effect the runtime. Additionally, the configuration of an application may impact the runtime as well. Optimizing the configuration of resources, the programming environment, or the application itself, are non-trivial problems on their own and a lot of research has been done in these areas.

A prototype of the proposed framework has been implemented and integrated in the Vienna Cloud Environment (VCE) [9], a versatile cloud environment for scientific applications, data sources, and scientific workflows. The VCE follows the Software as a Service (SaaS) model and relies on the concept of virtual appliances to provide a common set of generic interfaces to the user while hiding the details of the underlying software and hardware infrastructure. The adaptive framework is evaluated on top of a data-intensive application [10] from the field of high-throughput molecular systems biology [11], which has been Cloud-enabled with the VCE.

The remainder of this paper is organized as follows: The next section discusses related work followed by a section introducing the model for describing the different layers of the Cloud stack and presenting challenges regarding the configuration of these layers. Afterwards, the design of the proposed adaptive framework based on utility functions and autonomic computing concepts is delineated and the MAPE-K loop components are presented in detail. Subsequently, the adaptive utility-optimization process is described on the basis of a cloudified data-intensive application. Finally, a conclusion of the work including future work completes this paper.

Related work

The paper investigates how utility functions and adaptive technologies, namely the MAPE-K loop, can be utilized to configure the Cloud stack towards optimizing runtime and resource utilization for specific jobs. To place this in context, this section reviews work on utility-based optimization and adaptive methods for scheduling and resource allocation.

In adaptive systems relying on feedback loops, e.g. the MAPE-K loop, various concepts for managing knowledge are established and could be utilized (e.g., Concept of Utility, Reinforcement Learning, Bayesian Techniques) [6]. The basic idea is the provisioning of knowledge about the system and to use it in the process of decision-making. In autonomic computing decision-making has been classified in action policies, goal policies and utility function policies [12]. While action policies define specific actions taken in response to sensed information, goal policies identify actions potentially leading to the desired state of the system. Utility function policies are based on the concept of utility from economics and are used to measure and quantify the relative satisfaction of customers with goods.

The principle of utility functions has been applied to diverse problem statements for resource allocation in multiple domains. In [13], utility functions in autonomic systems are used to continually optimize the utilization of managed computational resources in a dynamic, heterogeneous environment. The authors describe a system that is able to self-optimize the allocation of resources to different application environments. In contrast to their approach, we try to reduce the costs (resource usage, runtime) for a single application by automatically configuring the environment. In [14], a utility-based resource allocation and scheduling process for wireless broadband networks is described. The approach uses utility-based resource management and QoS architecture enabling an optimization system where only the utility function has to be changed for new applications. In this sense, their approach is quite similar to the approach described herein. In [15] the authors present an architecture for the implementation of self-manageable Cloud services which in case of failures or environmental changes manage themselves to fulfill the guaranteed quality of service. Whereas they focus on the quality of service, our paper uses a similar approach to optimize the resource utilization and the runtime of applications in the Cloud. Research on QoS-aware scheduling for heterogeneous datacenters is presented in [16]. Their work is not based on utility functions but likewise our work, their approach leverages from information the system already has about applications.

In [12], the authors apply autonomic computing concepts and utility functions on adaptive resource allocation for concurrent workflows. They define utility based on response time and profit, realize dynamic and adaptive workflow optimization on top of Pegasus and DAGMan and present the feasibility of the approach on top of five workflow-based scenarios. In contrast to our approach, they focus on the assignment of specific workflow tasks to execution sites. Additional related work on utility-directed resource allocation has been published in [17]. They apply this approach in virtual desktop clouds with the objective of improving the user experience. Their approach deals with resource scheduling while the work presented herein tries to optimize the utility for single jobs by configuring the Cloud stack.

In [18], an adaptive resource control system is presented. It adjusts the resources to individual tiers in order to meet application-level Quality of Service (QoS) goals. That is, to increase the resource utilization in a data center by taking into account the application level QoS. The premier objective of our framework is to reduce the amount of utilized resources for individual jobs.

The Automat toolkit [19] is a community testbed architecture that targets research into mechanisms and policies for autonomic computing that are under closed-loop control. The toolkit enables researchers to instantiate self-managed virtual data centers and to define the controllers that govern resource allocation, selection, and dynamic migration.

Cloud stack configuration model

To achieve the goal of maximizing the utility for a specific job, the adaptive framework has to take into account the resource utilization as well as the runtime of the application. This approach assumes that both, utilization and runtime, depend on the configuration of the application, the execution environment (platform), as well

as the resources. This assumption raises the need for a generic model enabling the specification of layer-specific parameters to be taken into account during the utility-optimization process. Thus, we defined a model of the Cloud stack (see Figure 1) comprising three layers: the application layer (SaaS), the execution environment layer (PaaS), and the resource layer (IaaS). For each layer a declarative descriptor captures a set of configuration parameters that might impact the resource requirements and the runtime of an application by assuming that a finite parameter set is sufficient for optimizing the resource utilization. The definition of the concrete set of parameters at each layer, which should be configured adaptively, should be hidden from the end user but has to be done by experts on the specific layer (e.g. application or service provider). Specifically, defining a concrete set of parameters spanning the whole Cloud stack requires deep knowledge about resource allocation, resource and environment configuration, and application behaviour. Thus, this approach provides a flexible model enabling the definition of a variety of parameters, but promotes the minimization of the parameters defined with the objective to reduce the overall complexity.

Representation of descriptors

The application descriptor, the environment descriptor, as well as the resource descriptor are defined in a generic manner by enabling the definition of element-specific parameters. All descriptors are defined on the basis of XSD schemes which include generic key/value pairs for defining parameters. Additionally, the XSD schema supports the definition of the scope of each parameter to

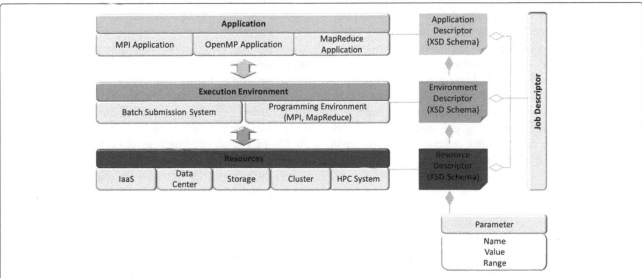

Figure 1 Layered Cloud stack model. Each layer (application, execution environment, resources) can include multiple elements, each describable by an XML descriptor. Each XML descriptor includes a list of parameters with a name, a value, and a range. A job descriptor consists of one or more application, environment, and resource descriptors.

be considered during job configuration. By following this approach, different applications, execution environments, and resources can be easily supported.

Application descriptors

The purpose of the application descriptor is to explicitly describe a set of application-specific parameters that should be tuned by the adaptive framework. Many applications provide a large set of configuration parameters enabling the tuning of an application regarding specific hardware resources. Moreover, experiments often rely on the execution of parameter studies which can be configured in different ways. Depending on the input parameters and the available resources, it may be appropriate to change the configuration of an application. The application descriptor has to be specified by the application provider by defining a specific set of parameters.

Environment descriptors

The execution of an application may require different execution environments depending on the application characteristics and underlying resources. On HPC systems and clusters, usually batch submission systems are utilized for allocating the computing resources. In case of a virtual cluster in the Cloud, a batch submission system can be configured on demand for scheduling the jobs dependent on the virtual execution appliances available. Thus, scheduling system-specific parameters that have to be set at job submission time can be defined via the environment descriptor.

For scientific applications usually a parallel execution environment such as MPI, OpenMP, or MapReduce is utilized. Most of these environments provide a huge set of configuration parameters that may impact the runtime of an application. For example, the Apache Hadoop framework supports an enormous set of parameters enabling to specify the number of map and reduce tasks, the configuration of the Java Virtual Machines, or how many tasks can be executed in parallel (on a single machine). The provisioning of a "good" configuration for such a system can be very complex. With our approach, those parameters that should be taken into account by the adaptive framework are defined in the environment descriptor and set upon job submission time to improve the behavior of the system for a specific job.

Resource descriptors

The purpose of the resource descriptor is to explicitly describe a set of computing and storage resource-specific parameters that should be taken into account by the adaptive framework. Within Cloud environments, often virtual clusters consisting of a variable set of computing resources with different CPUs and memory sizes are utilized during job execution. HPC systems provide different hardware architectures to consumers (e.g. multicore CPUs, GPUs) suitable for the execution of different applications. Resource descriptors enable an explicit description of the compute resources to be considered for the execution of a specific job.

Additionally, many applications require processing of large data sets, especially in the area of data-intensive computing. Storage environments, such as for example, the Hadoop Distributed File System (HDFS), provide a huge set of configuration parameters effecting the systems behavior. For example, the HDFS file system enables the definition of the block size of files (how a file is split across multiple distributed storage nodes) and the replication factor (how often the file is replicated). Adjusting these parameters is often not feasible for single jobs because their configuration is time-consuming. Nevertheless, these parameters effect the runtime of the application and have to be considered during the job configuration (e.g. changing the replication of a huge file in a distributed file system may require prohibitive data transfers), but they may impact the job configuration process. The resource descriptor supports the specification of these parameters.

Often, Cloud-based applications necessitate the configuration of a specific network stack, for instance a private virtual network provided by the Cloud offering. Currently, networking parameters are not in the scope of this work, but, by the generic design, resource descriptors are capable of representing different networking requirement.

Job descriptors

The purpose of the adaptive framework is to adaptively configure a job upon submission time on the basis of the application, the environment, and the resource descriptor(s). Therefore, a job descriptor comprises application, environment, and resource descriptors which consist all job-specific parameters to be configured. The current implementation of the Cloud stack configuration model is quite simple but very flexible due to the fact that any parameter can be represented and different types of descriptors are available to define diverse components of the Cloud stack including the application, multiple platforms, different resources (storage, compute, networking). Currently, consistency between the different descriptors is not assured by the system itself, but has to be taken into account by carefully defining the parameter set for all descriptors.

Design of the adaptive framework

On top of the Cloud stack model representing the configuration of all three layers, an adaptive framework for optimizing the utility of a specific job regarding these layers has been designed. The main objective of the adaptive framework is the optimization of the utility for a specific job which is achieved by adaptive configuration of these layers.

The adaptive framework is utilized for configuring the resource layers and for self-optimizing a specific job regarding runtime and resource utilization. Therefore, the design of the framework follows the MAPE-K loop [6], which is a well-established concept in autonomic computing. The MAPE-K loop comprises a monitoring, an analyzing, a planning, an execution, and a knowledge element and has the objective of designing systems with self-* characteristics (self-configuration, self-healing, self-protection, and self-optimization) [20]. The adaptive framework itself acts as autonomic manager of the different layers of the Cloud stack and the planning component relies on the utility function. The generic nature of the framework enables the adaption of the objective without changing the framework itself, but by defining different utility functions supporting varying target functions. The design of the framework is shown in Figure 2.

Managed resources

The adaptive framework has been designed to manage resources at all three Cloud stack layers involved. The framework provides sensor and effector interfaces, following the definition of the MAPE-K loop, for gaining actual information about resources and their utilization and for changing the state of the resources.

Multiple execution environments may be involved during the job execution including the scheduling system and the programming environment (e.g. MPI, MapReduce). Currently, the Hadoop Framework can be configured by changing the configuration files or by setting parameters at job execution time.

The management of the resource layer provides an interface to the computing and storage resources. Computing resources may be HPC resources and clusters managed by a batch scheduling system. In case of the Oracle Grid Engine (OGE), information about the allocatable resources can be retrieved via the Distributed Resource Management Application API (DRMAA) [21]. In case of private or public Cloud environments, the management can be done over the Cloud environment's API. Storage resources include distributed file systems, such as for example, the HDFS, and Cloud storage solutions as provided by Amazon (Amazon S3).

Knowledge

To realize a framework capable of adaptively configuring the application, the execution environment, and the resources, there is a need to integrate knowledge gained from previous configurations of the system. Following the concept of the MAPE-K loop, this knowledge is made available to the framework via the knowledge component and used in the process of decision-making. The knowledge is automatically revised during the execution by the

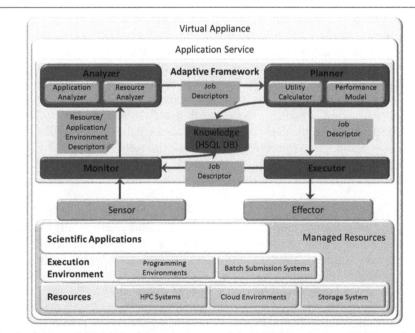

Figure 2 Design of adaptive framework. The design follows the concept of the MAPE-K loop for managing the configuration of the Cloud stack for a specific job. The framework monitors the managed resources, analyzes the state of the resources, generates an execution plan based on knowledge, and executes this plan on the resources.

adaptive framework by integrating new insights gained from additional runs of the application.

In this approach, the concept of utility, describing the usefulness of a specific configuration, is utilized for representing knowledge. This enables the representation of varying goals from different stakeholders by defining different utility functions. For example, a specific configuration may have a different utility for the researcher or for the service provider depending on their goals.

The utility U of a job [22] is defined as $U(A, E, R)$, where $A = \{a_1, \ldots, a_n\}$, $E = \{e_1, \ldots, e_m\}$, and $R = \{r_1, \ldots, r_k\}$ represent the parameter set at the application layer, the execution environment layer, and the resource layer, respectively. Different configurations are ranked on the basis of their utility. If $U_c(A_c, E_c, R_c) > U_{c'}(A_{c'}, E_{c'}, R_{c'})$, then configuration C is ranked higher than configuration C'. The configuration with the highest utility is chosen for job execution. The utility of a configuration is normalized in the range [0, 1]. The utility function itself is defined as Sigmoid function depending on a function $f(A, E, R)$. This function f is scenario-specific and has to be defined by domain experts. The equation of the utility function is depicted in the following:

$$U(f) = -e^{-5e^{-0.5*f}} + 1 \tag{1}$$

A Sigmoid function has been chosen because it highlights a small set of "good" configurations, slopes promptly, and settles down on a low value. Hence, the function (1) fits the problem of accentuating good job configurations.

The knowledge itself is captured within a database system which stores application-, environment-, and resource-descriptors of previous application executions. In our framework we utilize a HSQL database system for the knowledge base following a generic database schema. For each job, the runtime of the job, the utility of the job, and estimated values for runtime and utility (during planning phase) are stored and made available to the framework. A `parameter` table is used to store parameters specific to the managed resources. After a job has been finished, the utility of this job is calculated based on the runtime of the job, and both values are added to the knowledge base.

Monitor

The monitoring component is responsible for sensing the involved managed resources and for providing this information to the autonomic manager. Sensing the resources results in the generation of actual application, environment, and resource descriptors. These descriptors refer to the actual configuration of the managed resource (e.g. OGE). The adaptive framework has to monitor multiple resources at the different layers (IaaS, PaaS, SaaS). Therefore, the monitor relies on a component-oriented architecture, which enables simple integration of new monitor components for monitoring specific resources (e.g., different set of resources).

The realization of the monitor relies on the DRMAA API [21] for communicating with OGE. By utilizing the Java API, the monitor retrieves information about free computing resources and their configuration (e.g. number of nodes). Additionally, information about free computing resources in the private Cloud environment are provided via the KVM API [23] on the Cloud nodes. Information about the HDFS storage resource, including the block size, replication factor, and the size of the file, is retrieved by utilizing the Hadoop API. The configuration of the Hadoop framework is available via the Hadoop configuration files. Application and job specific information is supplied by the user, including the number of input files and the needed database.

Analyzer

The analyzer is responsible for evaluating the actual configuration of all layers involved. The analyzer adopts a component-based architecture, as depicted in Figure 3, and can be composed of multiple specific analyzers, for analyzing the configuration of specific resources. The analyzer executes all specific analyzer components sequentially. The basic execution chain of analyzer components is bottom-up, starting from the resource layer, next the execution environment, and finally the application layer. The execution chain can be changed by the service provider if required. The analysis phase of the adaptive framework results in the provisioning of job descriptors depicting the possible configurations on all layers that should be taken into account by the planner.

Each analyzer component provides the same generic interface retrieving a set of actual job descriptions and the resource specific description and examines the layer-specific parameters to generate a set of corresponding job descriptors. For example, if the resource descriptor includes a virtual cluster consisting of ten virtual appliances, the resource analyzer component creates ten different job configurations describing the utilization of one up to ten virtual appliances. In order to limit the number of different configurations, the range of the different parameters has to be restricted by the service provider. The analyzing phase results in a set of feasible job configurations, each specifying a different configuration of the resources on each layer. One aspect with this approach is to balance the amount of parameters with the accuracy of the approach. On the one hand, we try to minimize the amount of generated job configurations by utilizing as less parameters as possible at each layer. On the other hand, the utilized parameters have to be chosen carefully to retrieve appropriate and accurate results. The parameter set has high impact on the complexity and the accuracy

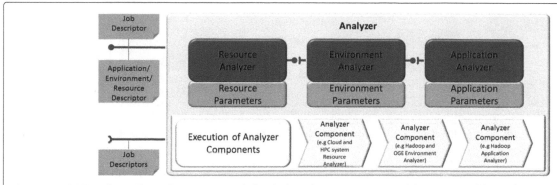

Figure 3 MAPE-K analyzer. The analyzer is comprised of multiple analyzer components, each being aware of the configuration of one managed resource. The execution of analyzer components is chained and has to be defined by the service provider. The default execution chain is depicted.

of the solution. Thus, we propose that parameters should be defined by experts in the whole system (Cloud stack model) and think about future extensions towards expert recommendation systems enabling automatic decisions on the parameters to use.

The complexity of the configuration scope can be explained as follows: n, m, k define the number of parameters $|A| = n$, $|E| = m$, $|R| = k$ and $a_i : u_i$, $e_i : v_i$, $r_i : w_i$ define the number of possible values per parameter. Thus, the number of possible configurations L is defined as $\prod_{i=1}^{n} u_i \prod_{j=1}^{m} v_j \prod_{j=1}^{k} w_l$. If we claim that $u_i, v_i, w_i \geq 2$ (saying that we have at least two possible values for each parameter), we can state that the number of configurations is exponential and at least $L \geq 2^n 2^m 2^k = 2^{nmk}$. Thus, reducing the problem scope is necessary for assuring acceptable runtime of the approach.

The prototype implementation of the adaptive framework includes an application-analyzer (application specific parameters), an environment-analyzer (Hadoop specific parameters), and a resource-analyzer (computing resource parameters). The resource-analyzer generates a set of job descriptors by utilizing information about the available computing resources (cluster and Cloud resources). Either cluster or Cloud resources are utilized by the system. The environment-analyzer provides job descriptors including different Hadoop configuration parameters. The basic implementation takes into account if compression should be utilized within Hadoop, and the number of Map and Reduce tasks which can be executed in parallel on one node. The application-analyzer configures the execution of parameter studies by evaluating the number of input files to be matched. The application-analyzer evaluates the possibility of splitting the input files to multiple jobs and generates a set of job descriptors including different configurations.

Planner

Within the MAPE-K loop, the planning component is responsible for acting on top of the information gained by the analyzer component. Herein, the planner is in charge of choosing the job configuration with the highest utility. This is done by means of knowledge and a planning strategy on the basis of the concept of utility.

According to the design, different planners could be implemented following different approaches for ranking the set of configurations. The approach utilized within this work is based upon a utility function, which enables ranking of different configurations based on the concept of utility, which is used in economics to describe the measurement of 'useful-ness' that a consumer obtains from any good [24].

In this approach, the planner uses internally a utility calculator component for estimating the utility of a specific job configuration. The utility calculator calculates the utility for a specific job configuration on the basis of the utility function. The utility function takes into account a set of parameters included in the job description and the runtime of the job. Thus, an application-specific performance model is needed to estimate the utility. Additionally, the parameter set changes due to different types of involved resources, execution environments, or applications. Therefore, the utility function has to be adapted according to the specific application scenario.

Regarding to the estimated runtime and job-specific parameters the utility for a job description is calculated and the planner ranks all job descriptions on this basis. The job configuration with the highest utility is chosen for execution.

The basic design of the planner including a utility calculator and an application-specific performance model is depicted in Figure 4.

Utility calculator

The utility calculator computes the utility of a job descriptor taking into account parameters within the application, environment, and resource descriptors as well as the estimated runtime as obtained with the performance model. The utility function depends on parameters from

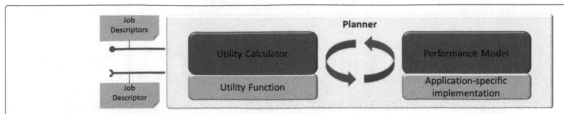

Figure 4 MAPE-K planner. The planner component consists of an application specific performance model and a utility calculator. The utility calculation is done on the basis of a utility function. The planner calculates the utility of each provided job description and ranks them afterwards by means of the utility.

the application A, the environment E and the resource R layer.

As specified, a scenario dependent function f considering the parameter sets available at the resource, execution environment, and application layer, has to be defined to be used in conjunction with the utility function. On the basis of the utility function (1) and the function f the utility of a job is estimated and different job configurations can be ranked. The prototype implementation of the adaptive framework focuses on a small sample set of parameters, specifically the parameters $n \in R$, the number of nodes, $d \in A$, the number of input files, $s \in R$ the database size, and $r \in A$ the estimated runtime of the job. Therefore, a scenario function $f(n, d, s, r)$, normalizing the parameters for the calculation of the utility, is defined in (2).

$$f(n, d, s, r) = w_f \frac{(w_n n)\ (w_r r)}{(w_d d)\ (w_s s)} \tag{2}$$

The function f is defined on the basis of the utilization of the resources (runtime and number of nodes) and the data transfer (database size and number of input files). Each value can be weighted with a factor $w_p (p \in f, n, d, s, r)$ for setting the importance of the parameter for calculation of the utility. According to initial experiments, these weighting factors have been set to $w_n = 0.3$, $w_d = 0.4$, $w_s = 0.6$, and $w_r = 0.7$. Additionally, the number of input files is normalized before applying the function. The size of the input files can have impact on the runtime of an application. Currently, this fact is not considered in the scenario dependent function due to the characteristics of the sample application. A scaling factor of $w_f = 20$ has been chosen to scale the function according to the utility function. The weighting factors within the function f have been chosen according to initial experimental results.

Performance model

Predicting the accurate runtime of an application usually is a complex, often not realistic task [25]. Similarly, a complete multidimensional regression including all parameters involved requires a large amount of test cases to deliver appropriate results. For these

reasons, we propose the utilization of a history-based performance model. Nevertheless, the generic design of the adaptive framework supports the utilization of different performance models dependent on the application.

The history-based performance model is realized on the basis of knowledge about previously run jobs with a similar configuration and of parameter-specific regression functions. Therefore, the prototype implementation defines regression functions for a subset of parameters of R (resource) and A (application), which are considered in this approach. The prototype focuses on three specific parameters including the number of nodes allocated for a specific job n, the size of the database s, and the number of input files to be compared d and has been evaluated within a case study. Therein we retrieved accurate results on different computing resources [22]. Following this, the performance prediction is based on historical execution time and regression functions. While the approach could be easily extended with support for additional parameters, it is shown that considering only a subset of parameters can results in appropriate estimations. Different types of computing resources implicate changes in the runtime of the application. Therefore, the regression functions are not completely independent of the utilized computing resources (Cloud or cluster resources), but have to be adapted with a weighting factor regarding the allocated computing resources.

Executor

The task of the executor is to configure the three Cloud stack layers according to the chosen parameter configuration and to execute the application job. First, the executor reserves and configures the computing and storage resources (or initializes them in case of a virtual cluster within a Cloud environment) regarding the resource parameters specified in the configuration. Then, the executor configures the attached execution environment as well as the application. After all three layers have been configured, the application is executed according to the defined job description.

After job completion, the executor evaluates the execution (runtime of job and recalculated utility) and stores the gained information in the knowledge base so that it can be utilized for planning of forthcoming job submissions.

Case study: adaptive configuration of a MapReduce application

A prototype of the adaptive framework including all introduced components has been implemented within the Vienna Cloud Environment (VCE) [9]. In the following we report on experiments with a MapReduce application from the domain of molecular systems biology [26,27].

At the application layer, support for the execution of the MoSys application [28], matching tryptic peptide fragmentation mass spectra data against the ProMEX database [11], has been implemented. The application supports the execution of parameter studies, in particular the comparison of hundreds of files against the database. The framework adaptively splits or combines these input files into multiple jobs and schedules their execution on different sets of computing resources. In the case study a private cloud environment and a cluster system have been utilized for executing the application. The cluster consists of eight compute nodes, each equipped with two Nehalem QuadCore processors, 24 GB of memory, and 6 TB of disk space, and is interconnected via Infiniband and Gigabit Ethernet. The private Cloud environment is connected via Gigabit Ethernet to the frontend and includes four computational nodes, each equipped with two 12-core AMD Opteron processors and 48 GB of main memory, 12 TB of storage and virtualized via KVM.

The job execution scenario is based on a test case executing a parameter study with 1000 input files against a 500 GB database. Following this scenario, the adaptive job configuration process within the adaptive framework is explained.

The job life cycle starts with a user who uploads the input files to the VCE application appliance via the Web service interface. Afterwards, the user starts the execution of the job via the application service's `start()` method and the service initiates the adaptive framework. Hence, the MAPE-K loop for this job is started, and the monitor queries the actual configuration of the application, the Hadoop environment, and the available computing resources. The monitor generates a *ResourceDescriptor* describing the available compute nodes on the cluster and the private Cloud. For this test case, it is assumed that eight compute nodes are allocatable on the cluster and up to twelve virtual machines, each containing eight virtual CPUs, can be started in the private Cloud. Additionally, an *ApplicationDescriptor* is generated including actual information about the job. Information stored in the *ApplicationDescriptor* includes the size of the database, and the number of input files.

Configuration of the job

The analyzer executes the chain of analyzer components consisting of a *ResourceAnalyzer*, an *EnvironmentAnalyzer*, and an *ApplicationAnalyzer*. Each component analyzes the parameters stored in one descriptor and generates a set of possible job descriptors.

The resource analyzer takes care of the resource descriptors provided by OGE and the private Cloud environment. The analyzer component generates eight different job configurations on the basis of the cluster resource descriptor setting the amount of compute nodes for this job between one and eight nodes. Additionally, the analyzer component creates twelve job configurations setting the amount of Cloud nodes to be allocated from one to twelve.

The *EnvironmentAnalyzer* sets Hadoop specific parameters according to the resource specific parameters. For example, the number of parallel map tasks on one node is set to eight, according to the number of cores per node.

Finally, the *ApplicationAnalyzer* evaluates the possibility to split the parameter study into multiple jobs. The test case job compares 1000 files against the database. In this case, the *ApplicationAnalyzer* generates job descriptors with one job matching 1000 input files, two jobs matching 500 input files, 4 jobs matching 250 input files, and so on. In order to simplify the procedure, the test case does not further discuss the job descriptors created by the *ApplicationAnalyzer* and explains the adaptive job configuration process on the basis of the generated resource descriptors.

The generated job descriptors are depicted in Table 1. Each line includes the Job ID, the number of input files, the database size (DB Size), the number of compute nodes including the type and the number of CPUs (Nodes(Type - CPU)), and the number of jobs generated (for the purpose of simplification all possible values are shown within one job descriptor).

Utility calculation

The planner ranks the job descriptors generated by the analyzer on the basis of the utility function and the underlying performance model. The planner estimates the performance of each job description following an application-specific performance model and information about previously run jobs stored in the knowledge base. Afterwards, the utility calculator is utilized for computing the utility of each job descriptor on the basis of the estimated performance. The planner ranks the job descriptors on the basis of the calculated utility and selects the descriptor with the highest utility for execution.

In the following the process of the utility calculation is explained in detail on the basis of the assumption that the knowledge base stores information about three historical jobs as shown in Table 2. The first job in the knowledge base has been a job matching 1000 input files against a 100

Table 1 Scope of job: this table depicts the job descriptors generated by the analyzer components (resource, environment, application) during the adaptive configuration of the test case

Job ID	Input Files	DB Size	Nodes (Type)	Number of Jobs
1	1000	500	8 (cluster - 8)	1,2,4,5,8,...,1000
2	1000	500	7 (cluster - 8)	1,2,4,5,8,...,1000
3	1000	500	6 (cluster - 8)	1,2,4,5,8,...,1000
4	1000	500	5 (cluster - 8)	1,2,4,5,8,...,1000
5	1000	500	4 (cluster - 8)	1,2,4,5,8,...,1000
6	1000	500	3 (cluster - 8)	1,2,4,5,8,...,1000
7	1000	500	2 (cluster - 8)	1,2,4,5,8,...,1000
8	1000	500	1 (cluster - 8)	1,2,4,5,8,...,1000
9	1000	500	12 (cloud - 8)	1,2,4,5,8,...,1000
10	1000	500	11 (cloud - 8)	1,2,4,5,8,...,1000
11	1000	500	10 (cloud - 8)	1,2,4,5,8,...,1000
12	1000	500	9 (cloud - 8)	1,2,4,5,8,...,1000
13	1000	500	8 (cloud - 8)	1,2,4,5,8,...,1000
14	1000	500	7 (cloud - 8)	1,2,4,5,8,...,1000
15	1000	500	6 (cloud - 8)	1,2,4,5,8,...,1000
16	1000	500	5 (cloud - 8)	1,2,4,5,8,...,1000
17	1000	500	4 (cloud - 8)	1,2,4,5,8,...,1000
18	1000	500	3 (cloud - 8)	1,2,4,5,8,...,1000
19	1000	500	2 (cloud - 8)	1,2,4,5,8,...,1000
20	1000	500	1 (cloud - 8)	1,2,4,5,8,...,1000

GB database and the second job compared one input file against a 500 GB database. Both jobs have been executed on cluster resources. The third job compared one input file against a 500 GB database by utilizing eight Cloud nodes.

The process is explained on the basis of the job configuration with Job ID 1 depicted in Table 1 (1000 input files, 500 GB, 8 Cluster Nodes). Both job configurations from the knowledge base, which have been executed on the cluster, differ in one parameter from job configuration one. Thus, the application-specific performance model is utilized to calculate the runtime of the job descriptor by using the runtime of both historical jobs. As a result an

Table 2 Knowledge base: this table depicts the job descriptors, including the utility and the runtime, stored in the knowledge base before the job execution starts

Job ID (KB)	# Input Files	DB Size	Nodes (Type)	Time	Utility
1 kb	1000	100	8 (cluster - 8)	1722	0.5908
2 kb	1	500	8 (cluster - 8)	1123	0.6458
3 kb	1	500	8 (cloud - 8)	2525	0.5266

estimated runtime of 8030.75 seconds is computed and used as basis for the calculation of the utility.

Afterwards, the utility function is applied to rank the job configurations regarding runtime and resource utilization. In Table 3 six assessed job configurations are shown. The planner choses the job configuration with the highest utility. In this case, the job configuration with eight cluster nodes and the utility of *0.6111* is chosen for execution. The job descriptors obtained during the planning phase, including the estimated runtime and the estimated utility, are shown in Table 3.

Job execution and results

Finally, the executor manages the execution of the job configuration. Therefore, eight nodes are allocated on the cluster and the Hadoop framework is initialized according to the chosen configuration. After the job has been finished, the information about the job in the knowledge base is updated with the actually measured runtime. The utility of this job configuration is recalculated on the basis of the runtime and stored accordingly. Table 3 shows the runtime and the utility of the executed job.

By comparing the estimated runtime with the real runtime of the job it can be seen that the best job configuration in terms of the runtime has been chosen by the framework for execution. Additionally, the behavior of the system can be changed by adapting the utility function to favor less resources instead of less runtime.

In this section, a prototype implementation of the adaptive framework has been presented. The realization has been based on MapReduce which is known for its scalability. Additionally, only three parameters have been taken into account in the performance model. Due to the characteristics of MapReduce, this approach delivers appropriate results in terms of resource utilization and job runtime. Nevertheless, utilizing this approach for different applications would require to specify application-specific performance models, which may not be possible for other applications, and a detailed analysis of how the utility is defined.

Conclusion

In this work, an approach towards an adaptive configuration of the Cloud stack regarding the optimization of the utility for a specific job is described. The utility of a job configuration is defined as its usefulness for a stakeholder with respect to the optimizing resource utilization and runtime. The delineated approach is based on the assumption that optimizing the utility for scientific applications in the Cloud relies on the configuration of all three Cloud layers: the infrastructure layer (IaaS), the execution layer (PaaS), and the application layer (SaaS). Therefore, the configuration has to consider the allocation of computing

Table 3 Planned job: this table depicts the job descriptors, including the utility and the runtime, created during the planning phase

Job ID	# Input Files	DB Size	Nodes (Type)	Time	Est. Time	Est. Utility	Utility
1	**1000**	**500**	**8 (cluster)**	**7855**	**8030.75**	**0.6111**	**0.6246**
2	1000	500	7 (cluster)	-	9178	0.608	
3	1000	500	6 (cluster)	-	10707.67	0.6038	
9	1000	500	12 (cloud - 8)	-	10683.33	0.6052	
13	1000	500	8 (cloud - 8)	-	16025	0.5905	
16	1000	500	4 (cloud - 8)	-	32050	0.547	

The job descriptor chosen for execution is highlighted and includes the runtime of the job inserted into the knowledge base after the job execution.

resources, the provisioning of the programming environment needed, and the configuration of the application itself.

To describe the configuration parameters on all three layers, a generic model representing the Cloud stack via descriptors has been defined. Therefore, declarative descriptors for the allocatable computing and storage resources (IaaS), the utilized programming and execution environments (PaaS), and the applications themselves (SaaS), have been defined.

On top of these descriptors, an adaptive framework, capable of optimizing the utility has been designed. The design of the adaptive framework has been done on the basis of well-established concepts from the domain of autonomic computing, especially the MAPE-K loop (monitor, analyzer, planner, knowledge), and a utility function. Thus, the adaptive framework manages the configuration of resources at all three layers (resource, environment, application) by utilizing the defined descriptors and generic implementations of a monitor, an analyzer, a planner, an executor, and a knowledge base component. Firstly, the monitor is utilized for retrieving information about the utilized resources, which includes the amount of allocatable computing resources, the configuration of the execution system, and the application. Secondly, the analyzer, following a component-based architecture, enables the chained execution of resource-specific analyzer components, and evaluates the possible configurations at all layers. Thirdly, the planner ranks the possible configurations on the basis of a utility function and an application specific performance model and choses the best configuration for execution. Finally, the executor component configures the application, the environment, as well as the computing resources and executes the application according to the chosen configuration.

Additionally, the adaptive framework has been evaluated within a case study on the basis of a MapReduce application from the domain of molecular systems biology. A prototype implementation of all application-specific components has been provided and described.

Sample parameters at all layers, including the configuration of parameter studies and scaling on different computing resources, have been chosen to evaluate the design. Additionally, an application-specific performance model has been implemented and is needed for the utility calculation process.

Finally, the adaptive job configuration process within the prototype framework has been explained on the basis of a sample job. The utility calculation, the performance estimation as well as the ranking of different job descriptions within the adaptive framework have been described in detail.

The developed Cloud stack configuration model enables the definition of scenario- and layer-specific parameters in a generic and flexible way for a not restricted set of applications, programming environments, and resources (compute, storage, network). The adaptive framework provides a modular reference implementation for adaptively optimizing the utility with respect to differing objectives (resource utilization, runtime). Nevertheless, this approach necessitates the specification of scenario-specific parameters and functions enabling the measurement of the utility for submitted jobs. This raises the need for future work towards automating and simplification of domain-specific definitions of parameters and functions.

Future work will include the evaluation of the framework with additional applications, execution environments, and resource types regarding scale, heterogeneity, and energy consumption which results in new research objectives. For instance, the area of green Cloud computing [29], emerging from green-IT [30], tackles the impact of the wide spread utilization of Clouds on the energy consumption regarding network and computing resources. Therefore, the optimization of energy consumption will be a promising future direction. Moreover, self-managing in Clouds has to consider the optimization of Quality of Service criteria relating to trust, security and privacy [2] which are increasingly important aspects, especially in Cloud computing.

Competing interests
The author declares that he has no competing interests.

Acknowledgements
I thank Siegfried Benkner, University of Vienna, who provided contributions in the conception of the work and in the acquisition of data. Additionally, I thank Norbert Brändle, AIT for proofreading.

References
1. Buyya R, Broberg J, Goscinski AM (2011) Cloud computing principles and paradigms. Wiley Publishing, New York
2. The Future Of Cloud Computing, Opportunities for European Cloud Computing Beyond (2010). http://cordis.europa.eu/fp7/ict/ssai/docs/cloud-report-final.pdf.
3. Waddington S, Zhang J, Knight G, Jensen J, Downing R, Ketley C (2013) Cloud repositories for research data–addressing the needs of researchers. J Cloud Comput: Adv Syst Appl 2(13):1
4. Petcu D, Martino B, Venticinque S, Rak M, Máhr T, Lopez G, Brito F, Cossu R, Stopar M, Šperka S, Stankovski V (2013) Experiences in building a mosaic of clouds. J Cloud Comput: Adv Syst Appl 2(12):1-22
5. Kephart JO, Chess DM (2003) The vision of autonomic computing. Computer 36:41–50
6. Huebscher MC, McCann JA (2008) A survey of autonomic computing - degrees, models, and applications. ACM Comput Surv 40:7–1728
7. Rappa MA (2004) The utility business model and the future of computing services. IBM Syst J 43:32–42
8. Dean J, Ghemawat S (2008) Mapreduce: simplified data processing on large clusters. Commun ACM 51:107–113
9. Köhler M, Benkner S (2011) VCE - A versatile cloud environment for scientific applications. In: Galis A, Dillenseger B (eds) The Seventh International Conference on Autonomic and Autonomous Systems (ICAS 2011), 22-27 May 2011, IARIA, Venice/Mestre, Italy, pp 81–87
10. Hey T, Tansley S, Tolle K (2009) The fourth paradigm: data-intensive scientific discovery. Microsoft Research, Redmond
11. Hummel J, Niemann M, Wienkoop S, Schulze W, Steinhauser D, Selbig J, Walther D, Weckwerth W (2007) Promex: a mass spectral reference database for proteins and protein phosphorylation sites. BMC Bioinformatics 8:216
12. Lee K, Paton NW, Sakellariou R, Fernandes AA (2011) Utility functions for adaptively executing concurrent workflows. Concurrency Comput: Pract Exp 23(6):646–666
13. Walsh WE, Tesauro G, Kephart JO, Das R (2004) Utility functions in autonomic systems. In: Werner B (ed) Proceedings of International Conference on Autonomic Computing. IEEE, New York, USA, pp 70–77
14. Song G, Li Y (2005) Utility-based resource allocation and scheduling in ofdm-based wireless broadband networks. Commun Mag IEEE 43(12):127–134
15. Maurer M, Brandic I, Sakellariou R (2013) Adaptive resource configuration for cloud infrastructure management. Future Generation Comput Syst 29(2):472–487. Special section: Recent advances in e-Science
16. Delimitrou C, Kozyrakis C (2013) Paragon: Qos-aware scheduling for heterogeneous datacenters. In: Proceedings of the eighteenth international conference on Architectural support for programming languages and operating systems, 16-20 March 2013. ACM, Houston, Texas, pp 77–88
17. Calyam P, Patali R, Berryman A, Lai AM, Ramnath R (2011) Utility-directed resource allocation in virtual desktop clouds. Comput Netw 55(18):4112–4130
18. Padala P, Shin KG, Zhu X, Uysal M, Wang Z, Singhal S, Merchant A, Salem K (2007) Adaptive control of virtualized resources in utility computing environments. ACM SIGOPS Oper Syst Rev 41:289–302
19. Yumerefendi A, Shivam P, Irwin D, Gunda P, Grit L, Demberel A, Chase J, Babu S (2007) Towards an autonomic computing testbed. In: Proceedings of the Second Workshop on Hot Topics in Autonomic Computing. ACM/IEEE, Jacksonville, FL, p 1
20. Kephart JO (2005) Research challenges of autonomic computing. In: Roman G-C (ed) ICSE '05: Proceedings of the 27th International Conference on Software Engineering, 15-21 May 2005. ACM, St. Louis, USA, pp 15–22
21. DRMAA - Distributed Resource Management Application API (2014). http://www.drmaa.org.
22. Köhler M, Kaniovskyi Y, Benkner S (2011) An adaptive framework for the execution of data-intensive MapReduce applications in the Cloud. In: Werner B (ed): The First International Workshop on Data Intensive Computing in the Clouds (DataCloud 2011). IEEE, Anchorage, Alaska, pp 1122–1131
23. Kernel Based Virtual Machine (2014). http://www.linux-kvm.org/page/Main_Page.
24. Principles of Economics/Utility (2014). http://en.wikibooks.org/wiki/Principles_of_Economics/Utility.
25. Bailey D, Snavely A (2005) Performance modeling: Understanding the past and predicting the future. In: Cunha J, Medeiros P (eds): Euro-Par 2005 Parallel Processing vol 3648, 1st edn. Springer, Berlin/Heidelberg, pp 620–620
26. Köhler M, Benkner S (2012) Design of an adaptive framework for utility-based optimization of scientific applications in the cloud. In: Bilof R (ed): The 2nd International Workshop on Intelligent Techniques and Architectures for Autonomic Clouds (ITAAC 2012), in Conjunction with The 5th IEEE/ACM International Conference on Utility and Cloud Computing (UCC 2012). IEEE/ACM, USA, pp 303–308
27. Köhler M (2012) A service-oriented framework for scientific cloud computing. PhD thesis, University of Vienna
28. Köhler M, Kaniovskyi Y, Benkner S, Egelhofer V, Weckwerth W (2011) A cloud framework for high troughput biological data processing. In: PoS (ed): International Symposium on Grids and Clouds, PoS(ISGC 2011 & OGF 31). Proceedings of Science, Taipei, Taiwan, p 69
29. Baliga J, Ayre RWA, Hinton K, Tucker RS (2011) Green cloud computing: balancing energy in processing, storage, and transport. Proc IEEE 99(1):149–167
30. Murugesan S (2008) Harnessing green it: principles and practices. IT Professional 10(1):24–33

7

Multi-cloud resource management: cloud service interfacing

Victor Ion Munteanu[1,2]*, Călin Şandru[1,2] and Dana Petcu[1,2]

Abstract

Cloud service abstractions are currently used to hide the underlying complexity given by existing technologies and services, in hope of facilitating the enacting of Cloud Federations and Marketplaces. In particular, resource management systems dealing with multiple Cloud providers need to expose an uniform interface for various services and to build wrappers for the Cloud service APIs. In this paper we discuss the solution adopted by a recent developed open-source and vendor agnostic platform-as-a-service for Multi-Cloud application deployment. The middleware includes a multi-agent system for automatic Cloud resource management. With a modular design, the solution provides a flexible approach to encompass new Cloud service offers as well as new resource types. This paper focuses on the modules which enable resource abstraction and automatized management.

Introduction

Offering rapid access to a large pool of available hardware and software resources to a large variety of users, the Cloud computing has been rapidly adopted by business and academic communities. The most preferred services are the ones from the Infrastructure-as-a-Service (IaaS) category and a large number of such services are available all over the world.

Currently, there are many reasons for the use of services from multiple Clouds. We can name here few scenarios: optimize costs or improve quality of services; react to changes in existing provider offers; follow constraints, like new locations or laws; avoid dependency on only one external provider; ensure backup-ups to deal with disasters or scheduled downtime; deal with the peaks in service and resource load by offloading on external ones, on demand basis; replicate applications/services by consuming services from different Clouds to ensure their high availability; act as intermediary; enhance own Cloud resource and service offers, based on agreements with other providers; consume different services for their particularities not provided elsewhere.

According to [1], a Multi-Cloud denotes the usage of multiple and independent Clouds by a client or a service. It does not imply interconnection and sharing between Clouds. The clients or their software representatives are responsible for managing resource provisioning. The selection of the best fitted place to deploy a Cloud application is a complex technical issue in a Multi-Cloud that requires the introduction of a Cloud resource management layer based on vendor-independent brokers and semi-automated tools (including knowledge-based selection methods for Cloud services). Such a resource management system should be able to hide the complexity of service selection procedures and to control the lifecycle of the resources and services allocated to a certain application.

The mOSAIC project consortium (http://www.mosaic-cloud.eu) has recently proposed and developed an open-source Platform-as-a-Service focusing on ensuring the portability of applications consuming Cloud resources from Private or Public Clouds (the acronym stands for Open-source API and Platform for multiple Clouds). It complies with the requirements of a Multi-Cloud resource management system. In order to achieve its goal to serve application developers, the PaaS relies upon artificial intelligence methods in the different procedures, like in the selection of the Cloud resources to be consumed.

mOSAIC, as a whole, is of modular design, allowing modules to be used as a whole or individually, individual modules servicing specific purposes. Previous papers about mOSAIC's platform have reported the

*Correspondence: vmunteanu@info.uvt.ro
[1] West University of Timişoara, Timişoara, Romania
[2] Institute e-Austria Timişoara, Timişoara, Romania

design and functionality of different architectural modules. In this paper we put a special focus on the platform modules which are allowing the connection to different Cloud resources to be consumed. The following sections describe them in detail as well as their integration within the whole platform.

The work carried out in this paper is of direct consequence of a general lack of support for common standards coming from Cloud Vendors, each of them having proprietary, closed source, implementations with custom interfaces and APIs. This in turn makes it difficult for cloud application developers to create provider independent cloud applications and forces them to spend time away from working on their applications to work on integrating various Cloud Vendor technologies.

This paper is an extension of the authors' paper presented at ITAAC 2012 [2]. The extension consists in the description of the interaction with the Cloud resources, as well as a the functionality of the tool designed as proof-of-concept.

The remainder of the paper is organized as follows. Section 'Short overview of mOSAIC's approach for interaction with Cloud services' gives a brief introduction to the mOSAIC's approach to the interaction with Cloud services. The main results are presented in Section 'Vendor module role and functionality' where our approach to Vendor Modules is detailed along with use cases for which the solution was designed and in Section 'Proof-of-concept implementation' a proof-of-concept implementation is presented. Finally, conclusions and future work are presented in Section 'Conclusions'.

Short overview of mOSAIC's approach for interaction with Cloud services

Triggered by the need of a solution for the portability problem, mOSAIC was designed to be an open-source and deployable middleware able to support applications which are consuming Private or Public Cloud services. An overview of the entire solution can be found in the recent paper [3].

Figure 1 captures mOSAIC's architecture as a series of grouped components. The top part represents proof of concept applications that were developed on top of mOSAIC. The bottom part is the mOSAIC PaaS which is composed of: an application support layer made up of APIs, tools and semantic support; software platform support which is behind the high level APIs and handles execution; infrastructure support which handles the management of the infrastructure; cloud adaptors which for the basis of the PaaS and communicate directly to various Cloud services and providers.

mOSAIC offers integration of Cloud services which is achieved through an interface that is instantiated in three forms:

1. an abstract entity (e.g. an object) in a programming language, mainly used at the design stage of the application;
2. a wrapper that allows the service to be integrated in the platform, mainly used at the run time by the platform as an intermediary for the application;
3. a representation in the service acquisition and SLA management processes, mainly at the deployment time of the support platform and the application.

In the next sections we will focus on the last case. The other two cases we present shortly in what follows.

Design time: language-dependent and vendor-independent abstraction of the Cloud services

The developer of a new application intended to run in Cloud environment is invited to describe the application in Java, Python and Erlang following the mOSAIC's API recommendations so that the application is not depending on a certain implementation of a Cloud service. An application can profit from the elasticity at the level of components (instead at a larger granularity level, as usual, at virtual machine level), if the component is able to scale. An event-driven programming style has been adopted to reduce the network traffic.

The first level of interface with the Cloud service (the abstraction layer) is done to the level of the language-dependent APIs through the so-called Cloudlets and Connectors. The first ones are expressing the reaction of the application to the events related to Cloud resource consumption. The second ones are generic in terms of operations allowed for a certain type of Cloud resource (e.g. key-value store, distributed file system, http gateway, or message passing system).

The latest detailed description of the mOSAIC's API can be found in [4].

Run time: wrappers of cloud service interfaces

An interoperability service of the mOSAIC's platform acts at run-time as a proxy between a vendor-agnostic and language-dependent Connector used by a certain application and a Driver of a certain type of Cloud resource (e.g. message queuing system, key value store, distributed file system). The Driver is wrapping the native API of the Cloud service in order to enable the service to interact with the other components of the platform or application. Deployable open-source services (like RabbitMQ as message queuing system, Jetty as web server, or Riak as key-value store) are used as Cloud resources available on the provisioned virtual machines on which the mOSAIC platform is deployed. The open-source code of the latest stable version includes more then ten drivers for various deployable or hosted services and is provided at https://

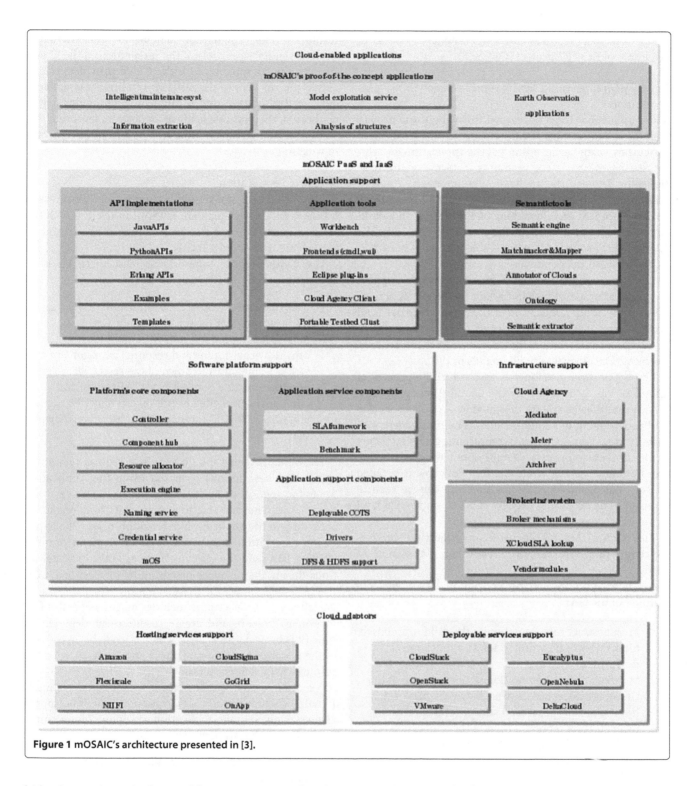

Figure 1 mOSAIC's architecture presented in [3].

bitbucket.org/mosaic. Some of them are mentioned in the next section (see the tables).

The platform that is deployable on virtual machines acquired from Private or Public Clouds includes core modules that ensure the deployment of the application, the control of the deployed components, the registration and discovery of new components. A web interface allows

manual start, destruction, replication or replacement of application components without stopping and restarting the application or the platform.

The latest detailed description of the platform functionality at run-time can be found in [5]. The platform is further developed to include monitoring facilities in the frame of the EC-FP7 project MODAClouds [6] and to improve security features and SLA compliance checks in the frame of EC-FP7 project SPECS [7].

Deployment time: cloud service representation for acquisition

The Application Tools developed throughout the project were designed to assist the developers in the deployment process by enabling the editing of the application descriptor stating the basic requirements in terms of the relationships between the application components. Another component, the Portable Testbed Cluster (PTC), allows the development and debugging of application on a desktop and then assist in its porting on a Private or Public Cloud. The Resource Allocator is able to acquire resources as described in the deployment descriptor.

The Semantic Engine and Service Discoverer support the application developer in finding the proper functionality for his or her application or the proper type of Cloud service (details in [8]). In order to tackle with the variety of terms and relationships between of them, a Cloud Resource Ontology was build (details in [9]).

The application developer is assisted in the process of Cloud service acquisition by the Cloud Agency (shortly, CA), a multi-agent system designed to support brokering and provisioning of Cloud services. The multi-agent system includes Vendor Agents representing the providers in the brokerage process. Details about the CA concept can be found in [10], while the full workflow is detailed in [11]. An overview of its architecture can be seen in Figure 2. The brokering process is based on service level agreements (details in [12]).

The Cloud Agency focuses on acquiring services for computing, storage or networking (i.e related to resources).

A Cloud resource can be present in the inputs and outputs of the CA:

1. in an abstract representation in the call for proposals for services to be acquired for an application deployment;
2. in an abstract representation in the response of the Cloud providers agents available in the platform leading to a proposal for a service level agreement;
3. in an abstract representation in the application deployment descriptor, after the approval of the service level agreement.

The interface with the Cloud service for resource acquisition is achieved through a so-called Vendor Module that is discussed in what follows.

Vendor module role and functionality

This section focuses on the Vendor Modules, as being relevant for the management system of multiple Cloud resources. The design requirements are related to the need of vendor agnosticism, the integration in the Cloud Agency, the compliance with the Cloud providers offers. While the answers to the last two requirements are specific for the solution that is build or the provider that is connected, the first one leads to an abstract level that can be of general interest, and therefore is described in details in what follows.

Supported applications

Taking a step back, we should first note that there are two business processes which are relevant in relation with the vendor agents: the resource provisioning and the resource management (Figures 3 and 4).

The Cloud Agency supports at least three kinds of applications:

1. ones that run on top of the Platform having CA as a resource provider for the Platform itself;
2. ones that run on the Cloud without Platform and CA provides provisioning and resource management as well as scaling up and down of the resources;
3. ones that include both mOSAIC API compliant components intended to run on top of the Platform and non-mOSAIC components to be serviced by the CA.

The Vendor Agents should be able to read and interpret application descriptions prepared using the Application Tools for applications addressing any of the three situations above. They are able to prepare the Cloud resources according to the application description rules. The application description together with other elements coming in place based on the user preferences and tools interactions during the resource provisioning process (e.g. SLA mechanisms) allows for the generation of a deployment descriptor. This descriptor includes all the needed information to prepare and create resources at deployment time (it is basically an artifact which is available at the end of the resource provisioning phase and is the base for the resource management phase).

A sample deployment descriptor is included in Listing 1. It mainly includes a set of descriptions for all the resource classes involved in the application to deploy. The example presents an application which needs:

1. the CA support, thus a CA Virtual Machine has to be available;
2. the Platform support, thus the Platform Control VM and Platform Execution VM should be available;
3. a storage for a platform Driver implementing a key-value storage;
4. the Web Server functionality presented as a distinct tier with all the resources at this tier being load balanced.

Listing 1 Deployment descriptor

```
<deployment_descriptor>
  <application>
    mOSAIC Application
  </application>
  <description>
    Requiring the CA, PaaS and a Web Server
  </description>
  <tiers>
   <tier>
    <id> CA </id>
    <resource_classes>
      <resource_class resource_type="compute" name="CA_VM">
              <provider>AMAZON</provider>
              <sla>SLA_1001</sla>
              <description>CA Virtual Machine</description>
              <url>deployed_image://CA.ami</url>
              <files>
              <file>*/*</file>
          </files>
              <run>
              <program>startCA.sh</program>
          </run>
              <max_instances>1</max_instances>
      </resource_class>
    </resource_classes>
   </tier>
   <tier>
    <id>mOSAIC Platform </id>
    <resource_classes>
      <resource_class resource_type="compute" name="PLATFORM_VM">
              <provider>AMAZON</provider>
              <sla>SLA_1002</sla>
              <description>PaaS Control VM</description>
              <url>deployed_image://PLATFORM.ami</url>
              <files>
                  <file>PLATFORM/*</file>
              </files>
              <run>
                  <program>init_paas.sh</program>
              </run>
              <max_instances>1</max_instances>
      </resource_class>
      <resource_class resource_type="storage" name="PLATFORM_KV_STORAGE">
              <provider>AMAZON</provider>
              <sla>SLA_1002</sla>
              <description>Platform KV storage</description>
              <url>storage://kv_bucket_name</url>
      </resource_class>
      <resource_class resource_type="compute" name="PLATFORM_EXEC_VM">
              <provider>AMAZON</provider>
              <sla>SLA_1002</sla>
              <description>PaaS Execution VM</description>
              <url>deployed_image://PLATFORM_EXEC.ami</url>
              <run>
                  <program>init_exec_platform.sh</program>
                  </run>
              <max_instances>5</max_instances>
```

```
    </resource_class>
   </resource_classes>
  </tier>
 <tier>
  <id>Web server</id>
   <resource_classes>
    <resource_class resource_type="compute" name="APP_WS_VM">
        <provider>AMAZON</provider>
        <sla>SLA_1003</sla>
        <description>App WS Tier VM</description>
        <url>deployed_{i}mage://WebService.ami</url>
        <files>
            <file>APP/WebService/*</file>
        </files>
        <run>
            <program>ca_monitor.sh</program>
            <program>tier1.sh</program>
        </run>
        <max_instances>3</max_instances>
        <load_balancing>
            <port>8080</port>
            <protocol>HTTP</protocol>
        </load_balancing>
    </resource_class>
   </resource_classes>
  </tier>
 </tiers>
</deployment_descriptor>
```

Use case

In their white paper "Architecture for Managing Clouds" [13], Distributed Management Task Force (DMTF) identify a series of cloud management use cases and depict these in close relation with the cloud service lifecycle, starting from NIST's definition of Cloud Computing [14], at the same time identifying relations between various actors.

Of the use cases presented by DMTF, the provisioning use case is the most important one as it essentially defines the work carried out in this paper. The provisioning use cases defines "the process of selecting, reserving, or creating an instance of a service offering" [13].

The normal steps for this use case are:

- Authentication – establishing the identity and permissions with the cloud provider;

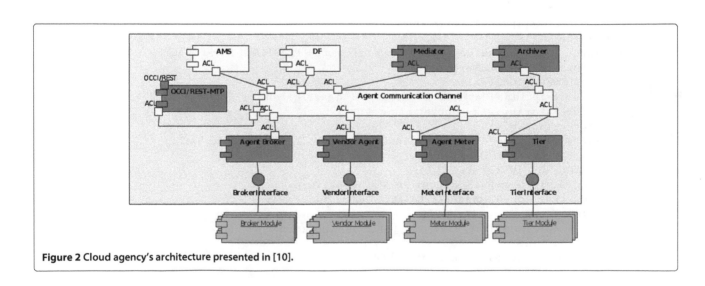

Figure 2 Cloud agency's architecture presented in [10].

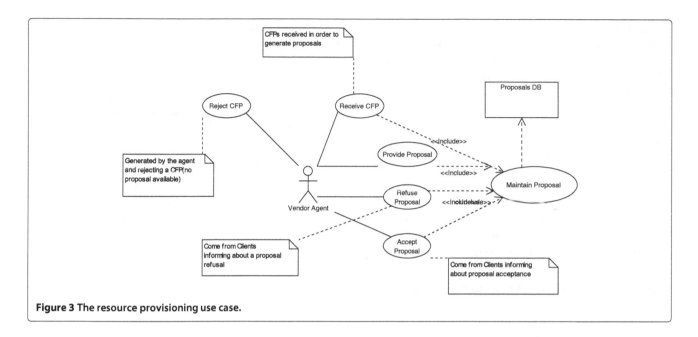

Figure 3 The resource provisioning use case.

- Offerings – evaluating and selecting from existing offerings;
- Provisioning – the actual provisioning of the desired resources;
- Provisioning monitoring – monitoring the activity of the provisioning process;
- Information retrieval – retrieving meta information about the provisioned resources;

The best example for this use case would be a company that has a cloud application composed of two components: one that runs on a public cloud and one that runs on a private cloud. When provisioning, the company must choose two cloud providers to match the components.

The ease of use provided by the CA enables the company to provision the resource for its application on desired cloud vendors as long as these vendors are supported through specific Vendor Modules.

Thus, having an unified interface provides a vendor agnostic approach to resource provisioning enables provisioning without knowing the intricacies of cloud vendor APIs, as well as it allows the addition of other cloud vendors with great ease.

Describing resources

A resource class is uniquely identified by a name and its type. After resource provisioning, it is tied to a specific provider and a specific SLA. Because of the nature

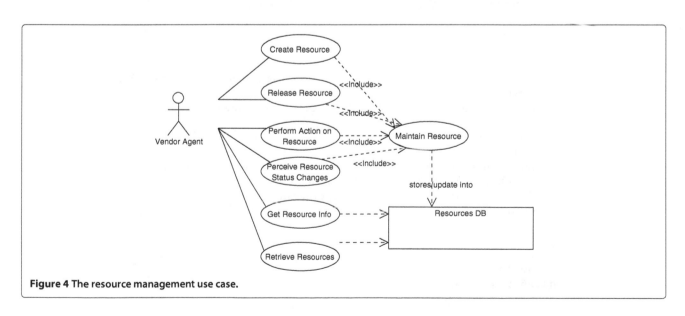

Figure 4 The resource management use case.

of SLAs, that of being cloud vendor specific, it is hard to find common ground between different vendors, and moreover it is hard to find common relationships between SLA metrics and provisioned resources. A clear example of this issue would be Amazon, the largest cloud provider, which only has 1 SLA metric: Monthly Uptime. The SLAs do not have to be the same for different resource classes. Depending of the class resources type, there are description tags which need to be specified in the class description. For example in the case of compute resources, the location of the image to use in order to create that VM is specified. In the same situation, there could be a set of files to be uploaded into that VM before using it. Also, one or more programs have to be executed at startup. All this information is present in the descriptor.

Listing 2 presents an example for the resource classes for the Platform part. There are three resource classes in the above descriptor extract:

1. Compute resources in order to run the VMs for the core Platform. Specific files have to be installed on the VMs and some programs to be run at the initialization time;
2. Compute resources in order to host the components of the Application which runs on top of the Platform. These VMs have to be properly initialized as well;
3. A storage to be used by the Platform core. It is to be attached to each core Platform VM, indication specified accordingly in the core VM descriptor.

Listing 2 Cloud Application Resource Descriptor

```
<tier>
      <id>mOSAIC Platform</id>
      <name>CA Part 2</name>
      <description>mOSAICPlatform</description>
      <resourceClasses>
        <resourceClass>
          <id>Platform_VM</id>
          <name>Platform VM</name>
          <description>Platform VM</description>
          <type>COMPUTE</type>
          <vendorId>AMAZON</vendorId>
          <slaId>
            <id>AMAZON_SLA_1342887364004_2</id>
            <cfpId>
              <id>CFP_1</id>
              <appDescriptorId>App_Dscr_Id</appDescriptorId>
            </cfpId>
          </slaId>
          <image_url>
          deployed_image://AMI_WITH_LINUX.ami?user-data=#!pkg:mosaic-node-boot
          </image_url>
          <filesToDeploy>
            <file>
              <localURL>
http://ftp.info.uvt.ro/mosaic/mos/bundle-installer/mosaic-tools-bundle-0.2.sh
              </localURL>
              <remotePath>mosaic-tools-bundle-0.2.sh</remotePath>
            </file>
          </filesToDeploy>
          <programsToRun>
            <program>sh mosaic-tools-bundle-0.2.sh standalone</program>
            <program>chroot /opt/mosaic/os</program>
            <program>/etc/init.d/mosaic start</program>
          </programsToRun>
          <firewall>
            <openPorts>
             <range>
              <min>0</min>
              <max>65535</max>
```

```
          </range>
          </openPorts>
        </firewall>
        <storage>Platform_Storage_Id</storage>
        <max_instances>3</max_instances>
      </resourceClass>
      <resourceClass>
        <id>Platform_Exec_VM</id>
        <name>Platform Execution VM</name>
        <description>Platform Execution VM</description>
        <type>COMPUTE</type>
        <vendorId>AMAZON</vendorId>
        <slaId>
          <id>AMAZON_SLA_1342887364004_2</id>
          <cfpId>
            <id>CFP_1</id>
            <appDescriptorId>App_Dscr_Id</appDescriptorId>
          </cfpId>
        </slaId>
        <image_url>deployed_image://AMI_WITH_LINUX.ami</image_url>
        <filesToDeploy>
          <file>
          <localURL>
http://ftp.info.uvt.ro/mosaic/mos/bundle-installer/mosaic-tools-bundle-0.2.sh
          </localURL>
            <remotePath>mosaic-tools-bundle-0.2.sh</remotePath>
          </file>
        </filesToDeploy>
        <programsToRun>
          <program>sh mosaic-tools-bundle-0.2.sh standalone</program>
      <program>chroot /opt/mosaic/os</program>
      <program>/etc/init.d/mosaic_exec_machine start</program>
        </programsToRun>
        <firewall>
         <openPorts>
          <range>
            <min>0</min>
            <max>65535</max>
          </range>
         </openPorts>
        </firewall>
        <max_instances>5</max_instances>
      </resourceClass>
      <resourceClass>
        <id>Platform_Storage_Id</id>
        <name>Platform KV Storage</name>
        <description>Platform KV Storage</description>
        <type>STORAGE</type>
        <vendorId>AMAZON</vendorId>
        <slaId>
          <id>AMAZON_SLA_1342887364004_2</id>
          <cfpId>
        <id>CFP_1</id>
        <appDescriptorId>App_Dscr_Id</appDescriptorId>
          </cfpId>
        </slaId>
      </resourceClass>
    </resourceClasses>
</tier>
```

To summarize it, Listing 2 contains a list of resource types that need to be provisioned (two compute resources and one storage). For the compute resources, information related to the vendor, sla, vm image, deployment information, security information are specified. Storage resource has only information related to the vendor and sla defined.

For compute resources, the maximum number of instances, open ports can be specified. Additionally, one can specify if they are load balanced using some load balancers, like in the case of the Web server tier described in Listing 1.

Generally speaking, deployment descriptors (e.g. Listing 1) contain information like: files to upload, commands to run, number of instances to start, and are mostly used in conjunction with compute resources.

The first distinction between Cloud resources is made by their traditional classification in the Cloud. We are interested in the following resource types:

1. COMPUTE : a Virtual Machine;
2. STORAGE : a volume to be attached (mounted) to a Virtual Machine;
3. NETWORK: networking for a compute resource;
4. LOAD BALANCER: a balancer associated with Virtual Machines;
5. MAP-REDUCE : a resource implementing the map reduce protocol;
6. CLUSTER: a set of COMPUTE resources being subject of auto-scaling.

A second distinction came from the fact that two compute resources (or, in general, resources of the same type) may require different credentials or are subject of different provisioning restrictions. We consider the concept of a resource class in order to cope with this distinction. In particular, resource types are important when asking for credentials and when creating resources as, for example, compute resources might require additional credentials (e.g. key pairs, ssh credentials) as opposed to storage resources. A resource identifier includes information about the resource class.

Cloud provider specifics

Different Vendor Agents are expected to have some common behavior which integrates with specific behavior. It is important to share common functions and their implementation between different Vendor Agents in order to minimize the development effort and to provide an uniform approach in the CA. The concept of Vendor Module was introduced therefore to encapsulate the specifics of Cloud providers. Such a module, pluggable into the Vendor Agent, is based on an Abstract Vendor Module entity intended to address all the common functionality of the vendor agents and their integration in the CA. The

Figure 5 presents the relationship between the Abstract Vendor Module and the Vendor Module.

As the Vendor Module is a component which is intended to address the specifics of a Cloud provider in terms of resource provisioning and resource management, Vendor Modules are necessary to be developed for each Cloud service provider. An API was designed therefore to support the fast development of Vendor Modules. The API includes an abstract behavior of the Vendor Modules, definitions and implementations of all the important concepts related to resources, resources provisioning and resources management. Also the API was concerned about the deployment of the applications on the Cloud infrastructures.

Because of the specifics of the Cloud providers affect Cloud resource management, common elements had to be identified and currently reflect in the design and implementation as they take into account important elements like the provided resources by a specific vendor, the operations available on resources (like COMPUTE, VOLUME and STORAGE), the way the credentials are managed, the available APIs or administrative operations. Such common elements are discussed in what follows, for twelve providers of hosted or deployable services (the ones connected with the mOSAIC's platform).

Provider resources
As can be seen in Table 1, COMPUTE and VOLUME resources are available to all providers.

Compute operations
Table 2 basically reflects the availability of the major operations on virtual machine for all the considered Cloud providers. However, there are some variations between providers as some of them directly start the virtual machine on creation or can only attach volumes after the virtual machine creation.

Storage operations
The volume operations basically involve the ability to create and delete drives (see Table 3). Then, the drives are attached to the compute resources either at the creation time or later.

Admin operations
Table 4 includes some common administrative operations performed on virtual machine images and on the credentials as they can be made using some API. In some cases there is an ability to upload virtual machine images, but most of the providers cannot do that. This is why the current API of the Vendor Module is avoiding this step and is relying on the users to upload the appropriate images on the providers.

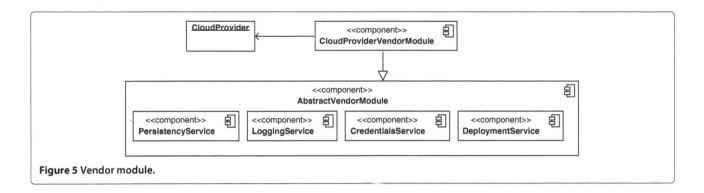

Figure 5 Vendor module.

Credentials management

The used credentials in order to manage resources vary across the Cloud providers (Table 5). In general, username/password authentication is possible. Amazon and Eucalyptus put this into the form of Access/Secret keys.

API

There is a wide range of options related to the API to use when accessing the services of a Cloud provider. The Table 6 provides a reference. The current vendor modules rely on Java libraries whenever available. In some cases there are Java libraries wrapping REST or SOAP communication.

Resource provisioning and management

The Abstract Vendor Module operations cover two important goals of the Vendor Agent: resource provisioning and resource management. The operations specific to the Vendor Module are presented in the Figure 6.

The operations outlined in the Abstract Vendor Module description falls into few categories which are not necessarily distinct:

1. public operations: are intended to be called in order to address client requests. They can be implemented at the level of the Abstract Vendor Module or Vendor Module (those also being abstract);
2. protected operations: are intended to be implemented by the Abstract Vendor Module (most of them) or by the Vendor Module (the ones which are also abstract: in italics);
3. abstract operations: are intended to be implemented by the specific Vendor Modules.

Provisioning

The resource provisioning is projected in Vendor Agents provisioning of proposals as answer to a Call for Proposal (CFP). Once a proposal is accepted, the resource classes involved in that proposal are prepared in order for resource services to be created/activated. The creation/activation of brokered SLA resources is not yet possible, as resources are intended to be created and destroyed when

needed; however, for certain resource classes, the preparation step may be required, for example, to make sure some image is available on the right place on the Cloud provider environment. Resource class preparation also involves ensuring the right credentials are in place before actually managing resources (as instances of resource classes).

Management

The resource management refers here to all the operations on resources once they are provisioned. The resource management starts with the accepting of a proposal. Then, the resource classes have to be prepared by obtaining the needed credentials and by performing any required step in order for the resources of that class to be created.

Vendor module services

There are four services in relation with the Vendor Module coping with persistency, credentials, logging and serialization. These services are passed to the Vendor Modules by the Vendor Agent at the module creation time, and they can be potentially reused across Vendor Modules.

Credentials management

Different Cloud providers use different authentication policies. Also, different resource types require specific credentials in order to be created and managed. The credentials are not directly available to the Vendor Agents and therefore the agents should query them from the application deployer at the deployment time. The credentials may no longer be requested at the execution time as the agents are deployed in the Cloud and the CA is decoupled by the deployment tools. A Credentials Service is therefore intended to manage all the needed credentials of the vendor agent in relation with the resource classes and SLAs. The Vendor Module can query the credentials for a resource class defined in relation with a specific SLA in order to perform operations on that resource class or its instances.

Persistence management

There are two kinds of entities which are identified to be subject of persistence: vendor proposals (SLAs) and

Table 1 Cloud resources

	Amazon	Flexiscale	CloudSigma	Eucalyptus	OpenNebula	NIIFI Cloud	OpenStack	VMware	OnApp	GoGrid	CloudStack	DeltaCloud
Compute	✓	✓	✓	✓	✓	✓	✓	✓	✓	✓	✓	✓
Storage	✓			✓			✓		✓	✓	✓	✓
Volume	✓	✓	✓	✓	✓	✓*	✓	✓		✓	✓	
MapReduce	✓											
Databases	✓											
Load balancing	✓						✓	✓	✓	✓	✓	
Firewall	✓	✓		✓			✓	✓		✓	✓	
Clusters	✓			✓								

*Not persistent (created and destroyed with the appropriate VM).

Table 2 Compute operations

	Amazon	Flexiscale	CloudSigma	Eucalyptus	OpenNebula	NIIFICloud	OpenStack	VMware	OnApp	GoGrid	CloudStack	DeltaCloud
Create	✓	✓	✓	✓	✓	✓	✓	✓	✓	✓	✓	✓
Destroy	✓	✓	✓	✓	✓	✓	✓	✓	✓	✓	✓	✓
Start	✓	✓	✓	✓	✓	✓	✓	✓	✓	✓	✓	✓*
Stop	✓	✓	✓	✓	✓	✓	✓	✓	✓	✓	✓	✓*
Reboot	✓	✓	✓	✓	✓		✓	✓	✓	✓	✓	✓*
Attach Volume	✓	○	○		○							
Detach Volume	✓	✓	✓	✓			✓	✓	✓	✓	✓	
List details	✓	✓	✓	✓		✓	✓	✓	✓	✓	✓	✓

○: onCreate; * depends on particular driver load.

Table 3 Storage operations

	Amazon	Flexiscale	CloudSigma	Eucalyptus	OpenNebula	NIIFI Cloud	OpenStack	VMware	OnApp	GoGrid	CloudStack	DeltaCloud
Create	✓	✓	✓	✓	✓	✓	✓	✓	✓	✓	✓	✓
Delete	✓	✓	✓	✓			✓	✓	✓	✓	✓	✓

Table 4 Administrative operations

	Amazon	Flexiscale	CloudSigma	Eucalyptus	OpenNebula	NIIFI Cloud	OpenStack	VMware	OnApp	GoGrid	CloudStack	DeltaCloud
Upload Image	✓	✓	✓	✓			✓	✓	✓	✓	✓	✓
Bundle Image	✓			✓					✓			
Download Image	✓		✓	✓			✓	✓	✓		✓	
Delete Image	✓	✓	✓	✓			✓	✓	✓		✓	✓
Manage Keys	✓	✓	✓	✓			✓	✓	✓		✓	✓

Table 5 Credentials management

	Amazon	Flexiscale	CloudSigma	Eucalyptus	OpenNebula	NIIFI Cloud	OpenStack	VMware	OnApp	GoGrid	CloudStack	DeltaCloud
Private/Public Key	✓						✓		✓		✓	✓*
Username/Password		✓	✓		✓	✓	✓	✓	✓	✓	✓	✓*
Access/Secret key	✓		✓	✓						✓	✓	✓*
External Authentication					✓						L	✓*

L - based on LDAP; * depends on the driver load and provider configuration.

Table 6 API

	Amazon	Flexiscale	CloudSigma	Eucalyptus	OpenNebula	NIIFI Cloud	OpenStack	VMware	OnApp	GoGrid	CloudStack	DeltaCloud
REST	✓		✓	✓	✓	✓	✓		✓	✓		✓
Java	✓			E	✓		✓	✓		✓	E	E
SOAP	✓	✓		✓								
Other	R,H,N				R,X	R,L						R,C
OCCI compliant					✓							✓
AWS compliant	✓			✓	P		✓				✓	P

E - external libs; P - EC2; R - Ruby; H - PHP; N - .NET; L - CLI; C - C/C++; X - XML-RPC.

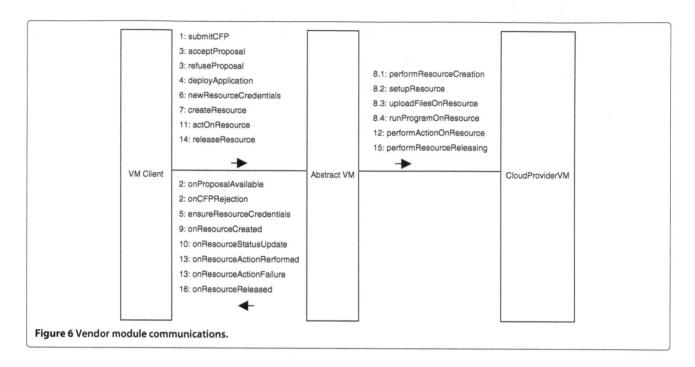

Figure 6 Vendor module communications.

Cloud resources. The Vendor Agents can refer to vendor proposals both when provisioning resources and when using resources. Therefore the proposals have to be stored and their status maintained in some persistent area. The proposals are related to the submitted CFP which may be stored as well. Once an SLA was agreed, the Vendor Agents maintain information about the resources classes and how they can be referred by the Cloud provider. For example, the AMAZON's Vendor Agent may keep a mapping between an AMI image and the resource class it is related to as this information comes from the deployment descriptor or as the Vendor agent itself may infer. When starting to create resources, the identifiers of these resources are also stored and mapped to resource descriptions and resource classes in order for future requests to be satisfied. The status of the resources is maintained as well based on the received requests from the clients and the received updates from the Cloud provider.

Logging

Logging events is sometimes useful and necessary. The Vendor Agent provides the Vendor Module with a logging service in order for the significant events to be logged at the level of the agency. There are different logging levels, in a similar way the Java language itself provide logging support.

Serialization

The CA uses its own protocol and serialization elements in order to transport messages and their parameters between agents. Once a message arrives to the Vendor Agent, it has to be split and its components transferred into an object oriented form in order for the agents' services' methods to be called. The serialization service is therefore tasked with message composition/decomposition as the objects are transmitted or received from the CA API.

Note that currently in the open-source repository of mOSAIC, on bitbucket.org, the codes of the Vendor Agents and Modules are available in `mosaic-vendor-vendors` sub-repository and are being maintained by their authors.

Support for brokering

Within the mOSAIC's Cloud Agency, it is the responsibility of the Vendor Agents to create an (SLA) offer in reply to a Call-for-proposal received from the user. These offers should contain a service description (hardware parameters of the virtual machines, storage, network, and/or any additional provider specific SLA related information) and a price (e.g. hourly fee of the offered infrastructure). The possible hardware configurations, and their price change from provider to provider. In the current implementation of the Vendor Modules, this information is either hardcoded in the corresponding module, or provided as configuration files which are read by the Vendor Modules. The main disadvantage of this solution is that whenever a provider changes its offered services, or its prices, the corresponding vendor module, or its configuration file has to be updated.

A more seamless integration could have been achieved, if the Vendor Modules could directly query the available hardware configurations and their prices from the providers. This method could be applied, if the providers exposed public Web services to publish such information. Unfortunately, none of the providers support this functionality entirely. The most complete functionality is provided by Flexiscale and CloudSigma. These providers publish Web service calls to query the available hardware configurations and the prices of certain services. For instance, one can query the price of the available VM configurations from Flexiscale, and the price of some network and software (license) resources from CloudSigma. The problem with these providers is that they do not expose these calls as a public service, the user has to have a username and a password to make such requests. Since brokering happens before deployment, the user will typically not have a password to these providers at brokering time.

An even lower level of service is provided by RackSpace (using the OpenStack API) and Arctur-1 (using the VMWare API). These providers do expose the available hardware configurations, but there is no way of querying the corresponding prices. Unfortunately, we expect the prices to change more frequently than the offered hardware configurations, therefore the configurations of the corresponding vendor modules have to be changed anyway. Finally, among the integrated vendors, Amazon and GoGrid was found to lack any support for automated brokering. Neither the offered hardware configurations, nor their prices can be queried. Until this situation changes, these vendor modules have to rely on the current off-line approach.

Migration

The CA deployment procedure involves an initial situation when the CA agents are deployed into a local environment, on the user's machine and a follow-up situation when the agents are migrated into a Cloud environment as part of the application deployment procedure.

There are few elements which concerns the Vendor Agents as part of this process. In the initial phase, the Vendor Agents only contribute to resource provisioning. The resource creation and the resource management is subject of the second phase when the agents are deployed in the Cloud. During the first phase the Vendor Agents acquire credentials for different resource classes and create content in the Proposals DB as it results from the provisioning process. The Resources DB may also be populated with resource class details. Apart of the information the Vendor Agents themselves directly manage, there are a set of application specific elements which have to be moved into the Cloud context in order to be accessible to the Vendor Agents at the resource creation time. Such elements include files as described in the Application Types to Support section.

The Vendor Agents are directly interested about such considerations as they are actually responsible to move the application and all the needed elements from the local context to the Cloud environment.

Proof-of-concept implementation

In order to make a preliminary validation of the design and to have a reference implementation, a SampleVendor Module was developed. Additional development was made in order to interact with the PTC (Portable Testbed Cluster) infrastructure by writing a specific Vendor Module. After the initial validation on PTC, the remainder of the vendor specific modules were developed, current implementation of the modules covering several Cloud providers including Amazon, CloudSigma, Eucalyptus, Flexiscale, GoGrid, Niifi Cloud, OpenNebula, OpenStack, PTC and VMWare and can be found on the BitBucket repository (https://bitbucket.org/mosaic/mosaic-agency-vendors/).

In order to support the development and testing of Vendor Modules, an Eclipse based tool was developed. This tool facilitates the creation and editing of the descriptors that are used throughout the provisioning and management of Cloud resources as well as enable the workflow patterns under which the Vendor Modules have been designed as follows:

- Cloud Application – enables creation and editing of the description of the Cloud application with its tiers and resources (Figure 7);
- Call for Proposal – enables generation of CfP from an existing Cloud Application description and allows customization of each resource attributes (Figure 8);
- Service Level Agreements – enables the brokering (simple resource brokering) of the CfP by sending it to enabled Cloud vendor modules and receiving from each the suitable SLAs and enables their visualization, acceptance and rejection (Figure 9);
- Resource Deployment Descriptor – upon SLA acceptance, this file is automatically created and its editing enables the preparation and creation of resources at the execution time.
- Resource management – based on the deployment descriptor, the tool allows the creation of one or several instances of brokered Cloud resources as well as their management (resource information, starting and stopping resources etc.).

Related work

As identified in [1] the Multi-Cloud middleware can be library-based or service-based. In the first case, a library facilitates a uniform way to access multiple services and resources, as well as the provisioning of services and

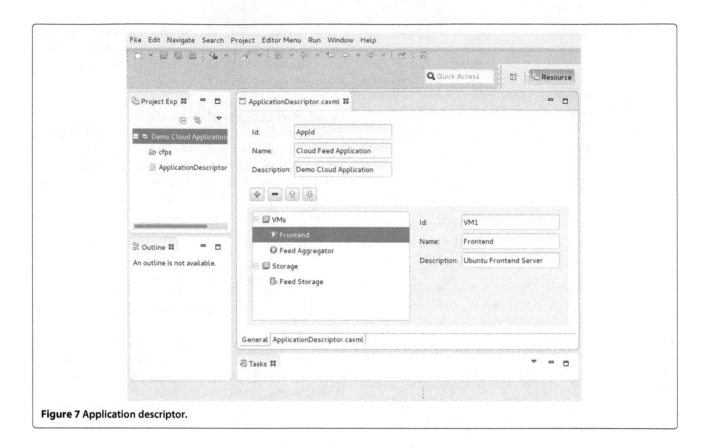

Figure 7 Application descriptor.

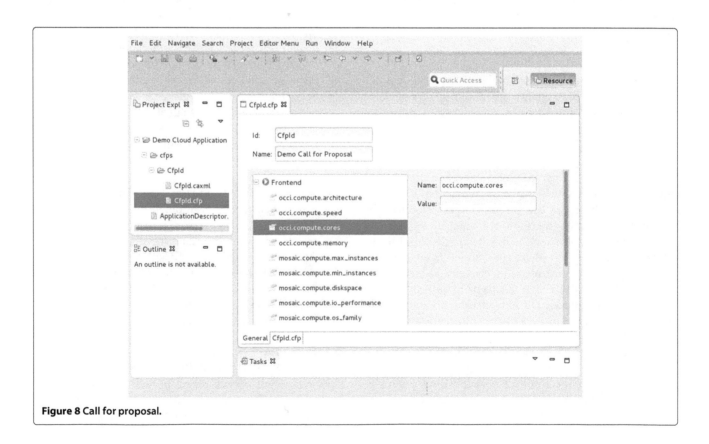

Figure 8 Call for proposal.

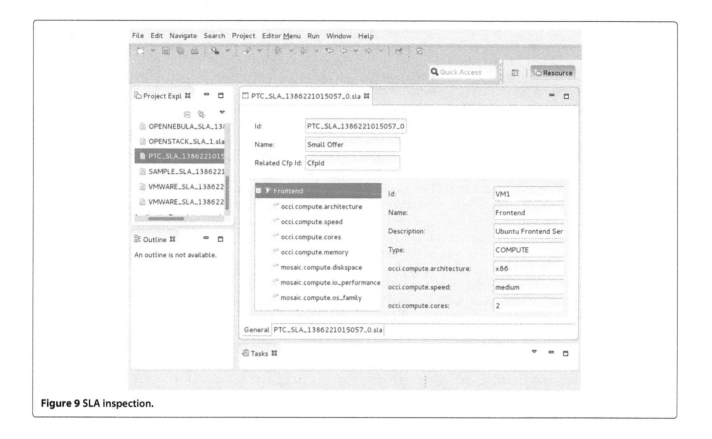

Figure 9 SLA inspection.

resources from multiple Clouds. In the second case, a special service is offering brokerage between multiple Clouds based on clients' service level agreements or provisioning rules and performs deployment, execution and monitoring.

The most known library-based approaches are jclouds, libcloud, and δ-cloud. Jclouds is an open source Java library designed to support the portability of Java applications, which allows the uniform access to the resources from various IaaS providers (jclouds.apache.org). Libcloud is a Python library that abstract the differences among the programming interfaces of Cloud services (libcloud.apache.org). δ-cloud is a REST-based API written in Ruby which allows also the connections to various Cloud resources (deltacloud.apache.org). These libraries are offering the common denominator of the underlying services, and are loosing their individuality [15]. Moreover, they are compliant with portability requirement only for off-line case (i.e. stopping the application in the current Cloud, and restarting it entirely and from the beginning in another Cloud). A more complex case is that in which the relocated application is decomposed and relocated over a new set of Clouds. Such use cases have been rarely reported until now.

In mOSAIC each of these libraries can be used as Driver interfaces with the Cloud services. The acquisition of the resources is not a subject for these libraries, nor for the Driver of mOSAIC (ensure only the second level of the interface with the Cloud service).

We classify the service-based approach for Multi-Cloud in two categories: hosted or deployable.

The most known hosted services are the commercial offers of RightScale, Kavoo and Enstratus. RightScale is offering a management platform for the control and administration of deployments in different Clouds (www.rightscale.com). Its Multi-Cloud Engine is able to broker capabilities related to virtual machine placement in Public Clouds. Kaavo allows the management of distributed applications and workloads in various Clouds (www.kaavo.com). Enstratius, allows the management, monitoring, automation and governance of resource consumption based on the services from various Cloud providers (www.enstratius.com).

Several deployable services are results of open-source projects like mOSAIC, Aoleus, Cloud4SOA or OPTIMIS. Aeolus is an open-source Cloud management software written in Ruby and provided for Linux systems by Red-Hat and it is based on the δ-cloud library (aeolusproject.org). Cloud4SOA is dealing with portability of applications between PaaSs by relying upon semantic technologies (www.cloud4soa.eu). OPTIMIS offers a deployable Platform (-as-a-Service) that allows Cloud service provisioning and the management of the life-cycle of the services (www.optimis-project.eu). It is more comprehensive than mOSAIC PaaS in terms of facilities for brokerage and run-time control, while mOSAIC offers more complex tools to support the application developers.

The Cloud brokers are playing an important role in both Multi-Cloud. The most known independent Cloud brokers are: SpotCloud, Scalr and Stratos. SpotCloud provides a marketplace for infrastructure service and a matching service with the client requirements (www.spotcloud.com). Scalr provides deployment of virtual machines in various Clouds and includes automated triggers to scale up and down (www.scalr.com). Stratos offers single sign-on and monitors resource consumption and the fulfillment of service level agreements and offers auto-scaling mechanisms (wso2.com/cloud/stratos). None of these brokers for Multi-Cloud are exposing their internal interfaces for the Cloud resource acquisition. Moreover, these brokers are not offering a complete solution for a Multi-Cloud, with the full stack from software development tools to run-time control; mOSAIC is trying to offer a proof-of-concept of such full stack.

A Multi-Cloud enabler is invited to follow the current Cloud standards. The current emerging standards, like OCCI [16-18], CDMI [19], CIMI [20,21], or TOSCA [22], along with others identified in [23] are still not adopted on large scale. One reason is their limited scope: at IaaS level, not yet for PaaS level [24].

In order to cope with the possible large adoption of the OCCI as standard for managing virtual machine mOSAIC is compliant with OCCI in the Call for Proposals [10]. Additional efforts were made for having a WS-Agreement [25,26] and SLA@SOI [27] compliant versions of the Call for Proposal and Service Level Agreement formats.

Conclusions

The variety of the Cloud services interfaces is a challenge to be dealt with by the Multi-Cloud resource management systems. Until standards in what concern these interfaces are are not adopted, practical approaches need to be found.

We presented one of such approach that was adopted by an open-source platform available as a deployable service and which intends to offer a proof-of-concept in what concerns the portability of Cloud-enabled applications. The approach is relying on the modularity of the platform architecture. The interfaces are different at the design, at run-time and at deployment stages.

Unlike other solutions which provide similar functionality, our focus was to provide an open source, modular solution which can be easily integrated and used due to unified interfaces without the unnecessary dependencies other solutions require.

Our approach alleviates developers of knowing the intricacies particular to cloud vendors (interfaces, APIs), thus dropping cloud application development time and allowing them to focus on more important aspects of their applications.

The focus of this paper was put on the deployment stage in which the variety of interfaces has the highest impact. We proposed to use Vendor modules to make the connection with the particular services which are following a given pattern in their description. Such modules are integrable in the broker system that was reported earlier. Moreover we proposed a pattern for describing the Cloud resource and the Cloud application that is compatible with current emerging standards, as proved by the proof-of-concept editor for application and resource description, shortly described in this paper.

Competing interests
The authors declare that they have no competing interests.

Authors' contributions
Approach for an unified interface with the Cloud services from multiple providers at deployment stage. Proof-of-concept implementation of the interface integrated in a brokerage system for Multi-Clouds. All authors read and approved the final manuscript.

Acknowledgments
The research reported in this paper was partially supported by Romanian grant PN-II-ID-PCE-2011-3-0260 (AMICAS), and refers to several parts of the platform developed in the frame of European Commission FP7-ICT-2009-5-256910 grant (mOSAIC). The tables that are included in this paper are improvements of the ones presented in the mOSAIC deliverables D2.5, D2.6 and D2.11. The team that has elaborate them is far from being reflected in the list of authors of this paper. We express our thanks in this context to Mariano Cecowksi and Miha Stopar (Xlab), Adrian Copie (Institute e-Austria Timişoara), Salvatore Venticinque (Second University of Naples), Támás Máhr (AITIA), Petr Škoda (Brno University of Technology), Jernej Južna and Vlado Stankosvki (University of Ljubljana).

References

1. Grozev N, Buyya R (2012) Inter-cloud architectures and application brokering: taxonomy and survey. Software Pract Ex. doi:10.1002/spe.2168
2. Şandru C, Petcu D, Munteanu VI (2012) Building an open-source platform-as-a-service with intelligent management of multiple cloud resources. In: 2012 IEEE Fifth International Conference on Utility and Cloud Computing (UCC), pp 333–338. doi:10.1109/UCC.2012.54
3. Petcu D, Martino B, Venticinque S, Rak M, Mahr T, Lopez G, Brito F, Cossu R, Stopar M, Sperka S, Stankovski V (2013) Experiences in building a mosaic of clouds. J Cloud Comput Adv Syst Appl 2(1): 12. doi:10.1186/2192-113X-2-12
4. Petcu D, Macariu G, Panica S, Craciun C (2013) Portable cloud applications-from theory to practice. Future Generat Comput Syst 29(6): 1417–1430. doi:10.1016/j.future.2012.01.009
5. Petcu D, Panica S, Crăciun C, Neagul M, Şandru C (2013) Cloud resource orchestration within an open-source component-based platform as a service. Concurrency Comput Pract Ex. doi:10.1002/cpe.3175
6. Ardagna D, Di Nitto E, Mohagheghi P, Mosser S, Ballagny C, D'Andria F, Casale G, Matthews P, Nechifor C-S, Petcu D, Gericke A, Sheridan C (2012) Modaclouds: A model-driven approach for the design and execution of applications on multiple clouds. In: 2012 ICSE Workshop on Modeling in Software Engineering (MISE), pp 50–56. doi:10.1109/MISE.2012.6226014
7. Rak M, Luna J, Petcu D, Casola V, Suri N (2013) Security as a service using an sla-based approach via specs. In: 2013 IEEE 5th International Conference on Cloud Computing Technology and Science (CloudCom), vol 2, pp 1–6, doi: 0.1109/CloudCom.2013.165

8. Cretella G, Di Martino B (2012) Towards a semantic engine for cloud applications development. In: 2012 Sixth International Conference on Complex, Intelligent and Software Intensive Systems (CISIS), pp 198–203. doi:10.1109/CISIS.2012.159

9. Moscato F, Aversa R, Di Martino B, Fortis T, Munteanu V (2011) An analysis of mosaic ontology for cloud resources annotation. In: 2011 Federated Conference on Computer Science and Information Systems (FedCSIS), pp 973–980

10. Venticinque S, Tasquier L, Di Martino B (2012) Agents based cloud computing interface for resource provisioning and management. In: 2012 Sixth International Conference on Complex, Intelligent and Software Intensive Systems (CISIS), pp 249–256. doi:10.1109/CISIS.2012.139

11. Venticinque S, Şandru C (2013) Agents based deployment of heterogeneous iaas clouds. Int J Comput Sci Eng 9. http://www.inderscience.com/info/ingeneral/forthcoming.php?jcode=ijcse.

12. Rak M, Aversa R, Venticinque S, Martino B (2012) User centric service level management in mosaic applications. In: Alexander M, et al. (eds) Euro-Par 2011: Parallel Processing Workshops Lecture Notes in Computer Science, vol. 7156. Springer, Berlin, pp 106–115. doi:10.1007/978-3-642-29740-3_13

13. Distributed Management Task Force (2010) Architecture for managing clouds. Distributed management task force. http://dmtf.org/sites/default/files/standards/documents/DSP-IS0102_1.0.0.pdf

14. NIST (2011) Cloud Architecture Reference Models: A Survey. http://collaborate.nist.gov/twiki-cloud-computing/pub/CloudComputing/Meeting4AReferenceArchtecture013111/NIST_CCRATWG_004v2_ExistentReferenceModels_01182011.pdf

15. Bermbach D, Kurze T, Tai S (2013) Cloud federation: effects of federated compute resources on quality of service and cost. In: 2013 IEEE International Conference on Cloud Engineering (IC2E), pp 31–37. doi:10.1109/IC2E.2013.24

16. Nyrén R, Edmonds A, Papaspyrou A, Metsch T (2011) Open Cloud Computing Interface - Core. http://www.ogf.org/documents/GFD.183.pdf

17. Metsch T, Edmonds A (2011) Open Cloud Computing Interface - Infrastructure. http://www.ogf.org/documents/GFD.184.pdf

18. Metsch T, Edmonds A (2011) Open Cloud Computing Interface - RESTful HTTP Rendering. http://www.ogf.org/documents/GFD.185.pdf

19. Storage Networking Industry Association (SNIA) (2012) Cloud Data Management Interface. http://snia.org/sites/default/files/CDMIv1.0.2.pdf

20. Distributed Management Task Force (DMTF) (2012) Cloud Infrastructure Management Interface - Common Information Model (CIMI - CIM). http://www.dmtf.org/sites/default/files/standards/documents/DSP0264_1.0.0.pdf

21. Distributed Management Task Force (DMTF) (2013) Cloud Infrastructure Management Interface (CIMI) Model and RESTful HTTP-baseds Protocol. http://www.dmtf.org/sites/default/files/standards/documents/DSP0263_1.1.0.pdf

22. Organization for the Advancement of Structured Information Standards (OASIS) (2013) Topology and Orchestration Specification for Cloud Applications. http://docs.oasis-open.org/tosca/TOSCA/v1.0/cs01/TOSCA-v1.0-cs01.pdf

23. Harsh P, Dudouet F, Cascella RG, Jégou Y, Morin C (2012) Using open standards for interoperability - issues, solutions, and challenges facing cloud computing. CoRR abs/1207.5949

24. Lewis GA (2013) Role of standards in cloud-computing interoperability In: 2013 46th Hawaii International Conference on System Sciences (HICSS), pp 1652–1661. doi:10.1109/HICSS.2013.470

25. Andrieux A, Czajkowski K, Dan A, Keahey K, Ludwig H, Nakata T, Pruyne J, Rofrano J, Tuecke S, Xu M (2011) Web Services Agreement Specification (WS-Agreement). http://www.ogf.org/documents/GFD.192.pdf

26. Venticinque S, Negru V, Munteanu VI, Sandru C, Aversa R, Rak M (2012) Negotiation policies for provisioning of cloud resources. In: Filipe J, Fred ALN (eds) 2012 4th International Conference on Agents and Artificial Intelligence (ICAART). SciTePress, pp 347–350. http://www.bibsonomy.org/bibtex/29a327c46d508a37eab3155ca147ac746/dblp.

27. Kearney KT, Torelli F, Kotsokalis C (2010) Sla*: An abstract syntax for service level agreements. In: 2010 11th IEEE/ACM International Conference on Grid Computing (GRID), pp 217–224. doi:10.1109/GRID.2010.5697973

8

An improved task assignment scheme for Hadoop running in the clouds

Wei Dai[*] and Mostafa Bassiouni

Abstract

Nowadays, data-intensive problems are so prevalent that numerous organizations in various industries have to face them in their business operation. It is often crucial for enterprises to have the capability of analyzing large volumes of data in an effective and timely manner. MapReduce and its open-source implementation Hadoop dramatically simplified the development of parallel data-intensive computing applications for ordinary users, and the combination of Hadoop and cloud computing made large-scale parallel data-intensive computing much more accessible to all potential users than ever before. Although Hadoop has become the most popular data management framework for parallel data-intensive computing in the clouds, the Hadoop scheduler is not a perfect match for the cloud environments. In this paper, we discuss the issues with the Hadoop task assignment scheme, and present an improved scheme for heterogeneous computing environments, such as the public clouds. The proposed scheme is based on an optimal minimum makespan algorithm. It projects and compares the completion times of all task slots' next data block, and explicitly strives to shorten the completion time of the map phase of MapReduce jobs. We conducted extensive simulation to evaluate the performance of the proposed scheme compared with the Hadoop scheme in two types of heterogeneous computing environments that are typical on the public cloud platforms. The simulation results showed that the proposed scheme could remarkably reduce the map phase completion time, and it could reduce the amount of remote processing employed to a more significant extent which makes the data processing less vulnerable to both network congestion and disk contention.

Keywords: Cloud computing; Hadoop; MapReduce; Task assignment; Data-intensive computing; Parallel and distributed computing

Introduction

We have entered the era of Big Data. It was estimated that the total volume of digital data produced worldwide in 2011 was already around 1.8 zettabytes (one zettabyte equal to one billion terabytes) compared to 0.18 zettabytes in 2006 [1]. Data has been generating in an explosive way. Back in 2009, Facebook already hosted 2.5 petabytes of user data growing at about 15 terabytes per day. And the trading system in the New York Stock Exchange generates around one terabyte of data every day. For many organizations, petabyte datasets have already become the norm, and the capability of data-intensive computing is a necessity instead of a luxury. Data-intensive computing lies in the core of a wide range of applications used across various industries, such as web indexing, data mining, scientific simulations, bioinformatics research, text/image processing, and business intelligence. In addition to large volume, Big Data also features high complexity, which makes the processing of data sets even more challenging. As a result, it is difficult to work with Big Data using most relational database management systems. And the solution is parallel and distributed processing on large number of machines.

MapReduce [2] is a parallel and distributed programming model and also an associated implementation for processing huge volumes of data on a large cluster of commodity machines. Since it was proposed by Google in 2004, MapReduce has become the most popular technology that makes data-intensive computing possible for ordinary users, especially those that don't have any prior experience with parallel and distributed data processing. While Google owns its proprietary implementation of MapReduce, an open source implementation named Hadoop [3] has gained great popularity in the rest of the world. Hadoop is now being used at

* Correspondence: wdai@knights.ucf.edu
School of Electrical Engineering & Computer Science, University of Central Florida, 4000 Central Florida Blvd., Orlando, Florida 32816, USA

many organizations in various industries, including Amazon, Adobe, Facebook, IBM, Powerset/Microsoft, Twitter, and Yahoo! [4]. Many well-known IT companies have been either offering commercial Hadoop-related products or providing support for Hadoop, including Cloudera, IBM, Yahoo!, Google, Oracle, and Dell [5].

The access to computer clusters of sufficient size is necessary for the parallel processing of large volumes of data. However, not every organization with data-intensive computing needs can afford or has the interest to purchase and maintain such computer clusters. The innovative concept of utility computing proposed a perfect solution to this problem, which eliminates both upfront hardware investment and periodical maintenance costs for cloud users. The combination of Hadoop and cloud computing has become an attractive and promising solution to parallel processing of terabytes and even petabytes datasets. A well-known feat of running Hadoop in clouds for data-intensive computing was the New York Times used 100 Virtual Machines (VM's) on Amazon Elastic Compute Cloud (EC2) [6] to convert 4 terabytes of scanned archives from the paper to 11 million articles in PDF format in less than 24 hours [7].

Although Hadoop has become the most prevalent data management framework for the processing of large volumes of data in clouds, there exist issues with the Hadoop scheduler that can seriously degrade the performance of Hadoop running in clouds. In this paper, we discuss the issues with the Hadoop task assignment scheme, and present an improved scheme, which is based on an optimal algorithm for minimum makespan scheduling and explicitly strives to shorten the duration of the map phase of MapReduce jobs. We conducted extensive simulations to evaluate the performance of the proposed scheme. The simulation results indicated that the proposed scheme could significantly improve the performance of Hadoop in terms of both the completion time of map phase and the amount of remote processing employed.

The rest of the paper is organized as follows. Background: MapReduce and Hadoop introduces the related background in MapReduce and Hadoop. Issues with the Hadoop task assignment scheme discusses issues with the Hadoop task assignment scheme in the context of the cloud environments. Related mathematical model introduces the related mathematical model on which our new scheme is based. The ECT task assignment scheme provides the details of the new scheme. Evaluation presents the simulation setup and results. Related work is introduced in Related work, and we conclude in Conclusion.

Background: MapReduce and Hadoop

In the programming model of MapReduce [2], the input of the computation is a set of key/value pairs, and the output is also a set of key/value pairs usually in a different domain from the input. Users define a map function which converts one input key/value pair to an arbitrary number of intermediate key/value pairs, and a reduce function which merges all intermediate values of the same intermediate key into a smaller set of values, typically one value for each intermediate key. An example of the application of the programming model is counting the number of occurrences of each word in a large collection of documents. The input < key/value > pair to the map function is < the name of certain document in the collection/contents of that document>. The map function emits an intermediate key/value pair of < word/1 > for each word in the document. Then the reduce function sums all counts emitted for a particular word to obtain the total number of occurrences of that word.

Hadoop [3] is currently the most mature, accessible, and popular implementation of the MapReduce programming model. A Hadoop cluster adopts the master–slave architecture, where the master node is called the Job-Tracker, and the multiple slave nodes TaskTrackers. Hadoop is usually supported by the Hadoop Distributed File System (HDFS), an open-source implementation of the Google File System (GFS). HDFS also adopts the master–slave architecture, where the NameNode (master) maintains the file namespace and directs client applications to the DataNodes (slaves) that actually store the data blocks. HDFS stores separate copies (three copies by default) of each data block for both fault tolerance and performance improvement. In a large Hadoop cluster, each slave node serves as both the TaskTracker and the DataNode, and there would usually be two dedicated master nodes serving as the JobTracker and the Name-Node respectively. In the case of small clusters, there may be only one dedicated master node that serves as both the JobTracker and the NameNode.

When launching a MapReduce job, Hadoop first splits the input file into fixed-sized data blocks (64 MB by default) that are then stored in HDFS. The MapReduce job is divided into certain number of map and reduce tasks that can be run on slave nodes in parallel. Each map task processes one data block of the input file, and outputs intermediate key/value pairs generated by the user defined map function. The output of a map task is first written to a memory buffer, and then written to a spill file on local disk when the data in the buffer reaches certain threshold. All the spill files generated by one map task are eventually merged into one single partitioned and sorted intermediate file on the local disk of the map task. Each partition in this intermediate file is to be processed by one different reduce task, and is copied by the reduce task as soon as the partition becomes available. Running in parallel, reduce tasks then apply the user defined reduce function to the intermediate key/value pairs associated with each intermediate key, and generate the final output of the MapReduce job.

In a Hadoop cluster, the JobTracker is the job submission node where a client application submits the MapReduce job to be executed. The JobTracker organizes the whole execution process of the MapReduce job, and coordinates the running of all map and reduce tasks. TaskTrakers are the worker nodes which actually perform all the map and reduce tasks. Each TaskTraker has a configurable number of task slots for task assignment (two slots for map tasks and two for reduce tasks by default), so that the resources of a TaskTraker node can be fully utilized. The JobTracker is responsible for both job scheduling, i.e. how to schedule concurrent jobs from multiple users, and task assignment, i.e. how to assign tasks to all TaskTrackers. In this paper, we only address the problem of map task assignment. The map task assignment scheme of Hadoop adopts a heartbeat protocol. Each TaskTraker sends a heartbeat message to the JobTracker every few minutes to inform the latter that it's functioning properly and also whether it has an empty task slot. If a TaskTracker has an empty slot, the acknowledgment message from the JobTracker would contain information on the assignment of a new input data block.

To reduce the overhead of data transfer across network, the JobTracker attempts to enforce data locality when it performs task assignment. When a TaskTraker is available for task assignment, the JobTracker would first attempt to find an unprocessed data block that is located on the local disk of the TaskTracker. If it cannot find a local data block, the JobTracker would then attempt to find a data block that is located on certain node that is on the same rack as the TaskTracker. If it still cannot find a rack-local block, the JobTracker would finally find an unprocessed block that is as close to the TaskTracker as possible based on the topology information on the cluster.

While map tasks have only one stage, reduce tasks consist of three: copy, sort and reduce stages. In the copy stage, reduce tasks copy the intermediate data produced by map tasks. Each reduce task is usually responsible for processing the intermediate data associated with many intermediate keys. Therefore, in the sort stage, reduce tasks need to sort all the intermediate data copied by the intermediate keys. In the reduce stage, reduce tasks apply the user defined reduce function to the intermediate data associated with each intermediate key, and store the output in final output files. The output files are kept in the HDFS, and each reduce task generates exactly one output file.

Hadoop fault tolerance mechanisms

Failures are mostly inevitable when Hadoop runs at large scales. Consequently, Hadoop is designed as a fault-tolerant framework that can handle various failures with minimum impact on the quality of service. There are three different failure modes, task failure, TaskTracker failure, and JobTracker failure. When the TaskTracker detects a task failure, it will mark the task attempt as *failed*, free the task slot on which the task is running, and notify the JobTracker of the failure in its heartbeat message. The JobTracker will then try to reschedule execution of that task on a different TaskTracker. The whole job will fail, if any task fails a configurable number of times (four times by default), which usually means the user code is buggy. TaskTracker failure occurs, when the JobTracker hasn't received any heartbeat message from certain TaskTracker for a configurable period of time (10 minutes by default). TaskTracker failure is a much more serious failure mode than task failure, because the intermediate output of all map tasks that previously ran and finished on the failed TaskTracker becomes inaccessible. In this case, the JobTracker will rerun all those completed map tasks, and reschedule any tasks in progress on other TaskTrackers. JobTracker failure is the most serious failure mode, but it is not likely to happen as the chance that a particular machine fails is low. In the case of JobTracker failure, Hadoop provides a configuration option that can attempt to recover all jobs that were running at the time the failure occurred.

More detailed discussions on various aspects of MapReduce and Hadoop can be found in [8] and [9].

Issues with the Hadoop task assignment scheme

Both MapReduce and Hadoop were originally designed for computer clusters instead of computer clouds. Clusters are mostly a homogeneous computing environment, where homogeneous nodes run in similar load conditions, and tasks of the same type tend to start and finish at roughly close times. However, the situation is completely different in the clouds. Cloud service providers employ virtualization technology to abstract physical resources, simplify their usage, improve hardware utilization, and provide user isolation for security purposes. Although current virtualization technology can isolate CPU and memory usage effectively, co-located VM's still have to compete for both network and disk bandwidth, especially in the case of I/O intensive workload, such as the MapReduce jobs. Even in homogeneous environments, network bandwidth is often a bottleneck, and it is more precious in the clouds due to the employment of virtualization technology. Consequently, a cluster of VM's in the clouds are mostly heterogeneous instead of homogeneous, and there exist two different sources of heterogeneity. First, when the cloud service user only uses small to medium numbers of VM's, most of these VM's would probably reside on distinct physical hosts, and hence would not compete with each other for the I/O resources. However, these VM's still have to compete with varying numbers of VM's belonging to other users running different applications, and hence face resource contention of different intensities that could change during the whole time period of data processing. Secondly, the even worse scenario is when the user runs Hadoop at large scales, and hence large numbers of VM's are allocated. In this case, most of the VM's belonging to the same user would not be isolated to each other anymore, and would have to compete with each other for I/O resources, which results in much higher heterogeneity in the VM cluster than in the first scenario. As an example, Zaharia et al. [10] conducted large scale experiments on Amazon EC2 to measure its heterogeneity. Their experimental results indicated that the performance difference can be of a factor of about 1.4 in the first scenario, and up to 2.7 in the second scenario due to the heterogeneity of the computing platform. To evaluate the performance of our proposed task assignment scheme, the above scenarios were resembled in the simulation as the slightly and highly heterogeneous environments.

The Hadoop task assignment scheme is simple and intuitive. Whenever a task slot becomes available, the scheme assigns a data block to it. Initially all slots only consume local blocks. After a while, certain slots, most likely the faster ones, would run out of local blocks, and as the data processing approaches the end of the map phase, more and more slots would so. The challenging question of how to utilize these task slots arises. The Hadoop scheme simply assigns a remote block to the slot to prevent it from becoming idle, which may not be appropriate for two reasons. First, task slots can process local blocks much faster than they can remote ones. Although the local slots have to start the processing later than the remote ones that are immediately available, the local slots may still be able to finish earlier than the remote ones. Therefore, it may not be necessary to assign data blocks to remote slots, even if the overhead of fetching remote data blocks is acceptable. Secondly, the utilization of remote slots comes at a price that may be high enough to offset or even outweigh its benefits. This is because reduce tasks start copying intermediate data produced by map tasks as soon as the data becomes available. In most cases, the copy stage accounts for the majority of the execution time of reduce tasks, and requires large amount of data transfer across network. Therefore, after the first batch of map tasks finish, all the reduce tasks would be running and fetching remote data across network. At this point, the network bandwidth would become the most precious resource within the cluster environment, especially if it is a VM cluster running in a cloud. Any map tasks processing remote blocks would increase the contention for network bandwidth, and slow down the copy stage of all running reduce tasks. Moreover, a remote map task also competes for the local disk bandwidth with all running local tasks, as the remote task needs to read the data block located on the local disk. The competition would slow down both local and remote tasks.

The second issue with the Hadoop scheme is about data locality. One rule works well in the context of data-intensive computing is moving processing to data, which is adopted by both MapReduce and Hadoop. The Hadoop scheduler always attempts to schedule a map task on a node that has a copy of the data block to be processed first. If it could not make it, the scheduler would instead schedule the task as close to a copy of the data block as possible based on the network topology information on the computer cluster. Nodes in a computer cluster are typically connected by high performance network, which means the network topology of the cluster is known and remain unchanged throughout the whole processing period. However, in the case of clouds, the VM's in a cluster are linked together by certain network topology that is completely unknown or at least obscure. And, cloud operators employ the technology of VM migration to balance load among physical servers or bring down certain servers for maintenance purposes, which means the network topology of a cluster of VM's could change during the whole period of data processing. Therefore, when running in the clouds, the Hadoop scheduler would not have sufficient information on the network topology of the VM cluster. As a result, the scheduler may schedule a map task on a VM to process certain data block located on another VM that could be many network hops away from the first one. Since the data block must be fetched across the network to be processed, that single map task could seriously slow down the data processing if any part of the network between those two VM's is congested.

The completion time of MapReduce jobs is an important performance metric of Hadoop, especially for the use cases of ad-hoc queries where users need to obtain the results as quickly as possible, and for the use cases of public clouds where users are charged according to the amount of time the provisioned resources are used. The Hadoop scheme is reactive instead of proactive, it doesn't make any explicit effort to shorten the Map Phase Completion Time (MPCT). Whereas, the MPCT is crucial to the job completion time of MapReduce jobs, because reduce tasks need to copy intermediate data produced by map tasks before they can start processing, and typically all reduce tasks need the intermediate data produced by each and every map task including the one that finishes the last, which stops at the MPCT.

Related mathematical model

Minimum makespan scheduling is one classical combinatorial optimization problem, where given a set of jobs and a cluster of machines, the scheduling is to assign jobs to machines so that the makespan (maximum completion time of all jobs) is minimized. There exist many variants of this problem, but the one that is specifically related to the map task assignment problem is scheduling identical jobs on uniform parallel machines. The scheduling problem can be defined as follows. A set of identical and independent jobs J_i ($i = 1, 2, \ldots, n$) need to be assigned to a set of uniform machines M_j ($j = 1, 2, \ldots, m$) running in parallel. Machines are uniform if they can process at most one job at a time, and do so at known processing speeds, which can be either the same or different for different machines. The scheduling objective is to minimize the makespan.

In 1990, Dessouky et al. [11] proposed an algorithm for solving the above scheduling problem, which is based on the Earliest Completion Time (ECT) rule. The algorithm maintains a priority queue of the completion times of the m machines' next job assignment. It selects jobs in sequential order and schedules each job on the machine that can complete it the earliest among all machines. And the earliest completion time in the priority queue is replaced by the updated completion time of the machine that is assigned the job. The procedure continues until all n jobs are assigned, and returns a series of job completion times of $t_1, t_2, \ldots, t_n$, where $t_1 \le t_2 \le \ldots \le t_n$. It is obvious that no job would be assigned to a machine in such a manner that its completion time can be reduced by the assignment of the job to another machine. Therefore, the Minimality Property can be directly reasoned out from the algorithm procedure, which asserts that there does not exist any other schedule with job completion times $t_1' \le t_2' \le \ldots \le t_n'$, such that $t_k' < t_k$ for any $k = 1, 2, \ldots, n$. In other words, the completion time of each job is the earliest possible time.

In spite of its simplicity, the ECT algorithm is optimal, which can be proved by the Minimality Property. Suppose we have another schedule with job completion times $t_1', t_2', \ldots, t_n'$ which can yield a smaller makespan. Whether the series of $t_1', t_2', \ldots, t_n'$ is in certain order or no order at all, we can always sort it to make it in the ascending order. The last completion time in this sorted series is the makespan of the schedule, which cannot be possibly smaller than t_n (the makespan of the schedule produced by the ECT algorithm) according to the Minimality Property.

The ECT task assignment scheme

Although the map task assignment problem is related to scheduling identical jobs on uniform parallel machines, the former is not identical to the latter for two reasons. First, each machine in the latter can process all jobs at the same speed. Whereas, in the former, machines can process local blocks faster than they can remote ones. Secondly, each machine in the latter has known and constant processing speed, nevertheless the processing

speeds of machines in the former are unknown and fluctuate over the whole processing period.

However, the ECT rule proposed by Dessouky et al. is still applicable in the map task assignment problem. Since all data blocks are of the same size, we assume all of them require the same amount of processing work to be processed. Therefore, in the context of map task assignment, the identical jobs are the input data blocks to be processed, and the machines are the task slots on VM's. The scheduler assigns a data block (job) to a task slot (machine) by scheduling a map task on that slot. The whole map phase of a MapReduce job can be considered as a multi-step process. The number of the steps is equal to the number of input data blocks to be processed. In each step, one single data block is processed by certain slot. If we can minimize the completion time of each step, we would be able to minimize the MPCT. Suppose we have a set of task slots S_i ($i \in \{1, 2, \ldots, m\}$) for the processing of input data blocks. Each task slot S_i has an available time T_i at which it would complete its current data block and be available to process its next data block. And if we know that it will take a task slot processing time P_i ($i \in \{1, 2, \ldots, m\}$) to process its next data block, then the completion time of its next data block will be $C_i = T_i + P_i$ ($i \in \{1, 2, \ldots, m\}$). The minimum value $C_j = \min\{C_i\}$ ($i, j \in \{1, 2, \ldots, m\}$) is the earliest possible completion time of the next step of the whole map phase, which means we can minimize the completion time of the next step by assigning a data block to the task slot S_j ($j \in \{1, 2, \ldots, m\}$). Therefore, the basic task assignment strategy of our new scheme is the ECT rule, i.e. the slot that can complete a data block (either a local or a REMOTE one) the earliest among all slots is assigned one. Note that this task slot doesn't have to be the earliest available slot, to which the Hadoop scheme would always assign the next data block. We call the new scheme ECT as it's based on the ECT rule. Figure 1 is a flowchart of the ECT scheme. The two concurrent processes: {When a slot becomes available, update its PTE} and {Initialize the priority queue of completion times} are modeled in the flowchart by a concurrent construct similar to the Fork symbol used in UML activity diagrams.

Since the processing speeds of slots fluctuate, ECT predicts the amount of time it takes a slot to process a data block by sampling the processing behaviors of that slot and averaging those samples into a Processing Time Estimate (PTE). For each slot, there are two types of PTE's, local and remote PTE's for the processing of local and remote blocks, respectively. In the simulation, the processing times of a slot were randomly generated within certain range, and hence the PTE was simply computed as the average of all processing time samples. Nevertheless, in practice, the PTE can also be calculated in a way

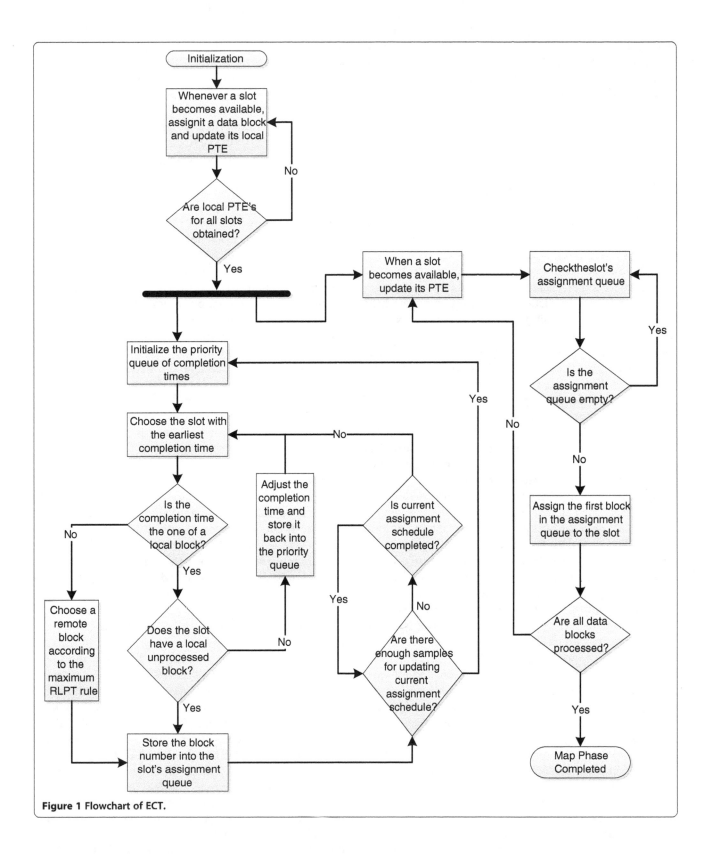

Figure 1 Flowchart of ECT.

that is similar to the way the round-trip time is estimated in network transport protocols to allow the PTE adapt to sample variance more quickly. Whenever a new sample is obtained, ECT can update the task slot's PTE according to the following formulas:

$$PTE_1 = S_1$$

$PTE_{j+1} = \alpha \times PTE_j + (1 - \alpha)S_{j+1}$ $(j = 1, 2, 3, ...)$, where PTE_j is the current PTE, PTE_{j+1} is the new estimate based on the new sample S_{j+1}, and α is a constant between 0 and 1 that controls how fast the PTE adapts to sample variance. The value of α can be set to higher ones for more variable computing environments, such as virtualized clouds, and lower ones for more stable computing environments, such as real clusters.

Before it can assign data blocks according to the ECT rule, ECT needs to obtain the local PTE of all task slots. Therefore, ECT assigns data blocks to slots whenever they become available in its first stage. After the local PTE is available for each slot, ECT starts assigning data blocks according to the ECT rule by working out an assignment schedule. ECT maintains a priority queue of the completion times of all slots' next data block based on their PTE's. At each step of the schedule calculation, ECT chooses the slot that can complete its next data block the earliest among all slots. The next data block can be either local or remote to the slot. Initially, all completion times in the priority queue are the ones of local blocks, as all slots would process local blocks first. At certain point, each slot would run out of its local blocks. The situation that needs special treatment is when there are no remaining local blocks to be assigned to certain slot that has the earliest completion time in the priority queue. Instead of assigning a remote block to the slot immediately, ECT needs to replace the slot's completion time in the priority queue, which is the completion time of its next LOCAL block, with the completion time of its next REMOTE block. Only when this updated completion time shows up as the earliest time in the priority queue, ECT will then assign a remote block to the corresponding slot. And, this remote assignment still minimizes the completion time of the corresponding processing step.

When it does need to assign a data block to a remote slot, ECT chooses a block on the local disk of the slot that has the maximum Remaining Local Processing Time (RLPT) to further reduce the amount of remote processing. The RLPT of a slot is calculated as the number of unprocessed local blocks times the current local PTE of the slot. For the slot having maximum RLPT, the assignment of its local blocks to remote slots is less likely (compared with other slots) to make it run out of local blocks before the map phase ends, and hence it is

less likely this slot would engage in remote processing at a later time.

ECT maintains an assignment queue for each slot to store the block numbers of all data blocks assigned to that slot. Task slots don't wait until the whole assignment scheme is calculated to receive their assignments. Instead, as soon as the first data block is assigned to a slot, the slot can start processing the data block. And a slot's data processing would not be interrupted, as long as its assignment queue is not empty.

The processing speed of any task slot always fluctuates, and ECT updates each slot's PTE whenever a new sample becomes available for that slot. ECT also updates the assignment schedule of data blocks to make it better reflect the changing computing environment. After a configurable number of processing time samples are obtained, ECT will work out a new assignment schedule to replace the current one. The update of assignment schedule also helps reduce the effect of estimation error, which is the difference between the PTE and the actual slot processing time. Estimation error will accumulate in the calculation of an assignment schedule, therefore the accuracy of the schedule decreases from the beginning to the end. If the schedule is frequently updated, only the beginning part of it, which is more accurate, will actually be executed.

Evaluation

We evaluated the performance of ECT compared with the Hadoop scheme by extensive simulation. We used Discrete-Event Simulation to model the operation of the map phase under both the Hadoop scheme and ECT. The discrete sequence of events is the completion of individual data blocks, each of which is completed at a particular instant in time and causes the change of state in the simulated map phase operation. After the state of the map phase operation has been updated, the current simulation time skips to the completion time of the data block that is to be completed next. The simulation procedure continues until all data blocks are processed. Various statistics are recorded during the simulation, and the ones of special interest are the MPCT, and the total Number of data Blocks Remotely Processed (NBRP). The simulation program also records the completion time of each data block for the generation of processing time traces. The common settings of all simulation scenarios are shown in Table 1.

We tested ECT in two different computing environments that were typical in the public clouds, the slightly and highly heterogeneous environments. To resemble the heterogeneous environment in the clouds, we assumed the base processing speeds of all 1000 task slots were evenly distributed within a fixed range, while the two slots on the same VM had identical base speed. In the simulation, we

Table 1 Common settings of all simulation scenarios

Total processing workload of input data	100,000 task slot × time units
Number of VM's	500
Number of map task slots on each VM	2 (Hadoop Default)
Duplication factor of data blocks	3 (Hadoop Default)
Speculation	No

Table 2 RPC and VPPT settings in the simulation

	Remote processing coefficient (RPC)	Variation percentage of processing time (VPPT)
Scenario One	1.5	± 2.5%
Scenario Two	2.5	± 5%
Scenario Three	4.0	± 10%
Scenario Four	1.0	± 2.5%

actually used slot processing times to represent slot processing speeds. There were two types of slot processing times, Local Processing Time (LPT) and Remote Processing Time (RPT), which indicated the amount of time it took a slot to process a local and remote block, respectively. LPT was randomly generated within the range $[(1\text{-VPPT})t, (1 + \text{VPPT})t]$, where t was the base processing time of the task slot, and VPPT was the Variation Percentage of Processing Time, which was used to reflect the fact that the actual slot processing times fluctuated during the whole processing period. Most MapReduce jobs belong to the relatively short and interactive category, so their job completion times are usually measured in minutes instead of hours. As a result, it is unlikely that the actual slot processing times would fluctuate significantly during the whole processing period. Therefore, we ran the simulation at three different VPPT values: 2.5%, 5% and 10%. The base processing time t's of slots on different VM's were assumed to be evenly distributed within the range $[(1\text{-P})T, (1 + P)T]$, where $T = 100,000$ / total number of data blocks. In the simulation, the value of P was set to 0.2 and 0.5 to resemble the slightly and highly heterogeneous environments respectively, which was based on the experimental results obtained on Amazon EC2 by Zaharia et al. [10]. The RPT consisted of two parts, the LPT and the amount of time it took the processing slot to fetch the data bock across the network. In the simulation, the RPT was calculated as $(\text{RPC} \times \text{LPT})$, where RPC was the Remote Processing Coefficient used to reflect the overhead of fetching remote data blocks and hence was greater than one. Since LPT was randomly generated within the range $[(1\text{-VPPT})t, (1 + \text{VPPT})t]$, RPT was randomly generated within the range $[\text{RPC}(1\text{-VPPT})t, \text{RPC}(1 + \text{VPPT})t]$.

For both slightly and highly heterogeneous environments, we ran the simulation at four typical combinations of RPC and VPPT values as shown in Table 2. Scenario one resembles the computing environment where the remote fetching overhead is low and background load on VM's is fairly stable. Scenario two resembles the environment where the remote fetching overhead is medium and background load is relatively stable. Whereas, in Scenario three, task slots experience network congestion (disk contention), and slot processing speeds fluctuate. Scenario

four is to evaluate the performance of ECT in the circumstance where there is no overhead of fetching remote data blocks.

For the performance comparison, we examined two metrics: the MPCT and the NBRP. Although minimum MPCT is one of the ultimate goals of all task assignment schemes, the NBRP is also an important metric in the sense that smaller NBRP values mean less remote processing employed, and thus it is less likely the data processing would be delayed by network congestion and/or disk contention. Furthermore, remote processing involves more factors than local processing, thus it is more likely to fail due to its complexity. Therefore, a task assignment scheme that employs less remote processing would be more favorable to one that employs more, if the MPCT's achieved by both schemes are close.

Slightly heterogeneous environment

For the slightly heterogeneous environment, it can be reasoned out from the simulation settings that the shortest possible processing time of one data block is $0.9 \times 0.8 \ T = 0.72 \ T$ time units, and the longest possible processing time $1.1 \times 1.2 \ T = 1.32 \ T$ time units, which is less than two times the shortest time. This means at the time the slowest slot finishes its first block and is assigned its second block, all other slots would be processing their second blocks. Consequently, ECT needs to assign the first 2000 data blocks to obtain the processing time estimates of all task slots, before it can assign the remaining data blocks according to the ECT rule. Therefore, for each of the four scenarios, we ran the simulation with the total number of data blocks taking on values of 2500, 3000, 3500, ... , 8000. The amount of processing work of one data block was adjusted according to the total number of data blocks (i.e. $T = 100,000/$total number of data blocks), so that the results of different total numbers of data blocks are comparable to each other.

Figures 2, 3 and 4 present the MPCT's achieved by both schemes at different total numbers of data blocks in scenarios one, two and three, respectively. It can be observed that ECT always achieves less MPCT than the Hadoop scheme, and the reduction is most significant in scenario three, where the remote fetching overhead is high. Simulation results of different total numbers of

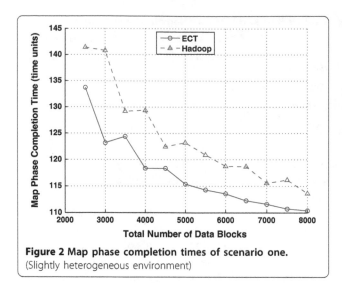

Figure 2 Map phase completion times of scenario one.
(Slightly heterogeneous environment)

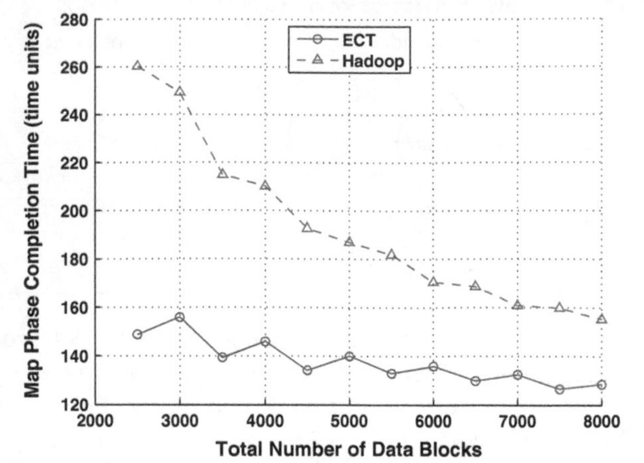

Figure 4 Map phase completion times of scenario three.
(Slightly heterogeneous environment)

data blocks in scenarios one, two and three are shown in Tables 3, 4 and 5, respectively. (Only partial results are included due to length limitation. All results are the average of ten simulation runs.) The average results of ALL different total numbers of data blocks for each scenario is shown in Table 6, which indicate that the average MPCT achieved by ECT is 5.6%, 15.3% and 28.6% less than the one achieved by the Hadoop scheme, and the average NBRP under ECT is 29.5%, 73.8% and 97.5% less than the one under the Hadoop scheme in scenarios one, two and three, respectively. The MPCT reduction of ECT is mostly attributed to its capability to reduce remote processing, which could seriously impair the MPCT performance. As mentioned earlier, ECT is designed based on an optimal algorithm, which assumes that all slot processing speeds remain the same throughout the whole processing period. If this assumption held, ECT would be able to yield the minimum possible

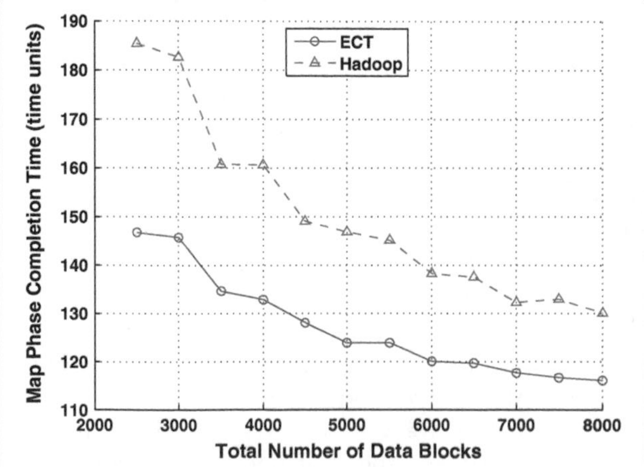

MPCT. Unfortunately, in the case of map task assignment, the slot processing speeds always fluctuate, and hence the optimal solution does not actually exist. However, since the remote fetching overhead is relatively high compared with the fluctuation of the slot processing times, ECT can still effectively reject unnecessary remote processing despite the estimation error of processing time.

It can also be observed from the simulation results that ECT is much more robust to network congestion and/or disk contention than the Hadoop scheme. As shown in Table 6, when the RPC increases from 1.5 to 4.0, the average MPCT of Hadoop rises remarkably from 124.2 to 192.5 time units (a 55.0% increase), whereas the average MPCT of ECT only rises from 117.2 to 137.5 time units (a 17.3% increase). The robustness of ECT is a result of its capability to reduce the NBRP accordingly when the remote fetching overhead rises. As shown in Table 6, when the RPC increases from 1.5 to 4.0, the average NBRP under ECT drops sharply from 226.6 to 7.5 (a 96.7% decrease), whereas the average NBRP under Hadoop only decreases slightly from 321.5 to 306.2 (a 4.8% decrease). As mentioned earlier, ECT projects and sorts all task slots' completion times of their next data block and assigns blocks to slots at the sorted order, from the earliest to the latest. When the remote fetching overhead increases, it becomes more and more unlikely that a data block would be assigned to a remote slot. In contrast, the Hadoop scheme doesn't consider either the remote fetching overhead or the MPCT when assigning data blocks. The decrease of the NBRP under Hadoop is actually related to the VPPT instead of the RPC, because when the fluctuation of slot processing times increases, the whole cluster of 1000 task slots becomes slightly less heterogeneous due to the fact that the base slot processing times are evenly distributed within a fixed range.

Figure 3 Map phase completion times of scenario two.
(Slightly heterogeneous environment)

Table 3 Simulation results of scenario one (Slightly heterogeneous environment, low remote fetching overhead, and stable slot processing speeds)

RPC = 1.5	Total number of data blocks						
VPPT = ± 2.5%	2500	3000	4000	5000	6000	7000	8000
Number of blocks assigned according to the ECT rule	500	1000	2000	3000	4000	5000	6000
MPCT of Hadoop (time units)	141.4	140.8	129.4	123.2	118.7	115.6	113.6
MPCT of ECT (time units)	133.7	123.2	118.4	115.4	113.5	111.6	110.4
ECT reduction in MPCT	5.4%	12.5%	8.5%	6.3%	4.4%	3.4%	2.8%
NBRP under Hadoop	297.3	85.7	222.4	315.2	375.5	413.9	449.9
NBRP under ECT	159.4	56.4	143.5	214.7	265.7	300.4	325.6
ECT reduction in NBRP	46.4%	34.2%	35.5%	31.9%	29.2%	27.4%	27.6%

Consequently, the average NBRP under Hadoop decreases insignificantly.

Another important observation from the simulation results is the total number of data blocks has a significant impact on the MPCT's achieved by both schemes. It can be seen from Figures 2, 3 and 4, in general, the MPCT decreases while the total number of data blocks increases for both schemes. The data processing proceeds at the highest speed before it enters the ending stage, because all slots run in parallel to process data blocks. After it enters the ending stage, the processing proceeds slower and slower, as more and more slots stop running. All slots would eventually stop and mostly they stop at different times. In general, the smaller the data blocks, the closer the stop times of different slots. When the total number of data blocks increases, the size of them decreases accordingly, thus overall the stop times of different slots get closer, which has the same effect as increasing the average speed of the data processing in the ending stage and hence decreases the MPCT. Although they can yield shorter MPCT's, larger values of the total number of data blocks will increase the amount of time it takes to duplicate the data blocks and distribute all the copies to different VM's, and will also increase the maintenance overhead of the Hadoop Distributed File System and the task assignment overhead of the JobTracker

in a Hadoop cluster, which necessitates a wise tradeoff between performance and overhead. Moreover, as the data blocks become smaller, the distinction of the MPCT performance between different task assignment schemes also gets smaller, because in general a bad decision on the assignment of a data block would increase the MPCT less than it would when the data block is bigger. Consequently, the MPCT reduction of ECT over the Hadoop scheme decreases when the total number of data blocks increases, as shown in Figures 2, 3 and 4 where the curves of both schemes approach to each other while stretching to the right.

The processing time traces of one typical case are shown in Figure 5. It can be seen that the time traces of both schemes match perfectly except for the tail part. This is because both schemes keep all slots running in parallel until the ending stage, when there are not enough remaining data blocks for the schemes to do so. And both schemes have fairly close block completion times as simulation results are the average of ten simulation runs. The two time traces diverge at the tail. While the ECT trace rises in slightly accelerated rate, the Hadoop trace rises sharply. Since there are less and less slots running in the ending stage, the data processing gradually slows down, which causes the accelerated rising of the ECT trace. On the other hand, the Hadoop scheme

Table 4 Simulation results of scenario two (Slightly heterogeneous environment, medium remote fetching overhead, and relatively stable slot processing speeds)

RPC = 2.5	Total number of data blocks						
VPPT = ± 5%	2500	3000	4000	5000	6000	7000	8000
Number of blocks assigned according to the ECT rule	500	1000	2000	3000	4000	5000	6000
MPCT of Hadoop (time units)	185.4	182.6	160.7	146.8	138.2	132.2	130.0
MPCT of ECT (time units)	146.8	145.7	132.9	123.8	120.0	117.6	116.0
ECT reduction in MPCT	20.8%	20.2%	17.3%	15.6%	13.2%	11.1%	10.8%
NBRP under Hadoop	285.2	89.6	214.1	306.9	365.5	411.2	443.1
NBRP under ECT	0.9	15.0	23.6	36.4	85.0	135.6	176.6
ECT reduction in NBRP	99.7%	83.3%	89.0%	88.1%	76.7%	67.0%	60.1%

Table 5 Simulation results of scenario three (Slightly heterogeneous environment, high remote fetching overhead, and less stable slot processing speeds)

RPC = 4.0	Total number of data blocks						
VPPT = ± 10%	2500	3000	4000	5000	6000	7000	8000
Number of blocks assigned according to the ECT rule	500	1000	2000	3000	4000	5000	6000
MPCT of Hadoop (time units)	260.1	249.1	210.0	186.9	170.5	160.8	155.3
MPCT of ECT (time units)	148.7	155.8	145.9	140.0	135.9	132.5	128.4
ECT reduction in MPCT	42.8%	37.4%	30.5%	25.1%	20.3%	17.6%	17.3%
NBRP under Hadoop	260.4	95.4	204.8	298.7	358.3	402.1	437.8
NBRP under ECT	0	0	0.1	1.7	6.6	14.6	26.6
ECT reduction in NBRP	100%	100%	100%	99.4%	98.2%	96.4%	93.9%

works reasonably well until most slots run out of local blocks. From this point on until the end of the map phase, the majority of the data blocks would be processed by remote slots, and large amount of remote processing causes the sharp rise of the Hadoop trace.

Table 6 also includes the standard deviations of all simulation results in addition to the averages. It can be observed that, in scenarios one, two, and three where there exists remote fetching overhead, the variance of ECT results is always lower than the one of Hadoop results for both MPCT and NBRP, and the higher the overhead, the bigger the difference. The most significant difference occurs in scenario three, where the standard deviation of ECT MPCT is 8.8 time units compared with Hadoop's 34.7 time units, and the standard deviation of ECT NBRP is 10.9 compared with Hadoop's 96.4. This is because ECT has the capability to automatically adapt to the congestion (contention) level of the cluster network (VM disks), which the Hadoop scheme doesn't have. When the remote fetching overhead is sufficiently high, remote processing of data blocks in

the ending stage is mostly rejected by ECT. As shown in Table 5, compared with the Hadoop scheme, ECT only allows very limited (if any) number of data blocks to be processed remotely at different total numbers of data blocks in scenario three, which causes much more stable NBRP and hence much more stable MPCT. The benefit of stable NBRP and MPCT is that better performance can be achieved by splitting the input file into less number of data blocks, and hence incurring less overhead.

Highly heterogeneous environment

For the highly heterogeneous environment, it can be reasoned out from the simulation settings that the shortest possible processing time of one data block is 0.9×0.5 T = 0.45 T time units, and the longest possible processing time 1.1×1.5 T = 1.65 T time units, which is larger than three times the shortest time. As a result, ECT needs to assign more data blocks during its first stage to obtain the processing time estimates of all slots than it does in the slightly heterogeneous environment. Therefore, for

Table 6 Simulation results of slightly heterogeneous environment

	Scenario			
	One	Two	Three	Four
RPC	1.5	2.5	4.0	1.0
VPPT	± 2.5%	± 5%	± 10%	± 2.5%
Average of Hadoop MPCT (time units)	124.2	150.1	192.5	111.9
Standard deviation of Hadoop MPCT (time units)	9.3	18.8	34.7	4.9
Average of ECT MPCT (time units)	117.2	127.1	137.5	110.4
Standard deviation of ECT MPCT (time units)	7.0	10.8	8.8	5.1
ECT reduction in average MPCT	5.6%	15.3%	28.6%	1.4%
Average NBRP under Hadoop	321.5	314.4	306.2	—
Standard deviation of NBRP under Hadoop	99.4	97.4	96.4	—
Average NBRP under ECT	226.6	82.4	7.5	—
Standard deviation of NBRP under ECT	80.7	60.2	10.9	—
ECT reduction in average NBRP	29.5%	73.8%	97.5%	—

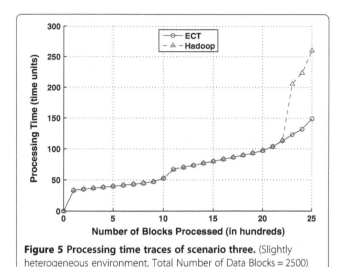

Figure 5 Processing time traces of scenario three. (Slightly heterogeneous environment, Total Number of Data Blocks = 2500)

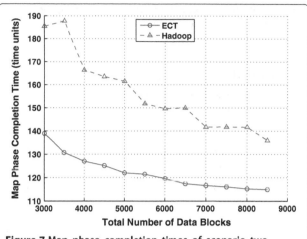

Figure 7 Map phase completion times of scenario two. (Highly heterogeneous environment)

each of the four scenarios, we ran the simulation with the total number of data blocks taking on values of 3000, 3500, 4000, … , 8500, which were slightly larger than the values in the slightly heterogeneous environment.

Figures 6, 7 and 8 present the MPCT's achieved by both schemes at different total numbers of data blocks in scenarios one, two and three, respectively. Simulation results of different total numbers of data blocks in scenarios one, two and three are shown in Tables 7, 8 and 9, respectively. (Only partial results are included due to length limitation. All results are the average of ten simulation runs.) The average results of ALL different total numbers of data blocks for each scenario is shown in Table 10, which indicate that the average MPCT achieved by ECT is 12.2%, 22.0% and 33.7% less than the one achieved by the Hadoop scheme, and the average NBRP under ECT is 11.4%, 31.4% and 53.7% less than the one under the Hadoop scheme in scenarios one, two and

three, respectively. Even in scenario four, where the remote fetching overhead is zero, the average MPCT achieved by ECT is still 7.0% less than the one achieved by the Hadoop scheme. The MPCT reduction in this case is solely attributed to the ECT rule, which can yield better results than the simple Hadoop strategy even when the slot processing speeds fluctuate over time. And, the stabler the slot processing speeds, the less the MPCT achieved by ECT is expected to be due to the optimality of the ECT rule.

When comparing the results in Table 10 with the ones in Table 6, we can see that both schemes assigned more data blocks to remote slots in the highly heterogeneous environment due to the increased heterogeneity. As a result, the average MPCT of the Hadoop scheme increases slightly in scenarios one, two and three, where there exists remote fetching overhead. There is no remote fetching overhead in scenario four, hence the faster slots would get assigned more remote blocks than they would

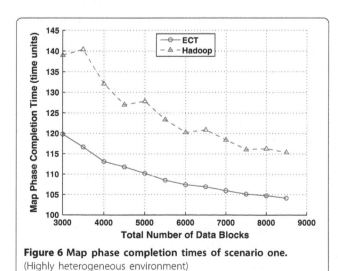

Figure 6 Map phase completion times of scenario one. (Highly heterogeneous environment)

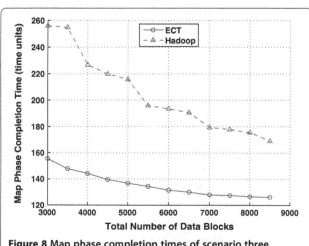

Figure 8 Map phase completion times of scenario three. (Highly heterogeneous environment)

Table 7 Simulation results of scenario one (Highly heterogeneous environment, low remote fetching overhead, and stable slot processing speeds)

RPC = 1.5	Total number of data blocks						
VPPT = ± 2.5%	3000	3500	4500	5500	6500	7500	8500
Number of blocks assigned according to the ECT rule	725.1	1225.5	2226.0	3224.3	4225.7	5227.8	6224.3
MPCT of Hadoop (time units)	139.0	140.4	127.0	123.3	120.9	116.1	115.3
MPCT of ECT (time units)	119.8	116.7	111.8	108.5	106.9	105.1	104.1
ECT reduction in MPCT	13.8%	16.9%	11.9%	12.0%	11.6%	9.4%	9.7%
NBRP under Hadoop	435.3	468.4	631.3	733.7	883.4	1030.4	1145.0
NBRP under ECT	394.0	459.0	558.3	664.0	780.4	879.2	993.6
ECT reduction in NBRP	9.5%	2.0%	11.6%	9.5%	11.7%	14.7%	13.2%

in the first three scenarios. In the ending stage of scenario four, most running slots would be those faster ones processing remote blocks. Since the faster slots in the highly heterogeneous environment are faster than the ones in the slightly heterogeneous environment due to the simulation settings, the average MPCT of the Hadoop scheme in the former is less. On the other hand, ECT achieves smaller MPCT's in all four scenarios in the highly heterogeneous environment than it does in the slightly heterogeneous environment. This is because, in the former, the slot base processing time t's are evenly distributed within a wider range compared with the latter, whereas the VPPT still takes on the same values in all four scenarios. As a result, the distinction of slot processing times in the former is larger. Consequently, the estimation error of slot processing time impairs the optimality of the ECT rule to a less extent when ECT projects and compares the completion times of different slots, which yields less MPCT's.

Simulation results of the highly heterogeneous environment confirm again that ECT is much more robust to network congestion (disk contention) than the Hadoop scheme. As shown in Table 10, when RPC increases from 1.5 to 4.0, the average NBRP under ECT drops sharply from 691.6 to 287.7 (a 58.4% decrease), and the average MPCT achieved by ECT rises from 109.5 to 135.6 time units (a 23.8% increase). In contrast, the average NBRP

under Hadoop only decreases from 780.6 to 621.8 (a 20.3% decrease), and the average MPCT achieved by Hadoop increases considerably from 124.7 to 204.5 time units (a 64.0% increase). The processing time traces of one typical case are shown in Figure 9, which exhibit the similar pattern as the ones in Figure 5 due to the same reason discussed in the previous section. Table 10 also includes the standard deviations of all simulation results in addition to the averages, which indicate again that the ECT results are more stable than the Hadoop results.

ECT limitations

The proposed ECT scheme has its limitations. First, the performance improvement of MPCT decreases when the total number of data blocks increases for the reason explained earlier. Secondly, the performance improvement of MPCT decreases when the remote fetching overhead decreases. As discussed earlier, after most task slots run out of local blocks, the Hadoop scheme will incur large amount of remote processing which accounts for most part of the MPCT performance difference between ECT and the Hadoop scheme. Therefore, when the remote fetching overhead decreases, the performance difference decreases as well. Finally, the performance improvement of NBRP decreases when the remote fetching overhead decreases. This is because ECT will assign more data blocks

Table 8 Simulation results of scenario two (Highly heterogeneous environment, medium remote fetching overhead, and relatively stable slot processing speeds)

RPC = 2.5	Total number of data blocks						
VPPT = ± 5%	3000	3500	4500	5500	6500	7500	8500
Number of blocks assigned according to the ECT rule	700.1	1199.5	2198.2	3200.3	4196.4	5200.1	6195.4
MPCT of Hadoop (time units)	185.4	187.8	163.5	151.8	149.9	141.8	135.9
MPCT of ECT (time units)	138.9	130.7	125.1	121.4	117.4	116.0	114.9
ECT reduction in MPCT	25.1%	30.4%	23.5%	20.0%	21.7%	18.2%	15.5%
NBRP under Hadoop	423.6	427.7	571.7	665.9	742.7	878.7	984.0
NBRP under ECT	241.2	273.3	378.4	455.3	527.5	625.1	699.8
ECT reduction in NBRP	43.1%	36.1%	33.8%	31.6%	29.0%	28.9%	28.9%

Table 9 Simulation results of scenario three (Highly heterogeneous environment, high remote fetching overhead, and less stable slot processing speeds)

RPC = 4.0 VPPT = ± 10%	Total number of data blocks						
	3000	3500	4500	5500	6500	7500	8500
Number of blocks assigned according to the ECT rule	645.2	1140.3	2138.2	3142.3	4140.6	5136.1	6139.9
MPCT of Hadoop (time units)	256.0	254.7	219.7	195.9	190.5	177.8	169.0
MPCT of ECT (time units)	155.5	147.8	139.5	134.2	129.9	127.4	125.9
ECT reduction in MPCT	39.3%	42.0%	36.5%	31.5%	31.8%	28.3%	25.5%
NBRP under Hadoop	417.9	418.9	536.8	607.6	672.7	758.4	845.8
NBRP under ECT	119.1	151.2	206.7	268.4	340.5	400.7	457.3
ECT reduction in NBRP	71.5%	63.9%	61.5%	55.8%	49.4%	47.2%	45.9%

to remote task slots when the remote fetching overhead decreases. Although the Hadoop scheme will do so as well, ECT is much more sensitive to the remote fetching overhead, and hence will assign more data blocks than the Hadoop scheme.

Related work

Dean et al. introduced the MapReduce programming model, implementation details, and various refinements in [2]. Their work served as the fundamental basis for the development of Hadoop, as well as all the following research on both MapReduce and Hadoop.

Jiang et al. presented a comprehensive performance study of Hadoop on Amazon EC2 in [12]. They identified certain design factors of Hadoop and discussed alternative methods for these factors. Their study indicated that the performance of Hadoop could be remarkably improved by tuning the design factors in a correct way. Lee et al. presented a comprehensive survey on MapReduce

in [13]. They discussed the merits and drawbacks of MapReduce, various improvement contributions in literature, and remaining open issues regarding parallel processing with MapReduce. Vijayalakshmi et al. introduced various implementations of MapReduce in [14] including Hadoop. They evaluated and compared the performance of different implementations. The insights and experimental results provided in the above papers are very helpful to the in-depth understanding of Hadoop as well as the further improvement on the framework.

Zaharia et al. [10] focused on the speculative execution mechanism of Hadoop to reduce the job completion time. They discussed all the Hadoop assumptions related to speculative execution, and explained why these assumptions broke down in the clouds. They suggested a new strategy of speculative execution, which always speculatively executed the task that was predicted to finish the farthest into the future. The strategy launched a speculative copy of any potential straggler tasks, before they

Table 10 Simulation results of highly heterogeneous environment

	Scenario			
	One	Two	Three	Four
RPC	1.5	2.5	4.0	1.0
VPPT	± 2.5%	± 5%	± 10%	± 2.5%
Average of Hadoop MPCT (time units)	124.7	156.4	204.5	108.1
Standard deviation of Hadoop MPCT (time units)	8.7	17.0	29.9	5.3
Average of ECT MPCT (time units)	109.5	122.1	135.6	100.5
Standard deviation of ECT MPCT (time units)	5.0	7.3	9.5	3.4
ECT reduction in average MPCT	12.2%	22.0%	33.7%	7.0%
Average NBRP under Hadoop	780.6	685.1	621.8	—
Standard deviation of NBRP under Hadoop	242.3	189.3	145.7	—
Average NBRP under ECT	691.6	469.7	287.7	—
Standard deviation of NBRP under ECT	195.4	151.6	113.1	—
ECT Reduction in Average NBRP	11.4%	31.4%	53.7%	—

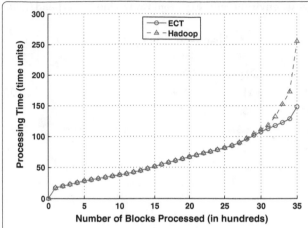

Figure 9 Processing time traces of scenario three. (Highly heterogeneous environment, Total Number of Data Blocks = 3500).

could actually prolong the completion of the whole MapReduce job at the expense of extra resource expenses. Whereas ECT works in a different way: it strives to minimize the completion time of each processing step of the map phase without any duplicated execution.

Pinedo discussed various deterministic scheduling models in the first part of [15], including the model of uniform parallel machines that was related to the map task assignment problem. Lawler et al. [16] pointed out that the problem of scheduling identical jobs on uniform parallel machines could be formulated as linear assignment problem and solved accordingly in polynomial time. Dessouky et al. [11] proposed a priority queue procedure for solving the same problem, which was an optimal and more efficient algorithm. The algorithm served as the basis of our improved task assignment scheme.

Conclusion

In this paper, we discussed the issues with the Hadoop task assignment scheme when Hadoop running in the clouds. We presented an improved scheme ECT based on an optimal algorithm for a related deterministic scheduling problem. We further conducted extensive simulation to evaluate the performance of ECT compared with the Hadoop scheme. The simulation results confirmed that ECT could significantly outperform the Hadoop scheme with respect to both the completion time of map phase and the amount of remote processing employed.

In future research, we plan to continue to address the map task assignment problem based on other related scheduling models. Also, we only focused on the task assignment aspect of Hadoop in this paper. We plan to address the job scheduling aspect, more specifically how to shorten the overall map phase completion time of multiple MapReduce jobs, which have different input data block sizes.

Competing interests
The authors declare that they have no competing interests.

Authors' contributions
The research presented in this paper is part of the Ph.D. dissertation of the first author under the supervision of the second author. The two authors read and approved the final manuscript.

Authors' information
Wei Dai received the Bachelor of Engineering degree in Computer Engineering in 1999 from Zhejiang University and the MS degree in Computer Engineering in 2009 from the University of Central Florida. He is currently a Ph.D. student in Computer Engineering at the University of Central Florida, Orlando. His research interests include cloud computing, data-intensive computing, and computer networks.
Mostafa Bassiouni received his BS and MS degrees in Computer Science from Alexandria University and received the Ph.D. degree in Computer Science from the Pennsylvania State University in 1982. He is currently a professor of Computer Science at the University of Central Florida, Orlando. His research interests include computer networks, distributed systems, real-time protocols and concurrency control. He has authored and coauthored over 190 papers published in various computer journals, book chapters and conference proceedings. His research has been supported by grants from ARO, ARPA, NSF, STRICOM, PM-TRADE, CBIS, Harris, and the State of Florida. He is an Associate Editor of the Computer Journal- Oxford University Press, Editor-in-Chief of Electronics-MDPI, and an Editorial Board Member of four other journals. He has served as member of the program committee of several conferences, as the program committee chair of CSMA'98 and CSMA'2000 and as the guest co-editor of a special issue of the Journal of Simulation Practice and Theory, 2002.

References
1. Gantz JF, Chute C, Manfrediz A, Minton S, Reinsel D, Schlichting W, Toncheva A (2008) The Diverse and Exploding Digital Universe: An updated forecast of worldwide information growth through 2011. IDC White Paper – sponsored by EMC, Framingham, MA, USA
2. Dean J, Ghemawat S (2004) MapReduce: Simplified Data Processing on Large Clusters. Proceedings of the 6th conference on Symposium on Operating Systems Design & Implementation, Berkeley, CA, USA
3. Official Apache Hadoop Website. http://hadoop.apache.org. Accessed 30 Sep 2013
4. Hadoop Wiki. http://wiki.apache.org/hadoop/PoweredBy. Accessed 30 Sep 2013
5. Wikipedia: Apache Hadoop. http://en.wikipedia.org/wiki/Hadoop. Accessed 30 Sep 2013
6. Amazon Elastic Compute Cloud (EC2). http://aws.amazon.com/ec2/. Accessed 30 Sep 2013
7. Gottfrid D (2007) Self-service, prorated supercomputing fun. http://open. blogs.nytimes.com/2007/11/01/self-service-prorated-super-computing-fun/. Accessed 30 Sep 2013
8. White T (2012) Hadoop: The Definitive Guide, 3rd edition. O'Reilly Media, Sebastopol, CA, USA
9. Lin J, Dyer C (2010) Data-Intensive Text Processing with MapReduce. Morgan and Claypool Publishers, San Rafael, CA, USA
10. Zaharia M, Konwinski A, Joseph A, Katz R, Stoica I (2008) Improving MapReduce Performance in Heterogeneous Environments. Proceedings of the 8th USENIX conference on Operating Systems Design and Implementation, Berkeley, CA, USA, pp 29–42
11. Dessouky M, Lageweg B, Lenstra J, van de Velde S (1990) Scheduling identical jobs on uniform parallel machines. Statistica Neerlandica 44:115–123
12. Jiang D, Ooi BC, Shi L, Wu S (2010) The performance of MapReduce: an in-depth study. Proc VLDB Endowment 3(1–2):472–483
13. Lee K, Lee Y, Choi H, Chung YD, Moon B (2011) Parallel data processing with MapReduce: a survey. ACM SIGMOD Rec 40(4):11–20
14. Vijayalakshmi V, Akila A, Nagadivya S (2012) The Survey on MapReduce. Int J Eng Sci Technol 4:07

15. Pinedo M (2012) Scheduling: Theory, Algorithms, and Systems. Springer, New York, NY, USA

16. Lawler E, Lenstra J, Rinnooy Kan A (1982) Recent Developments in Deterministic Sequencing and Scheduling. Deterministic and Stochastic Scheduling. Springer Netherlands, Dordrecht, Netherlands, pp 35–73

9

Genetic-based algorithms for resource management in virtualized IVR applications

Nadjia Kara[1*], Mbarka Soualhia[1], Fatna Belqasmi[2], Christian Azar[2] and Roch Glitho[2]

Abstract

Interactive Voice Response (IVR) is a technology that allows automatic human-computer interactions, via a telephone keypad or voice commands. The systems are widely used in many industries, including telecommunications and banking. Virtualization is a potential technology that can enable the easy development of IVR applications and their deployment on the cloud. IVR virtualization will enable efficient resource usage by allowing IVR applications to share different IVR substrate components such as the key detector, the voice recorder and the dialog manager. Resource management is part and parcel of IVR virtualization and poses a challenge in virtualized environments where both processing and network constraints must be considered. Considering several objectives to optimize the resource usage makes it even more challenging. This paper proposes IVR virtualization task scheduling and computational resource sharing (among different IVR applications) strategies based on genetic algorithms, in which different objectives are optimized. The algorithms used by both strategies are simulated and the performance measured and analyzed.

Keywords: Resource management; Cloud computing; Virtualization; IVR applications; Genetic algorithms

Introduction

Interactive Voice Response (IVR) is a technology that allows automatic human-computer interactions, via a telephone keypad or voice commands. Its key function is to provide end-users with self-service voice information [1]. IVR systems are widely used in many industries, including telecommunications and banking, to improve customer satisfaction, reduce cost, and ensure uninterrupted service. Examples of IVR applications include automated attendants, automated meter readers and IVR banking. The automated attendant transfers callers to the appropriate extensions automatically, without intervention by a receptionist; using automated meter readers, utilities customers can remotely enter their meter readings, while IVR banking allows end-users to consult their bank balance or last transactions, for instance.

Virtualization is a potential technology that can enable the easy development of IVR applications and their deployment on the cloud. It allows the abstraction and sharing of computer and network resources, as well as

the co-existence of entities on the same substrates [2]. Cloud computing is a multi-facet paradigm, which enables the easy introduction of new services, scalability and efficient resource usage. The main facets of cloud computing are Infrastructure as a Service (IaaS), Platform as a Service (PaaS), and Software as a Service (SaaS) [3]. IaaS provides the pool of virtualized resources that are used by applications provisioned (to end-users or other applications) as SaaS. The development and management of such applications are made easier through PaaS which adds one or more levels of abstraction to the infrastructures offered by IaaS providers.

IVR virtualization will enable efficient resource usage by allowing IVR applications to share different IVR substrate components such as key detectors, voice recorders and dialog managers. It will also ease the development and the management of IVR applications that can be offered as cloud-based services.

In a previous work [4,5], we proposed a virtualized infrastructure for IVR applications in the cloud. The proposed architecture is composed of three layers (substrate, infrastructure, and platform) and an IVR substrate repository (Figure 1). The substrate layer provides IVR substrates that can be composed and assembled on the fly to build IVR applications. These substrates are accessible via the

* Correspondence: Nadjia.kara@etsmtl.ca
[1]ETS, University of Quebec, 1100, Notre-Dame street West, Montreal, Quebec H3C 1K3, Canada
Full list of author information is available at the end of the article

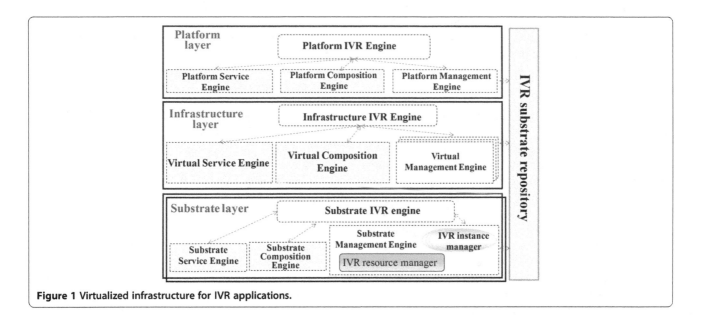

Figure 1 Virtualized infrastructure for IVR applications.

infrastructure layer. The platform layer for its part adds one or more abstractions and makes the substrates available to the IVR applications' developers while the IVR substrate repository is used to publish and discover existing IVR substrates.

The three layers communicate via three planes: service, composition and management. The service plane handles the service execution, including coordinating the execution of services that involve several substrates; the composition plane intervenes in the composition of the appropriate substrates to create a given IVR application and the management plane is responsible for the actual control and management of substrate resources. It allows the instantiation of IVR applications and related substrates, enables fault and performance monitoring, and performs accounting for charging purposes. Each layer includes one functional entity at each plane, and one key entity that coordinates the operation of the layer entities at the three planes. At the substrate layer for instance we have a substrate service, composition and management engines that are coordinated by the substrate IVR engine.

This paper focuses on the management plane, and more precisely on resource management at the substrate layer. Before a service provider can make an IVR application available to its end-users, he should develop such an application by discovering and (eventually) composing existing substrates. It then activates the application, a phase which includes the instantiation of the substrates required to run the application. It is only after this that the end-users can interact with the application.

To instantiate new substrates, the substrate management engine should identify the resources needed, verify resource availability and then allocate the appropriate resources. We

focus on two issues: computational resources sharing and task scheduling. In computational resource sharing, we examine the sharing of existing computational resources (e.g., virtual machines, processors) between different IVR applications optimally. Task sch\eduling relates to the assignment of the instantiation requests received.

Computational resource sharing and task scheduling in virtualized environments where both processing and network constraints must be considered are challenging issues. Considering several objectives to optimize the resource scheduling and usage makes them even more challenging.

Several research studies have focused on load balancing across processors or computers in both non-virtualized [6] and virtualized environments [7]. This paper proposes to address these issues for a specific application: IVR. It defines task scheduling and computational resource sharing strategies based on genetic algorithms, in which different objectives are optimized. We chose genetic algorithms because their robustness and efficiency for the design of efficient schedulers have been largely proven in the literature [8,9]. More specifically, we identify task assignments that guarantee maximum utilization of resources while minimizing the execution time of tasks. Moreover, we propose a resource allocation strategy that minimizes substrate resource utilization and the resource allocation time. We also simulated the algorithms used by the proposed strategies and measured and analyzed their performance.

The rest of the paper is organized as follows. Section "Assumptions and problems statement" presents the assumptions and the problem statement. Section "Resource management algorithms" discusses the proposed resource management algorithms. Sections "Computational resource sharing algorithm" and "Task scheduling" describe the computational resource sharing and instantiation request scheduling algorithms respectively. Section "Performance results and analysis" presents the main performance analysis. The state of the art review and the conclusion are given in sections "State of the art review" and "Conclusion" respectively.

Assumptions and problems statement

Assumptions

The substrate management engine (Figure 1) has two entities: the IVR resource manager and the IVR instance manager. The resource manager maintains and monitors the current state of resources and allocates resources for new IVR service substrates (ISSs). An ISS is the set of IVR substrate instances used by a single IVR application. Each ISS is managed by a separate IVR instance manager, which coordinates the process of ISS instantiation (i.e., ISS creation, configuration and activation).

We assume that each virtualization machine (i.e. a machine that hosts the substrate layer) has a fixed number of processors that are dedicated to the processing of the incoming instantiation requests, and a fixed amount of computational resources (e.g. virtual machines, processors, CPU, memory, disk space) that are used to run the different ISSs. The computational resources are shared among a set of ISSs, each having specific resource requirements evaluated in terms of CPU, memory, disk space and bandwidth. We assume that the virtualization machine capabilities are known in advance, while the ISSs' resource requirements are estimated at run time. In our case, the latter are estimated using a set of functions derived from observed measurements performed using a prototype of a virtualized infrastructure for IVR applications in the cloud [4].

When a resource manager receives an instantiation request, it verifies the availability of the substrate resources according to the ISS requirements. It then creates a new ISS and allocates the necessary resources. If no more substrate resources are available, the resource manager will reject all incoming instantiation requests.

We further assume that the service quality parameters required by each ISS are described by the IVR application provider using a service level agreement (SLA). In this work, we only consider as one SLA parameter; i.e. the satisfactory factor of the IVR application. This satisfactory factor is defined as the resources employed by a certain number of users over the allocated ISS resources. This parameter allows the control of the application status, such as ensuring that no ISS is under or over loaded and therefore guarantees pay-as-you-use access. To guarantee this quality parameter, the instantiation requests should specify the expected number of users as well as the users' arrival rate.

The IVR substrate management engine also allows the resizing of computing and network capacities, using the monitored ISS resource usage. If an ISS is over or under loaded for a certain interval of time, the resource control entity will notify the resource negotiation entity and the ISS computing and network resources are resized. The resource control and negotiation entities are out of the scope of this paper.

Problem statement

In this paper, the following notations are used:

- N is the expected number of users for a given IVR application.
- λ is the expected call arrival rate for an ISS. We should mention that λ is used in this paper only to determine the resources needed by an ISS, depending on the number of request/min that it is expected to support.
- t_n is the size in unit of time for the execution of a given instantiation request (task size). It is the time needed to instantiate, configure, and activate a new ISS.
- t_r is the time needed to compute the required resources for a given instantiation request. It is the time difference between the end of resource computation for task j and the arrival time of task j in processor queue.
- t_v is the time needed for the creation, configuration and activation of the appropriate virtual machine that will host a given ISS ($t_n = t_v + t_r$).
- m is the number of processors that can be used to handle the instantiation requests.
- (CPU_r, M_r, B_r, D_r) represents the required resources for a given ISS, in terms of CPU, memory, bandwidth and disk space, respectively.
- (CPU_c, M_c, B_c, D_c) represents the available capacities (i.e., the capabilities of the virtualization machine), in terms of CPU, memory, bandwidth and disk space, respectively.
- (τ_{cpu}, τ_M, τ_B, τ_D) represent the percentage of resource usage for a given ISS:

    ○ τ_{cpu} is the ratio of CPU_r over CPU_c.
    ○ τ_M is the ratio of M_r over M_c.
    ○ τ_B is the ratio of B_r over B_c.
    ○ τ_D is the ratio D_r over D_c.

Our objective is to propose two algorithms: computational resource sharing and task scheduling. These algorithms will be used by the IVR instance manager and the substrate IVR engine, respectively. The computational resource sharing algorithm should allow the selection of the required resources (CPU_r, M_r, B_r, D_r) for each ISS, while minimizing the amount of resources used as well as the resource allocation time, and maximizing the satisfactory factor of the ISS using a specific amount of resources. The task scheduling algorithm should minimize the execution time for the instantiation requests (i.e., t_n), by sharing the instantiation requests among the available processors as equally as possible. No processor should be underused while others are overloaded.

Both algorithms are executed during the ISS instantiation, meaning before the IVR application is ready to receive end-users' requests. The task scheduling is first performed by the substrate IVR engine to assign the set of instantiation tasks to a given number of processors, and then each processor will run the computational resource sharing algorithm to select the resources that should be assigned to each ISS to be created. These two algorithms are described in the next section.

Resource management algorithms

Our computational resource sharing and task scheduling algorithms are based on Genetic Algorithm (GA) [10]. In GA, a population of strings randomly generated from a set of potential solutions (represented by chromosomes) is used to create new populations, based on the fitness of each individual in the population and by applying different GA operators, such as selection, crossover and mutation. The algorithm ends when a targeted fitness level is reached for the population.

In this paper, GA is used to optimize 1) the computational resource sharing, and 2) the assignment of instantiation requests to different processors provided by the virtualization machine. For each algorithm, a specific fitness function and specific GA operators are used. In the computational resource sharing algorithm, a population is represented by the resources required by each ISS to instantiate. This population is of limited size (e.g., CPU, memory, bandwidth, disk space). In the task scheduling algorithm, a population is represented by the instantiation requests. The size of the population depends on the number of instantiation requests received by the substrate provider.

We first discuss the computational resource sharing, followed by the task scheduling.

Computational resource sharing algorithm

Each processor performs resource computation for the instantiation request that is assigned to it. As a first step in the definition of the computational resource sharing algorithm for IVR applications, we performed a set of experimental measurements to quantify the resources used by a given number of ISSs. This was done using the prototype from our previous work [4]. The measurements were then used as input to define the load measurement mathematical models and the resource computation algorithm to calculate the required resources for each instantiation request since we don't have access to real arrival rate data from IVR providers. We also defined a resource computation fitness function.

Load measurement

Load measurement allows the quantification of the ISS resource usage according to the number of users accessing the ISS. It is performed to identify the required resources (CPU_r, M_r, B_r, D_r) for each ISS. The measurements were executed on a system providing a set of ISSs, and that had the following capacity: $CPU_c = 1$ GHz, $M_c = 512$ MB, $D_c = 20$ GB and $B_c = 1$ Gbps bit rate. Knowing the system capacity, we measured the used resources (CPU_r, M_r, B_r, D_r) according to different call arrival rates. The results are given in Figures 2, 3, 4 and 5. From these observed data, we derived the functional models that fit these data and that describe the relationship between the number of users and the usage of each resource CPU, BW, Memory and Disk space. We started from the models given in Equation (1) where y_{CPU}, y_M, y_B and y_D are respectively the CPU, memory, bandwidth, and disk space consumption in percentage according to the call arrival rate (here the variable λ). We propose to use a linear regression to model CPU, Memory, disk space and Bandwidth.

$$\begin{cases} y_{CPU,M,D} = a_1\lambda^5 + a_2\lambda^4 + a_3\lambda^3 + a_4\lambda^2 + a_5\lambda + a_6 \\ y_B = a_1\lambda^4 + a_2\lambda^3 + a_3\lambda^2 + a_4\lambda + a_5 \end{cases}$$

$$(1)$$

For each model, we computed the R-square (coefficient of determination R_s^2) to assess the accuracy of the model and how well it fits the measured data. The closer the value of R_s^2 is to 1, the better the linear regression models the data. This led to the identification of the functional parameters a_i, $i = \{1,2,3,...,6\}$ presented in Equation (2).

$$\begin{cases} y_{CPU} \begin{cases} a_1 = 85 \times 10^{-14}, a_2 = -25.26 \times 10^{-10}, \\ a_3 = 28.91 \times 10^{-7}, a_4 = -14.48 \times 10^{-4}, \\ a_5 = 34.69 \times 10^{-2}, a_6 = 8.38 \\ R_s^2 = 0.9964 \end{cases} \\ y_M \begin{cases} a_1 = 13.30 \times 10^{-14}, a_2 = -361.93 \times 10^{-12}, \\ a_3 = 3670.03 \times 10^{-10}, a_4 = -17367.23 \times 10^{-8}, \\ a_5 = 489.26 \times 10^{-4}, a_6 = 12.21 \\ R_s^2 = 0.9958 \end{cases} \\ y_D \begin{cases} a_1 = -0.10 \times 10^{-14}, a_2 = 3.08 \times 10^{-12}, \\ a_3 = -19.10 \times 10^{-10}, a_4 = 8.14 \times 10^{-8}, \\ a_5 = 3.04 \times 10^{-4}, a_6 = 0.07 \\ R_s^2 = 0.9965 \end{cases} \\ y_B \begin{cases} a_1 = 16.92 \times 10^{-12}, a_2 = 73.49 \times 10^{-10}, \\ a_3 = -48.85 \times 10^{-6}, a_4 = 4.82 \times 10^{-2}, \\ a_5 = 11.75 \\ R_s^2 = 0.9843 \end{cases} \end{cases}$$

$$(2)$$

Resource computation

Resource computation allows the computation of the resources to be allocated for each ISS, in terms of CPU,

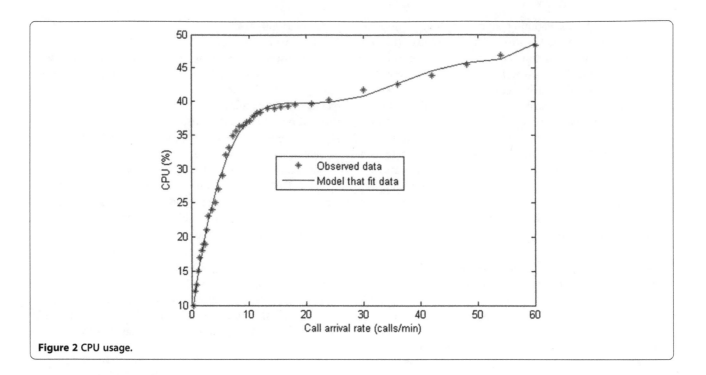

Figure 2 CPU usage.

memory, bandwidth, and disc space. It is performed using a GA-based method with the sliding window technique where two dimensional strings are used to represent the resource computation for each task in each processor.

Two dimensional strings are used to represent the resource computation for each task in each processor. One string identifies the resource combination types provided by the virtualization machine and the second identifies the required resources for each task. A resource combination type represents a possible configuration of a virtual machine that could be created by the virtualization machine. These resources can be selected separately to configure a virtual machine that will host an ISS.

In Figure 6, the resource string R_1 for instance refers to an assignment of (CPU = 1 GHz, M = 256 MB, B = 0.250

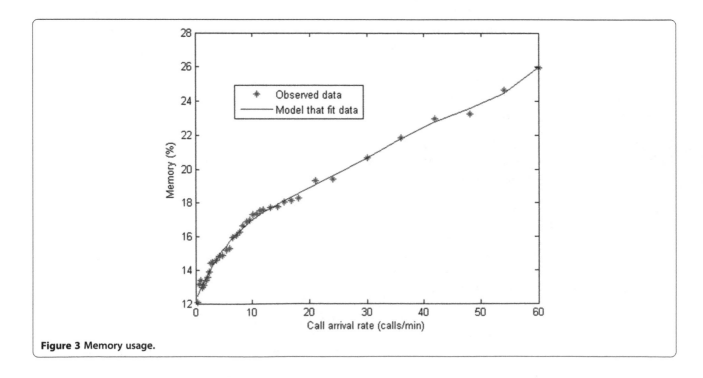

Figure 3 Memory usage.

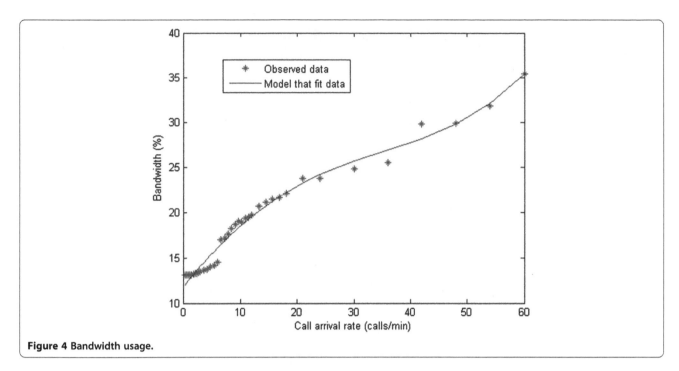

Figure 4 Bandwidth usage.

Gbps, D = 1 GB), as defined in Table 1. These are discrete values as offered by the substrate provider. A substrate provider may for instance allow to only reserving 256 MB and its multiples in terms of memory.

Figure 6 shows an example of two-dimensional strings, where each resource in the second string is identified by the resource values C_i^j , where i is the type of resource (CPU (1), memory (2), bandwidth (3) or disk space (4) and j is the resources allocated to the instantiation request. The resources to be allocated to each instantiation request

are identified using the resource computation selection, crossover and mutation methods described in section 5.4.

Two main objectives are defined and used by the resource computation fitness function. The first objective is to maximize the satisfactory factor of each ISS (τ_{cpu}, τ_M, τ_B, τ_D). These values are given by Equation (3). These satisfactory factors are used as fitness functions for the GA resource computation algorithm. The closer the satisfactory factors are to 1, the better the resource usage. If the satisfactory factors are less than 0.75 or greater than 1, the

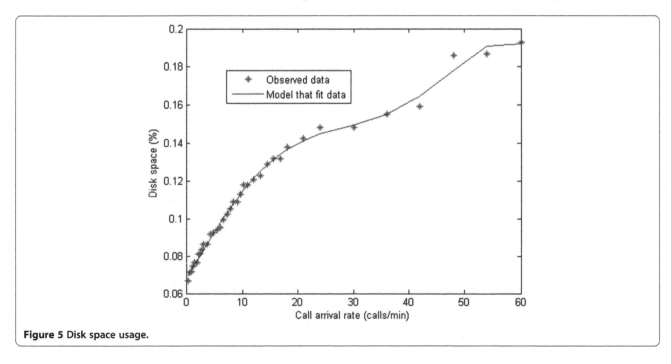

Figure 5 Disk space usage.

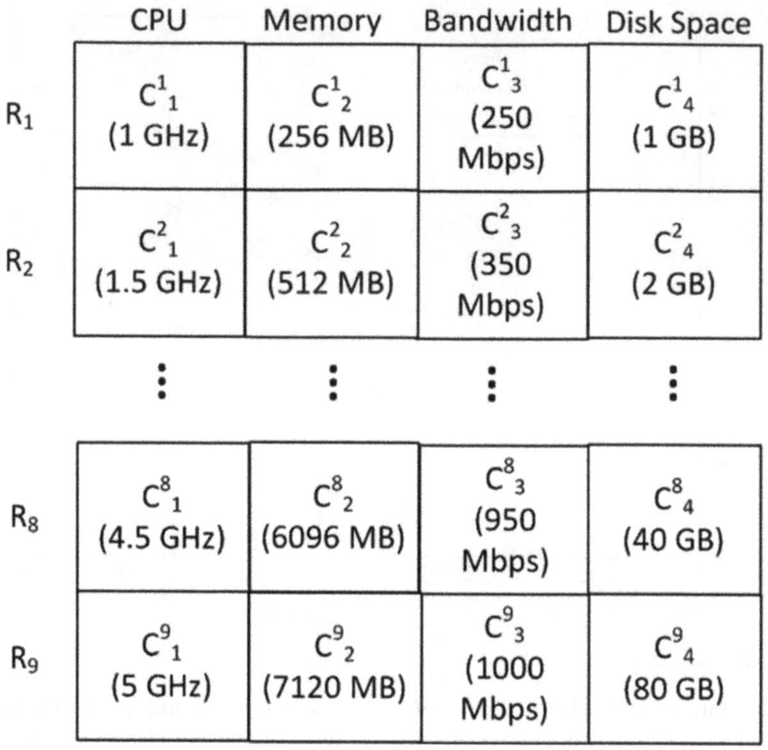

	CPU	Memory	Bandwidth	Disk Space
R_1	C^1_1 (1 GHz)	C^1_2 (256 MB)	C^1_3 (250 Mbps)	C^1_4 (1 GB)
R_2	C^2_1 (1.5 GHz)	C^2_2 (512 MB)	C^2_3 (350 Mbps)	C^2_4 (2 GB)
⋮	⋮	⋮	⋮	⋮
R_8	C^8_1 (4.5 GHz)	C^8_2 (6096 MB)	C^8_3 (950 Mbps)	C^8_4 (40 GB)
R_9	C^9_1 (5 GHz)	C^9_2 (7120 MB)	C^9_3 (1000 Mbps)	C^9_4 (80 GB)

Figure 6 Resource sharing.

resource is under or over loaded, respectively. The second objective is to minimize the time t_r to compute the resources to be allocated. The resource computation selection, crossover and mutation method proposed in section 5.4 satisfies this objective.

$$\tau_{cpu} = \frac{y_{cpu}}{C^j_1}, j = 1, ..., m$$
$$\tau_M = \frac{y_M}{C^j_2}, j = 1, ..., m$$
$$\tau_B = \frac{y_B}{C^j_3}, j = 1, ..., m \qquad (3)$$
$$\tau_D = \frac{y_D}{C^j_4}, j = 1, ..., m$$

Table 1 Example of resource combination types

Type	Capacity			
	CPU (GHz)	RAM (MB)	BW (Gbps)	Disk space (GB)
1	1	256	0.250	1
2	1.5	512	0.350	2
3	2	1024	0.450	4
4	2.5	2048	0.550	8
5	3	3072	0.650	10
6	3.5	4096	0.750	20
7	4	5072	0.850	30
8	4.5	6096	0.950	40
9	5	7120	1.000	80

Resource computation crossover and mutation

The selection of strings in a population is based on the models given in Equations (1–2). Knowing the expected call arrival rate λ for each ISS, the required resources for each task are estimated using these models. For instance, if the call arrival rate for a given ISS is $\lambda = 30$ requests/min, then the expected resource usage is:

$$y_{CPU} = 49.89\% \times 1\,GHz = 0.4989\,GHz$$
$$y_M = 20.6659\% \times 512\,MB = 105.8094\,MB$$
$$y_B = 25.31\% \times 1\,Gbps = 0.2531\,Gbps$$
$$y_D = 0.1629\% \times 20\,GB = 0.0326\,GB$$

$$(4)$$

The expected resource usage levels for small IVR systems are given in Table 2 (for small-size IVR system, $\lambda \leq 60$ requests/min). From these expected resource usage levels we derive the resources to be allocated for each instantiation request by selecting the appropriate strings in the population described in Figure 6. For instance, an instantiation request with $\lambda = 60$ requests/min requires 1.22 GHZ of CPU, 130.74 MB of memory, 0.35 Gbps of bandwidth and 0.12 GB of disk space. For this request, the string with the closest values is selected (i.e., R_1 CPU, memory, bandwidth and disk space values). We compute the fitness values using Equation (3). We find $\tau_{CPU} = 1.222$, $\tau_M = 0.51$, $\tau_B = 1.4$ and $\tau_D = 0.12$. The values of the allocated

Table 2 Required resources according to the call arrival rate

λ requests/min	Required resources			
	y_{CPU} (GHz)	y_M (MB)	y_B (Gbps)	y_D (GB)
15	0.41	92.35	0.21	0.02
30	0.50	105.81	0.26	0.03
45	0.76	118.17	0.27	0.05
54	0.99	123.80	0.32	0.08
60	1.22	130.74	0.35	0.12

resources should be reduced for fitness values less than 0.75 and increased for a satisfactory factor greater than 1. Therefore, the CPU and bandwidth values of string R_1 (1 GHz and 0.250 Gbps) are swapped with that of string R_2 (1.5 GHz and 0.35 Gbps) respectively. The memory and disk space of string R_1 remain unchanged because the allocated resources are the smallest values provided by the IVR substrate. The population derived from this mutation process will have a satisfactory factors τ_{CPU} = 0.81 and τ_B = 1. This new population will be selected to represent the resources to allocate to the received instantiation request that guarantee the best resource usage according to the resource combination types provided by the ISS substrate.

As a second example, let's consider the case of an instantiation request where λ = 160. This request requires 3.6 GHZ of CPU, 420 MB of memory, 1.05 Gbps of bandwidth and 0.3 GB of disk space. For this request, a virtual machine with resource type R6 will be selected to host the new ISS. The memory, bandwidth and disk space of string R_6 are swapped with that of strings R_2 (512 MB), R_9 (1 Gbps) and R_1 (1 GB) respectively, with satisfactory factors $\tau_{CPU} \cong 1$, τ_M = 0.82, $\tau_B \cong 1$ and τ_D = 0.3.

Task scheduling

The substrate IVR engine receives a set of instantiation tasks that should be assigned to a number of processors. We propose to adapt the task scheduling algorithm proposed in [6] for this purpose. Therefore, we propose to use a GA-based method to perform load balancing and a sliding window technique to initialize a population of tasks on which the GA will be applied [6]. This new algorithm is called ISI GA (Instantiation request scheduling for IVR based on GA). At each time, the tasks that are within the window are reordered using the GA selection, crossover and mutation methods described in Section Task representation selection, crossover and mutation and then assigned to the processors for execution. The window is dragged to the next group, for a repeat of the assignment process, when the tasks within the window are placed in processor queues [11]. We first introduce how the set of available processors and tasks are represented; we then describe our task scheduling fitness function, and end with the task scheduling algorithm.

Processor and task representation

The scheduling for parallel processors is represented by two-dimensional strings. One string identifies the processors and the other represents the scheduled tasks in each processor queue [11]. We identify each task with its task size $t_n = t_v + t_r$ in unit of time, preceded by the number n of tasks to be scheduled in the system (e.g. $2(t_v + t_r)$). For the example presented in Figure 7a, the processors' string will include the list of available processors. To perform the GA algorithm, the strings are converted from two-dimensional to one as shown in Figure 7b.

From the experimental measurements we carried out using the implemented prototype and 8 processors, we noticed that the t_v value is the same for all ISSs. However, the t_r differs from one ISS to another. This is one of the differences between the original scheduling and the adapted algorithms. In the original algorithm (proposed in [6] and [11]), the t_n value for each individual in a GA population is supposed to be known in advance and is the same for each individual in the population. For the ISS instantiation scheduling, the t_v is known in advance but t_r should be computed using our proposed computational resource sharing algorithm. This may result in a different t_n value for each individual in the same population.

Task representation fitness function

The fitness function allows the evaluation of the task scheduling performance according to specific objectives. The main goal here is to identify task assignments that guarantee maximum processors utilization, to balance the traffic load across processors and to guarantee minimum execution time of tasks.

In [6], the following objectives apply: 1) a minimization of the largest task completion time (i.e., Maxspan) across processors to guarantee that assignment tasks will be executed in the shortest time possible [8]; 2) increase of the average processor utilization based on the Maxspan value, and 3) optimization of the number of tasks in each processor queue, in order to ensure proper load balancing across the processors.

We propose to combine the first and the second objectives by defining the TaskSpan as the difference between the largest task completion time and the smallest task completion time among all the processors in the system. The TaskSpan is calculated as in Equation (5), where n is the number of tasks in each processor queue.

$$TaskSpan = \max_{i=1,\dots,m}\left(\sum_{j=1}^{n}(t_v + t_{rj})\right) - \min_{i=1,\dots,m}\left(\sum_{j=1}^{n}(t_v + t_{rj})\right)$$

(5)

In the example given in Figure 8, we assume that t_v is equal to 6 units of time and the times t_r to compute the

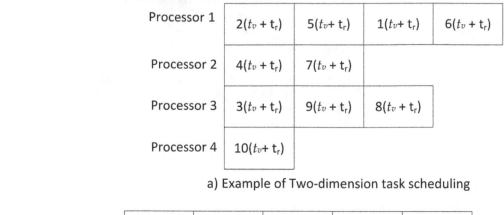

a) Example of Two-dimension task scheduling

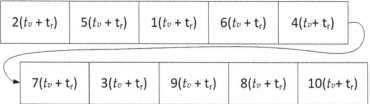

b) Example of one dimension task scheduling

Figure 7 Task scheduling: **(a)** two-dimensional task scheduling strings: one identifying the processors and the other the scheduled tasks. **(b)** Conversion of two-dimensional task scheduling strings into one dimensional string.

required resources for tasks 1 to 10 are respectively 4, 3, 8, 9, 8, 5, 7, 10, 8 and 12.

Then, the processor 1 will execute tasks 2, 5, 1 and 6 within 44 units of time. Tasks 4 and 7 will be executed on processor 2 within 28 units of time, while tasks 3, 9, 8 and 10 will be executed within 44 and 18 units of time, respectively. Therefore, the TaskSpan for this task schedule example is 26 (Equation (6)).

$$TaskSpan = \max_{i=1,\dots,4}(44, 28, 44, 18) - \min_{i=1,\dots,4}(44, 28, 44, 18) = 26$$

(6)

We propose to use the difference between the largest and the smallest task completion times rather than the MaxSpan value (as used in [6] and [8]) because guaranteeing a minimum TaskSpan value not only ensures a shorter task completion time but also a proper load balancing between all processors.

The second objective that we propose to define is the average processor utilization value. In [6], this value is the sum of all processor utilization levels by the total number of processors. Each processor utilization is calculated by dividing the task completion time by the MaxSpan value. The higher the average processor utilization, the better is the load balancing across the processors [6]. However, this objective does not guarantee that the load is well balanced across processors. We propose to define a

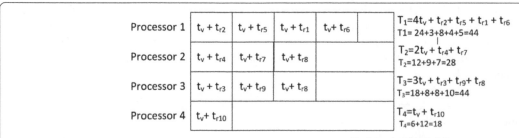

Figure 8 TaskSpan.

utilization factor U of all processors as the product of all processor utilizations.

$$U = \prod_{i=1}^{m} \left(\frac{\sum_{j=1}^{n}(t_v + t_{rj})}{MaxSpan} \right) \quad (7)$$

Using the example given in Figure 8, this will lead to:

$$\begin{cases} P_1 : \dfrac{\sum_{j=1}^{n}(t_v + t_{rj})}{MaxSpan} = \dfrac{24+3+8+4+5}{44} = \dfrac{44}{44} = 1 \\[3mm] P_2 : \dfrac{\sum_{j=1}^{n}(t_v + t_{rj})}{MaxSpan} = \dfrac{12+9+7}{44} = \dfrac{28}{44} = 0.64 \\[3mm] P_3 : \dfrac{\sum_{j=1}^{n}(t_v + t_{rj})}{MaxSpan} = \dfrac{18+8+8+10}{44} = \dfrac{44}{44} = 1 \\[3mm] P_4 : \dfrac{\sum_{j=1}^{n}(t_v + t_{rj})}{MaxSpan} = \dfrac{6+12}{44} = \dfrac{18}{44} = 0.41 \end{cases} \quad (8)$$

Therefore, the U for this task schedule will be 0.26 and the average utilization value as defined in [6] will be 0.76. If we assign task 6 to processor 4 rather than to processor 1 in order to better balance the load in term of task completion time, this lead to:

$$\begin{cases} P_1 : \dfrac{\sum_{j=1}^{n}(t_v + t_{rj})}{MaxSpan} = \dfrac{18+3+8+4}{44} = \dfrac{33}{44} = 0.75 \\[3mm] P_2 : \dfrac{\sum_{j=1}^{n}(t_v + t_{rj})}{MaxSpan} = \dfrac{12+9+7}{44} = \dfrac{28}{44} = 0.64 \\[3mm] P_3 : \dfrac{\sum_{j=1}^{n}(t_v + t_{rj})}{MaxSpan} = \dfrac{18+8+8+10}{44} = \dfrac{44}{44} = 1 \\[3mm] P_4 : \dfrac{\sum_{j=1}^{n}(t_v + t_{rj})}{MaxSpan} = \dfrac{12+12+5}{44} = \dfrac{29}{44} = 0.66 \end{cases} \quad (9)$$

The utilization factor is then equal to 0.31, but the average utilization value as defined in [6] will remain unchanged 0.76. Therefore, the greater the utilization factor, the better the load balancing.

TaskSpan and utilization factor U are the two main objectives used by the fitness function of the GA task scheduling algorithm we propose. This function is defined as follow:

$$f = \frac{U}{TaskSpan} \quad (10)$$

The higher the fitness function, the better is the task scheduling. The single objective function f derived from this multi-criterion optimization problem reduces the problem's complexity while satisfying the multiple objectives predefined. Using a single objective function also helps in meeting our requirement on minimizing the execution time for the instantiation requests, as multi-objective functions are known to require a longer processing time.

Task representation selection, crossover and mutation
We propose to reuse the selection, the crossover and the mutation methods described in [6]. The selection operator is based on the roulette wheel method [10]. In this method, the selection of strings in a population is based on their fitness values. These values are used to assign a probability of being selected to each string. These probabilities are computed by dividing the fitness of each string by the sum of the fitness values of the current set of strings in the population. The slots of the roulette wheel are created by adding the probability of the current string to the probability of the previous string. The probabilities are then assigned until the value of 1 is reached. Then, the strings are selected randomly by generating a random number between 0 and 1. To perform the crossover operation, the selected strings are then converted from two dimensions to one. We use this two dimensions string to balance the number of tasks across the processors. For instance, for 12 tasks and 8 processors, this procedure ensures that each processor will have at least one task, and no more than 2 tasks. Hence, 8 tasks are allocated to 8 processors and 4 tasks are randomly assigned to 4 processors. This will allow the GA to converge for a fixed number of generation cycles.

The crossover operator is based on the cycle crossover method [6]. In this case, two one dimension strings S_1 and S_2 are selected. The crossover operation begins by selecting a random starting point between *1* and the length of the strings S_1 and S_2. Let us assume that this starting point is $S_{1,n}$ which denotes the task at the position *n* in string *1*. This task is marked as finished, and its corresponding task at $S_{2,n}$ is then also marked off as finished. The task in S_1 position is the value of $S_{2,n}$ is marked as finished and its corresponding task in S_2 is then marked off as finished as well. This process ends when the starting point $S_{1,n}$ is reached once again. Then, the remaining tasks $S_{1,n}$ that were not marked off are swapped with their corresponding tasks in S_2 (e.g., $S_{1,4}$ is swapped with $S_{2,4}$). When all tasks in the two strings are crossed over, they are reordered and converted to a two-dimensional form to compute their new fitness values.

The third GA operator is based on swap mutation. It randomly selects and then swaps two tasks. Each task is taken on randomly selected processors which should be different in order to ensure that the two selected tasks are not the same. New fitness values are then computed using the population derived from this swapping mutation process.

Performance results and analysis

For the computational resource sharing algorithm, we propose to compare the required resources (CPU_r, M_r, B_r, D_r) with the allocated ones. The required resources are estimated based on Equations (1–2), whereas the allocated ones are estimated using the proposed GA computational resource sharing algorithm. The comparison will allow us to see if the example of resource combination types given in Table 2 and which is usually used in cloud computing environment is suitable to well manage the available resources (CPU_c, M_c, B_c, D_c).

For the instantiation request scheduling algorithm, we compute the total completion times and average processors utilization in order to compare the resource usage efficiency of the proposed fitness function with those analyzed in [6] (dynamic and random algorithms). We choose to compare with the dynamic algorithm because it is the basis of our algorithm which we enhanced; and with the random algorithm because the dynamic one was compared to it. The different proposed algorithms were simulated using Matlab and the results were measured via the same simulator.

Computational resource sharing

The required and allocated CPU, memory and bandwidth were computed according to the call arrival rate. As described in Table 2, the required resources for call arrival rates less than 60 requests/min are less than 1 GHZ of CPU, 256 MB of memory, 350 Mbps of bandwidth and 1GB of disk space. Because the performance measurements are too small for a small-sized IVR, we computed the required and allocated resources for a large-sized IVR (i.e., for $\lambda \geq 60$ requests/min).

For instance, for $\lambda = 60$ requests/min, the required CPU was almost 1.2 GHz and the estimated resource was 1.5 GHZ which represents a typical resource combination type provided by the virtualization machine. The required memory was almost 131 MB and the estimated resource was 256 MB. The required bandwidth was almost 350 Mbps and the estimated resource was 350 Mbps. For its part the required disk space was very small even for higher call arrival rates (e.g., $\lambda = 600$ requests/min) always staying under 1GB. This is due to the nature of the IVR applications, which need little disk space. The disk space measurements were therefore not included in this section because the estimated value was the same (i.e. 1 GB).

As shown in Figures 9, 10 and 11, the required and allocated resources increased as the call arrival rates were increased. These performances were expected because each IVR call requires specific ISS resources (CPU, memory and bandwidth) to be executed. In Figure 9, the difference between the required CPU and the allocated value was small and according to the CPU satisfactory factor (Figure 12) the resource usage percentage was greater than 90%.

For λ greater than 350 requests/min, this percentage was more than 95%. The required and the allocated

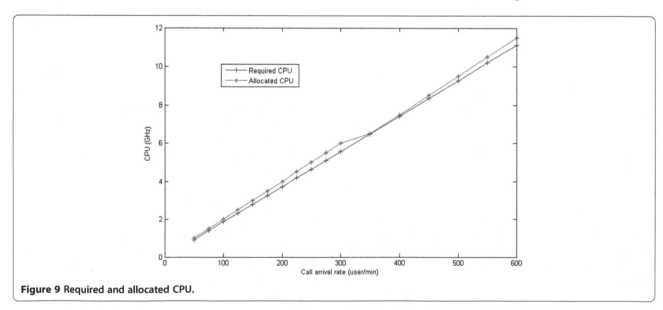

Figure 9 Required and allocated CPU.

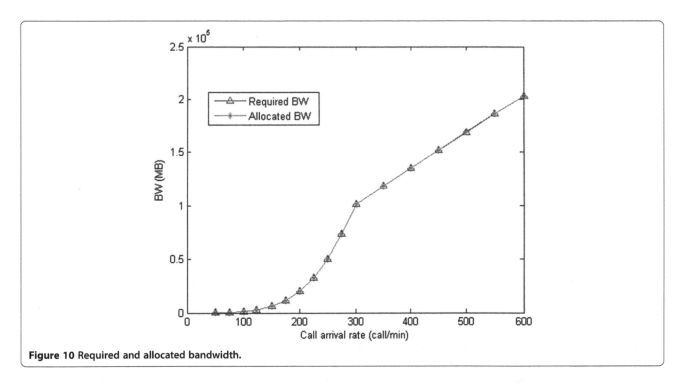

Figure 10 Required and allocated bandwidth.

bandwidth were almost the same and the bandwidth usage was almost 100% (Figure 12). The required and allocated memory measurements were different due to the fact that the sizes of the resource combination types were predefined 256, 512, 1024, etc. For instance, for $\lambda = 60$ requests/min the required memory was almost 131 MB while the allocated memory was 256. Only half the capacity memory was therefore used. For $\lambda = 100$ requests/min, the required memory was almost 500 MB and the

allocated memory was 512 MB, representing 97% memory usage. Therefore, for a large-sized IVR, the higher the instantiation request arrival rate, the higher the percentage of CPU and Bandwidth resource usage. Unlike the CPU and bandwidth performance improvement in terms of resource usage, Figures 11 and 12 show that the memory usage was efficient.

In fact, the memory resource needs for an IVR application are small. The difference between the required

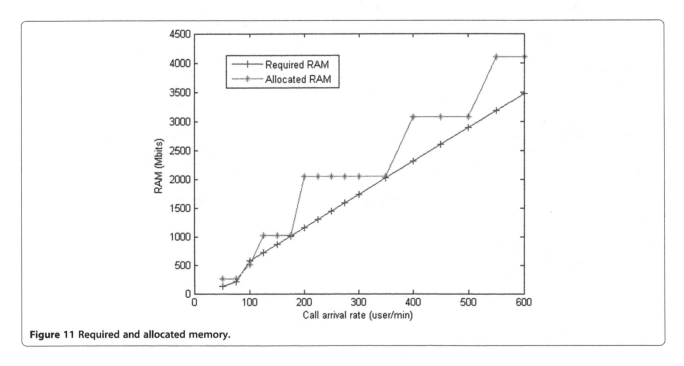

Figure 11 Required and allocated memory.

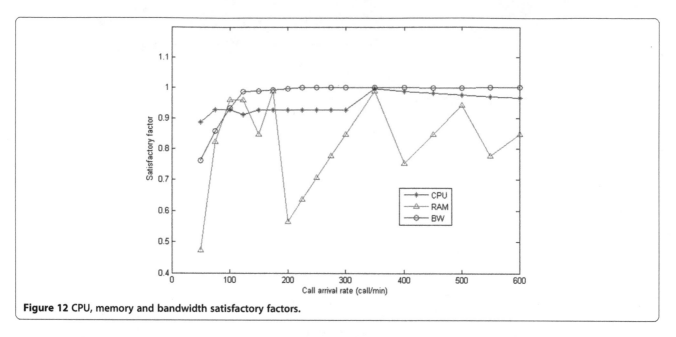

Figure 12 CPU, memory and bandwidth satisfactory factors.

memory and the allocated value varies according to the instantiation request arrival rate (Figure 11). The percentage of the resource usage varies from 50 to almost 100% for instantiation request arrival rates less than 250 requests/min and varies from 70% to 100% otherwise. We also compute the time required to allocate resources and to serve all the IVR instantiation requests. The computational resource sharing was fast because the slicing window technique allows reducing the total number of iteration of the GA algorithm. Table 3 gives some values of the required time according to the number of IVR instantiation requests.

As a conclusion, the resource combination types usually used in cloud environments do not allow for efficient resource usage. New combination types are therefore needed.

Instantiation request scheduling

We computed the total completion times and average processor utilization according to the number of tasks, the sizes of window and number of generation cycles. These performances were compared to dynamic GA as well as to random allocation strategies that were analyzed in [6].The dynamic algorithm is based on the selection, crossover and mutation methods described in 5.3.

A set of tests were performed using the following default values: 100 instantiation requests, 8 processors,

window size of 10 requests, generation cycles of 10 and population size of 10. As instantiation requests' length (t_n) we used 20 units of time for the following three reasons. First, this is the average time measured using the implemented IVR prototype: $t_v = 6$ ms and $t_r = 14$ ms in average given the prototype setup. The second reason is that we wanted to compare our algorithm to those of reference [6] which use the same task size for all of the individuals in the population. Third, using a fixed t_n value will not affect the performance of our algorithm. We have also tested the proposed algorithm for different numbers of generation cycles (10, 20, and 30) and we noticed very slight changes.

To compute the total completion time and the average processor utilization, the test parameters were set to the default values and we varied the number of tasks from 0 to 1500. These values are summarized in Table 4.

As shown in Figure 13, the total completion time for the three algorithms increased as the number of tasks increased.

Hence, the higher the number of tasks to be scheduled, the longer is the total completion time. Moreover, the instantiation request scheduling algorithm provided

Table 3 Time required allocating resources

Number of IVR instantiation requests	Required time (seconds)
14	0.38
18	0.46
22	0.62
24	0.86

Table 4 Default simulation values

	Variation of number of tasks	Variation of window size	Variation of generation size
Number of processors	8	8	8
Window size	10	10 to 60	10
Generation size	10	10	10 to 60
Number of tasks	0 to 1500	0 to 1500	0 to 1500

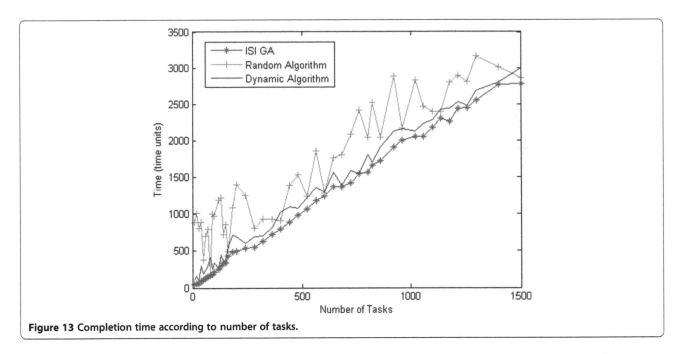

Figure 13 Completion time according to number of tasks.

a better performance than the two other algorithms. In Figure 14, the average processors utilization is much higher for instantiation request scheduling algorithm than for the dynamic and the random algorithms. The means of these utilizations were 0.83, 0.74 and 0.58 for instantiation request Scheduling, dynamic and random algorithms, respectively. These performance behaviors are due to the fact that the instantiation request scheduling algorithm provides a fitness function that guarantees a better processors utilization and the faster task execution times than those defined for

the dynamic and random algorithms. It therefore requires less processing.

We also computed the total completion time and the average processor utilization according to the window size. Figures 15 and 16 both illustrate these performances for 10 tasks.

The total completion time decreased as the window size was increased and the average processor utilization improved as the window size increased for instantiation request and dynamic algorithms. Moreover, the instantiation request scheduling algorithm outperformed the dynamic

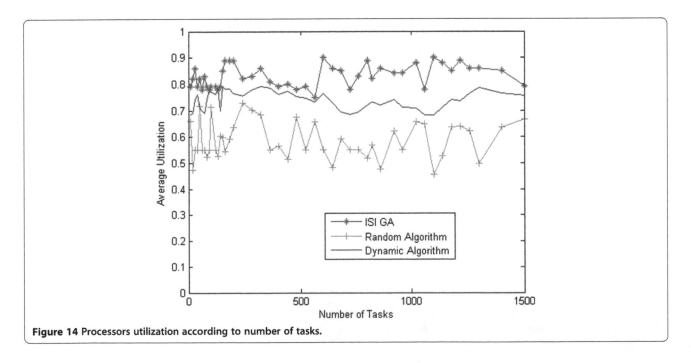

Figure 14 Processors utilization according to number of tasks.

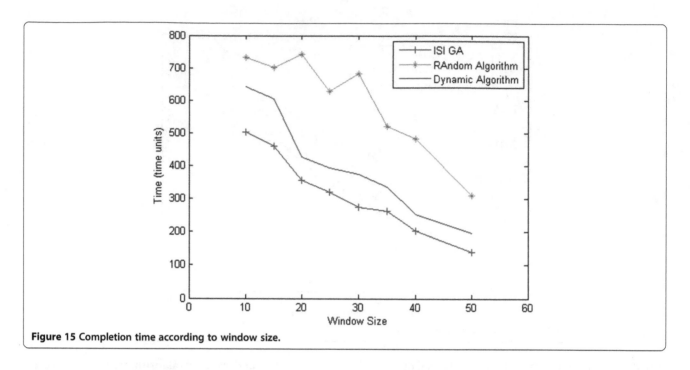

Figure 15 Completion time according to window size.

scheduling and random algorithms. This performance improvement shows that the increasing number of tasks to be scheduled was well handled by the 8 processors.

Furthermore, we analyzed the effect of the number of generation cycles on the instantiation request scheduling algorithm. We varied the number of generation from 0 to 60 for a 10 request window size and a task number of 10. Figures 17 and 18 show the total completion time and average processor utilization according to the number of generation cycles. The total completion time and

the average processor utilization decrease as the number of generation cycles increase. A significant reduction in completion time and improvement in processor utilization were noticed when varying the number of generation cycles from 10 to 30. These performances were expected because increasing the number of generation cycles improves the task assignment quality.

However, through the simulation we noticed that after a certain number of generation cycles (~25 cycles), the average processor utilization results are slightly different. This

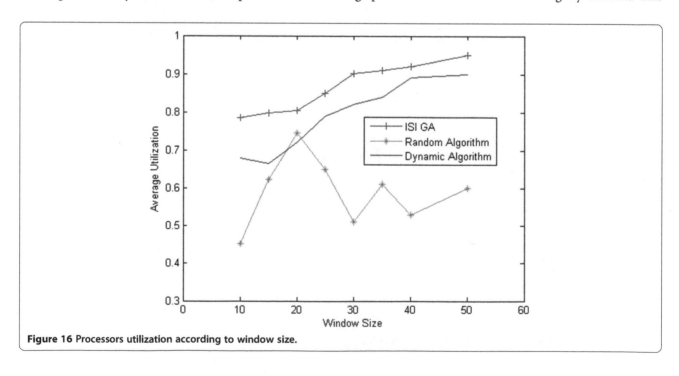

Figure 16 Processors utilization according to window size.

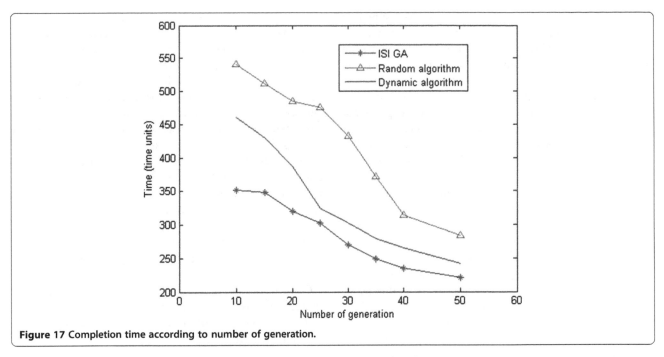

Figure 17 Completion time according to number of generation.

finding can be used to configure an upper limit for the generation cycles, in order to meet our requirement on minimizing the algorithm execution time. Moreover, the instantiation request scheduling performed better than the dynamic and random algorithms. As a conclusion, the proposed instantiation request scheduling algorithm outperforms the dynamic and random algorithms in almost all of the taken measurements. Furthermore, the algorithm performances are enhanced when the windows size is increased and the number of generation cycles increases.

State of the art review

This work joins many efforts devoted to task scheduling and load balancing across processors or computers in non-virtualized and virtualized environments. It complements them by defining new task scheduling and computational resource sharing strategies based on genetic algorithms for virtualized IVR application. Moreover, it proposes new task assignment that guarantees maximum utilization of resources while minimizing the execution time of tasks for virtualized IVR applications. We also propose a

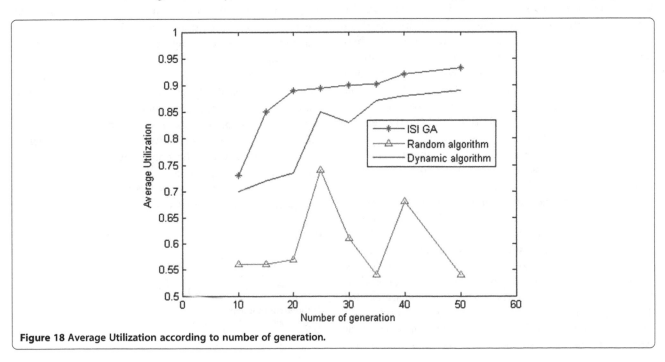

Figure 18 Average Utilization according to number of generation.

resource allocation strategy that minimizes substrate resource utilization and the resource allocation time.

The issue of load balancing based on genetic algorithm in non-virtualized environments has been addressed in [6-8]. It has been addressed by Y. Albert Zomaya et al. in [6] to propose a framework for using genetic algorithm to solve scheduling problem for parallel processor systems and to highlight the condition under which this algorithm outperform the ones based on heuristics. The genetic algorithms proposed in this paper are based on this framework.

In [11], authors propose task scheduling algorithm to achieve minimum execution time, maximum processor utilization and optimal load balancing across different processors by defining tree objective functions. In this work, we have demonstrated how two of these objective functions did not guarantee minimum execution time and maximum processor utilization and this independently of the virtualized application to which the scheduled tasks belong. We have proposed new objective functions that maximize resource utilization while minimizing task execution time. Several task scheduling methods based on modified genetic algorithm have been proposed [12-14]. In [12,13], authors propose to modify GA to control the task duplication and reduce the length of the processor queues. In [14], a modified genetic algorithm is proposed to handle task scheduling in parallel multiprocessor systems. Unfortunately, these modified algorithms yield to task scheduling time greater than that obtained with non-modified GA.

In [8], genetic-based algorithm has been proposed where a dedicated processor has been used to schedule tasks across processors. This paper has shown that this algorithm outperforms a genetic algorithm based on first-in first-out scheduling approach. However, these performances depend on the number and the distribution of tasks being executed. Moreover, it uses the same objective function as defined in [11]. We believe that this objective function that allows minimization of the largest task completion time does not guarantee the minimum execution time.

The load balancing issue based on genetic algorithm has also been addressed in virtualized computing environments [11,15,16]. In [11] and [15], authors propose to minimize task execution time by using an objective function that minimizes the largest task completion time as defined in [11] and [8].

In [16], author proposes task scheduling algorithm for Hadoop MapReduce framework. This framework is used to satisfy the data-processing needs in environments where high parallel computing and huge data storage are needed. The proposed genetic algorithm is based on statistical prediction model KCCA (Kenel Canonical Correlation Analysis) to identify the expect task execution time [16,17].

However, this paper neither describes how KCCA is used to predict the task execution time nor gives performance analysis of such algorithm. In [18], authors have described a non-genetic scheduling algorithm based KCCA and demonstrated that KCCA could be a good prediction mechanism. They stress the need for the task scheduling in Hadoop but not for optimizing resource usage in cloud environment (ex., CPU, memory, etc.). In our work, we have addressed this issue too. This issue has been also neglected by some research projects on grid computing [19,20]. Several research projects tackle the task scheduling issue in cloud for many applications like workflow and e-learning applications [21-24], but no resource optimization mechanism is provided in order to guarantee both efficient task scheduling and resource usage. Finally to the best of our knowledge, these two issues have been recently addressed in [25].

Our work is similar to this effort in that it considers the optimization of each required resource (CPU, memory, disk space, Bandwidth) according to specific applications needs: IVR application.

Conclusion

This paper proposes two resource management-related algorithms for virtualized IVR applications. The first algorithm concerns computational resource sharing, whereas the second relates to the scheduling of IVR application instantiation requests. Both algorithms are GA-based and they both consider several objectives regarding the optimization of resource usage and sharing at the substrate layer. The scheduling algorithm maximizes resources utilization while minimizing task execution time. The computational resource sharing algorithm minimizes the substrate resource utilization and the resource allocation time while maximizing the satisfactory factor of IVR applications.

The performance measurements conducted showed that the proposed algorithms are promising. Indeed, compared to dynamic and random algorithms, the proposed instantiation request task scheduling GA outperformed in terms of total completion time and average processors utilization. The computational resource sharing algorithm allows efficient CPU and bandwidth usage. However, due to the resource combination types used and because the memory resource needs are small for IVR applications, the memory resource usage was not that efficient.

Competing interests
The authors declare that they have no competing interests.

Authors' contributions
NK developed the proposed algorithms for computational resource sharing and task scheduling of virtualized IVR application, analyzed the obtained results and helped in the design of a virtualized IVR platform and wrote and

reviewed this manuscript. MS implemented and tested the proposed algorithms and helped in the development of a virtualized IVR platform. FB designed a virtualized IVR platform and helped in the development of this platform and in reviewing this manuscript. CA helped in the development of a virtualized IVR platform and in the implementation and the testing of the proposed algorithms. RG helped in the design of virtualized IVR platform and reviewing this manuscript. All authors approved the final manuscript.

Acknowledgment

NK would like to thank the research funding organization NSERC which helped us by giving us financial support to conduct this research.

Author details

[1]ETS, University of Quebec, 1100, Notre-Dame street West, Montreal, Quebec H3C 1K3, Canada. [2]Concordia University, 7141, Sherbrook street West, Montreal, Quebec H4B 1R6, Canada.

References

1. Xu S, Gao W, Li Z, Zhang S, Zhao J (2010) Design of Hierarchical and Configurable IVR System. Second International Conference on Computational Intelligence and Natural Computing Proceedings (CINC), pp 205–208
2. Khan A, Zugenmaier A, Jurca D, Kellerer W (2012) Network Virtualization: A Hypervisor for the Internet? IEEE Commun Mag 50(1):136–143
3. Vaquero LM, Rodero-Merino L, Caceres J, Lindner M (2009) A break in the clouds: towards a cloud definition. ACM SIGCOMM Comp Commun Rev 39(1):50–55
4. Belqasmi F, Azar C, Soualhia M, Kara N, Glitho R (2011) A Virtualized Infrastructure for Interactive Voice Response Applications in the Cloud. ITU-T Kaleidoscope the Fully Networked Human - Innovations for Future Networks and Services, pp 1–7
5. Belqasmi F, Azar C, Soualhia M, Kara N, Glitho R (2013) A case study of Virtualized Infrastructure and its accompanying platform for IVR Applications in Clouds. IEEE Network Mag 28(1):33–41
6. Zomaya YA, The YH (2001) Observation on using genetic algorithms for dynamic load-balancing. IEEE Trans Parallel Distributed Syst 12(9):899–911
7. Xhafa F, Carretero J, Abraham A (2008) Genetic Algorithm Based Schedulers for Grid Computing Systems. Int J Innovative Comput, Inf Control 3(5):1–19
8. Kidwell MD, Cook DJ (1994) Genetic Algorithm for Dynamic Task scheduling. Proc. IEEE 14th Annual International Phoenix conference on Computers and communications, pp 61–67
9. Carretero J, Xhafa F (2007) Genetic algorithm based schedulers for grid computing systems. Int J Innovative Comput, Inf Control 3(6):1–19
10. Goldberg DE (1989) Genetic algorithms in search, optimization, and machine learning", Reading, Mass. Addison-Wesley, ISBN 0201157675
11. Zomaya AY, Ward C, Macey B (1999) Genetic Scheduling for parallel processor systems: Comparative studies and performance issues. IEEE Trans Parallel Distributed Syst 10(8):795–812
12. Kaur K, Chhabra A, Singh G (2010) Heuristics based genetic algorithm for scheduling static tasks in homogeneous parallel system. Int J Comput Sci Secur 4(2):149–264
13. Omara FA, Arafa MM (2010) Genetic algorithms for task scheduling problem. J Parallel Distributed Comput 70(1):13–22
14. Probir R, Mejbah Ul Alam MD, Nishita D (2012) Heuristic based task scheduling in multiprocessor systems with genetic algorithm by choosing the eligible processor. Int J Distributed Parallel Syst (IJDPS) 3(4):111–121
15. Prabhu S (2011) Multi-Objective Optimization based on genetic algorithm in Grid Scheduling. Int J Advanc Res Technol 1(1):54–58
16. Tayal S (2011) Tasks scheduling optimization for the cloud computing systems. Int J Advanc Eng Sci Technol 5(2):111–115
17. Bach FR, Jordan MI (2003) Kernel independent component analysis. J Mach Learn Res 3:1–48
18. Ganapathi A, Kuno H, Daval U, Wiener J, Fox A, Jordan M, Patterson D (2009) Proceedings of IEEE International Conference on Data Engineering., pp 592–603
19. Ganapathi A, Chen Y, Fox A, Katz R, Katz R, Patterson D (2010) Statistics-driven workload modeling for the cloud. 26th IEEE International Conference on Data Engineering, pp 87–92
20. Gao Y, Rong H, Huang JZ (2005) Adaptive grid job scheduling with genetic algorithms. Elsevier J Future Generation Comp Syst 21(1):151–161
21. Kim S, Weissman JB (2004) A genetic algorithm based approach for scheduling decomposable data grid applications. International Conference on Parallel Processing, pp 406–413
22. Barrett E, Howley E, Duggan J (2011) A learning architecture for scheduling workflow applications in the cloud. 9th IEEE European Conference on Web Services, 83, pp 83–90
23. Yu J, Buyya R (2006) Scheduling scientific workflow applications with deadline and budget constraints using genetic algorithms. Sci Programming J 14(3):217–230
24. Morariu O, Morariu C, Borangiu T (2012) A genetic algorithm for workload scheduling in cloud based e-learning. In Proceedings of the 2th International Worshop on Cloud Computing Platforms., pp 1–6
25. Zhong H, Tao K, Zhang X (2010) An approach to optimized Resource scheduling algorithm for Open-Source Cloud Systems. The 5th Annual China Grid Conference, pp 124–129

10

Development of template management technology for easy deployment of virtual resources on OpenStack

Yoji Yamato*, Masahito Muroi, Kentaro Tanaka and Mitsutomo Uchimura

Abstract

In this paper, we describe the development of template management technology to build virtual resources environments on OpenStack. In recent days, Cloud computing has been progressed and also open source Cloud software has become widespread. Authors are developing cloud services using OpenStack. There are technologies which deploy a set of virtual resources based on system environmental templates to enable easy building, expansion or migration of cloud resources. OpenStack Heat and Amazon CloudFormation are template deployment technologies and build stacks which are sets of virtual resources based on templates. However, these existing technologies have 4 problems. Heat and CloudFormation transaction managements of stack create or update are insufficient. Heat and CloudFormation do not have sharing mechanism of templates. Heat cannot extract templates from existing virtual environments. Heat does not reflect actual environment changes to stack information. Therefore, we propose a new template management technology with 4 improvements. It has a mechanism of transaction management like roll back or roll forward in case of abnormal failure during stack operations. It shares templates among end users and System Integrators. It extracts templates from existing environments. It reflects actual environment changes to stack information. We implemented the proposed template management server and showed that end users can easily replicate or build virtual resources environments. Furthermore, we measured the performance of template extraction, stack create and update and showed our method could process templates in a sufficient short time.

Keywords: OpenStack; Cloud computing; IaaS; Template management server; Heat; CloudFormation

Introduction

In recent days, Cloud computing technologies such as virtualization and scale-out have been progressed and many providers have started Cloud services. Cloud services are divided into SaaS, PaaS and IaaS (Infrastructure as a Service). IaaS service provides hardware resources of CPU or Disk via a network. For examples, Amazon EC2 (Elastic Computing Cloud) [1] and Rackspace Cloud Servers [2] are production IaaS services. As IaaS infrastructure, RackSpace uses open source software OpenStack [3]. OpenStack and CloudStack [4] are major open source IaaS software and adoptions of open source IaaS software are increasing. Because OpenStack community is very active and open, we are also developing IaaS services on OpenStack.

With a spread of cloud services, technologies which deploy a set of virtual resources based on system environmental templates to enable easy building, expansion, migration of cloud virtual resources have emerged. For example, OpenStack Heat [5] and Amazon Cloud-Formation [6] are template deployment technologies and build stacks which are sets of virtual resources based on templates. However, these existing technologies have 4 problems. Heat and CloudFormation transaction managements of stack create or update are insufficient. Heat and CloudFormation do not have sharing mechanism of templates. Heat cannot extract templates from existing virtual environments. Heat does not reflect actual environment changes such as virtual machine deletion by OpenStack Nova API to stack information.

Therefore, we propose a new template management technology which has a mechanism of transaction management

* Correspondence: yamato.yoji@lab.ntt.co.jp
NTT Software Innovation Center, NTT Corporation, 3-9-11 Midori-cho, Musashino-shi 180-8585, Japan

like roll back or roll forward in case of abnormal failure during stack operations, template sharing among end users and System Integrators, template extraction from existing environments and reflection of actual environment change to stack information. We implemented the proposed template management (TM) server and showed that end users can easily replicate or build virtual resources environments. Furthermore, we measured the performance of template extraction, stack create and update and showed our method could process templates in a sufficient short time.

The rest of this paper is organized as follows. In Problems of existing template technologies, we review OpenStack architecture and clarify problems of existing template technologies for business use. In Proposal of template management technology, we propose a new template management technology which mediates users and OpenStack, and show how to resolve existing problems. In Template management server evaluation, we implement the TM server, confirm our proposed methods feasibility and evaluate the performance. We compare our work to related works in Related works. We summarize the paper in Conclusion.

Problems of existing template technologies
Outline of OpenStack
OpenStack, CloudStack and Eculayptus [7] are major open source IaaS software, and among them OpenStack community is active because many providers contribute developments and adopted services are rapidly increasing. Figure 1 shows architecture of OpenStack.

OpenStack is composed of the function blocks which manage logical/virtual resources deployed on physical resources, the function block which provides Single Sign On authentication among other function blocks and the function block which orchestrates a set of virtual resources. Neutron controls virtual networks. OVS

(Open Virtual Switch) [8] and other software switches can be used as a virtual switch. Nova controls virtual machines (VMs). KVM (Kernel based Virtual Machine) [9], Xen [10] and others can be used as hypervisors of VMs. Cinder manages block storages and can attach a logical volume to a VM like a local disk. Swift manages object storages. Glance manages Image files. Keystone is a base which performs Single Sign On authentications of these function blocks. Heat is an orchestration deployment function to create or update virtual resource instances using Nova, Cinder or other blocks based on a text template. Ceilometer is a metering function of virtual resource usage. The functions of OpenStack are used through REST (Representational State Transfer) APIs. There is also Web GUI called Horizon to use the functions of OpenStack.

OpenStack major version is released once a half-year. Henceforth Havana which is the latest version in Feb of 2014, the new functions to catch-up Amazon EC2 will be added.

Clarification of existing template technologies problems
OpenStack Heat and Amazon CloudFormation are technologies which deploy virtual resource instances based on templates which contain information of virtual resource environment and are described by JSON, YAML or other text format. The scope of Heat and CloudFormation are same and Heat supports CloudFormation-compatible API and template format. Both call a set of virtual instances which are deployed based on a template "stack" and provide APIs to operate stacks. However, these APIs provide primitive CRUD (Create, Read, Update and Delete) operations of stack and there are some insufficient points for business use. Here, we clarify 4 major problems of existing template technologies.

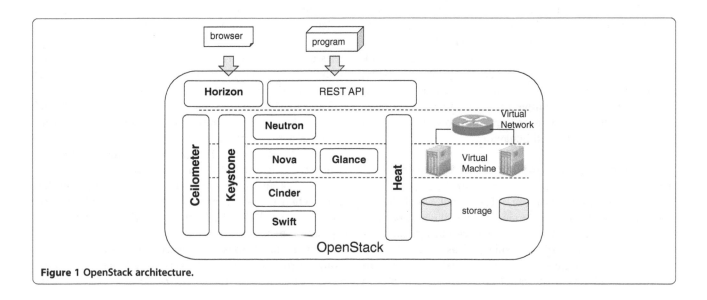

Figure 1 OpenStack architecture.

Insufficient transaction management of stack create, update or delete

Heat and CloudFormation transaction managements of stack create, update or delete are insufficient. When we create a stack, all resources need to be deployed successfully for business use. But Heat and CloudFormation sometimes fail some resources deployment and there is a possibility of end up with a half-finished stack creation. Moreover, when we update a stack, Heat and CloudFormation also fail some resources update and there is a possibility of end up with a half-finished stack update.

There is no template sharing mechanism

Templates sharing or re-use by other users are out of scope of Heat and CloudFormation. Users of Heat and CloudFormation need to describe and manage templates by themselves. However, users who do not have IT knowledge such as small business owners cannot create a template easily. It is preferable that System Integrators or distributers describe and verify templates, and end users only select templates and build virtual resource environments for their business demands.

Heat cannot extract templates from existing environments

Heat has a "template-show" API which gets a template from a stack but cannot extract a template from a non-stack environment. Thus, when users would like to replicate existing environments, they need to describe templates from the first. And because each resource belongs to only one stack in Heat specification, a template extraction is difficult for shared resources such as logical routers which connect VPN or the Internet not to belong multiple stacks.

Actual environment change is not reflected to stack information

Heat does not reflect non-Heat API operations to stack information. For example, when users shut down a VM via console or delete a VM via Nova API, there is a difference between an actual environment and stack information. When users call a stack update API, Heat checks a difference between a new template and a previous template. But in this example case, an actual environment is different from a previous template, so that there is a possibility of unexpected behavior.

Proposal of template management technology

To provide orchestration functions of OpenStack IaaS services to users, we propose a TM server which have a mechanism of transaction management like roll back or roll forward in case of abnormal failure during stack operations, template sharing among end users and System Integrators, template extraction from existing environments and reflection of actual environment change to

stack information. The TM server interprets Heat JSON or HOT (Heat Orchestration Template) format templates and calls OpenStack APIs such as Nova or Cinder. The TM server has a stack operation function, template sharing function, template extraction function and environmental change reflection function. Here, we explain how to resolve 1–4 problems by the TM server.

Transaction management of stack create, update and delete

Heat and CloudFormation transaction managements of stack create, update and delete are insufficient and may end up with a half-finished stack processing. It is not acceptable for some business users because some resources failures may lead critical problems. For example, if a VM creation is successful but a logical router security setting is failed, the VM may have a risk of abuse.

Therefore, when we create a stack, it is necessary to delete and roll back all resources in case of any failures of resource creation (All resources roll back). And when we delete a stack, it is necessary to retry and delete all resources in case of any failures of resource deletion (All resources roll forward).

When we update a stack, orchestration functions check a difference between previous template and new template, then create, delete or update resources to fill up the difference. Specifically, a resource which is in previous template and is not in new template is deleted, a resource which is not in previous template and is in new template is created, a resource which is changed from previous template to new template is created after deletion or updated. In OpenStack, some resources can be updated but some cannot be. (e.g. network connection change can be updated but VM RAM size change needs to delete VM once, then create new one).

In stack update case, individual resource creation, deletion and update may be operated, so that there may be a case we cannot roll back all operations. For example, a volume is deleted successfully then a VM creation is failed, we cannot roll back because the volume is already deleted. Therefore, in stack update case, the TM server tries to roll back or roll forward for each OpenStack API transaction (not all API transactions) when each OpenStack API processing is failed.

Figure 2 shows the transaction managements of stack create, delete and update. In stack create case, when there is a problem in logical router creation, the TM rolls-back all created resources. In stack delete case, when there is a problem in logical router deletion, the TM retries and deletes all resources. In stack update case, when there is a problem in logical load balancer deletion, the TM rolls-back the logical load balancer operation because it is a creation operation.

Heat template does not describe an order of each resource processing. Our TM server interprets Heat templates and process following orders for stack create,

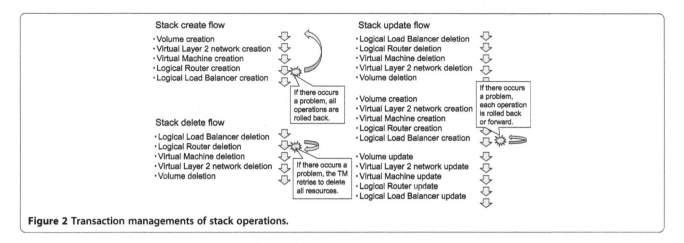

Figure 2 Transaction managements of stack operations.

delete and update. Regarding to stack create, the TM server creates resources in the following order; volume, virtual Layer 2 network, VM, logical router and logical load balancer. Regarding to stack delete, the order is logical load balancer, logical router, VM, virtual Layer 2 network and volume. Regarding to stack update, the TM server firstly deletes resources in the order same as stack delete case, secondly creates resources in the order same as stack create case and lastly updates resources in the order same as stack create case. Figure 2 also shows the orders of stack create, delete and update.

Following these orders, we can guarantee the precondition of resource creation in stack create case (e.g. a VM needs at least one volume). We can also prevent name duplication error or other precondition error in stack update case.

To follow these policies, the stack operation function of TM server manages orders of OpenStack API calls and those transactions. Because most of OpenStack APIs are asynchronous, the TM server retries a API or calls a purge API, or reverse API to decide state of OpenStack resource when a API transaction is failed. Note that a reverse API means the reverse process of each API (e.g. volume deletion API is a reverse API for volume creation). In this way, we can prevent a half-way state of stack during stack operations.

The function of stack transaction management can be generalized for deployment management with multiple resources. Resource deployment needs Create, Update and Delete transaction managements and also needs a valid order of each resource operation. Our proposal of stack transactions in case of failure and orders of each resource operation can be used also CloudStack, Eucalyptus and other Cloud platforms multiple resources provisioning because a virtual resource dependence (e.g. VM needs at least one volume) is almost same in IaaS platforms.

Template sharing

CloudFormation and Heat do not have a mechanism of template sharing. Our TM server provides a function to share templates and facilitate templates re-use. For example, when a small business owner would like to build a shopping site, a System Integrator provides a verified Web 3-tier structure template, then the small business owner selects the template and build the environment with one or two clicks. If we share templates unconditionally, there is a risk of malicious template spreading. Thus, it is necessary to limit a range of template sharing within contractual relationships. Here, we explain logics of template sharing.

- There are two methods to register a template: template extraction and template upload. The function described in Template extraction from existing tenant extracts a valid template in an extraction case. In the other side, the template sharing function validates a template in a template upload case because a template described by a user may have format or logical errors.

- Each template creator can set a scope of disclosure for each template. There are 3 options for disclosure; only the creator-self, all users who have contract with the creator and users selected by the creator. Service providers or System Integrators can share templates to subordinate users by setting a scope of disclosure. If System Integrators have multiple tier contractual relationships, there are 2nd tier subordinate users. In this case, 1st tier subordinate System Integrator downloads a template of upper tier System Integrator and registers it as its template. This is to restrict scope of disclosure within direct contractual relationships. Because each System Integrator prefers to sell its own brand, the template sharing function conceals templates upper than two tiers. Figure 3 shows an image of template sharing relations. A Cloud provider A creates and shares the template a to all users which have contracts. A System Integrator B and an End User C can use the template a. B also

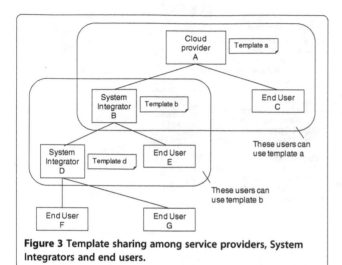

Figure 3 Template sharing among service providers, System Integrators and end users.

creates and shares the template b to users, so that D and E can use the template b.

- Users within scope of disclosure can download a template or create a stack using a template. If a template describes a reference of image ID to create a volume from the image, users also need to be able to use the image. Thus, template sharing function also manages a scope of disclosure for images. Specifically, when a user requests to create a stack, template sharing function represents to get Keystone token as upper System Integrator and create a user volume from an image of System Integrator.

In this way, users who do not have enough IT knowledge can select a shared template and build virtual resources environments easily.

The function of template sharing function shares a template among users. In Cloud services or hosting services, many System Integrators or resellers build and manage services for end users. The function of template sharing is generalized for multi-tier sharing model of cloud or hosting services. This can be used not only a text template file sharing but also restricted sharing of software with license such as OS images or restricted codes sharing for multi-vendor developments.

Template extraction from existing tenant

Heat main targets are operations of stacks and Heat cannot extract a template from non-stack environment. And there is a restriction that each virtual resource belongs to only one stack. Based on them, we propose logics to extract a template from an existing tenant.

- We extract whole virtual resources on an existing tenant to a template. If there is unnecessary resource in an extracted template, a user edits the template after downloading. This is because there is

no stack that we cannot restrict corresponding resources for extraction.

- Target resources to extract are volumes, virtual Layer 2 networks, VMs, logical routers and logical load balancers. Floating IPs are IP address resources that relate logical routers which connect the Internet. The Internet connected resources are shared by multiple stacks in general and VMs or logical load balancers which are assigned floating IPs may be shared by multiple stacks. Because a virtual resource only belongs to one stack, we do not include a floating IP to a template in extraction phase. Users can assign floating IPs after stack creation based on the extracted template. In the same way, shared virtual Layer 2 networks or logical routers (e.g. VPN connected routers) are out of scope for extraction because those are used by multiple stacks.
- When users extract a template, they also can select whether to acquire images from volumes of tenant or not. When users create a stack, these images are used to replicate volumes.
- During template extraction time, we block virtual resources operations in the tenant to prevent a change of target resources for extraction.
- Extracted templates are held in the template sharing function described in Template sharing. Extracted templates can be used for stack create, update or download to edit.

In this way, we can extract a template from an existing tenant and replicate an environment easily.

The function of template extraction extracts a template from an existing environment. Our implementation extracts JSON or HOT template and the extracted template can be deployed both by Amazon CloudFormation and OpenStack Heat because a template is abstract text information and does not depend on IaaS platform. To generalize and adapt extracted template format to other IaaS platforms, we can use this function for Cloud migration to another platform or Cloud federation on plural platforms.

Reflection of environment change to stack information

In case of stack update, orchestration functions check a difference between previous template and new template, then create, delete or update virtual resources to fill up the difference. However, Heat can only recognize an environment change by Heat API and does not know actual environment status.

Therefore, we reflect an environment change to stack information to guarantee stack update or delete behaviors as users expect.

There are four methods to change environments.

a) Stack create, update, delete by Heat Stack API
b) Individual resource create, update, delete by other OpenStack API (Nova, Cinder and so on)
c) Resource deletion by user's manual operation. (e.g. VM shutdown via console)
d) Resource deletion by unintentional physical or virtual server down.

Regarding to a), we do not have to care it because templates of Stack API are matched to actual environments after API process.

Regarding to b), when users call OpenStack API (not Heat API), the TM server hooks the requests as OpenStack API proxy and reflects the environment change to stack information. If proxy model is difficult, the TM server may poll OpenStack DB to confirm environment changes. But each OpenStack API does not have a parameter of stack ID so that individual resource creation is not reflected to stack information. If a user would like to add a resource to a stack, a user needs to call Heat stack update API including the resource.

Regarding to c), main case is a VM shutdown by user's manual operation. VM is operated by Libvirt [11] on KVM. Therefore, the TM server can reflect the VM down status to stack information by receiving notifications of Libvirt or other monitoring agents.

Regarding to d), the TM server reflects resources down to stack information by receiving a notification of each resource monitoring agent like c) case.

Based on reflected stack information on a)-d), the TM server can update or delete stacks as users expect. Table 1 shows a comparison of reflection of actual environment change to stack information in Havana Heat case and our TM server case. Havana Heat updates environment changes to stack information only in Stack API use. Our TM updates environment changes to it except for resource create by individual OpenStack API call.

The function of environment change reflection function is generalized to a difference resolve function of actual environment and management layer. The difference has a problem not only in a stack update case but also in an individual resource provisioning case. For example, OpenStack Neutron manages a resource state in OpenStack DB and does not care an actual completion of resource provisioning after it has written the requests to DB. Thus, there is a possibility that a VM is active but access control setting of a logical router to the VM is not available. Because a Cloud provider business is charging fees for provisioned resources, it is fatal to charge a resource not created yet. The function can be used for resolving these differences to collect actual environment information by monitoring modules such as Libvirt and Pacemaker or by hooking requests as a proxy.

Template management server evaluation

We implement the TM server with proposed 1–4 functions and confirm that it can be used for carrier IaaS services. We also evaluate the performance of implemented TM server.

Template management server implementation

Figure 4 shows function blocks of the TM server, OpenStack and related systems. The TM server has three outer interfaces, Web GUI, API and OpenStack communication process. Users can extract and share templates via Web GUI. API provides Heat stack operation APIs which receive requests of stack operations and other OpenStack APIs. OpenStack communication process calls individual OpenStack API such as Nova or Cinder, confirms the request status and asks roll-back or roll-forward in case of abnormal failure. The TM server has a stack information DB which manages stack information and a template sharing DB which manages shared templates. Proposed 3.1-3.4 functions are implemented on the function blocks 1)-4) described in Figure 4.

The stack operation function receives requests of stack create, delete and update via API, makes an order of OpenStack API calls and calls individual OpenStack API via OpenStack communication process. It manages transactions of stack operations, judges to roll-back or roll-forward and calls purge or reverse APIs via OpenStack communication process in case of a abnormal failure. The

Table 1 Reflection of actual environment change to stack information

Operation type		Havana heat	Our TM server
Heat stack API	stack create	✓	✓
	stack update	✓	✓
	stack delete	✓	✓
Other OpenStack API (Nova, Cinder and so on)	resource create		
	resource update		✓
	resource delete		✓
User manual operation (e.g. VM shutdown)	resource delete		✓
Physical or virtual server down	resource delete		✓

A tick mark means that a corresponding operation result is reflected to stack information.

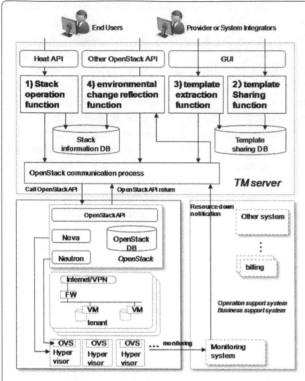

Figure 4 Function blocks of template management servers and related systems.

template sharing function retains templates which are extracted from existing environments or uploaded by users in template sharing DB. It also controls scope of disclosures of templates for users to search available templates. The template extraction function receives a request of template extraction via GUI, gathers information of current virtual resources from OpenStack DB and registers information of extracted template to template sharing DB. The environmental change reflection function behaves as a proxy for non-Heat OpenStack API such as Nova or Neutron API and reflects each resource status change to stack information DB. It also reflects virtual resources down to stack information DB when it receives a resource down notification from a monitoring system.

OpenStack has OpenStack DB, OpenStack modules such as Nova and OpenStack API. OpenStack receives a request via OpenStack API and controls a virtual resource using OpenStack modules like Nova or Neutron and retains virtual resource information in OpenStack DB. OSS (Operation Support System) and BSS (Business Support System) supports an operation of Cloud services. Monitoring system of OSS monitors virtual or physical resource availability and it sends a notification to the TM server when it detects a resource down.

We implemented the TM server on OpenStack Folsom. We implemented it on Ubuntu 12.04 OS and Apache Tomcat 6.0.36 by Java language (JDK1.6.0.38) and Python.

We confirmed 1–4 functions validity on a test environment of Figure 5. It is confirmed that stack is updated based on actual environment information and if there is an failure during stack operation, the TM server roll back or roll forward as expected. And it is also confirmed that System Integrators can extract a template from an existing tenant, share a template among users who have contracts to System Integrators and replicates a virtual resource environment to a user tenant using the template.

Performance evaluation of proposed method

The TM server mediates a user and OpenStack and manages a template processing. We measure the processing time of 3 type processings and confirm that an overhead of our proposed method is sufficient low. The graph values of processing time are average of 3 times measurements.

Performance measurement conditions

This subsection describes measurement conditions of what time is measured, what and how much resources are used and number of concurrent processing number in the measurements. We extract a template from a stack in the 1st measurement, create s stack using the extracted template in the 2nd measurement and update a stack by a new template in which some virtual resources are changed in the 3rd measurement.

The 1st measurement is a template extraction.

– Measured time: Template extraction processing time from a tenant.
– Extracted template: A tenant has 2 VMs, 4 volumes, 2 virtual Layer 2 networks, 1 logical router and 1 logical load balancer.
– Concurrent processing numbers: 1 and 3.

Note that processing time of Image acquisition from a volume is out of scope because it depends on network bandwidth between Cinder and Glance.

The 2nd measurement is a stack create.

– Measured time: Stack creation processing time.
– Template for stack creation: A template has 2 VMs, 4 volumes, 2 virtual Layer 2 networks, 1 logical router and 1 logical load balancer. (the same template in 1st measurement)
– Concurrent processing numbers: 1 and 3.

Note that processing time of volume creation from an image is out of scope because it depends on network bandwidth between Cinder and Glance.

The 3rd measurement is a stack update.

– Measured time: Stack update processing time.

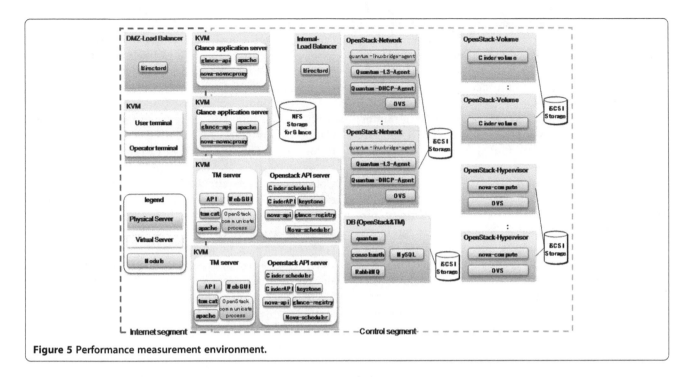

Figure 5 Performance measurement environment.

- Differences between a previous template and a new template: virtual resources numbers are same but 1 VM, 1 virtual Layer 2 network and 1 logical router in a previous template are removed and 1 VM, 1 virtual Layer 2 network and 1 logical router are newly added. Figure 6 shows parts of templates which are used for this measurement. Both templates have a VM but VM properties are different, so that a VM is deleted firstly and another VM is created secondly in stack update.
- Concurrent processing numbers: 1 and 3. Because concurrent update of one stack is blocked by the TM, we measure parallel 3 different updates in this experiment.

Performance measurement environment

Figure 5 is a performance measurement environment. It shows physical and virtual servers and modules in each server. For example in TM server case, a TM server is a virtual server, is in both Internet segment and Control segment and has modules of API, Web GUI, OpenStack communicate process, tomcat and apache. Two servers are for redundancy. Other servers are a user terminal and an operator terminal, Glance application servers for image upload, a NFS storage for image, OpenStack API servers, a DB for OpenStack and TM, OpenStack servers for virtual resources such as network, volume or VM and iSCSI storages and load balancers for load balancing. Figure 5 omits maintenance servers such as syslog or

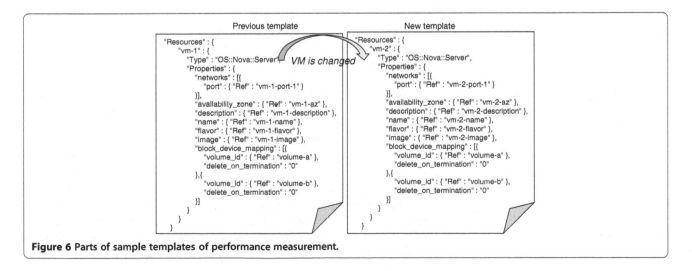

Figure 6 Parts of sample templates of performance measurement.

backup servers and redundant modules such as heartbeat. These servers are connected with Gigabit Ethernet.

Table 2 shows each server specification and usage. For example in DB case (6th row), the hardware is HP ProLiant BL460c G1, the server is a physical server, the name is DB, the main usage is OpenStack and TM DB, CPU is Quad-Core Intel Xeon 1600 MHz*2 and Core number is 8, RAM is 24 GB, assigned HDD is 72 GB and NIC (Network Interface Card) number is 4.

Performance measurement results
Template extractions need only DB checks and we can extract templates about 1–3 sec when concurrent processing numbers are 1 and 3. Because the design of system environment takes much time in general, we think quick template extraction is effective to replicate virtual resources environment.

Figure 7(a) shows the processing time of stack create. When concurrent processing number is 1, we can create a stack about 300 sec and when it is 3, it takes about 350 sec. Figure 7(b) shows divisions of resource creation times when concurrent processing number is 1. TM server processing takes 90 sec in orchestration and other times are OpenStack resources creation times (load balancer and VM creation take almost all time of OpenStack processing). Proposed TM server manages transactions of all virtual resources creation. We think an overhead of TM server transaction management is sufficient low. Note that actual stack create may need volume creation from an image and data transfer from Glance to Cinder may take 10–30 minutes.

Figure 8(a) shows the processing time of stack update. When concurrent processing number is 1, we can update a stack about 210 sec and when it is 3, it takes about 270 sec. Figure 8(b) shows divisions of resource update times when concurrent processing number is 1. TM server processing takes 90 sec in orchestration and other times are OpenStack resources update times (VM creation take much time of OpenStack processing). Proposed TM server manages transactions of updating virtual resources and judges roll back or roll forward for each OpenStack API processing. We think an overhead of TM server differential checks and transaction management is sufficient low. Note that actual stack update may need volume deletion and take 10–30 minutes because Cinder overwrites all data with zero for volume deletion.

Related works
Like OpenStack, OpenNebula [12], Ecalyptus [7] and CloudStack [4] are open source IaaS software. OpenNebula is a virtual infrastructure manager of IaaS building. OpenNebula manages VM, storage, network of company and virtualizes system resources to provide Cloud services. Eucalyptus characteristic is an interoperability of Amazon EC2, and Xen, KVM or many hypervisors can be used on Eucalyptus. Our group also contributes to developments of OpenStack itself. Functions of load balancer and some bug fixes of OpenStack are our group contributions.

Amazon CloudFormation [6] and OpenStack Heat [5] are two major template deployment technologies on IaaS platform. Our work has resolved 4 problems of these technologies. The paper [13] is a work of OpenStack federation using Heat and users need to describe a Heat template first. Because our work can extract templates from existing environments and reflects actual environment changes to stack information, users can replicate or federate virtual resource environments more easily. The paper [14] is a work to construct multitier cloud-based services. Our work provides a mechanism of template sharing in multi-tier contracts, so that end users can build virtual resource environments using templates of upper tier System Integrators. The paper [15] is a work to realize a transitional implementation of meta cloud (cloud abstraction layer) for solving cloud vendor lock-in problems. Our work also targets Cloud migration or transition and template extraction or template sharing function support it. Our work also faces transaction managements of resource deployment.

RightScale is a product for cloud service management which enables automatic operations of system monitoring, alert, auto scaling. ServerTemplates of RightScale [16] is an abstract template approach. When a user deploys a template to a Cloud such as Amazon Web Services or RackSpace Cloud Servers, RightScale sets a configuration adapting to each component of deployed Cloud. This concept is similar to our template extraction to enable easy Cloud migration or replication. However, RightScale ServerTemplates transaction managements or reflections of environment change depend on each Cloud and remain unresolved. Our work resolves them by the TM server. Amazon OpsWorks [17] is also a technology for cloud service management such as automatic scaling, scheduling, monitoring and deployment. Amazon recommends using OpsWorks in high layer management and using CloudFormation for low layer deployment. Support range of OpsWorks is limited in application oriented Amazon Web Services resources and support range of CloudFormation is much larger. Our work scope is low layer deployment and we will use current management technologies such as RightScale for high layer management.

The paper [18] is a research of dynamic resource allocation on OpenStack. As same as [18], our work is also a resource deployment technology on OpenStack but our work targets to resolve problems of plural resources deployment like stack operation transactions. There are some works of resource arrangement on hosting services to use physical server resources effectively [19]. We have

Table 2 Each server specification and usage

Hardware	Physical or VM	Name	Main usage	CPU Model name	Core	RAM (GB)	HDD Logical (GB)	NIC
HP ProLiant BL460c G6	Physical	KVM host		Quad-Core Intel Xeon 2533 MHz x 2	8	48	300	4
	VM	OpenStack API server	OpenStack stateless process such as API		assign: 4	assign: 8	assign: 60	
	VM	Template management server	Proposed template management server		assign: 4	assign: 8	assign: 60	
HP ProLiant BL460c G6	Physical	KVM host		Quad-Core Intel Xeon 2533 MHz x 2	8	48	300	4
	VM	Glance application server	Received requests related to glance		assign: 8	assign: 32	assign: 150	
HP ProLiant BL460c G1	Physical	DB (OpenStack & TM)	OpenStack and TM DB	Quad-Core Intel Xeon 1600 MHz x 2	8	24	72	4
HP ProLiant BL460c G1	Physical	OpenStack-Network	Used for OpenStack logical network resources	Quad-Core Intel Xeon 1600 MHz x 2	8	18	72	6
HP ProLiant BL460c G1	Physical	OpenStack-Volume	Used for OpenStack logical volume resources	Quad-Core Intel Xeon 1600 MHz x 2	8	18	72	6
HP ProLiant BL460c G1	Physical	OpenStack-Hypervisor	Used for OpenStack VM resources	Quad-Core Intel Xeon 1600 MHz x 2	8	24	72	4
IBM HS21	Physical	DMZ-Load Balancer	Load Balancer for internal access	Xeon E5160 3.0GHz x 1	2	2	72	1
IBM HS21	Physical	Internal Load Balancer	Load balancer for internal access	Xeon E5160 3.0GHz x 1	2	2	72	1
IBM HS21	Physical	KVM host		Xeon E5160 3.0GHz x 1	2	2	72	1
	VM	User VM	VM for user terminal		assign: 1	assign: 1	assign: 20	
	VM	Operator VM	VM for operator terminal		assign: 1	assign: 1	assign: 20	
EMC VNX 5300	Physical	iSCSI storage	iSCSI storage for user volume				500	
EMC VNX 5300	Physical	NFS storage	NFS storage for Image				500	

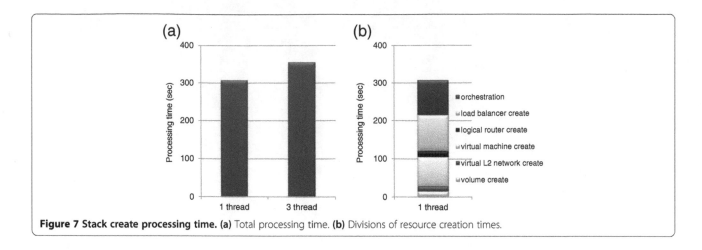

Figure 7 Stack create processing time. (a) Total processing time. **(b)** Divisions of resource creation times.

already developed a scheduler which determines an appropriate physical server for virtual resource deployment [20]. Because a stack has many virtual resources and need effective allocations to enhance total system performances, we will combine [20] and this work in the future.

Conclusion

In this paper, we proposed the template management technology for end users or System Integrators to build virtual resources environments on OpenStack. To resolve existing technologies problems, we designed the TM server which had a mechanism of roll back/roll forward in case of abnormal failure of stack operations, shared templates among end users and System Integrators, extracted templates from existing environments and reflected actual environment change to stack information. We implemented the proposed TM server on OpenStack Folsom, confirmed functions feasibilities and measured performances.

It was confirmed that the TM server prevented a half-finished stack because it rolled back all operations in case of abnormal failure of stack create and rolled back or rolled forward each operation in case of abnormal failure of stack update. Template sharing to end users who have contracts to System Integrators or providers can replicate virtual resource environments on new tenants easily. Our server extracted a template from non-stack environment except for shared resources. Users could update stack as expected because our server reflected actual environment change such as VM shut down or other OpenStack API operations to stack information. Moreover, we showed the effective performance of template management. Template extraction took 1–3 sec, stack create took 300 sec and stack update took 210 sec through experiments of sample templates with 10 virtual resources.

In the future, we will modify the TM server for OpenStack new versions. IceHouse or Juno is a new major version of OpenStack and provides new functions to catch up Amazon Web Services. We will also propose our technologies of transaction managements and reflections of actual environment change to stack information to community Heat. Furthermore, we will improve the software quality of the TM server and verify the feasibility of existing OSS / BSS interconnections to provide production carrier IaaS services based on OpenStack.

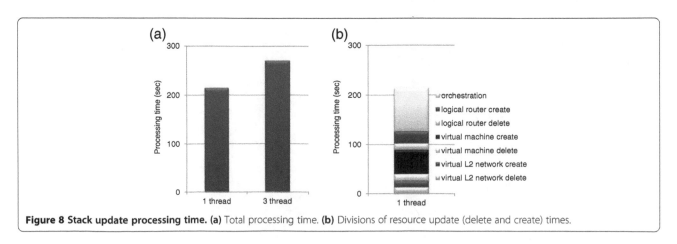

Figure 8 Stack update processing time. (a) Total processing time. **(b)** Divisions of resource update (delete and create) times.

Competing interests
The authors declare that they have no competing interests.

Authors' contributions
YY carried out the template management technology studies, participated in the design and implementation of the template management server, evaluated it, surveyed the related technologies and drafted the manuscript. MM, KT, MU participated in the design and implementation of the template management server. All authors have read and approved the final manuscript.

Authors' information
Yoji Yamato received his B. S., M. S. degrees in physics and Ph.D. degrees in general systems studies from University of Tokyo, Japan in 2000, 2002 and 2009, respectively. He joined NTT Corporation, Japan in 2002. Currently he is a RESEARCHER of NTT Software Innovation Center. There, he has been engaged in developmental research of Cloud computing platform, Peer-to-Peer computing, Service Delivery Platform. Dr. Yamato is a member of IEICE, Japan.
Masahito Muroi is a RESEARCHER of NTT Software Innovation Center, NTT Corporation.
Kentaro Tanaka is a RESEARCHER of NTT Software Innovation Center, NTT Corporation.
Mitsutomo Uchimura received his Bachelor's degree in Mechanical Engineering from University of Tokyo, Japan in 1997. He joined NTT Corporation, Japan in 1997. Currently he is a senior research engineer of NTT Software Innovation Center. There, he has been engaged in Cloud SE Project.

Acknowledgements
We thank Hiroshi Sakai and Hikaru Suzuki who are managers of this development.

References
1. Amazon Elastic Compute Cloud web site. http://aws.amazon.com/ec2/. Accessed 24 Jan 2014
2. Rackspace public cloud powered by OpenStack web site. http://www.rackspace.com/cloud/. Accessed 24 Jan 2014
3. OpenStack web site. http://www.openstack.org/. Accessed 24 Jan 2014
4. CloudStack web site. http://CloudStack.apache.org/. Accessed 24 Jan 2014
5. OpenStack Heat web site. https://wiki.openstack.org/wiki/Heat. Accessed 24 Jan 2014
6. Amazon CloudFormation web site. http://aws.amazon.com/cloudformation/. Accessed 24 Jan 2014
7. Nurmi D, Wolski R, Grzegorczyk C, Obertelli G, Soman S, Youseff L, Zagorodnov D (2009) The Eucalyptus Open-source Cloud-computing System. In: Proceedings of Cluster Computing and the Grid, 2009 (CCGRID '09). 9th IEEE/ACM International Symposium on., p 124
8. Pfaff B, Pettit J, Koponen T, Amidon K, Casado M, Shenker S (2009) Extending Networking into the Virtualization Layer. In: Proceedings of 8th ACM Workshop on Hot Topics inNetworks (HotNets-VIII), Oct. 2009
9. Kivity A, Kamay Y, Laor D, Lublin U, Liguori A (2007) kvm: the Linux virtual machine monitor. In: Proceedings of OLS '07: The 2007 Ottawa Linux Symposium. p 225
10. Barham P, Dragovic B, Fraser K, Hand S, Harris T, Ho A, Neugebauer R, Pratt I, Warfield A (2003) Xen and the art of virtualization. In: Proceedings of the 19th ACM symposium on Operating Systems Principles (SOSP'03). p 164
11. Libvirt web site. http://libvirt.org/. Accessed 24 Jan 2014
12. Milojicic D, Llorente IM, Montero RS (2011) OpenNebula: a cloud management tool. IEEE Internet Comput 15(2):11–14
13. Castillo L, Angel J, Mallichan K, Al-Hazmi Y (2013) OpenStack Federation in Experimentation Multi-cloud Testbeds. In: Technical reports of HP Laboratories, HPL-2013-58
14. Bahga A, Madisetti VK (2013) Rapid prototyping of multitier cloud-based services and systems. IEEE Comput 46(11):76–83
15. Satzger B, Hummer W, Inzinger C, Leitner P, Dustdar S (2013) Winds of change: from vendor lock-in to the meta cloud. IEEE Internet Comput 17(1):69–73
16. RightScale ServerTemplates web site. http://www.rightscale.com/blog/cloud-management-best-practices/rightscale-servertemplates-explained. Accessed 13 Apr 2014
17. Amazon OpsWorks web site. https://aws.amazon.com/opsworks/. Accessed 13 Apr 2014
18. Wuhib F, Stadler R, Lindgren H (2012) Dynamic resource allocation with management objectives - Implementation for an OpenStack cloud. In: Proceedings of Network and service management, 2012 8th international conference and 2012 workshop on systems virtualiztion management., p 309
19. Liu X, Zhu X, Padala P, Wang Z, Singhal S (2007) Optimal Multivariate Control for Differentiated Services on a Shared Hosting Platform. In: Proceedings of the IEEE Conference on Decision and Control., p 3792
20. Yamato Y, Yokozeki D, Hirai T, Yuhara M, Muroi M, Tanaka K (2013) Japanese patent application No. 2013–244205

11

An elastic virtual infrastructure for research applications (ELVIRA)

Alex Voss[1*], Adam Barker[1], Mahboubeh Asgari-Targhi[2], Adriaan van Ballegooijen[2] and Ian Sommerville[1]

Abstract

Cloud computing infrastructures provide a way for researchers to source the computational and storage resources they require to conduct their work and to collaborate within distributed research teams. We provide an overview of a cloud-based *elastic virtual infrastructure for research applications* that we have established to provide researchers with a collaborative research environment that automatically allocates cloud resources as required. We describe how we have used this infrastructure to support research on the Sun's corona and how the *elasticity* provided by cloud infrastructures can be leveraged to provide high-throughput computing resources using a set of off-the-shelf technologies and a small number of additional tools that are simple to deploy and use. The resulting infrastructure has a number of advantages for the researchers compared to traditional clusters or grid computing environments that we discuss in the conclusions.

Introduction

Many problems at the forefront of science, engineering, medicine, arts, humanities and the social sciences require the integration of large-scale data and computing resources at unprecedented scales to yield insights, discover correlations, and ultimately drive scientific discovery. The explosion of scientific data produced by simulations, network-connected instruments and sensors, as well as the increase in social and political data available to researchers, promises a renaissance in many areas of science. To meet the data storage and computing demands of such data-rich applications, users in industry and academia are looking to cloud computing [1-3], which promises to realise the long-held dream of computing as a utility with users accessing resources and applications hosted by a third-party data centre. This model has several potential key advantages that have aided its rapid adoption:

- upfront costs are eliminated as resources are rented from a third-party provider;
- users only pay for the computing resources they need on a short-term basis (e.g., CPU by the hour, storage by the day);

- resources are elastic in nature and can dynamically 'scale out' to meet increasing demands and 'scale in' when demand is reduced;
- the cost of managing the underlying hardware and networking infrastructure is shared by many users of the cloud service and is reduced through virtualisation and automation.

Predictions of rapid growth of the cloud computing market abound (cf. [4]) but so far it would seem that adoption is often limited to specific applications. For example, while a recent report for the European Commission [5] suggests that cloud computing may "contribute up to €250 billion to EU GDP in 2020 and 3.8 million jobs", the same report highlights the fact that adoption is currently very uneven and 'shallow' (limited to specific applications such as email) and growth is dependent on a number of barriers being overcome. We know from a previous study [6] that the uptake of grid computing and similar e-Infrastructures for research was similarly uneven with a number of early adopter communities making regular use of these resources and indeed driving their development and the development of underlying technologies. At the same time, there is a 'long tail' of researchers working with more modest resources even when their work could potentially benefit from the use of more advanced e-Infrastructures. The (lack of) usability of tools and fit

*Correspondence: alex.voss@st-andrews.ac.uk
[1] School of Computer Science, University of St Andrews, St Andrews, UK
Full list of author information is available at the end of the article

with users' working practices played a crucial role in limiting the uptake of grid computing but there was also lack of a pathway from the demonstration of benefits through to early stages of skills acquisition and adoption through to routine use [6]. There is a danger that the adoption of cloud computing for research purposes might be held back by similar issues and might be limited to those who are already users of advanced e-Infrastructures such as clusters, HPC resources or grid computing.

Clouds and scientific computing

A recent report by the e-Infrastructure Reflection Group [4] suggests two models of adoption of cloud computing: for those researchers who are already users of existing e-Infrastructure services, those services can be extended to make use of cloud computing resources, keeping the user interfaces and usage models that these users are familiar with intact. For this group of users, who collectively make use of significant resources, the economics of resource provision favour a hybrid model of provision where some resources are provided through the community of users or their institutions while peak usage is burst out to a cloud infrastructure. "The exact threshold when the investment in [one's] own hardware and staff is more cost efficient than the usage of public clouds depends on the application and its utilization" [4].

At the same time, cloud computing offers new opportunities for researchers who – for one reason or another – are not currently users of existing e-Infrastructure services and whose requirements can be met by cloud computing resources [4]. As existing e-Infrastructures such as clusters and grids are often tailored to specific user communities, researchers outside those communities often find the costs of uptake prohibitive or find that their applications do not match the requirements profiles assumed by the resource providers. Cloud computing resources allow users to select instance types that better match the characteristics of their applications and to build runtime environments tailored to their needs.

The performance of cloud computing resources does not reach that of specialised high-performance computing (HPC) resources such as those that make up the Top-500 list of HPC resources [7] and their multi-tenant architecture and limitations on I/O performance may not make them suitable candidates for workloads that spread computation across multiple nodes [8]. However, offerings targeted specifically at compute-intensive applications such as Amazon's Cluster instance types [9] are beginning to address the performance gap [8], in terms of the compute performance of individual nodes but also the IO bandwidth and low latency required, through higher-performance network interconnects and the introduction of the concept of 'placement groups'. From the point of view of a provider of compute services, clouds are therefore primarily of interest as a way to absorb peak loads (through 'cloud-bursting'), extending the capacity of the infrastructure while physical resources support the base loads.

From the point of view of individual researchers or projects, other criteria may be of equal or even higher importance than performance alone. One key advantage of many cloud environments is that they provide virtual machine instances that are under full control of the client, from the kernel upwards. This means that researchers have full control of the software stack installed, thus avoiding problems with conflicts and changing configurations. Images used to produce results can be archived, providing the opportunity to replicate results at a later point. Cloud resources have the advantage of being available on demand and provisioned rapidly within public clouds – although performance can vary [10] and by default resource provision in many clouds is limited to a given number of instances. The economic model of clouds means that in ideal circumstances, the costs of running n instances for an hour are similar to those for running a single instance for n hours – an effect called 'cost associativity', cf. [2]. In practice, overheads for instance creation and job submission as well as details of usage metering mean the costs will not be exactly the same [11]. However, in cases where a rapid turn-around time is desired, the on-demand and self-service nature of (public) clouds can be a signficant advantage over any alternative that cannot scale to the same levels or does not do so within the required timeframe.

Cloud computing interfaces

In principle the promise of cloud computing is a simple model of resource provision: virtual servers on demand. However, the practical issues involved in running research applications are significant. Current interfaces to Infrastructure as a Service (IaaS) clouds [2,3] are relatively low level and do not allow researchers to easily benefit from the elasticity that cloud infrastructures offer. The underlying logic for working with EC2-compatible clouds is the same in command-line tools such as the original EC2 tools [12], the equivalent Euca2ools [13] or graphical user interfaces such as the Amazon AWS Management Console [14] or Elasticfox [15]. Each of these interfaces deals with the same low-level concepts that are a direct representation of the EC2 cloud API. As a consequence, researchers have to deal with time-consuming and often error-prone tasks such as managing access credentials, selecting instance types, managing elastic IP addresses, as well as monitoring resource usage and starting, stopping and terminating instances in response.

In addition, the scientific applications and supporting components need to be deployed within instances and kept up-to-date. Input data needs to be staged in and output files retrieved. This keeps researchers from focusing directly on their scientific research. In essence, what is needed is not raw servers with a bare operating system but a runtime environment for the applications in question that is made available dynamically, on-demand and configured according to the researchers' needs; that is, IaaS needs to be turned into application-specific Platform-as-a-Service (PaaS) or Software-as-a-Service (SaaS).

Elastic virtual infrastructures for research applications

The Elastic Virtual Infrastructures for Research Applications project (ELVIRA, www.elvira-cloud.org) was funded under a joint EPSRC/JISC call for pilot projects for cloud computing in research. It set out to explore a novel way of using cloud resources by making use of the fact that clouds already provide a multi-tenant architecture that allows resource sharing between independent parties, opening up the possibility for the creation of *virtual private research environments* where groups of researchers can collaborate using relatively simple tools in an environment they have tailored to suit their specific requirements. This approach promises to avoid some of the problems often associated with traditional forms of sharing computational and storage resources such as the need for complex authentication and authorization mechanisms, restrictions on the available runtime environments, resource competition, delays in execution through job queueing as well as lack of support for interactive jobs.

In order to achieve this, we make use of functions already provided by cloud infrastructures rather than replicating them. Crucially, IaaS clouds provide a multi-tenant architecture at the infrastructure level using virtualisation and on-demand resource allocation. This is in contrast to grid infrastructures, which provide for multiple users at the operating system level and therefore give rise to issues of separating users, of allocating resources to them and of managing configurations (such as installed libraries). Using IaaS, we can move away from the model of a shared operating system environment and resources waiting for workloads to be submitted and instead create virtual private research environments on demand that are dedicated to a particular use and provide a user experience that differs in many important respects from that of current production grid infrastructures. Our aim in the project was to develop a set of tools, the ELVIRA tools, that enable the rapid creation of such research environments as high-level gateways to cloud resources.

In order to ensure that the development of the ELVIRA tools is informed by real-world requirements, we have worked closely with researchers from a number of disciplinary backgrounds. The case study we describe here involves the study of solar coronal loops but we have also supported computational algebra applications and studies

of the use of Twitter during the Summer riots in England in 2011 as well as during the 2012 Olympic and Paralympic Games. Below, we will briefly discuss the Alfvén Wave Turbulence Simulation application used to study solar coronal loops and the requirements it gives rise to. This application is a good example of the kinds of code that are the target for the ELVIRA project – developed by two researchers with a background in mathematics rather than programming and under constant development in line with the ongoing development of the science behind it. Tracking changes to the code, ensuring its quality and the provenance of the results as well as adapting the code to more powerful compute resources have been key concerns for the researchers involved. Following this, we outline the different components our virtual private research environment used to support this application and discuss our experiences with using these tools.

Alfvén wave turbulence simulation

Magnetic fields play an important role in the heating of the solar corona. The energy for coronal heating likely originates below the photosphere. At the photosphere, magnetic elements are continually moved about by convective flows on the scale of the solar granulation. This results in magneto-hydrodynamic (MHD) disturbances that propagate upward along the magnetic field lines and deposit their energy in the corona. In coronal loops the magnetic fields may become twisted or braided on small spatial scales, and thin current sheets may develop where most of the heating occurs. Alternatively, energy may be injected into the corona in the form of Alfvén waves, which can be dissipated in a variety of ways. Alfvén waves have indeed been observed in the photosphere, corona and solar wind, but the role of such waves in coronal heating has not been clearly demonstrated [16].

Recently, van Ballegooijen et al. [16] developed a three-dimensional (3D) MHD model describing the propagation and dissipation of Alfvén waves in active region loops. The model includes a detailed simulation of Alfvén waves in the coronal part of the loop, as well as in the lower atmospheres at the two ends of the loop. As in earlier studies, the waves are generated by interactions of convective flows with kilogauss flux tubes in the photosphere.

The Alfvén wave turbulence model predicts that the properties of the Alfvén waves depend strongly on the profile of the Alfvén speed $v_A(s)$ as a function of the position s along the loop. If the coronal Alfvén speed is very high, there will be strong reflection of waves at the transition region (TR), and the fraction of energy entering the corona will be reduced compared to the case of low Alfvén speed. The Alfvén speed in turn depends on coronal density. Therefore, it is important to determine the coronal density and wave heating rate so they are consistent with each other.

The purpose of this work [17] is to construct more realistic models of Alfvén wave turbulence for various coronal loops in an observed active region. We use data from instruments on the Solar Dynamics Observatory (SDO) satellite for an active region observed on 2010 May 5 shown in Figure 1. Coronal images obtained with the Atmospheric Imager Assembly (AIA) in several EUV passbands show the presence of coronal loops in this region with temperatures in the range 1 - 3 million kelvin (MK). Our goal is to determine whether these loops may be heated by Alfvén wave turbulence, and if so, to predict the observational signatures of such waves and turbulence.

For each loop in Figure 1, we repeat our computations five times to ensure that the temperature $T_0(s)$, density $\rho_0(s)$, and average heating rate $Q_0(s)$ are consistent with the condition of thermal equilibrium. The iterative process is illustrated in Table 1 for field line F6. The time resolution is about 0.1s and the waves are simulated for a period of 3000 seconds, which is much longer than the Alfvén wave travel time along the entire loop ($\sim$200s).

The software used is a combination of interactive tools written in IDL and a batch part for solving the partial differential equations of the model that is written in Fortran. Because of the memory requirements of the IDL code used for analysing the results of runs and because of the software license required, data analysis was conducted on a server at St Andrews, which has been upgraded to 96GB of main memory. The Fortran code initially was similarly

Table 1 Iterations for model F6

Iteration	m	Q_{min} erg/cm^3/s	$\overline{Q}_{cor}$ erg/cm^3/s	T_{max} MK	p_{cor} dyne/cm^2
1	0.524	7.99×10^{-4}	9.66×10^{-4}	2.28	1.65
2	0.567	8.15×10^{-4}	1.01×10^{-3}	2.29	1.68
3	0.532	8.38×10^{-4}	1.02×10^{-3}	2.31	1.71
4	0.514	8.22×10^{-4}	9.86×10^{-4}	2.30	1.69
5	0.553	8.41×10^{-4}	1.03×10^{-3}	2.31	1.72

memory intensive and jobs were running for up to five days, making it difficult to use in many production HTC infrastructures such as the UK's National Grid Service [18] without negotiating tailored service provision. As part of the ELVIRA project, we have made changes to the code to significantly reduce the memory footprint and through the use of OpenMP [19] we are also making progress in reducing the running time by using multiple CPU cores, see Table 2.

As a result of these changes we are now able to run the Fortran jobs on the St Andrews StACC cloud, which provides a range of instance types, the largest of which provides 4 CPU cores, 4 GB of RAM and 40GB of instance storage. Where necessary, we can configure the system to use the Amazon EC2 cloud. The code scales well, so the larger instance sizes available there allow us to achieve significantly better turn-around times than would be possible on our local resources. The cc2.8xlarge instance type in particular is of interest as it provides the best overall performance while c1.xlarge provides a cheaper price per job (see Table 3).

Requirements and functionality

In the following section we describe some of the key requirements for ELVIRA and show how they have been met for the case of the Astrophysics application using the ELVIRA tools, the functionality provided by cloud infrastructures and a number of additional off-the-shelf components. Figure 2 provides an overview of the architecture of the system.

Configuration management

Functionality is required to ensure that instances are equipped to meet the requirements of the research application. We can distinguish between configuration at the cloud level such as choice of an appropriate instance type, assignment of virtual storage volumes and configuration within the instance itself such as configuration of the operating system, deployment of dependencies such as libraries or creation of user accounts. In the case of the Astrophysics application, we need to ensure that a 64bit instance with sufficient memory or swap space is created and that the Portland Group Fortran libraries are

Figure 1 Ten magnetic field lines used for modeling Alfvén wave turbulence in coronal loops. The field lines were traced through the Non-Linear Force Free Field (NLFFF) model. The background image is from the AIA 193 Å channel.

Table 2 Running times of a short test run (with _t_=100) on a physical machine with 32 cores (AMD Opteron™ 6272, Bulldozer architecture, 2.1GHz)

Threads	1	2	4	8	10	12	14	16	20	24	32
Time (s)	1379	862	610	516	509	491	485	496	576	592	1350

installed. In order to support changing requirements we configure instances at runtime using the ELVIRA kickstart process rather than working with static images. Configuration scripts are managed in a Subversion repository and configuration data is passed into instances through the user-data mechanism provided by the EC2 API, allowing the instance configuration to be further contextualised. Bootstrap code in /etc/rc.local retrieves this code and executes it. Alternatively, Ubuntu's cloud-init system [20] can be used. The whole process is designed to be simple but to allow for expansion. In most cases where instances have a limited lifetime, the simple mechanism provided will be sufficient but it is possible to invoke other configuration management tools such as Chef [21] or Puppet [22] if required. The details of the process of providing configured instances are embedded in the ELVIRA tools so that users do not need to be concerned with them but can simply provide a list of required configuration options.

Job management

The execution of the actual workload requires job management functionality. In the simplest of cases there can be a one-to-one mapping between jobs and instances but this makes sense only if the overhead of creating an instance is negligible compared to the job running time and if the instance resources are fully utilised by the workload. The latter is particularly important when using a public cloud and quirks in the charging models of cloud service providers can make the question of efficient usage and costing more complex than it would appear at first sight [11]. As a consequence, a common approach taken is to deploy a traditional batch job submission system (e.g., [23-25]) or a workflow management system (e.g., [26,27]) into the cloud or to use cloud resources to

extend an existing cluster or grid into the cloud through 'cloud-bursting' (e.g., [28]).

A number of clustering and grid environments have been ported to cloud infrastructures, often provided as a set of instance images that can be deployed relatively easily. An example is StarCluster [29], a cluster computing toolkit that supports the deployment of a batch job submission system based on Sun's Grid Engine into Amazon's EC2 cloud. This approach is suitable for a multitude of workloads and user communities where researchers are already using batch job submission systems and are thus familiar with their interfaces.

Our aim was to explore an alternative approach that would utilise the fact that cloud computing infrastructures already support multi-tenancy. Instead of deploying a traditional middleware into the cloud or adapting existing applications to cloud computing, we looked for an alternative that would fit into the philosophy of ELVIRA of building virtual private research environments, of providing simple solutions by leveraging the affordances of cloud computing technologies and of reusing and adapting existing code where possible. We did not wish to re-write the scientific application code to adapt them to the cloud (e.g., to use a MapReduce pattern, cf. [30]) as this would have made development and maintenance more difficult for the code owners.

We decided to instead explore the possibility of adapting the continuous integration system Jenkins [31,32]) to the needs of the project. It has the advantage of providing rich functionality for the management of jobs, their execution history, their input and output data as well as supporting distributed job execution through slave nodes. Its web-based user interface is highly configurable yet relatively easy to use and the system provides a robust plugin mechanism as well as a RESTful API to support extensions.

Table 3 Running times for a test job on different cloud infrastructures and instance types

Cloud	Type	Cores	Threads	Time(s)	Cost($/h)	Cost per job ($)
StACC	m1.large	1	1	12734	N/A	N/A
	m1.xlarge	2	2	7549	N/A	N/A
	c1.xlarge	4	4	4310	N/A	N/A
EC2	c1.xlarge	8	8	3602	0.58	0.58
	cc2.8xlarge	16	16	1303	2.40	0.87
Local		32	14	1863	N/A	

Experiments were run to determine the optimum number of threads and best results are reported. StACC instances are running on Dell PowerEdge R610 nodes with 2xQuadCore Intel Xeon E5504 2GHz and 16GB RAM. The local machine is a dual Opteron™ 6272 2.1GHz. Costs are EC2 Linux US East on-demand prices as of 2nd June 2013, prices per job are for pure running-time, excluding instance creation and configuration overheads.

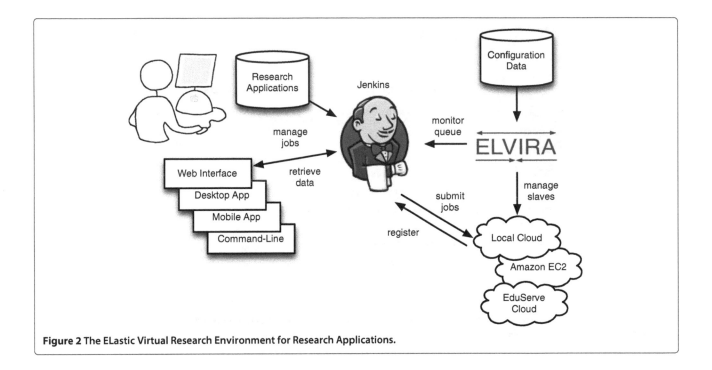

Figure 2 The ELastic Virtual Research Environment for Research Applications.

Jenkins comes with a wide range of plugins and additional tools such as mobile apps or integrations with integrated development environments are available.

Jenkins allows jobs to be configured through the web-based interface and it manages the relationship between these jobs and their execution histories ('builds'), capturing provenance information as well as input and output data. Jobs can be connected to each other so that they run in sequence and matrix jobs can be configured to produce parameter sweeps along a number of dimensions (cf. Figure 3). Matrices can be made sparse by supplying an expression that defines which elements of the matrix should be executed. Jobs can be configured to require a set of parameters including the option to upload input files. To control the environment in which a job executes, it can also be mapped to a specific worker or a set of workers that provide the specific runtime environment required by the job. Builds can be triggered manually by the user, through an external event such as a commit to a version control system or an update of a file or regularly through a `cron`-like scheduler.

Source code files for the application are hosted in a private `git` repository and a separate job exists to compile the sources for a range of processor architectures using the Portland Group Fortran [33] compiler. This step needs to run on a server at St Andrews that has a node-locked license for the compiler, so this job is locked to run on that server. The job execution script matches the CPU type used in the instance to the appropriate code. This is important as running times can differ significantly between unoptimised code and code optimised for the specific CPU architecture used in the cloud instance.

At any point in time, users can monitor what jobs are being executed on the worker nodes as well as what jobs are scheduled for execution. A real-time view of the job log files is available that includes the output the executing program produces on its standard output and error channels. This allows errors to be spotted during runtime and jobs to be terminated if necessary. The log output is archived after a job has executed together with the job's output files, which can be retrieved through the web front-end. The web-based front-end allows multiple users to collaborate in managing jobs and builds as well as giving them shared access to output and provenance data.

The input data is usually of negligible size (fieldline F6 being the largest at ca. 11MB) but the output data can be large (2GB in the case of F6). The output also does not compress well, so it is transfered to Jenkins as-is. While this does not normally take much time in a local environment, the transfer times from a public cloud can be significant and highly variable. The faster the computation the more this matters, especially since faster instances will be more expensive. By default, Jenkins stages data back synchronously at the end of a job and at the moment this is how data is staged back to the server at St Andrews. This problem can be avoided if staging the data back is relegated to a subsequent job that can run in parallel to the next compute job. Alternatively, output data can be uploaded to a storage service such as S3 instead of being sent back to the Jenkins node. From there it

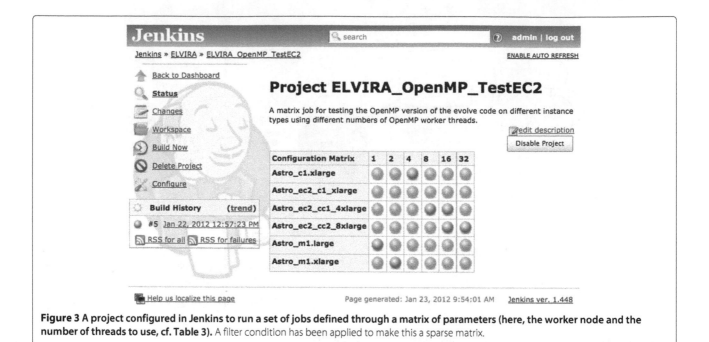

Figure 3 A project configured in Jenkins to run a set of jobs defined through a matrix of parameters (here, the worker node and the number of threads to use, cf. Table 3). A filter condition has been applied to make this a sparse matrix.

can be retrieved at a later point for analysis. Using S3 has other advantages such as providing an off-site, highly dependable archive for job output data.

Elastic scaling of resources

To allow resources to scale dynamically in response to the workload we have extended the Jenkins system by adding an external monitoring daemon that starts instances in response to changes in the build queue. Instance configurations are defined in the a central configuration file and assigned labels matching the labels defined in the job configurations in Jenkins. This allows a 1:n mapping between instance configurations and job definitions to be created so that different jobs can share instance configurations and instances.

The decision to create a new worker node is controlled by the formula given in Equation 1, which combines q, the number of jobs in the queue, w, the number of workers already running and i, the number of workers that are currently idle or still deploying. A factor f is used to adjust this relationship and a maximum m is defined for the number of instances that are turned on at each step. Figure 4 shows that if no instances are running and $n > m$ jobs are submitted, then m worker nodes will be started initially. The growth of the number of workers is limited but there is no maximum that is imposed although this would be easy to add. We assume cost associativity, i.e., that running n jobs in n instances in parallel costs as much as running n jobs sequentially in a single instance. This is roughly true for our jobs, which run for about 3 hours on a cc2.8xlarge instance and significantly longer

on other resources. For workloads with shorter running times, a parameter $p > 1$ can be introduced to represent the number of jobs to run per instance.

$$min(m, q) \text{ if } w = 0 \text{ else } min\left(q, m, \left\lfloor \frac{q}{f \times (w + i)} \right\rfloor\right) \quad (1)$$

Once created, instances register with the Jenkins server using the Swarm plugin [34] and start servicing the build queue. The Swarm plugin provides the necessary functionality for a client to register with Jenkins but it is the ELVIRA tools that manage the set of cloud instances, instantiate and terminate them, configure them to act as Swarm nodes and contextualise them to support the specific scientific application.

In contrast to the solution implemented by Strijkers et al. [23], our model does not take into account core counts. This is because we allow different configurations to match different workloads rather than trying to provide a generic clustering environment. Our model is a-historical, taking into account only the current state of the queue. This model is sufficient for us as our workloads are relatively long-running. For more general mixtures of workloads that include jobs with running times that are short compared to the queue poll frequency a history would probably need to be implemented as suggested in [23]. An additional extension that we are looking to implement is a scheme where we can automatically burst out from StACC into Amazon's EC2 service or a similar public cloud infrastructure.

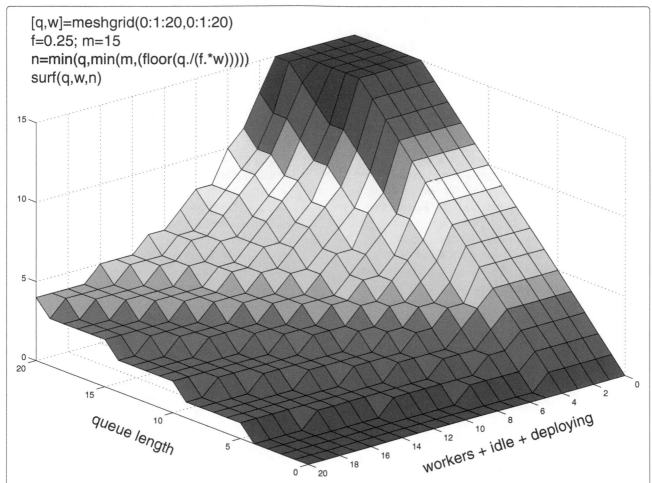

```
[q,w]=meshgrid(0:1:20,0:1:20)
f=0.25; m=15
n=min(q,min(m,(floor(q./(f.*w)))))
surf(q,w,n)
```

Figure 4 Matlab plot of equation 1. The growth of the number of worker nodes is limited by the number of workers already running, idle or deploying and there is an overall limit on the growth rate but no limit on the total number of workers.

Instance startup and configuration times

As both public and private clouds are shared infrastructures, instance startup times can be unpredictable. A recent study [10] has investigated this for three major public clouds. The findings show that instance creation time varies significantly between different instance launches. The mean launch time depends mainly on the instance image size and instance type. Launching multiple instances on Amazon EC2 does not increase the instance creation time on average [10].

In addition to the time it takes for the cloud infrastructure to provision an instance, configuration scripts that need to run also determine the time it takes for the instance to become available. To some extent, this time can be reduced by installing frequently required packages in the instance image used. For example, in the case of ELVIRA we installed OpenJDK in the instance image as well as the Swarm client .jar file to avoid having to download them every time an instance is created. The Portland Group Fortran libraries, in contrast, are staged in each time an instance is created since we wanted to keep the instance image generic.

To mitigate the time required for instance startup and configuration, it is important to ensure that instances are used to run a number of jobs, especially if the running time of the code is relatively short compared to the time it takes to provision a fully configured instance and register it with Jenkins. This ensures that the overheads are amortised across a larger workload. In contrast to the overheads of instance creation and configuration, the overhead of starting a job are negligible but the staging of output data back to the Jenkins server is not (see above).

Authentication and authorisation

Our virtual private research environment currently uses basic authentication based on a user database but Jenkins supports a number of different authentication options that allow it to be integrated with a number of different authentication options. Authentication between the Jenkins server and the worker nodes is via ssh keys, which are injected automatically by the ELVIRA configuration process. This means there is no need to set up a complete public key infrastructure (PKI) as in the case of Grid computing with all the key-management issues that go along with PKI such as the need for global trust, verification of identities and limited key lifetime. The comparative ease with which cloud-based resources can be established and shared within groups of collaborating researchers has also been pointed out by Wu et al. [35], who have developed a Science Gateway for Life Science applications.

Authorisation options are provided in Jenkins through an access control matrix per project, which allows fine-grained policies to be implemented that restrict the operations a user is allowed to invoke with respect to that project, the build history and the archived job data. We have used a single installation for a number of different projects using suitable authorisation settings. However, it is important to note that in environments where users cannot necessarily be trusted and are given permission to configure jobs it is necessary to deploy multiple instances of Jenkins using different Unix user accounts. In particular, it is important to ensure that the system is set up so that no jobs can be run under the Jenkins user account on the main server as this would give these jobs access to the Jenkins configuration information.

Conclusions

We have introduced the ELVIRA project and the concept of a *virtual private research environment*. The ELVIRA tools provide the necessary functionality to manage configurations of cloud resources that are tailored to researchers' needs and manage the elastic provision of these resources in response to workload demands. The researchers we have collaborated with are now able to utilise a virtual private research environment that allows them to manage the execution of their jobs, the resulting output data as well as provenance data through a web-based interface that is tried and tested. The ELVIRA tools provide the necessary extensions for the use of cloud resources but researchers do not need to worry about whether the resources used are provided through local physical resources, a local private cloud infrastructure or a public cloud like Amazon EC2.

Ease of use is important for the uptake of cloud computing for research applications. Ultimately, the success of cloud computing in research applications will depend on the creation of task-centric user interfaces to deal with the significant complexity involved in realising non-trivial applications. The approach we have taken has a number of advantages over alternatives:

- Direct control over the runtime environment used to run jobs allows users to configure it to their specific needs. Configuration here means configuration of the instances and other resources as well as the configuration of the operating system and any software installed. The ELVIRA tools use a central configuration file that can contain definitions for different clouds as well as ensembles of cloud resources to be used for different purposes. The repository of instance configuration scripts allows instances to be configured through declaring desired options rather than scripting.

- The elastic scaling functionality provided by ELVIRA adjusts the number of worker nodes to the current workload and through a set of parameters allows this scaling feature to be adjusted to fit the nature of the workload as well as the characteristics of the cloud environment used (e.g., a maximum number of instances). Different types of worker nodes can be configured for different workloads and jobs can be tied to these worker types.

- The fine-grained access control mechanisms provided by Jenkins allow research environments to be configured that allow researchers to collaborate by sharing access to builds. An annotation feature and the rigorous way that Jenkins uses to manage builds means that it is easy to refer to specific builds and their outputs, which is essential for collaborative research.

- The browser-based user-interface is relatively easy to use but provides access to rich functionality, allowing even complex jobs to be defined through the matrix build configuration option and workflows to be created through chaining jobs together.

- A seemingly trivial feature that is immensely important in practice is the log file viewer that allows the output of builds to be monitored in real-time through the web browser, allowing researchers to monitor build progress and health.

- The wealth of plugins and other extension of the Jenkins system allows the virtual private research environment to be tailored to the specific needs of a project or research group.

- Deployment of a Jenkins instance is very easy and well documented (e.g., in [31]). A basic installation that can be further configured and extended can be created in a cloud instance through the use of the ELVIRA tools, providing a starting point very rapidly. Maintenance is simplified through an integrated update mechanism and plugins to take care of tasks such as backups.

- The ELVIRA tools provide an interface to cloud instances that reduces the complexity by providing configurable defaults for a range of options that need to be provided for each operation with other cloud user interfaces. They make working with multiple clouds easier by providing these options per configured cloud infrastructure.

Our experience from previous projects shows that successul applications of e-Research infrastructures depend not just on more usable technologies but also crucially on the existence of a working division of labour that supports researchers and allows technological offerings to be adopted, appropriated and tailored to the specific needs of a research project [6]. We envisage the ELVIRA tools being used in a division of labour involving the researchers and system administrators. After all, providing a working runtime environment for research codes is non-trivial and there is no way to provide a generic solution to this, although trading configuration scripts and making them available through repositories may help. However, and more importantly, there are routine tasks to be done such as ensuring backups and generally ensuring secure operation that researchers would probably not want to be concerned with. At St Andrews, we run Jenkins on a server managed by our School's system administrators, who deal with day-to-day maintenance and monitoring while the researchers are free to build and manage the virtual private research environments they require and draw on cloud resources as needed. Our professional system administrators have also been crucial in initially setting up aspects of the runtime environment such as configuring server certificates (for https and authenticated SMTP for sending notification emails) and configuring Apache and Tomcat.

Finally, we wish to briefly touch on the issue of cost. While it is certainly possible to host an entire virtual private research environment in a cloud, we believe that given the current state of the art, in many cases it will be advantageous to host the Jenkins server, the repository for instance configurations and the ELVIRA daemon on a physical machine. Perhaps where a stable and well-managed private cloud exists, there will be a case for deploying onto virtual resources but the respective likelihood of downtimes needs to be assessed. The cloud's capacity for rapid recovery in the case of a resource failure can also be utilised in cases where a physical server is normally used. Hosting the parts of the system that are long-running in a public cloud is likely to incur significant costs and in a research environment it is likely that the full economic costs of hosting physical hardware will not be known. The case for deploying into a public cloud is therefore more likely to stem from the costs associated with transfering data across the boundaries of the cloud. If a significant proportion of the jobs are run in a public cloud then it will make sense to locate the whole research environment in that cloud and run all communication through the local IP addresses to avoid networking costs. It is certainly worthwhile modeling costs before making decisions about deployment [36] and it is important to take the cost of network traffic into account in addition to the cost of the cloud instances as this may be significant. In the UK,

through funding from the University Modernisation Fund, EduServ is offering a cloud computing service [37] that may well compare favourably to Amazon's EC2 service as it does not charge for traffic into the Janet network.

Future work

The work reported here is the result of a short eight month project. We are continuing to evaluate and use the resulting tools and hope to thereby add to the growing body of experience with the use of cloud computing for research applications. Our aim in this paper was to enable concrete production use of the cloud rather than providing benchmarks that are often the focus in other publications (e.g., [25]). An important factor in the use of cloud computing is the utilisation of multi-core and heterogeneous architectures. We are currently investigating the possibility of porting the MHD code to GPGPU resources such as Amazon's Cluster GPU instances. Utilising such resources in combination with the multiple cores that the CPU provides promises a further reduction in running times but it remains to be seen whether the speedup achieved will justify the higher cost of these instance types.

Competing interests
The authors declare that they have no competing interests.

Authors' contributions
IS was the ELVIRA project lead. AB was responsible for technical project management. AV was responsible for the implementation of the ELVIRA platform and liaison with the researchers using it. AvB and MAT were responsible for the substantive research on solar flares and for providing input to the requirements elicitation. All authors contributed to the writing of this article and all authors read and approved the final manuscript.

Acknowledgements
The work presented in this paper was funded by the UK's Engineering and Physical Sciences Research Council and JISC (EP/I034327/1). We would also like to thank Derek Wang, who has provided support for our use of the St Andrews Cloud Collaboratory. Our reviewers have provided useful comments that have helped to improve the paper significantly and we would like to thank them for this.

Author details
[1] School of Computer Science, University of St Andrews, St Andrews, UK.
[2] Harvard-Smithsonian Center for Astrophysics, Cambridge, MA, USA.

References
1. Foster I, Zhao Y, Raicu I, Lu S (2008) Cloud Computing and grid computing 360-degree compared. In: Grid computing environments workshop, 2008. GCE '08. IEEE, New York, pp 1–10
2. Armbrust M, Fox A, Griffith R, Joseph AD, Katz RH, Konwinski A, Lee G, Patterson DA, Rabkin A, Stoica I, Zaharia M (2009) Above the clouds: a Berkeley view of cloud computing. Tech. Rep. UCB/EECS-2009-28, EECS Department, University of California, Berkeley. http://www.eecs.berkeley.edu/Pubs/TechRpts/2009/EECS-2009-28.html
3. Badger L, Grance T, Patt-Corner R, Voas J (2011) DRAFT cloud computing synopsis and recommendations: recommendations of the National Institute of Standards and Technology. Tech. Rep. Special Publication 800-146, National Institute of Standards and Technology
4. Cloud Computing for research and science: a holistic overview, policy, and recommendations. Tech. rep., e-Infrastructure Reflection Group 2012.

http://www.e-irg.eu/images/stories/dissemination/e-irg_cloud_computing_paper_v.final.pdf

5. Bradshaw D, Folco G, Cattaneo G, Kolding M (2012) Quantitative Estimates of the Demand for Cloud Computing in Europe and the Likely Barriers to Uptake. Tech. Rep. SMART 2011/0045, D4 – Final Report, IDC. http://cordis.europa.eu/fp7/ict/ssai/docs/cloud-report-final.pdf

6. Voss A, Asgari-Targhi M, Procter R, Fergusson D (2010) Adoption of e-Infrastructure services: configurations of practice. Philos Trans A R Soc (368): 4161–4176

7. Top 500 Supercomputer Sites. http://www.top500.org

8. Iosup A, Ostermann S, Yigibasi MN, Prodan R, Fahringer T, Epema DH (2011) Performance analysis of cloud computing services for many-tasks scientific computing. IEEE Trans Parallel Distributed Syst 22(6): 931–945

9. Amazon EC2 GPU Instances. http://docs.aws.amazon.com/AWSEC2/latest/UserGuide/using_cluster_computing.html

10. Mao M, Humphrey M (2012) A performance study on the VM startup time in the cloud. 2012 IEEE Fifth Int Conf Cloud Comput 0: 423–430

11. Gillam L, Li B, O'Loughlin J, Tomar AP (2013) Fair Benchmarking for cloud computing systems. J Cloud Comput: Adv, Syst Appl 2(6). Springer, doi:10.1186/2192-113X-2-6

12. Amazon EC2 API Tools. http://aws.amazon.com/developertools/351

13. Eucalyptus 3.2.2 Command Line Interface Reference Guide. http://www.eucalyptus.com/docs/3.2/cli/

14. AWS Management Console. http://aws.amazon.com/console/

15. Firefox Extension for Amazon EC2. http://sourceforge.net/projects/elasticfox

16. van Ballegooijen AA, Asgari-Targhi M, Cranmer SR, DeLuca EE (2011) Heating of the solar chromosphere and corona by Alfvén wave turbulence. Astrophysical J 736: 3. doi:10.1088/0004-637X/736/1/3

17. Asgari-Targhi M, van Ballegooijen AA (2012) Model for Alfvén wave turbulence in solar coronal loops: heating rate profiles and temperature fluctuations. Astrophysical J 746: 81. doi:10.1088/0004-637X/746/1/81

18. UK National Grid Service (NGS). http://www.ngs.ac.uk

19. The OpenMP® API specification for parallel programming. http://openmp.org

20. Ubuntu CloudInit. https://help.ubuntu.com/community/CloudInit

21. Opscode Chef. http://www.opscode.com/chef/

22. Puppet. http://puppetlabs.com

23. Strijkers R, Toorop W, Av Hoof, Grosso P, Belloum A, Vasuining D, Laat Cd, Meijer R (2010) AMOS: using the cloud for on-demand execution of e-science applications. In: Proceedings of the 6th IEEE International Conference on e-Science. IEEE Computer Society, Washington, pp 331–338. http://dx.doi.org/10.1109/eScience.2010.15

24. Glenis V, McGough AS, Kutija V, Kilsby C, Woodman S (2013) Flood modelling for cities using cloud computing. J Cloud Comput: Adv, Syst Appl 2(7). Springer, doi:10.1186/2192-113X-2-7

25. Cohen J, Filippis I, Woodbridge M, Bauer D, Hong NC, Jackson M, Butcher S, Colling D, Darlington J, Fuchs B, Harvey M (2013) RAPPORT: running scientific high-performance computing applications on the cloud. Philos Trans A R Soc 371(1983): 1471–2962

26. Juve G, Deelman E, Vahi K, Mehta G, Berriman B, Berman B, Maechling P (2009) Scientific workflow applications on Amazon EC2. In: 5th IEEE International Conference on e-Science: Workshops IEEE, pp 59–66

27. Nagavaram A, Agrawal G, Freitas M, Telu K, Mehta G, Mayani R, Deelman E (2011) A cloud-based dynamic workflow for mass spectrometry data analysis. In: Proceedings of the 7th IEEE international conference on e-science. IEEE, New York, pp 47–54

28. Humphrey M, Hill Z, van Ingen C, Jackson K, Ryu Y (2011) Assessing the value of cloudbursting: a case study of satellite image processing in windows azure. In: Proceedings of the 7th, IEEE international conference on e-Science. IEEE, pp 126–133

29. StarCluster. http://web.mit.edu/star/cluster

30. Dalman T, Dörnemann T, Juhnke E, Weitzel M, Smith M, Wiechert W, Nöh K, Freisleben B Metabolic Flux Analysis in the Cloud In: Proceedings of the 6th IEEE conference on e-science. IEEE, pp 57–64

31. Smart J (2011) Jenkins: the definitive guide. 1st edition. O'Reilly

32. Jenkins Continuous Integration Server. http://www.jenkins-ci.org

33. The Portland Group. http://www.pgroup.com/

34. Jenkins Swarm Plugin. https://wiki.jenkins-ci.org/display/JENKINS/Swarm+Plugin

35. Wu W, Zhang H, Li Z, Mao Y (2011) Creating a cloud-based life science gateway In: Proceedings of the 7th IEEE international conference on e-science. IEEE, New York, pp 55–61

36. Khajeh-Hosseini A, Greenwood D, Smith J, Sommerville I (2011) The cloud adoption toolkit: supporting cloud adoption decisions in the enterprise. Software: Practice and Experience: 447–465

37. Eduserv Cloud IaaS. http://www.eduserv.org.uk/services/cloud

12

A secure user authentication protocol for sensor network in data capturing

Zhou Quan[1,2]*, Tang Chunming[1,2], Zhen Xianghan[3] and Rong Chunming[4]

Abstract

Sensor network is an important approach of data capturing. User authentication is a critical security issue for sensor networks because sensor nodes are deployed in an open and unattended environment, leaving them possible hostile attack. Some researchers proposed some user authentication protocols using one-way hash function or using biometric technology. Recently, Yel et al. and Wenbo et al. proposed a user authentication protocols using elliptic curves cryptography. However, there are some security weaknesses for these protocols. In the paper, we review several proposed user authentication protocols, with a detail review of the Wenbo et al.'s user authentication protocol and a cryptanalysis of this protocol that shows several security weaknesses. Furthermore, we propose a secure user authentication protocol using identity-based cryptography to overcome those weaknesses. Finally, we present the security analysis, a comparison of security, computation, and performance for the proposed protocols, which shows that this user authentication protocol is more secure and suitable for higher security WSNs.

Keywords: Data capturing; Wireless sensor networks; User authentication; Identity-based cryptography

Introduction

With the application of big data, there are some base manipulation processes: data capturing, data transport, data storage, data extraction & integration, data analysis & interpretation and data application. In the data capturing, using all kinds of devices and methods to collect data, such as smart devices, sensors, Web. So there are three important approaches of data capturing: Internet, Internet of Things (IoT) and sensor network [1]. Wireless Sensor networks (WSNs) is an open environment distributed network, which is an important approach of data capturing for big data. Nevertheless, with the application of dig data, the requirement of real-time data from WSNs is increasing highly. In some situations the gateway impossibly does force a user to access the sensor node directly. In such case the security and reliability to inquire and data disseminate are very important. Only when every client (remote sensor node, remote user) in the WSNs proves his/her identity can he/she be allowed to join the WSNs and access to resource, such as real-time data. Thus, a key security requirement for WSNs is user authentication [2-5].

In 2004, Sastry et al. [2] proposed a security scheme using access control lists (ACL) for IEEE 802.15.4 networks in the gateway node. An ACL would be maintained in gateway node and sensor nodes. Watro et al. [6] proposed a user authentication protocol using RSA and Differ-Hellman algorithm, but which was open to hostile attack by a user masquerading.

In 2005, Benenson et al. [7] proposed a user authentication protocol based on elliptic curve discrete logarithm problem (ECDLP) to handle the sensor node capture attack, which relied on a trusted third party.

In 2006, Wong et al. [8] proposed a dynamic user authentication scheme for WSNs based on a light-weight strong password using hash function, which included three phases: registration phase, login phase and authentication phase. Nonetheless, Tseng et al. [9] and Das [10] pointed out that this protocol had some weaknesses in protecting against replay attack, forgery attack, stolen-verifier attack, sensor node revealing and exposing the password to the other node and no updating user's password. In 2007, Tseng et al. [9] proposed an enhanced user authentication protocol by adding an extra phase (password changing phase) on Wong et al.'s phases. However,

* Correspondence: zhouqq@gzhu.edu.cn
[1]Key Laboratory of Mathematics and Interdisciplinary Sciences of Guangdong Higher Education Institutes, Guangzhou University, Guangzhou, China
[2]School of Mathematics and Information Science, Guangzhou University, Guangzhou, China
Full list of author information is available at the end of the article

in 2008 Ko [11] showed the Tseng et al.'s protocol was still insecure and did not provide mutual authentication.

In 2009, Das [10] proposed a two-factor user authentication protocol based on password and smart card against stolen-verifier attack. Nevertheless, Nyang et al. [12] showed there were some security weaknesses in offline-password guessing attacks.

In 2010, Vaidya et al. [13] demonstrated the Tseng et al.'s protocol, Wong et al.'s protocol and Ko's protocol were still not strong enough to protect again replay attack, stolen-verifier attack and man-in-the-middle attack. Khan et al. [14,15] pointed out the Das's protocol did not provide mutual authentication, and against by passing attack and privileged insider attack. Moreover, Chen et al. [16] also demonstrated the Das's protocol did not provide mutual authentication between the gateway node and the sensor node. And Chen et al. proposed a more secure and robust two-factor user authentication scheme for WSNs.

In 2011, Yeh et al. [17] found that the Chen et al.'s protocol failed to provide a secure method for updating password and insider attack. And Yeh et al. proposed a new user authentication scheme for WSNs using elliptic curve cryptography (ECC). Unfortunately, Han [18] found this protocol still had some weaknesses: no mutual authentication, no key agreement between the user and the sensor node, and no prefer forward security. Meanwhile, Yuan et al. [19] proposed a biometric-based user authentication for WSNs using password and smart card in 2010. Unfortunately, in 2011 Yoon et al. [20] showed the integrity problem of the Yuan et al.'s protocol and proposed a new biometric-based user authentication scheme without using password for WSNs.

In 2012, Ohood et al. [21] pointed out Yoon et al.'s scheme still had some drawbacks, such as no key agreement, no message confidentiality service, no providing against DoS and node compromise attack. Moreover, Ohood et al. [22] proposed an efficient biometric authentication protocol for WSNs.

Recently, Wenbo et al. [23] in 2013 proposed a new user authentication protocol for WSNs using elliptic curve cryptography to overcome the security weaknesses of Yeh et al.'s protocol. Although they suggested security improvements of Yeh et al.'s protocol, there were some security weaknesses in their protocol, e.g. no mutual authentication between the user and sensor node, no protecting against insider attack, forgery attack and DoS (denial of service) attack.

To address all of the issues raised in the above studies, we propose a secure user authentication protocol using identity-based cryptography on the basis of our previous studies to trusted management and trusted architecture of WSNs [24-26]. Our proposal addresses the key security issues.

The remainder of this paper is organized as follows: in Section Related works, we review the Wenbo et al.'s protocol and a detail cryptanalysis; next we present our user authentication protocol based on identity-based encryption in Section Proposed protocol; in Section Security and performance analysis, a security and performance analysis of the related protocol is presented; in Section Conclusion, we provide some conclusion remarks.

Related works
Notation
In Table 1, some notations used throughout this paper and their corresponding definitions are shown.

Review of Wenbo's scheme
In the Wenbo's protocol, the gateway GW held two master keys (x and y). And it was assumed that the gateway and the sensor nodes shared a long-term common secret key, $SK_{GS} = h(S_n||y)$. The Wenbo's protocol involves the registration phase, login phase, authentication phase and password update phase, which can be briefly described as follows.

Registration phase
In this phase, a user U submits his/her ID_u and a hash of his/her password to GW via a secured channel. Then, GW issues a license to U. The steps are described as follows.

Step 1: $U \rightarrow GW$: $\{ID_u, PS'\}$.

U enters an identity, selects a random number br and a password PS. And U computes $PS' = h(PS \oplus br)$. Then U sends message $\{ID_u, PS'\}$ to GW via a secured channel.

Step 2: $GW \rightarrow$ a smart card of U: $\{Bu, Wu, h(.)\}$.

GW computes $Ku = h(ID_u||x) \times P$, $Bu = h(ID_u \oplus PS')$, and $Wu = Bu \oplus Ku$, where x is a master key of GW. Then the GW stores (Bu, Wu) into a smart card and sends it to U.

Login phase
When U access Sn, U needs enter his ID_u and PS. And the smart card must confirm the validity of U via the following steps.

Step 1: Validate U.

The smart card check whether $Bu = h(ID_u \oplus h(PS \oplus br))$ hold. If the answer is no, the U's identification validation fails and the smart card will terminate this request. Otherwise, the smart card continues to execute the next step.

Step 2: U's smart card generates a random number r_u, calculates X and a. $X = r_u \times P$, $X' = r_u \times (Bu \oplus Wu)$, and $a = h(ID_u||X||X'||T_u)$, where T_u is the curren time of U's system.

Step 3: $U \rightarrow Sn$: $\{ID_u, X, T_u, a\}$.

The $\{ID_u, X, Tu, a\}$ is submitted to Sn via public channel.

Table 1 Notations

Symbol	Define
p	A big prime number
F_p	A finite field
E	An elliptic curve in F_p with a large order
P	A point on elliptic curve E with order q that is a big prime number
U	A remote user
ID	An identity
PS	A user password
GW	Gateway of WSNs
S_n	Sensor node of WSNs
Q_{id}	Public key of id
d_{id}	Private key of id
P_{set}	A system parameter set of PKG
$h(.)$	A public secure one-way hash function
$H_1(.)$	A public function: $\{0,1\}^* \rightarrow G_1$, the G_1 is a group $G_1 = \{NP \mid n \in \{0,1 \ldots q\text{-}1\}\}$
$H_2(.)$	A public function $G_2 \rightarrow \{0,1\}^*$, G_2 is subgroup with an order q of $GF (p^2)*$
$f(.)$	A public function: $G_1 \rightarrow \{0,1\}^*$
$\hat{e}(.)$	An admissible pairing: $G_1 \times G_1 \rightarrow G_2$
$E_k(m)$	Encrypt message m with key k
$D_k(c)$	Decrypt message c with key k
$\|$	A string concatenation operation
$\oplus$	A XOR operation

Authentication phase

The authentication phase includes: *Sn* checking the validity of the request message of *U*, *GW* authenticating *Sn* and *U*, *Sn* authenticating *GW* and *U*, *U* authenticating *Sn* and *GW*.

Sn checks the validity of the request message of *U*

When receiving the login message $\{ID_u, X, T_u, a\}$ at time T', *Sn* checks and generates request message which is sent to *GW* for authentication. *Sn* executes the following steps.

Step 1: Checks T_u.

Sn checks if $(T'\text{-}T_u) \leqq \Delta T$ holds, where ΔT denotes the expected time interval for transmission delay. If the answer is yes, the validity of T_u can be assured, and *Sn* executes the next step. Otherwise *Sn* rejects the login request.

Step 2: Picks a random number r_s and calculates Y and b.
$Y = r_s \times P$, $b = h(\text{SK}_{GS} \| ID_u \| X \| T_u \| a \| ID_{Sn} \| Y \| T_s)$, where T_s denotes the current request time of the *Sn* system.

Step 3: $Sn \rightarrow GW$: $\{ID_u, X, T_u, a, ID_{Sn}, Y, T_s, b\}$.

The $\{ID_u, X, T_u, a, ID_{Sn}, Y, T_s, b\}$ is submitted to *GW* via public channel.

GW authenticates *Sn* and *U*

When receiving the request message that sent by *Sn* at time T'', *GW* checks and validates *Sn* and *U*, and generates the response message that will be sent to *Sn*. *GW* executes the following steps.

Step 1: Validates if T_s and T_u.

GW checks whether $(T''\text{-}T_s) \leqq \Delta T$ and $(T''\text{-}T_u) \leqq \Delta T$ hold. If the answer is yes, the validity of T_s and T_u can be assured and *GW* executes the next step. Otherwise *GW* rejects this request message.

Step 2: Calculates b^*.

$$b^* = h(SK_{GS} \| ID_u \| X \| T_u \| a \| ID_{Sn} \| Y \| T_s).$$

Step 3: Confirms whether $b = b^*$ and validates *Sn*.

GW checks if $b = b^*$ holds. If the answer is yes, *GW* accepts this request message and executes the next step. Otherwise, *GW* rejects this request message.

Step 4: Calculates X' and a^*.

$X' = h(ID_u \| x) \times X$, $a^* = h(ID_u \| X \| X' \| T_u)$, where x denotes a master key of *GW*.

Step 5: Confirms whether $a = a^*$.

GW checks if $a = a^*$ holds. If the answer is yes, *GW* accepts this request message and executes the next step. Otherwise, *GW* rejects the request message.

Step 6: Calculates y and l.

$$y = h(SK_{GS} \| ID_u \| X \| T_u \| a \| ID_{Sn} \| Y \| T_G),$$

$$l = h(ID_u \| X \| X' \| T_u \| Y \| T_s),$$

where T_G denotes the current response time of *GW*.

Step 7: $GW \rightarrow S_n$: $\{T_G, y, l\}$

The $\{T_G, y, l\}$ is submitted to *Sn* via public channel.

Sn authenticates *GW*

When receiving the response message that sent by *GW* at time T''', *Sn* checks and validates *GW*, and generates the message that will be sent to *U*. *Sn* executes the following steps.

Step 1: Validates T_G.

Sn checks if $(T'''\text{-}T_G) \leq \Delta T$ holds. If the answer is yes, the validity of T_G can be assured and *Sn* executes the next step. Otherwise *Sn* rejects the response message.

Step 2: Calculates y^*.

$$y^* = h(SK_{GS} \| ID_u \| X \| T_u \| a \| ID_{Sn} \| Y \| T_G).$$

Step 3: Validates y.

Sn checks if $y = y^*$ holds. If the answer is yes, *Sn* accepts this response and executes the next step. Otherwise, *Sn* rejects this response message.

Step 4: Calculates K_{SU}, g and session key sk.

$$K_{SU} = r_s \times X, g = h(Y \| T_s \| l \| K_{SU}), \ sk = h(X \| Y \| K_{US}).$$

Step 5: $S_n \rightarrow U$: $\{Y, T_s, l, g\}$

The $\{Y, T_s, l, g\}$ is submitted to *U* via public channel.

U authenticates GW and Sn When receiving the response message that sent by Sn at time T'''', U checks and validates GW and Sn. U executes the following steps.

Step 1: Validates Ts.

U checks if $(T''''-Ts) \leq \Delta T$ holds. If the answer is yes, the validity of T_S can be assured and U executes the next step. Otherwise, U rejects the response message.

Step 2: Calculates K_{US}, l^* and g^*.

$$K_{SU} = r_u \times Y, \quad l^*$$
$$= h(ID_u||X||X'||T_u||Y||T_s)), \quad and g^*$$
$$= h(Y||T_s||l||K_{SU}).$$

Step 3: Confirms l and g.

U checks if $l = l^*$ and $g = g^*$ hold. If the answer is yes, U accepts the response message and executes the next step. Otherwise, U rejects the response message.

Step 4: Calculates session key sk.

$$sk = h(X||Y||K_{US}).$$

Password update phase

When U wants to update his/her old password, U and the smart card execute the following steps.

Step 1: U inserts his/her smart card into the smart terminal and enters his/her identify ID_u, the old password PS and the new password PSn.

Step 2: The smart card calculates $PS' = h(PS \oplus br)$, and checks whether $Bu = h(ID_u \oplus PS')$ holds. If it does not hold, the smart card stops U's request. Otherwise, the smart card continues to compute $Ku = h(ID_u||PS') \oplus Wu$, $PSn' = h(PSn \oplus br)$, $Bu' = h(ID_u \oplus PSn')$ and $Wu' = Bu' \oplus Ku$. Finally, the smart card replaces (Bu, Wu) with (Bu', Wu').

Cryptanalysis of Wenbo's protocol
Security requirements in WSNs

(1) Secure user authentication in WSNs should be based on full mutual authentication.
(2) Secure user authentication in WSNs should resist masquerade, replay, forgery and DoS attacks.
(3) Secure user authentication in WSNs should resist internal attack (compromise attack).
(4) Secure user authentication in WSNs with smart card should reject Virus Injection attack.

No full mutual authentication

Because Wenbo's protocol does not authenticate U during the authentication phase (**Sn checks the validity of the request message of U**), a malicious user can attack Sn and GW by means of forging. The attack could be accomplished as follows:

(1) The attacker sends a forging message $\{ID_a, X_a, Tu_a, a_a\}$ to Sn.
(2) Sn sends a message $\{ID_a, X_a, Tu_a, a_a, ID_{Sn}, Y, T_s, b\}$ to GW for authenticating the user when receiving the forging message.

During the above process, since Sn does not authenticate the user, Sn directly generates authenticating request message for GW to authenticate the user. When GW receives this request message, GW can finish the process from Step 1 to Step 4 of authentication phase (**GW authenticates Sn and U**). This is because there is no mechanism for Sn to be assured that U is real user of WSNs. Thus, the Wenbo's protocol does not provide mutual authentication between U and Sn. There is no full mutual authentication between Sn and U. This protocol cannot reject DoS attack to Sn and GW.

No protection against forgery attack

Because the confidential information (Bu, Wu) is not encrypted to be stored, the attacker can masquerade as a legal user U. In the case that an attacker steals the (Bu, Wu) from the smart card via some a Virus or a Trojan in the user terminal, he/she maybe try to impersonate user U to access resource in WSNs. The attack can be accomplished via the following means.

(1) The attacker steals the $(Bu, Wu)\}$ via some methods, such as Virus software, Trojan.
(2) The attacker could compute $Ku = Bu \oplus Wu$ and gain the secret Ku.
(3) The attacker picks a random number R_u.
(4) The attacker could computes $X_a = R_u \times P$, $X_a' = R_u \times Ku$, and $a_a = h(ID||X_a||X_a'||T_a)$ because the point P on elliptic curve E is public.
(5) The attacker sends the request message $\{ID_u, X_a, T_a, a_a\}$ to the Sn via public channel.
(6) Sn can finish the authentication phase processes. And GW also can accomplish the authentication phase processes.

After GW and Sn finish to authenticate, the attacker can gains the session key sk. The attacker continues to access Sn. Thus, the Wenbo's protocol does not provide sufficient protection against forgery attack.

No protection against insider attack

In the Wenbo's protocol, U uses a single password for accessing Sn. It is convenient for a user. Nevertheless, if the system manager or a privileged user of GW obtains (Bu, Wu) of U during U registration phase, he/she maybe try to impersonate U to access the resource in WSNs. The attacking processes are the same as the forgery attack. Thus, the Wenbo's protocol does not provide sufficient protection against an insider attack on GW by a privileged user.

No protection against compromise attack

In the Wenbo's protocol, the gateway and the sensor nodes shared a long-term common secret key SK_{GS}. If an attacker captures some a sensor node, he/she can attain the shared secret key SK_{GS} via some methods since the SK_{GS} is not encrypted. So it is very easy to impersonate a sensor node in WSNs. Even the attacker may make many sensor nodes to impersonate the sensor nodes of in WSNs.

Proposed protocol

To solve the security weaknesses of the Wenbo's protocol, we propose a new user authentication protocol for WSNs using identity-based cryptography. First, we review the fundamentals of identity-based cryptography, and then survey the identity-based cryptography which is suitable for our design of a secure authentication protocol for WSNs. In the proposed protocol, GW integrates the trusted and reputation scheme [24,26]. The proposed five phases are described in detail later.

Identity-based cryptography

Identity-based cryptography is a kind of public-key based scheme. The public key is the unique identity of the user. The private key is generated by a third party called a Private Key Generator (PKG) with its master secret and user's identity. In the identity-based cryptography system, firstly, the PKG must create a master public key and a master private key. Then any user may use this master public key and also use the user's identity to generate the user's public. The user's private key is created by the PKG with the user's identity.

For every two parties using in identity-based cryptography, it is easy to calculate a shared secret session key between them using its own private key and public key of another party. For example, a sensor node Sn with public key Q_{Sn} and private key d_{Sn}, and a user U with public key Q_u and private key d_u can calculate their shared secret session key by computing key $= \hat{e}(Q_u, d_{Sn}) = \hat{e}(d_u, Q_{Sn})$.

In the proposed protocol, GW is the PKG. GW selects a random number $s \in Z_q^*$ that is kept secret. GW computes $K_{pub} = s \times P$. This public-private key pair $< K_{pub}, s >$ is the master key pair of GW. And GW computes $Q_{GW} = H_1 (ID_{GW})$, $d_{GW} = s \times Q_{GW}$. Q_{GW} is the authentication public key of GW. d_{GW} is the authentication private key of GW.

Registration phase

In the registration phase, Sn and U register to GW. The processes are the follow as.

Sensor node registration

In the WSNs, all sensor nodes must register to GW before being deployed. GW creates a private key for every sensor node. And the system parameters P_{set}, the public functions and the private key are stored in the sensor node. GW completes the following steps.

Step 1: Creates the public key Q_{Sn}.

GW uses the identity ID_{Sn} of Sn to generate the public key Q_{Sn}, $Q_{Sn} = H_1(ID_{Sn})$.

Step 2: Generates the private key d_{Sn}.

GW uses the master key s and the public key Q_{Sn} to create the private key d_{Sn}, $d_{Sn} = s \times Q_{Sn}$.

Step 3: Installs system parameters, public functions and private key of Sn.

GW installs the system parameters P_{set}, d_{Sn} and other public functions into Sn. That is to say, $\{P_{set}, d_{Sn}, h(.), f(.), H_1(.), e(.)\}$ is stored into the Sn.

User registration phase

Before accessing a sensor node in WSNs, any user must register to GW and gains a set P_{set} and other parameters. The registration phase is shown in the Figure 1.

Step 1: $U \rightarrow GW$: $\{ID_u, \text{Reg-inf}, T_1\}$.

U sends the register request message $\{ID_u, \text{Reg-inf}, T_1\}$ to GW at the time T_1.

Step2: $GW \rightarrow U$: $\{ID_{GW}, P, xP, h(.), a_1, T_2\}$.

When receiving the register request message of U at the time T', firstly GW checks whether $(T'-T_1) \leq \Delta T$ holds. If the answer is no, GW rejects the register request message of U. Otherwise, GW selects a random number $x \in Z_q^*$ and computes $xP = x \times P$. Then GW calculates $a_1 = h(ID_{GW}||ID_u||xP||T_2)$, where T_2 is the current time of GW. Finally, GW sends the register response message $\{ID_{GW}, P, xP, h(.), a_1, T_2\}$ to U.

Step 3: $U \rightarrow GW$: $\{ID_u, E_k (PS'), yP, b, T_3\}$.

When receiving the register response message $\{ID_{GW}, P, xP, h(.), a_1, T_2\}$ at the time T', U checks whether $(T'-T_2) \leq \Delta T$ holds. If the answer is no, U rejects the register response message. Otherwise, U computes $a_1' = h(ID_{GW}||ID_u||xP||T_2)$ and checks whether $a_1' = a_1$ holds. If the answer is no, U rejects the register response message. Otherwise, U picks a random number $y \in Z_q^*$ and computes $yP = y \times P$. And U selects a password $PS \in Z_q^*$ and a random number $br \in Z_q^*$. U calculates $PS' = h(PS \oplus br)$ and $k = h(y \times xP)$. Then U encrypts PS' with the session key k, $E_k(PS')$. Finally, U computes $b = h(ID_u||ID_{GW}||E_k(PS')||yP||T_3)$, where T_3 is the current times of U. And U sends a message $\{ID_u, E_k(PS'), yP, b, T_3\}$ to GW.

Step 4: $GW \rightarrow U$: $\{ID_{GW}, P_{set}, E_\Theta(\Theta, M), a_2, T_4\}$.

Receiving the message $\{ID_u, E_k(PS'), yP, b, T_3\}$ at the time T', GW firstly checks whether $(T'-T_3) \leq \Delta T$ holds. If the answer is no, GW rejects this message. Otherwise, GW computes $b' = h(ID_u||ID_{GW}||E_k(PS')||yP||T_3)$ and

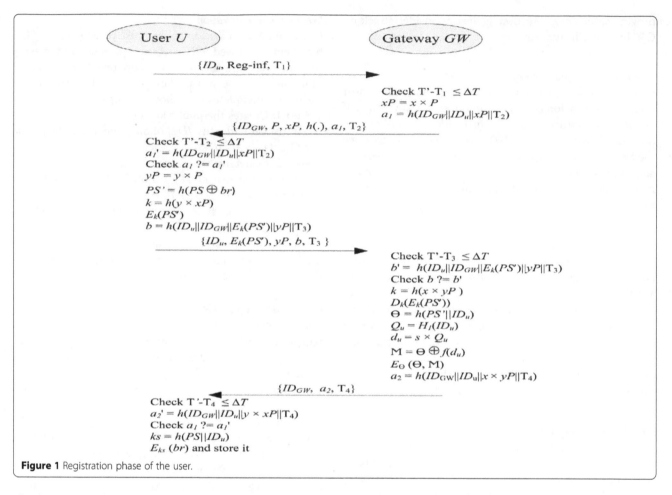

Figure 1 Registration phase of the user.

checks whether $b' = b$ holds. If the answer is no, GW rejects this message. Otherwise, GW generates the session key k and decrypts $E_k(PS')$, $k = h(x \times yP)$, $D_k(E_k(PS'))$ to gain PS'. Then GW computes $\Theta = h(PS'||ID_u)$, $Q_u = H_1(ID_u)$ and $d_u = s \times Q_u$. And GW also calculates $M = \Theta \oplus f(d_u)$. GW encrypts the (Q_u, M), $E_\Theta(\Theta, M)$ and computes $a_2 = h(ID_{GW}||ID_u||xyP||T_4)$. At last GW stores $(P_{set}, E_\Theta(\Theta, M), h(.), f(.), H1(.), \hat{e}(.))$ into a smart card that is sent to U. Moreover GW sends the register acknowledge message $\{ID_{GW}, a_2, T_4\}$ to U.

Step 5: U encrypts and stores br.

When receiving the register acknowledge message $\{ID_{GW}, a_2, T_4\}$ at the time T', U firstly checks whether $(T'-T_4) \le \Delta T$ holds. If the answer is no, U rejects this message. Otherwise U computes $a_2' = h(ID_{GW}||ID_u||yxP||T_4)$ and checks whether $a_2' = a_2$ holds. If the answer is no, U rejects this message. Otherwise, U computes $ks = h(PS||ID_u)$ and encrypts br, $E_{ks}(br)$. Finially U stores $E_{ks}(br)$.

Login phase and authentication phase

Accessing the data in Sn, U must login Sn and be authenticated by GW and Sn. And U must complete the login phase and authentication phase. Login phase and authentication phase are shown in Figure 2.

Login phase

U must enter his ID_u and password PS firstly. Then, after the smart card validates U via the following steps, the smart card sends the access request message to Sn.

Step 1: Gains br.

U enters his identity ID_u and password PS to the smart terminal. And the smart terminal computes $ks = h(PS||ID_u)$, and $D_{ks}(E_{ks}(br))$ to gain br.

Step 2: Validate U.

The smart card computes $PS' = h(PS \oplus br)$, $\Theta' = h(PS'||ID_u)$ and $D_{\Theta'}(E_\Theta(\Theta, M))$ to gain the (Θ, M). The smart card checks whether $\Theta = \Theta'$ holds. If the answer is no, the smart card stops and alarms. Otherwise, the smart card continues to execute the next step.

Step 3: Computes Q_{Sn}, Q_{GW}, d_u, X and Y.

$$Q_{Sn} = H_1(ID_{Sn}), \quad Q_{GW} = H_1(ID_{GW}), \quad d_u = H_1(M \oplus \theta),$$
$$X = \hat{e}(d_u, Q_{Sn}) \text{ and } Y = \hat{e}(d_u, Q_{GW}).$$

Step 4: Generates a, b and encrypts (a, b).

The smart card calculates $a = h(ID_u||ID_{GW}||Y||T_u)$, $b = h(ID_u||ID_{Sn}||X||a||T_u)$ and $E_X(a, b)$, where T_u is the current time of the smart terminal system.

Step 5: $U \rightarrow Sn$: $\{ID_u, ID_{Sn}, E_X(a, b), T_u\}$.

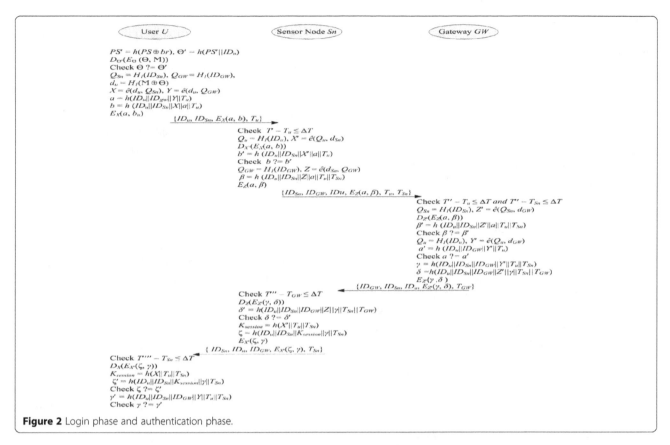

Figure 2 Login phase and authentication phase.

The smart card sends the login request message $\{ID_u, ID_{Sn}, E_X(a, b), T_u\}$ to the Sn.

Authentication phase

The authentication phase includes Sn authenticating U and GW, GW authenticating Sn and U, U authenticating Sn and GW. The authentication phase can complete the mutual authentication.

Sensor node Sn authenticates user U When receiving the login request message $\{ID_u, ID_{Sn}, E_X(a, b), T_u\}$ sent by U at time T', Sn firstly checks the validity of the request message. Then Sn authenticates U.

Step 1: Validates login request message.

Sn checks whether $(T'-T_u) \leq \Delta T$ holds. If the answer is no, Sn rejects the login request of U. Otherwise, it continues to perform the next step.

Step 2: Decrypts $E_X(a, b)$.

S_n computes $Q_u = H_1(ID_u)$, $X' = \hat{e}(Q_u, d_{Sn})$ and $D_{X'}(E_X(a, b))$ to gain (a, b).

Step 3: Computes $b' = h(ID_u||ID_{Sn}||X'||a||T_u)$.

Step 4: Validates U.

S_n checks if $b = b'$ holds. If the answer is yes, the validity of U can be assured and Sn continues to perform the next step. Otherwise, it rejects the login request message of U.

Step 5: Computes Q_{GW}, Z, β and encrypts.

$Q_{GW} = H_1(ID_{GW})$, $Z = \hat{e}(d_{Sn}, Q_{GW})$ and $\beta = h(ID_u||ID_{Sn}||Z||a||T_u||T_{Sn})$, where T_{Sn} is the current time of Sn system. And Sn encrypts (a, β), $E_Z(a, \beta)$.

Step 6: $S_n \rightarrow GW$: $\{ID_{Sn}, ID_{GW}, IDu, E_Z(a, \beta), T_u, T_{Sn}\}$

Sn sends a request message $\{ID_{Sn}, ID_{GW}, ID_u, E_Z(a, \beta), T_u, T_{Sn}\}$ to GW.

Gateway GW authenticates sensor node Sn When receiving the request message $\{ID_{Sn}, ID_{GW}, ID_u, E_Z(a, \beta), T_u, T_{Sn}\}$ at time T'', GW checks the validity of this message firstly. And GW authenticates Sn and U. Finally, GW creates a response message for Sn and U.

Step 1: Validates request message of Sn.

GW checks whether $(T''-T_u) \leq \Delta T$ and $(T''-T_{Sn}) \leq \Delta T$ hold. If the answer is no, GW rejects the request message. Otherwise, GW continues to perform the next step.

Step 2: Computes Q_{Sn}, Z' and gains (a, β).

GW computes $Q_{Sn} = H_1(ID_{Sn})$, $Z' = \hat{e}(Q_{Sn}, d_{GW})$ and $D_{Z'}(E_Z(a, \beta))$ to gain (a, β).

Step 3: Computes $\beta' = h(ID_u||ID_{Sn}||Z'|a||T_u||T_{Sn})$.

Step 4: Validates Sn.

GW checks if $\beta' = \beta$ holds. If the answer is yes, the validity of Sn can be assured and GW continues to perform the next step. Otherwise, it rejects the request message.

Step 5: Computes Q_u, Y' and a'.

GW computes $Q_u = H_1(ID_u)$, $Y' = \hat{e}(Q_u, d_{GW})$ and $a' = h(ID_u||ID_{GW}||Y'||T_u)$.

Step 6: Validates U.

GW checks if $a' = a$ holds. if the answer is yes, the validity of U can be assured and GW continues to perform the next step. Otherwise, GW rejects the request message.

Step 7: $GW \rightarrow Sn:\{ID_{GW}, ID_{Sn}, ID_u, E_{Z'}(\gamma, \delta), T_{GW}\}$.

GW generates the response message for Sn and U. GW calculates: $\gamma = h(ID_u||ID_{Sn}||ID_{GW}||Y'||T_u||T_{Sn})$ and $\delta = h(ID_u||ID_{Sn}||ID_{GW}||Z'||\gamma||T_{Sn}||T_{GW})$, where T_{GW} is the current time of GW's system. And GW encrypts (γ, δ) with the key Z', $E_{Z'}(\gamma, \delta)$, and sends the response message $\{ID_{GW}, ID_{Sn}, ID_u, E_{Z'}(\gamma, \delta), T_{GW}\}$ to Sn.

Sensor node Sn authenticates gateway GW When receiving the response message $\{ID_{GW}, ID_{Sn}, ID_u, E_{Z'}(\gamma, \delta), T_{GW}\}$ sent by GW at time T''', Sn checks and authenticates GW via the following steps.

Step 1: Validates the response message.

Sn checks if $(T'''-T_{GW}) \leq \Delta T$ holds. If the answer is no, Sn rejects this response message. Otherwise, Sn continues to perform the next step.

Step 2: Gains (γ, δ).

Sn decrypts the $E_{Z'}(\gamma, \delta)$ with the key Z, $D_Z(E_{Z'}(\gamma, \delta))$, to gain (γ, δ).

Step 3: Computes δ'.

$$\delta' = h(ID_u||ID_{Sn}||ID_{GW}||Z||\gamma||T_{Sn}||T_{GW}).$$

Step 4: Validates GW.

Sn checks if $\delta' = \delta$ holds. If th answer is yes, the validity of GW can be assured and S_n continues to execute the next step. Otherwise, it rejects the response message.

Step 5: Generates $K_{session}$, ζ and encrypts.

Sn computes $K_{session} = h(X||T_u||T_{Sn})$,

$$\zeta = h(ID_u||ID_{Sn}||K_{session}||\gamma||T_{Sn}) \text{ and } E_X(\zeta, \gamma).$$

Step 6: $Sn \rightarrow U$: $\{ID_{Sn}, ID_u, ID_{GW}, E_X(\zeta, \gamma), T_{Sn}\}$.

Sn sends the response message $\{ID_{Sn}, ID_u, ID_{GW}, E_X(\zeta, \gamma), T_{Sn}\}$ to U.

User U authenticates sensor node Sn When U receives Sn's response message $\{ID_{Sn}, ID_u, ID_{GW}, E_X(\zeta, \gamma), T_{Sn}\}$ at time T'''', U checks this message and authenticates Sn and GW. U performs the following steps.

Step 1: Validates the response message.

U checks whether $(T'''''-T_{Sn}) \leq \Delta T$ holds. If the answer is no, U rejects this response message. Otherwise, it continues to perform the next step.

Step 2: Gains (ζ, γ).

U computes $D_X(E_X(\zeta, \gamma))$ to decrypt $E_X(\zeta, \gamma)$ with the key X to gain (ζ, γ).

Step 3: Generates $K_{session}$ and ζ'.

U computes $K_{session} = h(X||T_u||T_{Sn})$, and $\zeta' = h(ID_u||ID_{Sn}||K_{session}||\gamma||T_{Sn})$

Step 4: Validates Sn.

U checks whether $\zeta = \zeta'$ holds. If the answer is yes, the validity of Sn can be assured and U continues to execute the next step. Otherwise, U rejects the response message.

Step 5: Computes $\gamma' = h(ID_u||ID_{Sn}||ID_{GW}||Y||T_u||T_{Sn})$.

Step 6: Validates GW.

U checks whether $\gamma' = \gamma$ holds. If the answer is yes, the validity of GW can be assured and U accepts this response message. Otherwise, U rejects this response message.

After U authenticates Sn and GW, U will access the data of the Sn with the session key $K_{session}$.

Password update phase

When U updates his password, U enters his ID_u, old password PS and news password PSn to the smart terminal or a update password program. The smart card must compute a new password value, which is encrypted and stored in the smart card. The user password update phase includes the following steps.

Step 1: U enters his ID_u, old password PS and news password PSn to the smart terminal or a update password program.

Step 2: The smart terminal computes $ks = h(PS||ID_u)$ and $D_{ks}(E_{ks}(br))$ to gain br firstly. Then it computes $PS' = h(PS \oplus br)$, $PSn' = h(PSn \oplus br)$. The smart terminal sends $\{ID_u, PS', PSn'\}$ to the smart card.

Step 3: The smart card computes $\Theta' = h(PS'||ID_u)$ and $D_{\Theta'}(E_{\Theta}(\Theta, M))$ to gain (Θ, M).

Step 4: The smart card checks whether $\Theta' = \Theta$ holds. If the answer is no, the smart card rejects the password update and alarms. Otherwise, the smart card continues to perform the next step.

Step 5: The smart card calculates $\Theta_n' = h(PSn'||ID_u)$ and $M' = \Theta_n' \oplus (\Theta \oplus M)$.

Step 6: The smart card encrypts the new sensitive password value (Θ_n', M') with the key Θ_n', $E_{\Theta n'}(\Theta_n', M')$, and replaces the $E_{\Theta}(\Theta, M)$ with $E_{\Theta n'}(\Theta_n', M')$.

Security and performance analysis

The proposed protocol provides message confidentiality service

Proof

Message confidentiality service against eavesdropping attack is performed by data encryption service. Our proposed protocol can provide sufficient confidentiality for sensitive data stored and transmitted with encrypting data (e.g. $E_k(PS')$, $E_{\Theta}(\Theta,M)$, $E_X(a, b)$, $E_Z(a, \beta)$, $E_{Z'}(\gamma, \delta)$ and $E_X(\zeta, \gamma)$. More specifically, these sensitive information are confidential against the attacker. If the sensitive data is stored or transmitted without encryption in the public channel , the attacker maybe view the plaintext data. This attack maybe occur in Wenbo's protocol and Yoon and Yoo's protocol [15]. Moreover, in Wenbo's protocol the sensitive (Bu, Wu) that was not encrypted was stored in the smart card and the long-term shared secret key SK_{GW} was not also encrypted in the Sn. In the [15] Sn's response message that was not encrypted was sent to U by a public channel directly.

The proposed protocol resists an integrity attack
Proof
The data integrity attack includes data modification attack, data corruption attack and data insertion attack. The integrity service assures the transmitted data is not modified by an unauthorized entity.

In our proposed protocol, Sn can guarantee the login request message $\{ID_u, ID_{Sn}, E_X(a, b), T_u\}$ from U has not been modified by an unauthorized entity via decrypting $E_X(a, b)$, recomputing and checking b. GW can also guarantee the authentication request message $\{ID_{Sn}, ID_{GW}, IDu, E_Z(a, \beta), T_u, T_{Sn}\}$ from Sn has not been modified by an unauthorized entity via decrypting $E_Z(a, \beta)$, recomputing and checking a, β. Similarly, Sn can guarantee the authentication response message $\{ID_{GW}, ID_{Sn}, ID_u, E_{Z'}(\gamma, \delta), T_{GW}\}$ from GW has not been modified by an unauthorized entity via decrypting $E_{Z'}(\gamma, \delta)$, recomputing and checking δ. Moreover, U uses the same way to guarantee the authentication response message $\{ID_{GW}, ID_{Sn}, ID_u, E_{X'}(\zeta, \gamma), T_{Sn}\}$ from Sn has not been modified.

The proposed protocol resists a denial attack
Proof
This type of attack is that the participating entity denies in all of the operations or part of its. However, in our proposed protocol, we assume that GW is a trusted party. And GW creates the unique private key for every entity (sensor node, user) . Although GW does not store the private key of an entity, it can trace the entity operations with the entity's public key and HMAC. Therefore, the entity cannot deny that he/she performed all participation.

The proposed protocol resists a DoS Attack
Proof
The DoS attack can be occurred by the attacker who transmitting the large number of request messages to Sn or GW in the login phase or in the authentication phase. In our proposed protocol, since every message associates with a timestamp T and is authenticated, the unauthenticated message or the timeout message is rejected. So the proposed protocol can reject DoS attack.

The proposed protocol resists a sensor node compromise attack
Proof
Since WSNs is normally deployed in an open environment, the attacker is easy to capture a sensor node and may attempt to get some information stored in the sensor node. When the attacker gets the secret from the capturing sensor node, he/she can attack the WSNs. If the authenticating user and data access from the sensor node are allowed directly to the user without the license of gateway, this attack is very high, which occurs in Watro et al.'s scheme [19].

In our proposed protocol, And U does not access data from Sn until it is authorized by GW and Sn. And U's request message must be authenticated by Sn firstly, and the request message must be authenticated by GW. After that GW sends the license of U's to Sn and U. Only U can access the data of sensor node when his/her license from GW is the same as Sn's from GW. Moreover, in our proposed protocol GW can monitor whether a sensor node is captured with the trusted and reputation management scheme [24,26]. If some a sensor node is captured by an attacker, GW can detect and isolate it.

The proposed protocol resists a replay attack
Proof
The replay attacks are impossible if the previous information is not reused again. In our proposed protocol, the login message and the authentication message are validated by checking timestamps. When an attacker eavesdrops the communication between U and Sn or between Sn and GW, he/she does not reusable again. We assume if an adversary intercepts a login request message $\{ID_u, ID_{Sn}, E_X(a, b), T_u\}$ and attempts replaying the same message for login to Sn. The verification of the login request fails because of $(T_a-T_u) > \Delta T$, where T_a denotes the time when Sn receives the replaying message. Similarly, if an adversary intercepts $\{ID_{Sn}, ID_{GW}, ID_u, E_Z(a, \beta), T_u, T_{Sn}\}$ and attempts to replay it to GW, he/she cannot pass the verification of GW because the time expires (i.e. $(T_b-T_{Sn}) > \Delta T$ and $(T_b -T_u) > \Delta T$), where T_b denotes the time when the replaying message is received by GW. Also if an adversary intercepts $\{ID_{GW}, ID_{Sn}, ID_u, E_{Z'}(\gamma, \delta), T_{GW}\}$ and attempts replaying the same message to Sn, he/she cannot pass the verification of Sn because of $(T_c-T_{GW}) > \Delta T$, where T_c denotes the time when Sn receives the replaying response message. Moreover, if an adversary intercepts $\{ID_{GW}, ID_{Sn}, ID_u, E_{X'}(\zeta, \gamma), T_{Sn}\}$ and attempts replaying the same message to U, he/she also cannot pass the verification of U because of $(T_d-T_{Sn} > \Delta T)$, where T_d denotes the time when U receives the replaying response message.

The proposed protocol resists an impersonation attack
Proof
In our proposed protocol, all sensitive information that is transmitted is encrypted with some a key. Additionally, the messages are validated and authenticated. Only when an attacker knows the master key s or solves

Bilinear Differ-Hellman Problem can he/she attain the private key. It is impossible for an attacker.

In the login phase, only when an attacker knows U's private key d_u can he/she generate a legal login request message $\{D_u, ID_{Sn}, E_X(a, b), T_u\}$ to impersonate the U. Moreover it is impossible that an attacker gains the sensitive key material (Θ, M) that is encrypted to only be stored in the smart card without the user U's password. Thus it is not possible to compute X without d_u for an attacker. And as long as an attacker does not possess Sn's private key d_{Sn}, he/she cannot generate a legal authentication request message $\{ID_{Sn}, ID_{GW}, IDu, E_Z(a, \beta)$, $T_u, T_{Sn}\}$ and $\{ID_{GW}, ID_{Sn}, ID_u, E_{X'}(\zeta, \gamma), T_{Sn}\}$ to impersonate Sn. This is because that the attacker cannot compute the key Z and the key X' without d_{Sn}. Similarly, an attacker also cannot generate a legal response message $\{ID_{GW}, ID_{Sn}, ID_u, E_{Z'}(\gamma, \delta), T_{GW}\}$ to impersonate GW. This is due to that an attacker does not know the private key d_{GW} of GW.

The proposed protocol resists a stolen verifier attack
Proof

An attacker who has stolen U's private key materials $E_\Theta(\Theta, M)$ from the smart terminal or the smart card via the Trojan or other intruding methods cannot obtain any useful information. This is due to that the private key materials are encrypted. The attacker cannot decrypt $E_\Theta(\Theta, M)$ to gain (Θ, M) without U's password PS. And the attacker also cannot attain any useful private key information of U from GW because U's private key materials are not stored in the GW database.

The proposed protocol resists a stolen smart card attacks
Proof

The attacker who has stolen U's smart card cannot impersonate this user to access S_n. Because the attacker does not know U's password, the smart card does not validate the login request and rejects the access request of the attacker.

The proposed protocol resists an insider attack
Proof

The insider attack is intentionally misused by authorized entities. In our proposed protocol, the gateway manager or system administrator cannot attain U's password PS because in the registration phase U transmits $E_k(PS')$ to GW instead of the plain password PS, and any sensitive key material information of U and any verifier table are not stored in GW. Additionally, the smart terminal manager or administrator also cannot attain the useful information of U's key from the smart card and the smart terminal because of the sensitive key material encrypted. Therefore, the proposed protocol can resist the privileged insider attacks.

The proposed protocol resists a man-in-the-middle attack
Proof

The man-in-the-middle attack is that an attacker intercepts the communication between the legal user and other entity (e.g. sensor node, gateway) and successfully masquerades as the user or other entity by some methods. In our proposed protocol, U is authenticated by Sn in the login phase, Sn and U are authenticated by GW in the authentication

Table 2 Security comparison

	Benenson et al. [7]	Das [10]	Chen and Shih [16]	Yuan et al. [19]	Yeh et al. [17]	Yoon and Yoo [20]	Ohood et al. [21]	Wenbo and Peng [22]	Ours
Data Confidentiality	NP	NP	NP	NP	NP	NP	P	NP	P
Data Integrity	NP	P	P	NP	NP	P	P	P	P
Password Update	NR	NP	R	NP	P	NR	NR	P	P
Key Agreement	NP	NP	NP	NP	NP	NP	P	P	P
Mutual Authentication	NP	NP	P	NP	NP	P	P	NP	P
Denial Attack	No	No	No	Yes	No	Yes	Yes	No	Yes
DoS Attack	No	No	No	No	No	No	Yes	No	Yes
Compromise Attack	Yes	No	No	No	No	No	Yes	Yes	Yes
Replay Attack	Yes	Yes	Yes	Yes	No	Yes	Yes	No	Yes
Impersonation Attack	No	Yes	Yes	No	No	Yes	Yes	No	Yes
Insider Attack	Yes	No	No	No	No	Yes	Yes	Yes	Yes
Forgery Attack	Yes	No	Yes	Yes	Yes	Yes	Yes	No	Yes
Stolen-Verifier Attack	Yes	Yes	Yes	Yes	No	Yes	Yes	Yes	Yes
Guessing Attack	Yes	Yes	Yes	Yes	Yes	Yes	Yes	Yes	Yes
Man-in-the-Middle Attack	No	No	Yes	No	No	Yes	Yes	No	Yes

Yes: Resist Attack, No: Not Resist Attack, P: Provided, NP: Not Provided, R: Required, NR: Not Required.

Table 3 Computation performance comparison

	Benenson et al. [7]	Das [10]	Chen and Shih [16]	Yeh et al. [17]	Yoon and Yoo [20]	Ohood et al. [21]	Yuan et al.[19]	Wenbo et al. [22]	Ours
Registration Phase	$1Texp$	$1Th$	$1Th$	$4Th + 2Tmp$	$3Th$	$2Th$	$4Th$	$3Th + 1Tpm$	$4Th + 4Tpm + 3Taes$
Login and Authentication Phase	$2nTh + 3nTexp$	$5Th$	$7Th$	$11Th + 4Tpa + 8Tpm + 2Te$	$10Th$	$4Trc + 8Th$	$9Th$	$15Th + 6Tpm$	$14Th + 6Tpair + 8Taes$
Total	$2nTh + 3nTexp + 1Texp$	$6Th$	$8Th$	$15Th + 4Tpa + 10Tpm + 2Te$	$13Th$	$4Trc + 10Th$	$13Th$	$18Th + 7Tpm$	$18Th + 4Tpm + 11Taes + 6Tpair$

request phase, and Sn also authenticates GW in the authentication response phase, U validates Sn and GW in the authentication response phase. That is to say, our proposed protocol can provide complete mutual authenticate among entities and resists the man-in-the-middle attack.

Table 2 shows the security functionality comparisons between our proposed protocol and the related protocols. According to the Table 2, although the Ohood et al.'s protocol presents the same security as ours, the Ohood et al.'s protocol needs some complicated biometric equipments. Compared against each other, our protocol provides is more security services than the other protocols.

Performance analysis The section summarizes the performance results of the proposed protocol. We define the notation Th as the hash function computation cost, $Texp$ as the modular exponential computation cost, Tpm as the elliptic curve point multiply cost, Tpa as the elliptic curve point addition cost, $Tpair$ as pairing computation cost, Trc as RC5 computation cost, $Taes$ as AES computation cost, Te as the elliptic curve polynomial computation cost. The comparison of related protocols is illustrated in the Table 3.

According to Table 3, Chen et al.'s protocol needs eight hash function computations, Yoon el at.'s needs thirteen hash function computations, Yuan et al.'s also need thirteen hash function computations, Das's protocol needs six hash function computations. And Benenson et al.'s protocol needs 2n hash function computations and $3n + 1$ modular exponential computations [22]. Ohood et al.'s biometric authentication protocol needs four RC5 computations and ten hash function computations. Yeh et al.'s protocol needs fifteen hash function computations, four elliptic curve point addition computations , ten elliptic curve point multiply computations and two elliptic curve polynomial computations. Wenbo et al.'s protocol needs eighteen hash function computations and seven elliptic curve point multiply computations. Our proposed protocol needs eighteen hash function computations, four elliptic curve point multiply computations, eleven AES computations and six pairing computations. Although our protocol needs more computations than their protocols, their protocols suffer from security issues or need complicated biometric equipments. Our protocol addressed these

issues and provides better security and more security services than the other related protocols.

Conclusion

In the paper, we discussed an approach of data capturing for big data that is data collecting via sensor networks and its user authentication protocol. We have analyzed Wenbo et al.'s user authentication protocol for WSNs. The Wenbo's protocol, which does not provide mutual authentication between user and sensor node and confidentiality service, is susceptible to insider, replay, denial, compromise, forgery, man-in-the-middle and DoS attacks. We have also reviewed the protocols of Yeh et al., which does not provide mutual authentication and protect against insider, denial, compromise, man-in-the-middle and DoS attacks, of Das, which is vulnerable to forgery, denial, compromise, DoS, man-in-the-middle attacks, of Benenson et al., which susceptible to denial, compromise, DoS, man-in-the-middle attacks, of Chen et al. which is vulnerable to denial, insider, compromise and DoS attacks, of other biometric authentication protocols. Since WSNs need more secure mutual authentication method in an insecure network environment, we use the IBE mechanism to design a news user authentication protocol. Our protocol can prevent all the problems of the former schemes. Furthermore, it enhances the WSNs authentication with higher security than the other protocol. Therefore, the protocol is more suited to open and higher security WSNs environment in despite of more computation cost.

Competing interests
The authors declare that they have no competing interests.

Authors' contributions
ZQ designed the user authentication protocol and analyzed performance. TC implemented the security analysis for protocol. ZX analyzed the security of Wenbo's protocol. RC coordinated the whole study. All authors read and approved the final manuscript.

Acknowledgements
This work was supported in part by the National Natural Science Foundation of China under Grant No. 11271003, the National Research Foundation for the Doctoral Program of Higher Education of China under Grant No.20134410110003, High Level Talents Project of Guangdong, Guangdong Provincial Natural Science Foundation under Grant No.S2012010009950 and No. S2012040007370, the Project of Department of Education of Guangdong Province under Grant No 2013KJCX0146, and the Natural Science Foundation

of Bureau of Education of Guangzhou under Grant No. 2012A004. We sincerely thank all the researchers in our references section for the inspiration they provide.

Author details
[1]Key Laboratory of Mathematics and Interdisciplinary Sciences of Guangdong Higher Education Institutes, Guangzhou University, Guangzhou, China. [2]School of Mathematics and Information Science, Guangzhou University, Guangzhou, China. [3]College of Mathematics and Computer Science, Fuzhou University, Fuzhou, China. [4]Faculty of Science and Technology, University of Stavanger, Stavanger, Norway.

References
1. Kenneth NC, Viktor MS (2013) The rise of big data: how It's changing the way we think about the world. Fortuna's Corner in cloud computing, Cybersecurity, Dow, Intelligence Community, Internet, Markets, national security, S & P, Uncategorized, US Military, April 24, 2013
2. Sastry N, Wagner D (2004) Security considerations for IEEE 802.15.4 networks. In Proceedings of the ACM Workshop on Wireless Security (WiSe'04). 32–42
3. WG802.15 (2003) IEEE Standards for 802.15.4, Part 15, Amendment 4. Wireless medium access control and physical layer specifications for low-rate wireless personal area networks. IEEE, Washington, DC, USA
4. Das ML, Saxena A, Gulati VP (2004) A dynamic ID-based remote user authentication scheme. IEEE Trans Consum Electron 50(2):629–31
5. Leung KC, Cheng LM, Fong AS, Chan CK (2003) Cryptanalysis of a modified remote user authentication scheme using smart cards. IEEE Trans Consum Electron 49(4):1243–5
6. Watro R, Kong D, Cuti S F, Gardiner C, Lynn C, Kruus P (2004) TinyPK: securing sensor networks with public key technology. In Proceedings of the ACM Workshop on Security of Ad Hoc and Sensor Networks (SASN'04), 59–64
7. Benenson Z, Gedicke N, Raivio O (2005) Realizing robust user authentication in sensor networks. In Real-World Wireless Sensor Networks (REALWSN), 14
8. Wong KHM, Yuan Z, Jiannong C, Shengwei W (2006) A dynamic user authentication scheme for wireless sensor networks. In Proceedings of the IEEE International Conference on Sensor Networks, Ubiquitous, and Trustworthy Computing, 244-251
9. Tseng HR, Jan RH, Yang W (2007) An improved dynamic user authentication scheme for wireless sensor networks. In Proceedings of the 50th Annual IEEE Global Telecommunications Conference (GLOBECOM'07), 986–990
10. Das ML (2009) Two-factor user authentication in wireless sensor networks. IEEE Trans Wirel Commun 8(3):1086–90
11. Ko KC (2008) A novel dynamic user authentication scheme for wireless sensor networks. In Proceedings of the IEEE International Symposium on Wireless Communication Systems, ISWCS'08, 608–612
12. Nyang DH, Lee MK (2009) Improvement of Das's two-factor authentication protocol in wireless sensor networks. Available via DIALOG. http://eprint.iacr.org/2009/631.pdf. Accessed 15 Jan 2014.
13. Vaidya B, Rodrigues JJ, Park JH (2010) User authentication schemes with pseudonymity for ubiquitous sensor network in NGN. Int J Communication Syst 23(9–10):1201–22
14. Khan MK, Alghathbar K (2010) Cryptanalysis and security improvements of 'two-factor user authentication in wireless sensor networks'. Sensors 10(3):2450–9
15. Khan MK, Alghathbar K (2010), Security Analysis of Two-Factor Authentication In Wireless Sensor Networks. In Proceedings of Advances in Computer Science and Information Technology: AST/UCMA/ISA/ACN 2010 Conferences, 55–60
16. Chen TH, Shih WK (2010) A robust mutual authentication protocol for wireless sensor networks. ETRI J 32(5):704–12
17. Yeh HL, Chen TH, Liu PC, Kim TH, Wei HW (2011) A secured authentication protocol for wireless sensor networks using elliptic curves cryptography. Sensors 11(5):4767–79
18. Han W (2013), Weakness of a secured authentication protocol for wireless sensor networks using elliptic curves cryptography. Available via DIALOG. http://eprint.iacr.org/2011/293. Accessed 15 May 2014.
19. Yuan J, Jiang C, Jiang Z (2010) A biometric-based user authentication for wireless sensor networks. Wuhan Univ J Nat Sci 15(3):272–6
20. Yoon EJ, Yoo K Y(2011) A new biometric-based user authentication scheme without using password for wireless sensor networks. In Proceedings of the 20th IEEE International Workshops on Enabling Technologies: Infrastructure for Collaborative Enterprises, 279–284
21. Ohood A, Mznah AR, Abdullah AD (2013) An efficient biometric authentication protocol for wireless sensor networks. Int J Distributed Sensor Networks 4:1–13
22. Wenbo S, Peng G (2013) A new user authentication protocol for wireless sensor networks using elliptic curves cryptography. Int J Distrib Sens Netw 3:1–7
23. Quan Z (2011) Trusted transmission model of wireless sensor networks, Ph. d. Theis. South China Agricultural University, China
24. Quan Z, Gui F, Deqin X, Jiuhao L (2010) trusted transport model based cluster-merkle-tree for WSNs. in Processing of 2010 IEEE International Conference on Computer Application and System Modeling V1, 564 -568
25. Quan Z, GUI F, Deqin X, Yi T (2012) Trusted architecture for farmland WSNs. in Processing of 2012 Forth IEEE International Conference on Cloud Computing Technology and Science, 782–787
26. Boneh D, Franklin M (2001) Identity based encryption from the Weil pairing. in processing of Advances in Cryptology. Lect Notes Computer Sci 2139:213–29

13

Performance analysis model for big data applications in cloud computing

Luis Eduardo Bautista Villalpando[1,2*], Alain April[2] and Alain Abran[2]

Abstract

The foundation of Cloud Computing is sharing computing resources dynamically allocated and released per demand with minimal management effort. Most of the time, computing resources such as processors, memory and storage are allocated through commodity hardware virtualization, which distinguish cloud computing from others technologies. One of the objectives of this technology is processing and storing very large amounts of data, which are also referred to as Big Data. Sometimes, anomalies and defects found in the Cloud platforms affect the performance of Big Data Applications resulting in degradation of the Cloud performance. One of the challenges in Big Data is how to analyze the performance of Big Data Applications in order to determine the main factors that affect the quality of them. The performance analysis results are very important because they help to detect the source of the degradation of the applications as well as Cloud. Furthermore, such results can be used in future resource planning stages, at the time of design of Service Level Agreements or simply to improve the applications. This paper proposes a performance analysis model for Big Data Applications, which integrates software quality concepts from ISO 25010. The main goal of this work is to fill the gap that exists between quantitative (numerical) representation of quality concepts of software engineering and the measurement of performance of Big Data Applications. For this, it is proposed the use of statistical methods to establish relationships between extracted performance measures from Big Data Applications, Cloud Computing platforms and the software engineering quality concepts.

Keywords: Cloud computing; Big data; Analysis; Performance; Relief algorithm; Taguchi method; ISO 25010; Maintenance; Hadoop MapReduce

Introduction

According to ISO subcommittee 38, the CC study group, Cloud Computing (CC) is a paradigm for enabling ubiquitous, convenient, on-demand network access to a shared pool of configurable cloud resources accessed through services which can be rapidly provisioned and released with minimal management effort or service provider interaction [1].

One of the challenges in CC is how to process and store large amounts of data (also known as Big Data BD) in an efficient and reliable way. ISO subcommittee 32, Next Generation Analytics and Big Data study group, refers Big Data as the transition from structured data

and traditional analytics to analysis of complex information of many types. Moreover, the group mentions that Big Data exploits cloud resources to manage large data volume extracted from multiple sources [2]. In December 2012, the International Data Corporation (IDC) stated that, by the end of 2012, the total data generated was 2.8 Zettabytes (ZB) (2.8 trillion Gigabytes). Furthermore, the IDC predicts that the total data generated by 2020 will be 40 ZB. This is roughly equivalent to 5.2 terabytes (TB) of data generated by every human being alive in that year [3].

Big Data Applications (BDA) are a way to process a part of such large amounts of data by means of platforms, tools and mechanisms for parallel and distributed processing. ISO subcommittee 32 mentions that BD Analytics has become a major driving application for data warehousing, with the use of MapReduce outside and inside of database management systems, and the use of self-service data marts [2]. MapReduce is one of the

* Correspondence: ebautistav@yahoo.com
[1]Department of Electronic Systems, Autonomous University of Aguascalientes, Av. Universidad 940, Ciudad Universitaria, Aguascalientes, Mexico
[2]Department of Software Engineering and Information Technology ETS, University of Quebec, 1100 Notre Dame St., Montreal, Canada

programming models used to develop BDA, which was developed by Google for processing and generating large datasets.

Sometimes, anomalies and defects found in platforms of Cloud Computing Systems (CCS) affect the performance of BDA resulting in degradation of the whole system. Performance analysis models (PAM) for BDA in CC, should propose a means to identify and quantify normal application behaviour , which can serve as a baseline for detecting and predicting possible anomalies in the software (i.e. applications in a Big Data platforms) that may impact BDA itself. To be able to design such PAM for BDA, methods are needed to collect the necessary base measures specific to performance, and a performance framework must be used to determine the relationships that exist among these measures.

One of the challenges in designing PAM for BDA is how to determine what type of relationship exists between the various base measures and the performance quality concepts defined in international standards such as ISO 25010 [4]. For example, what is the extent of the relationship between the amounts of physical memory used by a BDA and the performance quality concepts of software engineering such as resource utilization or capacity? Thus, this work proposes the use of statistical methods to determine how closely performance parameters (base measures) are related with performance concepts of software engineering.

This paper is structured as follows. Related work and background sections present the concepts related to the performance measurement of BDA and introduces the MapReduce programming model. In addition, background section presents the Performance Measurement Framework for Cloud Computing (PMFCC), which describes the key performance concepts and sub concepts that the best represent the performance of CCS. Analysis model section, presents the method for examining the relationships among the performance concepts identified in the PMFCC. An experimental methodology based on the Taguchi method of experimental design, is used and offers a means for improving the quality of product performance. Experiment section presents the results of an experiment, which analyzes the relationship between the performance factors of BDA, Cloud Computing Platforms (CCP) and the performance concepts identified in the PMFCC. Finally, conclusion section presents a synthesis of the results of this research and suggests future work.

Related work

Researchers have analyzed the performance of BDA from various viewpoints. For example, Alexandru [5] analyzes the performance of Cloud Computing Services for Many-Task Computing (MTC) system. According to

Alexandru, scientific workloads often require High-Performance Computing capabilities, in which scientific computing community has started to focus on MTC, this means high performance execution of loosely coupled applications comprising many tasks. By means of this approach it is possible to demand systems to operate at high utilizations, like to current production grids. Alexandru analyzes the performance based on the premise if current clouds can execute MTC-based scientific workload with similar performance and at lower cost that the current scientific processing systems. For this, the author focuses on Infrastructures as a Service (IaaS), this means providers on public clouds that are not restricted within an enterprise. In this research, Alexandru selected four public clouds providers; Amazon EC2, GoGrid, ElasticHosts and Mosso in which it is performed a traditional system benchmarking in order to provide a first order estimate of the system performance. Alexandru mainly uses metrics related to disk, memory, network and cpu to determine the performance through the analysis of MTC workloads which comprise tens of thousands to hundreds of thousands of tasks. The main finding in this research is that the compute performance of the tested clouds is low compared to traditional systems of high performance computing. In addition, Alexandru found that while current cloud computing services are insufficient for scientific computing at large, they are a good solution for scientists who need resources instantly and temporarily.

Other similar research is performed by Jackson [6] who analyzes high performance computing applications on the Amazon Web Services cloud. The purpose of this work is to examine the performance of existing CC infrastructures and create a mechanism to quantitatively evaluate them. The work is focused on the performance of Amazon EC2, as representative of the current mainstream of commercial CC services, and its applicability to Cloud-based environments for scientific computing. To do so, Jackson quantitatively examines the performance of a set of benchmarks designed to represent a typical High Performance Computing (HPC) workload running on the Amazon EC2 platform. Timing results from different application benchmarks are used to compute the Sustained System Performance (SSP) metric to measure the performance delivered by the workload of a computing system. According to the National Energy Research Scientific Computing Center (NERSC) [7], SSP provides a process for evaluating system performance across any time frame, and can be applied to any set of systems, any workload, and/or benchmark suite, and for any time period. The SSP measures time to solution across different application areas and can be used to evaluate absolute performance and performance relative to cost (in dollars, energy or other value propositions). The results show a strong correlation between the percentage of time an application spends communicating, and its overall performance on EC2. The more communication there is, the worse the performance becomes. Jackson also concludes that the communication pattern of an application can have a significant impact on performance.

Other researchers focus their work on the performance analysis of MapReduce applications. For example, Jin [8] proposes a stochastic model to predict the performance of MapReduce applications under failures. His work is used to quantify the robustness of MapReduce applications under different system parameters, such as the number of processes, the mean time between failures (MTBF) of each process, failure recovery cost, etc. Authors like Jiang [9], performs a depth study of factors that affect the performance of MapReduce applications. In particular, he identifies five factors that affect the performance of MapReduce applications: I/O mode, indexing, data parsing, grouping schemes and block level scheduling. Moreover, Jiang concludes that carefully tuning each factor, it is possible to eliminate the negative impact of these factors and improve the performance of MapReduce applications. Other authors like Guo [10] and Cheng [11] focus their works on improving the performance of MapReduce applications. Gou explodes the freedom to control concurrency in MapReduce in order to improve resource utilization. For this, he proposes resource stealing which dynamically expands and shrinks the resource usage of running tasks by means of the benefit aware speculative execution (BASE). BASE improves the mechanisms of fault-tolerance managed by speculatively launching duplicate tasks for tasks deemed to be stragglers. Furthermore, Cheng [11] focuses his work on improving the performance of MapReduce applications through a strategy called maximum cost performance (MCP). MCP improves the effectiveness of speculative execution by means of accurately and promptly identifying stragglers. For this he provides the following methods: 1) Use both the progress rate and the process bandwidth within a phase to select slow tasks, 2) Use exponentially weighted moving average (EWMA) to predict process speed and calculate a task s remaining time and 3) Determine which task to backup based on the load of a cluster using a cost-benefit model.

Although these works present interesting methods for the performance analysis of CCS and improving of BD applications (MapReduce), their approach is from an infrastructure standpoint and does not consider the performance from a software engineering perspective. This work focuses on the performance analysis of BDA developed by means of the Hadoop MapReduce model, integrating software quality concepts from ISO 25010.

Background

Hadoop MapReduce

Hadoop is the Apache Software Foundation s top level project, and encompasses the various Hadoop sub projects. The Hadoop project provides and supports the development of open source software that supplies a framework for the development of highly scalable distributed computing applications designed to handle processing details, leaving developers free to focus on application logic [12]. Hadoop is divided into several sub projects that fall under the umbrella of infrastructures for distributed computing. One of these sub projects is MapReduce, which is a programming model with an associated implementation, both developed by Google for processing and generating large datasets.

According to Dean [13], programs written in this functional style are automatically parallelized and executed on a large cluster of commodity machines. Authors like Lin [14] point out that today, the issue of tackling large amounts of data is addressed by a divide-and-conquer approach, the basic idea being to partition a large problem into smaller sub problems. Those sub problems can be handled in parallel by different workers; for example, threads in a processor core, cores in a multi-core processor, multiple processors in a machine, or many machines in a cluster. In this way, the intermediate results of each individual worker are then combined to yield the final output.

The Hadoop MapReduce model results are obtained in two main stages: 1) the Map stage, and 2) the Reduce stage. In the Map stage, also called the mapping phase, data elements from a list of such elements are inputted, one at time, to a function called Mapper, which transforms each element individually into an output data element. Figure 1 presents the components of the Map stage process.

The Reduce stage (also called the reducing phase) aggregates values. In this stage, a reducer function receives input values iteratively from an input list. This function combines these values, returning a single output value. The Reduce stage is often used to produce summary data, turning a large volume of data into a smaller summary of itself. Figure 2 presents the components of the Reduce stage.

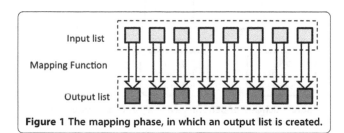

Figure 1 The mapping phase, in which an output list is created.

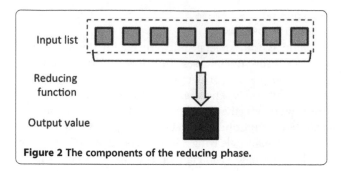

Figure 2 The components of the reducing phase.

According to Yahoo! [15], when a mapping phase begins, any mapper (node) can process any input file or part of an input file. In this way, each mapper loads a set of local files to be able to process them. When a mapping phase has been completed, an intermediate pair of values (consisting of a key and a value) must be exchanged between machines, so that all values with the same key are sent to a single reducer. Like Map tasks, Reduce tasks are spread across the same nodes in the cluster and do not exchange information with one another, nor are they aware of one another s existence. Thus, all data transfer is handled by the Hadoop MapReduce platform itself, guided implicitly by the various keys associated with the values.

Performance measurement framework for cloud computing

The Performance Measurement Framework for Cloud Computing (PMFCC) [16] is based on the scheme for performance analysis shown in Figure 3. This scheme establishes a set of performance criteria (or characteristics) to help to carry out the process of analysis of system performance. In this scheme, the system performance is typically analyzed using three sub concepts, if it is performing a service correctly: 1) responsiveness, 2) productivity, and 3) utilization, and proposes a measurement process for each. There are several possible outcomes

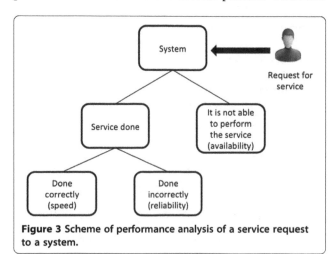

Figure 3 Scheme of performance analysis of a service request to a system.

for each service request made to a system, which can be classified into three categories. The system may: 1) perform the service correctly, 2) perform the service incorrectly, or 3) refuse to perform the service altogether. Moreover, the scheme defines three sub concepts associated with each of these possible outcomes, which affect system performance: 1) speed, 2) reliability, and 3) availability. Figure 3 presents this scheme, which shows the possible outcomes of a service request to a system and the sub concepts associated with them.

Based on the above scheme, the PMFCC [16] maps the possible outcomes of a service request onto quality concepts extracted from the ISO 25010 standard. The ISO 25010 [4] standard defines software product and computer system quality from two distinct perspectives: 1) a quality in use model, and 2) a product quality model. The product quality model is applicable to both systems and software. According to ISO 25010, the properties of both determine the quality of the product in a particular context, based on user requirements. For example, performance efficiency and reliability can be specific concerns of users who specialize in areas of content delivery, management, or maintenance. The performance efficiency concept proposed in ISO 25010 has three sub concepts: 1) time behavior, 2) resource utilization, and 3) capacity, while the reliability concept has four sub concepts: 1) maturity, 2) availability, 3) fault tolerance, and 4) recoverability. The PMFCC selects performance efficiency and reliability as concepts for determining the performance of CCS. In addition, the PMFCC proposes the following definition of CCS performance analysis:

> *The performance of a Cloud Computing system is determined by analysis of the characteristics involved in performing an efficient and reliable service that meets requirements under stated conditions and within the maximum limits of the system parameters .*

Once that the performance analysis concepts and sub concepts are mapped onto the ISO 25010 quality concepts, the framework presents a model of relationship (Figure 4) that presents a logical sequence in which the concepts and sub concepts appear when a performance issue arises in a CCS.

In Figure 4, system performance is determined by two main sub concepts: 1) performance efficiency, and 2) reliability. We have seen that when a CCS receives a service request, there are three possible outcomes (the service is performed correctly, the service is performed incorrectly, or the service cannot be performed). The outcome will determine the sub concepts that will be applied for performance analysis. For example, suppose that the CCS performs a service correctly, but, during its execution, the service failed and was later reinstated. Although the service was

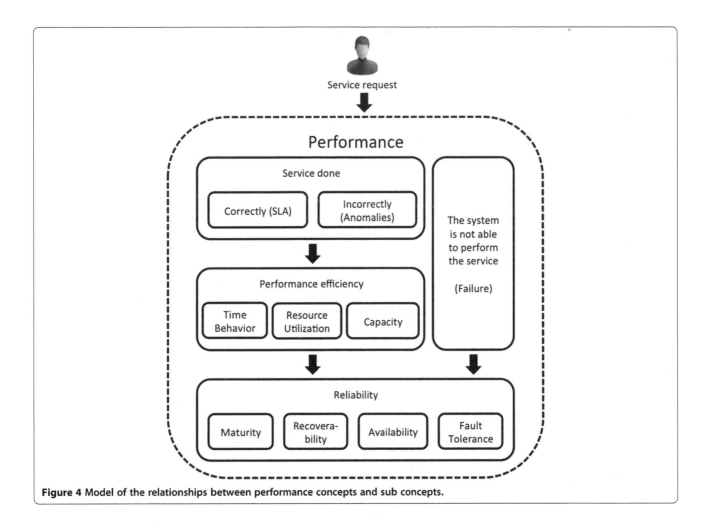

Figure 4 Model of the relationships between performance concepts and sub concepts.

ultimately performed successfully, it is clear that the system availability (part of the reliability sub concept) was compromised, and this affected CCS performance.

Performance analysis model for big data applications
Relationship between performance measures of BDA, CCP and software engineering quality concepts

In order to determine the degree of relationship between performance measures of BDA, and performance concepts and sub concepts defined in the PMFCC (Figure 4), first it is necessary to map performance measures from the BDA and CCP onto the performance quality concepts previously defined. For this, measures need to be collected by means of extracted data from MapReduce log files and system monitoring tools (see Table 1). This data is obtained from a Hadoop cluster, which is the cloud platform in which the CCS is running.

Once the performance measures are collected, they are mapped onto the performance concepts defined in the PMFCC by means of the formulae defined in the ISO 25023. ISO 25023 - Measurement of system and software

product quality, provides a set of quality measures for the characteristics of system/software products that can be used for specifying requirements, measuring and evaluating the system/software product quality [17]. It is important to mention that such formulae were adapted according to the different performance measures collected from the BDA and CCP in order to represent the different concepts in a coherent form. Table 2 presents the different BDA and CCP performance measures after being mapped onto the PMFCC concepts and sub concepts.

Selection of key PMFCC concepts to represent the performance of BDA

Once the performance measures extracted from the BDA and CCP are mapped onto the performance quality concepts (see Table 2), the next step is to select a set of key sub concepts of PMFCC that best represent the performance of BDA. For this, two techniques for feature selection are used in order to determine the most relevant features (PMFCC sub concepts) from a data set. According to Kantardzic [18], feature selection is a set of techniques that select relevant features (PMFCC sub

Table 1 Extract of collected performance measures from the BDA and CCP

Measure	Source	Description
jobs:clusterMapCapacity	Jobs of MapReduce	Maximum number of available maps to be created by a job
jobs:clusterReduceCapacity	Jobs of MapReduce	Maximum number of available reduces to be created by a job
jobs:finishTime	Jobs of MapReduce	Time at which a job was completed
jobs:JobSetupTaskLaunchTime	Jobs of MapReduce	Time at which a job is setup in the cluster for processing
jobs:jobId	Jobs of MapReduce	Job ID
jobs:launchTime	Jobs of MapReduce	Time at which a job is launched for processing
jobs:Status	Jobs of MapReduce	Job status after processing (Successful or Failed)
jobs:submitTime	Jobs of MapReduce	Time at which a job was submitted for processing
disk:ReadBytes	Virtual Machine System	Amount of HD bytes read by a job
disk:WriteBytes	Virtual Machine System	Amount of HD bytes written by a job
memory:Free	Virtual Machine System	Amount of average free memory on a specific time
memory:Used	Virtual Machine System	Amount of average memory used on a specific time
network:RxBytes	Virtual Machine System	Amount of network bytes received on a specific time
network:RxErrors	Virtual Machine System	Amount of network errors during received transmission on a specific time
network:TxBytes	Virtual Machine System	A mount of network bytes transmitted on a specific time
network:TxErrors	Virtual Machine System	Amount of network errors during transmission on a specific time

concepts) for building robust learning models by removing most irrelevant and redundant features from the data. Kantardzic establishes that feature selection algorithms typically fall into two categories: feature ranking and subset selection. Feature ranking ranks all features by a specific base measure and eliminates all features that do not achieve an adequate score while subset selection, searches the set of all features for the optimal subset in which selected features are not ranked. The next subsections present two techniques of feature ranking which are used in the PAM for BDA in order to determine the most relevant performance sub concepts (features) that best represent the performance of BDA.

Feature selection based on comparison of means and variances

The feature selection based on comparison of means and variances is based on the distribution of values for a given feature, in which it is necessary to compute the mean value and the corresponding variance. In general, if one feature describes different classes of entities, samples of two different classes can be examined. The means of feature values are normalized by their variances and then compared. If the means are far apart, interest in a feature increases: it has potential, in terms of its use in distinguishing between two classes. If the means are indistinguishable, interest wanes in that feature. The mean of a feature is compared in both cases without taking into consideration relationship to other features. The next equations formalize the test, where

A and B are sets of feature values measured for two different classes, and n_1 and n_2 are the corresponding number of samples:

$$SE\ A\text{--}B\quad \sqrt{\left(\frac{\text{var } A}{n_1}\quad \frac{\text{var } B}{n_2}\right)} \qquad 1$$

$$Test: \frac{|mean\ A - mean\ B|}{SE\ A\text{--}B} > threshold\_value \qquad 2$$

In this approach to feature selection, it is assumed that a given feature is independent of others. A comparison of means is typically a natural fit to classification problems. For k classes, k pair wise comparisons can be made, comparing each class with its complement. A feature is retained if it is significant for any of the pair wise comparisons as shown in formula 2.

Relief algorithm

Another important technique for feature selection is the Relief algorithm. The Relief algorithm is a feature weight-based algorithm, which relies on relevance evaluation of each feature given in a training data set in which samples are labeled (classification problems). The main concept of this algorithm is to compute a ranking score for every feature indicating how well this feature separates neighboring samples. The authors of the Relief algorithm, Kira and Rendell [19], proved that ranking score becomes large for relevant features and small for irrelevant ones.

The objective of the relief algorithm is to estimate the quality of features according to how well their values distinguish between samples close to each other. Given a training data S, the algorithm randomly selects subset of samples size m, where m is a user defined parameter. The algorithm analyses each feature based on a selected subset of samples. For each randomly selected sample X from a training data set, it searches for its two nearest neighbors: one from the same class, called nearest hit H, and the other one from a different class, called nearest miss M.

The Relief algorithm updates the quality score $W(Ai)$ for all feature Ai depending on the differences on their values for samples X, M, and H as shown in formula 3.

$$W_{new} A_i \quad \frac{W_{old} A_i - (diff\ X A_i , H A_i)^2 \quad diff\ X A_i , M A_i)^2)}{m}$$

3

The process is repeated m times for randomly selected samples from the training data set and the scores $W(Ai)$ are accumulated for each sample. Finally, using threshold of relevancy τ, the algorithm detects those features that are statistically relevant to the target classification, and

Table 2 BDA and CCP performance measures mapped onto PMFCC concepts and sub concepts

PMFCC concept	PMFCC sub concepts	Description	Adapted formula
Performance efficiency			
Time behavior	Response time	Duration from a submitted BDA Job to start processing till it is launched	submitTime - launchTime
Time behavior	Turnaround time	Duration from a submitted BDA Job to start processing till completion of the Job	finishTime submitTime
Time behavior	Processing time	Duration from a launched BDA Job to start processing till completion of the Job	finishTime-launchTime
Resource utilization	CPU utilization	How much CPU time is used per minute to process a BDA Job (percent)	100 cpuIdlePercent
Resource utilization	Memory utilization	How much memory is used to process a BDA Job per minute (percent)	100 memoryFreePercent
Resource utilization	Hard disk bytes read	How much bytes are read to process a BDA Job per minute	Total of bytes read per minute
Resource utilization	Hard disk bytes written	How much bytes are written to process a BDA Job per minute	Total of bytes written per minute
Capacity	Load map tasks capacity	How many map tasks are processed in parallel for a specific BDA Job	Total of map tasks processed in parallel for a specific BDA Job
Capacity	Load reduce tasks capacity	How many reduce tasks are processed in parallel for a specific BDA Job	Total of reduce tasks processed in parallel for a specific BDA Job
Capacity	Network Tx bytes	How many bytes are transferred while a specific BDA Job is processed	Total of transferred bytes per minute
Capacity	Network Rx bytes	How many bytes are received while a specific BDA Job is processed	Total of received bytes per minute
Reliability			
Maturity	Task mean time between failure	How frequently does a task of a specific BDA Job fail in operation	Number of tasks failed per minute
Maturity	Tx network errors	How many transfer errors in the network are detected while processing a specific BDA Job	Number of Tx network errors detected per minute
Maturity	Rx network errors	How many reception errors in the network are detected while processing a specific BDA Job	Number of Rx network errors detected per minute
Availability	Time of CC System Up	Total time that the system has been in operation	Total minutes of the CC system operation
Fault tolerance	Network Tx collisions	How many transfer collision in the network occurs while processing a specific BDA Job	Total of Tx network collisions per minute
Fault tolerance	Network Rx dropped	How many reception bytes in the network are dropped while processing a specific BDA Job	Total of Rx network bytes are dropped per minute
Recoverability	Mean recovery time	What is the average time the CC system take to complete recovery from a failure	Average recovery time of CC system

these are the features with $W(Ai) \geq \tau$. The main steps of the Relief algorithm are formalized in Algorithm 1.

Algorithm 1 Relief Algorithm
Initialize $W(A_j) = 0$; $i = 1, 2, ..., n$ (where n is the number of features)
For $i = 1$ to m

> Randomly select X from training data set S
> Find nearest hit H and nearest miss M samples
>
> *For $j = 1$ to n*
>> $W(A_j) = W(A_j)-(\text{diff}(X[A_j],H[A_j])^2+\text{diff}(X[A_j],M[A_j])^2)/m$
>
> *End*

End
Output: Subset of feature where $W(A_j) \geq \tau$

Choosing a methodology to analyze relationships between performance concepts

Once that a subset of the most important features (key performance sub concepts) has been selected, the next step is to determine the degree of relationship that exist between such subset of features and the rest of performance sub concepts defined by means of PMFCC. For this, the use of Taguchi s experimental design method is proposed: it investigates how different features (performance measures) are related, and to what degree. Understanding these relationships will enable us to determine the influence each of them has in the resulting performance concepts. The PMFCC shows many of the relationships that exist between the base measures, which have a major influence on the collection functions. However, in BDA and more specifically in the Hadoop MapReduce application experiment, there are over a hundred possible performance measures (including system measures) that could contribute to the analysis of BDA performance. A selection of these performance measures has to be included in the collection functions so that the respective performance concepts can be obtained and, from there, an indication of the performance of the applications. One key design problem is to establish which performance measures are interrelated and how much they contribute to each of the collection functions.

In traditional statistical methods, thirty or more observations (or data points) are typically needed for each variable, in order to gain meaningful insights and analyze the results. In addition, only a few independent variables are necessary to carry out experiments to uncover potential relationships, and this must be performed under certain predetermined and controlled test conditions. However, this approach is not appropriate here, owing to the large number of variables involved and the considerable time and effort required. Consequently, an analysis method that is suited to our specific problem and in our study area is needed.

A possible candidate method to address this problem is Taguchi s experimental design method, which investigates how different variables affect the mean and variance of a process performance characteristics, and helps in determining how well the process is functioning. This Taguchi method proposes a limited number of experiments, but is more efficient than a factorial design in its ability to identify relationships and dependencies. The next section presents the method to find out the relationships.

Taguchi method of experimental design

Taguchi s Quality Engineering Handbook [20] describes the Taguchi method of experimental design which was developed by Dr. Genichi Taguchi, a researcher at the Electronic Control Laboratory in Japan. This method combines industrial and statistical experience, and offers a means for improving the quality of manufactured products. It is based on a robust design concept, according to which a well designed product should cause no problem when used under specified conditions.

According to Cheikhi [21], Taguchi s two phase quality strategy is the following:

- Phase 1: The online phase, which focuses on the techniques and methods used to control quality during the production of the product.
- Phase 2: The offline phase, which focuses on taking those techniques and methods into account before manufacturing the product, that is, during the design phase, the development phase, etc.

One of the most important activities in the offline phase of the strategy is parameter design. This is where the parameters are determined that makes it possible to satisfy the set quality objectives (often called the objective function) through the use of experimental designs under set conditions. If the product does not work properly (does not fulfill the objective function), then the design constants (also called parameters) need to be adjusted so that it will perform better. Cheikhi [21] explains that this activity includes five (5) steps, which are required to determine the parameters that satisfy the quality objectives:

1. Definition of the objective of the study, that is, identification of the quality characteristics to be observed in the output (results expected).
2. Identification of the study factors and their interactions, as well as the levels at which they will be set. There are two different types of factors: 1) control factors: factors that can be easily managed or adjusted; and 2) noise factors: factors that are difficult to control or manage.
3. Selection of the appropriate orthogonal arrays (OA) for the study, based on the number of factors, and their levels and interactions. The OA show the

various experiments that will need to be conducted in order to verify the effect of the factors studied on the quality characteristic to be observed in the output.

4. Preparation and performance of the resulting OA experiments, including preparation of the data sheets for each OA experiment according to the combination of the levels and factors for the experiment. For each experiment, a number of trials are conducted and the quality characteristics of the output are observed.

5. Analysis and interpretation of the experimental results to determine the optimum settings for the control factors, and the influence of those factors on the quality characteristics observed in the output.

According to Taguchi s Quality Engineering Handbook [20] the OA organizes the parameters affecting the process and the levels at which they should vary. Taguchi s method tests pairs of combinations, instead of having to test all possible combinations (as in a factorial experimental design). This approach can determine which factors affect product quality the most in a minimum number of experiments.

Taguchi s OA can be created manually or they can be derived from deterministic algorithms. They are selected by the number of parameters (variables) and the number of levels (states). An OA array is represented by Ln and Pn, where Ln corresponds to the number of experiments to be conducted, and Pn corresponds to the number of parameters to be analyzed. Table 3 presents an example of Taguchi OA L12, meaning that 12 experiments are conducted to analyze 11 parameters.

An OA cell contains the factor levels (1 and 2), which determine the type of parameter values for each experiment. Once the experimental design has

been determined and the trials have been carried out, the performance characteristic measurements from each trial can be used to analyze the relative effect of the various parameters.

Taguchi s method is based on the use of the signal-to-noise ratio (SNR). The SNR is a measurement scale that has been used in the communications industry for nearly a century for determining the extent of the relationship between quality factors in a measurement model [20]. The SNR approach involves the analysis of data for variability in which an input-to-output relationship is studied in the measurement system. Thus, to determine the effect each parameter has on the output, the SNR is calculated by the follow formula:

$$SN_i \quad 10\log\frac{\bar{y}_i^2}{S_i^2} \qquad 4$$

Where

$$\bar{y}_i \quad \frac{1}{N_i}\sum_{u\ 1}^{N_i} y_{i,u}$$

$$S_i^2 \quad \frac{1}{N_i-1}\sum_{u\ 1}^{N_i}\left(y_{i,u}-\bar{y}_i\right)$$

i=Experiment number
u=Trial number
N_i=*Number of trials for experiment i*

To minimize the performance characteristic (objective function), the following definition of the SNR should be calculated:

$$SN_i \quad -10\log\left(\sum_{u\ 1}^{N_i}\frac{y_u^2}{N_i}\right) \qquad 5$$

To maximize the performance characteristic (objective function), the following definition of the SNR should be calculated:

$$SN_i \quad -10\log\left[\frac{1}{N_i}\sum_{u\ 1}^{N_i}\frac{1}{y_u^2}\right] \qquad 6$$

Once the SNR values have been calculated for each factor and level, they are tabulated as shown in Table 4, and then the range R (R = high SN - low SN) of the SNR for each parameter is calculated and entered on Table 4.

According to Taguchi s method, the larger the R value for a parameter, the greater its effect on the process.

Table 3 Taguchi s Orthogonal Array L12

No. of Experiments (L)	P1	P2	P3	P4	P5	P6	P7	P8	P9	P10	P11
1	1	1	1	1	1	1	1	1	1	1	1
2	1	1	1	1	1	2	2	2	2	2	2
3	1	1	2	2	2	1	1	1	2	2	2
4	1	2	1	2	2	1	2	2	1	1	2
5	1	2	2	1	2	2	1	2	1	2	1
6	1	2	2	1	2	2	1	2	1	2	1
7	1	2	2	2	1	2	2	1	2	1	1
8	2	1	2	1	2	2	2	1	1	1	2
9	2	1	1	2	2	2	1	2	2	1	1
10	2	2	2	1	1	1	1	2	2	1	2
11	2	2	1	2	1	2	1	1	1	2	2
12	2	2	1	1	2	1	2	1	2	2	1

Table 4 Rank for SNR values

Level	P1	P2	P3	P4	P5	P6	P7	*	P11
1	$SN_{1,1}$	$SN_{2,1}$	$SN_{3,1}$	$SN_{4,1}$	$SN_{5,1}$	$SN_{6,1}$	$SN_{7,1}$		$SN_{11,1}$
2	$SN_{1,2}$	$SN_{2,2}$	$SN_{3,2}$	$SN_{4,2}$	$SN_{5,2}$	$SN_{6,2}$	$SN_{7,2}$		$SN_{11,2}$
3	$SN_{1,3}$	$SN_{2,3}$	$SN_{3,3}$	$SN_{4,3}$	$SN_{5,3}$	$SN_{6,3}$	$SN_{7,3}$		$SN_{11,3}$
4	$SN_{1,4}$	$SN_{2,4}$	$SN_{3,4}$	$SN_{4,4}$	$SN_{5,4}$	$SN_{6,4}$	$SN_{7,4}$		$SN_{11,4}$
Range	R_{P1}	R_{P2}	R_{P3}	R_{P4}	R_{P5}	R_{P6}	R_{P7}		R_{P11}
Rank	**Rank$_{P1}$**	**Rank$_{P2}$**	**Rank$_{P3}$**	**Rank$_{P4}$**	**Rank$_{P5}$**	**Rank$_{P6}$**	**Rank$_{P7}$**		**Rank$_{P11}$**

*Corresponding values for parameters P8, P9 and P10.

Experiment

Experiment setup

The experiment was conducted on a DELL Studio Workstation XPS 9100 with Intel Core i7 12-core X980 processor at 3.3 GHz, 24 GB DDR3 RAM, Seagate 1.5 TB 7200 RPM SATA 3Gb/s disk, and 1 Gbps network connection. We used a Linux CentOS 6.4 64-bit distribution and Xen 4.2 as the hypervisor. This physical machine hosts five virtual machines (VM), each with a dual-core Intel i7 configuration, 4 GB RAM, 20 GB virtual storage, and a virtual network interface type. In addition, each VM executes the Apache Hadoop distribution version 1.0.4, which includes the Hadoop Distributed File System (HDFS) and MapReduce framework libraries, Apache Chukwa 0.5.0 as performance measures collector and Apache HBase 0.94.1 as performance measures repository. One of these VM is the master node, which executes NameNode (HDFS) and JobTracker (MapReduce), and the rest of the VM are slave nodes running DataNodes (HDFS) and JobTrackers (MapReduce). Figure 5 presents the cluster configuration for the set of experiments.

Mapping of performance measures onto PMFCC concepts
A total of 103 MapReduce Jobs (BDA) were executed in the virtual Hadoop cluster and a set of performance measures were obtained from MapReduce Jobs logs and monitoring tools. One of the main problems that arose after the performance measures repository ingestion process was the cleanliness of data. Cleanliness calls for the quality of the data to be verified prior to performing data analysis. Among the most important data quality issues to consider during data cleaning in the model were corrupted records, inaccurate content, missing values, and

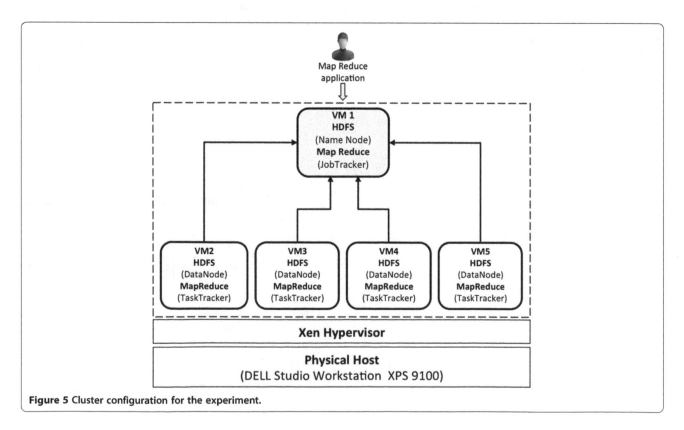

Figure 5 Cluster configuration for the experiment.

formatting inconsistencies, to name a few. Consequently, one of the main challenges at the preprocessing stage was how to structure data in standard formats so that they can be analyzed more efficiently. For this, a data normalization process was carried out over the data set by means of the standard score technique (see formula 7).

$$Xnorm_i \quad \frac{X_i - \mu_i}{S_i} \qquad 7$$

where

X_i=Feature i
μ_i=Average value of Xi in data set
S_i=Range of feature i ($MaxX_i$-$MinX_i$)

The normalization process scaled the values between the range of [-1, 1] according to the different collected performance measures which are expressed in different units and dimensions. For example the measure processing time is expressed in minutes while the measure memory utilization is expressed in Mbytes. Table 5 presents an extract from the different collected performance measures after the process of normalization.

Note: Table 5 shows that values related to network measures are equal to zero because the experiment is performed in a Hadoop virtual cluster. This means that real transmission over a physical network does not exist leaving out the possibility of errors. In addition, other measures such as mean time between failure and mean recovery time are also equal to zero because during the experiment duration Hadoop virtual cluster never failed.

Selection of key measures to represent the performance of BDA

One of the challenges in the design of the PAM for BDA is how to determine a set of key sub concepts which have more relevance in the performance compared to others. For this, the application of feature selection is used during the process for knowledge discovery. As previously mentioned, two techniques used for feature selection are: means and variances, and the Relief algorithm. The means and variances approach assumes that the given features are independent of others. In the experiment a total of 103 Hadoop MapReduce Jobs were executed storing their performance measures. A MapReduce Job may belong to one of two classes according to its status; failed or successful (0 or 1) (see Table 5).

Thus, applying means and variances technique to the data set, the feature Job Status classifies each Job records into two classes 0 and 1. First, it is necessary to compute a mean value and variance for both classes and for each feature (PMFCC sub concept measure). It is important to note that test values will be compared with the highest set

Table 5 Extract of collected performance measures after process of normalization

Performance measure	138367812000-job_201311051347_0021	1384366260-job_201311131253_0019	1384801260-job_201311181318_0419
Time of CC System Up	−0.4534012681	−0.4158208360	0.1921547093
Load map tasks capacity	−0.0860196415	−0.0770106325	−0.0860196415
Load reduce tasks capacity	−0.0334295334	−0.0334295334	−0.0334295334
Network Rx bytes	−0.0647059274	0.4808087278	−0.0055927073
Network Tx bytes	−0.0779191010	0.3139488890	−0.0613171507
Network Rx dropped	0.0	0.0	0.0
Network Tx collisions	0.0	0.0	0.0
Rx network errors	0.0	0.0	0.0
Tx network errors	0.0	0.0	0.0
CPU utilization	−0.0950811052	0.5669416548	−0.0869983066
Hard disk bytes read	−0.0055644728	0.0196859057	−0.0076297598
Hard disk bytes written	−0.0386960610	0.2328110281	−0.0253053155
Memory utilization	0.1956635952	0.4244033618	−0.0341498692
Processing time	−0.1838906682	0.8143236713	0.0156797304
Response time	0.0791592524	0.1221040377	−0.1846444285
Turnaround time	−0.1838786629	0.8143213555	0.0156595689
Task MTBF	0.0	0.0	0.0
Mean recovery time	0.0	0.0	0.0
Job Status	1.0	0.0	1.0

of values obtained after the ranking process (0.9) because this distinguished them from the rest of results. Results are shown in Table 6.

The analysis shows that measures *job processing time and job turnaround* have the potential to be distinguishing features between the two classes because their means are far apart and interest in such measures increases, this means their test values are greater than 0.9. In addition, it is important to mention that although between the second and third result (hard disk bytes written) there is a considerable difference; the latter is also selected in order to analyze its relationship with the rest of measures because it also has the potential, in terms of their use, to stand out from the rest of the measures and give more certainty to the analysis of relationships. Thus, the measures *job processing time, job turnaround and hard disk bytes written* are selected as candidates to represent the performance of the BDA in the Hadoop system.

In order to give more certainty to the above results, the Relief algorithm technique was applied to the same data set. As previously mentioned, the core of Relief algorithm estimates the quality of features according to how well their values distinguish between samples (performance measures of MapReduce Job records) close to each other. Thus, after applying the Relief algorithm to the data set, results are presented in Table 7 where the algorithm detects those features that are statistically relevant to the target classification which are measures with highest quality score.

Table 6 Results of means and variances

Performance measures	Test values
MapReduceJob_ProcessingTime[*]	**9.214837**
MapReduceJob_TurnAround[*]	**9.214828**
SystemHDWriteBytes_Utilization[*]	**8.176328**
SystemUpTime	7.923577
SystemLoadMapCapacity	6.613519
SystemNetworkTxBytes	6.165150
SystemNetworkRxBytes	5.930647
SystemCPU_Utilization	5.200704
SystemLoadReduceCapacity	5.163010
MapReduceJob_ResponseTime	5.129339
SystemMemory_Utilization	3.965617
SystemHDReadBytes_Utilization	0.075003
NetworkRxDropped	0.00
NetworkTxCollisions	0.00
NetworkRxErrors	0.00
NetworkTxErrors	0.00

[*]Distinguishing features between the two classes with the highest set of values obtained after the ranking process.

Table 7 Relief algorithm results

Performance measure	Quality score (W)
MapReduceJob_ProcessingTime[*]	**0.74903**
MapReduceJob_TurnAround[*]	**0.74802**
SystemHDWriteBytes_Utilization[*]	**0.26229**
SystemUpTime	0.25861
SystemCPU_Utilization	0.08189
SystemLoadMapCapacity	0.07878
SystemMemory_Utilization	0.06528
SystemNetworkTxBytes	0.05916
MapReduceJob_ResponseTime	0.03573
SystemLoadReduceCapacity	0.03051
SystemNetworkRxBytes	0.02674
SystemHDReadBytes_Utilization	0.00187
NetworkRxDropped	0.00
NetworkTxCollisions	0.00
NetworkRxErrors	0.00
NetworkTxErrors	0.00

[*]Distinguishing features between the two classes with the highest quality scores obtained after applying the Relief algorithm.

The Relief results show that the performance measures *job processing time and job turnaround*, have the highest quality scores (*W*) and also have the potential to be distinguishing features between the two classes. In this case the performance measure hard disk bytes written is also selected by means of the same approach as in the means and variance analysis: in other words, this has in terms of their use to stand out from the rest of the measures and give more certainty to the analysis of relationships. Thus, the measures *job processing time, job turnaround and hard disk bytes written* are also selected as candidates to represent the performance of BDA in the Hadoop system.

The results show that Time behavior and Resource utilization (see Table 2) are the PMFCC concepts that best represent the performance of the BDA. The next step is to determine how the rest of performance measures are related and to what degree. Studying these relationships enables to assess the influence each of them has on the concepts that best represent the BDA performance in the experiment. For this, Taguchis experimental design method is applied in order to determine how different performance measures are related.

Analysis of relationship between selected performance measures

Once that a set of performance measures are selected to represent the performance of BDA, it is necessary to determine the relationships that exist between them and the rest of the performance measures. These key measures are defined as quality objectives (objective functions) according to

Table 8 Experiment factors and levels

Factor number	Factor name	Level 1	Level 2
1	Time of CC system up	< 0.0	≥ 0.0
2	Load map tasks capacity	< 0.0	≥ 0.0
3	Load reduce tasks capacity	< 0.0	≥ 0.0
4	Network Rx bytes	< 0.0	≥ 0.0
5	Network Tx bytes	< 0.0	≥ 0.0
6	CPU utilization	< 0.0	≥ 0.0
7	Hard disk bytes read	< 0.0	≥ 0.0
8	Memory utilization	< 0.0	≥ 0.0
9	Response time	< 0.0	≥ 0.0

Taguchis terminology. According to Taguchi [20], quality is often referred to as conformance to the operating specifications of a system. To him, the quality objective (or dependent variable) determines the ideal function of the output that the system should show. In our experiment, the observed dependent variables are the following:

- Job processing time,
- Job turnaround and
- Hard disk bytes written

Each MapReduce Job record (Table 5) is selected as an experiment in which different values for each performance measure is recorded. In addition, different levels of each factor (see Table 3) are established as:

- Values less than zero, level 1.
- Values greater or equal to zero, level 2.

Table 8 presents a summary of the factors, levels, and values for this experiment.

Note. The factor set consisting of the rest of performance measures after the key selection process. In addition, it is important to mention that it is feasible to have values less than 0.0; this means negative values because the experiment is performed after the normalization process.

Using Taguchis experimental design method, selection of the appropriate OA is determined by the number of factors and levels to be examined. The resulting OA array for this case study is L12 (presented in Table 3). The assignment of the various factors and values of this OA array is shown in Table 9.

Table 9 shows the set of experiments to be carried out with different values for each parameter selected. For example, experiment 3 involves values of time of system up fewer than 0, map task capacity fewer than 0, reduce task capacity greater than or equal to 0, network rx bytes greater than or equal to 0, and so on.

A total of approximately 1000 performance measures were extracted by selecting those that met the different combination of parameter values after the normalization process for each experiment. Only a set of 40 measures met the experiment requirements presented in Table 9. This set of 12 experiments was divided into three groups of twelve experiments each (called trials). An extract of the values and results of each experiment for the *processing time* output objective is presented in Table 10 (the same procedure is performed to developed the experiments of *job turnaround and hard disk bytes written* output objectives).

Taguchis method defined the SNR used to measure robustness, which is the transformed form of the performance quality characteristic (output value) used to analyze the results. Since the objective of this experiment is to minimize the quality characteristic of the

Table 9 Matrix of experiments

Experiment	Time of system up	Map tasks capacity	Reduce tasks capacity	Network Rx bytes	Network Tx bytes	CPU utiliza-tion	HD bytes read	Memory utilization	Response time
1	< 0	< 0	< 0	< 0	< 0	< 0	< 0	< 0	< 0
2	< 0	< 0	< 0	< 0	< 0	≥ 0	≥0	≥ 0	≥ 0
3	< 0	< 0	≥ 0	≥ 0	≥ 0	< 0	< 0	< 0	≥ 0
4	< 0	≥ 0	< 0	≥ 0	≥ 0	< 0	≥ 0	≥ 0	< 0
5	< 0	≥ 0	≥ 0	< 0	≥ 0	≥ 0	< 0	≥ 0	< 0
6	< 0	≥ 0	≥ 0	< 0	≥ 0	≥ 0	< 0	≥ 0	< 0
7	< 0	≥ 0	≥ 0	≥ 0	< 0	≥ 0	≥ 0	< 0	≥ 0
8	≥ 0	< 0	≥ 0	< 0	≥ 0	≥ 0	≥ 0	< 0	< 0
9	≥ 0	< 0	< 0	≥ 0	≥ 0	≥ 0	< 0	≥ 0	≥ 0
10	≥ 0	≥ 0	≥ 0	< 0	< 0	< 0	< 0	≥ 0	≥ 0
11	≥ 0	≥ 0	< 0	≥ 0	< 0	≥ 0	< 0	< 0	< 0
12	≥ 0	≥ 0	< 0	< 0	≥ 0	< 0	≥ 0	< 0	≥ 0

Table 10 Trials, experiments, and resulting values for *job processing time* output objective

Trial	Experiment	Time of system up	Map tasks capacity	Reduce tasks capacity	Network Rx bytes	Network Tx bytes	CPU utilization	a	Job processing time
1	1	−0.44091	−0.08601	−0.03342	−0.04170	−0.08030	−0.00762	a	**−0.183902878**
1	2	−0.34488	−0.07100	−0.03342	−0.02022	−0.18002	0.16864	a	**−0.170883497**
1	3	−0.49721	−0.08601	0.79990	0.01329	0.02184	−0.03221	a	**−0.171468597**
1	4	−0.39277	0.01307	−0.03342	0.02418	0.08115	−0.02227	a	**−0.13252447**
b	b	b	b	b	b	b	b	b	b
2	1	−0.03195	−0.08601	−0.03342	−0.06311	−0.09345	−0.17198	a	**0.015597229**
2	2	−0.01590	−0.19624	−0.03342	−0.06880	−0.01529	0.06993	a	**0.730455521**
2	3	−0.11551	−0.07701	0.79990	0.05635	0.09014	−0.02999	a	**−0.269538778**
2	4	−0.04868	0.80375	−0.20009	0.00585	0.01980	−0.07713	a	**−0.13252447**
c	c	c	c	c	c	c	c	c	c
3	1	−0.06458	−0.08601	−0.03342	−0.06053	−0.08483	−0.14726	a	**0.015597229**
3	2	−0.04868	−0.19624	−0.03342	−0.07017	−0.01789	0.07074	a	**0.730455521**
3	3	−0.29027	−0.07100	0.79990	0.049182	0.06387	−0.07363	a	**−0.264375632**
3	4	−0.06473	0.91398	−0.03342	0.00892	0.02461	−0.05465	a	**−0.13252447**
d	d	d	d	d	d	d	d	d	d

[a]Corresponding values for HD bytes read and Memory utilization.
[b]Corresponding values for the set of experiments 5 to 12 of trial 1.
[c]Corresponding values for the set of experiments 5 to 12 of trial 2.
[d]Corresponding values for the set of experiments 5 to 12 of trial 3.

output (amount of processing time used per a map reduce Job), the SNR for the quality characteristic the smaller the better is given by formula 8, that is:

$$SN_i = -\left(\sum_{u=1}^{N_i} \frac{y_u^2}{N_i}\right) \qquad 8$$

The SNR result for each experiment is shown in Table 11. Complete SNR tables for the *job turnaround and hard*

disk bytes written experiments were developed in order to obtain their results.

According to Taguchi's method, the factor effect is equal to the difference between the highest average SNR and the lowest average SNR for each factor (see Table 4). This means that the larger the factor effect for a parameter, the larger the effect the variable has on the process, or, in other words, the more significant the effect of the factor. Table 12 shows the factor effect for each variable studied in the experiment. Similar

Table 11 Processing time SNR results

Experiment	Time of system up	Map tasks capacity	Reduce tasks capacity	Network Rx bytes	*	Processing time trial 1	Processing time trial 2	Processing Time trial 3	SNR
1	< 0	< 0	< 0	< 0	*	−0.1839028	0.5155972	0.4155972	−0.999026
2	< 0	< 0	< 0	< 0	*	−0.1708835	0.7304555	0.7304555	−0.45658085
3	< 0	< 0	≥ 0	≥ 0	*	−0.1714686	−0.269538	0.2643756	1.25082414
4	< 0	≥ 0	< 0	≥ 0	*	−0.1325244	−0.132524	−0.132524	15.7043319
5	< 0	≥ 0	≥ 0	< 0	*	−0.1856763	−0.267772	−0.269537	1.39727504
6	< 0	≥ 0	≥ 0	< 0	*	−0.2677778	−0.269537	−0.185676	1.39727504
7	< 0	≥ 0	≥ 0	≥ 0	*	−0.1714686	−0.174542	−0.174542	3.98029432
8	≥ 0	< 0	≥ 0	< 0	*	−0.2688839	−0.267712	−0.268355	5.32068168
9	≥ 0	< 0	< 0	≥ 0	*	0.81432367	0.8143236	0.8143236	15.7761839
10	≥ 0	≥ 0	≥ 0	< 0	*	−0.1325244	−0.132524	−0.132524	15.7043319
11	≥ 0	≥ 0	< 0	≥ 0	*	−0.1837929	−0.182090	−0.269544	1.24567693
12	≥ 0	≥ 0	< 0	< 0	*	−0.1714686	−0.269538	−0.269538	1.23463636

[*]Corresponding parameter configuration for Network Tx bytes, CPU utilization, HD bytes read, Memory utilization and Response time.

Table 12 Factor effect rank on the job processing time output objective

	Time of system Up	Map tasks capacity	Reduce tasks capacity	Net. Rx bytes	Net. Tx bytes	CPU utilization	HD bytes read	Memory utilization	Response time
Average SNR at Level 1	3.18205	4.1784165	5.4175370	3.3712	3.8949	6.57901	5.11036	2.005514	4.011035
Average SNR at Level 2	7.85630	5.8091173	4.8417803	7.5914	6.0116	3.58260	5.15667	8.253802	6.248281
Factor effect (difference)	4.67424	1.6307007	0.5757566	4.2202	2.1166	2.99641	0.04630	6.248288	2.237245
Rank	2	7	8	3	6	4	9	1	5

factor effect tables for *job turnaround time and hard disk bytes written* output values were also developed to obtain their results.

Results

Analysis and interpretation of results
Based on the results presented in Table 12, it can be observed that:

- *Memory utilization* is the factor that has the most influence on the quality objective (*processing time used per a MapReduce Job*) of the output observed, at 6.248288, and
- *Hard disk bytes read* is the least influential factor in this experiment, at 0.046390.

Figure 6 presents a graphical representation of the factor results and their levels for *processing time* output objective.

To represent the optimal condition of the levels, also called the *optimal solution of the levels*, an analysis of SNR values is necessary in this experiment. Whether the aim is to minimize or maximize the quality

characteristic (*job processing time* used per a MapReduce Job), it is always necessary to maximize the SNR parameter values. Consequently, the optimum level of a specific factor will be the highest value of its SNR. It can be seen that the optimum level for each factor is represented by the highest point in the graph (as presented in Figure 6); that is, L2 for time of system up, L2 for map task capacity, L1 for reduce task capacity, etc.

Using the findings presented in Tables 11 and 12 and in Figure 6, it can be concluded that the optimum levels for the nine (9) factors for *processing time* output objective in this experiment based on our experimental configuration cluster are presented in Table 13.

Statistical data analysis of job processing time
The analysis of variance (ANOVA) is a statistical technique typically used in the design and analysis of experiments. According to Trivedi [22], the purpose of applying the ANOVA technique to an experimental situation is to compare the effect of several factors applied simultaneously to the response variable (quality characteristic). It allows the effects of the controllable factors to be separated from those of uncontrolled variations. Table 14 presents the results of this ANOVA analysis of the experimental factors.

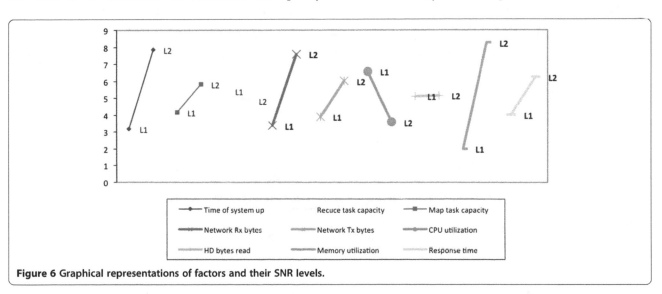

Figure 6 Graphical representations of factors and their SNR levels.

Table 13 Optimum levels for factors of the processing time output

Factor number	Performance measure	Optimum level
1	Time of CC System Up	≥ 0 (L2)
2	Load map tasks capacity	≥ 0 (L2)
3	Load reduce tasks capacity	< 0 (L1)
4	Network Rx bytes	≥ 0 (L2)
5	Network Tx bytes	≥ 0 (L2)
6	CPU utilization	< 0 (L1)
7	Hard disk bytes read	≥ 0 (L2)
8	Memory utilization	≥ 0 (L2)
9	Response time	≥ 0 (L2)

As can be seen in the contribution column of Table 14, these results can be interpreted as follows (represented graphically in Figure 7):

- *Memory utilization* is the factor that has the most influence (almost 39% of the contribution) on the processing time in this experiment.
- *Time of CC system up* is the factor that has the second greatest influence (21.814% of the contribution) on the processing time.
- *Network Rx bytes* is the factor that has the third greatest influence (17.782% of the contribution) on the processing time.
- *Hard disk bytes read* is the factor with the least influence (0.002% of the contribution) on the processing time in the cluster.

In addition, based on the column related to the variance ratio F shown in Table 14, it can be concluded that:

- The factor *Memory utilization* has the most dominant effect on the output variable.

- According to Taguchis method, the factor with the smallest contribution is taken as the error estimate. So, the factor *Hard disk bytes read* is taken as the error estimate, since it corresponds to the smallest sum of squares.

The results of this case study show, based on both the graphical and statistical data analyses of the SNR, that the *Memory utilization* required to process a MapReduce application in our cluster has the most influence, followed by the Time of CC system up and, finally, Network Rx bytes.

Statistical data analysis of job turnaround

The statistical data analysis of job turnaround output objective is presented in Table 15.

As can be seen in the contribution column of Table 15, these results can be interpreted as follows (represented graphically in Figure 8):

- *Load reduce task capacity* is the factor that has the most influence (almost 50% of the contribution) on the job turnaround in this experiment.
- *Load map task capacity* is the factor that has the second greatest influence (almost 21% of the contribution) on the job turnaround.
- *Hard disk bytes read* is the factor that has the third greatest influence (16.431% of the contribution) on the job turnaround.
- *CPU utilization* is the factor with the least influence (0.006% of the contribution) on the job turnaround in the cluster system.

In addition, based on the column related to the variance ratio F shown in Table 15, it can be concluded that:

- The factor *Time of CC system up* has the most dominant effect on the output variable.

Table 14 Analysis of variance of job processing time output objective (ANOVA)

Factors	Degrees of freedom	Sum of squares (SS)	Variance (MS)	Contribution (%)	Variance ration (F)
Time of CC system up	1	21.84857	21.84857	21.814	101.87
Load map tasks capacity	1	2.659185	2.659185	2.655	12.39
Load reduce tasks capacity	1	0.331495	0.331495	0.330	1.54
Network Rx bytes	1	17.81038	17.81038	17.782	83.04
Network Tx bytes	1	4.480257	4.480257	4.473	20.89
CPU utilization	1	8.978526	8.978526	8.964	41.86
Hard disk bytes read	1	0.002144	0.002144	0.002	0.001
Memory utilization	1	39.04110	39.04110	38.979	182.04
Response time	1	5.005269	5.005269	4.997	23.33
Error	0	0.0000	0.0000		
Total	9	100.15		100	
Error estimate	1	0.0021445			

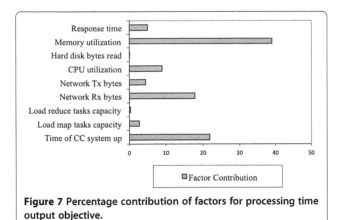

Figure 7 Percentage contribution of factors for processing time output objective.

- According to Taguchis method, the factor with the smallest contribution is taken as the error estimate. So, the factor *CPU utilization* is taken as the error estimate, since it corresponds to the smallest sum of squares.

The results of this case study show, based on both the graphical and statistical data analysis of the SNR, that the *Load reduce task capacity* into which is used by the Job in a MapReduce application in our cluster has the most influence in its job turnaround measure.

Statistical data analysis of hard disk bytes written patients

The statistical data analysis of hard disk bytes written output objective is presented in Table 16.

As can be seen in the contribution column of Table 16, these results can be interpreted as follows (represented graphically in Figure 9):

- *Time of CC system up* is the factor that has the most influence (37.650% of the contribution) on the hard disk bytes written output objective in this experiment.

- *Hard disk bytes read* is the factor that has the second greatest influence (32.332% of the contribution) on the hard disk bytes written.
- *CPU utilization* is the factor that has the third greatest influence (18.711% of the contribution) on the hard disk bytes written.
- *Memory utilization* is the factor with the least influence (0.544% of the contribution) on the hard disk bytes written in the cluster system.

In addition, based on the column related to the variance ratio F shown in Table 16, it can be concluded that the following:

- The factor *Time of CC system up* has the most dominant effect on the output variable.
- According to Taguchis method, the factor with the smallest contribution is taken as the error estimate. So, the factor *Memory utilization* is taken as the error estimate, since it corresponds to the smallest sum of squares.

The results of this experiment show, based on both the graphical and statistical data analysis of the SNR, that the *Time of CC system up* while a Job MapReduce application is executed in our cluster has the most influence in the hard disk written.

Summary of performance analysis model

To summarize, when an application is developed by means of MapReduce framework and is executed in the experimental cluster, the factors *job processing time, job turn around,* and *hard disk bytes written,* must be taken into account in order to improve the performance of the BDA. Moreover, the summary of performance concepts and measures which are affected by the contribution performance measures is shown in Figure 10.

Table 15 Analysis of variance of job turnaround output objective (ANOVA)

Factors	Degrees of freedom	Sum of squares (SS)	Variance (MS)	Contribution (%)	Variance ration (F)
Time of CC system up	1	1.6065797	1.6065797	11.002	174.7780
Load map tasks capacity	1	3.0528346	3.0528346	20.906	0.020906
Load reduce tasks capacity	1	7.2990585	7.2990585	49.984	0.049984
Network Rx bytes	1	0.0176696	0.0176697	0.121	0.000121
Network Tx bytes	1	0.1677504	0.1677504	1.148	0.001148
CPU utilization	1	0.0009192	0.0009192	0.006	0.62E-05
Hard disk bytes read	1	2.3993583	2.3993583	16.431	0.064308
Memory utilization	1	0.0521259	0.0521259	0.357	0.000356
Response time	1	0.0064437	0.0064437	0.044	0.000044
Error	0	0.0000	0.0000		
Total	9	14.602740		100	
Error estimate	1	0.0009192			

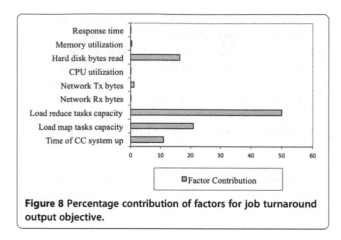

Figure 8 Percentage contribution of factors for job turnaround output objective.

Figure 10 shows that the performance on this experiment is determined by two sub concepts; *Time behavior and Resource utilization*. The results of the performance analysis show that the main performance measures involved in these sub concepts are: *Processing time, Job turnaround and Hard disk bytes written*. In addition, there are two sub concepts which have greater influence in the performance sub concepts; *Capacity and Availability*. These concepts contribute with the performance by means of their specific performance measures which have contribution in the behavior of the performance measures, they are respectively: *Memory utilization, Load reduce task, and Time system up*.

Conclusion

This paper presents the conclusions of our research, which proposes a performance analysis model for big applications   PAM for BDA. This performance analysis model is based on a measurement framework for CC,

which has been validated by researchers and practitioners. Such framework defines the elements necessary to measure the performance of a CCS using software quality concepts. The design of the framework is based on the concepts of metrology, along with aspects of software quality directly related to the performance concept, which are addressed in the ISO 25010 international standard.

It was found through the literature review that the performance efficiency and reliability concepts are closely associated with the performance measurement. As a result, the performance analysis model for BDA which is proposed in this work, integrates ISO 25010 concepts into a perspective of measurement for BDA in which terminology and vocabulary associated are aligned with the ISO 25010 international standard.

In addition, this research proposes a methodology as part of the performance analysis model for determining the relationships between the CCP and BDA performance measures. One of the challenges that addresses this methodology is how to determine the extent to which the performance measures are related, and to their influence in the analysis of BDA performance. This means, the key design problem is to establish which performance measures are interrelated and how much they contribute to each of performance concepts defined in the PMFCC. To address this challenge, we proposed the use of a methodology based on Taguchis method of experimental design combined with traditional statistical methods.

Experiments were carried out to analyze the relationships between the performance measures of several MapReduce applications and performance concepts that best represent the performance of CCP and BDA, as for example CPU processing time and time behavior. We found that

Table 16 Analysis of variance of hard disk bytes written output objective (ANOVA)

Factors	Degrees of freedom	Sum of squares (SS)	Variance (MS)	Contribution (%)	Variance ration (F)
Time of CC system up	1	2.6796517	2.6796517	37.650	69.14399
Load map tasks capacity	1	0.0661859	0.0661859	0.923	0.009299
Load reduce tasks capacity	1	0.0512883	0.0512883	0.720	0.007206
Network Rx bytes	1	0.1847394	0.1847394	2.595	0.025956
Network Tx bytes	1	0.4032297	0.4032297	5.665	0.056655
CPU utilization	1	1.3316970	1.3316970	18.711	0.187108
Hard disk bytes read	1	2.3011542	2.3011542	32.332	0.323321
Memory utilization	1	0.0387546	0.0387546	0.544	0.005445
Response time	1	0.0605369	0.0605369	0.850	0.008505
Error	0	0.0000	0.0000		
Total	9	7.1172380		100	
Error estimate	1	0.0387546			

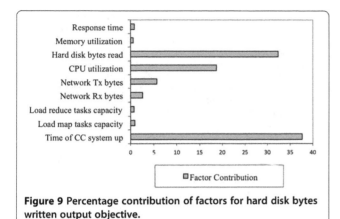

Figure 9 Percentage contribution of factors for hard disk bytes written output objective.

when an application is developed in the MapReduce programming model to be executed in the experimental CCP, the performance on the experiment is determined by two main performance concepts; Time behavior and Resource utilization. The results of performance analysis show that the main performance measures involved in these concepts are: *Processing time, Job turnaround and Hard disk bytes written*. Thus, these measures must be taken into account in order to improve the performance of the application.

Finally, it is expected that it will be possible, based on this work, to propose a robust model in future research that will be able to analyze Hadoop cluster behavior in a production CC environment by means of the proposed analysis model. This would allow real time detection of anomalies that affect CCP and BDA performance.

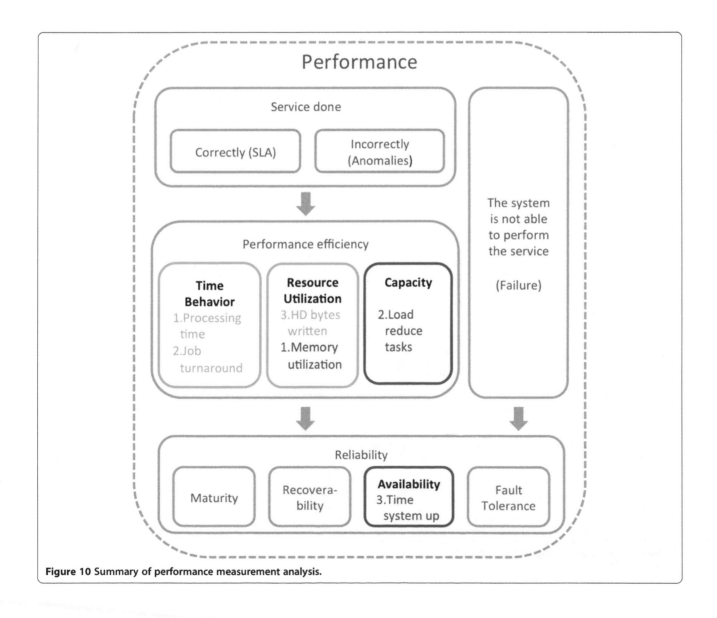

Figure 10 Summary of performance measurement analysis.

Competing interests
The authors declare that they have no competing interests.

Authors contributions
All the listed authors made substantive intellectual contributions to the research and manuscript. Specific details are as follows: LEBV: Responsible for the overall technical approach and model design, editing and preparation of the paper. AA: Contributed to requirements gathering and evaluation for designing the performance measurement framework for CC. Led the work on requirements gathering. AA: Contributed to requirements gathering and evaluation. Contributed to the design of methodology for analysis of relationship between performance measures. Contributed to the analysis and interpretation of the experiment results. All authors read and approved the final manuscript.

References
1. ISO/IEC (2012) ISO/IEC JTC 1 SC38: Cloud Computing Overview and Vocabulary. International Organization for Standardization, Geneva, Switzerland
2. ISO/IEC (2013) ISO/IEC JTC 1 International Organization for Standardization. ISO/IEC JTC 1 SC32: Next Generation Analytics and Big Data study group, Geneva, Switzerland
3. Gantz J, Reinsel D (2012) THE DIGITAL UNIVERSE IN 2020: Big Data, Bigger Digital Shadows, and Biggest Growth in the Far East. IDC, Framingham, MA, USA
4. ISO/IEC (2011) ISO/IEC 25010: Systems and Software Engineering-Systems and Software Product Quality Requirements and Evaluation (SQuaRE)-System and Software Quality Models. International Organization for Standardization, Geneva, Switzerland
5. Alexandru I (2011) Performance analysis of cloud computing services for many-tasks scientific computing. IEEE Transactions on Parallel and Distributed Systems 22(6):931 945
6. Jackson KR, Ramakrishnan L, Muriki K, Canon S, Cholia S, Shalf J, Wasserman HJ, Wright NJ (2010) Performance Analysis of High Performance Computing Applications on the Amazon Web Services Cloud. In: IEEE Second International Conference on Cloud Computing Technology and Science (CloudCom). IEEE Computer Society, Washington, DC, USA, pp 159 168, doi:10.1109/CloudCom.2010.69
7. Kramer W, Shalf J, Strohmaier E (2005) The NERSC Sustained System Performance (SSP) Metric. Lawrence Berkeley National Laboratory, California, USA
8. Jin H, Qiao K, Sun X-H, Li Y (2011) Performance under Failures of MapReduce Applications. Paper presented at the Proceedings of the 11th IEEE/ACM International Symposium on Cluster Computing, Cloud and Grid. IEEE Computer Society, Washington, DC, USA
9. Jiang D, Ooi BC, Shi L, Wu S (2010) The performance of MapReduce: an in-depth study. Proc VLDB Endow 3(1-2):472 483, doi:10.14778/1920841.1920903
10. Guo Z, Fox G (2012) Improving MapReduce Performance in Heterogeneous Network Environments and Resource Utilization. Paper presented at the Proceedings of the 2012 12th IEEE/ACM International Symposium on Cluster, Cloud and Grid Computing (ccgrid 2012). IEEE Computer Society, Washington, DC, USA
11. Cheng L (2014) Improving MapReduce performance using smart speculative execution strategy. IEEE Trans Comput 63(4):954 967
12. Hadoop AF (2014) What Is Apache Hadoop? Hadoop Apache. http://hadoop.apache.org/
13. Dean J, Ghemawat S (2008) MapReduce: simplified data processing on large clusters. Commun ACM 51(1):107 113, doi:10.1145/1327452.1327492
14. Lin J, Dyer C (2010) Data-Intensive Text Processing with MapReduce. Manuscript of a book in the Morgan & Claypool Synthesis Lectures on Human Language Technologies. University of Maryland, College Park, Maryland
15. Yahoo! I (2012) Yahoo! Hadoop Tutorial. http://developer.yahoo.com/hadoop/tutorial/module7.html - configs. Accessed January 2012
16. Bautista L, Abran A, April A (2012) Design of a performance measurement framework for cloud computing. J Softw Eng Appl 5(2):69 75, doi:10.4236/jsea.2012.52011
17. ISO/IEC (2013) ISO/IEC 25023: Systems and software engineering   Systems and software Quality Requirements and Evaluation (SQuaRE)   Measurement of system and software product quality. International Organization for Standardization, Geneva, Switzerland
18. Kantardzic M (2011) DATA MINING: Concepts, Models, Methods, and Algorithms, 2nd edn. IEEE Press & John Wiley, Inc., Hoboken, New Jersey
19. Kira K, Rendell LA (1992) The Feature Selection Problem: Traditional Methods and a New Algorithm. In: The Tenth National Conference on Artificial Intelligence (AAAI). AAAI Press, San Jose, California, pp 129 134
20. Taguchi G, Chowdhury S, Wu Y (2005) Taguchi s Quality Engineering Handbook. John Wiley & Sons, New Jersey
21. Cheikhi L, Abran A (2012) Investigation of the Relationships between the Software Quality Models of ISO 9126 Standard: An Empirical Study using the Taguchi Method. Software Quality Professional Magazine, Milwaukee, Wisconsin, Vol. 14 Issue 2, p22
22. Trivedi KS (2002) Probability and Statistics with Reliability, Queuing and Computer Science Applications, 2nd edn. Wiley, New York, U.S.A.

14

Virtual machine introspection: towards bridging the semantic gap

Asit More* and Shashikala Tapaswi

Abstract

Virtual machine introspection is a technique used to inspect and analyse the code running on a given virtual machine. Virtual machine introspection has gained considerable attention in the field of computer security research. In recent years, it has been applied in various areas, ranging from intrusion detection and malware analysis to complete cloud monitoring platforms. A survey of existing virtual machine introspection tools is necessary to address various possible research gaps and to focus on key features required for wide application of virtual machine introspection techniques. In this paper, we focus on the evolution of virtual machine introspection tools and their ability to address the semantic gap problem.

Keywords: Virtual machine introspection

Introduction

Security and safety are two principal factors governing future cloud computing research and development. Research in virtualisation technology has fuelled cloud computing growth and directly contributed to its development. Our work of reviewing virtual machine introspection (VMI) techniques predominantly targets cloud computing enabler virtualisation, with security as its major concern.

VMI is a technique initially suggested by [1] in 2003. They defined VMI as a method of inspecting a Virtual Machine (VM) from the 'outside' for analysing the software running on the machine. Over the past few years, VMI has seen concrete contributions, and various methods have been suggested to inspect VM data from the outside. The difficulty in interpreting the low level bits and bytes of a VM into a high level semantic state of a guest Operating System (OS) is called the "semantic gap problem" [2]. To interpret the low-level binary state information about the VM, a virtual machine monitor (VMM) must incorporate knowledge of the hardware architecture or guest OS [3].

In majority of VMI techniques, VM which is observing the results of introspection is different than the VM being introspected. The main motivation behind VMI is to analyse every possible change taking place in a guest OS due to the deployment of a given set of code over its entire lifecycle. It is also possible that in presence of monitoring code, deployed code may behave differently than its legitimate behaviour. Presence of monitoring code on a guest VM puts some limitations on execution of monitoring code like, VMI code could start after OS being loaded properly and it could continue till guest OS starts its shut down routine. Introspection from outside the guest VM addresses one or more of the above stated issues. Hence, introspection from different VM is preferred over the other options.

VMI, which has its roots in cloud enabling technology virtualisation, has the potential to change security deployment in cloud environments. The last couple of years have seen considerable progress in exploring various techniques for VMI. Path-breaking applications of VMI have been developed in relation to cloud security, cloud intrusion detection and cloud access management. There are evidences of intrusion detection systems and rootkit detection methods which have been proved effective only because of use of VMI in their implementation [4-6].

The contributions of this paper are as follows:

- It thoroughly inspects VMI techniques and outlines their advantages and weaknesses.

*Correspondence: asit_5@yahoo.com
ABV- Indian Institute of Information Technology & Management, Gwalior 474015, India

- It summarises various possible attacks and threats to VMI techniques.
- It proposes a VMI technique based on microprocessor architecture features.

We expect the following outcomes from our manuscript. We believe that it will provide a guide for future developers of VMI tools looking to develop various applications for cloud security and malware detection based on VMI. This paper is organised as follows: Section 'An overview' describes the basics of virtualisation and provides an illustration of the semantic gap problem. The later part of this section is dedicated to the taxonomy that we used to classify VMI tools. Section 'Characteristic properties of VMI' reveals the properties of an ideal VMI technique. Section 'Memory introspection' describes memory introspection, Section 'I/O Introspection' defines I/O introspection, and Section 'System call introspection' covers system call introspection. Section 'Process introspection' is dedicated to process introspection, and Section 'Other techniques' describes a range of possible techniques for VMI. Section 'Proposed architecture for VMI' describes the proposed architecture for VMI. Section 'VMI applications & future' outlines some predominant VMI applications. Section 'Security issues in VMI' discusses possible attacks on VMI techniques and the VMI architecture. Section 'Conclusion' presents the conclusion to our survey. Table 1 provides at a glance comparison of VMI techniques reviewed in this document.

An overview

Different terminologies are applied to the virtualisation framework. We adopt the following terminology throughout this paper: A *Guest VM* is a virtual machine running on a given hypervisor. The Guest OS is an OS system running on a particular guest VM. A *Secure VM* is a VM dedicated to security applications. Unless otherwise stated, the guest VM introspection is done through the same secure VM.

Virtualisation & hypervisors

The virtualisation technique is used to create a virtual environment for computing by virtualising hardware, I/O and processors. This virtual environment is possible with the help of a special layer of software named a VM monitor (VMM) or hypervisor. The VMM is the interface between the hardware and the VMs running on the system. Depending on the logical position of VMM in operating system architecture, VMMs are distinguished into two major types.

- Type I Hypervisor
- Type II Hypervisor

Type I hypervisors run directly on available hardware, eliminating the need for other layers, such as an OS, and providing high efficiency compared to its counterpart. Xen [7], VM Ware ESX [8] and Microsoft HyperV [9] are well-known Type I hypervisors. As these hypervisors run directly over hardware, they are also known as "bare metal hypervisors".

Type II hypervisors have the in-between interface of the OS to communicate with hardware. They usually depend on an OS to provide device drivers for hardware interaction. KVM [10], QEMU [11] and the VMWare workstation [12] are well-known examples of this type of hypervisor.

Semantic gap problem

The semantic gap problem in virtualisation was first stated by [2]. To extract meaningful information about the current state of a VM, detailed knowledge of the workings of the guest OS is required. It is very difficult to derive a complete view of a guest OS from outside a guest VM due to the highly dynamic nature of modern OSes. Various features, such as demand paging, parallel computing and multithreading, make the architecture of an OS very complex and volatile. View creation becomes extremely complex. This problem is known as the semantic gap problem. The preliminary aim of VMI is to generate a complete view of a guest VM. Hence, the evolution of VMI has been guided by the question: "How efficiently can the given VMI technique bridge the problem of semantic gap".

Characteristic properties of VMI

VMI is applied in widespread domains. With some listed in Section 'Introduction', Section 'VMI applications & future' details additional applications. It is obvious that some properties of VMI are application domain specific. Still, there are a few important properties that all VMI tools should possess, irrespective of their application domain. Some of the properties are listed below:

- **Minimum performance impact:** The main goal in virtualisation is to share resources between available guests. The implementation of introspection techniques should place as little burden as possible on the operation of the existing system. Introspection techniques should not place a burden on the hypervisor and real hardware resources.
- **Minimum modifications to hypervisor:** Introspection techniques should work independently and make minimum modifications to the hypervisor code. This is important in the application of VMI during minor revisions and in future versions of the VMM.
- **No modifications to guest OS:** Real-world hypervisors provide support to almost every possible

Table 1 Comparison of VMI techniques

Category	Technique	Location of code			VMM transparency	VMM alteration	Guest support	Advantages
		Guest VM	Secure VM	VMM				
Memory introspection	Using Xen Libraries	N	Y	Y	No	Required	PV Guests	Safety of VMI code
I/O Introspection		N	N	Y	No	Required	All Types	Driver and I/O access inspection
System call introspection	Using VT support	N	Y	Y	No	Required	All Types	Processor support makes introspection less complicated
	By Hardware Rooting	N	Y	N	No	Required	All Types	Protection from DKSM attacks
Process introspection	Using Hooks	Y	Y	Y	Yes	Required	All Types	Reverse remote control possible
	Using Shadow Page Tables	Y	N	Y	Yes	Required	All Types	Trusted Introspection code execution
	Using CFG	Y	N	Y	Yes	Required	All Types	Novel approach for code malfunction detection
Other techniques	Code Injection	Y	N	Y		Required	All Types	Secure and less prone to attacks
	Function Call Injection	Y	Y	Y	No	Required	All Types	Novel approach
	Page Flag Inspection	Y	Y	N	No	No	PV guests	Detects packed & encrypted malwares
	Process Out-grafting	Y	Y	Y	Yes	Required	All Types	A novel approach
	Live Kernel Data Redirection	Y	Y	Y	Yes	Required	All Types	Choice of selection for introspection programme
Proposed technique	Event Injection	Y	N	Y	Yes	Required	All Types	Secure & almost every introspection code can be used

OS as a guest. If the introspection code needs to be modified for each guest OS, its widespread applicability becomes questionable. Even minor revisions and periodical patches to a particular OS may create problems.

- **Transparency in operation:** The operation of VMI technique should be transparent to the hypervisor, the guest VM and any program on the guest VM.
- **Hypervisor independence:** The VMI technique should not depend on any exclusive feature of the hypervisor architecture. It should be applicable to any type of hypervisor, irrespective of its implementation technology.
- **No side effects:** The implementation of introspection tools should not generate any unwanted results, which may lead to malicious behaviour of system components. VMI tools should also not produce any extraordinary results, which may lead in the detection of its existence.
- **Security of monitoring component:** VMI modules can be located in the hypervisor, guest VM or secure VM. These modules must be secure from external attacks. If a VMI module is present in a guest VM, special protection must be provided to preserve its integrity.

Taxonomy of VMI

There are different possible events related to a guest VM and a guest OS running on it. These events can be grouped to have introspection at various degrees A brief overview is given below:

1. Memory Introspection
2. System Events Introspection

   (a) System Call introspection
   (b) Interrupt Requests Introspection
   (c) I/O Device Driver Introspection

3. Live Process Introspection

Based on the above-mentioned classification, we have divided the introspection techniques according to different types. Figure 1 describes a possible taxonomy for VMI.

Memory introspection

Memory introspection deals with live memory analysis. When the OS is running, all the important data structures are in the main memory. The main memory contains process control blocks (PCBs), registry entries, loadable kernel modules, kernel data structures and page tables, etc. The main memory also contains pages related to data segments and code segments of the process being executed. Information related to the OS can be retrieved by examining the content of the main memory. The majority of malware analysis tools inspect program behaviour by examining main memory contents of the given program. A variety of VMI techniques are available to access the main memory of a guest VM from a secure VM. These can be used for tasks such as intrusion detection or process analysis of the guest VM. A range of memory-based VMI techniques are summarised in the remainder of this section.

Introspection using Xen libraries

A guest VM can be introspected from a privileged domain (Dom 0) associated with a Xen hypervisor [7]. Dom 0 is a control domain of Xen, and it provides access to every data structure, driver and library implemented by Xen. *libxc* is a control library for Xen. The memory of the guest VM can be monitored using the function *xc_map_foreign_range()*, which belongs to the same library. A special high-performance disk driver named *blktap* made for Xen's paravirtualised guest VMs monitors disk access and data transfer. In the case of a guest VM, memory access needs to address translation from the virtual to the physical address and then again from the physical to the machine address. Xen has implemented shadow page tables for the same purpose. The introspection of a paravirtualised guest VM is possible using libxc, a blktap driver and the xen store library .

Xen_Access [13] is a good demonstration of memory and disk introspection with the Xen hypervisor. The introspection code remains safe, as it resides in a secure

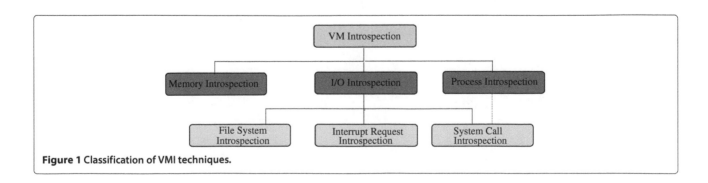

Figure 1 Classification of VMI techniques.

VM (Dom 0). However, there is a possibility that malware could change the kernel data structure, causing Xen_Access to produce irrelevant results. Xen_Access has achieved performance improvement in memory access by caching Xen Store mapping on a least recently used (LRU) basis, which is analogous to translation look-aside buffers (TLB). Xen Access provides very limited traces of file access, with only the creation and the deletion of a file traceable. Xen_Access also provides very limited support for hardware virtualisation machine (HVM) domains. This restricts its widespread application to OSs.

I/O Introspection

I/O introspection deals with device drivers and other utility hardware communications. dAnubis [14] is the technique suggested for VM introspection from outside of it. This method is the successor of Anubis and exclusively monitors Windows device drivers and kernel behaviour. It generates a detailed report of malware activities on machines running Windows. It is claimed that it detects kernel patching, call hooking and direct kernel object manipulation (DKOM). For kernel-side malicious code, the analysis needs to be performed at a higher privileged level than the privilege level of the kernel itself. It is only possible via out of the VM analysis as a hypervisor is available at the higher privileged level than a kernel of the guest OS.

The focus of dAnubis is on monitoring all communication channels between the rootkit (device driver affected by a rootkit) and the rest of the system. All necessary information, such as exported symbols, data structure and layouts are extracted from the Windows OS. To reconstruct the necessary information, kernel symbols and data structures are extracted from the Windows OS by using a technique mentioned by [15]. dAnubis has been proposed for detailed analysis of rootkits. This tool is capable of conducting memory analysis and detecting attacks, such as call table hooking, DKOM, runtime patching and hardware access.

Stimulator: Malware is activated by some triggering event. dAnubis has a stimulator engine that generates such events. dAnubis works only on Windows OS. It is a malware analysis engine and not a malware detection engine.

System call introspection

The system call is a request by program for service from the kernel. The service is generally something that only the kernel has the privilege to perform, such as doing I/O. Hence, system calls play a very important role in events such as context switching, memory access, page table access and interrupt handling. In case of the virtualisation technology (VT) support [16] enabled processors, the transition of a guest VM to the hypervisor and vice

versa is managed by special system calls. To maintain the integrity of the system, specific system calls are banned from execution by a guest VM.

Introspection using virtualization support

It has already been shown [13,17] that VT microprocessor support features can be used for introspection activities. Useful information related to guest VM implementation can be retrieved by monitoring the VM control structure (VMCS) of the processor. This region is dedicated to handling virtualisation support. Intel's VT-supported microprocessors have two modes of operation: VMX root operation and VMX non-root operation. The VMX root operation is intended for hypervisor use. The VMX non-root operation provides an alternative IA-32/64 environment controlled by a hypervisor. There are two transitions associated with these two operation modes: 1) a transition from the VMX root operation to the VMX non-root operation (i.e. from the hypervisor to the guest VM) called *hypervisor entry* and 2) a transition from the VMX non-root operation to the VMX root operation (i.e. from a guest to the hypervisor) called *hypervisor exit*.

The CR3 register is responsible for holding the page table address for currently running processes. Access to the CR3 register by the guest VM causes hypervisor exit. The hypervisor-based VMI module handles the hypervisor exit. A communication channel is opened between the VMI module in a secure VM and the VMI module in the hypervisor by setting a covert channel for communication. The channel is set through the VMCS region using an I/O bitmap. On receiving the CR3 change signal, the VMI module obtains access to the page tables. This enables tracking of current processes that are being executed.

Aquarius demonstrates the application of Intel VT and AMD technologies for effective out of VM introspection. Bit Visor [18] hypervisor was used for introspection purposes. Some modifications were made to the Bit Visor to inspect the guest's system call activities.

Introspection by hardware rooting

An introspection approach that relies only on guest OS knowledge might face attacks that change the architecture of the guest OS. Hardware rooting offers a solution to this type of attack, preventing malware from ever changing the structures of virtual hardware. Any trace which begins from hardware assistance has very less probability of such attacks. The hardware rooting mechanism thwarts possible kernel data structure attacks mentioned in Section 'Kernel structure manipulation'.

Hardware rooting exploits system call trapping using an interrupt descriptor table register (IDTR) and an interrupt descriptor table. The IDTR value is set by the processor. Genuine interrupt descriptor table gets accessed using system call trapping. Every time the value of the CR3 register needs to be changed, an interrupt needs to be generated. The VMI method traces this interrupt to detect process switching. In this way, the value of the CR3 register, along with the value of the first valid entry in the corresponding top-level page directory, is accessed. The value of CR3 register is unique for every process. It helps to identify the required process executing inside the VM.

Nitro [3] is another tool based on the hardware rooting technique. Nitro claims to work on any operating system and have defined rules for OS portability. The unique feature of Nitro is its rule set. Simple changes in a rule set enable it to work with almost any available OS. These rules have provision for determining locations of system call arguments, variables, etc. The locations of these arguments is variable according to the implementation of the OS. Generally, they reside in stack or CPU registers.

Nitro has modified QEMU [11], which is a monitor for KVM VMM [10]. All administrative commands to Nitro are given through the same monitor that is used by the KVM hypervisor. It is stealthier to direct kernel structure manipulation (DKSM) [19] types of attacks, as it depends on CPU data structures. Importantly, its performance is dramatically improved compared to its predecessor, Ether [20]. The major drawback of Nitro is that it supports only the x86 Intel 64-bit architecture.

Process introspection

Many application domains of VMI are limited to monitor specific processes. A process could range from any legitimate code, such as API, user application or test code, to malicious code, such as like malware and rootkit. Process introspection should be able to debug any process at any point of time during its entire execution cycle. It should also be able to detect invocation of a specific module or code snippet. Process introspection helps in the analysis of code. Process introspection is also useful for malware behaviour analysis, debugging, etc.

Introspection by hooks

Generally, this type of VMI technique comprises two separate parts. The design goal is to use a guest VM for only a minimum amount of essential code and to use a hypervisor layer or a secure VM for the remaining code. It consists of two modules, a guest module and an out of guest module described below:

- Guest module: It includes hooks for intercepting guest OS events and a small specially crafted trampoline code to pass events signalled by the hooks to the hypervisor. A hook is a jump mechanism, and it is generally associated with OS system calls. This ensures that whenever some system call is invoked by a process, the hook is activated. Hook transfers the control flow of a process to another kernel

component named the trampoline. The trampoline is a module that acts as a bridge for communication between hooks in a guest VM and a security driver running in a secure VM. It also receives commands from a secure VM.

- Out of guest module: It resides in a secure VM. This module is responsible for processing signals received from the trampoline. It consists of memory monitoring and Intrusion Detection System (IDS) tools, which inspect processes and memory on receiving calls from hooks. It also consists of various tools that analyse signals and makes decisions about the fate of running processes. Based on the decision, commands are issued to the guest OS to take preventive steps/measures.

The Lares [21] is made up of two distinct modules. High level implementation of the Lares is shown in Figure 2.

The Lares utilises a Xen hypervisor. Lares uses various features of Xen, including split device drivers and memory address translation, to provide a robust and secure introspection tool. It is appropriate for IDS or antivirus software development where immediate reverse action is needed upon detection of vulnerability. The trampoline mechanism distinguishes Lares from other introspection tools. However, the use of trampolines is a security bottleneck of Lares. Even the authenticity of calls generated by hooks is questionable because malware aimed at consuming system resources can invoke multiple false calls. False calls may lead to disturbances in working of legitimate programs.

An excellent feature of Lares is the availability of a reverse path from a secure VM to a guest VM. This feature is absent in almost every other existing VMI technique. The trampoline in Lares makes it possible to send signals to a guest VM resident code. This feature is referred to here as *reverse remote control*.

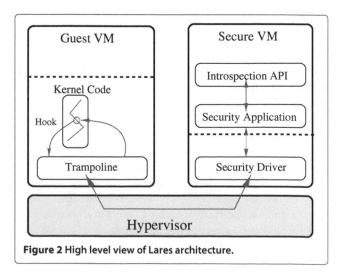

Figure 2 High level view of Lares architecture.

Introspection using shadow page tables

The hypervisor uses shadow page tables to convert a guest VM physical address to an actual machine address. Shadow page tables are accessible from the hypervisor and can be manipulated easily. The introspection code can be secured from guest VM-based applications using shadow tables and Intel VT technology features. Intel's VT support and virtual memory protection can be used to secure the monitoring code.

SIM [22] makes use of the above-mentioned techniques. A protected address space is allocated to a guest VM using memory mapping techniques. All methods and data related to the SIM are located in a special memory region, which is only accessible to the hypervisor. This region includes the following elements: a gate for transferring kernel calls, the SIM code and data, a separate copy of kernel code and data that are only read access and special call invocation checkers, which protect the SIM from attacks. Figure 3 shows the high-level architecture of the SIM. The gate is a special mechanism used by the SIM to enter and exit a protected address space (PAS). A separate copy of the kernel code is retained by the PASs because malware can easily infect kernel libraries. The SIM's introspection code uses its own copy of kernel libraries rather than trusting libraries provided by a guest OS. Hooks are placed within the kernel code to transfer a call made to the SIM module. On invocation of hooks, a hypervisor component of the SIM traces that call, and context transfer is done using the *SIM_SHADOW* page table. A *CR3_TARGET_LIST* is used to switch between page tables. A separate hypervisor level page table named *SIM_SHADOW* is created to replace the original shadow page table. A page table address of this shadow table is replaced inside the CR3 register to allow access to the SIM address space. The guest component of the SIM code is loaded onto the guest VM as a device driver.

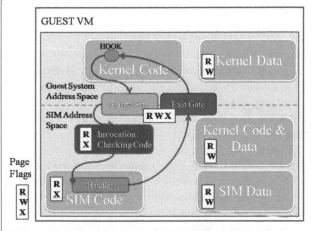

Figure 3 High Level Overview of SIM IN-VM monitoring. Page flags {R-Read, W-Write, X- Execute}.

SIM ensures that no code from a nontrusted address space can be executed while introspection is ongoing. This method proved to be a milestone in VM monitoring. Robustness and efficiency are the main advantages of IN-VM monitoring tools.

Introspection using CFG

Another technique known as PsycoTrace, which monitors the processes running on a guest VM, was introduced by [23]. PsycoTrace [23] is a unique method that utilises context-free grammar (CFG) for process activity monitoring and detecting malware attacks. The technique consists of two phases.

The first phase makes use of some static tools and acts from inside the guest VM and utilises the guest VM. These tools are responsible for capturing the legitimate workings of the process to be monitored. A CFG for processes is generated using a *grammar generating algorithm* developed for PsycoTrace. The CFG was developed according to custom-made rules (e.g. system call invocation is considered a terminating symbol). Bison [24] was modified to use C code and system calls as an input and to generate a CFG for a given process.

In the next phase, the kernel of the guest VM is modified and injected with a module named HiMod. Himod is responsible for monitoring system calls generated by a given process. It stores parameters of every system call and notifies the analyst module. The analyst module is associated with a secure VM. Communication between the HiMod and the analyst module takes place via a communication channel. The analyst module validates every system call with CFG to detect malware infection.

Although PsycoTrace has a very innovative way of detecting malware attacks, it has some weaknesses. It is not capable of handling processes that use multiple threads, and the kernel modification code is not well secured from detection and attacks. PsycoTrace, on successful malware detection, lacks malware counter-defence mechanisms. However, PsycoTrace has zero possibility of false positives, which is an achievement. The major drawback limiting the use of PsycoTrace is its initial run, during which the source code of the process has to be monitored.

Other techniques

It is very difficult to classify some VMI techniques in the categories mentioned above. Although some have the capabilities to introspect two or more regions, few have the additional capability to introspect system calls and introspect interrupt requests from devices. This is possible with hypervisors like Xen that use a special data structure called an event channel for passing interrupts and system calls and techniques such as process monitoring of system calls and memory. These abilities of hypervisors help in monitoring allied fields.

Introspection using code injection

Introspection is possible by implanting an introspection process (monitoring code) inside a guest VM with the help of the hypervisor. This implanted process is hidden under existing legitimate process. This technique is similar to camouflaging. The system consists of a victim process, which is used as a camouflage to hide the monitoring process. The victim process is a process or any user program that is used to replace itself by introspection process. The introspection process is a special program capable of executing certain code, which inspects system variables, parameters and the environment as per the introspection needs.

This introspection process resides in the address space of a secure VM. The hypervisor monitors every context switch to detect the loading of the victim process. On detection of the context switch to a desired victim process, it replaces all necessary pointers, such as the start processor instruction pointer (SIP). It ensures that instead of running the victim process, the monitoring code is initiated and run on a guest VM.

The memory required by the introspection process is provided by a secure VM at runtime. This ensures the address space of the monitoring process is hidden from processes running on the guest OS. It also ensure that the address space cannot be detected by malware programs running on the victim machine.

Although introspection using code injection looks promising, this method has the potential to alert malware that it is being monitored due to the reasons outlined below.

1. Every monitoring process is given explicit root privilege, enabling it to monitor all user-level applications.
2. The monitoring process exits on the request of the hypervisor or the secure VM. This is achieved by the hypervisor setting a control bit in a covert channel created exclusively for message passing.
3. An unkillable flag is used in the monitoring process, so that it cannot be killed in between the introspection process. This flag is set only for *init processes*.
4. *Fork* calls are blocked during execution of the monitoring process.

Gu et al. [25] implemented a similar technique and took various precautions to ensure the security of this technique. In the approach they used, all OS libraries needed by the monitoring process are compiled statically to avoid the use of guest VM libraries, which are possible baits for a malware. There is no restriction on the choice of

monitoring processes: It can be a malware catcher or user code, which, in turn, can inspect processes running inside a guest VM. This achievement is remarkable.

The introspection technique rectified almost all security vulnerabilities detected with the process implantation technique Virtuoso [25]. Virtuoso restricts the selection of the monitoring process, and it can only use tools provided by the OS [25]. The advantage of using Virtuoso is that the user needs very limited knowledge of OSs, and little effort is required to build OS-specific introspection routines. The process implantation technique is divided into two phases.

The first phase is the training phase in which the monitoring process is executed repeatedly. This phase is small and runs parallel on the guest programme and calculates the data required by the monitoring process. A slicing algorithm and a trace logging algorithm are used to analyse this monitoring code for different loops, jumps and conditional statements. These algorithms reproduce the monitoring programme, with almost the exact instruction code sequence. Whenever introspection is required, this newly created code segment is mounted on guest VM environment by the VMM.

According to the authors [25] , Virtuoso has been tested on various OSs, such as Windows XP SP2 (kernel version 5.1.2600.2180), Ubuntu Linux 8.10 (kernel version 2.6.27-11) and Haiku R1 Alpha 2. However, it has a serious drawback: It requires continuous human intervention. In addition, if any loop or conditional flow was not exercised during training, there are chances of generating instruction sequences from such loops/conditional flows, which may lead to ambiguous execution. Moreover, the slicing algorithm cannot deal with interrupts, page faults and external references to remote addresses. However, Virtuoso is secure and much less susceptible to malware detection and attacks. Repeated execution of the training phase has shown excellent results in monitoring code generation.

Introspection with function call injection (FCI)

Function call injection is the amendment to code injection technique. This method utilises the APIs of secure VM OS to ensure the security from code manipulation. When the introspection application residing in the guest VM is called, the hypervisor and the introspection mechanism patch these calls with equivalent function of a secure VM. This makes this technique applicable to almost every OS having APIs for monitoring. It removes the need for hooks inside the guest and a trampoline. The API is called from the secure VM, thereby strengthening the overall security of function call injection.

Function call injection monitors guest data structures and API locations. By pausing the Virtual Central Processing Unit (VCPU) state, a special jump is introduced to secure the API of the VM. This API is the code for VM introspection. As the API resides inside a secure VM, there is no possibility of malware infecting the API. This ensures that the monitoring code of the API has access to the data structures of the guest VM. This monitoring code generates the introspection results in a secure VM.

Before invoking the monitoring process, VMM runs another process named localised shepherding. The role of the localised shepherding process is to ensure the integrity of API monitoring. The shepherding process avoids switches in between the execution of the monitoring process. It is responsible for atomic execution of the monitoring process.

Syringe [26] is based on the function call injection technique. It utilises a VMWare ESX [8] server platform and the introspection tool VMWare VMSafe. VMSafe has a unique ability to debug guest VM execution during Syringe implementation. Syringe provides flexibility in terms of OSs and the selection of introspection tools. Syringe has no possibility of dynamic code outrage unlike its sibling Virtuoso. Syringe places a single VCPU restriction on guest VMs because placing multiple VCPU restrictions raises the possibility of the code being detected by malware. Keeping performance degradation in mind, atomic execution of the monitoring process is not always favourable.

Introspection using page flag inspection

The dependence of process implantation technique [27] on APIs of OS for introspection may lead to limited access to guest information. Malware that is either encrypted or packed (compressed) is very difficult to detect. Packed malware is generally stored in data pages as user data. Malware that resides in data pages will need to be page faulted, and NX flag[a] (in the case of x86 and DX in the case of AMD) needs to be set to make such pages executable.

Maitland [28] uses the Xen store utility and page flags for accessing NX flags. Maitland observes each page fault and makes these pages accessible to a security VM. The secure VM is equipped to detect malware signatures and inspects the shared pages for symptoms of malware. Maitland uses a split device driver utility, which it uses for paravirtualised guests of Xen. The application of Maitland to HVM (fully virtualised) guests requires major reforms in split device drivers. This restricts its use on Windows-based guest VMs. In turn, Maitland needs very little changes to the VMM, and its monitoring code for page faults consumes little resources. Even the code running on the guest VM incurs very little overheads. However, this code is easily detectable by malware, something that raises serious concerns with regard to its widespread adoption.

The design goal of Maitland is to develop a lightweight introspection tool. Maitland focuses on the detection of

encrypted and packed malware over the cloud on VM guests.

Introspection using process out-grafting

Many past VMI solutions are sensitive to version of OSs, with even a simple patch for an OS having an adverse effect on their operation. Numerous attempts have been made to inject a function/process in guest VMs. Process out-grafting proposes a solution for monitoring specific processes from a number of guest VM processes. The approach used here is exactly the reverse of that used conventionally. Instead of grafting the monitoring process running on a guest VM, process out-grafting relocates the specific process on-demand from a guest to a secure VM. The advantage of out-grafting is that monitoring tools do not need any modification. They essentially view it a normal process running in a secure VM.

The way in which "on demand grafting" works is very interesting. It monitors the state of the VCPU of a guest VM for user mode execution. Out-grafting begins when VCPU is switched to user mode. Process grafting can be achieved by transfer of the execution context (e.g. registers) and memory page frames. For memory page frames, it depends on memory virtualisation support by the processor. Process grafting is achieved by directly marking an NX flag of the corresponding pages in the EPT[b] kernel state of a guest VM that is maintained during out-grafting, and page tables are synchronised with a secure VM.

Srinivasan et al. [29] used a similar method to process out-grafting called mode-sensitive split execution for introspection. The system calls by the out-grafted process are redirected back to the guest VM. The same is achieved by coordinating between the stub residing on the guest VM and a helper module residing on a secure VM in a loadable kernel module (LKM) mode. Only user mode instructions are executed in a secure VM, and all kernel mode instructions are redirected back to the guest VM. The file system of the guest VM is in read only mode to aid monitoring activity. This helps in tracing the system call execution of the out-grafted process.

Although the guest process is out-grafted, a secure VM is needed to handle system call migration, page fault handling and kernel mode execution. All these events are executed by the guest VM. The *exec_ve* calls from the process have to be executed by the guest VM. In short, only user mode execution is monitored by a secure VM. The fate of out-grafting depends upon the efficient application of the NX bit of the process pages. Malware that could mask the NX bit could easily evade process out-grafting technique. Another disadvantage of process out-grafting is that if the kernel of a guest VM is compromised, then entire process becomes vulnerable. Nevertheless, natural support to any monitoring tool without any modification is remarkable.

Introspection using live kernel data redirection

As mentioned in Section 'Introspection using code injection', introspection using code injection has been suggested as a novel approach for VMI. However, it is not fully automated, and it requires the intervention of human experts. In the case of code injection, a monitoring code is generated by repeated analysis. In contrast, in kernel data redirection, the monitoring code remains fixed, and the data required by the monitoring code are provided by the corresponding guest VM that is to be introspected.

The concept behind kernel data redirection is very simple. It consists of a secure VM with all leading introspection tools installed. The guest VM that is to be introspected shares its memory with a secure VM. This is achieved by mounting the guest memory on a secure VM, using VMM. The secure VM uses its own code to introspect the guest VM using data available from its shared memory.

The VM space traveller (VMST) [30], utilises kernel data redirection. VMST automates the introspection process. The secure VM deploys a separate module named the *syscall execution context identification module*. It is used for identification of introspection-related system calls. Another module named the *redirectable data identification module* is responsible for redirecting the required data of the guest VM to the monitoring process. To retrieve data from the memory of the guest OS, it exploits well-known taint analysis techniques [31,32]. A detailed overview of the VMST is given in Figure 4.

VMST provides a very novel approach to VMI, with secure execution of the monitoring process. It is transparent to use on most Linux kernels. The user needs to select and install a kernel (OS) and then install the memory in read only mode on a secure VM. With VMST, any system API/programme can be used for introspection. It also requires no user intervention, and the user can develop a tailored introspection programme. VMST only depends on a guest VM for memory access. Moreover,

unlike Virtuoso, it does not need to mask interrupts and context switches.

Proposed architecture for VMI

We have already seen that VMI has very large scope with regard to security and privacy. VT-based processors provide additional support to hypervisors. Our proposed architecture for VMI is based on Intel VT technology. According to Intel's VT [33] architecture, if the valid bit in the *VM_entry_interruption _information_field* of VMCS is 1, a logical processor delivers an event to a guest OS after all the components of a guest VM state have been loaded. For delivering an event, a vector is used that points to a descriptor of a guest IDT.

This type of entry covers software interrupts, privileged software exceptions and traps. The VMM or introspection software running on a VMM can easily generate these types of interrupts. We have introduced a novel technique, which utilises this interrupt. Figure 5 represents the architecture of our proposed technique.

Our technique is divided into three modules residing at three different physical locations. Their operation is explained as follows:

- Controller Module: This resides on a secure VM. Whenever introspection is required, a command is given through this module. It is responsible for sending requests to a hypervisor-based module. As this module is part of a secure VM, it is part of a trusted computing base (TCB) and thus is secure.
- Injector Module: This module is located in the hypervisor layer. It listens for requests from the controller module. On receipt of an introspection request, it waits for the next VM entry. It detects the next *VM Entry* and introduces an artificial software interrupt by an event injection. The injection takes place after loading the IDT on a guest VM. The module is responsible for putting a particular vector entry in an event injection call. It corresponds to the

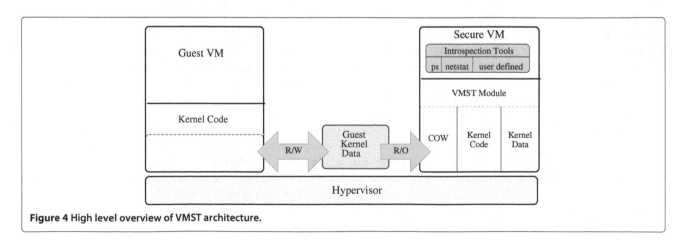

Figure 4 High level overview of VMST architecture.

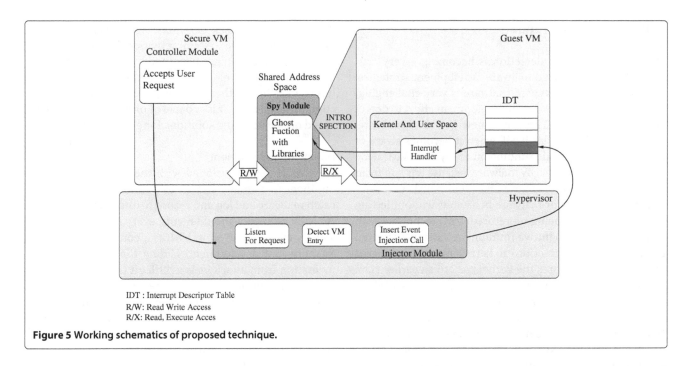

Figure 5 Working schematics of proposed technique.

user- defined interrupt descriptor in the IDT of a guest VM. Thus far, we have defined a single IDT entry, which corresponds to a single interrupt handler routine.

- Spy Module: This module has two parts. The first consists of an installation patch, which installs our own IDT entry and defines the interrupt handler routine for that IDT entry. The second part is hidden from the guest VM. The interrupt handler has a single role: It redirects every call to a ghost function. The *ghost function* contains the introspection code. The address space of the ghost function is different to that of the guest VM. The address space is mounted on the guest VM in read only and executable mode by the hypervisor, only after the controller module has invoked the introspection signal. The function first selects the required introspection type from the available options and then executes it. This function is pre-compiled, and the binary code of the function contains the libraries that are required during execution. This ensures the integrity of the code, preventing tampering . The results generated by this ghost function are saved in another part of the address space shared with the guest VM.

Salient features of our technique are as follows:

- Minimum Performance Impact: This VMI technique is invoked on demand i.e. if the valid bit in the VM entry interruption information field in VMCS region is 1, a logical processor delivers an event to a guest OS after all the components of a guest VM state have

been loaded. This will trigger the Spy module and it will start the introspection. This ensures that no script or agent will be running on hypervisor or inside the guest VM for the entire lifecycle of VM. The code will be invoked on-demand and it will terminate on completion of its execution.

- Minimum hypervisor modification: The technique is based on Intel VT technology and solely depends upon it for functioning. Hence requires very few modifications to hypervisor.

- Transparency in operation: This technique makes very few changes to the hypervisor and also do not make any change in guest OS which makes this technique transparent in operation.

- No side effects: The technique does not produce any unwanted results and outputs. The laboratory testing revealed that the execution of guest OS with and without VMI technique had no effect on a hypervisor and guest OS execution. This ensures that there will not be any unwanted site effect on existing setup.

- Security of monitoring code: Our VMI technique is divided in three parts. Controller and Injector module works from Secure VM and Hypervisor respectively. These two modules are never exposed to Guest VM and to the entities inside it (i.e. Softwares, applications and even malware running in Guest VM). Spy Module interacts with Guest VM and runs various custom scripts as per the user need, on Guest VM. It is stored in a separate memory area which is not part of the address scape of a Guest VM. This ensures that entities on Guest VM cannot implicitly access, modify this introspection code, making it secure.

VMI applications & future

Malware detection

Day by day, malware detection is becoming a very crucial task, with advanced malware development strategies. The detection of encrypted malware is very challenging. Maitland [28] is a VMI-based development effort to detect encrypted malware. There is a new breed of malware, which successfully hides itself, when it becomes aware of malware detection code running on the system. VMI code is not usually detectable by malware because it is run from out of a guest VM most of the time . It also makes it easier to detect and monitor malware behaviour without letting malware detect it's being monitored. VMI techniques can help in providing cognitive immunity to systems affected by malware. On detection of kernel modifying rootkit infection, VICI restores the kernel back to an earlier state to provide cognitive immunity [34]. VICI exploits VMI for infection detection and restoration.

Another threat to security is through malware generation capable of attacking not only victim machines but also capable of detecting system execution environment . Such malware is equipped with techniques to detect whether a given OS is running on a VMM or bare hardware. This type of malware attacks VMMs and cloud setups. Such type of malware could also be detected using VMI techniques.

Hidden process monitoring

Many advanced malwares have the capability to hide themselves behind a legitimate OS process. It can cause greater infection, by detaching itself from a process tree or a process node structure maintained by an OS. Such type of malware may be present on the memory of an OS but not detectable by an OS data structure enquiry using legitimate tools, such as *ps*. Hidden process detection and monitoring is possible using Aries [35], which utilises VMI to detect hidden malware process. The application of process monitoring has been extended to different domains, such as web service monitoring [36]. It could be used to record client and service communication over a service oriented architecture (SOA). The interaction trace allows a human or software agent to analyse, replay or debug the code that was executed.

File system/memory management

It is possible to trace every possible activity between a guest OS and hardware using VMI. Lares [13] has already reported preliminary efforts in tracing file system access. Major problem in secondary memory access tracing is, involvement of primary memory (main memory) and the semantic gap problem. The OS loads files from the secondary memory to the main memory . All operations on file are performed at file copy on the main memory. Disk drivers (secondary memory) are included only in create, delete and write back activities. This restriction limits introspection of file system activities. However, the use of disk introspection has benefited by the development of trusted domain development policy [37]. PsycoTrace [38] has tried to bridge the semantic gap involved in file operation introspection. It is capable of providing access rights based on file handling solutions for guest VM users.

Honeypot development

Honeypots were developed with the intention of exposing them to as many attacks as possible. Their aim is to catch malware and log and record features of the malware. An ideal honeypot should record every possible event and activity taking place on it. VMI is a considerable solution for honeypot development. Hiding the honeypot implementation from attackers is a difficult task, and it is a key problem in the majority of honeypot implementations. The productivity of the honeypot depends entirely on it remaining undetected. The chances of detection are much lower when VMI-based monitoring is employed. Similar type of work is possible using VMI. The Qemu Honeypot [39] is an example of using VMI for honeypots. VMI was used in more elaborate ways in honeypot development [40] using a Xen_Access library [13]. Lengyel et al. [40] also provided a good example of the potential use of VMI for honeypots.

Security issues in VMI

It is clear from Section 'VMI applications & future' that the majority of VMI applications are related to the security domain. As stated in Section 'Characteristic properties of VMI', transparency remains a key feature for VMI techniques, specially for those applications of VMI which are developed for the security and privacy. In this section, we have summarise possible attacks on VMI techniques.

Kernel structure manipulation

VMI tools that depend upon memory analysis are victims of kernel structure manipulation. Memory introspection tools derive information on the state of a guest's OS state and related information by analysing the memory of the guest VM. These tools rely upon underlying data structures used by the kernel. In kernel structure manipulation, some changes are intentionally made to kernel data structures. There are three types of modifications possible:

- Syntax manipulation: Certain fields of kernel data structure are modified or changed.
- Semantic manipulation: The semantics of the data structure are changed. Although they might not show any malfunction, the results produced by VMI will be irrelevant.
- Combination of semantic and syntactic manipulation: This type of modification can result in VMI failure.

The above mentioned attacks can be implemented in various ways, as demonstrated previously by [19].

As stated in Section 'Characteristic properties of VMI', ideal VMI techniques should place minimum overheads on the operation on the hypervisor and the involved system. This is important not just for performance but also for security. Recent malware and attack scripts have examined request-response parameters to detect underlying VMI installation. Timing-based attacks have tried to target out-of-bound memory and query system resources to record hypervisor replies . In many instances, the original drivers are faster than the drivers that are patched for the VMI technique. Such changes to the drivers by VMI techniques, may get noticed by malware and could be used as an alarm to take note of presence of VMI technique on VM.

Conclusion

Beginning with an introduction to the semantic gap problem, we have summarised distinct techniques developed for VMI. VMI has grown steadily over the past years. Based on the analysis of VMI techniques presented herein, it appears that the use of VMI is dominant in the security domain. In turn, this makes VMI susceptible to attacks. In the coming years, the security weaknesses of VMI will need to be addressed to enable widespread adoption by the industry.

VMI has great potential in the future development of malware detection tools and intrusion detection systems. Even cloud platforms could benefit from the use of VMI in imposing access right mechanisms.

Existing VMI tools have limited introspection capabilities. No one tool can provide process, memory, file and I/O introspection. In addition, the introspection capabilities of these tools are mostly dependent on the underlying hypervisor architecture. These architectural features are modified or replaced over time, making the application of these tools questionable in the current scenario.

Very limited work has been done to fully introspect HVM guests. Some performance improvement features of HVM guests, such as *pass through drivers*, place limitations on VMI implementation. Introspection using VT support has tremendous potential to enable VMI but requires additional work. The VMI technique based on VT support described in the current paper could be used in the security domain.

Endnotes

[a]The NX bit, which stands for Never eXecute, is a technology used in CPUs to segregate areas of memory for use by either storage of processor instructions (or code) or for storage of data

[b]Extended page table: This page table is part of the memory virtualisation support of the microprocessor. It contains maps of guest-physical addresses to host-physical addresses.

Competing interests
The authors declare that they have no competing interests.

Authors' contributions
Both the authors made substantive intellectual contributions to the research and manuscript. AM carried out the survey of the available literature and drafted the manuscript. He is responsible for the overall technical approach and architecture, editing and preparation of the paper. ST provided insight and guidance in developing the VMI technique. She edited and revised the final manuscript. Both authors read and approved the final manuscript.

Acknowledgements
Authors are grateful to the reviewers of this manuscript for their expert advice. Authors are thankful to Indian Institute of Information Technology & Management, Gwalior (IIIT, Gwalior) for support.

References
1. Garfinkel T, Rosenblum M (2003) A virtual machine introspection based architecture for intrusion detection. In: NDSS. The Internet Society, San Diego, California, ISBN 1-891562-15-0. http://www.isoc.org/isoc/conferences/ndss/03/proceedings/papers/13.pdf
2. Chen PM, Noble BD (2001) When virtual is better than real. In: Hot Topics in Operating Systems, 2001. Proceedings of the Eighth Workshop on. IEEE Computer Society, Los Alamitos, CA. p 0133. http://doi.ieeecomputersociety.org/10.1109/HOTOS.2001.990073
3. Pfoh J, Schneider C, Eckert C (2011) Nitro: hardware-based system call tracing for virtual machines. In: Proceedings of the 6th International Conference on Advances in Information and Computer Security, IWSEC'11. Springer-Verlag, Berlin, Heidelberg. pp 96–112. ISBN 978-3-642-25140-5 http://dl.acm.org/citation.cfm?id=2075658.2075669
4. Carbone M, Conover M, Montague B, Lee W (2012) Secure and robust monitoring of virtual machines through guest-assisted introspection. In: Balzarotti D, Stolfo SJ, Cova M (eds). Research in attacks, intrusions, and defenses. Lecture Notes in Computer Science. Springer, Berlin Heidelberg Vol. 7462. pp 22–41. http://dx.doi.org/10.1007/978-3-642-33338-5_2
5. Butt S, Lagar-Cavilla HA, Srivastava A, Ganapathy V (2012) Self-service cloud computing. In: Proceedings of the ACM Conference on Computer and Communications Security. Raleigh, North Carolina. ACM, Raleigh, New York, NY. pp 253–264. http://doi.acm.org/10.1145/2382196.2382226
6. Harrison C, Cook D, McGraw R, Hamilton JA (2012) Constructing a cloud-based IDS by merging VMI with FMA. In: Trust, Security and Privacy in Computing and Communications (TrustCom), 2012 IEEE 11th International Conference on. IEEE, Liverpool. pp 163–169. doi:10.1109/TrustCom
7. Xen (2012) Xen homepage. http://www.xen.org/. Accessed date 15 March 2013
8. Ware VM (2012) Vmware esx homepage. http://www.vmware.com/files/pdf/VMware\discretionary-ESX\discretionary-and\discretionary-VMware\discretionary-ESXi\discretionary-DS\discretionary-EN.pdf. Accessed date 15 March 2013
9. Microsoft (2012) Microsoft hyper -v homepage. http://www.microsoft.com/en-us/server-cloud/hyper-v-server/default.aspx. Accessed date 15 March 2013
10. KVM (2012) Linux kvm homepage. http://www.linux-kvm.org/page/Main_Page. Accessed date 15 March 2013
11. Qemu (2012) Qemu homepage. http://wiki.qemu.org/Main_Page. Accessed date 15 March 2013
12. Ware VM (2012) Vmware workstation overview. http://www.vmware.com/products/workstation/overview.html. Accessed date 15 March 2013
13. Payne BD, de Carbone MDP, Lee W (2007) Secure and flexible monitoring of virtual machines. In: Computer Security Applications Conference, 2007. ACSAC 2007. Twenty-Third Annual. IEEE, Miami Beach, FL. pp 385–397. doi:10.1109/ACSAC.2007.10

14. Neugschwandtner M, Platzer C, Comparetti P, Bayer U (2010) danubis – dynamic device driver analysis based on virtual machine introspection. In: Kreibich C, Jahnke M (eds). Detection of Intrusions and Malware, and Vulnerability Assessment, volume 6201 of Lecture Notes in Computer Science. Springer, Berlin Heidelberg. pp 41–60. ISBN 978-3-642-14214-7. doi:10.1007978-3-642-14215-4_3 http://dx.doi.org/10.1007/978-3-642-14215-4_3

15. Jiang X, Wang X, Xu D (2007) Stealthy malware detection through vmm-based "out-of-the-box" semantic view reconstruction. In: Proceedings of the 14th ACM conference on Computer and communications security, CCS '07. ACM, New York, NY, USA. pp 128–138. ISBN 978-1-59593-703-2. doi:10.1145/1315245.1315262 http://doi.acm.org/10.1145/1315245.1315262

16. Intel (2012) Intel virtualization technology. http://www.intel.com/technology/virtualization

17. Pfoh J, Schneider C, Eckert C (2010) Exploiting the x86 architecture to derive virtual machine state information. In: Proceedings of the 2010 Fourth International Conference on Emerging Security Information, Systems and Technologies SECURWARE '10. IEEE Computer Society, Washington, DC, USA. pp 166–175. ISBN 978-0-7695-4095-5. doi:10.1109/SECURWARE.2010.35 http://dx.doi.org/10.1109/SECURWARE.2010.35

18. Bitvisor (2012) Bitvisor hypervisor home page. http://www.bitvisor.org/. Accessed date 15 March 2013

19. Bahram S, Jiang X, Wang Z, Grace M, Li J, Srinivasan D, Rhee J, Xu D (2010) DKSM: subverting virtual machine introspection for fun and profit. In: Proceedings of the 2010 29th IEEE Symposium on Reliable Distributed Systems, SRDS '10. IEEE Computer Society, Washington, DC. pp 82–91. doi:10.1109/SRDS.2010.39. http://dx.doi.org/10.1109/SRDS.2010.39

20. Dinaburg A, Royal P, Sharif M, Lee W (2008) Ether: malware analysis via hardware virtualization extensions. In: Proceedings of the 15th ACM conference on Computer and communications security, CCS '08, ACM, New York, NY, USA. pp 51–62. ISBN 978-1-59593-810-7. doi:10.1145/1455770.1455779 http://doi.acm.org/10.1145/1455770.1455779

21. Payne BD, Carbone M, Sharif M, Lee W (2008) Lares: an architecture for secure active monitoring using virtualization. In: Proceedings of the 2008 IEEE Symposium on Security and Privacy. IEEE Computer Society, Washington, DC. pp 233–247. doi:10.1109/SP.2008.24. http://dx.doi.org/10.1109/SP.2008.24

22. Sharif MI, Lee W, Cui W, Lanzi A (2009) Secure in-vm monitoring using hardware virtualization. In: Proceedings of the 16th ACM conference on Computer and communications security, CCS '09. ACM, New York, NY, USA. pp 477–487. ISBN 978-1-60558-894-0. doi:10.1145/1653662.1653720 http://doi.acm.org/10.1145/1653662.1653720

23. Baiardi F, Maggiari D, Sgandurra D, Tamberi F (2009) PsycoTrace: virtual and transparent monitoring of a process self. In: Proceedings of the 2009 17th Euromicro International Conference on Parallel, Distributed and Network-based Processing. IEEE Computer Society, Washington, DC. pp 393–397. doi:10.1109/PDP.2009.45. http://dx.doi.org/10.1109/PDP.2009.45

24. Bison (2012) Bison - gnu parser generator. http://www.gnu.org/software/bison/. Accessed date 15 March 2013

25. Gu Z, Deng Z, Xu D, Jiang X (2011) Process implanting: a new active introspection framework for virtualization. In: Proceedings of the 2011 IEEE 30th International Symposium on Reliable Distributed Systems, SRDS '11. IEEE Computer Society, Washington, DC, USA. pp 147–156. ISBN 978-0-7695-4450-2. doi:10.1109/SRDS.2011.26 http://dx.doi.org/10.1109/SRDS.2011.26

26. Carbone M, Conover M, Montague B, Lee W (2012) Secure and robust monitoring of virtual machines through guest-assisted introspection. In: Proceedings of the 15th international conference on Research in Attacks, Intrusions, and Defenses, RAID'12. Springer-Verlag, Berlin, Heidelberg. pp 22–41. ISBN 978-3-642-33337-8. doi:10.1007/978-3-642-33338-5_2 http://dx.doi.org/10.1007/978-3-642-33338-5_2

27. Dolan-Gavitt B, Leek T, Zhivich M, Giffin J, Lee W (2011) Virtuoso: narrowing the semantic gap in virtual machine introspection. In: Proceedings of the 2011 IEEE Symposium on Security and Privacy, SP '11. IEEE Computer Society, Washington, DC, USA. pp 297–312. ISBN 978-0-7695-4402-1. doi:10.1109/SP.2011.11 http://dx.doi.org/10.1109/SP.2011.11

28. Benninger C, Neville SW, Yazir YO, Matthews C, Coady Y (2012) Maitland: Lighter-weight VM introspection to support cyber-security in the cloud. In: Cloud Computing (CLOUD) 2012 IEEE 5th International Conference on. IEEE, Honolulu, HI. pp 471–478. doi:10.1109/CLOUD.2012.145

29. Srinivasan D, Wang Z, Jiang X, Xu D (2011) Process out-grafting: an efficient "out-of-vm" approach for fine-grained process execution monitoring. In: Proceedings of the 18th ACM conference on Computer and communications security, CCS '11. ACM, New York, NY, USA. pp 363–374. ISBN 978-1-4503-0948-6. doi:10.1145/2046707.2046751 http://doi.acm.org/10.1145/2046707.2046751

30. Fu Y, Lin Z (2012) Space traveling across vm: Automatically bridging the semantic gap in virtual machine introspection via online kernel data redirection. In: Security and Privacy (SP) 2012 IEEE Symposium on. IEEE, doi:10.1109/SP.2012.40. pp 586–600

31. Chow J, Pfaff B, Garfinkel T, Christopher K, Rosenblum M (2004) Understanding data lifetime via whole system simulation. In: Proceedings of the 13th conference on USENIX Security Symposium - Volume 13, SSYM'04. USENIX Association, Berkeley, CA, USA. pp 22–22. http://dl.acm.org/citation.cfm?id=1251375.1251397

32. Newsome J (2005) Dynamic taint analysis for automatic detection, analysis, and signature generation of exploits on commodity software. In: Proc. of the 14th Annual Network and Distributed System Security Symposium (NDSS'05). The Internet Society, San Diego, California

33. Intel (2005) Intel® Virtualization Technology Specification for the IA-32 Intel® Architecture

34. Fraser T, Evenson MR, Arbaugh WA (2008) VICI virtual machine introspection for cognitive immunity. In: Computer Security Applications Conference, 2008. ACSAC 2008, Annual. IEEE, Anaheim, CA. pp 87–96. doi:10.1109/ACSAC.2008.33

35. Wen Y, Zhao J, Wang H, Cao J (2008) Implicit detection of hidden processes with a feather-weight hardware-assisted virtual machine monitor. In: Mu Y, Susilo W, Seberry J (eds). Information Security and Privacy, volume 5107 of Lecture Notes in Computer Science. Springer, Berlin Heidelberg. pp 361–375. ISBN 978-3-540-69971-2. doi:10.1007/978-3-540-70500-0_27 http://dx.doi.org/10.1007/978-3-540-70500-0_27

36. Vaculin R, Sycara K (2008) Semantic web services monitoring: An owl-s based approach. In: Hawaii International Conference on System Sciences. IEEE Computer Society

37. Ando R, Kadobayashi Y, Shinoda Y (2008) An enhancement of trusted domain enforcement using VMM interruption mechanism. In: Young Computer Scientists, 2008. ICYCS 2008. The 9th International Conference for. IEEE, Hunan. pp 2222–2229. doi:10.1109/ICYCS.2008.341

38. Zhao F, Jiang Y, Xiang G, Jin H, Jiang W (2009) Vrfps: a novel virtual machine-based real-time file protection system. In: Software Engineering Research, Management and Applications, 2009. SERA '09. 7th ACIS International Conference on. IEEE, Haikou. pp 217–224. doi:10.1109/SERA.2009.23

39. Tymoshyk N, Tymoshyk R, Piskozub A, Khromchak P, Pyvovarov V, Novak A (2009) Monitoring of malefactor's activity in virtualized honeypots on the base of semantic transformation in Qemu hypervisor. In: Intelligent Data Acquisition and Advanced Computing Systems: Technology and Applications, 2009. IDAACS 2009. IEEE International Workshop on. IEEE, Rende. pp 370–374. doi:10.1109/IDAACS.2009.5342958

40. Lengyel A, Neumann J, Maresca S, Payne BD, Kiayias A (2012) Virtual machine introspection in a hybrid Honeypot architecture. In: Presented as part of the 5th Workshop on Cyber Security Experimentation and Test. USENIX, Berkeley, CA. https://www.usenix.org/conference/cset12/workshop-program/presentation/Lengyel

15

Notes on Cloud computing principles

Thomas Sandholm[1,2]* and Dongman Lee[2]

Abstract

This letter provides a review of fundamental distributed systems and economic Cloud computing principles. These principles are frequently deployed in their respective fields, but their interdependencies are often neglected. Given that Cloud Computing first and foremost is a new business model, a new model to sell computational resources, the understanding of these concepts is facilitated by treating them in unison. Here, we review some of the most important concepts and how they relate to each other.

Keywords: Resource allocation; Provisioning; IT-economics

Introduction

Imagine that you have to go on a trip to meet a friend in a different city. There are many modes of transportation available to you. You can drive there by car, take a taxi, share a ride in a van, take a bus or a train, or even fly there in an airplane. Your choice is determined by your general preference for these options. In particular, your choice depends on the economics and convenience of these alternatives given the characteristics of the trip, including distance to destination and time available. The cost of the choice you make in turn is related to how many other people are sharing the same mode of transportation, and how expensive it is to operate the transportation vehicle and infrastructure.

Now compare this choice to the choice of energy supplier that people faced in the early 20th century. You could buy your own electric generator, but it was not very cost efficient if your needs varied diurnally or seasonally. As it became apparent that electricity was as invaluable of a commodity as gas, water and the telephone, utility companies and national electrical grids that could aggregate and distribute electricity on demand replaced the privately owned generators.

Cloud computing [1] could be seen as an effort to commoditize computing, and distribute and operate it as efficiently as the electrical grid while still offering consumers the plethora of alternatives known from the transportation domain. The pre-cloud era could be compared to everyone driving around in their own car and using their own generators. The cloud era allows computing to be used similarly to public transportation and makes it possible to tap into computing power with the same ease that you plug in your appliances to the electrical grid at home. To distinguish the Cloud from its predecessors it is often defined as a use of computing resources that are delivered as a service over a network. The way in which you provision these services holds the key to the innovation.

Cloud services need to be scalable, fault-tolerant, highly available, high-performance, reliable and easy to use, manage, monitor, and provision efficiently and economically. One early realization by Cloud computing pioneers was that meeting all these requirements for services handling massive amounts of data and huge numbers of concurrent users called for innovation in the software stack as opposed to the highly specialized hardware layer. The hardware is reduced to a commodity and the Quality of Services (QoS) are instead provided by a fully integrated and hardware agnostic software stack. Virtualization became the new silver bullet.

As the demand for computing power increased with more users coming on-line and more data being published on-line it became apparent that some drastic architectural changes had to be introduced to provision compute resources more efficiently. The most prominent enabler for efficient resource provisioning was data center consolidation. Instead of using spare cycles from arbitrary privately owned nodes in a network[a], it was more cost effective to provide high QoS by consolidating computing in highly streamlined data centers packed with low-cost dedicated compute and storage clusters in a highly reliable

*Correspondence: thomas.e.sandholm@hp.com
[1] HP Labs, 1501 Page Mill Rd, 94304 Palo Alto, CA, USA
[2] Department of Computer Science, KAIST, 291 Daehak-ro, 305-701 Daejeon, Korea

and fast network. These data centers were also frequently deployed in areas where energy and labor were cheap to further cut operational costs.

Data-center consolidation and more aggressive sharing of compute resources lead to the following key benefits of Cloud computing:

1. Lower cost of using compute resources
2. Lower cost of provisioning compute resources
3. Reduced time-to-market

The first benefit can be attributed to only paying for the resources when you use them. When you do not use them, the provider can allocate them to other users. Being able to host multiple users or tenants on the same infrastructure allows the provider to utilize the resources more efficiently and thereby increase the return on investment (ROI). This win-win relationship between users and providers is the reason why most companies switch to Cloud architectures. The growth and sudden popularity of Cloud computing was, however, not fueled by traditional, established companies. Start-ups were the pioneering users of Cloud technology as it reduced their time-to-market and provided them with less up-front risk to stand up a demo or beta version. If the users did not flock, not much harm was done, you just stopped paying for the resources. If there was an unexpected flash crowd of people bombarding the service, you would just pay for more resources. This type of usage is often referred to as the elasticity of the Cloud. The Cloud allows you to scale down as easily and as quickly as you scale up.

Below we will review some of the fundamental concepts of distributed computing at scale, and then relate these concepts to economic principles that help us understand the trade-offs governing their deployment. The main motivation for studying these economic principles is that solely maximizing systems metrics, such as, throughput, response time and utilization may not always be the most profitable strategy for a Cloud provider.

Before delving into these principles we will first take a look back at technologies that predated Cloud computing to see how the architecture of this new computing paradigm evolved into its current state.

Historical evolution

The vision of organizing compute resources as a utility grid materialized in the 1990s as an effort to solve grand challenges in scientific computing. The technology that was developed is referred to as Grid Computing [2], and in practice involved interconnecting high-performance computing facilities across universities in regional, national, and pan-continent Grids. Grid middleware was concerned with transferring huge amounts of data, executing computational tasks across administrative domains, and allocating resources shared across projects fairly. Given that you did not pay for the resources you used, but were granted them based on your project membership, a lot of effort was spent on sophisticated security policy configuration and validation. The complex policy landscape that ensued hindered the uptake of Grid computing technology commercially. Compare this model to the pay-per-use model of Cloud computing and it then becomes easy to see what, in particular, smaller businesses preferred. Another important mantra of the Grid was that local system administrators should have the last say and full control of the allocation of their resources. No remote users should have full control or root access to the expensive super computer machines, but could declare what kind of software they required to run their jobs. Inherently in this architecture is the notion of batch jobs. Interactive usage or continuous usage where you installed, configured and ran your own software, such as a Web server was not possible on the Grid. Virtual machine technology [3] released the Cloud users from this constraint, but the fact that it was very clear who pays for the usage of a machine in the Cloud also played a big role. In summary, these restrictions stopped many of the Grid protocols from spreading beyond the scientific computing domain, and also eventually resulted in many scientific computing projects migrating to Cloud technology.

Utility computing [4] refers to efforts in the industry around the turn of the millennium to improve manageability and on-demand provisioning of compute clusters. At this time, companies were very skeptical to running their confidential workloads off premise and thus utility computing was often sold on a cluster-by-cluster basis and installed on a company-by-company or organization-by-organization basis. This deployment model made it very expensive to get up and running, which ironically had been one of the key claimed benefits of utility computing. Nevertheless, it started to become clear around this time that virtualization was the key to on-demand provisioning of compute resources. Web services and Service-Oriented Architectures [5] were touted as the solution to many of the problems seen in the earlier efforts of Utility and Grid computing. Providing a standard API would allow infrastructure to be allocated programmatically based on demand. The APIs and protocols were borne out of the evolution of the World Wide Web (WWW) that started to provide more dynamic and interactive content on Web pages leading to the phenomenon of mashups. Mashups in the early days essentially scraped HTML from various Web pages to dynamically create a value-adding service on a new Web page. As this was error prone, it was quickly realized that APIs were needed and the first Web services protocols, such as SOAP [6], were designed.

By the time Amazon launched their Elastic Compute Cloud (EC2) service in 2006, both Web service APIs and virtualization technology (e.g. Xen[3]) were mature enough to form a compelling combination or a perfect storm to deliver the first real public utility computing service that had been envisioned a decade earlier.

In summary, the vision of the Grid combined with Virtual Machine technology and Web service APIs were the essential characteristics of the first Clouds. Next, we will review the fundamental distributed systems principles underlying today's Cloud systems.

Computational principles

Next, we provide a brief recap of the most important computational systems principles related to the new Cloud computing era. These concepts have been presented in-depth in many pre-existing review articles, so here we only cover them at a level of detail that helps the reader appreciate the economic implications discussed in the second part of this letter. A reader already familiar with the systems-related principles of Cloud computing may skip forward to the section on Economic principles. However, to avoid confusion about taxonomy, this section may be revisited as a reference for technical definitions of these widely referred-to concepts.

Multi-tenancy

A tenant in the Cloud context is a user of Cloud infrastructure, i.e. Infrastructure-as-a-Service (IaaS) services [7]. A VM owner is an example of a tenant and if multiple VM owners are allocated on the same physical machine it is an example of multi-tenancy [8]. The difference between a multi-(end)-user service and a multi-tenant service is that a multi-user offering may benefit from having users know about each other and explicitly share social content to promote the network effect. A multi-tenant solution could internally benefit from shared physical resources but must give the impression of an exclusive offering to each of the tenants. As an example, hosting the Facebook service on a Web server in the Cloud would be an example of a multi-user service, but hosting both a Twitter Web server and a Facebook Web server in the same Cloud data center would be an example of multi-tenancy. From this definition, it is clear that the IaaS provider needs to provide mechanisms to isolate the tenants from each other.

Multiple tenants need to be isolated in terms of privacy, performance and failure:

- **Privacy Isolation.** Multiple tenants must not have access to each other's data. This may seem like an easy requirement to meet but in a typical file system there may be traces left after a file even after removing it, which would violate this property.
- **Performance Isolation.** Multiple tenants must not be effected by each other's load. If one tenant starts

running a CPU intensive task and other tenants see a drop in performance as a result, then this property is violated.

- **Failure Isolation.** If a tenant either inadvertently or maliciously manages to crash its compute environment, it should not effect the compute environment of other users. Imagine a Java VM hosting multiple applications such as a Tomcat Servlet engine. Now, if one servlet Web app crashes the VM, then the other apps in the same VM would also crash. This failure would in that case be a violation of the failure isolation property. Virtual machines offer a popular technique to ensure isolation, but in some cases the overhead of virtualization, of e.g. IO and network, is too high so a trade-off has to be made between isolation level and performance.

Ensuring these levels of isolation is closely related to the strategy used to allocate resources to tenants, which we will discuss next.

Statistical multiplexing

One major benefit related to data center consolidation that we discussed in the introduction is statistical-multiplexing [9]. The idea behind statistical multiplexing is that bursty workloads that are consolidated on the same Cloud infrastructure may in aggregate display a less bursty pattern. Figure 1 shows an example of statistical multiplexing with two workloads exhibiting complementing demand over time.

1. Without an elastic Cloud infrastructure, the most common way of provisioning resources to tenants is to allocate resources that meet the peak demand of each workload. Clearly, this leads to a major waste in resources for the majority of the time. Statistical multiplexing allows an allocation that is substantially lower than the sum of the peaks of the workloads.
2. Ideally if statistical multiplexing is applied on a large number of independent workloads, the aggregate will be stable, i.e. a straight line in the demand chart. If this is the case, it is enough to just allocate the sum of the averages of resource demand across all workloads.
3. Now assuming that we are in an elastic Cloud environment and we can slice resource allocations by time akin to how an OS time-shares CPU between processes. In this scenario, further reductions in resource allocations may be achieved by simply allocating the sum of resource demand across all workloads in each time slice.
4. Finally if each time slice only has a single workload active at any point in time, the allocation reduces to just the maximum demand across the workloads.

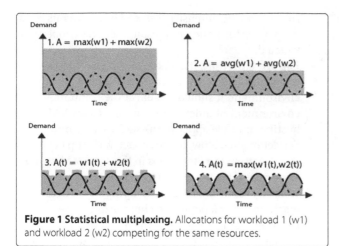

Figure 1 Statistical multiplexing. Allocations for workload 1 (w1) and workload 2 (w2) competing for the same resources.

This model of perfect statistical multiplexing is hard to achieve in practice. The main reason for this is that workloads tend to be correlated. The effect is known as self-similarity. Self-similar workloads have the property that aggregating bursty instances will produce an equally bursty aggregate, something that is often observed in practice. However, there are many techniques to recreate the effects of statistical multiplexing without having to hope for it to occur organically. For instance, you could measure the correlation between workloads and then schedule workloads that are complementing on the same resources. These techniques are sometimes referred to as optimal packing of workloads or interference minimization [10]. Poor statistical multiplexing tends to lead to low utilization, or unmet demand, as we will discuss further when we review the economic principles governing under and over-provisioning.

Horizontal scalability

An application or algorithm that runs in the Cloud will not be able to scale up and down with the infrastructure unless it can run at least in part in parallel. Execution in the Cloud requires efficient scaling across machines, referred to as horizontal scalability. A local program running on a single machine on the other hand only needs to scale vertically, i.e. run faster as local resources such as CPU, memory, and disk are added. How well a program scales is thus related to the parallelizability of its algorithms. This effect is formalized in what is called Amdahl's Law [11]:

$$T(n) = T(1)(B + (1 - B)/n) \qquad (1)$$

Amdahl's Law predicts the expected speed-up of a program or algorithm when run over multiple machines. $T(n)$ is the time taken to run on n machines. B is the fraction of the program that needs to run serially, i.e. that cannot be parallelized. Note that several disjoint sections in the

execution path may need to run serially to collect, distribute or synchronize parallel computations. It is clear that minimizing B maximizes the speedup. However, the most important consequence of Amdahl's Law is that it sets a theoretical cap on how many machines a program will benefit from running on, beyond which point adding new machines will not make the program run faster. If B is close to negligible we can expect *linear scalability*. Adding x machines will make the program run x times faster. If the program speedup grows at a slower rate than the number of machines added, which is the common case due to various overheads of distribution, we refer to *sublinear scalability*. The program may also speedup at a faster rate than the machines being added, in which case the program is said to exhibit *superlinear scalability* (see Figure 2). This effect may happen if there is some common resource like a shared cache that benefits from more usage, e.g., more cache entries and fewer cache misses.

Many advances in the database community have emerged, and been popularized, to achieve horizontal scalability when processing massive amounts of data in Clouds. The most prominent concepts include: data partitioning and sharding [12]; consistent hashing and distributed hashtables (DHT) [13,14]; and eventual and quorum consistency [15,16].

Economic principles

Now, we discuss the economic implications of the new Cloud systems principles to see how economic theories may help with various systems trade-offs that from a pure computational perspective seem insurmountable to overcome without fine-tuning heuristics and trial and error.

Over and under provisioning

As we alluded to in the section on statistical multiplexing, over-provisioning is a common strategy for allocating resources across tenants. Here we discuss the economic dilemma of over (Figure 3) versus under-provisioning (Figure 4) resources.

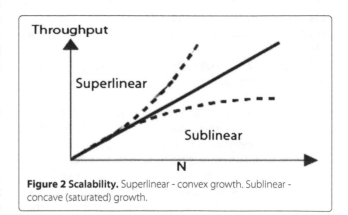

Figure 2 Scalability. Superlinear - convex growth. Sublinear - concave (saturated) growth.

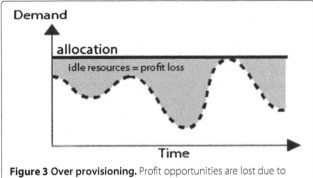

Figure 3 Over provisioning. Profit opportunities are lost due to many idle resources.

We can see that over-provisioning leads to a large area of idle resources over time. In financial terms this means high-operational cost, and lost opportunities to increase profit. To increase profit the IaaS provider may be tempted to lower the allocation to reduce the operational cost as seen in Figure 4. However, this leads to an even more severe drawback, unmet demand. Unmet demand means revenue loss, and can have long-term negative effects as customers who are denied access to a resource despite being willing to pay for it may not return. For this reason over-provisioning is more popular than under-provisioning. However, neither the IaaS provider nor the tenant may be able to perfectly predict the peaks, after all that is why they are running in the Cloud in the first place. In this case under-provisioning may occur inadvertently.

Hence, over-provisioning versus under-provisioning involves making a trade-off between profit and revenue loss.

Variable pricing

Given all the issues of allocating resources to bursty demand, it is natural to ask whether this burstiness can be suppressed somehow as opposed to being accommodated. That is exactly the idea behind variable pricing or demand-driven pricing. The idea is to even out the peaks and valleys with incentives. If the demand is high we increase the price. This leads to tenants who cannot afford the higher price to back-off and thereby demand is reduced. On the other hand, if the demand is low, a price drop may encourage tenants who would otherwise not have used some resources to increase their usage and thereby demand. The end result is a stable aggregate demand as in the statistical multiplexing scenario. The key benefits to IaaS providers include the ability to cash in on peak demand by charging premiums, and a mechanism to increase profit during idle times. Now, how can we ensure that the price is a good representation of demand? Here, microeconomic theory of supply and demand [17] helps.

If we plot the quantity of goods a supplier can afford to produce given a price for the good we get the supply curve. If we plot the quantity of goods requested by consumers given a price for the good we get the demand curve. The price at the point where the supply and demand curves meet is called the efficient marker price as it is a stable price that a market converges towards (see Figure 5). To see why this is the case, consider the gray dot on the supply curve in Figure 5. In this case the supplier observes a demand that is higher than the current quantity of goods produced. Hence, there is an opportunity for the supplier to increase the price of the good to afford to produce more goods to meet this demand. Conversely, considering the black dot on the demand curve, we can see that the demand is higher than the volume of goods that the supplier can produce. In this case the demand will naturally go down and the consumers are likely to be willing to pay a higher price to get their goods.

In general, variable pricing allows a provider to allocate resources more efficiently.

Price setting

There are many ways to set prices for goods in a market. The most commonly known are various forms of auctions,

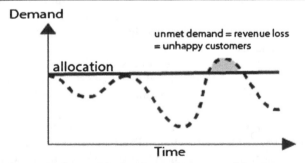

Figure 4 Under provisioning. Demand is unmet and therefore revenue opportunities are lost. Service downtime may also lead to long-term revenue loss due to lost customers.

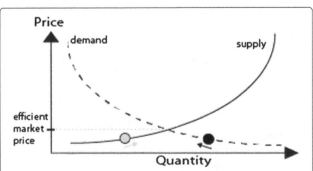

Figure 5 Supply and demand curves. The efficient market price is where the supply and demand curves meet. Pricing below may lead to shortage of supply. Increasing the price towards the market price will take the demand down to a point were it can be met.

spot prices and reservations. In auctions, bidders put in offers to signal how much they are willing to pay for a good. In double actions, there are also sellers who put in asks denoting how much they are willing to sell the good for. The stock market is an example of a double auction. In computational markets, second price sealed bid auctions are popular since they are efficient in determining the price, i.e. reflect the demand, without too much communication. All bidders put in secret bids and the highest bidder gets the good for the price equalling the second highest bid.

In the case where there is not a completely open market price, and there is just a single provider selling off compute resources, spot pricing is a common way of setting demand based prices. The spot price is computed on a running basis depending on the current level of demand. There could for instance be a base pay that is discounted or hiked based on demand fluctuations. A spot market differs from a futures market in that goods are bought and consumed immediately. Futures markets such as options are less common in practical computational markets today.

Purchasing resources on a spot market involves a high risk of either having to pay more for the same allocation or being forced to reduce the allocation to stay within budget (see the section on Predictability below). A common way to reduce the risk for consumers is to offer a reservation market. A reservation market computes the expected spot demand for some time in the future and adds a premium for uncertainty to arrive at a reservation price. Essentially you have to pay for the provider's lost opportunity of selling the resources on the spot market. This way the risk is moved from the consumer of compute resources, the tenant, to the provider. I.e., the provider's actual cost or revenue when providing the resource may vary, whereas the cost for the tenant is fixed. If there is an unexpected hike in the demand and all resources have already been promised away in reservations there is no way for the provider to cash in on this demand, which constitutes a risk for the provider.

The research field of computational economies have tackled these problems as far back as the 1960s and 70s [18-20]. More recent computational market designs include [21-23]. Reviews of some of these designs can be found in [24,25].

In summary, reservation markets move the risk of uncertain prices from the tenant to the provider as uncertain demand.

The tragedy of the commons

The next principle we will discuss is a social dilemma referred to as the tragedy of the Commons [26]. The dilemma was introduced in a paper in 1968 by Garrett Hardin, where the following scenario was outlined.

Imagine a public, government-owned piece of land with grass, in the UK referred to as a Common. Now, a number of shepherds own sheep that they need to feed on this Common to keep alive. The shepherds will benefit economically from the sheep because they can, for instance, sell their wool. Each shepherd faces the financial decision whether it would be more profitable to purchase another sheep to feed on the Common and extract wool for, or provide more food to each sheep by sticking with the current herd. Given that it is free to feed the sheep on the Common and the reduction in available food is marginal, it turns out that it is always optimal for a selfish shepherd trying to optimize his profit to buy another sheep. This has the effect of driving the Common into a slump where eventually no more grass is available and all sheep die and all shepherds go bankrupt.

One could argue that less selfish shepherds who are wary of the benefits of the group of shepherds as a prosperous community will not let the situation end in tragedy. However, there are many examples of communities that have gone extinct this way. In general what these communities have in common is that there is a high degree of free-riders, i.e. community members who take more from the common resources of the community than they give back. Sometimes the effects are temporal and not as obvious since no one purposefully abuses the community. One example is the PlanetLab testbed [27] used by systems researchers in the US. The testbed is distributed across a large number of organizations to allow wide area and large-scale experiments. The weeks leading up to major systems conferences such as OSDI, NSDI, SOSP and SIGCOMM see extreme load across all machines in the testbed typically leading to all researchers failing to run their experiments.

The opposite of free-riding is referred to as altruism. Altruists care about the community and are the backbone of a sustainable and healthy community. A good example of this is the Wikipedia community with a small (compared to readers) but very dedicated group of editors maintaining the order and quality of the information provided. The opposite of the tragedy of the Commons is the network effect where more users lead to greater benefits to the community, e.g. by providing more content as in the Wikipedia case.

The balance between free-riders and altruists as well as the regulations and pricing of resource usage determines whether the tragedy of Commons or the network effect prevails.

This concept is closely related to what economists refer to as externality [28], individual actions impose an unforeseen positive or negative side-effect on the society. The archetypical example is factory pollution. Such side-effects are mainly addressed in the Cloud by various infrastructure isolation designs such as virtual machines, or virtual private networks (see discussion in the section on Multi-tenancy above).

Incentive compatibility

One of the most frequently overlooked aspects of distributed systems is incentive compatibility [29]. Yet it is a property that all successful large-scale systems adhere to, the Cloud being no exception, and it is very often the main reason why proposed systems fail to take off. It is a concept borrowed from game-theory. In essence, an incentive compatible system is a system where it is in the interest of all rational users to tell the truth and to participate. In a systems context, not telling the truth typically means inserting incorrect or low quality content into the system to benefit your own interests. Incentive to participate is closely related to the notion of free-riding. If there is no incentive to contribute anything to a common pool of resources, the pool will eventually shrink or be overused to the point where the system as a whole becomes unusable. That is, the system has converged to a tragedy of the Commons. Ensuring that the system cannot be gamed is thus equivalent to ensuring that there is no free-riding and that all users contribute back to the community the same amount of valuable resources that they take out. A new, untested, system with a small user base also has to struggle with a lack of trust, and in that case it is particularly important to come out favorable in the individual cost-benefit analysis, otherwise the potential users will just pick another system. Tit-For-Tat (TFT) is an example of an incentive compatible algorithm to ensure a healthy and sustainable resource sharing system.

If Cloud resources are sold at market prices it ensures incentive compatibility, .i.e. ensuring that the price is following the demand (in the case of a spot market) or the expected demand (in the case of a reservation market) closely has the effect of providing an incentive for both suppliers and consumers to participate in the market. Earlier systems such as the Grid and P2P systems that did not have an economic mechanism to ensure incentive compatibility has historically had a much harder time of sustaining a high level of service over a long period of time due to frequent intentional and non-intentional free-riding abuses. Hence, demand-based pricing helps ensure incentive-compatibility.

Computational markets that have demand-driven pricing may however still not be incentive compatible. If it for instance is very cheap to reserve a block of resources ahead of time and then cancel it before use, it could lead to an artificial spike in demand that could dissuade potential customers from using the resource. This in turn would lead to the spot market price being lower, which could benefit the user who put in the original reservation maliciously. In economic terms, it is a classic example of someone not telling the truth (revealing their true demand in this case) in order to benefit (getting cheaper spot market prices). Another classic example is an auction where the bidders may overpay or underpay for the resource, just to make sure competitors are dissuaded to participate or to falsely signal personal demand.

Efficiency

Shared resource clusters such as the Grid are commonly monitored and evaluated based on systems metrics such as utilization. A highly utilized system meant the resources typically funded by central organizations such as governments were being efficiently used. This type of efficiency is referred to as computational efficiency. It is a valuable metric to see whether there are opportunities to pack workloads better or to re-allocate resources to users who are able to stress the system more, i.e. a potential profit opportunity (see the section above on Over and under provisioning). In a commercial system such as the Cloud it is also important to consider the value that the system brings to the users, because the more value the system brings to users the more they are willing to pay and the higher profit the Cloud provider is able to extract from a resource investment. This trade-off becomes apparent when considering a decision to allocate a resource to a user who is willing to pay $0.1 an hour for some resource and utilize at close to 100% versus another user who is willing to use the same resource over the same period of time but at 90% utilization and paying $0.5 an hour. There is likely more idle time and unused resources if the second user is accommodated but the overall profit will be higher (0.5-0.1=$0.4/hour).

To evaluate the economic efficiency [30] one therefore often goes beyond pure system metrics. In economics, utility functions are used to capture the preferences or the willingness of a user to pay for a resource. Maximizing the overall utility across competing users is then a common principle to ensure an overall healthy and sustainable ecosystem. This sum of utilities across all users is referred to as the *social welfare* of the system. To compare two systems or two resource allocation mechanisms for the same system one typically normalizes the social welfare metric by comparing the value to an optimal social welfare value. The optimal social welfare value is the value obtained if all users (in the case of no contention) or the highest paying user receive all the resources that they desire. Economic efficiency is defined as the optimal social welfare over the social welfare obtained using an actual allocation strategy. A system with an economic efficiency of 90%, for instance have some opportunity, to allocate resource to higher paying users and thereby extract a higher profit.

In essence, ensuring economic efficiency involves optimizing social welfare.

There is however an argument to be made that always allocating to the highest paying user does not create a healthy sustainable ecosystem, which we will discuss next.

Fairness

Consider the case where some user constantly outbids a user by $.0001 every hour in a competitive auction for resources. An economically efficient strategy would be to continuously allocate the resource to the highest bidder. The bidder who keeps getting outbid will however at some point give up and stop bidding. This brings demand down and the resource provider may lose out on long term revenue. It is hence also common practice to consider the fairness of a system. In economics, a fair system is a defined in terms of envy between users competing for the same resource [31]. Envy is defined as the difference in utility that a user received for the actual allocation obtained compared to the maximum utility that could have been obtained across all allocations for the same resource to other users. The metric is referred to as envy-freeness and a fair system tries to maximize envy freeness (minimize envy). Having high fairness is important to maintain loyal customer, and it may in some cases be traded off against efficiency as seen in the example above. Fairness may not be efficient to obtain in every single allocation instance, but is commonly evaluated over a long period of time. For example a system could keep track of the fairness deficit of each user and try to balance it over time to allocate resources to a user that has the highest fairness deficit when resources become available.

In addition to fairness considerations, there could be other reasons why a resource seller may want to diverge from a pure efficiency-optimizing strategy. If information is imperfect and the seller needs to price goods based on the expected willingness to pay by consumers, it may be a better long-term strategy to set the price slightly lower to avoid the dire effects of losing trades by setting the price to high. Another reason may be that some consumers have less purchasing power than others, and giving them benefits, so they can stay in the market, improves the overall competitiveness (and liquidity, see below) of the market, which in turn forces the richer consumers to bid higher.

Liquidity

The central assumption in variable pricing models (see the section above on Variable pricing) is that the price is a proxy or a signal for demand. If this signal is very accurate, allocations can be efficient and incentives to use versus back off of resources are well aligned. If there are too few users competing for resources the prices may plummet and the few users left may get the resource virtually for free. It is therefore critical for a provider to have enough competing users and to have enough purchases of resources for all the market assumption to come into play. In particular, this means ensuring that the second part of incentive compatibility is met, i.e. users have an incentive to participate. Most providers fall back on fixed pricing if there is too little competition, but that may lead to all the inefficiency that variable pricing is designed to address. In economics, this volume of usage and competition on a market is referred to as liquidity [32]. Lack of liquidity is a very common reason for market failure, which is why many financial and economic markets have automated traders to ensure that there is a trade as long as there is a single bidder who sets a reasonable price. A provider may, for instance, put in a daemon bidder to ensure that resources are always sold at a profit.

Predictability

The biggest downside of variable pricing models is unpredictability. If the price spikes at some time in the future, the allocation may have to drop even though the demand is the same to avoid breaking the budget. Exactly how much budget to allocate to resources depends on the predictability of the prices, i.e. the demand. If the demand is flat over time, very little excess budget has to be put aside to cope with situations where resources are critically needed and demand and prices are high. On the other hand, if some application is not elastic enough to handle resource variation, e.g. nodes being de-allocated because the price is too high, a higher budget may need to be allocated to make sure the application runs at some minimal level of allocation.

Essentially users as well as applications have different sensitivity to risk of losing resource allocations or resources being more expensive. In economics the attitude towards risk is described in the risk-averseness or risk attitude property of a user. There are three types of users that differ in how much they are willing to spend to get rid of risk (variation) [33]. Risk-averse users will spend more money than the expected uncertain price (i.e. hedge for future spikes c.f. the discussion on over-provisioning and under- provisioning) [34]. Risk-neutral users will spend exactly the expected price. Finally, risk-seekers will put in a lower budget than the expected price to meet their allocation needs (see Figure 6). An application that is perfectly elastic and that may scale down or up over time as long as the long term performance is guaranteed may choose a risk neutral strategy. Risk seekers are less common in computational markets, but they may be bettering on demand going down in the future. Risk-averse users are the most common group, and the premium they pay above the expected price is a good indicator for how much a resource provider can charge for reservations, which essentially eliminates this uncertainty.

In summary, the elasticity of a Cloud application is highly related to the risk-aversion of the resource purchase, i.e. how much to pay to hedge uncertainty.

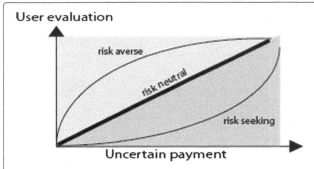

Figure 6 Risk attitudes. Risk averseness is the amount of money you are willing to pay to remove risk. Risk neutral people will always be willing to pay the same amount for a lottery ticket as the expected outcome or gain of the lottery.

Discussion

Even though many of the economic approaches to computational resource allocation have been known since the 1960s, the adoption has been very slow. One of the reasons may be the assumption of instant, low-latency scaling and friction-less allocation, a.k.a. elasticity assumed by the economic models. Another, may be the limited opportunities to large-scale sharing and co-location of workloads, as many private firms are very sensitive to share their computational resources with others. The success of Public Clouds, such as Amazon EC2, has brought many of these economic concepts back into mainstream usage again. One example is the now fully operational Amazon Spot Market. There have been a multitude of attempts in the past to deploy such markets, but they do not start providing tangible benefits to consumers and providers until the markets reach a certain level of maturity and liquidity. It is informative to study when Amazon thinks Spot instances should be used [35]. The key stated reasons include, scaling out large, low-risk computations whenever either the market demand is low, and thus prices are low, or when large computations need to run unexpectedly and the planned capacity is not sufficient.

Another recent example of a more sophisticated computational market is the Deutsche Börse Cloud Exchange [36]. This exchange allows IaaS providers to sell resources at a centralized exchange to avoid vendor lock-in and to spur competition for more efficient pricing of commodity Cloud resources. The main argument to sellers is that their sales volume would increase, and to consumers that the prices would be lower. Trust is also an important factor that would allow smaller providers to sell through a well-known stock exchange. As these markets and others mature, the Economic principles discussed here will start having a bigger impact on how we provide, consume, and design Cloud resource infrastructure in the future.

Summary

We have discussed some computational principles underlying the efficient design of Cloud computing infrastructure provisioning. We have also seen how economic principles play a big role in guiding the design of sustainable, profitable, and scalable systems. As Cloud computing becomes more commonplace and more providers enter the market, the economic principles are likely to play a bigger role. The sophistication of the market designs depends very much on the level of competition and usage, a.k.a. as the liquidity of a market.

The key to a successful market design is to align the incentives of the buyers and sellers with those of the system as a whole. This will ensure participation and liquidity. Most computational principles in the Cloud are governed by the notion that large scale distributed systems see failures so frequently that failover and recoverability must be an integral part of the software design. In order to failover successfully one needs to have full programmatic control from hardware to end-user application. An ongoing trend has been to develop platforms and cloud operating systems that offer this level of software control of hardware to automate administration, management, and deployment dynamically based on demand.

Endnote

[a]done in many P2P networks at the time.

Competing interests

The authors declare that they have no competing interests.

Authors' contributions

This text is based on a distributed systems class co-taught and co-developed by the authors at KAIST during the fall of 2013. TS contributed mostly to the economics section, and DL contributed mostly to the systems section. Both authors read and approved the final manuscript.

Acknowledgements

This work was partially supported by the IT R&D program of MSIP/KEIT. [10045459, Development of Social Storyboard Technology for Highly Satisfactory Cultural and Tourist Contents based on Unstructured Value Data Spidering]. We thank the students in the class, which this text is based on, for their feedback. We also thank Bernardo Huberman for influencing many of the ideas presented in the sections on Economic principles. Finally, we would also like to thank Filippo Balestrieri for reviewing early drafs of this letter.

References

1. Armbrust M, Fox A, Griffith R, Joseph AD, Katz R, Konwinski A, Lee G, Patterson D, Rabkin A, Stoica I, Zaharia M (2010) A view of cloud computing. Commun ACM 53(4):50–58. doi:10.1145/1721654.1721672
2. Kesselman C, Foster I (1998) The grid: Blueprint for a new computing infrastructure. Morgan Kaufmann Publishers, Inc, San Francisco, CA, USA
3. Barham P, Dragovic B, Fraser K, Hand S, Harris T, Ho A, Neugebauer R, Pratt I, Warfield A (2003) Xen and the art of virtualization. In: Proceedings of the Nineteenth ACM Symposium on Operating Systems Principles. SOSP '03, ACM, New York, NY, USA, pp 164–177. doi:10.1145/945445.945462. http://doi.acm.org/10.1145/945445.945462
4. Rolia J, Friedrich R, Patel C (2002) Service centric computing - next generation internet computing. In: Calzarossa M, Tucci S (eds).

Performance Evaluation of Complex Systems: Techniques and Tools. Lecture Notes in Computer Science, vol. 2459. Springer-Verlag Berlin Heidelberg, Germany, pp 463–479. doi:10.1007/3-540-45798-4_19. http://dx.doi.org/10.1007/3-540-45798-4_19

5. Gottschalk K, Graham S, Kreger H, Snell J (2002) Introduction to web services architecture. IBM Syst J 41(2):170–177. doi:10.1147/sj.412.0170
6. Box D, Ehnebuske D, Kakivaya G, Layman A, Mendelsohn N, Nielsen HF, Thatte S, Winer D (2000) Simple Object Access Protocol (SOAP) 1.1. W3c note, World Wide Web Consortium. See http://www.w3.org/TR/SOAP/ Accessed 1/12/2014
7. Lenk A, Klems M, Nimis J, Tai S, Sandholm T (2009) What's inside the cloud? an architectural map of the cloud landscape. In: Proceedings of the 2009 ICSE Workshop on Software Engineering Challenges of Cloud Computing. CLOUD '09. IEEE Computer Society, Washington, DC, USA, pp 23–31. doi:10.1109/CLOUD.2009.5071529. http://dx.doi.org/10.1109/CLOUD.2009.5071529
8. Wilder B (2012) Cloud Architecture Patterns: Using Microsoft Azure. O'Reilly Media, Beijing Cambridge Farnham Köln Sebastopol Tokyo
9. Knightly EW, Shroff NB (1999) Admission control for statistical qos: theory and practice. Netw IEEE 13(2):20–29. doi:10.1109/65.768485
10. Delimitrou C, Kozyrakis C (2014) Quasar: resource-efficient and qos-aware cluster management. In: Proceedings of the 19th International Conference on Architectural Support for Programming Languages and Operating Systems, ACM, New York, NY, USA, pp 127–144
11. Amdahl GM (1967) Validity of the single processor approach to achieving large scale computing capabilities. In: Proceedings of the April 18-20, 1967, Spring Joint Computer Conference. ACM, New York, NY, USA, pp 483–485
12. Stonebraker M (1986) The case for shared nothing. IEEE Database Eng Bull 9(1):4–9
13. Karger D, Lehman E, Leighton T, Panigrahy R, Levine M, Lewin D (1997) Consistent hashing and random trees: Distributed caching protocols for relieving hot spots on the world wide web. In: Proceedings of the Twenty-ninth Annual ACM Symposium on Theory of Computing. ACM, New York, NY, USA, pp 654–663
14. Stoica I, Morris R, Karger D, Kaashoek MF, Balakrishnan H (2001) Chord: A scalable peer-to-peer lookup service for internet applications. In: ACM SIGCOMM Computer Communication Review, vol. 31. ACM, New York, NY, USA, pp 149–160
15. Vogels W (2009) Eventually consistent. Commun ACM 52(1):40–44
16. Lamport L (2001) Paxos made simple. ACM Sigact News 32(4):18–25
17. Mas-Collel A, Whinston MD, Green J (1995) Microeconomic theory. Oxford university press, Oxford
18. Sutherland IE (1968) A futures market in computer time. Commun ACM 11(6):449–451. doi:10.1145/363347.363396
19. Nielsen NR (1970) The allocation of computer resources–is pricing the answer? Commun ACM 13(8):467–474
20. Ellison CM (1975) The utah tenex scheduler. Proc IEEE 63(6):940–945
21. Waldspurger CA, Hogg T, Huberman BA, Kephart JO, Stornetta WS (1992) Spawn: a distributed computational economy. Softw Eng IEEE Trans 18(2):103–117
22. Chun BN, Culler DE (2000) Rexec: A decentralized, secure remote execution environment for clusters. In: Network-Based Parallel Computing. Communication, Architecture, and Applications. Springer-Verlag Berlin Heidelberg, Germany, pp 1–14
23. Rogers O, Cliff D (2012) A financial brokerage model for cloud computing. J Cloud Comput 1(1):1–12
24. Sandholm T (2008) Statistical Methods for Computational Markets. Doctoral Thesis ISRN SU-KTH/DSV/R–08/6–SE, Royal Institute of Technology, Stockholm
25. Yeo CS, Buyya R (2006) A taxonomy of market-based resource management systems for utility-driven cluster computing. Soft: Pract Exp 36(13):1381–1419
26. Hardin G (1968) The tragedy of the commons. Science 162(3859):1243–1248. doi:10.1126/science.162.3859.1243. http://www.sciencemag.org/content/162/3859/1243.full.pdf
27. Chun B, Culler D, Roscoe T, Bavier A, Peterson L, Wawrzoniak M, Bowman M (2003) Planetlab: an overlay testbed for broad-coverage services. ACM SIGCOMM Comput Commun Rev 33(3):3–12
28. Buchanan JM, Stubblebine WC (1962) Externality. Economica 29(116):371–384
29. Arrow KJ (1977) 1921- Studies in resource allocation processes. edited by Kenneth J. Arrow, Leonid Hurwicz. Cambridge; New York: Cambridge University Press, xiv, 482 p.ill. 24 cm. HB135 .A79 ISBN: 0521215226
30. Papadimitriou C (2001) Algorithms, games, and the internet. In: Proceedings of the Thirty-third Annual ACM Symposium on Theory of Computing. ACM, New York, NY, USA, pp 749–753
31. Varian HR (1974) Equity, envy, and efficiency. J Econ Theory 9(1):63–91
32. Keynes JM (1965) A Treatise on Money, Vol. 1: The Pure Theory of Money. Macmillan, London, UK
33. Pratt JW (1964) Risk aversion in the small and in the large. Econometrica 32(1/2). doi:10.2307/1913738
34. Arrow KJ (1965) Aspects of the Theory of Risk-bearing. Yrjö, Helsinki, Finland
35. Amazon EC2 Spot Instances. http://aws.amazon.com/ec2/purchasing-options/spot-instances/. (Accessed 17/11/2014)
36. Jaeger H (2014) A new era in sourcing. Technical report, Deutsche Börse Cloud Exchange http://www.dbcloudexchange.com/wp-content/uploads/2014/08/A-new-era-in-sourcing_290813.pdf (Accessed 1/12/2014)

16

Clouds in Space: Scientific Computing using Windows Azure

Steven J Johnston[*], Neil S O'Brien, Hugh G Lewis, Elizabeth E Hart, Adam White and Simon J Cox

Abstract

In this paper we report upon the cloud-based solution that we designed and implemented for space situational awareness. We begin by introducing the background to the work and to the area of space situational awareness. This concerns tracking the hundreds of thousands of known objects in near-Earth orbits, and determining where it is necessary for satellite operators to conduct collision-avoidance manoeuvres to protect their satellites. We also discuss active debris removal, which would be necessary to stabilise the debris population at current levels. We examine the strengths that cloud-based solutions offer in general and how these specifically fit to the challenges of space situational awareness, before describing the architecture we designed for this problem. We demonstrate the feasibility of solving the space situational awareness problem with a cloud-based architecture and note that as time goes on and debris levels rise due to future collisions, the inherent scalability offered by a cloud-based solution will be invaluable.

Background

A variety of software and infrastructure solutions are referred to as cloud products, and although there is not a formal definition for cloud computing, the solutions tend to have much in common. Most cloud providers, such as Apple, Amazon, Google and Microsoft offer a pay-as-you-go pricing model for software and infrastructure, which is often referred to as a utility pricing model. Many cloud products offer a finished software solution rather than just infrastructure; for example, Microsoft, Google and Apple offer cloud based services, such as Hotmail, Gmail and iCloud respectively, directly to end users. The key cloud-based solutions can be divided into three categories: Infrastructure as a Service (IaaS) *e.g.* virtual machines, Platform as a Service (PaaS) *e.g.* a managed OS, and Software as a Service (SaaS) *e.g.* email services. The variety of available cloud-based architectures combined with a utility pricing model makes using a cloud-based architecture applicable to many scientific and engineering problems.

In this paper we use a case study from aerospace engineering to showcase the applicability of a cloud-based architecture. The case study looks at the issue of space situational awareness (SSA). SSA involves looking at near

*Correspondence: sjj698@zepler.org
Faculty of Engineering and the Environment, University of Southampton, Southampton, UK

Earth objects and understanding the risk they pose to Earth. This has been highlighted in the news by many events including the Upper Atmosphere Research Satellite (UARS) re-entry in 2011, the International Space Station having to perform a collision-avoidance manoeuvre in 2010, and the collision between Iridium-33 and Cosmos-2251 in 2009. Figure 1 shows the orbits of these two satellites, and the debris produced by their collision.

The UARS NASA satellite was launched in 1991 as an orbital observatory and its mission was to study the Earth's atmosphere. UARS was decommissioned in 2005 and in 2010 the International Space Station had to perform a manoeuvre to avoid colliding with this debris. UARS gained considerable attention when it re-entered the Earth's atmosphere in 2011 with NASA predicting that large parts could reach the Earth's surface.

The "Clouds in Space" project demonstrated how a cloud-based architecture can be applied to SSA to produce an active debris removal solution. This paper begins by giving a more detailed introduction to the field of SSA, before discussing the strengths of cloud computing. The application of cloud-based architectures to SSA is then discussed in terms of these areas of strength. Next, we describe the cloud-based architecture that we designed for SSA. We then detail some of the observations made while architecting, implementing and demonstrating the solution, and finish with discussion and conclusions.

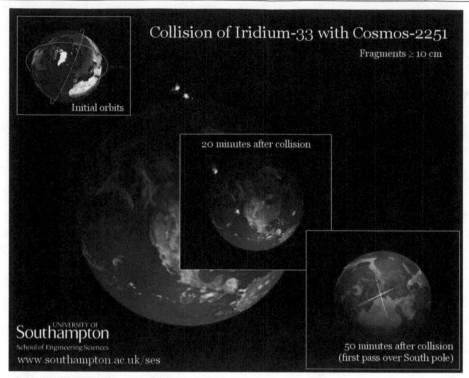

Figure 1 Iridium-33 and Cosmos-2251 collision in 2009.

Space situational awareness

Within the last two decades, the downstream services provided by space-based assets have become a ubiquitous component of everyday life within the European Union and internationally, from satellite television and navigation to environmental monitoring. The European Space Agency (ESA) and European national space agencies currently rely on information from outside sources to form an awareness of these assets and the environment in which they operate. In the near future, this awareness will be provided by a European space situational awareness (SSA) system, which will provide *"a comprehensive knowledge, understanding and maintained awareness of the population of space objects, the space environment, and the existing threats and risks"*(User Expert Group of ESA SSA requirement study, 2007).

Through its SSA Programme (and its Preparatory Programme), ESA aims to provide key services and information regarding the space environment. The SSA system will comprise three main segments:

1. Space surveillance and tracking (SST) of man-made space objects,
2. Space weather (SWE) monitoring and forecasting,
3. Near-Earth object (NEO) surveillance and tracking.

The provision of timely, high quality data via the space surveillance and tracking segment is required to maintain an awareness of operational space assets as well as the population of debris objects in Earth orbit. This awareness provides key knowledge that supports space missions and includes the detection of conjunction events, the detection and characterisation of in-orbit fragmentations and the re-entry of risk objects. In addition, knowledge of overall space traffic is required to understand the evolution of the space (debris) environment and to support space debris mitigation and remediation activities.

Space debris represents a significant risk to satellite operations, particularly in the low Earth orbit (LEO) region. Approximately 19,000 objects larger than 10 cm are known to exist, with around 500,000 larger than 1 cm. The number of smaller particles likely exceeds tens of millions [1]. Conjunctions between satellite payloads and other catalogued objects occur at an average rate of 2,400 per day, with operators having to perform collision avoidance manoeuvres in cases where the risk cannot be reduced to an acceptable level by dedicated tracking campaigns [2]. Whilst mitigation guidelines have been adopted and measures implemented by space-faring nations, predictions made by computer models of the space debris environment indicate that the population of orbiting objects will continue to grow even in the absence of future space launches [3]. The remediation of the near-Earth space environment is now widely accepted as a requirement for the long-term, sustainable use of this vital resource. A reliable and robust SSA infrastructure will be essential for the development and operation of any remediation technology.

The computational and data-intensive challenges presented by the requirements of a SSA system can be met using a cloud-based computational approach. In this work, we establish the applicability of a cloud-based architecture for space surveillance and tracking, algorithm development and comparison.

Application of cloud computing to space situational awareness

In this section, we first introduce the strengths of cloud computing in general terms. We then go on to illustrate how the problem of space situational awareness is naturally suited to take advantage of all of the areas of strength that are inherent in a cloud-based architecture. We discuss how SSA could benefit both in terms of the available computational power and data storage opportunities offered by cloud providers, and how financial economies may be found by opting to use this approach rather than locally-provided data centres. This provides the background for the next section, in which we will introduce the architecture we designed for the SSA problem.

Strengths of cloud computing

Cloud-based computing allows Internet-based resources, software, data and services to be provisioned on demand using a utility pricing model. Where solutions are architected for scalability, a cloud-based architecture can provide the ability to trade computation time against costs. This is readily applicable to applications that require frequent bursts of computational activity. Many individuals and businesses use cloud-based services for email, web searching, photo sharing and social networking. Scientists and engineers use a similar paradigm to make use of massive amounts of compute and data handling resources provided by companies such as Amazon, Microsoft and Google.

Central to a cloud-based architecture is the ability to purchase compute and storage resources using a flexible, on-demand billing model, much like the way traditional utilities (*e.g.* electricity) are purchased. This utility pricing model changes the way compute and storage can be exploited, encouraging scalable architectures and shifting the focus to almost unlimited, instant and on-demand resources with a direct monetary cost. Provisioning resources from a cloud provider is fast (typically taking times on the order of 1 min to 1 hour) and there is usually no minimum rental period, reducing or eliminating the need for large capital expenses as projects start-up or expand.

Cloud providers benefit from economies of scale; bulk purchasing hardware and electricity, and optimising machine administration. When combined with a flexible on-demand billing model, cloud providers can operate data centres very efficiently, in theory resulting in cost savings for end users. Owning and maintaining a data centre or cluster of machines is costly; hardware which is not being utilised is wasted (and probably wasting energy), so it is important to keep the hardware utilisation as high as possible to get best value from the hardware. Using cloud resources ensures that hardware utilisation is high, as un-utilised resources can be returned to the provider (for use by others) and no longer incur a cost.

One of the key architecture patterns for cloud computing is to decouple a problem into independent discrete operations, and implement each with a *worker*. A worker consumes messages from a queue, completes the work stored in the message and then outputs a message to a different queue, as shown in Figure 2. Each message is a discrete piece of work which can result in data being created or consumed from storage (tables, SQL, blobs); the output message indicates work that has been completed and can easily become the input for another worker. This architecture is very flexible as workers can be reordered or substituted to achieve different objectives, or as a queue starts to get too long more workers of the same type can be created, speeding up the overall process. The key benefits of using a cloud-based architecture are described below [4].

- Data dissemination
  Cloud offerings are inherently global, highly available and have large bandwidth capabilities, making them ideal for data aggregation and dissemination. Often sharing data involves copying the data (perhaps multiple times) to ensure that the data and compute reside near each other; but using a cloud-based resource, sharing can be as simple as changing access permissions. Once a dataset resides in a globally accessible cloud resource it too becomes a valuable resource [5] suitable for third party data mashups [6,7]. The data owner can provide access to a third party, who can purchase compute resources with the same cloud provider and immediately start processing the data set. The data owner is responsible for data storage costs but the third party is responsible for their own computational resource costs.
- Burst capability
  Figure 3 shows how a data centre copes with predictable demand (top left) and unpredictable demand (top right). When sizing a data centre for such a scenario it has to be able to cope with the peak load; for the majority of the time this hardware remains unused. Where the data centre can cope with demand, the end user applications are unaffected. Once the demand exceeds the capability of the data

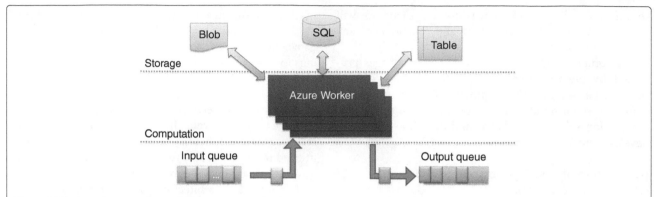

Figure 2 Windows Azure worker architecture pattern. Workers consume messages from input queues, and write data to storage systems and output queues. This pattern enables a dynamic number of workers to process queue messages.

centre, the under-resourced demand has a negative impact on the end user application. Moving such an application to a cloud provider ensures that you only incur costs for the resources utilised, whilst enabling rapid scaling to deal with a variable demand level.

- Super-Scalability
  It is difficult to judge the demand of an application, so there is an inherent need to make applications scalable. In addition to the application scaling the underlying resources need to scale. As with the burst capability, cloud computing offers near-instant

scalability (quicker than purchasing physical machines [8]) allowing an application to scale beyond what is easily achievable with in-house data centres, as shown in Figure 3. In addition, as an application workload declines or plateaus, cloud computing permits the scaling back of resources; currently this is very difficult to accomplish with physical hardware.

- Algorithm development
  Procuring hardware on-demand ensures that the most appropriate hardware is utilised throughout algorithm development and validation. Where a test

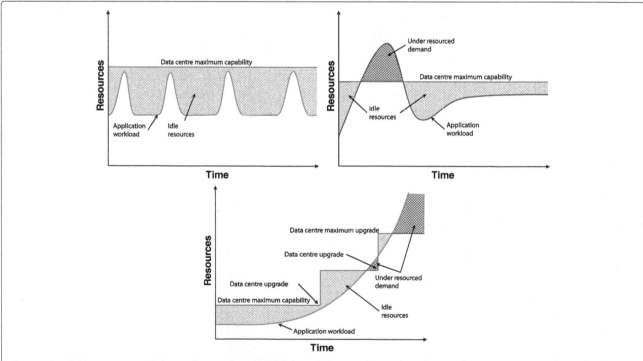

Figure 3 Available resource and demand curves for several data centre scenarios. Under utilisation of compute resources for predictable demand (top left), unpredictable demand with insufficient resources available (top right) and scaling of an application and the data centre that hosts it, with alternating periods of excess and insufficient available resources (lower) [4].

or validation dataset becomes sufficiently large or requires large computational resources a cloud-based architecture can reduce the overall algorithm development time. Cloud-based architectures also encourage a modular design which is ideal for comparing different algorithms as they can be run side-by-side and output data can easily be compared [9].

Applicability of cloud computing to space situational awareness

In the previous section, we highlighted four key benefits of using a cloud-based architecture in general. Now we will discuss in more detail how the SSA challenge specifically fits into these categories.

- Data dissemination
  ESA currently depends on the space catalogue provided by the US Department of Defence (DoD), through its Space Surveillance Network (SSN), for an awareness of space objects. The DoD catalogue contains orbital data for all objects > 10cm and for some objects > 5 cm (approximately 20000 objects). An independent, European catalogue, derived from measurements using European sensor systems, is likely to provide similar capability. However, as new detection hardware is incorporated in the future, the increase in sensitivity will result in a several-fold increase in the number of catalogued objects. The catalogue will also increase in size as space launches are sustained and fragmentation events continue (albeit at a reduced rate as a result of mitigation measures). In particular, collisions between large, intact objects are likely to generate several thousand fragments larger than 10 cm and tens of thousands of fragments larger than 1 cm. For example, the Iridium 33-Cosmos 2251 collision in February 2009 added 1900 objects to the catalogue whilst more than 2000 debris of the order 10 cm or larger were identified by the US SSN in the year following the intentional destruction of the Fengyun 1-C satellite in January 2007 [10]. Whilst a significant number of conjunctions between space objects involve intact spacecraft, nearly half of all conjunctions occurring in August 2009 involved debris from these recent major fragmentation events (Figure 4), illustrating the importance of the timely detection and characterisation of break-ups [2]. A cloud-based storage solution could offer an excellent way to store this increasingly large amount of data. The advantage of storing in a cloud-based resource is the ability to share data between trusted partners and to co-locate data and compute. For example, this could enable satellite operators to securely share precise orbital

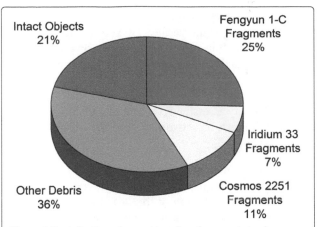

Figure 4 Contribution of recent breakup fragments to close approaches. (data: Centre for Space Standards and Innovation, generated at 13:33 on 15 August 2009).

data and to understand possible conjunctions whilst each person pays for their own storage and compute requirements.
- Burst capability
  Every object in the debris catalogue requires processing (e.g. for conjunction analysis) and as the catalogue grows, the demand for computational power increases. New launches increase the catalogue size in a predictable manner but conjunctions can unpredictably add thousands of new objects, then as the debris orbits decay, the number of entries reduces. A cloud-based architecture would facilitate the rapid procurement of processing power to process the debris orbital data and the characterisation of the conjunction event in a timely fashion. This is a fundamental component of the SST segment. As debris in the catalogue decays out of orbit, excess computational resources can be released, thus not incurring a cost. The burst capability of a cloud-based architecture offers rapid expansion and reduction of computational resources making it ideal for scenarios such as SSA.
- Super-Scalability
  The current debris catalogue size is limited by the ability to track distant or small objects. As detection methods improve we can expect to track a wider range of debris. This will vastly increase the debris catalogue. Currently the catalogue contains approximately 20000 objects but there are millions of objects that could be tracked [1]. This ability to purchase additional compute power in a flexible way means that a cloud-based infrastructure can be scaled to provide a continuity of awareness as the population of space objects and the SST measurement hardware evolve over time.

- Algorithm development
  The development, verification and tuning of complex SST algorithms can be accelerated using using cloud-based technologies. *e.g.* running two different propagators to predict orbits side by side and then comparing the output or comparing collision probability assessment algorithms. Developing such algorithms is an active area of research (see, *e.g.* [11-13]).

The requirement to monitor compliance with space debris mitigation guidelines and the increasingly strong focus on the remediation of the near-Earth environment within the space community will require considerable support in the form of an awareness of overall space traffic. In this way, SSA has a key role to play. The ability of a cloud-based architecture to combine this service-oriented infrastructure with support for research and algorithm development offers a way to generate future space debris and space traffic solutions in a manner that is consistent, reliable and allows for full international collaboration. The development of active debris removal (ADR) technologies and the design of ADR missions fit within this paradigm. As such, we have selected the development of an algorithm for optimising ADR mission delta-vs as an illustration of the utility of a cloud-based computing approach.

A cloud-based architecture solution to the SSA case study
Recent computer modelling studies have suggested that the LEO debris population may be stabilised at current levels through the removal of five large, intact objects per year [14]. Whilst this approach can only be successful if the objects that are targeted would otherwise contribute to future collision activity, it does provide a more cost-effective approach to remediation than the removal, en masse, of all debris objects. However, this leads to a requirement that future collisions are forecast to a sufficient accuracy. In addition, to limit the generation of more debris and to reduce costs further, it is likely that an ADR mission will aim to remove more than one debris object. Consequently, mission requirements include orbital transfers between targets in addition to manoeuvres in close proximity to these uncontrolled objects.

In the light of these requirements, a key concern in the design of an ADR mission will arise from the choice of propulsion system. The choice will be determined, in part, by the energy required to remove debris targets from orbit and to transfer to subsequent targets. The required energy also provides an additional constraint on the selection of removal targets, as it is also linked to mission cost, such that the determination of the route between target destinations becomes an important optimisation task in ADR

mission design. This optimisation problem, known as the travelling purchaser problem (TPP), forms the basis of the demonstration of a cloud-based computing approach. Figure 5 shows the cloud-based architecture for the example ADR mission. The architecture is implemented on Microsoft Windows Azure and each numbered block in the figure is a worker type which can be launched as multiple instances if required.

In our example, an ADR mission with a chemical propulsion system performs a rendezvous manoeuvre to attach a solid rocket motor to a target object, which subsequently fires under remote command to de-orbit the target. The ADR vehicle then uses its primary chemical propulsion to transfer to the next target. Removal targets are identified and ranked using a fast, pair-wise collision algorithm based on the Cube approach employed by the LEO-to-GEO Environment Debris Model (LEGEND) [15] and applied to all objects in the US SSN catalogue. The approach determines the collision probability for each object using Monte Carlo (MC) simulation, whereby the number of MC samples effectively determines the amount of compute time required within the cloud-based solution.

An overview of the ADR workflow architecture is shown in Figure 5. The entire workflow is a single instance of the ADR analysis for a given point in time and it is possible to run multiple workflows in parallel; they do not require inter-process communications. In this paper we only run a single ADR instance, which is comprised of seven different worker types. The workers are synchronised using cloud based queues to identify which unit of work requires processing, and all the data is stored in cloud storage. The storage and queues are designed to be super scalable and are part of the cloud fabric. A cloud based architecture affords us the ability to vary the number of worker instances dynamically, thus we can easily add more hardware to speed up parallel tasks. This is not the case for all workers as some are single instance, shown as a single worker in Figure 5. For example the 1st worker is a data importer that monitors a particular location for new TLE data and therefore only requires one worker. If there were multiple TLE sources it would be possible to run multiple workers to import the data.

The 2nd worker in the ADR architecture is the main propagator and collision detector, which consumes a full TLE catalogue and runs an MC simulation to calculate the probability of a collision between each piece of debris. The bespoke numerical orbital propagator features Earth gravity harmonics up to order 20, solar radiation pressure, luni-solar and atmospheric drag perturbations (using the NRLMSIS-00 atmospheric model) [2]. The propagation and collision algorithms are implemented as a single worker within the cloud-based architecture so that multiple instances (multiple MC samples) can be created for each debris pair. Propagation and collision detection are

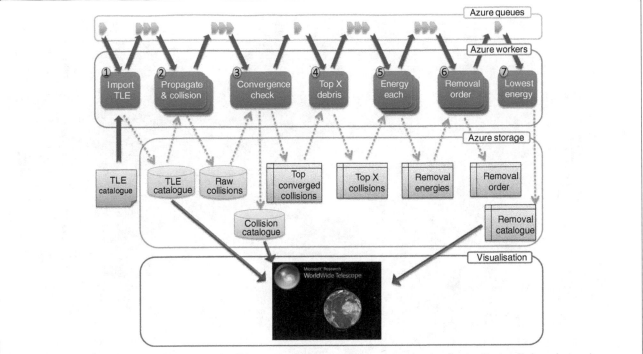

Figure 5 Windows Azure active debris removal architecture. Worker types and sample output data for visualisation. Each worker can have multiple instances demonstrating the scalability and burst capability of a cloud-based architecture.

the main computational workload and are used to identify the debris which has the potential to cause the most disruption in the future. Many instances of this worker are run in parallel, each outputting an ordered list of debris and probability of collision.

The 3rd worker reads these lists of collision probabilities and checks to see when the order of debris in the collision list has stabilised, at which point the MC simulation has converged with the most problematic debris at the top of the list. The 4th worker is a single instance worker that identifies the top ranked objects according to collision probability (and other physical characteristics), normally around 10 pieces of debris. This table of debris is consumed by the 5th multiple instance worker, which computes the delta-v required by each solid rocket motor to de-orbit a selected target object, the optimum route between target objects, and the delta-v required to transfer between these objects. In our preliminary implementation, the TPP is solved using a 'brute force' approach whereby the delta-vs required for every route permutation are calculated by the 6th worker, and we assume Hohmann transfers are employed. The 7th and final worker outputs a list of problematic debris as well as the removal order which requires the lowest energy.

A Hohmann transfer is a transition between two coplanar circular orbits of different altitudes, first described by Walter Hohmann in 1925 [16]. The manoeuvre is accomplished by firing a spacecraft's engine to accelerate it from the first circular orbit into an elliptical orbit, chosen to touch both the initial and destination circular orbits. At the intercept between the transfer orbit and the destination orbit, the engine is fired again to accelerate the spacecraft into a circular orbit. To transfer to a larger circular orbit the acceleration is applied along the spacecraft's current direction of travel; to transfer to a smaller orbit, it is in the opposite direction.

The ADR architecture shown in Figure 5 generates data which is stored in cloud-storage. Accessing the raw data from cloud-storage is trivial and we utilise World Wide Telescope (WWT) [17] to visualise the input, output and intermediate files. WWT has a rich API which supports importing data via a REST interface or from Excel, and is used to visualise data directly from Windows Azure as shown in Figure 6.

In Figure 5 the workers depicted with a single block are single instance workers, where as those with multiple blocks are parallel workers. The propagation and collision worker consumes the largest computational resources but is highly parallel, however the convergence checker cannot start until the propagator has completed. Currently, convergence is checked after the propagator has run for a set number of times, but future implementations will run a convergence checker which can terminate the propagation once converged (to save computational resources).

Figure 6 World Wide Telescope displaying a full TLE catalogue.

This limits the minimum computational wall clock time: if each propagation and collision MC simulation was run with its own worker, the minimum time to complete a full run is bounded below by the time taken by a single propagation (this could be accelerated by using more powerful hardware). The 'energy each' and 'removal order' workers have to wait for the top debris list, but can then process the entries in parallel. Using cloud storage and queues reduces the communication bottlenecks and failure overheads as they are transactional and fault-tolerant.

Cloud observations

The SSA example discussed provides an insight into the generic capabilities of a cloud-based architecture. These are applicable and transferable to many disciplines and are worthy of discussion. For example the generic worker pattern shown in Figure 2 is a pattern commonly applied to a cloud-based architecture.

Cloud based applications may be scaled by either or both of two methods: scaling up by procuring a more powerful computational resource, and scaling out by procuring more instances of a computational resource, each of which offer some distinct advantages.

Scaling up is the most common method to improve performance, but is restricted by the capabilities of the most powerful hardware; the evolution of hardware performance should also be considered. Migrating existing solutions to more powerful hardware is a well understood

problem and is particularly applicable where the task cannot easily be decomposed into smaller units of work. In the SSA example, each worker performs a unit of work that would be difficult to decompose, and satisfactory performance is within the capability of existing hardware.

In order to benefit by scaling out, an understanding of the computation is required as the algorithm has to be decomposed to take advantage of parallel operations. Scale-out often requires more development effort than migrating to a scale-up method. Dividing a task across multiple computational resources incurs an overhead, thus limiting the theoretical improvement in performance as more resources are added. In the SSA example, complex units of work consume tasks from a queue, which makes scaling-out easier since the number of workers consuming tasks from a queue can be varied with the length of the queue.

Using Microsoft Windows Azure was advantageous in this example as this is a PaaS, negating the need to maintain, patch and update the underlying OS. The environment also supports queues, various types of storage, including an SQL server and even includes a data market place to monetise datasets. One key advance which emerged during this work is a cloud-based high performance compute (HPC) cluster. Although not incorporated into this example architecture, HPC is a very powerful asset that ensures legacy MPI applications can seamlessly migrate into a cloud-based architecture.

Throughout this example it became obvious that cloud providers are offering powerful, cost effective infrastructures, but harnessing the power and migrating existing applications is often painful and just out of reach of most application scientists. Cloud providers are still evolving their offerings, and as migration scenarios and remote debugging capabilities improve we can expect to see scientists consuming more cloud resources.

Using workers as an individual unit of computation and feeding them individual tasks using a cloud based queue works well as it is easy to scale-out. Each item in the queue incurs a monetary cost as well as a retrieval time, thus when the computation for each task is short and the queue large, it is preferable to retrieve multiple tasks from the queue in one go, or better still, for each message in the queue to contain multiple tasks.

In this work we have demonstrated a cloud capability, but further work is required to optimise the workflow. For example, the number of worker instances is set at the start, and the workers do not terminate if there is a shortage of work. Likewise, as the queue for a particular worker increases in size, the number of instances does not automatically increase. It is possible to increase worker instances manually, but some work is required for taking them off-line.

Much of this work was carried out using the development environment for Windows Azure, which includes an emulator that can be run on a single development machine. This is a very powerful tool as we were able to test each worker and the entire workflow using a sample TLE dataset. Once we were satisfied with the results, simply deploying the workers on Azure resulted in a working system which could process complete TLE catalogues.

Further work is required to see how scaling-up can benefit the workflow; Microsoft Windows Azure workers come in different sizes and are billed proportionally. Buying larger, more powerful instances does not always improve the performance at the same rate as the instance cost. This is partly dependent upon the type of task – for example, whether it is computationally or IO intensive. It is no longer sufficient to look at overall performance, but rather performance per monetary cost.

Discussion

The space surveillance and tracking segment of ESA's space situational awareness (SSA) system will provide vital security for space assets due to the increased awareness of the risks posed by space debris. The requirements of the SSA system will grow as the population of space objects — and the threat they pose — increases into the future. In this work, we have shown the relevance of a cloud-based architecture to SSA. In particular, the cloud-based architecture is able to manage unpredictable computational demands, in response to a break-up event, in addition to the predictable requirements associated with the regular processing of a space object catalogue. The solution can grow to include more physical computational and storage resources, thereby scaling with the demands of a catalogue of space objects which is rapidly increasing in size due both to conjunctions which introduce new debris, and the introduction of new measurement hardware which can provide information on increasingly smaller debris.

The cloud-based solution provides additional advantages, including the ability to share data with trusted partners simply, rapidly and securely. The partners, at their option, could then fund additional compute resources located close to the data to perform further analysis. The data marketplace provided by Windows Azure is also potentially advantageous, in that it extends the concept of readily and securely sharing data to include the option for the data owner to monetise the data set, the income from which could fund additional analysis, for example.

Further, we have illustrated the applicability of the cloud-based architecture to the development of algorithms that support the long-term sustainable use of outer space. The modular architecture pattern that a cloud-based solution promotes is ideal for this purpose, since a new algorithm could be implemented as a new worker type, and could be run in parallel with existing algorithms on the same data. The compute resources required to try out a novel algorithm and compare its results to those from an established code could be rented just for the time that they are required, making this an economical way to proceed.

In conclusion, not only have we shown how a cloud-based architecture using Microsoft Windows Azure can be successfully applied to an active debris removal mission design task, we have also developed a modular architecture which will be used in the future to support other SSA activities. The modular, cloud-based nature of this solution gives it some unique advantages over alternative architectures due to the rapid availability of huge computational and data storage resources; due to the simplicity that it brings to securely sharing raw or processed data; and due to the ease with which it facilitates the side-by-side comparison of alternative algorithms.

Competing interests
The authors declare that they have no competing interests.

Authors' contributions
SJJ, NSOB, AW and EEH have all contributed to the Clouds in Space project, taking part in migrating existing algorithms into Azure workers, designing the architecture and debugging the solution. HGL was responsible for the underlying SSA algorithms, contributing towards the paper, and proofreading. SJJ and NSOB were responsible for drafting the paper. SJC was the principal investigator on the project; he contributed to the cloud architecting, the paper and proofreading. All authors read and approved the final manuscript.

Acknowledgements
We are grateful to EPSRC and JISC for funding this work through EP/I034009/1. We thank Microsoft for providing access and resource on Windows Azure.

References

1. NASA (2009) Orbital Debris Frequently Asked Questions. NASA Orbital Debris Program Office http://orbitaldebris.jsc.nasa.gov/faqs.html
2. Lewis HG, Swinerd G, Newland R (2011) The space debris environment: future evolution. Aeronautical J 115: 241–247
3. Liou JC, Johnson NL (2006) PLANETARY SCIENCE: Risks in Space from Orbiting Debris. Science 311(5759): 340–341
4. Johnston SJ, Cox SJ, Takeda K (2011) Grid and Cloud Database Management. In: Aloisio G Fiore S (eds). Springer, chap. 9: Scientific computation and data management using Microsoft Azure, pp 169–192. http://www.springer.com/computer/database+management+%26+information+retrieval/book/978-3-642-20044-1
5. Hey T, Tansley S, Tolle K (eds) (2009) The Fourth Paradigm: Data-Intensive Scientific Discovery. In: Jim Gray's Fourth Paradigm and the Construction of the Scientific Record. Microsoft Research, 1 edition October, 177
6. Peenikal S (2009) Mashups and the enterprise. Strategic white paper [Mphasis white paper]. http://www.mphasis.com/pdfs/Mashups_and_the_Enterprise.pdf
7. Hinchcliffe D (2008) An Executive Guide to Mashups in the Enterprise. Executive white paper [Jackbe.com Accessed 23 Aug 2010]. http://mdc.jackbe.com/downloads/Jackbe_Mashups_in_the_Enterprise_White_Paper.pdf
8. Lin G, Fu D, Zhu J, Dasmalchi G (2009) Cloud Computing: IT as a Service. IT Professional 11(2): 10–13
9. O'Brien NS, Johnston SJ, Hart EE, KDjidjeli, Cox SJ (2011) Exploiting cloud computing for algorithm development. CyberC 1: 336–342. doi:10.1109/CyberC.2011.60
10. Johnson NL, Stansbery E, Liou J, Horstman M, Stokely C, Whitlock D (2008) The characteristics and consequences of the break-up of the Fengyun-1C spacecraft. Acta Astronautica 63(1-4): 128–135
11. Yi-yong L, Huai-rong S, Zhi L (2009) Faster algorithm of debris cloud orbital character from spacecraft collision breakup. Adv Space Res 43(10): 1527–1531
12. Lewis H, Swinerd G, Newland R, Saunders A (2009) The fast debris evolution model. Adv Space Res 44(5): 568–578
13. Alarcón-Rodríguez J, Martínez-Fadrique F, Klinkrad H (2004) Development of a collision risk assessment tool. Adv Space Res 34(5): 1120–1124
14. Liou JC (2011) An active debris removal parametric study for LEO environment remediation. Adv Space Res 47(11): 1865–1876
15. Liou JC, Hall DT, Krisko PH, Opiela JN (2004) LEGEND - a three-dimensional LEO-to-GEO debris evolutionary model. Adv Space Res 34(5): 981–986. [Space Debris]
16. Hohmann W (1960) Die Erreichbarkeit der Himmelskörper. Munich and Berlin: R. Oldenbourg 1925. [NASA Technical Translation F-44: The attainability of heavenly bodies, http://archive.org/details/nasa_techdoc_19980230631]
17. Fatland DR, JFay, Fay D (2011) Geoscience Visualization with World Wide Telescope. Microsoft Research Technical Report

Permissions

List of Contributors

Ernest Sithole
Networking and Computing Technologies Laboratory, University of Ulster at Coleraine, Coleraine - BT52 1SA Northern Ireland, United Kingdom

Aaron McConnell
Networking and Computing Technologies Laboratory, University of Ulster at Coleraine, Coleraine - BT52 1SA Northern Ireland, United Kingdom

Sally McClean
School of Computing and Information Engineering, University of Ulster at Coleraine, Coleraine - BT52 1SA Northern Ireland, United Kingdom

Gerard Parr
School of Computing and Information Engineering, University of Ulster at Coleraine, Coleraine - BT52 1SA Northern Ireland, United Kingdom

Bryan Scotney
School of Computing and Information Engineering, University of Ulster at Coleraine, Coleraine - BT52 1SA Northern Ireland, United Kingdom

Adrian Moore
School of Computing and Information Engineering, University of Ulster at Coleraine, Coleraine - BT52 1SA Northern Ireland, United Kingdom

Dave Bustard
School of Computing and Information Engineering, University of Ulster at Coleraine, Coleraine - BT52 1SA Northern Ireland, United Kingdom

Dana Petcu
Institute e-Austria Timişoara and West University of Timişoara, Timişoara, Romania

Beniamino Di Martino
Second University of Naples, Aversa, Italy

Salvatore Venticinque
Second University of Naples, Aversa, Italy

Massimiliano Rak
Second University of Naples, Aversa, Italy

Tamás Máhr
AITIA International Inc, Budapest, Hungary

Gorka Esnal Lopez
Industrial Systems Unit, Tecnalia, San Sebastian, Spain

Fabrice Brito
Terradue SRL, Rome, Italy

Roberto Cossu
Earth Observation Science, Applications and Future Technologies Department, ESRIN, European Space Agency, Frascati, Italy

Miha Stopar
XLAB d.o.o., Ljubljana, Slovenia

Svatopluk Šperka
Brno University of Technology, Brno, Czech Republic

Vlado Stankovski
University of Ljubljana, Ljubljana, Slovenia

Katarina Grolinger
Department of Electrical and Computer Engineering, Faculty of Engineering, Western University, London, ON N6A 5B9, Canada

Wilson A Higashino
Department of Electrical and Computer Engineering, Faculty of Engineering, Western University, London, ON N6A 5B9, Canada
Instituto de Computação, Universidade Estadual de Campinas, Campinas, SP, Brazil

Abhinav Tiwari
Department of Electrical and Computer Engineering, Faculty of Engineering, Western University, London, ON N6A 5B9, Canada

Miriam AM Capretz
Department of Electrical and Computer Engineering, Faculty of Engineering, Western University, London, ON N6A 5B9, Canada

Sanjeev Kumar Pippal
Department of Computer Science and Engineering, MNNIT Allahabad, Allahabad, India

Dharmender Singh Kushwaha
Department of Computer Science and Engineering, MNNIT Allahabad, Allahabad, India

Marc Mosch
Technische Universität Dresden, Department of Computer Science, Chair of Computer Networks, D-01062 Dresden, Germany
Technische Universität Dresden, Faculty of Civil Engineering, Institute of Construction Informatics, Dresden, Germany

Stephan Groß
Technische Universität Dresden, Department of Computer Science, Chair of Computer Networks, D-01062 Dresden, Germany

Alexander Schill
Technische Universität Dresden, Department of Computer Science, Chair of Computer Networks, D-01062 Dresden, Germany

Martin Koehler
Mobility Department, Austrian Institute of Technology (AIT), Giefinggasse 2, 1210 Vienna, Austria

Victor Ion Munteanu
West University of Timi,soara, Timi,soara, Romania
Institute e-Austria Timi,soara, Timi,soara, Romania

C lin ,Sandru
West University of Timi,soara, Timi,soara, Romania
Institute e-Austria Timi,soara, Timi,soara, Romania

Dana Petcu
West University of Timi,soara, Timi,soara, Romania
Institute e-Austria Timi,soara, Timi,soara, Romania

Wei Dai
School of Electrical Engineering & Computer Science, University of Central Florida, 4000 Central Florida Blvd., Orlando, Florida 32816, USA

Mostafa Bassiouni
School of Electrical Engineering & Computer Science, University of Central Florida, 4000 Central Florida Blvd., Orlando, Florida 32816, USA

Nadjia Kar
ETS, University of Quebec, 1100, Notre-Dame street West, Montreal, Quebec H3C 1K3, Canada.

Mbarka Soualhia
ETS, University of Quebec, 1100, Notre-Dame street West, Montreal, Quebec H3C 1K3, Canada.

Fatna Belqasmi
Concordia University, 7141, Sherbrook street West, Montreal, Quebec H4B 1R6, Canada

Christian Azar
Concordia University, 7141, Sherbrook street West, Montreal, Quebec H4B 1R6, Canada

Roch Glitho
Concordia University, 7141, Sherbrook street West, Montreal, Quebec H4B 1R6, Canada

Yoji Yamato
NTT Software Innovation Center, NTT Corporation, 3-9-11 Midori-cho, Musashino-shi 180-8585, Japan

Masahito Muroi
NTT Software Innovation Center, NTT Corporation, 3-9-11 Midori-cho, Musashino-shi 180-8585, Japan

Kentaro Tanaka
NTT Software Innovation Center, NTT Corporation, 3-9-11 Midori-cho, Musashino-shi 180-8585, Japan

Mitsutomo Uchimura
NTT Software Innovation Center, NTT Corporation, 3-9-11 Midori-cho, Musashino-shi 180-8585, Japan

Alex Voss
School of Computer Science, University of St Andrews, St Andrews, UK

Adam Barker
School of Computer Science, University of St Andrews, St Andrews, UK

Mahboubeh Asgari-Targhi
Harvard-Smithsonian Center for Astrophysics, Cambridge, MA, USA

Adriaan van Ballegooijen
Harvard-Smithsonian Center for Astrophysics, Cambridge, MA, USA

Ian Sommerville
School of Computer Science, University of St Andrews, St Andrews, UK

Zhou Quan
Key Laboratory of Mathematics and Interdisciplinary Sciences of Guangdong Higher Education Institutes, Guangzhou University, Guangzhou, China
School of Mathematics and Information Science, Guangzhou University, Guangzhou, China

Tang Chunming
Key Laboratory of Mathematics and Interdisciplinary Sciences of Guangdong Higher Education Institutes, Guangzhou University, Guangzhou, China
School of Mathematics and Information Science, Guangzhou University, Guangzhou, China

Zhen Xianghan
College of Mathematics and Computer Science, Fuzhou University, Fuzhou, China

Rong Chunming
Faculty of Science and Technology, University of Stavanger, Stavanger, Norway

Luis Eduardo Bautista Villalpando
Department of Electronic Systems, Autonomous University of Aguascalientes, Av. Universidad 940, Ciudad Universitaria, Aguascalientes, Mexico

Alain April
Department of Software Engineering and Information Technology ETS, University of Quebec, 1100 Notre-Dame St., Montreal, Canada

Alain Abran
Department of Software Engineering and Information Technology ETS, University of Quebec, 1100 Notre-Dame St., Montreal, Canada

Asit More
ABV- Indian Institute of Information Technology & Management, Gwalior 474015, India

Shashikala Tapaswi
ABV- Indian Institute of Information Technology & Management, Gwalior 474015, India

Thomas Sandholm
HP Labs, 1501 Page Mill Rd, 94304 Palo Alto, CA, USA
Department of Computer Science, KAIST, 291 Daehak-ro, 305-701 Daejeon, Korea

Dongman Lee
Department of Computer Science, KAIST, 291 Daehak-ro, 305-701 Daejeon, Korea

Steven J Johnston
Faculty of Engineering and the Environment, University of Southampton, Southampton, UK

Neil S O'Brien
Faculty of Engineering and the Environment, University of Southampton, Southampton, UK

Hugh G Lewis
Faculty of Engineering and the Environment, University of Southampton, Southampton, UK

Elizabeth E Hart
Faculty of Engineering and the Environment, University of Southampton, Southampton, UK

Adam White
Faculty of Engineering and the Environment, University of Southampton, Southampton, UK

Simon J Cox
Faculty of Engineering and the Environment, University of Southampton, Southampton, UK